# 500

*Frommer's*®

## places to see before they disappear

*1st Edition*

*by Holly Hughes*

*with Larry West*

**WILEY**

Wiley Publishing, Inc.

# Contents

Published by:

# Wiley Publishing, Inc.

111 River St.
Hoboken, NJ 07030-5774

ISBN 978-0-470-18986-3

Editor: William Travis
Production Editor: Heather Wilcox
Photo Editors: Richard Fox & William Travis (with special thanks to Julia Fuchs & Joanna Kata)
Interior book design: Melissa Auciello-Brogan
Production by Wiley Indianapolis Composition Services

Front cover photo: Amboseli National Park, Kenya: Elephant family in foreground, Mount Kilimanjaro in distance.
Back cover photo: Aphrodisias, Turkey: Medusa's head; Holbrook, Arizona: Wigwam Motel; France: Camargue horse running; Kathmandu, Nepal: prayer flags wave in the breeze at Swayambhunath Temple

For information on our other products and services or to obtain technical support, please contact our Customer Care Department within the U.S. at 800/762-2974, outside the U.S. at 317/572-3993 or fax 317/572-4002.

Wiley also publishes its books in a variety of electronic formats. Some content that appears in print may not be available in electronic formats.

Manufactured in the United States of America

5 4 3 2

## About the Author

Holly Hughes has traveled the globe as an editor and writer—she's the former executive editor of Fodor's Travel Publications, the series editor of Frommer's Irreverent Guides, and author of *Frommer's New York City with Kids* and *500 Places to Take Your Kids Before They Grow Up*. She's also written fiction for middle graders and edits the annual *Best Food Writing* anthology. New York City makes a convenient jumping-off place for her travels with her three children and husband.

## About the Consultant

Larry West is a professional writer who covers environmental issues for About.com (http://environment.about.com), which is part of The New York Times Company and one of the world's leading online sources of news and consumer information. During his previous career as a newspaper journalist, he was part of an investigative team whose work was nominated for the Pulitzer Prize and received the Edward J. Meeman Award for environmental reporting from the Scripps-Howard Foundation. An avid and experienced traveler, he currently divides his time between Oregon and Panama.

## An Invitation to the Reader

In researching this book, we discovered many wonderful places. We're sure you'll find others. Please tell us about them, so we can share the information with your fellow travelers in upcoming editions. If you were disappointed with a recommendation, we'd love to know that, too. Please write to:

> *Frommer's 500 Places to See Before They Disappear,* 1st Edition
> Wiley Publishing, Inc. • 111 River St. • Hoboken, NJ 07030-5774

## An Additional Note

Please be advised that travel information is subject to change at any time—and this is especially true of prices. We therefore suggest that you write or call ahead for confirmation when making your travel plans. The authors, editors, and publisher cannot be held responsible for the experiences of readers while traveling. Your safety is important to us, however, so we encourage you to stay alert and be aware of your surroundings. Keep a close eye on cameras, purses, and wallets, all favorite targets of thieves and pickpockets.

## Frommer's Icons

We use four feature icons to help you quickly find the information you're looking for. At the end of each review, look for:

 Where to get more information

 Nearest airport

 Nearest train station

 Recommended kid-friendly hotels

# A Letter from the Author

## Why These 500 Places?

Nailing Jell-O to a wall—that's what writing this book felt like at times. I have been haunted by that fact that, between the time this book was being written and the time it would appear in stores—let alone by the time you finally read it—any of these threatened destinations could have radically changed. That came with the territory, so to speak—you can't call a book 500 Places to See Before They Disappear without assuming that the places you're going to write about are on the brink of extinction. I became afraid to open the newspaper in the morning. The 2008 one-two punch of the cyclone in Myanmar and the Sichuan earthquake in China is a perfect example of how perilous the fate of our planet seems these days.

If you've bought this book, you don't need me to tell you that. Those of us concerned about earth's survival already hear the warning alarms around us on a daily basis. But when all is said and done, this book is, above all, meant to be a travel guide, not a scientific treatise or an eco-sermon. What you'll find in these pages is a carefully chosen list of destinations for travelers to enjoy. That verb "enjoy" is crucial—for in the process of cherishing these natural and cultural wonders, we renew our commitment to preserving them.

Naturally, as travelers we don't want to visit only ruins and devastation—so whenever possible, I've steered you to those spots where now-rare species *are* surviving, where special landscapes *are* still intact, where unique cultural artifacts *have* been preserved. (Who wants to devote a week's precious vacation to dive at a dying coral reef, when there are still healthy ones to glory over?) And as you visit these places, hopefully my suggestions will help you do so with sustainable travel habits—choosing nonpolluting, fuel-efficient transportation, supporting local suppliers, and leaving as few traces as possible on the land.

## We Can Make a Difference

Here's the good news. At the outset, I feared that this project would be infinitely depressing. Yet over the months I spent researching and writing, I discovered more positive developments than I expected. Some of the destinations I've included in this book are already on the road to being saved, usually because they've been championed by preservationists with a will to make a difference. And even in cases where a site has been lost, or irrevocably damaged, it often has become a rallying point for activists, inspiring them to fight on so that the same mistakes aren't made again. Many of the case studies in this book are reasons for hope, not despair, and the more support we can lend them, the better.

The litany of environmental concerns is familiar to all of us by now—global warming, pollution, deforestation, desertification, melting ice caps and glaciers, rising oceans, acid rain, invasive species, loss of biodiversity. Though many situations were caused by human arrogance or ignorance, others are inevitable cyclical developments, and many others are reversible. Sometimes even small changes can arrest the decline of an ecosystem, something as simple as letting a river revert to its natural course or not suppressing beneficial forest fires. So many of the 500 case studies in this book prove that we *can* make a difference.

Though this book was originally conceived as a handbook for eco-tourists, it soon became clear that we couldn't separate natural and man-made attractions. After all, historical and cultural landmarks are part of the environment, too. The destruction of an entire city like New Orleans is as much as a natural disaster as the destruction of an entire biosphere like the Amazonian rainforest; the same concerns affect the Acropolis as the giant redwoods. If changes in the natural environment have threatened the piping plover, the Tasmanian devil, and the mountain gorilla, so too have changes in our cultural environment threatened classic amusement parks, ballparks, and movie palaces. Our planet is the poorer every time we allow something beautiful to die.

## A Note on Hotels & Tours

You'll also find at the end of every write-up useful information about visitors bureaus, transportation options, tour operators, and **hotel recommendations.** I wish I'd had space to give you full-blown reviews, but you can rely on these choices being solid values with an eco-friendly dimension. (You don't need my help in finding the poshest hotel in town—what's hard to find is the small locally owned hotel with no advertising budget.) The three **price ranges** I note—$$$ (expensive), $$ (moderate), and $ (inexpensive)— are all relative to the local market. A $125-per-night motel room in South Dakota would seem expensive, but if you can find something clean and safe at that price in London, snap it up! Similarly, in more far-flung destinations I've listed local tour specialists who can package your visit for you, whenever possible choosing operators with a sustainable travel focus. For fuller descriptions (and other useful travel info), please consult the corresponding Frommer's guides for these destinations. Note that any **phone numbers** listed are what you'd dial from outside the country—for local dialing in non-U.S. destinations, drop the country code and add a 0 before the first number.

Five hundred disappearing destinations—that's a lot. Inevitably, some of them won't survive, or will only survive in a diminished, damaged version. If reading about any of these sights inspires you to experience them for yourself, don't put it off—start booking your trip **now.**

## Acknowledgments

I'd like to thank the devoted corps of Frommer's writers who alerted me to looming crises on their various turfs. You're the real experts in your various parts of the world, and I'm beholden to you. And a special thanks goes out to my husband and three children, who put up with all my lectures on recycling and energy saving and animal welfare while I was in the throes of writing this book. Hopefully they enjoyed our trips to the desert, the volcanoes, the rainforest, and the seashore anyway. And hopefully most of these 500 places will somehow survive, so that my children can take their children there someday, too.

# Frommers.com

Now that you have this guidebook to help you plan a great trip, visit our website at **www. frommers.com** for additional travel information on more than 4,000 destinations. We update features regularly to give you instant access to the most current trip-planning information available. At Frommers.com, you'll find scoops on the best airfares, lodging rates, and car rental bargains. You can even book your travel online through our reliable travel booking partners. Other popular features include:

- Online updates of our most popular guidebooks

- Vacation sweepstakes and contest giveaways

- Newsletters highlighting the hottest travel trends

- Podcasts, interactive maps, and up-to-the-minute events listings

- Opinionated blog entries by Arthur Frommer himself

- Online travel message boards with featured travel discussions

# 1 Big Pictures

*Los Glaciares National Park.*

# The Everglades
## *Choking the River of Grass*
### Southern Florida

A THRIVING ECOSYSTEM FILLED WITH RARE SPECIES, THE EVERGLADES HAS LOST APPROXIMATELY 50% of its land due to agriculture and urban development. Dwindling water levels and pollution have severely compromised what remains. The number of bird species has fallen by 93%, and many of the fish that remain show high mercury levels.

There's nothing else like it on the planet: a vast marshy river that's 40 miles (64km) wide but rarely more than knee deep. Endangered species such as manatees, hawksbill turtles, panthers, American crocodiles, roseate spoonbills, snowy egrets, great egrets, wood storks, snail kites, the Cape Sable seaside sparrow, and the big black Anhinga bird thrive in its murky backwaters. It's the only place in the world where alligators and crocodiles live side by side.

An estimated half of the Everglades has already disappeared over the past century, as land is filled in for farms and residential developments for booming south Florida. The natural flow of water into the wetlands is diverted for drinking water, sewers, and irrigation, and what water does flow in is often contaminated. Though $8 billion was appropriated in 2000 to build new reservoirs, filter marshes, and dismantle disruptive canals, most of those engineering projects are stalled. The state has failed to enforce pollution limits; to date only half the acreage earmarked for preservation has been acquired.

Swooping into the Everglades.

In this unique ecosystem, even a slight water-level drop in the winter dry season radically alters the topography of this shallow plain, affecting nesting areas and food supply. Cattails aggressively root in the marshlands, clogging waterways when the rains return; the balance between saltwater and freshwater in the park's southern estuaries gets out of whack, killing the seagrass that shelters so many marine species.

Still, though, you can explore this delicate ecosystem in a variety of ways. Hikers and bird-watchers strike out on boardwalk trails from the Flamingo Visitor Center, which lead through mangrove swamps, coastal prairies shaded by buttonwood trees, and around freshwater ponds. Trails from the Gulf Coast Visitor Center explore saw-grass marsh, forests of pines and palmettos, and hammocks of tropical hardwood trees such as mahogany and gumbo-limbo. From the Shark Valley Visitor Center, there's excellent cycling through the saw-grass prairie, as well as tram tours.

But to my mind, the best way to experience the Everglades is on the water—and no, not on one of those heavily promoted Everglades tours on noisy powered airboats that operate outside the park limits. The national park's longest "trails" are designed for canoe travel, where you can really feel the gentle surging of the park's waters. You can rent canoes at the Gulf Coast Visitor Center in Everglades City or the Flamingo Lodge by the Flamingo Visitor Center. Better yet, book a guided canoe tour; contact **Everglades National Park Boat Tours** (② **800/445-7724**) at the Parks Docks on Chokoloskee Causeway (Hwy. 29) in Everglades City, or **North American Canoe Tours** at the Ivey House (see "Lodging," below). With a guide in the prow of your canoe, you'll know just where to look to uncover the secrets of this amazing terrain.

ⓘ **Everglades National Park** (② **305/ 242-7700**; www.nps.gov/ever). Visitor centers: Ernest Coe, 40001 State Rd., Homestead. Flamingo, Hwy. 9336, west of Florida City. Gulf Coast, Hwy. 29, Everglades City. Shark Valley, 36000 SW 8th St., Miami.

✈ Miami International Airport

🛏 $$ **Best Western Gateway to the Keys,** 411 S. Krome Ave. (U.S. 1), Florida City (② **305/246-5100**; www.bestwestern. com). $$ **Ivey House B&B,** 107 Camellia St., Everglades City (② **239/695-3299**; www.iveyhouse.com).

**2** One-of-a-Kind Landscapes

# The Grand Canyon
## *Where the Earth Splits Open*
### Tusayan, Arizona

Rising metal and mineral prices worldwide have sparked a new wave of prospecting in the Old West. The number of mining claims near the Grand Canyon increased from 10 in 2003 to more than 1,100 in 2008, bringing with them the risk of stream and groundwater contamination from cyanide and other chemicals.

Postcards just don't do justice to this classic American panorama, a majestic 277-mile-long (446km) canyon of the Colorado River, a primeval, titanic gash in the earth's crust. Gaze down into its depth from the rim and you'll see striated bands of

The Grand Canyon.

multicolored rock, a living history of geo-logic periods unfolding at your feet. Descend into it, on foot or mule back, and you'll pass through no less than four distinct climate zones, as if you began your day in Mexico and ended it in Alaska. Ride those raging whitewaters on a raft and you'll experience how one river could carve such a monumental chasm out of the sandstone desert.

On such an iconic stage, environmental battles are fiercely waged. The increase of mining claims and its potential threat are ongoing concerns, but the outcome is still up in the air. Nearly half of the river's endemic fish species have disappeared in recent years, but careful wildlife management appears to have turned the tide for the endangered humpback chub.

But as part of the greater Colorado River system, the Grand Canyon's fate hinges on so many factors beyond the park boundaries. The Glen Canyon Dam, constructed upriver in 1964 to manage the canyon's flood levels and trap sediments, recently adjusted its seasonal water-level variations, a useful strategy to mimic natural flood cycles. But as sediments build behind the dam, Lake Powell—a popular recreational area created by the dam—could silt up. Even worse, the Glen Canyon Dam could burst, releasing a catastrophic flood to pummel the canyon and crest on into Lake Mead, threatening Hoover Dam as well.

Grand Canyon attracts a staggering number of tourists every year—4.5 to 5 million visitors—many of whom simply view the panorama from the North or South Rim viewpoints and then drive on. A fair number also buzz overhead in sight-seeing planes and helicopters, launched from nearby Tusayan or Las Vegas; tour companies claim that these flights impact the environment less than other modes of exploration, but their intrusive noise is an ongoing source of concern.

To really explore the canyon, it's best to either hike or ride down by mule; it's a mile (1.6km) deep, but with switchbacks, the trails are 7 to 9 miles (11–15km) long. The full descent requires an overnight stay, either at the Bright Angel Campground or the rustic, bare-bones **Phantom Ranch** (reserve up to 23 months in advance at *C* **888/297-2757**). For mule-back expeditions, contact **Canyon Trail Rides** (*C* **928/638-9875;** www.canyonrides.com). If taking on the whitewater is more your style, check the park website for a list of approved commercial outfitters; rafting trips run from 3 to 18 days and range from placid floats to heart-stopping rides.

(i) Grand Canyon National Park, Grand Canyon, AZ (*C* **800/638-7888** or 928/638-7888; www.nps.gov/grca)

✈ Grand Canyon Airport

🛏 $$$ **El Tovar Hotel,** South Rim (*C* **928/638-2631**). $$ **Grand Canyon Lodge,** North Rim (*C* **928/638-2611**). Reservations for either (*C* **888/297-2757**).

# The Redwood Forests of California
## *Earth's Largest Living Things*
### Crescent City, California

CLIMATE CHANGE THREATENS TO UPSET THE ECOLOGICAL BALANCE IN THE TEMPERATE RAINFOREST environment where giant redwoods have thrived for millennia. And although redwoods are naturally resistant to fire, rising temperatures are putting the stately trees at serious risk of death by forest fire for the first time.

Respect must be paid to the giant redwood trees, and it must be paid now. Perhaps the planet's most ancient living things—some are dated at more than 2,200 years old—these massive conifers grow only in temperate rainforests. And one of the last few temperate rainforests left on the earth is here, on the Pacific Coast of the United States.

It's hard to explain the feeling you get striding between the immense trunks of these old-growth forests—the word "awe" doesn't begin to capture it. Everything is huge, misty, and primeval: Flowering bushes cover the ground, 10-foot-tall ferns line the creeks, smells are rich and musty, and an ancient unhurried silence reigns. Sheathed in rough reddish bark, the stout straight trunks shoot up 100 feet (30m) or more before a canopy of branches begins, arching overhead like the roof of a Gothic cathedral.

For many years, the redwoods and their cousins, the giant sequoias, thrived in peace on this relatively isolated coast. Miraculously fire-resistant, the trees could

Towering Redwoods.

withstand most forces that threatened other local timber. But as human development spread, by 1968 the federal government realized the need to create a haven for them in Redwood National Park (nowadays combined with three state redwood parks).

In an earlier age of tourism, an unfortunate number of tacky attractions (the hollow Chimney Tree; One-Log House, a small dwelling built inside a log; the Shrine Drive-Thru Tree) were built along the **Avenue of the Giants,** a 33-mile (53km) stretch of U.S. 101 through the Humboldt Redwoods State Park (© **707/946-2263;** www.humboldtred woods.org). More respectful landmarks include **Founders Grove,** honoring those who started the Save the Redwoods League in 1918, and the 950-year-old **Immortal Tree.** Short walking loops lead into the woods from most parking areas.

Some 100 miles (160km) farther north, there are grander views on two roads that parallel 101: the **Newton B. Drury Scenic Parkway,** passing through redwood groves and meadows where Roosevelt elk

graze, and **Coastal Drive,** which has sweeping views of the Pacific. Pick up a park map to find your way to **Tall Trees Trail,** a 3¼-mile (5.2km) round-trip to a 600-year-old tree often touted as the world's tallest (get a permit at the Redwood Information Center in Orick); the self-guided mile-long (1.6km) **Lady Bird Johnson Grove Loop;** the short, very popular **Fern Canyon Trail;** or the quarter-mile-long (.4km) **Big Tree Trail,** a paved trail leading to—what else?—a big tree.

---

ⓘ **Redwood National and State Park,** 1111 Second St., Crescent City, CA (© **707/464-6101,** ext. 5064; www.nps.gov/redw)

✈ Crescent City Airport

🛏 $$$ **Lost Whale Bed & Breakfast,** 3452 Patrick's Point Dr., Trinidad (© **800/677-7859** or 707/677-3425; www.lostwhale inn.com). $ **Curly Redwood Lodge,** 701 Redwood Hwy. S. (U.S. 101), Crescent City (© **707/464-2137;** www.curlyredwood lodge.com).

## One-of-a-Kind Landscapes 4

# Death Valley
### *Extreme Junction*
#### Furnace Creek, California

IN DEATH VALLEY, HUNDREDS OF SPECIES THRIVE IN ITS INHOSPITABLE LANDSCAPE OF ROCK, sand, and sun. But rising temperatures due to climate change could tip the balance of their precarious existence and push them over the edge. A more immediate threat is toxic pollution from increased mining and mineral exploration in the area.

Harsh, yes. Remote, yes. But there's something compelling about this below-sea-level desert valley, cut off by mountain ranges from the rest of California. A freak of nature, birthed by seismic faults, it is a stark landscape of scalding sand flats, jagged canyons, and glittering outcrops of crystals left behind by withered lakes. Despite scorching temperatures (think 120°F/49°C in summer) and next-to-no rainfall (1.9 in./4.8cm a year, on average),

more than a million tourists come each year to marvel at this extreme landscape.

The historic name memorializes the Forty-Niners who perished here en route to the California gold fields. Life was hardly easier for the borax miners with their 20-mule wagon teams during a brief boom in the late 1880s. But once it was designated a national monument in 1933, the region's harsh desert beauty became its strongest selling point.

Death Valley.

Along Highway 190 lies a string of attractions. **Badwater** is the lowest spot in North America, 282 feet (85m) below sea level; the visual contrast between it and 11,049-foot (3,315m) **Telescope Peak,** only 15 miles (24km) away, is stunning. A 9-mile (15km) driving loop called **Artist's Palette** displays a wind-chiseled range of hills in a spectrum of mineral hues. For camera-ready panoramas, visitors stop at either **Zabriskie Point** or **Dante's View.** But as polluted air increasingly drifts into the valley from metropolitan areas, high temperatures convert it into haze that can obstruct those famous views. Dust thrown up by cars on unpaved park roads, or even people walking on the fragile crust of the salt pan, compounds the problem.

Death Valley also has its own bizarre sand dunes—drifted piles of fine, loose quartz granules eroded from the surrounding rocks and trapped in the valley's isolated trough. The cracked, bleached saltpan at the bottom of the valley is usually devoid of vegetation, but hunt further and you'll find nearly 1,000 species of plants rooted here, some 50 of them endemic. Wildflowers such as desert star, blazing star, desert gold, mimulus, encelia, poppies,

verbena, evening primrose, and phacelia carpet the valley floor from mid-February to early April (check park website for seasonal wildflower predictions).

Most native mammals here are small—gophers, mice, rats—and nocturnal, foraging only after the cruel sun has gone down. Believe it or not, Death Valley even has fish—five species of pupfish, including the endangered Devil's Hole pupfish in western Nevada, 37 miles (60km) east of Furnace Creek. At Salt Creek, just north of Furnace Creek, a boardwalk nature trail allows you to view the tiny Salt Creek pupfish, wriggling in the trickling stream. Even this severe landscape nurtures life, if you just know where to look—there's a message of hope for the planet.

---

ⓘ **Death Valley National Park,** Box 579, Death Valley, CA (✆ **760/786-3200;** www.nps.gov/deva)

✈ Las Vegas

🛏 $$–$$$ **Furnace Creek Inn & Ranch,** Hwy. 190 (✆ **800/236-7916;** www.furnace creekresort.com). $ **Sunset Campground,** Furnace Creek (✆ **800/365-2267;** www. recreation.gov).

# Columbia Icefields
## *End of the Ice Age?*
### Alberta, Canada

GLOBAL WARMING IS MELTING THE COLUMBIA ICEFIELDS, A VITAL SOURCE OF FRESH WATER FOR North America. The glaciers that comprise the Columbia Icefields are receding more each year, and the annual runoff to the major rivers they supply has declined dramatically in the last half century.

The Columbia Icefields straddle the top of the North American continent like a great crystalline mother embracing her children. Massive amounts of pure, century-old ice and snow lie packed in around these peaks, in some spots 750m (2,500 ft.) thick. Covering some 325 sq. km (125 sq. miles), this is the world's largest nonpolar ice mass, a vast frozen dome mantling the eastern face of the Canadian Rockies. But the ice mother's arms seem to clutch her children ever closer, as the edges of the ice field recede an ominous 10m (30 ft.) per year. And what this means for the North American watershed is anybody's guess.

Whereas the Arctic and Greenland ice caps are made of saltwater, the Columbia Icefields are freshwater ice. Melt from its outlying sections creates what's known as a hydrologic apex, a major source of water for North America, eventually flowing into three different oceans (Atlantic, Pacific, and Arctic). It's true that the ice field is so massive, it's not going to vanish completely anytime soon. The hydrologic apex,

Columbia Icefields.

however, may already be critically compromised. The melt at present is ancient snow, free from modern pollutants, but once the melt reaches 20th-century snows, its water quality may be drastically different.

The most accessible section of the ice field is the Athabasca Glacier in Jasper National Park, where the Icefield Visitor Center is set in a valley that was buried in the glacier a century and a half ago. An outdoor timeline here demonstrates where the ice edge lay at various milestone dates in the past. Rocky debris left behind by the melting glacier lies in all-too-evident scraggy piles. From the lodge beside the visitor center you can book a 90-minute ride onto the surface of the glacier with **Brewster Snocoach Tours** (✆ **403/762-6735**), which uses a specially designed bus with balloon tires. Hiking on the glacier's surface is the highlight of these tours, a literally dazzling opportunity to stand on a glittering expanse of solid ice and feel its frosty exhalations.

The drive to get here is spectacular in itself: the 287km (178-mile) **Icefields Parkway,** a majestic stretch of highway between Banff and Jasper national parks that climbs through deep river valleys; beneath soaring, glacier-notched mountains; and past dozens of hornlike peaks shrouded with permanent snowcaps. Along the way, visit the jewel-like resort town of Lake Louise, set on a vivid turquoise lake cupped in a dramatic bowl of glaciers. Don't panic when you see the unearthly greenish color of the lake; it's not caused by pollution, but rather by the way that minerals deposited by glacier melt refract the sunlight. This beautiful land of ice transforms everything.

---

ⓘ **Sunwapta Pass,** Alberta, Canada (✆ **780/852-7030**)

✈ Calgary

🛏 $$$ **Columbia Icefields Center,** Sunwapta Pass (✆ **780/852-7032**). $$ **Becker's Chalets,** Hwy. 95, Jasper (✆ **780/852-3779;** www.beckerschalets.com).

# The Burren
## *Ireland's Stony Wilderness*
### County Clare, Ireland

THE BURREN'S STONY LANDSCAPE IS A FRAGILE ENVIRONMENT THREATENED BY BOTH TOO much and too little human attention. Every year, thousands of people hike the Burren's rocky paths and marvel at the stone relics of its ancient inhabitants. And as small farms continue to dwindle, leaving too few sheep and cattle to graze between the rocks, scrub plants invade and displace native species that once protected the Burren from wind and rain.

The very name Ireland evokes a postcard image of soft, intensely green countryside—so what is this harsh limestone scree doing there? It's as weird as if you had just stepped onto the moon. The name "Burren" comes from the Irish word *boirreann,* which means "a rocky place"—what an understatement.

The coach tours that overrun the Cliffs of Moher trundle through here, too, but most day-trippers merely stare out the windows at the Burren and move on. It's one thing to drive along corkscrewing R480 between Corofin and Ballyvaughan through the heart of the landscape, and another thing entirely to get out of your

The Burren.

car and hike along portions of the 42km (26-mile) **Burren Way** footpath signposted from Ballyvaughan to Liscannor. These massive sheets of rock and jagged boulders quickly reveal caves, deep hidden potholes, and even tiny lakes and rushing streams. It even has its own terminology—the deep cracks riven in the rock are known as "grikes," the chunks of rock between them as "clints."

And then you've got to look even closer. The Burren is a botanical freak, one of the few places on the earth where alpine, arctic, and Mediterranean plants thrive side by side, clinging stubbornly to whatever soil they find in this uniquely cool, moist, bright coastal climate. There is always something blooming here, even in winter, from fern and moss to orchids, rock roses, milkwort, wild thyme, geraniums, violets, and fuchsia. The blue spring gentian—normally an alpine species—is so common, it's the region's unofficial mascot. Some species are relics of the warmer climate this region knew before the last ice age; others are descendants of seeds

dropped by the same glaciers that grooved and striated the karst so dramatically.

Close as it is to western Ireland's most popular tourist sites, the Burren could easily be overrun by tourists, and locals have had to fight off proposals for car parks and attractions. It seems hypocritical to keep out visitors altogether, though, for the Burren is hardly untouched by man. It's been inhabited since megalithic times, as the wealth of dolmens, wedge tombs, and ring forts attest. Cattle and sheep grazed for centuries on the stubborn tufts of grass between the rocks, but as farms were abandoned during the famine, hazel scrub quickly invaded, and the naked stone lay open to pelting Irish rains and scouring winds.

A wide swath bordered by Corofin, Lahinch, Lisdoonvarna, Ballyvaughn, and Boston has been designated the **Burren National Park,** but don't expect an official entrance or acres of parking lot. The Burren is already paved by nature—why add to that?

ⓘ Visitor centers: the **Burren Exposure,** Galway Rd., .4km (¼ mile) north of Ballyvaughan (📞 **353/65/707-7277**). The **Burren Centre,** R476 to Kilfenora (📞 **353/65/708-8030**).

✈ Shannon International Airport

🚌 Ennis or Galway

🛏 $$ **Hylands Burren Hotel,** N67, Ballyvaughan (📞 **353/65/707-7037;** www.hylandsburren.com). $ **Carrigann Hotel,** Lisdoonvarna (📞 **353/65/707-4036**).

**7** One-of-a-Kind Landscapes

# The Dead Sea
## *Doing the Dead Sea Float*
### Israel

THE DEAD SEA IS DRYING UP BECAUSE IT NO LONGER RECEIVES ENOUGH WATER FROM THE Jordan River and other sources to offset the rapid evaporation caused by Israel's arid climate. To save the Dead Sea from going completely dry within just a few decades, a sustainable balance between water flowing in and evaporating out will have to be restored.

Lying at the lowest point on the earth—a remarkable 417m (1,367 ft.) below sea level—the Dead Sea is anything but dead. Granted, no fish live in this salt-saturated inland lake, less than an hour's drive from Jerusalem, but a certain green algae do just fine, plus lots of red archaebacteria. The water looks slightly greenish, and also milky from all its rich minerals—magnesium, calcium, bromine, potassium. For centuries Dead Sea mud has been touted for its healing powers.

But while the Dead Sea is fed by water from several sources, notably the Jordan River, water doesn't flow out, it just evaporates. And with Jordan River waters increasingly diverted to irrigation projects upstream, there isn't enough water flowing in these days to offset the rapid evaporation caused by this dry climate. Rocky coves all along the shore are edged with snowy encrustations of salt, and lately the water level has been dropping at the alarming rate of a meter (3¼ ft.) every year. Within 3 decades, the Dead Sea could be completely dry.

And with it would go an incredible, unique experience. The sensation of floating in the Dead Sea is so freaky, you keep testing it again and again—releasing your body into that incredibly saline water and popping up to the surface, as buoyant as if you were weightless. Not only that, the Dead Sea air contains 10% more oxygen than normal, making you feel relaxed and

The Dead Sea.

energized. It's hot (up to 107°F/41°C in summer) but dry, and thanks to an extra layer of atmosphere caused by evaporation, the sun's UV rays are filtered, making it a fairly safe place to sunbathe.

Although the desert ridges around the sea look sand scoured and fierce, along the lakeside highway you'll find a few lush oases, many of them with sulfur hot springs that give rise to a booming spa industry. Two main beach areas thrive along the Israeli shore: one at **Ein Gedi,** where you'll find a rather crowded public beach, a kibbutz with a good hotel and spa, and a botanic garden planted with rare trees and shrubs from all over the world. At Ein Gedi kibbutz, you can book a

desert jeep safari, a Bedouin feast in a tent, or an hour-long cruise on the Dead Sea in an eccentric wooden double-deck boat called Lot's Wife. Further down the coast, past the ancient fortress of **Masada,** you'll reach **Ein Bokek,** where there are several hotels and free public beaches.

ⓘ **The Living Dead Sea** (✆ **972/8/668-8808;** www.deadsea.co.il)

✈ Ben-Gurion International Airport

🛏 $$$ **Golden Tulip Dead Sea Hotel,** Ein Bokek (www.fattal-hotels-israel.com). $$ **Kibbutz Ein Gedi Resort Hotel,** Ein Gedi (✆ **800/844-4007** or 972/8/659-4222; www.ngedi.com/guest_house.htm).

One-of-a-Kind Landscapes 8

# The Vredefort Dome
## *Scar of an Ancient Asteroid*
### Parys, South Africa

THE VREDEFORT DOME IN SOUTH AFRICA OFFERS A UNIQUE RECORD OF THE EARTH'S GEOLOGICAL history, which is crucial to our understanding of the planet's evolution. Erosion and geological activity that have destroyed other asteroid-impact sites also threaten the integrity of the Vredefort Dome.

As if there weren't enough earthly forces to worry about, don't forget the threats that come from outer space. Take this gentle ring of hills rising from the South Africa plains—who would have guessed that it was caused by a giant asteroid, walloping the earth some 2 billion years ago? We can only guess how huge the asteroid was; geologists estimate it was some 10km (6¹/₄ miles) in diameter. The mark of its forcible landing is what geologists call an "impact structure"—and the one at Vredefort is not only the largest, it's the oldest one on the earth.

The village of Vredefort, which nestles within the dome, lies 100km (62 miles) southwest of Johannesburg, just off the N1 highway to Cape Town. Actually, this ring of hills, some 180km (112 miles) across, isn't the entire crater; it's a secondary spot

at the crater's center where the earth's surface sprang back violently. (The original crater, long eroded away, may have been 250–300km/155–186 miles in diameter.) The asteroid itself was simply vaporized by the ruthless blast. Such enormous energy was released in this cataclysm, it must have triggered major global changes, perhaps even altering the course of evolution. No, this wasn't the one that killed the dinosaurs—that meteor hit the earth many years later, in Mexico. The Vredefort collision was even more important—it kicked the earth's oxygen levels up to a threshold that would finally sustain multicellular life.

Designated a World Heritage Site in 2005, the Vredefort Dome is still relatively undeveloped as a tourist destination, though plans are afoot to lay out interpretive hiking trails and organize sightseeing flights over the crater. Given all that primeval furor, the Vredefort Dome today presents a surprisingly placid, pastoral face. Rich in birds and butterflies, the land shelters rare rooikats, aardwolves, leopards, and the endangered rock dassie, not to mention the world's largest olive-tree forest. The rounded, eroded hills are mantled in veldt grass, with erratic outcrops of granite. But where the rock has broken away, you can see a distinctive pattern of turbulence: blobs of light gray granite trapped within an ancient flow of molten dark-gray granite. The magnetic field hereabouts remains so severely affected, it

sets compasses spinning. Earth hasn't forgotten its ancient injury—and neither should we.

ⓘ **Parys Tourism** (✆ **27/56-811-2000;** www.parysinfo.co.za)

✈ Johannesburg

🛏 $$$ **The Westcliff,** 67 Jan Smuts Ave., Westcliff (✆ **800/237-1236** in U.S. or 27/11-646-2400; www.westcliff.orient-express.com). $ **Otter's Haunt,** Kopeskraal Rd., Parys (✆ **27/82-475-8767** or 27/84-245-2490; www.otters.co.za). $ **Thwane Bush Camp,** Schoemansdrif Rd., Parys (✆ **27/56-811-2345;** thwane@parysinfo.co.za).

---

**9**     One-of-a-Kind Landscapes

# Mount Kilimanjaro
## *Snow Today, But Tomorrow?*
### Tanzania

THE FAMOUS SNOWS OF KILIMANJARO ARE MELTING AND MAY SOON BE GONE. A COMBINATION of evaporation, too little snowfall, and internal heat from the dormant volcano have reduced the mountain's ice and snow cover by 90% from historic levels—and it continues to retreat about 1m (3¼ ft.) a year.

The Masai tribesmen called it *Oldoinyo Oibor,* or "White Mountain." In Swahili, it's *Kilima Njaro,* or "Shining Mountain." Ernest Hemingway titled his famous short story "The Snows of Kilimanjaro." Clearly, those majestic snow-capped peaks are what make this the most famous mountain in Africa, along with the fact that it's the continent's highest peak. That snowy plateau, rising 4,600m (15,100 ft.) above the Tanzanian plains just south of Kenya, is a mesmerizing sight indeed—here, in equatorial Africa, standing all by itself, is a mountaintop with snow.

As world-class peaks go, it's a relatively easy climb, though it takes several days round-trip to reach the summit; climbers overnight at a series of huts on the mountain. Nearly 30,000 climbers a year attempt it, though at least a quarter of that number fails to reach the top. Ascending, you pass

through four radically different climate zones. First comes the lush, steamy Kilimanjaro Forest Reserve surrounding the base; then the grassy moorlands of the shouldering slopes; above 3,900m (13,000 ft.), the mountain suddenly becomes steeper and more barren, with rocky scree underfoot. Last of all, you hit glacial ice fields, dazzling in the reflected African sun. It's not a technical climb, but it's a strenuous steep hike, and the extreme altitude makes it physically challenging if your body hasn't acclimated properly.

There are several routes to the summit. One of the most popular, the **Western Breach,** has already been closed due to rock slides caused by receding ice. The 5-day **Marangu Route**—nicknamed the Coca-Cola Trail—is currently most popular; it starts from the Marangu Park Gate. The **Lemosho Trail,** which takes off from

Mount Kilimanjaro.

Londorossi Gate, is easier and more scenic, though it takes 9 days. Whichever route you take, you must obtain park permits and hut reservations in advance (available through a licensed tour operator or local hotels in Moshi); at the park gate you'll hire a guide, and possibly a porter (you won't be allowed on the mountain without a guide). Park fees are substantial, but they include hut accommodation on the mountain; guides and porters ask ridiculously low wages, hoping for generous tips on top. If you book with a tour operator (which I recommend), most of this, along with a cook to prepare all meals en route, is included in your package. Standing on the snow-capped summit? That's priceless.

ⓘ **Kilimanjaro National Park,** Tanzania (www.tanzaniaparks.com/kili.htm)

✈ Kilimanjaro International

**TOUR Destination Africa Tours** (www.climbingkilimanjaro.com). **Roy Safaris,** Arusha, Tanzania (✆ **255/27/2502115;** www.roysafaris.com). **Tanzania Serengeti Adventure,** Arusha, Tanzania (✆ **255/27/2544609;** www.habari.co.tz/tsa).

One-of-a-Kind Landscapes **10**

# The Amazon Rainforest
## *Paradise Lost?*
### Manaus, Brazil

SINCE 1970, SCIENTISTS ESTIMATE, AS MUCH AS 20% OF THE AMAZON BASIN'S RAINFOREST may have disappeared, at the mercies of clear-cut logging and subsequent cattle ranching. It is said that .6 hectares (1½ acres) are lost every second. And a recent series of droughts has pushed the basin closer and closer to irretrievable desiccation and death.

"Save the rainforest!" became a conservation rallying cry in the early 1980s, a cliché for environmental awareness. You'd think by now we would have saved it.

But the crisis is by no means past for this amazing tropical wilderness. The Amazon—the world's largest river—courses through the world's biggest forest, a dense green jungle that shelters myriad endangered and endemic species, on its way to the Atlantic Ocean. This lush environment is, as one catchphrase calls it, the "lungs of the earth," producing more than 20% of the world's fresh oxygen. It also shelters an enormous number of species, including 20% of the world's plants, many of which are thought to be unique sources for lifesaving medicines. In all, the total number of species can only be estimated because so many remain unrecorded.

For the traveler, though, this fertile wilderness is one of the most beautiful and exotic paradises on earth, a spellbinding scene of draping vines, waxy blossoms, and leafy canopies, with a soundtrack of chattering monkeys and twittering parakeets. Gaze upwards and you'll find comical toucans and iridescent parrots in the trees; peer into the river's mysterious depths and you'll spot furtive anacondas and flitting tetra fish. In the past few decades, an entire eco-tourism industry has sprung up in the Amazon, offering new economic hope for natives who formerly depended on destructive logging. While the tourism infrastructure is still limited, Amazon basin travel improves every year.

The usual starting point is **Manaus,** the largest city in the region, located on the shores of the Rio Negro. Just downstream from Manaus lies the momentous **Meeting of the Waters (Encontra das Aguas),** which every visitor should see, either by boat or sightseeing plane. As the dark slow waters of the Rio Negro meet the fast muddy brown waters of the Rio Solimões—officially becoming the capital-A Amazon—differences in velocity, temperature, and salinity actually keep the two rivers from blending. You can see the distinct colors of their currents running side by side for miles past the junction, a stunning natural phenomenon.

Plenty of operators run boat trips of varying lengths out of Manaus, either offering overnight accommodations on board or traveling to Amazon lodges set in their own jungle preserves. Whether you're sleeping on the water or on land, these package tours generally include common features: canoe excursions up smaller tributaries, sunset and sunrise tours, wildlife-watching walks under the leafy canopy of the rainforest, piranha fishing, and nighttime caiman spotting. See also the separate entry on the Anavilhanas Ecological Station (p. 98).

For a more adventurous option, try **Amazon Mystery Tours** (✆ 55/92/633-7844; www.amazon-outdoor.com), whose tours explore the deeper reaches of the rainforest via kayak, jungle hiking, and camping out. Some of their itineraries even include climbing up into the rainforest canopy, and guides can tailor excursions to focus on special interests: Bird-watching, orchid hunting, medicinal plants—the Amazon's fascinations are endless.

---

ⓘ **Manaus Tourist Center Tourist Service** (✆ 55/92/3231-1998; www.amazonastur.am.gov.br)

✈ Eduardo Gomes in Manaus

🛏 $$ **Hotel Tropical de Manaus,** Av. Coronel Texeira 1320, Ponta Negra, Manaus (✆ 55/800/701-2670; www.tropicalhotel.com.br). $$ **Holiday Inn Taj Mahal,** Av. Gentúlio Vargas 741, Manaus (✆ 55/800/925-333).

**TOUR Viverde** (✆ 55/92/248-9988; www.viverde.com.br). **Amazon Clipper Cruises** (✆ 55/92/656-1246; www.amazonclipper.com.br). **Swallows and Amazons** (✆ 55/92/622-1246; www.swallowsandamazonstours.com). Lodging included in tour packages.

# The Pantanal
## *Off Road & Under Water*
### Southwestern Brazil

THE PANTANAL HOSTS THE GREATEST CONCENTRATION OF PLANTS AND WILDLIFE IN SOUTH America. However, recreational fishing and rampant poaching are swiftly decimating the Pantanal's wildlife population, and toxic runoff from agriculture and gold mining upstream have all undermined the Pantanal's unique ecosystem.

The Amazon rainforest may grab all the headlines, but here's a little-known secret: The best place in South America to see wildlife is right here, on this flat, treeless savanna. The world's largest freshwater flood plain (equal to the size of France), the Pantanal may not have as many species as the rainforest does, but nowhere else in the world are the flora and fauna so densely packed. In the rainy season, December through March, the waters may rise as much as 3m (10 ft.), covering up to 80% of the region—and leaving an incredibly fecund landscape in its wake.

Despite the overwhelming stresses this superbly adapted ecosystem faces, the government has done little to protect it; less than 2% has been set aside for conservation, only one small national park (Parque Nacional do Patanal Mato-Grossense, near Poconé in the north Pantanal), and a handful of private preserves.

Capybaras, caimans, jaguars, maned wolves, jaibiru, Brazilian tapirs, giant otters, Hyacinth macaws—the Pantanal offers endangered critters everywhere you look. They're incredibly easy to spot, too. In the rainy season, you'll find mammals clustered on the few remaining humps of dry land while fish and aquatic birds slosh happily through the water. In dry season, the reverse happens: The plain dries up, and animals can be found around the few freshwater pools.

There's no point in building many roads here—even the Transpantaeira, a gravel road meant to traverse the entire region,

was abandoned after the northern 143km (89 miles). (Just as well—the roadway would have brutally bisect the region's idiosyncratic natural drainage system.) But that unfinished Transpantaeira functions as a splendid nature trail, taking visitors into the heart of north Pantanal. Its roadside ditches are favorite feeding grounds for kingfishers, egrets, jibiru storks, and more than four varieties of hawks and three different kinds of kites. Beneath the many rickety bridges are small rivers or pools where caimans lurk by the hundreds.

Ruled by the rhythms of its waters, ranchers graze their cattle in the dry season and retreat to higher ground in the floods. With eco-tourism on the rise, however, many of the region's cattle ranches *(fazendas)* have created accommodations and gone into business as the Brazilian version of dude ranches. While local lodges may offer short rides around their properties, you can also book entire tour packages based on exploring the flood plain by horse (see "Tour," below). Ramble far from settled areas, where the local wildlife wanders otherwise undisturbed; rein in your mount and observe a flock of herons fishing in the rich floodwaters, then take off with a splash at a full gallop, startling alligators and snakes underfoot. Unspoiled corners can still be found all over the Pantanal . . . but the clock is ticking.

ⓘ Praça da República 131, Cuiabá (ⓒ **55/ 65/624-0960**)

✈ Cuiabá in the north, Campo Grande in the south

🛏 $$$ **Araras Eco Lodge,** Transpantaeira Hwy. (© **55/65/682-2800;** www.araraslodge.com.br). $$$ **Refugio Caiman,** near Miranda (© **55/11/3079-6622;** www.caiman.com.br).

**TOUR Pantanal Explorer,** for northern Pantanal excursions (© **55/65/682-2800;** www.araraslodge.com.br). **Open Door,** for southern Pantanal excursions (© **55/67/721-8303;** www.opendoortur.com.br).

## 12 One-of-a-Kind Landscapes

# Antarctica
## *The Frozen Continent*
### Antarctica

IN ANTARCTICA, GLOBAL WARMING IS RAISING SEA TEMPERATURES, MELTING SEA ICE, AND threatening marine life and four penguin species by destroying habitat and disrupting the food chain. Antarctica has also become an increasingly popular destination for cruise ships, and the resulting pollution is adding to the continent's woes.

Here at the literal bottom of the earth, be prepared for ice like you've never seen it. Monumental peacock-blue icebergs tower in surreal formations; craggy glaciers drop crashing chunks into the sea. Narrow canals knife between sheer ice-encrusted walls, and jagged peaks jut out of icy fields.

Antarctica has long exerted a magnetic pull on those who crave adventure. Mapmakers didn't even know it was a continuous continent until the 19th century. The first explorers only reached the South Pole in 1911, when Norwegian Roald Admunsen

reached the pole a scant 33 days ahead of rival British captain Robert Scott, whose party tragically died returning to their ship. Irish explorer Ernest Shackleton tried (and failed) to cross the continent 4 years later.

Unless you're a scientist posted to a research station, you'll most likely come to Antarctica these days on an expedition cruise (though a few travelers do book expensive air treks from Punta Arenas, Chile). Starting in the 1990s, when Russian research ships were retrofitted to bring the first leisure travelers here, Antarctica travel

Antarctica.

has grown exponentially, turning what used to be a rugged adventure trip into a luxury cruise. Nearly 40,000 travelers visited the region in the 2006–2007 season—and matters may have reached a tipping point. While the first tour ships were svelte icebreakers, ever larger cruise ships now shoulder through the region's unpredictable ice floes. The sinking of the Canadian vessel M/S *Explorer* in November 2007 underscored the importance of limiting Antarctic travel before too many ships jostle around Antarctica's seas, releasing fuel and waste into the water and negatively impacting the very wildlife that the passengers have paid so much to observe.

Ice covers more than 98% of the continent year-round, but it can only be visited in summer (Nov–Mar) when the surrounding sea ice melts enough to let ships reach the landmass. Itineraries vary in length, depending on which subantarctic islands are included en route to the Antarctic Peninsula (all tours include the wildlife-rich South Shetland Islands). Longer tours may venture inside the polar circle or circle around to the iceberg alleys of the continent's west side.

On those long polar days, passengers are diverted with natural-history lectures and shore excursions. One day you may scuba dive, scale a frozen peak, or kayak through calving ice; the next you may observe penguins, seals, or whales, or soak in thermal springs. Bird-watchers spend hours training their binoculars on a variety of unique seabirds, including petrels and albatrosses.

It's an ethical dilemma: Join the swelling ranks of cruisers, or pass up the chance to experience this icebound Eden. By choosing a responsible tour operator, and then supporting measures to regulate Antarctic routes more tightly, you just may be able to have your ice cream and eat it too.

ⓘ www.70south.com, www.antarctic connection.com

✈ Ushuaia, Argentina

**TOUR Polar Cruises** (ⓒ **888/484-2244**; www.polarcruises.com). **Lindblad Expeditions** (ⓒ **800/397-3348** or 212/765-7740; www.expeditions.com). **Quark Expeditions** (ⓒ **800/356-5699** or 203/656-0499; www.quarkexpeditions.com). **Adventure Network International** (ⓒ **866/395-6664** or 561/347-7523; www.adventure-network.com).

## One-of-a-Kind Landscapes  13

# Uluru–Kata Tjuta National Park
## *A Sacrilege at the Sacred Red Rocks*
### Northern Territory, Australia

THE ULURU–KATA TJUTA NATIONAL PARK IS ONE OF THE MOST SIGNIFICANT ARID-LAND ecosystems in the world. The park attracts hundreds of thousands of visitors every year, but while increasing tourism helps the regional economy, it also presents an ongoing challenge of how to balance conservation of the natural landscape and cultural values with the needs of tourists.

The native Anangu call tourists *minga*— little ants—because that's what they look like, crawling up the red sandstone flanks of Uluru, central Australia's most storied monolith. Despite often-ferocious winds and withering heat, some visitors still feel compelled to spend 2 to 4 hours scrambling up the great rock. Yes, the views from the top are impressive, but the tourists are committing sacrilege: Uluru is a sacred spot in the Tjukurpa/Wapar belief system. Even more sacred is Kata Tjuta ("Many Heads"), 36 momentous red domes bulging out of the earth 50km (31 miles) to the west.

Anangu leaders have reestablished the historic names Uluru (instead of the colonial name Ayers Rock) and Kata Tjuta (instead of the Olgas), but they haven't banned either rock climbers or sightseeing flights over Uluru—they simply request climbers to refrain from violating the sacred site. Focused on scaling the rock, climbers rarely take time to experience the monolith's richness—the wildlife that thrives in the potholes and overhangs of the red rock surface, the little coves hiding water holes and Aboriginal rock art. But you can see all this on a paved 9.7km (6-mile) **Base Walk** around Uluru, or an easy 1km (.5-mile) round-trip loop from the **Mutitjulu** parking lot. Even better is the free daily 90-minute **Mala Walk** with a ranger—often an Aborigine—who can explain the significance of the rock art and the Creation narrative related to Uluru. It's no coincidence that this hike is named after the mala, or rufous hare-wallabies; the Anangu consider them important ancestral guardians, and recently an enclosure has been built nearby in the park for a group of ranger-bred mala. Extinct in the wild, the species are to be reintroduced to a landscape they haven't inhabited since the mid-1900s.

Though it looks like a giant meteorite, Uluru did not fall from the sky; it is a mass of hardened sediment heaved upward from the floor of an ancient inland sea. The same seismic forces created the domes of Kata Tjuta, but their conglomerate rock yielded far more dramatically to the sculpting power of rain and temperature. At Kata Tjuta, there are two routes winding through the other-worldly domes: the 7.4km (4.5-mile) **Valley of the Winds** walk or an easy 2.4km (1.5-mile) **Gorge** walk.

Just gazing upon Uluru should be enough—there's something undeniably spiritual in its massive shape, heaving powerfully upward from the dunes, changing color dramatically depending on the slant of the sun. The best time to visit is sunset, when gaudy oranges, peaches, pinks, reds, and then indigo and deep violet creep across its face as if it were a giant opal. But there's something to be said, too, for experiencing the rosy spectacle of Uluru gradually unveiled by dawn, hailed by a chorus of twittering birdsong.

---

ⓘ **Uluru-Kata Tjuta Cultural Centre** (✆ **61/8/8956 3138**)

✈ Ayers Rock (Connellan) Airport

🛏 $$$ **Emu Walk Apartments,** Yulara Dr., Ayers Rock Resort (✆ **61/8/8957 7888;** www.voyages.com.au). $$ **Outback Pioneer Hotel and Lodge,** Yulara Dr., Ayers Rock Resort (✆ **61/8/8957 7888;** www.voyages.com.au).

---

**14** One-of-a-Kind Landscapes

# Purnululu National Park
## *The Kimberly's Striped Secret*
### The Kimberly, Western Australia

Purnululu National Park encompasses a landscape so culturally rich and geologically unique that protecting it is considered a national priority. Although the Australian government closely controls tourist access, the stark beauty of the Bungle Bungle Mountains has attracted more visitors every year to this pristine wilderness area, which puts the fragile environment at risk. When you go, tread lightly.

Rising out of the vast and lonely landscape of the Kimberly, the Bungle Bungle Mountains are so stunning, it's a wonder that they aren't on everybody's must-see list. Yet their very existence wasn't even known until the early 1980s—that's how rarely people travel to this sparsely inhabited, forgotten corner of Western Australia.

But perhaps that's why these fragile sandstone marvels have held up so well. Soon after they were discovered, this national park was created to protect them. It's promptly closed every year during the January to March rainy season, known here simply as the Wet, and in the dry season, the only access is by four-wheel-drive vehicles. The park has a rich repository of Aboriginal art and burial sites, but they're kept off limits to casual visitors. Purnululu's park management—a joint effort by white Australians and the local Aboriginal people—has evidently benefited from the mistakes other, older parks have made in managing their natural wonders. Let's hope they got it right this time.

Geologists get excited talking about this unique range of sandstone domes (*purnululu* means "sandstone" in the local language). They're rare examples of cone karst formations made of sandstone rather than limestone, heaved up from the floor of an ancient sea. Etched by erosion into filigreed beehives, they're also vividly striped in contrasting orange and gray bands by ancient algae trapped inside the permeable stone. (Layers of sandstone containing more clay attracted bacteria that colored that stone orange.) The domes rise 200 to 300m (650–1,000 ft.) high, and cover an area of 45,000 hectares (111,150 acres), punctuated by knifelike gorges and palm-draped pools.

The domes look spectacular from the air—that's the way most people see them, on 2-hour sightseeing flights from Kununurra. In fact, during the Wet, a plane is your only option. Once the waters subside, however, hikers take over the park, heading for spectacular Cathedral Gorge, the rock pool at Frog Hole Gorge, and palm-filled Echidna Chasm. Stark as the landscape looks from the air, on foot you'll find it's full of wildlife, particularly birds (rainbow bee-eaters, budgerigars), the rare nail-tailed wallaby, and a kangaroo cousin known as the euro. For all the effort it takes to get here, the rewards are spectacular.

ⓘ Visitor center (✆ **61/8/9168 7300**)

✈ Kununurra

🛏 $$ **Bungle Bungle Wilderness Lodge,** Purnululu National Park (✆ **61/1800/ 889 389** or 61/3/9277 8555; www.kimberly wilderness.com.au). $$$ **El Questro Homestead,** Gibb River Rd, Accor (✆ **61/1300/ 65 65 65,** or 800/221-4542 in the U.S. and Canada; www.elquestro.com.au). **Country Club Hotel,** 47 Coolibah Dr., Kununurra (✆ **61/1800/808 999** or 68/9168 1024; www.countryclubhotel.com.au).

**TOUR East Kimberly Tours** (✆ **61/88/ 9168 2213;** www.eastkimberleytours. com.au). **Slingair Heliwork** (✆ **61/1800/ 095 500** or 61/08/9169 1300). **Alligator Airways** (✆ **61/1800/632 533** or 61/8/9168 1333).

Islands 15

# The Galápagos Islands
## *Nature's Laboratory*
### Offshore Ecuador

LEGIONS OF TOURISTS WHO VISIT THE GALÁPAGOS EACH YEAR HAVE HELPED AND HURT THE islands' delicate ecosystem. But despite laws to protect the Galápagos, increased land and sea tourism, population growth (which brings pollution and habitat destruction), and invasive species continue to threaten the wildlife here. Fishing and poaching also threaten the survival of native marine life.

Sea lions on the Galápagos.

Everybody knows the Galápagos, thanks to Charles Darwin. Ever since that upstart English scientist visited in 1835 as a ship's doctor—or at least ever since he described its incredible wildlife in his 1859 book *On the Origin of Species*—this isolated Pacific archipelago has been famous for its natural wonders. If it hadn't been for their extreme location, 966km (600 miles) off the west coast of Ecuador, mass tourism would have spoiled the islands years ago.

Well, don't speak too soon. Tourism has become Ecuador's fourth-largest industry and the Galápagos its most popular tourist draw by far, with the number of tourists mounting by 12% a year. Immigrant workers have smuggled in goats and pigs that compete with native species for food; invader rats come ashore with cruise ships. The sleepy main town, Puerto Ayora, is rife with trendy hotels and restaurants. Visitors are often a new breed of tourist, zipping around in pick-up trucks madly snapping photos of everything they see. Ecuador's president has declared the islands at risk and may put a cap on the number of visitors (expect prices to rise if that happens). The pristine Galápagos wildlife experience may already be a thing of the past.

What's most remarkable about Galápagos's wildlife is how little they fear humans—and why would they, since they've never had to worry about predators. Young sea lions will show off their best moves as you snorkel among them; mockingbirds will peck at your shoelaces; the blue-footed boobie will perform its famous two-stepped mating dance right under your nose.

An astounding number of unique species thrive on these 19 small volcanic islands (plus about 40 islets); boat travel is essential to view them all. At the **Darwin Research Station** in Puerto Ayora (© **593/5/526146**) on Santa Cruz, the most populated island, visitors can get an up-close view of the gentle giant tortoises that have captured public imagination ever since Darwin first wrote about them. Santiago's rocky tide pools are home to rare fur sea lions and many beautiful heron species; Española has albatrosses and blue-footed boobies; in Fernandina there are vivid marine iguanas and flightless cormorants; Isabela is home to Galápagos's penguins (the world's only tropical penguins); Genovesa has frigate birds and red-footed boobies; and San Cristobal is where California sea lions, red crabs, and lava gulls reside.

Taking a cruise to the Galápagos is a popular option—departing from Guayaquil, you'll sleep and dine on the cruise boat and take small dinghies to the islands by day for naturalist-led hikes, climbs, kayak trips, or snorkel outings to the best wildlife viewing spots. But choose your tour operator with care, if you want an eco-conscious wildlife visit. And don't put it off, or it just may be too late.

---

ⓘ **Galápagos Islands National Park,** Ecuador (© **593/5/526-189**)

✈ Baltra (near Santa Cruz Island)

🛏 $$$ **Royal Palm Hotel,** Via Baltra Km 18, Isla Santa Cruz (© **800/528-6069** in U.S. or 593/5/5527-409; www.royalpalmhotel.net). $$ **Finch Bay Hotel,** Pinta Estrada, Island Santa Cruz (© **593/5/5526-297**; finchbayhotel@spsinter.net).

**TOUR** **Ecoventura,** 6404 Blue Lagoon Dr., Miami (© **800/633-7972**). **KLEIN Tours,** Av. Eloy Alfaro and Caralina Aldaz, Quito, Ecuador (© **888/50-KLEIN** [505-5346] in the U.S.; www.kleintours.com).

# Madagascar
## *Land of the Lemurs*
### Island of Madagascar

For generations, the practice of slashing and burning forest land has been an accepted way for impoverished locals to create farmland and feed their families. But this practice has decimated Madagascar's interior forests, and the tropical rainforest is quickly disappearing. The resulting loss of habitat threatens many of Madagascar's unique wildlife species, and some are already gone.

Fourth-largest island in the world? That's impressive to start with. But now consider that a hefty 5% of the world's species live on this Indian Ocean island, off Africa's east coast—and nearly 75% of those species live nowhere else. That's why Madagascar is such a vital destination for any nature lover.

You'll see the glorious yellow comet moth with its 20cm (8-in.) tail, the sticky-pawed tomato frog, neon-green day geckoes, petite chameleons less than an inch long, spiny insect-gobbling tenrecs, and leathery-winged flying foxes. Though Madagascar has only 258 bird species, nearly half of them are also unique to the island, including the pheasantlike ground birds known as couias. The only amphibians here are frogs—but there are 300 species of them, nearly all endemic.

Lemurs of Madagascar.

Madagascar has cornered the market on lemurs; no other country has any lemurs whatsoever. In Madagascar, though, lemurs seem to drip from the trees, both in the rainforest and the western dry forest. They come in all shapes and color and sizes, resembling pandas, raccoons, monkeys, rats, bats, whatever you can imagine. It's truly mind boggling.

But like many other undeveloped countries, Madagascar has seen wide deforestation and the ravages of slash-and-burn agriculture (coffee, sugar cane, and vanilla are its main exports). The interior's dense woods have mostly been leveled, and the tropical rainforest areas are rapidly following suit. With their habitats reduced, those one-of-kind species are increasingly endangered. Several species have already been lost due to human depredation—pygmy hippos, the stately elephant bird, giant tortoises, and lemurs. Now here's the good news: President Marc Ravalomanana has been turning the tide with new aggressive conservation programs. By investing half of park entrance fees back into local communities, he's giving natives a direct economic incentive to protect the environment, to attract eco-tourism revenues. The world watches hopefully.

Andasibe-Mantadia National Park, a 3-hour drive from the country's capital Antananarivo, is the most accessible wildlife preserve, known especially for the black-and-white lemur called the indri, whose cry sounds uncannily like a whale song. Farther south along Route 7 lies the country's most developed rainforest park, Ranomafana (60km/37 miles from Fianarantosa), a romantic terrain of rocky slopes, waterfalls, and moss-draped trees. Continue south for L'Isalo National Park, where you can hike around tapia forests, narrow canyons, and sheer sandstone crags. On the east coast near Morondava you can gape at the Avenue of the Baobabs, a remarkable collection of those upside-down tropical trees, another of Madagascar's specialties.

Even if you're normally a go-it-alone traveler, it's advisable to take an organized tour to Madagascar, especially if you want to move around the countryside. Local roads are spotty at best, and booking hotels can be a gamble. You'll need local guides, anyway—how else will you tell all the different lemurs apart?

✈ Antananrivo

**TOUR Madagascar Travel** (✆ **44/20 7226 1004** in the U.K.; www.madagascar-travel.net). **Ilay Tours** (✆ **33 1 55 46 85 95** in France or 20 22 390 35; http://madagascar ilaytours.com).

---

**17** Islands

# Kangaroo Island
## *The Purity of Island Living*
### South Australia

NATIVE ANIMAL SPECIES PROLIFERATE IN KANGAROO ISLAND'S UNIQUE, SELF-CONTAINED environment with its lack of natural predators. But Kangaroo Island has a fragile balance that must be protected. Koalas, not native to the island, were introduced in the 1920s and the population is thriving, threatening native gum trees and destroying the habitats of endangered birds.

To understand the virtues of island isolation, look no further than Kangaroo Island. Lying just across the strait from metropolitan Adelaide, this Southern Hemisphere ecosystem flourishes in a miraculously unspoiled state. No foxes or rabbits were

A Kangaroo Island koala.

ever introduced to prey on the island's inhabitants—the koalas, kangaroos, and wallabies that are Australia's iconic wildlife. (The kangaroos here, however, are a distinct species from the mainland's.) The island was also never colonized by the dingo, Australia's "native" dog that's really a feral scavenger introduced from Asia some 4,000 years ago. Even along the roadsides, the underbrush is mostly native eucalypt scrub.

To preserve all this, strict regulations monitor what visitors bring on and off the island. Tourists are asked to wash the soil off their shoes and car tires to prevent the spread of fungus. Bushwalkers are required to stay on marked paths and not to feed the wildlife; drivers are encouraged to drive slowly, especially at dusk, when koalas, echidnas, bandicoots, and kangaroos may wander onto the roads.

Of the many preserves on the island (about one third of the island is conservation area), you'll score the most wildlife

sightings at **Flinders Chase National Park** on the western end of the island. Birders have recorded at least 243 species here, including the endangered glossy black cockatoo; koalas are so common they're almost falling out of the trees (the government has in fact had to take steps to reduce the koala population). Kangaroos, wallabies, and brush-tailed possums are so tame that a barrier was erected around the Rocky River Campground to stop them from carrying away picnickers' sandwiches. Platypuses have been sighted, too, but they're elusive—you might need to wait next to a stream in the dark for a few hours.

At Cape du Couedic, the southern tip of the park, the hollowed-out limestone promontory called Admiral's Arch is home to a colony of some 4,000 New Zealand fur seals (despite the name, a legitimately native species). Rangers at the southern coast's **Seal Bay Conservation Park** (✆ 61/8/8559 4207) lead guided tours along boardwalks through the dunes to a beach where you can hobnob with Australian sea lions.

Up on the north coast, **Lathami Conservation Park,** just east of Stokes Bay, is a superb place to spot wallabies in the low canopy of casuarina pines. If you want to see little penguins—tiny animals that stand about a foot high—the **National Parks & Wildlife South Australia** (✆ 61/8/8553 2381) conducts tours of their colonies around Nepean Bay at both Kingscote and Penneshaw. Last but not least, **Clifford's Honey Farm** (✆ 61/8/8553 8295) is the home of the protected Ligurian honeybee, found nowhere else on earth but on this seemingly magical island.

ⓘ **Tourism Kangaroo Island,** Howard Dr., Penneshaw (✆ 61/8/8553 1185; www.tourkangarooisland.com.au)

✈ Kangaroo Island

🛏 $$$ **Ozone Seafront Hotel,** The Foreshore, Kingscote (✆ 61/8/8553 2011; www.ozonehotel.com). $$ **Kangaroo Island Lodge,** Scenic Rd., American River (✆ 61/8/8553 7053; www.kilodge.com.au).

# Iceland
## *World of Fire & Ice*
Landmannalaugar, Iceland

WITH MORE THAN 200 ACTIVE VOLCANOES, ICELAND IS ONE OF THE MOST VOLCANICALLY active countries in the world. In some areas, basaltic sandy beaches, which result from volcanic eruption, threaten to overrun green areas, and wind erosion affects native habitats. Overgrazing, once a serious problem, is now somewhat controlled, and many landscapes have returned to their green origins.

When you get off the plane at Keflavik Airport, it's clear right away: You've entered another world. Steam whiffs out of cracks in the treeless basalt plain; the air has a definite sulphuric tang. Iceland is perched right on a geologic hot spot, with its active geysers of the Atlantic shifting and reshaping its stony terrain. As recently as the late 18th century, an eruption wiped out a quarter of the population. Talk about sitting in the hot seat.

Nowhere is this geothermal instability more striking than in the central highlands of Iceland. It's like a world that is still being created—a world of shapes and colors you've only seen in dreams. The earth steams and bubbles; conical volcanoes rise like islands in a sea of black sand. Twisted lava, cracked and cooled in a thousand grotesque shapes, seems to have eyes that follow you wherever you go. It's a landscape so lunar, NASA astronauts trained here in preparation for landing on the moon. And of the many awesome spots in Iceland's unearthly interior, none is more spectacular than the hot springs of Landmannalaugar.

One-day bus trips roll out from Reykjavik in summer to Landmannalaugar, quickie excursions that leave time for nothing but a look around and a brief dip in the bathtub-warm natural thermal pools. Yet one look at the nearby mountains, undulating like folds of silk and tinted with rare mineral colors—blues, yellows, bright reds, even shocking pink—and you'll itch to explore them. So give yourselves time to hike into those bewitching mountains, along the marked trails of the surrounding Fjallabak Nature Reserve, staying overnight at one of the mountain huts run by the Iceland Touring Association (Ferdafélag Islands). In July and August they book up far in advance, so plan accordingly.

If you're up for more than short forays, try the 3- to 4-day walk from Landmannalaugar to Þórsmörk, sleeping in mountain huts along the route. It's the premier hike in Iceland, through a stark terrain of snow, ice, and rock. At the far end, the designated nature reserve of Þórsmörk is a welcome contrast, a softer landscape with woods and grass nestling among mountains and glaciers. Ah, that's the magic of Iceland.

---

ⓘ **Icelandic Tourist Board** (✆ 212/885-9700; www.visiticeland.com)

✈ Reykjavik

# Wrangel Island Reserve
## *Arctic Circle Refuge*
### Chukchi Sea, Russia

HUNTING ALMOST DECIMATED THE SNOW GOOSE POPULATION AND THREATENED POLAR BEAR mothers and cubs. Imported reindeer herds have thrived but have trampled delicate summer vegetation. Along with global warming, which threatens the icy habitat of polar bears and other species, the area's military base, mining operations, and scientific facilities also endanger the reserve.

Northwest of the Bering Strait, the arctic winters are long, and I mean loooooong. For 2 months, from November 22 to January 22, the sun never rises at all. A lonely landmass in the Chukchi Sea, Wrangel Island lies shrouded in snow until June, an icy wind moaning overhead.

And yet the sun does return every spring, and when it does, it's miraculous. Tens of thousands of migratory birds—black-legged kittiwakes, pelagic cormorants, glaucous gulls—arrive to nest on the jagged cliffs. Ringed seals and bearded seals dip their snouts through holes in the ice, hungry for fish. Walruses lumber out onto narrow spits to give birth. Female polar bears emerge drowsily from their winter dens, newborn cubs snuffling in their wake. Arctic foxes scavenge the rocky beaches, where snowy owls swoop down on unsuspecting lemmings.

A few months later, in the summer, the tundra teems with life. Rivers, swelled with snowmelt, gush through the narrow valleys, and the last remaining Russian population of snow geese paddles around glacial lakes in the island's interior. Brilliantly colored arctic wildflowers mantle the slopes in shades of pink and yellow.

Shaggy musk oxen browse sedges and grasses of the ancient tundra, a relic of the Ice Age. The walruses bask on ice floes and rocky spits, going through their annual breeding rituals. It's a sight to see—but very few travelers ever get the chance.

Located 193km (120 miles) off the coast of Siberia, right on the 180-degree line that divides the Western and Eastern hemispheres, Wrangel Island became a nature reserve (or *zapovednik*) in 1976 to protect the delicate arctic ecosystem, in particular the snow geese and polar bear, which were being hunted to death. There are no lodgings on the island—a small research island is the only habitation—so the only way to visit is on a ship (and an icebreaker at that), with smaller craft for shore visits. On your way through the Bering Strait, you'll also have a good chance of sighting minke, gray, and even beluga whales. These are long, expensive, summer-only expeditions, and few companies run them—if you see one offered (there was one in June–July 2008), jump on it.

---

**TOUR Polar Cruises** (✆ **888/484-2244** or 541/330-2454; www.polarcruises.com)

# Fraser Island
## *Rainforest on the Dunes*
### Queensland, Australia

WITH LITTLE AGRICULTURAL DEVELOPMENT AND A CAREFULLY MANAGED ECO-TOURISM business, Fraser Island has escaped some of the problems that plague other nature preserves. The island's biggest threats are animal and plant predators, which have migrated on their own or were introduced by people. Cane toads, rodents, and non-native weeds are among the serious threats to this ecosystem's delicate balance.

Sand is just sand, right? Well, Fraser Island may change your mind about that. Lying just south of the Great Barrier Reef, this is the world's biggest sand island, an ecological marvel where ancient eucalyptus rainforest actually grows out of the dunes. With dunes as high as 240m (787 ft.), and gorgeous ocher-colored cliffs dramatically sculpted by erosion, it's a unique ecosystem—and still evolving, with strong southeasterly winds visibly shifting the dunes a couple meters every year.

With no towns and few facilities, apart from low-profile eco-tourism resorts, Fraser Island is maintained as a no-frills destination for folks who love wildlife better than the wild life. It's a place for camping out, bird-watching, and bush walking through eucalyptus woods and low-lying "wallum" heaths that offer a spectacular wildflower display every spring and summer. Its fringing wetlands feature pristine mangrove colonies, seagrass beds, and up to 40,000 shorebirds, an important migratory rest stop on the route to Siberia. Rare, vulnerable, or endangered species include dugongs, turtles, Illidge's ant-blue butterflies, and eastern curlews; possums and swamp wallabies thrive in its swamps. Some 354 different species of birds have been recorded here, including the rare ground parrot, easily spotted in the heathlands.

It's also a place for swimming, with more than 100 little freshwater lakes dotting the island's interior, ringed with dazzling white sand that's pure silica. Some, like brilliant blue Lake McKenzie, sprang up when water filled hardened hollows in the dunes; others, like emerald-green Lake Wabby, were created when shifting dunes dammed up a stream. The astonishing purity of these inland waters (the major pollution source is tourists' sunscreen) ironically make them a poor environment for fish.

At 75-Mile Beach, a surf-pounded Pacific beach running the length of the island, treacherous offshore currents and shoals full of sharks make it a risky swimming spot, but the rippling sand here is as hard-packed as cement, making it ideal for

Fraser Island's *Maheno* shipwreck.

driving four-wheel-drive vehicles (the only cars allowed on this island) and for landing small sightseeing planes. A rusted wrecked luxury steamship, the *Maheno*, sits right on the beach, which you can explore—a rare chance for nondivers to see a shipwreck up close. At the northern end of the beach, you can dip into the ocean in the spalike bubbling waters of the Champagne Pools (also called the Aquarium for their tide-pool marine life), shallow pockets of soft sand protected from the waves by a natural rock barrier.

From August through October, Fraser Island is one of Australia's best sites for seeing humpback whales returning to Antarctica with their calves in tow (book whale-watch tours, as well as dolphin- or manatee-spotting tours, from local resorts). Dingos run wild here, one of the purest populations anywhere—what's more Australian than that?

---

ⓘ **Fraser Island,** Australia (www.fraser island.net)

✈ Hervey Bay

🛏 $$$ **Kingfisher Bay Resort,** west coast (✆ **61/1800/072 555** or 61/7/4120 3333; www.kingfisherbay.com). $$ **Fraser Island Retreat,** Happy Valley (✆ **61/7/ 4127 9144;** www.fraserislandco.com.au).

## Islands 21

# Bali
## *Trouble in Shangri-La*
### Indonesia

ONLY ABOUT 38% OF INDONESIA'S PRISTINE FORESTS REMAIN, AND MUCH OF THE DESTRUCTION has taken place in the past few years due to wholesale burning by businesses and locals to create farmland and make charcoal. Peat-bog burning, to make room for palm oil farms, releases thousands of tons of carbon dioxide into the atmosphere.

What a canny choice of location for the December 2007 U.N.-sponsored conference on global warming. White sand beaches, sparkling blue seas, lush gardens, and a wide assortment of luxury resorts—a perfect setting for those environmental delegates, for if they began to get depressed about the fate of the planet, all they had to do was look out the window and they'd feel just fine.

Bali seems to have it all—exotic Southeast Asian culture, tropical Pacific natural beauty, and a tourism infrastructure that can coddle even the most finicky Western travelers. But on closer inspection, Bali also has degraded offshore coral reefs, a deforested interior, waterways polluted and clogged by plastic waste, and a location right in prime tsunami territory, at the mercy of rising oceans. The December 2004 tsunami that laid waste to Sumatra and southern Thailand could just have easily have swept over Bali, which lies close to the same fault line. The government is finally addressing its internal issues, with aggressive measures to promote recycling and to reclaim damaged mangrove stands and upland forests. But when it comes to global warming, the problems require international action—it's more than one little Indonesian Shangri-La can solve on its own. Unfortunately, if action isn't taken soon, destinations like Bali will pay the price first.

It's not as if the resort developers haven't discovered Bali. You can stay at a five-star property in the manicured beach resort enclave of Nusa Dua and have no idea that you're in a foreign country at all. But stay inland instead in the town of Ubud and you'll have more contact with the Balinese people, as well as a better sense of the island's volcanic topography. River rafting on the Ayung River, through phosphorescent rice paddies and deep-cut jungle gorges, is one tempting option; day hikes to neighboring villages and into the hills are also popular. Animal lovers may want to visit **Elephant Safari Park,** Jalan Bypass Ngurah Rai, Pesanggaran (✆ **361/ 721480**) or **Monkey Forest** (at the end of Monkey Forest Rd., naturally), although both attractions are a bit zoolike and hokey; even better, try a bird-watching walk with **naturalist Victor Mason** (✆ **361/ 975009** or 812/3913801) to study some of Bali's 100 tropical species.

Day trips to the active volcanoes of Gunung Agung and/or Gunung Batur give a fascinating insight into this region's geothermal instability. Ubud's also within handy distance of resortlike activities such as surfing at Kuta or lolling on the wide beach at Jimbaran Bay. After all, what's the point of visiting Shangri-La without at least a little hedonism?

ⓘ www.bali-paradise.com. www.indo. com. www.baliguide.com.

✈ Ngurah Rai

🛏 $$$ **Maya Ubud,** Gulung Sari Peliatan, Ubud (✆ **62/361/977888;** www. mayaubud.com). $$ **Alam Sari,** Keliki, Tromoi Pos 03, Kantor Pos Tegallalang, Ubud (✆ **62/361/240308;** www.alamsari. com).

**TOUR Bali Adventure Tours** (✆ **62/361/ 721480;** www.baliadventuretours.com)

---

**22** Islands

# The Falkland Islands
## *Penguin Paradise*
### Off the Coast of Argentina

Sᴇᴡᴀɢᴇ ᴀɴᴅ ɢᴀʀʙᴀɢᴇ ᴅᴜᴍᴘᴇᴅ ʙʏ ʟᴏᴄᴀʟ sᴀɴɪᴛᴀᴛɪᴏɴ ᴄᴏᴍᴘᴀɴɪᴇs, ᴛʜᴇ sʜɪᴘᴘɪɴɢ ɪɴᴅᴜsᴛʀʏ, and fishing boats threaten marine life in the Falkland Islands. Penguin, elephant seal, and sea lion populations have declined and are increasingly vulnerable to pollution, discarded fishing equipment, and oil slicks; they often either ingest or become entangled in plastic rope, soda can holders, and plastic bottles.

Say "Falkland Islands" and most folks will recall late-night comedians joking over Argentina's quixotic 1982 invasion of this virtually unknown British possession. But say "Falkland Islands" to an ornithologist and he'll see something way different: a sunny vision of penguins, seals, and albatrosses, frolicking on unspoiled rocky islands.

Sketch in an image of offshore oil rigs, though, and it's a darker picture indeed. One of the reasons Britain fought to retain this offshore territory was the promise of oil here, 482km (300 miles) off Argentina's Atlantic coast. As plans to develop that oil proceed apace, environmentalists scramble to assess the impact on the islands' extraordinary wildlife. One thing is sure: It won't be good.

Often lumped into an Antarctic cruise itinerary (see Antarctica, p. 17), the Falklands—also known as the Malvinas—deserve a visit on their own merits. Individual tourists (and there aren't many) can fly in from Santiago, Chile, though there is also a weekly RAF charter from the U.K. Instead of daredevil glacier climbing, Falklands visitors enjoy more contemplative pursuits such as photography, birding, cross-country tramping, and trout fishing. Penguins are the stars of the show, with no fewer than five varieties colonizing the islands' white sandy beaches: gentoo (chinstrap), Magellanic (jackass), macaroni, rockhopper, and king penguins. Sea lions, fur seals, and elephant seals hide in the tall tussock grass, alongside tiny spiky tussock birds; rare seabirds such as the black-browed albatross, the giant petrel, and the striated caracara (known here as the Johnny rook) roost on tiny rocky sanctuaries scattered around the two main islands. Local tour companies will help you organize the 4WD vehicles or small planes you may need to reach the more remote wildlife spots.

The Falklands have their own defiantly unglitzy charm, the no-nonsense air of a distant outpost where the settlers simply soldier on. Residents cling to a sense of empire, with the Union Jack proudly on display; the port town of Stanley has a Victorian air, though most houses sport gaily colored tin roofs that look more like Reykjavik than Dover. Southerly as they are, the Falklands are still in the temperate zone, with temperatures similar to London's; even in the depths of winter the sun shines at least 6 hours a day. The landscape is a scrubby, hardy terrain of eroded peat and rocky scree, where dwarf shrubs stand in for trees. But those penguins, they think the island is paradise—and naturalists would like to keep it that way.

ⓘ **Falkland Islands Tourist Board** (✆ **500/22215;** www.visitorfalklands.com)

✈ Mount Pleasant

🛏 $$ **Malvina House Hotel,** 3 Ross Rd., Stanley (✆ **500/21355**). $$ **Upland Goose Hotel,** 22 Ross Rd., Stanley (✆ **500/21455**).

**TOUR** **Falkland Islands Holidays** (✆ **500/22622;** www.falklandislandsholidays.com). **International Tours and Travel** (✆ **500/22041;** www.falklandstravel.com). **Polar Cruises** (✆ **888/484-2244;** www.polarcruises.com).

---

Islands **23**

# Assateague Island
## *Do the Pony on the Eastern Shore*
### Eastern Shore, Maryland & Virginia

MOST OF THE PROBLEMS FACING ASSATEAGUE ISLAND ARE MAN-MADE: POPULATION GROWTH in neighboring areas, which affects water quality, marine life, and vegetation in the bay and ocean; threats from recreational boaters and clam fishermen; and jetties that inhibit the natural flow of sediment.

Legend has it that the ponies swam ashore from a shipwrecked Spanish galleon centuries ago, washing up on this barrier island off of Virginia's Eastern Shore. The truth may be a little more prosaic; more likely they were put there in the late 1600s by English settlers who found the island a natural corral, but at this point it hardly matters. They're shaggy, sturdy little wild horses, running free on this one narrow barrier island. How cool is that?

*Misty of Chincoteague* was one of my favorite books as a child—it's practically required reading for any girl in her "horse phase"—and as every Misty-lover knows, they may be called Chincoteague ponies but they are really from Assateague Island. Neighboring Chincoteague Island comes into the picture because every July, Chincoteague townsfolk row over to uninhabited Assateague, round up the tough feral ponies, make them swim across the narrow channel separating the two islands, and sell the foals to raise money for the local fire department.

Assateague ponies.

But 37-mile-long (60km) Assateague is also a prime Atlantic flyway habitat where peregrine falcons, snow geese, great blue heron, and snowy egrets have been sighted. Dolphins swim off shore; bald eagles soar overhead. Like most of the Eastern Shore, it's a tranquil, wind-ruffled shoreland with a lot of wildlife refuges and weather-beaten charm. Lying close to heavily populated areas, however, its delicate coastal environment is threatened by recreational boating, commercial clam fishery, and agricultural runoff pollution. Every year the island moves closer to the mainland, as its oceanward beaches erode and sediment fills in the landward shore.

A causeway connects Chincoteague to the mainland, and another causeway leads to Assateague, though a strict quota system controls the number of cars on Assateague at any one time. Since the island lies partly in Maryland, partly in Virginia, half of the horses live in a state park on the Maryland side, while the other half live in Virginia's national wildlife refuge. It's the herd from this refuge that supplies ponies for the annual Chincoteague roundup, which sustains the herd at a manageable size; the Maryland herd, unculled, exerts constant pressure on its marshy grazing lands.

Wildlife cruises operate from either Chincoteague or nearby Ocean City, Maryland, taking visitors to explore the coasts of the island. Narrated bus tours also run along a paved 4¹/₂-mile (7.2km) Wildlife Drive through the marshes of the Chincoteague refuge (you can also walk or cycle along the road, or drive your own car after 3pm). At the end of the main road, you come to the Assateague National Seashore, a pristine beach with bathhouses, lifeguards, and a visitor center. It's a great place to settle on the sand, feel the wind in your face, and imagine the ghost of a wrecked Spanish galleon.

ⓘ **Chincoteague National Wildlife Refuge,** Assateague Island, VA (✆ 757/336-3696; www.nps.gov/asis)

✈ Norfolk

🛏 $$$ **Island Motor Inn Resort,** 4391 N. Main St., Chincoteague (✆ **757/336-3141;** www.islandmotorinn.com). $$ **Refuge Inn,** 7058 Maddox Blvd., Chincoteague (✆ **888/868-6400** or 757/336-5511; www.refugeinn.com).

# The San Juan Islands
## *Nature's Patchwork Marvel in Puget Sound*
### Washington State

POPULATION GROWTH IN THE SAN JUAN ISLANDS HAS INCREASED GROUND AND WATER pollution, while legions of commercial and private whale-watchers disturb whales and other marine creatures. Overfishing and habitat destruction have severely limited (in some cases to extinction) wild runs of salmon, which force whales and other marine mammals to deplete local fish resources or leave the area to find food.

Standing on the deck of a Puget Sound ferryboat, gazing at the snowcapped peaks of the Olympic Peninsula, it seems odd to imagine the thickly strewn San Juan Islands surrounding your boat as mountain peaks themselves. But today this ancient range, submerged at the end of the last ice age, is simply dwarfed by those towering youngsters across the way.

Now here's the twist: The Olympic range casts what's called a "rainshadow" over the sound, blocking the rainfall that soaks most of the Northwest. As a result, the San Juan Islands are a rare mosaic of microclimates, some rainforest, some desert, often on the same islands. Here you'll find rare and endangered plants, such as the brittle cactus, the naked broomrape, and the golden paintbrush, alongside patches of ferns, mosses, and lichens, and old-growth forests of cedar, hemlock, yew, and alder. These tiny specialized habitats are often unrecognized, tucked away in crevices of coastal cliffs, in a patch of grassland or small stand of trees. They're not big enough to be marked as nature preserves—but they need to be preserved all the same.

The San Juan archipelago has 175 islands big enough to be given names; another 500 or so smaller outcroppings punctuate the waters in between, accessible only by boat. Ferries visit only four islands (San Juan, Orcas, Lopez, and Shaw), and only those first three have tourist accommodations. For years, the San Juans preserved unspoiled habitats, with approximately 83 islands designated wildlife refuges. The San Juans have the largest breeding population of bald eagles in the United States, and they're a magnet for migrating wildlife—not only orcas and minke whales (whale-watching expeditions set out from all the main harbors June–Sept), but also trumpeter swans, snow geese, and salmon. You're likely to spot dall porpoises, Steller sea lions, harbor seals, and brown river otters, too, especially if you venture around in a kayak.

Unfortunately, all this natural beauty may be the islands' undoing. The word is out, and San Juan County has attracted so many new residents, its population has almost tripled since 1990. As more and more homes are crowded onto the islands, less land is open to shelter those fragile microclimates. Alien species such as red foxes and rabbits overrun some islands, crowding out native species. An upsurge in tourism is also a problem, as more hikers tramp through its parks and venture too close to seabird-nesting areas or the rocky coves where harbor seals bask. The popularity of boating around these islands has begun to wreak havoc with its offshore eelgrass and kelp beds, so vital for sustaining marine life.

Visit the San Juan Islands if at all possible—but be the best sort of visitor you can. Stay on walking paths, observe beach closures, moor your boat only at designated sites, and deal with eco-conscious tour groups. It's the least a nature lover can do.

**25** Islands

# Isle Royale National Park
## *Lake Woods Wilderness by Design*
### Michigan

CLIMATE CHANGE HAS PUT ISLE ROYALE'S MOOSE AND WOLF POPULATIONS AT RISK. RISING summer temperatures and thriving ticks weaken moose and limit their appetite, making it harder for them to survive the harsh winters. Fewer moose mean less food for wolves. Air pollution, rising mercury levels in fish, and federal policies that divert funds away from restoration also contribute to a decline in this national landmark.

In most other national parks, you have to worry about whether the parking lot is full. At Isle Royale, you worry about low lake levels. If boats can't maneuver past Lake Superior's treacherous rocks, you just can't get here.

Inaccessibility is part of the deal at Isle Royale—that's why it's so unspoiled. This 45-mile-long (72km) island gets fewer visitors in an entire season than Yosemite may get in just 1 day. Since 1976 it's been a designated wilderness area, which specifies that 99% of the island must remain undeveloped, roadless backcountry; in 1980, it was designated an International Biosphere Reserve. There's an oasis of creature comforts at Rock Harbor, with its rustic resort hotel and limited services at a couple other ports around the island; only a few steps from those areas you plunge deep in Northwoods solitude.

Thick forests cover the island today, but that's deceptive; it's anything but virgin wilderness. Native Americans mined copper here since time immemorial; French fur trappers exploited its wealth of beaver; a 19th-century copper boom sank numerous

The rocky Isle Royale coast.

pits into its bedrock. Yet nature has a way of reclaiming its territory, and Isle Royale stands as a pristine example of how wilderness can be resurrected. These may be second-growth forests, but they're so dense and rich with wildlife, it doesn't matter. The predominant species used to be lynx and caribou, which are now extinct, but in their place Isle Royale has moose and wolves, introduced from the mainland—the only place in the world where these two populations coexist in such balance. Bears and raccoons, common on the nearest mainland, never arrived here, but mink, ermines, and otters, as well as the native red squirrel, thrive. Grebes and loon breed in its wetlands, while great horned owls, pileated woodpeckers, and yellow-bellied sapsuckers nest in the forest tops.

Glaciers left this outcropping of land—the largest island in the world's largest freshwater lake—pocked with lakes and bogs, carving ancient volcanic rock into one long jagged ridge along its spine. Canoes and kayaks can be rented at Rock Harbor or Windigo to explore the shoreline or penetrate the wilderness. Anglers fish in its teeming inland lakes; scuba divers scout out numerous wrecks off

shore, testament to Lake Superior's dangerous shoals. Park rangers lead daily walks ranging from bird-watching to visiting the many lighthouses that protect Isle Royale's shores.

Ferries run from Copper Harbor (the *Isle Royale,* ℂ **906/289-4437**) and Houghton, Michigan (the *Ranger III* icebreaker, ℂ **906/482-0984,** which can carry smaller boats); and Grand Portage, Minnesota (the *Voyageur II* and *Wenonah,* ℂ **888/746-2305** or 715/392-2100). Seaplanes can be booked out of Houghton, Michigan (Royale Air Service, ℂ **877/359-4753** or 218/721-0405; www.royaleairservice.com). These services, however, only run from late spring through early fall. The rest of the year, Isle Royale is left to the wolves and the moose—as it should be.

ⓘ **Isle Royale National Park,** 800 E. Lakeshore Dr., Houghton, MI (ℂ **906/482-0984;** www.nps.gov/isro)

⊨ $$$ **Rock Harbor Lodge,** Isle Royale National Park (ℂ **906/337-4993** in summer, ℂ 866/644-2003 in winter; www.rockharborlodge.com)

---

Islands  **26**

# Santa Catalina Island
## *Snorkeling for Dear Life*
### Southern California

DESPITE BEING BANNED DECADES AGO, TOXIC CHEMICALS THAT WERE DUMPED IN THE CHANNEL continue to contaminate the natural habitat of birds, fish, and mammals, and disrupt their ability to breed. Sewage pollution and climate change–related weather events have increased ocean temperatures and now threaten native food supplies.

When chewing-gum magnate William Wrigley, Jr., fell in love with Catalina Island in 1915, he did what any self-respecting tycoon would do: He built an Art Deco resort town and invited A-list friends like Laurel and Hardy, Cecil B. DeMille, John Wayne, and even Winston Churchill to enjoy it with him. But, luckily, Wrigley was

also a nature lover. Determined to preserve his own private Eden, he kept 88% of the island off limits to development.

Wrigley's forethought ensured that this little island, only 22 miles (35km) off the Southern California coast, would feel like another world from the Los Angeles metro sprawl. The elegant Art Deco and

Spanish-Mediterranean architecture of car-free Avalon, with its relaxed resort vibe, is nicely complemented by the well-preserved native Californian landscape of its rugged, hilly interior. In 1975 Wrigley's estate deeded most of the interior outright to the **Catalina Island Conservancy** (© 310/510-2595; www.catalinaconservancy.org), which has vigorously protected his legacy. But these days the conservancy has its hands full.

Sewage pollution, sea otter hunting, sea urchin grazing, and elevated temperatures caused by El Niño events have reduced the lush stands of giant kelp that make this one of the West Coast's best snorkeling sites. (Luckily, marine reserves had already been set up at **Lover's Cove, Casino Point, Toyon Bay,** and **Blue Cavern Point,** where the snorkeling is still superb.) There are too many mule deer—a non-native species introduced years ago as wild game—and not enough of the native foxes. Wildfire—an inescapable part of nature's cycle in Southern California—devastated 4,750 acres (1,922 hectares) of the island in May 2007. But the worst problem is much more intractable: 25 years of DDT and PCBs being dumped across the channel that separates it from Los Angeles. Though the dumping was stopped in the early 1970s, tons of DDT and PCBs still lie on the ocean floor off the Palos Verde peninsula. Artificial reefs have been created around the island to protect its fish, and conservancy naturalists zealously protect the nesting sites of native eagles. Whether they can turn the tide is still uncertain.

To get to Catalina, depart from either San Pedro or Long Beach on the **Catalina Express** ferryboat (© 800/481-3470; www.catalinaexpress.com) or **Island Express** helicopters (© 800/2-AVALON [228-2566]; www.islandexpress.com). Arriving in resortlike Avalon, the island's port and only town, be sure to visit the **Wrigley Botanical Garden** in Avalon (© 310/510-2288), which is like a mini-course in the botany of California's coastal islands. To explore the interior, you'll need to hike or mountain bike (Catalina stringently limits the number of cars on its roads), or take a 4-hour tour with **Discovery Tours** (© 800/626-1496; www.scico.com), which also runs underwater tours of the kelp forest and nighttime trips to observe flying fish. Don't be surprised if you see buffalo roaming the range, the offspring of a few movie-prop bison imported in 1929—just another of the quirks that makes Catalina so special.

(i) **Catalina Island Visitors Bureau,** Green Pleasure Pier, Avalon, CA (© 310/510-1520; www.catalina.com)

✈ Los Angeles International

🛏 $$ **Hotel Vista Del Mar,** 417 Crescent Ave. (© 310/510-1452; www.hotel-vistadelmar.com). $ **Hotel Catalina** (© 800/540-0184 or 310/510-0027).

---

**27** **Ecosystems in Transition**

# The Adirondacks
## *Getting Wet & Wild*
### Upper New York State

WHEN ADIRONDACK STATE PARK WAS CREATED IN 1892, THE STATE CONSTITUTION DECLARED its public lands would be "forever kept as wild forest land." Today, the park is interlaced by developed areas, heavily used by nature lovers, and under assault by non-native species, but area residents are working with conservation groups to keep its remaining wild areas pristine.

The Adirondacks.

Yes, the Adirondacks has several ski resorts and has hosted two Winter Olympic games. Yes, it has strips of motels and lakefronts crowded with vacation homes. But this New York State park covers 6 million acres (2.5 million hectares); there's plenty of room left for woods and wilderness. And the heart of the park are its lakes, some 3,000 lakes and ponds that are deliberately left inaccessible, connected not by highways but by 1,500 miles (2,414km) of rivers.

Naturally, it's difficult to police such a large water system. Inevitably, some recreational boat or piece of fishing gear will enter a lake bearing fragments of some invasive species, and it doesn't take much to set off an epidemic. Take, for example, the Eurasian watermilfoil, a scraggly herb which not only crowds out native species on the lake bottom, it can tangle boat propellers and trap swimmers. First spotted in Lake George, the watermilfoil has spread to more than 45 of the Adirondacks' over 3,000 lakes, including such jewels as Shroon Lake and Saranac Lake.

Adirondack residents are declaring war, doing everything from introducing grass carp (sterile ones that won't breed and create a new invasion) to stretching sheets of plastic over the watermilfoil beds to block out the sunlight they need to grow.

The best way to appreciate this huge park is to canoe through it, slipping along quiet rivers onto forested lakes. The only sounds you may hear are birdcalls and the dip of your paddle as it slices through the glassy water. Keep an eye out for white-tailed deer, red fox, and beaver; if you're really lucky, you may surprise a moose. The three connected Saranac lakes are good for day trips, and in the Tupper Lake area, there's a popular route along the Raclette River. The classic Adirondacks canoeing experience, however, is the Seven Carries Route through the gorgeous St. Regis Canoe Wilderness north of Saranac Lake, visiting all three of the St. Regis lakes and several secluded ponds, a trip that may take 3 or 4 days (free campsites are plentiful along most of these routes for overnight stays). If you need more of an adrenaline rush, the 17-mile-long (27km) Hudson River Gorge near Indian Lake offers some spectacular whitewater rafting. And if dropping a line into a mirror-calm lake isn't enough for you, put on some hip waders and cast your fly into the churning rapids of the Ausable River. How you use the water is up to you—but enjoy its pristine beauty while you can.

---

ⓘ **Adirondack Regional Tourism Council** (② **518/846-8016;** www.adirondacks. org)

✈ Saranac Lake

🛏 $$ **Hotel Saranac,** 101 Main St., Saranac Lake (② **800/937-0211** or 518/ 891-2200; www.hotelsaranac.com)

**CAMPING Saranac Lake Islands** (② **518/ 891-3170;** www.dec.ny.gov/outdoor/ 24496.html), accessible only by canoes

**TOUR Adirondack Lakes and Trails Outfitters,** 168 Lake Flower Ave., Saranac Lake (② **518/891-7450;** www.adirondack outfitters.com). **St. Regis Canoe Outfitters,** 9 Dorsey St., Saranac Lake (② **518/ 891-1838;** www.canoeoutfitters.com).

# Apalachicola Bluffs & Ravines Preserve
## *Flooding the Florida Plain*
### Bristol, Florida

THIS CAREFULLY RESTORED LANDSCAPE, HOME TO MANY RARE SPECIES OF PLANTS AND animals—some found nowhere else on earth—and its environmental riches are threatened on all sides by a maelstrom of competing commercial and residential demands. Preserving it for future generations will be an ongoing challenge.

Everybody wants a piece of the Apalachicola River. Fishermen want it to provide them with largemouth bass, striped bass, and catfish. Boaters want it to float their houseboats and river cruisers. The seafood industry wants it to feed the productive oyster beds in Apalachicola Bay. Naturalists want it to nurture waterfowl and endangered mussels and sturgeon. Communities along the entire river system—which stretches from northwest Georgia along the Flint and Chattahoochee rivers to the Florida border, where they merge underneath Lake Seminole and become the 106-mile-long (171km) Apalachicola—want it to provide clean drinking water, not to mention water for irrigation and hydropower.

Even in good years, these conflicting needs compete, and it doesn't help that three different states (Georgia, Alabama, and Florida) are all involved. In a drought year (like 2007), it can be a fight to the death.

The Apalachicola, like most rivers, is threatened by pollution and by the impact of upriver dams on its natural seasonal levels. Plus, years of dredging by the Army Corps of Engineers has smothered shore habitats with dredged-up sand and gravel. The Corps's intention was to improve the river for navigation, but few commercial barges really use the river, and there's surprisingly little recreational boating either.

Featured in the film *Ulee's Gold,* the lower Apalachicola—Florida's largest floodplain—is an area known not only for

bass fishing and quail hunting but for raising tupelo honey, a precious variety made by bees who feed around the increasingly rare tupelo tree. Today it encompasses several protected areas: Apalachicola National Forest, Torreya State Park, Tates Hell State Forest, the Apalachicola Wildlife and Environmental Area, and the **Apalachicola Bluffs and Ravines Preserve,** which is run by the Nature Conservancy.

At the preserve, a 3.8-mile (6km) nature trail—aptly named the Garden of Eden trail—winds through a mix of rare habitats. First comes a recently restored longleaf pine/wiregrass uplands (look for Florida yew trees, once of the world's rarest evergreens, as well as the magnolias and oak-leaf hydrangea). Then you'll pass through dramatic steephead ravines, a rare geological feature that nurtures unique species such as the Apalachicola dusky salamander. On the sand hills, in spring you'll see wildflowers like trillium, wild ginger, and Gholson's blazing star; in fall, toothed basil and lopsided Indian grass.

The trail ends on a panoramic bluff 135 feet (41m) above the Apalachicola River, where bald eagles, Mississippi kites, and swallowtail kites swoop overhead. It's a breathtaking view of a landscape painstakingly preserved. Will politics prevent saving the rest of it? Stay tuned.

---

ⓘ **Apalachicola Bluffs and Ravines Preserve,** off State Rd. 12, Bristol, FL (✆ **850/643-2756**)

# 10 Places to See the Last Healthy Coral Reefs

Scuba divers will testify—there's no more jaw-dropping sight than a healthy coral reef, with its vivid colors, mazy shapes, quicksilver fish, and dreamy anemones. But a quarter of the world's coral reefs are now dead, and marine biologists estimate that 70% could be gone by 2020. We wouldn't just lose those coral palaces; the species they shelter will have no other home (one quarter of all fish species dwell only in coral reefs). Sure, some reefs are more imperiled than others, but make no mistake—they are all at risk.

These 10 still-pristine reefs argue persuasively for saving the rest:

**29 Biscayne National Park** Pulsing with parrotfish and angelfish, gently rocking sea fans, sea turtles, and dolphins, Biscayne Bay's reef shelters some 512 species, all told. Daily snorkel/dive tours and glass-bottomed boat tours are offered by **Biscayne National Underwater Park, Inc.** (✆ **305/230-1100**). *Biscayne National Park.* ✆ *305/230-7275. www.nps.gov/bisc.*

**30 Bonaire** Thanks to the pioneering Bonaire Marine Park—which includes 80-plus dive sites along with permanent boat moorings and attentive rangers—this Caribbean island's reefs remain in prime condition. It's a haven for over 355 species from beautiful parrotfish and damselfish to huge groupers and tough moray eels. Operators include **Dive II** (✆ **599/717-8285**) and **Bonaire Dive and Adventures** (✆ **599/717-2229**). *InfoBonaire.* ✆ *800/BONAIRE [266-2473]. www.infobonaire.com.*

**31 Saba** Saba may look tiny and rocky above the water, but undersea it's got a wealth of dive sites, especially around a number of spiky offshore pinnacles, richly encrusted with coral and sponges. The protected **Saba Marine Park,** Ford Bay (✆ **599/416-3295**), circles the entire island, including four seamounts (underwater mountains), more than two dozen marked and buoyed dive sites, and a snorkeling trail. Operators include **Sea Saba Dive Center** in Windwardside (✆ **599/416-2246**) and **Saba Deep Dive Center** in Fort Bay (✆ **599/416-3347**). *Saba Tourist Bureau. www.sabatourism.com.*

**32 Cozumel** Off the Yucatan coast, Cozumel is often rated the top dive site in the Western Hemisphere, with spectacular reefs built up by a strong (and somewhat tricky) coastal current. Known for its dramatic underwater topography of steep drop-offs and underground caverns, it's best navigated with seasoned dive operators like **Aqua Safari** (✆ 52/987/872-0101; www.aquasafari.com) or **Liquid Blue Divers** (✆ 52/987/869-0593; www.liquidbluedivers.com). *Cozumel Official Site (www.islacozumel.com.mx).*

Cozumel.

**33 Great Barrier Reef** Australia's Great Barrier Reef is so immense, it's visible from the moon. Snorkelers can view the reef's profuse marine life in the shallow waters around the coral cay of **Green Island** or sandy **Beaver Cay,** an hour's boat ride from Mission Beach, south of Cairns. Scuba divers may prefer the dazzling reef architecture out on the rainforested islands of the Outer Reef: Base yourself in the **Whitsunday Islands,** where operators such as **Reef Dive** (✆ 61/7/4946 6508) and **Kelly Dive** (✆ 61/7/4946 6122) explore the Great Barrier Reef Marine Park. *Great Barrier Reef Visitors Bureau. ✆ 07/3876 4644. www.great-barrier-reef.com.*

**㉞ Tumbalen**   Perhaps the most diverse coastal environment in the world lies on the east end of Bali, where divers spot many small, fugitive species that exist nowhere else on earth. The most spectacular reefs are offshore from Amuk Bay and the Lombok Strait harbor. Base yourself in the small resort town of Candi Dasa, where storefront dive operators abound, or the nearby fishing village Padangbai, the base of **Geko Divers** (✆ 62/363/41516; gekodive@indosat.net.id). *Bali Paradise Online (www.bali-paradise.com).*

**㉟ Wakatobi National Marine Park**   Set up in the mid-1990s in southeast Sulawesi, Indonesia, this remote four-island marine preserve is reachable only from the Wakatobi Dive Resort. It's a spectacular reef with astonishing diversity and some truly beautiful coral formations, both hard and soft. More than 40 dive sites are available, many of them quite shallow. ✆ *62/868/121 22355.*

**㊱ Rock Islands, Palau**   Thanks to a decade-old ban on commercial fishery, threatened shark, barracuda, and wrasse species thrive off the deep drop-offs of this Pacific chain of limestone islands, some 805km (500 miles) west of the Philippines. Of its 76 dive sites, 20 feature shipwrecks. Operators include **Fish and Fins** (✆ 680/488-2637; www.fishnfins.com) and **Neco's Marine** (✆ 680/488-1755; www.necomarine.com).

**㊲ The Maldives**   Scattered around this low-lying Indian Ocean chain of coral islands, several relatively isolated atolls offer unspoiled diving around technicolored reefs. Barracuda, batfish, unicornfish, fusiliers, and harlequin sweetlips patrol the warm, remarkably clear water. Live-aboard boats let you explore the more remote sites: Try the **MV *Sea Queen*** or **MV *Sea Spirit*** (✆ **44 845 130 7210;** www.scubascuba.com), or the ***Manthiri*** (✆ **960/332-5634;** www.manthiri.com). *www.maldives.com.*

The Maldives' underwater reefs.

**㊳ Cape Verde Islands**   Tourism hasn't yet overwhelmed this Portuguese colonial outpost in the Atlantic, west of Africa. Its lava shoal reefs—many of which formed around shipwrecks—are rich in marine life, including manta rays, sharks, tuna, dolphins, and turtles, not to mention underwater flora and surprising caves. Humpback and gray whale migrations in March and April are an added attraction. *www.caboverde.com.*

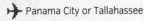 Panama City or Tallahassee

🛏 $$ **Gibson Inn,** 51 Ave. C, Apalachicola (✆ **850/653-2191;** www.gibsoninn.

com). $$$ **Apalachicola River Inn,** 123 Water St., Apalachicola (✆ **850/653-8139;** www.apalachicolariverinn.com).

## Ecosystems in Transition  39

# The Okefenokee Swamp
## *The Murky Mysteries of Georgia's Wet Wilderness*
### Georgia

THE OKEFENOKEE SWAMP IS WILD, BUT FAR FROM UNTOUCHED. HUMAN ACTIVITIES FROM logging to upstream development have unbalanced the swamp's delicate ecosystem. Peat is filling in the wetlands, threatening to destroy the natural habitat of countless plants and animals.

Over the years man has tried to tame the great Okefenokee Swamp—and always the swamp prevailed. Paddling around its inky backwaters, you'll see a few abandoned farmsteads, a half-built drainage canal, and ghostly remains of major logging operations. Stumps of half-century-old cypress trees thrust out of the murk, surrounded by the slim black gum and bay trees that defiantly sprang up to replace them.

But human meddling inevitably has thrown the ecosystem out of whack. In 1960, for example, sinking water levels were raised again by the Suwanee River Sill to such levels that no fires can cyclically clear out ground vegetation. Without the fires, increased vegetation eventually creates peat buildups, which could turn to solid land, altering the wetlands forever.

Meandering over 650 square miles (906 sq. km) of southeastern Georgia, cut off by Trail Ridge from the coastal plain, this vast wilderness is a watery mosaic of various habitats—wet prairies, peat marsh, pine uplands, hardwood hammocks, small lakes and "gator holes," and floating mats of peat that have become their own islands. No wonder the Creek Indians called it "Land of the Trembling Earth." To keep the various interconnected habitats in balance, 80% has been set aside as a national wildlife refuge, which shelters endangered and threatened species such as the wood stork, the sandhill crane, the red-cockaded woodpecker, the indigo snake, the carnivorous parrot pitcher plant, and the Florida black bear. Bobcats prowl, marsh hares skitter for cover, and possums (the models for the comic-strip character Pogo) cling to tree trunks. And yes, venomous snakes and alligators add their notes to the deliciously creepy atmosphere.

While a few park areas have been developed around the edges, with interpretive centers, nature trails, and canoe-rental facilities, no roads traverse the wilderness itself. But there are 225 miles (362km) of marked canoe trails, mirrorlike dark waterways where you can glide under low-hanging trees while keeping an eye out for alligators and an ear tuned for the rat-tat-tat of a woodpecker or the agile slither of an otter. For guided canoe expeditions, try the **Suwanee Canal Recreation Area,** GA Spur 121, Folkston (✆ **912/496-7156**); on the eastern fringe of the wilderness contact **Okefenokee Adventures** (✆ **866/ THESWAMP** [843-7926] or 912/496-7156; www.okefenokeeadventures.com). If you want to camp deep in the wilderness, you'll need to make reservations 2 months in advance with the **U.S. Fish and**

Wildlife Service (© 912/496-3331). Being lulled to sleep by a chorus of a dozen different kinds of frogs—that's when you know you've had the prime Okefenokee experience.

---

ⓘ **Okefenokee National Wildlife Refuge,** Rte. 2, Folkston (© 912/496-7156; www.fws.gov/okefenokee). **Okefenokee**

**Swamp Park,** GA 177, Waycross (© 912/283-0583). **Stephen C. Foster State Park,** GA 177, Fargo (© 912/637-5274).

✈ Jacksonville, FL

⊨ $$ **Holiday Inn,** 1725 Memorial Dr. (© 912/283-4490; www.holiday-inn.com). $ **Stephen C. Foster State Park,** GA '77, Fargo (© 912/637-5274).

---

**Ecosystems in Transition**

**40**

# The Greenbrier Valley
## *Appalachian Twists & Turns*
### Lewisburg, West Virginia

ENVIRONMENTAL DAMAGE FROM MANY YEARS OF MINING, LOGGING, AND POORLY PLANNED development still threatens West Virginia's most vulnerable ecosystems, including the wild caves and limestone shale barrens in and around the Greenbrier Valley. The caverns and the shale barrens both support many rare native species, which may be lost if the state is unable to summon enough resources and political will to save them.

Blessed with some of the most spectacular mountain scenery in the United States, West Virginia is also plagued by its own hillbilly reputation. Driving along winding back roads, you'll see an awe-inspiring Appalachian vista one moment—and the next, a dilapidated shack with a rusted pickup in the yard and an immense satellite dish on the roof.

Below the surface is a similar story. For under the Appalachian mountains in southeastern West Virginia, some 500 limestone caves harbor many vulnerable plant and animals species—bats, beetles, spiders, millipedes, shrimplike crustaceans, crayfish, salamanders, you name it. (Little known fact: Half of all the most vulnerable plant and animal species in the 48 contiguous United States are found only in caves.) Yet these caves get treated with little respect. Entire caverns have been gobbled up by quarries, and highway and building construction leads to cave-ins, causing contaminated groundwater to seep in; even cave mouths are often

plugged up with trash. Vigilant spelunkers and cavers have saved many, but valuable habitat is lost daily. The area's two major commercial caverns, **Lost World Caverns** on Fairview Road in Lewisburg (© 304/645-6677; www.lostworldcaverns.com), and **Organ Cave** on Route 63 in Ronceverte (between rtes. 293 and 60; © 304/645-7600; www.organcave.com), both offer wild cave tours to investigate relatively unspoiled cave habitat. If that's not adventurous enough for you, caving expeditions with **ACE Adventures** (www.cave-wv.com) can take you to little-known caves on private property.

Above ground, the limestone karst does other weird things, too. Some of the state's rarest ecosystems are shale barrens—dry, desertlike mountainside habitats with flaky surface rock and few trees, which harbor a number of sun-loving endemic flora. Those species actually resemble desert plants from the American West much more than they do their Appalachian forest neighbors. Botanists and geologists treasure the shale barrens, but most West Virginians see these crumbling steep slopes as worthless; roads and utility lines bisect them, and adjacent pastures often introduce aggressive, invasive weeds (like the multiflora rose, first introduced to stop erosion). **Kate's Mountain,** in the Greenbrier State Forest, has some spectacular shale barrens; you'll find them near the high point of the 2.1-mile (3.4km) Rocky Ridge Trail, accessible either by hiking or by car. Several rare wildflowers were first identified by botanists on Kate's Mountain, including—naturally—the Kate's Mountain clover.

The Greenbrier State Forest is just one section of the 79-mile (127km) **Greenbrier River Trail** (www.greenbrierrivertrail. com), a packed gravel trail that follows an old C&O railroad bed along the Greenbrier River. It's a spectacular place for hiking or mountain biking; interpretive signs point out natural features along the way. West Virginia's made great strides in restoring its natural wonders (just see what they've done with the nearby New River Gorge in Fayetteville)—may the trend continue!

ⓘ **Greenbrier State Forest,** Caldwell, WV (✆ **304/536-1944;** www.greenbriersf. com)

✈ Greenbrier Valley, Lewisburg

🛏 $$$ **The Greenbrier,** 300 W. Main St., White Sulphur Springs (✆ **800/624-6070** or 304/536-1110; www.greenbrier. com). $$ **Old White Inn,** 865 E. Main St., White Sulphur Springs (✆ **304/536-2441**). $ **Greenbrier State Forest** (campsites and cabins), exit 175 off I-64, White Sulphur Springs (✆ **304/536-1944;** www. greenbriersf.com).

---

**Ecosystems in Transition** 41

# Lake Mead
## *Playing God with the Colorado Watershed*
### Boulder City, Nevada

LAKE MEAD HAS ALWAYS BEEN SOMETHING OF A MIRACLE——AN ENORMOUS FRESHWATER LAKE in the middle of the desert—but the miracle may soon be a memory. Climate change combined with ongoing drought conditions, upstream diversion of the Colorado River, and escalating downstream demands for water are draining the lake and threatening to turn it into desert again.

That wide band of rocky bleached shelf that surrounds Lake Mead—where did that come from? After 9 years of drought, in 2007 the lake stood half empty, and water management officials faced the grim possibility that this isn't just a cyclical pattern.

It wasn't part of the original plan, that's for sure. When Hoover Dam was completed in 1935, harnessing the mighty Colorado River to provide electricity and water for booming California and Arizona, the creation of Lake Mead was icing on the cake. At 110 miles (177km) long, it would be the largest artificial lake in the United States, a fantastic site for fishing and boating carved out of what had been desert. Cupped in a basin of rainbow-colored rock just above the gigantic concrete dam, Lake Mead shimmers like a blue mirage under the fierce Nevada sun.

Fed by melting snows from the western Rockies, the Colorado River has long been a lifeline for the arid west. In the early 1920s, Secretary of Commerce Herbert Hoover, a civil engineer himself, urged the Southwestern states to dam Boulder Canyon, not only to generate power but to manage scarce water resources. The idea

Lake Mead.

became even more attractive during the Depression, when huge government projects like this created vital jobs.

Is it possible that Lake Mead's condition is due to something more than drought? Some observers suggest long-term climate change is to blame; others point out that adding the Glen Canyon Dam 490 miles (789km) upriver in the 1960s (thereby creating Lake Powell) may have strained the Colorado's capacity. (Lake Mead's level fell noticeably for a couple of years while Lake Powell was filling.) The mushrooming growth of Las Vegas, only 30 miles (48km) west, is an obvious factor, but that's only the tip of the iceberg. Given the Southwest's population growth, there are a lot of golf courses to be watered downstream from Lake Mead.

Meanwhile, on Lake Mead, sportsmen and boat operators continue as before—launching from new docks, built at the current water line. Paddlewheeler cruises from **Lake Mead Cruises** (✆ **702/293-6180;** www.lakemeadcruises.com) depart from the Nevada side of Hoover Dam, giving a running commentary on the lake's

wildlife and history (though they never mention the word "drought"). If you're piloting your own boat (rentals are available at marinas around the lake), keep an extra careful eye out for reefs and rocks, and that goes double for water-skiers.

Drive along the Northshore Drive to get another perspective on the fragile Mojave Desert environment—several short nature trails are marked, including the .5-mile (.8km) **Redstones Trail** loop at Mile 27. Threading around its red sandstone monoliths, watch for ground squirrels, lizards, scorpions, and other desert denizens—just one more reminder that nature never intended Lake Mead to be here.

ⓘ **Lake Mead National Recreation Area** (✆ **702/293-8906;** www.nps.gov/lame)

✈ Las Vegas

🛏 $$ **Boulder Dam Hotel,** 1305 Arizona St., Boulder City, NV (✆ **702/293-3510;** www.boulderdamhotel.com). $$ **Lake Mead Resort,** Lakeshore Scenic Dr. (✆ **800/752-9669;** www.sevencrown.com).

# Sweet Grass Hills, Montana
## *Sacred Mountains Sacrificed*
### Hi-Line, Montana

RICH MINERAL DEPOSITS HAVE CAUSED TROUBLE IN THE SWEET GRASS HILLS SINCE GOLD WAS first discovered there in the 1880s. Pegasus Gold Corporation started using cyanide leach mining here during the 1990s, posing serious threats to water supplies, public health, and wildlife habitat.

Looking at the three buttes towering serenely over the Montana plains, you can almost imagine the Blackfeet Indians standing on the heights, searching for bison herds to hunt. Rising nearly 2,000 feet (610m) from the grassy plain, the hills are visible from 50 miles (80km) away, yet as you drive toward them on Highway 2, the backbone of the Montana Hi-Line, the buttes never seem to get closer. They look like orphans that wandered away from the Rocky Mountains and got lost (indeed, the Blackfeet myth claims that the creator Napi used leftover stones from the Rockies to make them).

The Blackfeet weren't the only Native American peoples to hold these hills sacred—the Chippewa-Cree, Gros Ventre, Salish, Kootenai, and Assiniboine tribes all have a spiritual connection to them. Young warriors were sent here for their vision quests; ancient tipi rings, eagle-catching pits, and stone cairns are hidden in its recesses. But in 1885 gold was struck near Middle Butte, and the U.S. government, which had ceded the land to the Blackfeet, instead declared the Sweet Grass Hills "public land." Over the next few years, companies hauled away gold, silver, iron, copper, and marble; in the 1920s, oil was discovered near West Butte, setting off another little boom. Ranchers took over the surrounding slopes, turning their cattle to graze on the lush buffalo grass and sage.

By the 1990s, commercial activity had mostly died down; rippling grass covered the hills' scars. Then a new threat arose. Another mining company filed a claim to mine for gold—this time using cyanide leach, a much more devastating open-pit process. Environmentalists sprang into action, joining with Blackfeet tribal leaders from the nearby reservation. Through lawsuits they managed to impose a 20-year moratorium, but the legal battle is not over yet.

The Sweet Grass Hills aren't just a sacred site for Native Americans; they provide habitat for the endangered peregrine falcon, and for threatened elk and deer. Located between the Canadian border and the Milk River, the buttes and their attendant hills guard the headwaters of the Marias River, the only aquifer that provides drinking water for this part of northern Montana. While the Middle Butte, also known historically as Gold Butte, is grassy and open, East and West buttes are lightly forested with lodgepole, Douglas fir, ponderosa pine, and limber pine, alternating with meadows of prairie wildflowers. Hawks and curlews ride the updrafts, and gleaming trout muscle around the scattered ponds.

Drive up the gravel road from Lothair to Whitlash, park your car, and hike into the trackless hills on your own vision quest. What you'll find there will be worth more than gold.

---

ⓘ **Sweet Grass Hills,** between Shelby and Havre

✈ Great Falls

🛏 $$ **Comfort Inn,** 455 McKinley, Shelby (✆ **406/434-2493;** www.choicehotels.com). $ **Crossroads Inn,** 1200 Hwy. 2, Shelby (✆ **800/779-7666** or 406/434-5134).

# Hell's Canyon
## *Turning Back the Wilderness Clock*
### Snake River, Idaho/Oregon

HELL'S CANYON NATIONAL RECREATION AREA HAS BEEN GRADUALLY RECLAIMED AND RETURNED to wilderness status after many years as farmland and pasture. But environmental threats come in many forms. Today, Hell's Canyon is under attack by noxious weeds such as the yellow star thistle, which chokes out native plants, deprives 350 bird and animal species of food and habitat, and can spread up to 7 miles (11km) in a single year.

River rafters know Hell's Canyon, the deepest gorge in North America, as a great stretch of Class III–IV whitewater along the Snake River, tracing the border between Idaho and Oregon. Churning through forested canyon walls a full mile and a half (2.4km) high, the Snake builds up quite a head of steam, heading toward the Columbia River in Washington State.

But believe it or not, when the Hell's Canyon National Recreation Area (HCNRA) Act was enacted in 1975, plans were afoot to harness the Snake River with hydroelectric dams. Luckily, the interests of wildlife won out.

If Hell's Canyon was going to be a wilderness, park management had years of abuse to undo. Looking today at this hilly wilderness, it's hard to imagine it as farmland. Yet that's what it was, as far back as the 1730s when the Nez Perce grazed their horses and cattle here. Nineteenth-century homesteaders snapped up the level benchlands for hayfields and orchards, while sheep and cattle were pastured on the slopes. Native elk, deer, mountain goats, and bighorn sheep were driven away, unable to compete with the domestic herds.

Overgrazed to exhaustion, the land was set aside as a wildlife reserve in 1905, but the number of grazing allotments was only gradually reduced. By the 1970s, when the NRA was set up, there was finally room to reintroduce species. The deer and elk populations rebounded, but, mysteriously, not the bighorn sheep. It took another decade before scientists realized that bighorns were contracting a deadly parasite from the remaining domestic sheep. In 1994, the last sheep grazing allotments were removed. Slowly but surely, the bighorns have come back—look for them on the upper peaks and plateaus as you explore this quintessential Western park.

The standard 3-day rafting trip covers about 36 miles (58km), but it's not rapids all the way—there are plenty of placid sections where rafters can relax and enjoy stunning views of the Seven Devils Mountains and the Summit Ridge. When you're not rafting, there's plenty else to do—trout fishing, swimming, short hikes to view Native American pictographs on canyon walls, or to find the abandoned cabins of those early 1900s settlers. There are also 900 miles (1,448km) of riding trails, through mountain meadows and timbered draws, down steep trails to the canyon floor.

With such dizzying elevation changes, native flora and fauna in Hell's Canyon range from mountain goats and Ponderosa pine on the heights to prickly-pear cactus and rattlesnakes on the desertlike canyon floor. Far from being hell, it's a bit of heaven on earth—and to think we almost lost it!

ⓘ **Hell's Canyon National Recreation Area,** 88401 Hwy. 82, Enterprise, OR (✆ **541/426-5546**; www.nps.gov/heca)

✈ Lewiston, ID

**TOUR Northwest Voyageurs** (✆ **800/ 727-9977**; www.voyageurs.com). **O.A.R.S.** (✆ **800/346-7277;** www.oars.com). **Zoller's Outdoor Odysseys** (✆ **800/366-2004** or

509/493-2641; www.snakeraft.com). **Back-country Outfitters** (✆ **888/420-7855;** www.backcountryoutfittersinc.com). **Steens Wilderness Adventures** (✆ **541/ 432-6545;** www.steens-packtrips.com).

**Ecosystems in Transition**  44

# Glacier National Park
## *Melting Under the Big Sky*
### West Glacier, Montana

GLOBAL WARMING IS MELTING THE GLACIERS THAT GIVE GLACIER NATIONAL PARK ITS NAME and much of its spectacular scenery. By 2030, they all could be gone. Meanwhile, the retreating ice is dramatically altering the alpine ecosystem, making it more vulnerable to fire and threatening the habitat of the park's numerous wildlife species, including large populations of bighorn sheep, mountain goats, and grizzly bears.

Blackfeet tribes call this northern stretch of the Continental Divide "the spine of the

Glacier National Park.

world," which, as you no doubt remember from geography class, is the ridge of the Rockies from which all rivers flow either east or west. When the Ice Age ended millennia ago, retreating ice floes revealed a stunning valley gouged out of what is now the state of Montana and lower Alberta, Canada. Majestic mountain crags loom above the valley, their crevices hiding lakes and ponds that are really just melted glacial leftovers. Icy waters spill over the crags in spectacular waterfalls.

The glaciers are still receding—faster than ever, in fact, adding opalescent runoff to those mountain lakes and exposing rocky slopes that haven't seen the sun for eons. In 1850, early European explorers documented some 150 glaciers draping the limestone peaks; by the early 1960s, aerial surveys showed 50 glaciers; by 1998, there were only 26. Scientists estimate they may be gone entirely in 25 years. With the ice dwindling, the ecosystem is in the grip of radical, rapid change. Trees, foliage, and meadows take over, creating a habitat that's increasingly vulnerable to fire (Glacier Park's white bark pine trees are rapidly disappearing) and prone to more avalanches in winter. Avalanches carve out meadows of low scrubby growth, hospitable to bighorn sheep (Glacier has a booming population), nimble snow-white mountain goats, and birds, including predatory hawks and golden eagles. Meadow berries make good food for foraging grizzly bears as well, of which Glacier has more than its share.

Between late May and mid-September, you can circle the park on the spectacular 50-mile (80km) **Going-To-The-Sun Road,** running from the West Glacier park entrance (U.S. Hwy. 2 near Columbia Falls, MT) to the St. Mary visitor center at the eastern edge of the park. You'll wind dramatically up 3,400 feet (1,036m) into the mountains (keep an eye out for circling hawks) to the **Logan Pass** visitor center, open summers only; there's a popular turnout for **Jackson Glacier** (once connected to neighboring Blackfoot Glacier, now a separate and much smaller entity).

With more than 700 miles (1,127km) of hiking trails, Glacier is a park that truly

rewards getting out of the car to explore on foot. Visitors do everything from day hikes and rafting on the Flathead River to cross-country skiing in winter and week-long backcountry camping trips; for more info contact **Glacier Guides, Inc. (**©**800/521-RAFT** [7238]; www.glacierguides. com). Climb through alpine meadows spangled with glacier lilies, cool off in new-growth conifer woods, scramble over rock faces striated from glacial grind, and hope you don't encounter grizzlies.

ⓘ **Glacier National Park (**©**406/888-7800;** www.nps.gov/glac)

✈ Kalispell

🛏 $$$ **Lake McDonald Lodge,** on Lake McDonald (©**406/892-2525;** www. glacierparkinc.com). $$ **Glacier Campground,** 12070 U.S. Hwy. 2, West Glacier (©**888/387-5689** or 406/387-5689).

**45** Ecosystems in Transition

# Pinnacles National Monument
## *Preserving Life on the Fault Edge*
Paicines, California

AN UNUSUAL BLEND OF DIFFERENT ECOSYSTEMS AND HOME TO SEVERAL RARE SPECIES, INCLUDING the California condor, Pinnacles National Monument is in danger of being loved to death by visitors who come to hike and climb but leave behind littered landscapes and polluted streams. Natural forces, such as wind and rain erosion, also threaten the area's distinctive geography.

It's like a textbook study of the forces of nature. Chapter 1: The Power of Plate Tectonics—just look at these jagged crags, spires, and hoodoos, carried an amazing 195 miles (314km) north from the Mojave Desert by grinding shifts along the San Andreas Fault. Chapter 2: Ecosystem Dynamics—just see how biodiverse this landscape is, with species thriving on the intersections of overlapping habitats.

Set among the rolling brown hills of California, only 80 miles (128km) south of

San Francisco, it's not surprising that the Pinnacles National Monument is one of the most popular weekend climbing spots in central California year-round—some weekends it seems every spire and monolith has a climber clinging to its surface. But the Pinnacles is more than just a popular climbing area. In 1908, these freakish rock formations inspired local nature lovers to lobby for protection, making Pinnacles one of the first parks in the national system, an early victory for environmental activists.

Pinnacles National Monument.

Here, where tectonic plates grind against each other, several ecosystems also meet—chaparral, grassland, woodland, riparian, rocky scree—but instead of clashing, they stimulate each other. Besides the rare big-eared kangaroo rat, Gabilan slender salamander, Pinnacles shield-back katydid, and Pinnacles riffle beetle, the park has the world's highest bee diversity—nearly 400 distinct species buzzing around its high chaparral and grasslands. Talus caves—narrow stream canyons roofed over with tumbled boulders—make the park a haven for bats as well, including the rare Townsend's big-eared bats. And then there are the extremely rare California condors, more than a dozen of which were released to the wild here. An early-morning hike up the strenuous High Peaks trail gives you your best chance of seeing one of these endangered scavengers.

With so many visitors, the Pinnacles faces several challenges. Carelessly discarded litter and human waste jeopardize the streams that are vital for survival in this dry microclimate. The condors, which are carrion eaters, have tested for high lead levels after feasting on contaminated carcasses. The seeds of exotic species like the yellow star thistle, carried in on hiking boots, threaten to overrun the native plants. To mimic the region's natural cycles, park management has to set occasional controlled wildfires. Wind and erosion continue to exert their force on the pinnacles, which are still moving $3/4$ to $1 1/4$ inches (2–3cm) a year. A century of protected status has preserved this unique landscape remarkably—but even so, constant vigilance is required.

ⓘ **Pinnacles National Monument,** 5000 Hwy. 146, Paicines, CA (✆ **831/389-4485;** www.nps.gov/pinn)

✈ Monterey Peninsula Airport

🛏 $ **Pinnacles Campground,** off CA 25 near the eastern entrance (✆ **831/389-4485,** ext. 267)

# Hawaii Volcanoes National Park
*Where There's Smoke . . .*
Volcano, Hawaii

HAWAII VOLCANOES NATIONAL PARK IS A LANDSCAPE IN MOTION—OFTEN QUITE LITERALLY as two of the world's most active volcanoes, Kilauea and Mauna Loa, continue to erupt and pour molten lava into the sea. Volcanic eruption continually alters and reshapes the island of Hawaii, and the park provides a spectacular view of nature at work—one that may change as you watch.

Dormant volcano? Think again. Since 1983, the Big Island's Kilauea volcano has been erupting all the time. Although these are "quiet"' eruptions—gas escaping slowly instead of exploding violently—you can often see its slow-moving red lava oozing over the landscape, sometimes even over the park roads; at other times the lava flows through underground tubes that spill out miles away. Over the past 2 decades, some $100 million worth of property has been destroyed by Kilauea's

eruptions—yet the lava flow has also added 560 acres (227 hectares) of new land. It's a landscape in continual, violent flux, and where it'll end up is anybody's guess.

Near the park's visitor center, you can view the **Kilauea Caldera,** a 2½-mile-wide (4km), 500-foot-deep pit with wisps of steam rising from it. Going counterclockwise on Crater Rim Road, you'll drive past the Sulphur Banks, which smell like rotten eggs, and the Steam Vents, fissures where

Lava flow in Hawaii.

trails of smoke, once molten lava, escape from the inner reaches of the earth. At the **Thomas A. Jaggar Museum** there's a viewpoint for Halemaumau Crater, which is half a mile (.8km) across but 1,000 feet (300m) deep; walk right to the rim to gape at this once-fuming old fire pit, which still gives off some fierce heat out of its vents. Near the Iki Crater, the .5-mile (.8km) **Devastation Trail** is a sobering look at how a volcanic eruption wreaked havoc in 1959. At **Puu Loa,** an ancient site considered sacred to the volcano goddess, Pele, a .5-mile (.8km) boardwalk loop trail reveals thousands of mysterious Hawaiian petroglyphs.

If the volcano is actively erupting, call the visitor center for directions to the best locations for night viewing—it's quite a

sight to see, as brilliant red lava snakes down the side of the mountain and pours into the sea. Blue Hawaiian Helicopter (*©* **800/745-BLUE** [2583] or 808/886-1768; www.bluehawaiian.com) runs several tours right over the bubbling caldera, for a bird's-eye view you'll never forget.

---

ⓘ **Hawaii Volcanoes National Park,** Hawaii Belt Rd. (Hwy. 11), Volcano, HI (*©* **808/985-6000;** www.nps.gov/havo)

✈ Hilo

🛏 $$ **Killauea Lodge,** Old Volcano Rd., off Hwy. 11. (*©* **808/967-7366;** www. kilauealodge.com). $ **Volcano House,** inside Hawaii Volcanoes National Park (*©* **808/967-7321;** www.volcanohouse hotel.com).

## Ecosystems in Transition  47

# The Jungfrau
## *Europe's Dwindling Ice Cap*
### Bernese Highlands, Switzerland

GLOBAL WARMING OVER THE PAST 150 YEARS HAS BEEN MELTING SWITZERLAND'S FAMOUS glaciers, and recent heat waves in Europe have accelerated the loss of glacial ice. As the glaciers continue to melt, scientists predict increased flooding along major rivers and a sharp reduction in the amount of fresh water stored in the frozen reaches of the Bernese Highlands.

A trio of peaks loom here, the Jungfrau ("Maiden"), the Eiger, and the Mönch ("Monk")—their very names bespeaking purity, aloofness, and icy solitude. The Bernese Highlands hold the largest glacier in Europe, or for that matter, in all Eurasia—but like glaciers all over the world, it's shrinking every day.

Alpine glaciers may have lost half their mass between 1850 and 1980; in the heat wave of 2003 alone, they lost 10%. Under an atmosphere of trapped greenhouse gases, warming global temperatures will only accelerate the process. Photographs reveal that the Jungfrau's Aletsch glacier

has retreated 1.4km (1 mile) since 1950. The pace of retreat lately has been more like 30m (100 ft.) a year; new vegetation creeps ever further up newly exposed slopes. By 2050, 75% of Switzerland's glaciers could very well disappear. Even the great Aletsch could conceivably be gone by 2100.

Besides ruining the Swiss skiing industry (resorts have already started to emphasize summer activities), increased glacier melting will drastically alter Europe's water supply system. Water levels in major rivers from the Rhine and the Rhone to the Danube are likely to rise over the next several years, flooding historic cities and landscapes. In the long run, though, smaller glaciers will mean less fresh water to nourish Europe.

It's still hard to believe this as you hike in summer through the Swiss Alps, where slow-moving ancient ice continues to wind between the peaks. You'll get an awesome view from the **Jungfraubahn,** the highest rack railway in Europe (begin at Interlaken, taking one train to Lauterbrunnen and another to Kleine Scheidigg, where the Jungfraubahn tunnel starts). At the Eismeer stop, get out to peer through windows cut into the rock at the vast Eismeer, or "Sea of Ice." At the top, go to the Sphinx Terraces observation deck to see the Aletsch Glacier in its full glory. The Eispalast ("Ice Palace"), at the Jungfraubahn terminus, is a kitschy but historic attraction boasting several rooms hewn out of the ice, 20m (65 ft.) below the glacier's surface.

In the resort town of **Grindelwald,** 22km (14 miles) south of Interlaken, the **Bergsteigerzentrum** (☎ 033/853-52-00; www.bergsteigerzentrum.ch) hiking center organizes walks and hikes of various lengths and difficulty levels out onto the glacier. You can study the striated ravine at the base of the Lower Grindelwald glacier, at an observation deck just outside of town, or take a half-day hike to the base of the Upper Grindelwald Glacier, following the Milchbach River (so named because it looks milky from minerals in the melting glacier's ice). At the receding snout of the glacier, you can visit the ice-carved chamber of the Blue Ice Grotto.

Drive northeast from Interlaken to the village of **Brienz** to trace the course of the glacier's melting snows; they plunge downhill at dramatic Geissbach Falls, then flow into Lake Brienz and eventually into the Mediterranean. It reminds us that the glaciers' fate isn't just a Swiss problem—not at all.

ⓘ **Interlaken Tourist Office** (☎ 41/33/826-53-00)

✈ Bern

🛏 $$ **Royal St. Georges,** Höheweg 139, Interlaken (☎ 41/33/823-30-75). $$ **Romantik Hotel Schweizerhof,** Grindelwald (☎ 41/33/853-22-02; www.hotel schweizerhof.com).

---

**48** Ecosystems in Transition

# Torres del Paine
## *A Second Act in the Andes Highlands*
### Chile

FIFTY YEARS AGO, THE CHILEAN GOVERNMENT RECLAIMED THE TORRES DEL PAINE IN SOUTHERN Chile and began to transform the exhausted and overgrazed ranchland into a stunning wilderness area that supports a diverse group of plants and animals—even in the harsh climate of Patagonia. Unfortunately, climate change is causing glaciers in the area to melt and recede at a rapid rate, which could radically alter the ecosystem.

Not so very long ago, the Torres del Paine was just ranchland—and worn-out ranchland at that. Rare beech forests were burned down to expand pastureland, and vast herds of sheep had grazed the steppes down to the soil.

Since the Chilean government took over the land in 1959, however, nature's done a

Torres del Paine.

salmon-colored granite peaks, wind-eroded giants that soar from sea level to upward of 2,800m (9,184 ft.). Paine is the Tehuelche Indian word for "blue," referring to the blue lakes of the surrounding glaciers.

Its Argentine neighbor Los Glaciares (see below) may be easier to reach, but there's more to do in Torres del Paine, starting with the obvious choice, hiking. The classic day hike leads from the Hosteria Las Torres to the Torres formations, but another popular route follows the shores of Lago Grey for spectacular up-close views of the gigantic blue iceberg feeding the lake; day hikes across the surface of Glacier Grey, prowling through its frosty caverns, are also available. Serious backpackers can do overnight treks from 4 to 11 days, depending on your route, staying along the way in tents or cabinlike refugios (© **56/61/226054** for reservations; Sept–Apr). Horseback treks are another population option. If glaciers are your thing, you can also book a cruise on an open Zodiac boat past the glaciers Tyndall and Geike to the Torres del Paine entrance and up the Rio Serrano to the knifelike Serrano Glacier, where you can hike around the surface before sailing back to Puerto Natales.

Think of Torres del Paine as a Chilean version of Yellowstone or Yosemite. Sure, it takes more effort to get here, but the bonus is major glacier action—at least for as long as they last.

remarkable turnaround. Nowadays hikers tramp through leafy forests, golden pampas, and along the shores of startling blue lakes, their waters turned milky by glacial melt. Native populations of guanacos, flamingoes, pumas, and the ostrichlike rhea birds have rebounded from near extinction; Andean condors roost on its remote peaks. Besides the three towering granite formations the park is named after, its other most striking feature is its glaciers, and while they are rapidly receding (as much as 19m/56 ft. a year), it's fascinating to see how quickly new vegetation sprouts on the exposed rock left behind.

As extreme bits of land go, they don't get more extreme than Patagonia. Down here where Chile and Argentina divide the narrow tail of South America, fierce winds whip down from the crest of the Andes, and even in summer (Jan–Feb) the weather can be chilly. The "Torres" in the name means towers, as in the three namesake

(i) **Parque Nacional Torres Del Paine** (www.torresdelpaine.com)

✈ Puerto Natales

╞═══ $$ **Hotel CostAustralis,** Pedro Montt 262, Puerto Natales (© **56/61/ 412000;** www.australis.com). $$$ **Hosteria Las Torres** (© **56/61/226054**).

**TOUR** **Aventour** (© **56/61/410253**). **Onas** (© **56/61/412707;** www.onaspatagonia. com). **Bigfoot Expeditions** (© **56/61/ 414611;** www.bigfootpatagonia.com). **Andes Mountain** (© **56/61/415749;** www.andesmountain.cl).

# Kakadu National Park
## *Crocodile Dundee Territory*
### Northern Territories, Australia

KAKADU NATIONAL PARK ENCOMPASSES A HIGHLY SPECIALIZED LANDSCAPE WITH MANY unusual species that have adapted to its extreme seasonal changes. Owned by the Aborigines but managed by the Australian government, the parkland surrounds a functioning uranium mine and pressure is growing to open more mines, which could put the local environment at high risk from toxic pollution.

Freshwater crocodiles are mild mannered and relatively harmless; it's the vicious saltwater ones you have to worry about. But despite the name, saltwater crocodiles mainly live in fresh water, and you'll see both kinds lurking in the rivers and lagoons of Kakadu National Park. Confused yet?

Contradictions like this are what make Kakadu so fascinating. Located in the less touristy Northern Territories, Australia's largest national park is also technically Aborigine land. The government converted it to parkland to give the Aborigines an alternative to their traditional livelihood of raising water buffaloes, which had overgrazed the land for centuries. The water buffaloes, an imported species from Asia, are mostly gone now, but a new threat hovers: government factions eager to exploit the land's rich uranium deposits. One original mine is still operating, near the area's only town, Jabiru, and Kakadu's Aborigine owners and park administrators continue to spar over whether to allow more.

This is one destination where it really pays off to have a guide. Kakadu's habitats range from bushland and wetlands to stony escarpment and pockets of monsoon forest, from red cliffs and waterfalls to lush lagoons, each with its own panoply of rare plants to identify. What's more, because the difference between wet and dry seasons is so radical, only experienced guides know where the wildlife can be found at any given time.

Those seasonal extremes require tough, specially adapted vegetation—resurrection grasses, sedges, and spear grass, as well as banyans and kapok trees and freshwater mangroves, help stabilize the ground when it's completely underwater. Mammals here are mostly nocturnal; frogs and reptiles go dormant during the dry season, yet that's the best time for viewing other wildlife, especially birds, as all animal life clusters around the shrinking waterholes. During the Wet, many tour companies simply close down—you may want to opt for a scenic flyover instead, where you can see the swollen rivers and waterfalls and see the floodplain turn lush green.

With so much park to cover, plan your trip carefully. Kakadu can be breathtaking for bird-watchers, with 275 species, one third of all Australia's bird species. Birders gravitate to the various wetlands, such as the Mamukala wetlands, near Jabiru, where you can observe swarms of magpie geese; or the yellow water billabong, near Cooinda, where narrated cruises let you watch sea eagles, kites, and kingfishers hunt for fish among the mangrove roots and waterlilies. Those with anthropological curiosity will want to hike to the preserved examples of Aborigine rock art at sites like Nourlangie and Ubirr. In the eastern section of the park, two waterfalls spill dramatically from the red stone escarpment—Jim Jim Falls and Twin Falls. Many park visitors like to take a swim in the deep pools at their bases, but if that's on your agenda, just remember—watch out for those crocs.

(i) **Bowali Visitor Center,** Kakadu Hwy. (*C* **61/8/8938 1120;** www.deh.gov.au/parks/kakadu). Jabiru Travel Centre, shop 6, Tasman Plaza, Jabiru (*C* **61/8/8979 2548**).

✈ Darwin

🛏 $$$ **Gagudju Crocodile Holiday Inn,** 1 Flinders St., Jabiru (*C* **800/465-4329** in U.S. and Canada, 44/800/405060 in U.K.,

61/1300/666 747 in Australia). $–$$ **Gagudju Lodge Cooinda,** Kakadu Hwy, Jim Jim (*C* **800/835-7742** in U.S. and Canada, 44/800/897 121 in U.K., 44/800/500 401 in Australia; www.gagudjulodgecooinda.com.au).

**TOUR** Gagudju Lodge Cooinda (*C* **61/8/8979 0145**)

---

**Ecosystems in Transition**  **50**

# Parque Nacional Los Glaciares
## *A Patagonian Balancing Act*
### Argentina

IN GENERAL, THE GLACIERS OF THE SOUTHERN PATAGONIAN ICEFIELD ARE SHRINKING JUST LIKE their Northern Hemisphere counterparts. But when it comes to the Perito Moreno glacier in Argentina's Los Glaciares National Park—massive chunks of ice shearing off a glacier and dropping into turquoise Lago Argentina with a thundering crash—appearances can be deceiving.

Few natural wonders in South America are as spectacular or as easily accessed as this 3,000-year-old glacier, nicknamed the "White Giant." Situated in a rugged section of the Andes, close to the Chilean border, it's a jagged wall of ice measuring 5km (3 miles) across and roughly 60m (200 ft.) above the channel that connects the two halves of Lago Argentina. Instead of receding, the Perito Moreno actually adds around 2m (6 ft.) every day, reaching toward the other shore of the lake. The new glacier is formed by gravity, pushing old compacted ice outward in response to the weight of new snow, which falls almost constantly up on the crest of the Andes several miles away.

As the ice face expands, however, huge chunks calve off the face, a few every day—there's a good chance to see it happen while you're there, if you're patient. The whole glacier remains in equilibrium, losing as much ice as it gains. Even though periodically it dams up the channel completely—most recently in March 2006—the lake water finally blasts through the ice

dam, carrying off a spectacular mass of frozen debris.

There are 48 glaciers in this park in the southern tip of Argentina, but this one's the easiest to get to, only 80km (50 miles) from the town of El Calafate. From the parking lot on the peninsula, walkways with frequent observation platforms descend to the glacier's face. Several operators offer guided treks onto the glacier itself, starting with a boat ride across the lake. On the way, you'll pass through harsh rocky steppe and a rare beech forest. Scramble around for a couple hours on rough surface of the ancient ice and peer deep into sapphire-hued crevices—it's an exhilarating experience, to say the least.

---

(i) **Punto Calafate** (www.elcalafate.com.ar)

✈ El Calafate

🛏 $$$ **Los Notros,** Parque Nacional Los Glaciares (*C* **54/11/4814-3934;** www.losnotros.com). $$ **Hotel Posada Los**

**Alamos,** Gobernador Moyano at Bustillo, El Calafate (℗ **54/2902/491144;** www. posadalosalamos.com).

**TOUR Caltur** (℗ **54/2902/491368;** www. cultur.com.ar)

# Kuranda Village
## *Packaging the Rainforest Experience*
### Queensland, Australia

AT KURANDA VILLAGE, THE ONCE WILD RAINFOREST IS QUICKLY BECOMING LITTLE MORE THAN a theme park. Native plants and animals are protected, and the rainforest is no longer at risk from mining and logging interests that once threatened its trees and streams. But the tourism that saved the rainforest near Kuranda is transforming it into something it was never meant to be.

If you were really pressed for time, you could just go to the Rainforest Dome atop the Hotel Sofitel Reef Casino in Cairns and see 100 rainforest species in one tidy artificial environment. But it only takes a day to visit the actual rainforest just outside of Cairns, a lush green landscape of waterfalls, steep ferny slopes, and rare primeval cycad jungle. You won't escape tourists altogether, but it's an intriguing case study in how eco-tourism can save habitat.

An influx of hippies in the 1970s saved the mountain village of Kuranda from having to resort to mining, logging, or coffee growing for economic survival. It still has a bohemian vibe, with markets selling locally made arts and crafts, fresh produce, boomerangs, T-shirts, and the like. Tourism is the mainstay of the local economy these days, which means that preserving what's left of the surrounding rainforest is high on every Kurandan's agenda.

Naturally, you have to climb the mountain to see it. There are two scenic ways to do this: on the Skyrail Rainforest Cableway (℗ **61/7/4038 1555;** www.skyrail.com.au), the world's longest gondola cableway; and on the **Kuranda Scenic Railway** (℗ **61/7/ 4036 9249;** www.kurandascenicrailway. com.au). Luckily, combination packages are available so you can enjoy both on one round-trip. The gondola hoists over the foothills of the coastal range until the

dense green rainforest canopy takes over beneath you, full of wild orchids and rare butterflies; at two intermediate stops, **Red Peak** and **Barron Falls,** you can stroll around for ground-level views of the rainforest (guided walks available). The steam train affords magnificent vistas of the Barron Gorge and its huge waterfalls, which were harnessed for hydroelectric power in the 1930s. Either way, the ride takes 90 minutes and ends at Kuranda station, which is so draped in ferns, you'll be in no doubt that you're in the rainforest.

The main eco-site in Kuranda is the 40-hectare (99-acre) **Rainforestation Nature Park,** Kennedy Highway (℗ **61/7/ 4085 5008;** www.rainforest.com.au), where you can take a 45-minute narrated ride into the rainforest on a World War II amphibious Army Duck. The tour includes a performance by Aboriginal dancers and koala-cuddling activities in the wildlife park, but every ticket sold ensures that flora and fauna will remain protected. You can also walk through either of two aviaries—**Birdworld** (℗ **61/7/4093 9188),** behind the Heritage markets off Rob Veivers Drive, or **the Aviary,** 8 Thongon St. (℗ **61/ 7/4093 7411)**—or visit **Australian Butterfly Sanctuary** (8 Rob Veivers Dr.; ℗ **61/ 7/4093 7575;** www.australianbutterflies. com). To go farther afield, take a 45-minute river cruise with **Kuranda Riverboat**

**Tours** (✆ **61/7/4093 7476** or 61/412/159212). Yes, it's only a quick taste of the Australian rainforest—but it's a better way to sell the rainforest than to level it for timber.

---

ⓘ **Kuranda Tourist Office,** Centenary Park (✆ **61/7/0493 9311;** www.kuranda.org)

🛏 $$ **Hotel Sofitel Reef Casino,** 35–41 Wharf St., Cairns (✆ **800/221-4542** in the U.S. and Canada, 44/20/8283 4500 in the U.K., 61/1800/808 883 in Australia; www.accorhotels.com). $$ **The Reef Retreat,** 10–14 Harpa St., Palm Cove, Cairns (✆ **61/7/4059 1744;** www.reefretreat.com.au).

# Rotorua
## *Land of Mists*
### North Island, New Zealand

MOUNT TARAWERA IS AN ACTIVE VOLCANO, AND THE LANDSCAPE IN AND AROUND ROTORUA is a hotbed of geothermal activity. The hot springs have made Rotorua famous as a spa, but the same forces that make the area attractive to tourists also make it unstable and unpredictable. The landscape here is in flux and still being formed.

There's something unsettling about the landscape around Rotorua—the sulfuric aroma, the steam hissing out of fissures in

Hell's Gate in Rotorua.

the earth, the volcano peak of Mount Tarawera in the hazy distance. In this case, human actions aren't to blame for the fluctuations in the environment; it's just life as usual on the North Island of New Zealand.

Rotorua has been a spa destination since the 19th century, when the Te Arawa people (the local population is still about one-third Maori) began guiding visitors to the picturesque Pink and White Terraces, spectacular limestone formations—some called them the "Eighth Wonder of the World"—on the shores of silica-rich Lake Rotomahana. Afterward, tourists "took the waters" at the region's many hot springs. Then came the big event of 1886, when Mount Tarawera erupted, spewing much more lava than the 1980 Mount St. Helens eruption. The Terraces were annihilated, the local landscape radically reshaped. Tarawera is still visible 24km (15 miles) southeast of town, a massive hump of lava domes clearly cleft down the middle by the force of the 1886 eruption. **Volcanic Air Safaris** (✆ **64/7/348-9984;** www.volcanicair.co.nz) offers helicopter rides over the crater.

While the spas are still popular, these days it's geothermal attractions that make Rotorua a hot destination (no pun intended). Right in town, there's the **Whakarewarewa Thermal Reserve,** Hemo Road (✆ **64/800/494-252** or 64/7/348-9047; www.nzmaori.co.nz), a rocky landscape full of mud pools and the prolific Pohutu Geyser, which shoots upward 16 to 20m (50–60 ft.) 10 to 25 times a day. South of town on Highway 5, you can see the **Buried Village of Te Wairoa,** excavated after the 1886 eruption; **Waimangu Volcanic Valley,** with the world's largest hot-water spring and the mysterious rising and falling turquoise lake in Inferno Crater; and **Waiotapu,** where you can see the Lady Knox Geyser, New Zealand's largest bubbling mud pool, and arsenic-green Devils' Bath. The fiercest of the thermal valleys, though, is northeast of town on Highway 30: the Maori-owned **Hell's Gate,** which has hot-water lakes, sulfur formations, Rotorua's only mud volcano, and the largest boiling whirlpool in New Zealand.

Perhaps the most sobering sight is in the middle of the city: **Kuirau Park,** off Pukuatua and Ranolf street. As recently as 2000 a spontaneous eruption blasted the park; you can still see the dead trees in a cordoned-off area. There are still active vents smoldering up at Tarawera. Take nothing for granted.

---

ⓘ ✆ **64/7/348-5179;** www.rotorua.co.nz.

✈ Rotorua

🛏 $$ **Rydges Rotorua,** 272 Fenton St. (✆ **64/800/367-793** or 64/7/349-0900; www.rydges.com). $$ **Wylie Court Motor Lodge,** 345 Fenton St. (✆ **64/800/100-879** or 64/7/347-7879; http://new.wyliecourt.co.nz).

**53** Ecosystems in Transition

# Sundarbans National Park
## *Man-Eaters in the Mangroves*
### Ganges Delta, Bangladesh/India

SUNDARBANS NATIONAL PARK FACES TWO SERIOUS RISKS. RISING SEA LEVELS DUE TO GLOBAL warming could flood the park and threaten the tigers, wild birds, and other native species. And the River Ganges, which feeds the delta where the park is located, is so polluted from industrial outflow, raw sewage, human remains, and naturally occurring arsenic that the water is no longer safe for humans or animals to drink.

Sundarbans is used to dancing on the edge—on the edge between India and Bangladesh, on the edge between the saline Bay of Bengal and the three freshwater rivers that feed it, on the edge between monsoon floods and a dry season that's not all that dry. And now, as if rising sea levels and upstream dams aren't bad enough, tectonic shifts are actually tilting the Bangladesh half of this vast delta, further disrupting the balance between fresh and salt waters that bred this unique ecosystem in the first place.

Traditionally, Sundarbans—despite a name that means "beautiful forest"—was considered a dangerous wasteland. Now it's recognized as a World Heritage Biosphere, home to threatened species like water monitor lizards, olive ridley turtles, Gangetic dolphins, spotted chital deer, and macaques, as well as such amazing birds as brown-winged kingfishers, gray-headed lapwings, Pallas's fish eagles, and mangrove whistlers. And what other place in the world has a fish like the mudskipper, which actually climbs trees?

And then there are the native Bengal tigers. It's unclear why they're so much more aggressive than other Bengal tigers; it could be the saltwater they drink while swimming between the scattered mangrove islands, or the fact that shifting tides obliterate the scents that help them mark their territory, or inherited behavior from generations of scavenging on drowned humans during monsoon floods. Whatever it is, they're renowned man-eaters, and Sundarbans visitors must always be on their guard while cruising the intricate tidal waterways by boat, observing wildlife from enclosed watchtowers, or wearing face masks on the back of their head to confuse the tigers, which prefer to attack humans from behind.

But dealing with tigers is part of the excitement when visiting this sprawling system of parks bridging Bangladesh and West Bengal, India. The Sundarbans is not necessarily unspoiled wilderness; you'll see local residents harvesting the sundri trees for timber or charcoal, using trained otters to fish for the shrimp that shelter within the mangrove roots, hunting for beehives in honey season (Apr–May). But there is something inherently untamable about the place that calls out to adventurers. There are only a few basic accommodations within the park; many visitors come on a government-organized 2- to 3-day tour (the best season is Nov–Mar), which ferries guests around on boats to sites such as the Sajnakhali Bird Sanctuary, the Bhagatpur Crocodile Project, or the ridley turtles' nesting site at Kanak.

Yes, there could be a crocodile basking on that next muddy bank, or a tiger lurking in the tangled understory of a mangrove island. But just as easily you could be delighted by a rhesus monkey chattering in the thick green treetop canopy, or a stately heron promenading through the shallows. Hold your breath, stay alert, and you're sure to be surprised.

✈ Kolkata

🛏 $$ **Sunderban Tiger Camp,** Dayapur, India (✆ **32935749** or 9331092632; www.sunderbantigercamp.com). $$ **Sundar Chital Tourist Lodge,** Sajnakhali, India, c/o West Bengal Tourism Development (✆ **033 2485917;** www.wbtourism.com). $ **Hiron Point Rest House,** Bangladesh (✆ **404 071**).

**TOUR Bangladesh Ecotours** (✆ **880/ 189-318345** or 880/171-264827; www.bangladeshecotours.com). **Safari Plus** (✆ **880/2-8858736** or 880/2-8831695; www.safariplus.net). **Oriental Tours and Travel** (www.wildlifeindiatour.com).

Ecosystems in Transition  54

# Nilgiri Biosphere Reserve
## *Forest upon Forest upon Forest*
### Kerald/Karnakata/Tamil Nadu, India

EFFORTS TO CONSERVE THE FORESTS OF THE NILGIRI HILLS HAVE ALTERED THE LIVES AND undermined the livelihoods of indigenous peoples who have hunted and farmed and grazed the region for thousands of years. And now increased tourism poses risks to conservation. A proposed railway to carry tourists through the area would cut through a rare expanse of elephant habitat, endangering thousands of elephants.

In the clamor to protect endangered species, who's watching out for the species homo sapiens? The Nilgiri Hills of south India shelter over a million individuals from various indigenous peoples, hunter-gatherers and forest dwellers who depend upon the forests for their survival. What we call poaching and illegal logging are simply ancient, honorable ways of life to them.

Balancing these interests is an ongoing debate here in south India. Named an International Biosphere Reserve in 1986, the 5,520-sq.-km (2,131-sq.-mile) Nilgiri preserve spreads across the intersection of three states—Karnataka, Kerala, and Tamil Nadu. The forests that blanket the steep slopes of the western Ghats constitute a spectrum of forest habitats, rainforest giving way to moist evergreens, then thorn forest and scrub, morphing into grassland and the short, dense Shola forest—often referred to as "living fossils"—atop the plateau. The various phases offer everything you'd expect in a tropical forest: Mosses, ferns, and orchids grow thickly; heavy lianas drape from the canopy; and buttresses support the giant trunks. Along with tigers and elephants, it's a protected home for the Nilgiri tahr, the glossy black Nilgiri langar, and the endangered lion-tailed macaque. Of its 3,330 species, 1,232 are endemic.

Just south of Mysore, three superb wildlife sanctuaries—Bandipur National Park, Nagarhole National Park, and **Mudumalai National Park**—show off tigers and elephants and leopards to nearly 200,000 visitors a year. Other parks within the reserve are known for their bird-watching or for their rare orchids; the hilltop park **Mukurthi in Tamil Nadu** gets migrating birds from the Himalayas November to March, and there's even a narrow-gauge train climbing to the charming old hill station of Ooty. This humid tropical wilderness is so rich in flora and fauna, cameras and binoculars can barely catch it all.

Meanwhile, peoples such as the Todas, the Malasars, Sholigas, Paniyas, various subgroups of Kurumbas, and the nearly extinct primitive Cholanaikens hunt small game; weave baskets; and forage spices, honey, and medicinal plants from the forest. Those who once herded buffalo have seen their grasslands dwindle; those who lived by slash-and-burn agriculture depend now on wage work on local tea and teak plantations, or on government handouts. New jobs may be created by increased tourism, but will they spoil the traditional cultural practices?

The newest threat to the region is a proposed 156km (97-mile) broad-gauge railway from Chamarajanagar to Mettupalayam, cutting a broad swath through the Sathyamangalam forests, a corridor of woodlands that's home to some 2,500 elephants. It's all in the name of tourism development, of course—but since when was destroying elephant habitat good for tourism?

✈ Bangalore

⊨ $$ **Jungle Retreat,** Masinagudi, Tamil Nadu (① **91/423/2526469;** www.jungleretreat.com). $$ **Bandipur Safari Lodge,** Bandipur National Park, Karnakata (www.junglelodge.com).

**TOUR Ecomantra Nature Adventures** (① **91/22/65248646;** www.ecomantra.org)

---

55 **Ecosystems in Transition**

# Fiordlands National Park
## *Middle-earth Under the Ozone Hole*
### South Island, New Zealand

THE HOLE IN THE OZONE LAYER THAT HAS THREATENED SOUTH ISLAND FOR DECADES HAS started to close, but the danger isn't over yet. While the human-produced chemicals that weakened the ozone layer have been banned or heavily restricted, it will take many years for the damage to be entirely reversed.

Fiordlands National Park.

The entrance to the Fiordlands' most dramatic fiord, 23km-long (14-mile) Milford Sound, is so narrow, Captain Cook missed it completely when he first sailed around New Zealand some 200 years ago. Plenty of tourists have discovered it since, though—scenic planes and helicopters do regular flyovers, tour buses clog up the stunningly scenic Milford Road from Te Anau, and sightseeing cruises chug around the water. Head instead for the largest fiord in the park, Doubtful Sound, which is much more peaceful and remote. Real Journeys (see "Tour," below) leads day sails on catamarans or overnight cruises on the *Fiordland Navigator;* out on the water you're likely to have the bottlenose dolphins, frisky fur seals, and rare crested penguins all to yourselves.

The quintessential Fiordlands experience, though, is reserved for hikers, who can study the striations of its glacially carved rocks, discover delicate alpine wildflowers and mossy hollows, and feel the waterfalls' spray on their skin. New Zealand's Department of Conservation closely regulates the number of hikers on the famous Milford Track from Laek Te Anau to Milford Sound's Sandfly Point. It's a 4-day tramp, offered late October to mid-April only, and you must get permission from the park center's Great Walk Booking Desk, Box 29, Te Anau (© **64/3/ 249-8514;** greatwalksbooking@doc.govt. nz). For a guided option, go with Milford Track Guided Walk or get a 1-day sample with Trips 'n' Tramps (see below for both). Hobbit sightings are few and far between, but there're plenty of other wonders to compensate.

When it came to those intensely green, mist-shrouded Middle-earth landscapes, the *Lord of the Rings* movies didn't need stage sets or computer animation: Director Peter Jackson simply shot the films in New Zealand. The South Island's Fiordlands are perfect examples of that primeval *Lord of the Rings* look, with plunging waterfalls, pristine lakes, virgin forest, and steep peaks surrounding deep-gouged fiords. It's spectacularly different from the geothermal spots like Rotorua that travelers used to associate with New Zealand.

In the 1980s, however, New Zealand faced an environmental crisis: A hole in the ozone layer, discovered in the 1980s over Antarctica, was letting in dangerous levels of UV radiation. Not only would this expose humans to higher risks of developing skin cancer, vegetation could be damaged, and ocean plankton could die off. For the South Island, which lay closest to the ozone hole, it was scary news indeed. But thanks to widespread bans on the refrigerants, solvents, and aerosol sprays that did most of the damage, the hole seems to be growing smaller with each Antarctic summer, though it may take another 50 or 60 years for the ozone layer to be completely restored.

✈ Te Anau

**TOUR Real Journeys** (© **64/3/249-7416;** www.realjourneys.co.nz). **Fiordland Ecology Holidays,** Manapouri (© **64/3/249- 6600;** www.fiordland.gen.nz). **Milford Track Guided Walk** (© **64/3/441-1138;** www.milfordtrack.co.nz). **Trips 'n' Tramps** (© **64/3/249-7081;** www.milfordtours walks.co.nz).

# The Aysen Wilderness
## *Damming Patagonia*
### Baker & Pascua Rivers, Chile

ECONOMIC AND ENVIRONMENTAL PRIORITIES COLLIDE IN THE AYSEN REGION OF SOUTHERN Chile. Electricity supplies Chile's cities and powers the industries that drive the nation's economy, but the cost of damming rivers and running transmission lines through this pristine wilderness may be measured in species lost as well as dollars spent.

Starved for energy, the Chilean government thought it had an ideal solution. Why not dam up a couple of rivers down in Patagonia, that southern Chilean region where hardly anybody lives anyway?

Well, hardly anybody lives there except rare endemic species—like the torrent duck, the southern river otter, the culpeo fox, the endangered puma, and the Andean huemul deer, not to mention unique beech, conifer, and cypress forests. And while the Aysen region is mostly wilderness, unexplored until the late 19th century, its glacier panoramas and unspoiled temperate rainforest have increasingly become a top draw for adventure hiking, biking, rock climbing, trout fishing, rafting, and kayaking. With those rivers dammed, Chile may end up losing more than it gains.

Only one road—the Carreterra Austral—strings through this sparsely populated region, a ragged coastline deeply indented by fjords and milky-blue glacial lakes, including Lago General Carrera (South America's second-largest lake) and Lago O'Higgins (Chile's deepest lake). Between Cohaique and Puerto Natales, towns are few and between; adventure tourists generally fly into the region rather than drive. The proposed locations of the $4-billion project's five dams are along the turbulent Pascua River and the Baker River, Chile's largest, which run through a pristine landscape of rugged valleys and ice-capped mountain peaks. The waters of both are exceptionally pure—mostly meltwater from the Patagonian IceField, the largest expanse of permanent ice outside Antarctica and Greenland.

Not only will the dammed rivers flood nearly 6,000 hectares (15,000 acres) of biodiverse rainforest, the plan also requires clear-cutting the world's longest power corridor through that forest, thus leaving a 91m-wide (300-ft.) scar punctuated with 5,000 metal towers, stringing high-tension cables for 2,317km (1,440 miles) north to Chile's largest cities and copper mines. Some 14 national parks and protected reserves may be radically affected by the project.

Chile desperately needs energy—the country currently imports up to 70% of its energy, and skyrocketing oil prices and a reduction of natural gas imports from neighboring Argentina have hit hard. The five hydroelectric plants planned by the international conglomerate HidroAysen would increase Chile's power supply by 20%; it would take seven coal-fired plants to produce that amount, which would otherwise release 16 million tons of greenhouse gases.

International environmental organizations, however, have banded together under the name Chilean Patagonia Defense Council (CPDP) to urge Chile's president, Michelle Bachelet, to seek more renewable energy sources. Hydroelectric plants are not the only possible solution to Chile's energy problems, these activists insist. In terms of economic development, there might be far more to gain in the long run by tapping the eco-tourism potential of this region. Once those dams are built and that power corridor slashed, the Aysen's wilderness's beauty will be damaged forever.

ⓘ www.nrdc.org. www.international rivers.org.

✈ Balmaceda/Puerto Natales

🛏 $$ **Hotel CostAustralis,** Pedro Montt 262, Puerto Natales (© **56/61/ 412000;** www.australis.com). $$ **El Reloj,**

Baquedano 828, Coyhaique (© **56/67/ 231108**).

**TOUR Mountain Travel Sobek** (© **888/ 831-7526;** www.mtsobek.com). **H2O Patagonia** (© **866/525-2395** in the U.S. or 800/772-05820 in Europe; www.h2o patagonia.com). **Patago** (© **800/373-5360** or 970/416-7411; www.patago.com).

## Ecosystems in Transition · 57

# The Three Gorges
## *The Rising River*
### Central Yangtze River, China

ONCE COMPLETE AND FULLY OPERATIONAL, THIS CONTROVERSIAL DAM IS EXPECTED TO GENERATE as much energy as 15 nuclear power plants and control downstream flooding. However, the Three Gorges Dam is altering entire ecosystems, threatening traditional fisheries, and posing serious risks to human life and health for the millions of people who live in its shadow.

Look at it one way and China's massive Three Gorges Dam—the world's largest hydroelectric plant—will be a boon to the environment. This showcase project, a stupendous curtain of concrete sealing off the Yangtze River at Mount Wushan, will supply the vast central Yangtze basin with clean electric power, much less polluting than the oil or coal power previously used. The area's stunning scenic views of mountain peaks towering over steep chasms—celebrated in Chinese poetry and paintings since the 5th century A.D.—will still attract sightseeing riverboats, officials predict; the river will just be wider, and the peaks won't seem quite so high.

But that's by no means the only view of this controversial dam. To many Chinese, damming the Three Gorges is a sacrilege on the scale of filling up the Grand Canyon or turning off Niagara Falls. Though it was first proposed by Sun Yat-Sen in 1919, the project was hotly debated for years. Despite considerable dissent, it was finally pushed through the National People's Congress in 1992. As work on the dam progressed, environmental red flags have been raised continually.

On the cultural side, several towns were flooded over, a million-and-a-half people relocated, and many archaeological sites submerged. With the Yangtze widened above the dam, shipping traffic is increasing on the already-congested river. The dam's role in preventing seasonal floods (like the disasters of 1911, 1931, 1935, 1954, and 1998) has also been questioned, since the basin's draining network of tributary rivers and more than 100 freshwater lakes was compromised by haphazard erection of earlier dams and dykes. Massive deforestation has left the riverbanks vulnerable to erosion and landslides; silt that used to be deposited downstream in the delta may now plug up the reservoir. The dam's location on a seismic fault troubles many observers, though it did successfully weather the disastrous May 2008 earthquake.

Already the reservoir is grossly polluted, full of backed-up toxins and effluents from upstream areas, especially industrialized Hubei. The impact on wildlife is incalculable. The critically endangered Siberian crane has lost its principal winter habitat as wetlands above the dam are being wiped out. Four endemic Yang- tze species teeter on the verge of extinc- tion—the Chinese alligator, the Chinese paddlefish, the Chinese finless porpoise, and the baiji or Chinese river dolphin (which has already been ruled extinct). With the river's reduced flow of fresh water, algae are blooming at a fearsome rate downstream, and fishermen already report drastically smaller catches.

It's too late to turn back now; most of the dam's 26 hydroturbines are already in operation, and the reservoir is filling up. Belatedly, however, Chinese top officials have sought to distance themselves from the project, and they're hastily slapping bandages on the ravaged landscape. A new nature reserve in the Tian'ezhou oxbow lake has been stocked with the last few finless porpoises, as well as a herd of 600 Pere David's deer, formerly native to the Yangtze wetlands and long extinct in China. Dykes have been removed,

reconnecting lakes to the Yangtze; trees are being replanted on denuded river- banks; waste treatment plants are being installed in populous urban areas. But is all this too little, too late?

---

ⓘ **Hubei Tian'e-zhou Oxbow Wetland Center** (✆ **86/27/8274-3845**). **Interna- tional Rivers** (✆ **510/848-1155;** www. internationalrivers.org).

🛏 $$$ **Xierdun Jiudian (Hilton),** Zhongshan San Lu 139, Chongqing (✆ **800/ 820-0600** or 86/23/6903-9999; www. hilton.com). $$ **Qing Chuan Jiari Jiudian (Riverside Holiday Inn),** Xima Chang Jie 88, Wuhan (✆ **86/27/8471-6688;** www. sixcontinentshotels.com).

**TOUR Yangtze River Cruise** (✆ **800/305- 1213** or 86/717/625-1390; www.china- tourism.org). **China Odyssey Tours** (✆ **800/773-0862;** www.chinaodyssey tours.com).

---

**58** Ecosystems in Transition

# The Windmills of Kinderdijk
## *The Dutch War Against the Elements*
### Alblasserwaard, South Holland, the Netherlands

THE HISTORIC WINDMILLS AT KINDERDIJK, BUILT TO PUMP EXCESS WATER FROM LAND THE Dutch had reclaimed from the sea, are retired now, but the ocean still threatens the low country of the Netherlands. Although the Netherlands has the world's most sophisti- cated flood-control system, the nation is particularly vulnerable to rising sea levels caused by global warming; about 65% of its land is already below sea level.

This is what you get when you start fooling around with nature. The very name "Neth- erlands" means "low country," and nowhere else has man so radically trans- formed the landscape. As every school- child knows, ever since the Middle Ages dikes have been built here to turn coastal marshes into solid arable land. But it isn't just a question of stealing terrain for agri- culture; in this flat, treeless region, vast inland seas rise and fall, peninsulas turn into islands and then submerge com- pletely, and even in the 19th and 20th

centuries, disastrous floods have periodi- cally gushed in to reclaim the land.

Once the Dutch began to play with nature, an inevitable cycle of events began to play out. As people drained swampland for agricultural use, the layers of boggy peat would eventually compress and the ground level drop even further, requiring further drainage—making the underlying peat compress even more. (It didn't help that peat was also being dug up, dried, and used for fuel, up until the 19th c.) Whereas in other countries, mills were built to grind corn or power factories; however, the chief purpose of Holland's iconic windmills was to control seasonal fluctuations in water level, pumping excess water from the below-sea-level polder lands to protect its settlements from destruction.

To appreciate this arrangement, come to the tidy Dutch village of Kinderdijk, on the Alblasserwaard polders near Rotterdam. Kinderdijk (the name means "children's dike") has 19 historic windmills—all dating from around 1740—set in a windmill park along a branching canal. Their powerful mill sails (each sail is around 14m/46 ft. long) harness the force of the wind to turn large paddlewheels, which scoop up water and sluice it into the canals, draining into a reservoir and then the nearby River Lek. One windmill's interior has been fitted with period furnishings; a miller is on hand to operate the mill and explain its technology. Though they're turned on for effect on summer Saturdays, the windmills were retired during World War II, after diesel-driven pumping engines built in the 1920s took over the job.

Half-hour canal cruises drift through the windmill park April to September, but you'll get a better perspective up close by cycling along the canal paths, laid out along the absolutely flat polder embankments. It's an evocative sight, worthy of the Dutch masters, with the flat North Sea sunlight shimmering on the polders' vivid green grass under a mackerel-colored sky. Peaceful, rural, traditional—who knows what this land would have been like otherwise? It hardly matters whether those Dutch ancestors ever had a right to master the sea like this; it's been going on too long for them to turn back now.

---

✈ Rotterdam

🛏 $$$ **Westin Rotterdam,** Weena 686, Rotterdam (℃ **31/10/430-2000;** www. westin.com). $ **Hotel Kinderdijk,** Westkinderdijk 361, Albasserdam (℃ **31/78/ 691-2425**). $ **Het Wapen van Alblasserdam,** Dam 24, Alblasserdam (℃ **31/78/ 691-4711**).

# 2 Sea & Stream

Mono Lake.

# Delaware Bayshores
## *Atlantic Flyway Hot Spot*
### New Jersey/Pennsylvania/Delaware

SHORELINE EROSION, INVASIVE REEDS, OIL SPILLS, FARMING, AND HUMAN AND ANIMAL ACTIVITY at popular beaches all threaten nesting and foraging habitat for migratory birds on this major migration route. While much of this region is protected, remaining areas are increasingly threatened by urban sprawl.

For more than a million neotropical birds, migrating every spring from South America to Canada, the Delaware Bayshores beckons like a big Holiday Inn. Special buffet tonight: tiny green horseshoe crab eggs, freshly laid and served right on the beach! Every May and June the birds feast greedily, doubling their weight before heading on to higher latitudes.

But now this great migratory rest stop along the Atlantic Flyway is in trouble. Once it held one of the country's greatest oyster beds; ravaged in the 1950s and 1990s by parasites, the bay's oyster population is still in critical condition. Horseshoe crabs, more abundant here than anywhere else in the U.S., have been so drastically overharvested that migrating birds dependent on their eggs (most notably the endangered red knot) are dying off. The recent arrival of the alien Chinese mitten crab threatens to push out what's left of the crabs. Residential development around the bay reduces habitat and pollutes the water. And then there's climate change, with milder winters and rising sea levels throwing traditional migratory patterns out of whack.

Lying between the Delmarva Peninsula ("del" for Delaware, "mar" for Maryland, "va" for Virginia) and New Jersey's southern shore, Delaware Bay is not as big as its neighbor, Chesapeake Bay, but it's the culmination of a vast watershed that runs upstream through Pennsylvania to Hancock, New York, the longest undammed main-stem river east of the Mississippi (and spawning grounds for species such as the American eel, American shad, Atlantic sturgeon, and shortnose sturgeon). This great interdependent water system doesn't care where state boundaries fall. But thanks to coordination by the U.S. Fish and Wildlife Service, the Nature Conservancy, and local Audubon society chapters, a patchwork of local parks preserves as much of this landscape as possible—not an easy task in this thickly settled Northeast corridor.

A mile from Philadelphia International Airport lies the shimmering tidal marsh of the **John Heinz National Wildlife Refuge,** 8601 Lindbergh Blvd., Philadelphia (*©* **215/365-3118,** http://heinz.fws.gov). Two major wildlife refuges in Delaware State are at **Bombay Hook,** 2591 Whitehall Neck Rd., Smyrna (*©* **302/653-9345,** http://bombayhook.fws.gov), whose tidal salt marshes are prime nesting grounds for wood ducks, bluebirds, purple martins, barn owls, and eastern screech owls; and 10,000-acre (4,046-hectare) **Prime Hook,** 11978 Turkle Pond Rd., Milton (*©* **302/684-8419,** http://primehook.fws.gov), with its wide mix of woodland and wetland habitats where bald eagles nest, peregrine falcons stop over, and the endangered Delmarva fox squirrel makes its last stand. Also, check out the New Jersey Audubon Society's online guide to popular birdwatching sites in the state's marshlands, forests, and beaches (www.njwildlifetrails.org/dbloops.htm), including Cape May.

**60** **At Water's Edge**

# Cape Cod National Seashore
## *Turtle Time on the Outer Cape*
### Chatham to Provincetown, Massachusetts

AS HOUSING GROWTH ON THE CAPE CONTINUES TOWARD CAPACITY, PESTICIDES, NITRATES, and phosphates leaching from residential septic systems and other pollution have taken a toll on threatened species such as the diamondback terrapin, along with hundreds of other native species. However, efforts are underway to restore more than 2,500 estuaries that were degraded by salt-marsh ditching and dikes.

In the old children's tale, "slow and steady wins the race"—but slow and steady hasn't worked so well for turtles lately. Complex factors—habitat loss, pollution, disease, global climate change—have reduced their numbers, both in the U.S. and around the world. Although several marine turtles swim offshore (loggerheads, leatherbacks, ridleys, hawksbills, green turtles), Cape Cod naturalists are more concerned about the turtles who live on the edge of the Atlantic, where beach meets estuary meets creek—hibernating in tidal mudflats in winter, mating in the salt marshes in spring, nesting in the sand dunes come summer (that is, if raccoons don't steal their eggs). On this narrow, low-lying barrier strip, bisected by busy Route 6, just imagine how hard it is for a little spotted turtle to cross from ocean to bay without becoming road kill.

Running for 30 miles (48km) along the Atlantic coast of Cape Cod, the Cape Cod National Seashore was set aside in 1961 to preserve the magnificent white sands of the Outer Cape, where the dunes stand 50 to 150 feet (15–46m) high. A string of

awesome beaches, all well marked off of Route 6, include Coast Guard and Nauset Light beaches in Eastham, Marconi Beach in Wellfleet, Head of the Meadow Beach in Truro, and Provincetown's Race Point and Herring Cove beaches. You can also bicycle up the Cape Cod Rail Trail, which goes as far as Wellfleet, and walk onto the beach.

Severed from the mainland by the Cape Cod Canal, Cape Cod has a limited range of habitats, and in general has fewer species than the mainland does. Yet just yards away from white sand and surf lies a whole other natural world, with its own meditative rhythms: a rich wilderness of marsh and wetlands tucked away behind the beach. Here, the seashore's rangers carefully monitor not only the threatened northern diamondback terrapin and eastern box turtle, but even common freshwater species like painted turtles and snapping turtles, and the less common pond-dwelling musk turtle and spotted turtle.

At the Salt Pond Visitor Center (just east of Rte. 6 in Eastham), you can pick up a brochure identifying the turtles, then walk the splendid **Nauset Marsh Trail,** where you're likely to spot painted turtles basking on logs. The **Wellfleet Bay Wildlife Sanctuary,** off Route 6, South Wellfleet (✆ **508/349-2615;** www.wellfleetbay.org), a 1,000-acre (405-hectare) refuge run by the Massachusetts Audubon Society, has no fewer than 5 miles (8km) of trails through pine forests, moors, and salt marsh, a favored habitat for diamondback terrapins. And for box turtles, who prefer fields and forest, the town of Wellfleet has set aside a 6½-acre (2.6-hectare) parcel in the middle of the intertidal marsh, designated—what else?—Box Turtle Woods.

---

ⓘ **Cape Cod National Seashore** (✆ **508/255-3421;** www.nps.gov/caco)

✈ Hyannis

🛏 $$ **Viking Shores Motor Lodge,** Rte. 6, Eastham (✆ **800/242-2131;** www.vikingshores.com). $$ **Even'tide,** 650 Rte. 6, South Wellfleet (✆ **800/368-0007** or 508/349-3410; www.eventidemotel.com).

**At Water's Edge** **61**

# Blowing Rocks Preserve
## *If These Rocks Could Talk . . .*
### Hobe Sound, Florida

OCEAN POLLUTION AND DUMPING ARE A SERIOUS THREAT TO THE SURVIVAL OF REMAINING SEA turtle populations. Closer to home, pollution, eroding dunes, marauding predators such as dogs and birds, and beachfront lighting (which confuses the hatchlings) all contribute to the demise of these endangered species. Asian snakewood, an aggressively invasive plant, threatens native vegetation.

Up at the north end of the Miami sprawl, nature finally gets room to breathe again—and that's good news for endangered sea turtles. On the beaches of North Palm Beach County, the turtles swim ashore to lay clutches of eggs from May to August, burying them in the warm sand. It's hard to believe that this all happens only 20 miles (32km) away from glitzy Palm Beach, but it does—and preservationists are determined to keep those nesting beaches safe from high-rise developers.

The **Marinelife Center of Juno Beach,** 14200 U.S. 1, Juno Beach (✆ **561/627-8280**), will quickly get you up to speed on the local habitats with its hands-on exhibits about Florida's tropical ecosystems. Visitors can also walk interpretive trails through the sand dunes; in June and July, the peak of turtle-breeding season, guided walks take you to a nearby beach where the nests are laid. These walks are so popular, they often book up as soon as reservations are taken, beginning May 1, so call early.

North of Jupiter lies a protected sliver of barrier island between the Atlantic and Indian River Lagoon. This sanctuary is named **Blowing Rocks** after its distinctive limestone ridge, formed from compacted seashells and sand, that guards the ocean shore. In rough weather, waves forced through erosion holes in the rock are sent whistling sky high—quite a dramatic sight. Despite this wall, some 600 loggerhead turtles crawl onto the beach in summer to lay their eggs; nesting areas are roped off and must be strictly observed.

Entering through a tunnel of thick evergreen sea grapes, you can take a mile-long (1.6km) hike along the ridge through the oceanfront dunes. Coastal hammocks are planted with local sabal palms and the distinctive gumbo-limbo tree (nicknamed the "tourist tree" because its peeling red bark looks like a sunburned tourist), gradually replacing the invasive Australian pines that overran the beach before it was donated to the Nature Conservancy in 1969. Across the highway the preserve backs onto the Indian River Lagoon, a threatened estuary 156 miles (251km) long that is slowly being coaxed back to health after decades of pollution and overdevelopment. Here a boardwalk trail passes mangrove wetlands and oak hammock, which shelter fiddler crabs and, occasionally, manatees. It's like a mini-course in Florida habitats; there's even a butterfly garden featuring native plants.

Though many visitors come here in summer to see the loggerheads, Blowing Rocks is also delightful in the fall, when the southward bird migration flies through—warblers, offshore pelagic birds, hawks, and falcons stop off to feast on the abundant sea grapes' juicy berries. Springtime buzzes with butterflies and hummingbirds visiting beach wildflowers. It's generally a cool place to hang out anytime of year—just ask the turtles.

ⓘ **Blowing Rocks Preserve,** 574 S. Beach Rd., State Rd. A1A (✆ **561/744-6668**)

✈ Palm Beach

🛏 $$$ **Jupiter Beach Resort,** 5 N. A1A, Jupiter (✆ **800/228-8810** or 561/746-2511; www.jupiterbeachresort.com). $ **Baron's Landing Motel,** 18125 Ocean Blvd., Jupiter (✆ **561/746-8757**).

---

**62** **At Water's Edge**

# Cape Hatteras National Seashore
## *A Battered Barrier Island*
### Outer Banks, North Carolina

CLIMATE CHANGE HAS INCREASED OCEAN LEVELS AND STORM SEVERITY, CONTRIBUTING TO THE increasing erosion of these fragile beaches. As many as 2,200 vehicles park on Outer Banks beaches during the peak summer season, driving through nesting shorebird habitat on the way—and contributing to an 86% decline in shorebird populations over the past decade. Some species are no longer seen in the area.

Rising oceans and eroding beaches—they go hand in hand, and anyone who's ever stood on the barrier islands of North America's Atlantic coast knows how fragile those strips of sand seem, frail bits of land holding off the pounding surf. Add to that the increasing frequency of tropical storms and hurricanes ravaging this part of the world, and those barrier islands could disappear any day now. Oh, solutions have been proposed—there was a plan in 2001, for instance, to dredge offshore sand and pump it back onto Nags Head Beach—but they're expensive, may

not have any long-term effect, and could damage fragile seashore ecosystems.

On this 70-mile (113km) strand of Outer Banks barrier islands—also known as "the Graveyard of the Atlantic" for its treacherous waters and shifting shoals—summer thunderstorms can sweep in at a moment's notice. Its riptides and currents are so strong, dabbling in the surf is better than really swimming. But repeat visitors are hooked on the land's-end vibe of the Outer Banks, its edgy wind-scoured beauty and promise of drama.

Cape Hatteras Seashore is an informal, barefoot hangout—you can easily beach

Cape Hatteras Lighthouse.

seabeach amaranth; and leatherback, loggerhead, and green sea turtles (pay attention to beach closures during nesting season). At the north end, on Bodie Island, guided ranger walks along Coquina Beach explore this delicate ecosystem, home to blue crabs and sea turtles. Across the bridge on Hatteras Island, you can bird-watch on a nature trail at the **Pea Island Wildlife Refuge** (© **252/473-1131**); on Ocracoke Island, you can visit the island's wild ponies, just like those up the coast on Assateague Island.

As you'd expect, each island has its own substantial lighthouse, the tallest being the black-and-white diagonally striped Cape Hatteras Lighthouse, built in 1870. At 208 feet (63m), it's the tallest brick lighthouse in the United States; visitors can climb 268 steps to the top for an awesome view. In 1999, however, the beach had eroded to within 100 feet (30m) of the lighthouse. To protect it, engineers moved the lighthouse inland 2,900 feet (884m)—only to lose another 1,400 feet (427m) of sand since then, mostly due to 2003's Hurricane Isabel. The lighthouse now stands 1,500 feet (457m) from the water. But for how long?

(i) **Hatteras Island Visitor Center,** Buxton (© **252/995-4474;** www.nps.gov/caha)

✈ Norfolk International

🛏 $$ **Cape Hatteras Bed & Breakfast,** 4223 Old Lighthouse Rd., Buxton (© **800/252-3316**). $$ **Okracoke Harbor Inn,** 135 Silver Lake Rd., Okracoke (© **888/456-1998** or 252/928-5731; www.ocracoke harborinn.com).

hop, pulling into one of many beach-access parking lots, crossing a small boardwalk over dunes of sea oats, and plopping down in the tawny sand. North Carolina Highway 12 runs along the national seashore, linking its four long narrow islands—from north to south, Bodie Island, Hatteras Island, Ocracoke, and Cedar Island (a car ferry links Hatteras to Ocracoke and Ocracoke to Cedar Island). Among the endangered species that thrive here are piping plovers;

# The Shores of Biscayne Bay
## *Last Stand of the Mangroves*
### Homestead, Florida

MANGROVES ARE A CRUCIAL ELEMENT OF FLORIDA'S ECOSYSTEM. MANGROVE STANDS USED TO line the coast, until hotel developers started ripping them out to gain access to the shores for high-rises and swimming beaches. Today, it's illegal to cut down mangroves, but the damage is already done. Biscayne's forest is one of the last great stands in the state.

Snorkelers and scuba divers are so eager to get down to Biscayne Bay's enormous coral reef, they often miss the park's most spectacular secret: its shoreline. In these surprisingly shallow waters—Biscayne Bay is actually an estuary, a gradual transition zone from freshwater to saline sea—an overwhelming variety of life thrives in pillowy seagrass beds and tangled mangrove stands.

Mangroves love estuaries; they are uniquely adapted to handle saltwater, through either salt-blocking root systems or leaves that secrete excess salt. Canoe or kayak along the western shore of Biscayne Bay and you'll see three species—red, black, and white mangroves—all with distinctive arching prop roots, cigar-shaped seed pods, and thick-bladed leaves. Those dense above-water roots trap the waters flowing into the bay and let sediment settle out; they also shelter the smallest marine organisms, which feed on disintegrated leaves (and then provide food themselves for fish, pink shrimp, crabs, and the Florida spiny lobster—it's the circle of life). The treetops create a canopy where many birds, including the endangered brown pelican, breed and nest.

Sediments settling onto the shallow floor of the bay make an ideal base for flowering seagrasses, which depend on the shallows' plentiful sunlight. Seagrass beds produce loads of oxygen and stabilize sediments; they also feed and shelter myriad sea creatures, especially juveniles that aren't ready for open water. Even from a kayak, you can look down through the amazingly clear water and identify the three major types of seagrasses: shoal grass in the shallowest waters; wide-leaved turtlegrass, the most common; and cylindrical-leaved manatee grass. Packed white-sand floors may be great for swimming beaches, but these oozy bottoms are a vital source of marine health.

If you don't bring your own canoe or kayak, **Biscayne National Underwater Park, Inc.** (✆ **305/230-1100**) rents them for use within sight of the Convoy Point visitor center. Some small creeks and channels just north of Convoy Point are fun to explore, prime spots for glimpsing an American crocodile or manatee. An even better option for exploring the shoreline may be **ranger-led canoe tours** (✆ **305/230-1100** for information).

Unlike land-based parks, which can erect barriers to keep out invaders and pollutants, an underwater park like Biscayne has to deal with whatever flows in. The mangroves and seagrass can only do so much to clean south Florida's water. As it is, imagine what would have happened if developers had been allowed to dredge the bay and build resorts in the early 1960s. Instead, conservationists fought to preserve the bay and its 44 tiny islands as a national park. Their victory was a win for all of us.

(i) **Biscayne National Park,** 9700 SW 328th St., Homestead, FL (✆ **305/230-7275;** www.nps.gov/bisc)

✈ Miami International

🛏 $$$ **Sonesta Beach Resort Key Biscayne,** 350 Ocean Dr., Key Biscayne

(✆ **800/SONESTA** [766-3782] or 305/361-2021; www.sonesta.com). $$ **Indian Creek Hotel,** 2727 Indian Creek Dr., Miami Beach (✆ **800/491-2772** or 305/531-2727; www.indiancreekhotel.com).

At Water's Edge  **64**

# The Mink River Estuary
## *Blending the Great Lakes Shore*
### Door County, Wisconsin

A MIGRATORY STOPOVER FOR MORE THAN 200 SPECIES OF BIRDS, THIS AREA IS ALSO HOME TO two species on the U.S. Fish & Wildlife Service's threatened and endangered list: the Hine's emerald dragonfly and the dwarf lake iris. Saved by government and conservation groups from residential and commercial development, the Mink River Estuary is being protected as one of the most pristine estuaries in the struggling Great Lakes region.

Some estuaries lie between fresh and salt water, but not up in the Great Lakes. Here, they're a vital transition point between freshwater river and freshwater lake. The salinity of the water may not vary, but their ebb and flow still makes them dramatic, dynamic places—and often very fragile. In a popular vacation destination like Door County, tourist development has put such pressure on shoreline habitats that the Mink River—one of the last and most pristine estuaries—is more important than ever. Where else can lake fish come to spawn? Where else would migrating birds rest before and after crossing those huge lakes?

For such a significant body of water, the Mink River isn't very long, running from alkaline springs in the central Door Peninsula just a few miles to Rowley's Bay on Lake Michigan. Most of it is estuary, where the lake and river waters surge and flush together. At some seasons it's an expanse

of flooded marshes; at others, the marshes are dry, with just a few distinct spring channels running through. Whatever grows here must be adaptable—like the sedges, bluejoint grass, and reed grass at the marshy river's edge, backed by taller water-loving shrubs like willows, red osier dogwood, and alder. Going deeper into the marsh, you'll fight your way through thick stands of bulrushes, wild rice, narrow-leaved cat-tail, and bur-reed. The wettest areas display waterlilies and water milfoil. A low-lying white cedar swamp borders the marshes, and a small beach runs along Rowley's Bay, where threatened dune thistle clings to the sand.

Numerous birds nest in these wetlands—bitterns, loons, ducks, great blue herons, marsh hawks, and threatened species like the yellow rail, black duck, black tern, black-crowned night heron, northern harrier, and—rarely—a sandhill crane or two. In late summer and fall, you may even spot double-crested cormorants and red-breasted mergansers on their seasonal visits. And then there are, of course, the sort of mammals that thrive happily at water's edge—beaver, porcupine, and muskrat.

There are few trails through this soggy landscape, but the best way to explore it is by canoe. Pause often to let the silence descend around you, to hunt for birds with your binoculars. Let yourself lap and drift with the water, feeling the subtle interchange of waters. That's what an estuary's all about.

ⓘ **Wisconsin's Nature Conservancy** (ℂ **608/251-8140**)

✈ Green Bay

⊨ **$ Wagon Trail Resort & Campgrounds,** 1041 C. Rd. ZZ, Ellison Bay (ℂ **888/559-2466,** 920/854-2385 lodge, or 920/854-4818 campground; www.wagontrail.com)

---

**65** **At Water's Edge**

# Golden Gate National Recreation Area
## *Where San Francisco Left Its Heart*
### San Francisco, California

SANDWICHED BETWEEN SOME OF THE COUNTRY'S MOST EXPENSIVE REAL ESTATE, THE LARGEST urban park in the United States aims to save native habitat and no less than 33 threatened or endangered species. Climate change, pollution, surrounding development, and recreational activities are some of the stressors that this urban sanctuary faces every day.

Now this is a national park that's focused on saving the environment. Just a stone's throw from bustling San Francisco, the Golden Gate National Recreation Area (GGNRA) is a surprising biological hot spot—and saving it has become the GGNRA's top priority.

Most of the GGNRA consists of narrow strips of coastal naturelands, snapped up before real-estate development could ruin them. It includes the Presidio, Land's End, and Ocean Beach in San Francisco itself; Angel Island; oceanfront points and ridges down in San Mateo County; and across the Golden Gate Bridge, the Marin headlands, Stinson Beach, Muir Woods, and an inland corridor bordering Point Reyes National Seashore. The "R" in GGNRA stands for recreation, however, and considering the huge urban population, these sites get a lot of traffic. With habitat destruction the biggest factor in species loss here, GGNRA rangers have to be vigilant about keeping visitors on roadways and trails, controlling predators like foxes and feral cats, and organizing volunteer crews to do beach clean-ups and habitat replanting.

Five of the birds on the GGNRA's watch list are water birds—the marsh-dwelling California clapper rail, shore-dwelling western snowy plover, California least tern, marbled murrelet, and brown pelican. The northern spotted owl, which requires old-growth conifers like Muir Woods' magnificent redwoods, rounds out the avian list. The brown pelican in particular looks to be on its way back from near extinction caused by industrial DDT

Stellar sea lions.

runoff in Southern California; on any coastal drive you should see these long-winged, long-billed birds flapping lazily around the shoreline. Of course, the list also includes six fishes: tidewater goby, Coho salmon, two species of Chinook salmon, and two species of steelhead, which winter in the Pacific before their spring or summer spawning runs up central California rivers. Southern sea otters and Steller sea lions bask on the rocky shores year-round, while the magnificent humpback whale sails past on its annual migrations.

But besides seashore, the Golden Gate area includes marshes and grasslands, where you'll find the salt-marsh harvest mouse, the San Francisco garter snake, the California red-legged frog, and three types of butterflies—the delicate Mission

blue, the gaudy bay checkerspot, and the dusty-brown San Bruno elfin. Those brown hills just north of the Golden Gate Bridge are spangled with wildflowers in spring, no less than 11 of them threatened species. From beachy dune flowers (California seablite, San Francisco lessingia) to desert-like plants (fountain thistle, Tiburon paintbrush) to tiny hillside blossoms of yellow (San Mateo woolly sunflower) or pink and white (white-rayed pentachaeta, Marin dwarf-flax, Presidio Clarkia, San Mateo thornmint), these surviving flowers take a little time to spot but are worth the effort.

There's only one plant left of the Presidio Manzanita, and because it doesn't self-pollinate, it's most likely the last of its species. But then, the 2-foot-tall (.6m) showy Indian clover was considered extinct in the wild, and now it's been rein-troduced to these Marin County slopes. Anything is possible.

(i) www.nps.gov/goga

✈ San Francisco International

**At Water's Edge**

**66**

# Kenai Fjords
## *Where Mountains Slide into the Sea*
### Seward, Alaska

EARTHQUAKES, RISING OCEAN TIDES, AND THE RELENTLESS SEA ARE CHANGING THE TOPOGRAPHY of the Kenai Mountains. Environmental disasters, such as Exxon Valdez oil spill in 1989, are a constant threat. Strong population growth has increased logging and residential, commercial, and recreational development, which are destroying the habitat of many native species, including the Kenai Peninsula brown bear.

It's hard to imagine anything more perma-nent than a mountain—unless you're talking about the Kenai Mountains in south-central Alaska. Right at this very minute, colliding tectonic plates are pulling the Kenai range into the sea. And the deep coastal fjords that make this area a must-see Alaska cruise stop were once alpine valleys, with glaciers nes-tled inside. In the spring of 1964, an earth-quake dropped this dynamic bit of Alaska shoreline 6 feet (1.8m) further underwater in just 1 day.

The glaciers in the Alps and the Rockies are valley or piedmont glaciers; in Kenai Fjords National Park you'll see much rarer tidewater glaciers, massive cliffs of ice as high as 1,000 feet (305m), dropping abruptly into the icy Gulf of Alaska. Huge chunks of ice sheer off frequently, with puffs of frozen mist mixed with sea spray. As they break off, they resound with a boom that can be heard 20 miles (32km) away. Though Kenai Fjords has inland glaciers, too—notably Exit Glacier

and the vast Harding Icefield—which you can hike up to (Exit Glacier can even be reached by car), the coastal glaciers are the star attraction.

To view this dramatic coast from the water, several companies offer day tours out of nearby Seward Harbor. These tours are the best way to see a lot of wildlife in a short time—nesting colonies of black-legged kittiwakes, cormorants, murres, and puffins; frolicking sea lions and sea otters; resident orcas and Dall's porpoises; migrating humpback and gray whales. (Half-day tours stick to Resurrection Bay, where you'll see much of the same wildlife but no tidewater glaciers.) Those who want a little more adventure can explore by sea kayak. To kayak around the fjord glaciers, take a water taxi or charter boat from Seward to Aialik Bay or Northwestern Lagoon and then launch your kayak; other-wise stay in Resurrection Bay, because it's not a good idea to round turbulent Aialik

Cape in such a small craft. Along the coastline, there's another sobering sight: "ghost forests" of dead trees, still standing, whose roots were submerged in saltwater during the tumult in 1964.

The drive to Kenai Fjords is memorable in itself, taking the scenic Seward Highway with its jaw-dropping views of Turnagain Arm, Kenai Lake, glaciers, wetlands, and rugged mountains. It takes about 2½ hours from Anchorage. There's also a scenic train ride on the Alaska Railroad, which takes 4 hours from Anchorage. Kenai Fjords is open year-round, but most services shut down between October and April. The only part of the park accessible by road is Exit Glacier, and that road is only open in summer—the rest of the year you'll need skis, a snowmobile, or a dogsled.

ⓘ **Kenai Fjords National Park,** Seward (ⓒ **907/224-7500;** www.nps.gov/kefj)

✈ Anchorage

🛏 $$$ **Seward Windsong Lodge,** Mile 0.5, Herman Leirer Rd. (ⓒ **888/959-9590** or 907/265-4501; www.sewardwindsong.com). $$ **Holiday Inn Express,** Seward Harbor, 1412 4th Ave., Seward (ⓒ **888/465-4329** or 907/224-2550; www.ichotelsgroup.com).

**TOUR Major Marine** (ⓒ **800/764-7300,** 907/274-7300, or 907/224-8030; www.majormarine.com). **Renown Tours** (ⓒ **888/514-8687** or 907/224-3806; www.renowntours.com). **Kayak Adventures Worldwide** (ⓒ **907/224-3960;** www.kayakak.com). **Sunny Cove Sea Kayaking Co.** (ⓒ **907/224-8810;** www.sunnycove.com).

---

**At Water's Edge**  **67**

# The Birds of Lyme Bay
## *Oil Hits Jurassic Coast*
### East Devon/Dorset, England

LYME BAY IS A VICTIM OF COMMERCE. THE *NAPOLI* OIL SPILL IS AN EXTREME EXAMPLE OF THE pollution and devastation that threaten any region near a shipping channel. In addition, some of the bay's famed coral reefs have been ravaged by scallop-dredging operations.

It would have been an environmental horror story no matter where it happened—the wreck of a huge commercial container ship carrying 3,500 tons of oil. But what made it even worse was where the *Napoli* went down in January 2007: right off the pebbled coast of Dorset and East Devon, England's foremost World Heritage Site.

After its hull split in an English Channel storm, the foundering *Napoli* was being towed to Portland for salvage when it began to leak so badly, it was deliberately run aground on Branscome Beach in Lyme Bay—a baffling decision, considering Lyme Bay's importance as a wildlife habitat. Leaking oil formed a 8km (5-mile) slick, and the air reeked of gasoline, residents reported. Hundreds of guillemots, gulls, and razorbills were washed ashore covered in tarry oil; five dolphins were found dead; and mounds of rotting fish and oil-coated debris accumulated on beaches.

The oil slick was sprayed with dispersant and the rest of the ship's oil was eventually pumped out, but the long-term effects on local wildlife are incalculable. This stretch of English coastline is often called the Jurassic Coast because of the wealth of fossils in its rocky shingle beaches and colorful cliffs— red Triassic-era cliffs, darker gray cliffs from the swampy Jurassic Age, and white chalk cliffs formed underwater in the Cretaceous era. But it's also a haven for seabirds, especially around the Exe estuary, just west of the wreck site. At low tide, the Dawlish Warren Nature Reserve's enormous mudflats are vital feeding grounds for all sorts of shorebirds; ringed plovers and Sandwich terns breed on the shore, and larks and linnets nest in the reserve's dunes and grasslands. Footpaths through the Exminster and Bowling Green marshes along the river are breeding grounds for waders such as lapwings and redshanks, as well as winter homes for wigeons, curlews, and godwits.

Along the bay's eastern curve lies the grand panorama of Chesil Beach, a 29km-long (18-mile) pebbled bank that shelters a large brackish lagoon. Known as the Fleet, it's one of Europe's most important tidal and semitidal natural habitats. Telescopes at the **Chesil Beach Centre** (✆ 01305/ 760579) let visitors study from a distance the little terns, ringed plovers, Brent geese, and hosts of other birds who breed or winter in the Fleet; check for guided tours as well. Just east of Chesil Bank, the spectacular sea cliffs of the Isle of Portland are riddled with shelves where gulls, guillemots, and kittiwakes nest; it's such an ornithological hot spot, the old lighthouse here has been converted to a bird-watching center (see "Lodging," below). Walking atop the sea cliffs, fragrant with rare wildflowers and butterflies, is a glorious experience indeed. It's no wonder the birds like it here—if they can survive.

ⓘ **The Jurassic Coast World Heritage Site** (www.jurassiccoast.com)

🚊 Dorchester or Axminster

🛏 **The Royal Lion Hotel,** Broad St., Lyme Regis (✆ **44/1297/445622;** www. royallionhotel.com). **Portland Bird Observatory,** the Old Lower Light, Portland Bill (✆ **44/1305/820553;** www.portlandbird obs.org.uk).

---

**68** At Water's Edge

# iSimangaliso Wetlands Park
## *Zulu Zoo Supreme*
### Zululand, South Africa

iSIMANGALISO WETLANDS PARK, SOUTH AFRICA'S FIRST WORLD HERITAGE SITE, IS A HAVEN FOR many species of threatened and endangered plants and animals, although climate change threatens the fragile balance in the park's five ecosystems. Park rangers are working to stop illegal poaching of black and white rhinos, both endangered species.

iSimangaliso means "miracle" in Zulu— that's how King Shaka's trusted advisor Ujeqe described this stretch of coastland when he first wandered into it (on the run from his enemies, but that's another story). Formerly known as the Greater St. Lucia Wetlands Park, iSimangaliso truly is a miraculous, Noah's Ark sort of place. Tropical Africa merges into subtropical Africa here, yielding five distinct ecosystems; it also sits on several migration routes, adding up to a mind-boggling total of species— over 100 different butterflies and some 530 types of birds alone.

At the park's heart lies Lake St. Lucia, which is really a vast estuary—Africa's largest—teeming with hippos, Nile crocodiles, and flamingos. Even when severe drought hits the rest of Africa, there's water here, so it's a vital bird migration spot. You can take guided tours on the **Santa Lucia** lake cruiser (✆ **035/590-1340**), and at the mouth of the St. Lucia River, visit the **Crocodile Centre,** McKenzie Street, St. Lucia Village (✆ **035/590-1387**)—it's not just some tourist trap but a significant research center with fine exhibits about Africa's many crocodile species.

On the lake's western shores you can drive into the Mkhuze savanna and thornveld, where kudu, nyala, impala, duiker, and reedbuck roam. Even more unusual are the wooded hills on the lake's eastern shores—the world's largest vegetated sand dunes. Conservationists recently fought to prevent mining companies from digging up the rich titanium and zirconium deposits under these rare dunes; follow a trail through their peaceful dusky gloom and marvel at what might have been lost. At the end of that road is Cape Vidal beach, where you can watch migrating whales from an observation tower from July to November. Scuba divers head farther north for warm Sodwana Bay, which has almost as many varieties of fish as the Great Barrier Reef; north of there, the mineral-rich sands of Kosi Bay Nature preserve are protected nesting grounds in summer (Dec–Mar) for loggerhead and leatherback

sea turtles, endangered elsewhere by poaching and by 4-wheel-drive vehicles on beaches (banned here since 2006).

If bird-watching is your passion, head for the **Mkhuze Game Reserve** (✆ **035/573-9004**), where at least 430 species of birds have been recorded. Mkhuze is like a greatest-hits version of the rest of the park, with a little of every habitat: mountain slopes, acacia savanna, swamps, riverine forest. In winter (June–Sept) you can settle into game viewing hides next to the Kubube, Kamasinga, and Kwamalibala watering holes and see black and white rhinoceros, elephant, giraffe, blue wildebeest, warthog, and myriad antelopes. Two bird hides at Nsumo Pan afford a spectacular year-round view of pelicans, ducks, and geese on the waterway; from here you can also take a guided walk through the lovely, rare Mkhuze Fig Forest. Ujeqe had it right—the whole place is a miracle indeed.

ⓘ **St. Lucia Publicity Association** (✆ 27/35/550-4059)

✈ Richard's Bay

🛏 $$$ **Makakatana Bay Lodge** (✆ 27/35/550-4189; www.makakatana.co.za). $ **Cape Vidal Camp,** c/o KZN Wildlife (✆ 27/33/845-1000; www.kznwildlife.com).

# Shiretoko National Park
## *Japan's Last Frontier*
### Hokkaido, Japan

HARSH WEATHER CONDITIONS PROTECT THIS REGION FROM THE RAVAGES OF HUMAN DEVELOPMENT, and it provides such abundant resources that a wide range of species, including the brown bear, are able to thrive in small habitats. But the fragile balance between terrestrial and marine ecosystems is dependent upon the stability of sea ice, which climate change may affect.

The ancient Ainu people called it Shiretoko, "End of the Earth," and that's what this peninsula still feels like—remote, rugged, uninhabited, set at the farthest tip of Japan's farthest north island. Its virgin forests are home to Yezo sika deer and one of the last large populations of Hokkaido brown bears (watch out for them in spring, when they grumpily emerge from hibernation); its extensive wetlands attract droves of migratory birds. Cormorants, white-tailed sea eagles, and the Blackiston's fish owl hover watchfully over its waters, while seals and seal lions flop around its rocky coves.

Though most visitors come here in summer, what makes Shiretoko unique is the sea ice drifting offshore in winter in the Sea of Orkhost—it's the farthest south that ice floes are found in the Northern Hemisphere. The combination of sea ice and a relatively temperate latitude makes it a virtual resort destination for marine mammals like fur seals and Steller's sea lions; whales frequently circle around the headlands.

There are no roads at all in the northern quarter of the peninsula—to explore its beauty, you need to hike and camp, or else take a boat tour around the western coast, leaving from the gateway town of Utoro. While the western coast's dramatic waterfalls can be viewed on any of the various tours, the longer cruises—3 to 4 hours—go all the way to the tip of the peninsula, where your wildlife-spotting opportunities are best.

It would be a shame, though, to come here and not walk through the picturesque woodlands, even if you don't attempt a strenuous wilderness trek. Easy walking trails circle the peaceful forested Five Lakes, only 15km (9 1/3 miles) from Utoro. An even more special experience is wading up a warm mountain stream to Kamuikukka Falls, where you can bask in the hot springs basin at its base. Even if you don't reach the main falls—stretches of the river may be closed due to falling rocks—slipping around the algae-coated rocks and plunging into warm pools along the way is exhilarating.

Rugged volcanic ridges kept out human settlers for centuries, protecting the wildlife; nowadays it's up to park management to protect this rare marine/alpine ecosystem. And sometimes politics intrude—UNESCO has informed Japan and Russia that they're jointly responsible for one hotly disputed section, the offshore Kurile Islands, which the former Soviet Union invaded 2 weeks after V-J Day ended World War II. Territorial disputes or not, this wildlife haven must be kept pristine. It's one of those frontier spots that nobody paid attention to for years—which is just what makes it so worth saving.

ⓘ www.shiretoko.or.jp

✈ Metambetsu

🛏 $$$ **Hotel Shiretoko,** 37 Utoroka-gawa, Shari Cho (ⓒ **81/152/24-2131**). $ **Shiretoko-Iwaobetsu Youth Hostel,** at Iawaobetsu bus stop (ⓒ **81/152/24-2311**).

# 10 Disappearing Beaches

When seas rise, beaches disappear. And even setting climate change aside, scientists predict a 10- to 12-inch (25–30cm) rise in ocean levels by the end of this century. And for each inch (2.5cm) the ocean rises, a beach gets on average 3¼ feet (1m) narrower. Add to that sinking coastal lands, increasing violent storms, and humans interfering with natural beach architecture by dredging channels and building seawalls and jetties, and it's a recipe for disaster.

Here are 10 notable beaches in need of saving:

**⑩ The Hamptons, New York** Although the beaches in the Hamptons are only eroding half a foot per year—less than most Atlantic beaches—with its multimillion-dollar beachfront retreats the impact of coastal storms on Long Island's south shore gets plenty of press. A key problem has been groynes (beach-stabilizing jetties) in Georgica Pond, which block sand migration to down-current beaches. Warning signs include dwindling dunes from Sagaponack to Westhampton and storm damage to houses now sitting only 50 feet (15m) from the high tide line. *www.hamptonsweb.com/beaches.*

**⑪ Cape May Beach, New Jersey** Jetties built at the mouth of the Cape May Channel have accelerated sand deposits at busy North Wildwood, making it New Jersey's widest beach; but meanwhile south of the jetty, charming Cape May, America's oldest seaside resort, has had to restock the sand on its quiet beaches—an expensive, and generally short-term, remedy. *www.njcapemay.com.*

**⑫ Miami Beach, Florida** Really a barrier island, Miami Beach has been pumping up its high-profile beach since 1976, spending millions of dollars to preserve the 10-mile-long (16km) strand lined with high-rise hotels. Tropical storms are a constant concern, but years of building seawalls and "borrowing" sand from the sea floor have accelerated beach erosion. *www.ecomb.org.*

Galveston beach.

**⑬ Galveston, Texas** On the hurricane-prone Gulf Coast, Galveston has monitored beach width ever since a disastrous 1900 storm drowned more than 6,000 people. A historic 10-mile (16km) seawall protects the resort town's Victorian architecture, but the soft tan sand of its public beaches—a major weekend getaway for Houstonians—has suffered serious erosion, as has two-thirds of Texas's 350-mile (563km) coastline. *www.galveston.com.*

**⑭ Santa Barbara, California** The "American Riviera," Santa Barbara is known for its Spanish-Mediterranean architecture and well-groomed, palm-lined, white beaches. But battered by periodic El Niño events, armored with seawalls that only intensify wave action, and robbed of replenishing sediments by several upriver dams, Santa Barbara's beaches are in trouble. Goleta Beach Park has been severely reduced, and in a domino effect, Arroyo Burro Beach is following suit. *www.santabarbaraca.gov.*

**75 Playa del Carmen, Mexico** Protected by offshore coral reefs, the northern stretch of the Yucatan's Caribbean coast naturally develops lovely beaches wherever there are gaps in the reefs. But because a unique confluence of changing winds and strong offshore currents make this coast's beaches dwindle or grow almost on a day-to-day basis, the inviting beach pictured in resort brochures may not be there when you arrive. If the one by your hotel has turned narrow and rocky, you may need to head north, to less developed beaches with more sand—and more entangling seagrass. *www.playadelcarmen.com.*

**76 Negril, Jamaica** Starting in the 1970s, a wave of resort building along Negril's popular Seven-Mile Beach capitalized on its glorious sand. But degraded offshore coral reefs and the dredging of seagrass beds left the existing sand vulnerable to wave erosion. Tropical storms periodically pummel this flat, low-lying area, and every year, natural processes have a harder time replenishing the slowly-but-steadily eroding beach. *www.negril.com.*

**77 The Holderness Coast, Northeast England** The fastest-eroding coastline in Europe is this 62km (39 miles) stretch north of the Humber Estuary, where soft clay cliffs are battered by powerful North Sea waves. Beaches at the foot of those low crumbling cliffs lose nearly 2m (6 ft.) per year. Groynes and other manmade revetments protect the holiday sands at resort towns like Hornsea and Mappleton, but steal sand from other areas. *www.i-know-yorkshire. co.uk.*

Holderness Coast.

**78 Gold Coast, Australia** Ever since 1967, Australia's heavily developed Gold Coast—an artificially maintained 69km (43-mile) barrier strip south of Brisbane—has battled beach erosion. An oceanfront boulder wall protects shoreline buildings, but prevents production of new sand; after storms, inland waterways are dredged for sand to be pumped back onto the beaches. However, a new technique was pioneered in 1999: An artificial reef was built to stabilize the beach at Narrowneck, which happily also created a new surfing spot—always a plus here in this surfing mecca. *www.goldcoastaustralia.com.*

**79 Banda Aceh, Indonesia** The worst-hit spot in the December 2004 tsunami was this city on the north tip of Sumatra. With beaches submerged, coastal villages flooded, and mud deposited everywhere, the disaster required massive rebuilding. But while buildings and roads were reconstructed on the same vulnerable coastal areas—often on raised roadbeds or stilts—damaged offshore reef and shoreline mangroves, which provide protection from further storms, still need to be restored. *www.indonesia-tourism.com/aceh.*

# Peninsula Valdés
## *A Home Where the Guanacos Roam*
### Argentina

AN ESTIMATED 50% OF THE WORLD'S ENDANGERED SOUTHERN RIGHT WHALES PASS THROUGH these waters each year along with a year-round population of orcas, and conservationists are concerned about the impact of water pollution, increased oil tanker traffic, and tourism on whale habitat and breeding. The area is also an important habitat for the southern elephant seal and native penguins.

Snuggled into the long curve of Argentina's Atlantic coast, far south of Buenos Aires and a long way from desolated Tierra Del Fuego, Peninsula Valdés—virtually an island, connected to the mainland by the slenderest of isthmuses—is not the sort of destination travelers stumble onto accidentally. Those who do come have one item on their agenda: viewing wildlife.

At first you may be shocked by how barren this peninsula seems. You can drive the gravel roads for hours through the relatively treeless coastal plateau without seeing another soul. Oh, you'll spot guanacos, the llama's small Patagonian cousins, running in panic away from your car. You may see choiques (ostrichlike birds); the strange-looking mara, a hare that runs on four legs like a dog; armadillos and foxes; and lots of grazing sheep, property of the few family-run ranches still permitted to operate here. In the middle of the peninsula, three giant salt flats appear like mirages on the horizon.

But it's the coasts you've come for, the rugged cliffs and gravelly beaches that meet the unusually calm, mild gulfs sheltered by the peninsula on either side. Five kilometers (3 miles) past the park entrance, which has an excellent interpretive exhibit, you head down a track to Isla de los Pájaros, where you can observe an important seabird colony through binoculars. Another 20km (12 miles) east on Ruta 2, the tiny village of Puerto Pirámides is home base for whale-watching tours, from April to late December. Once nearly hunted to extinction, southern right whales come to these protected gulfs to breed after feeding for 3 months in Antarctic summer seas.

From Puerto Pirámides, head either east to Punta Delgada or north to Caleta Valdés to see beaches swarming with elephant seals from mid-June to late December. The rest of the year, when the seals decamp, head for the northeastern tip of the peninsula, Punta Norte, where hundreds of sea lions congregate from January to June. Just west of Punta Norte, **Estancia San Lorenzo** (© **54/2965/458-444**) offers tours of a huge colony of Magellan penguins September to March. As for the orcas—well, they tend to lurk offshore year-round, shifting their hunting to wherever vulnerable babies are being tended: off Punta Norte for sea lions in March and April, and off Caleta Valdes in September, waiting for young elephant seals.

Because different species show up at different seasons, timing is critical if you're intent on viewing one particular species. All things considered, the ideal time to visit is October or November, when the penguins are guarding their nests, whales and their new calves are swimming in the bays, and the elephant seals mass on the beaches with their pups. But there's always something happening on the beaches of Peninsula Valdés—it just takes a little traveling to get here, that's all.

(i) www.peninsulavaldes.org.ar

✈ Puerto Madryn

🛏 $$$ **Faro Punta Delgada Country Hotel,** Punta Delgada (✆ **54/2965/458-444;**

www.puntadelgada.com). $$$ **Estancia La Elvira,** inland from Caleta Valdés (✆ **54/2065/474-248;** www.laelvira.com.ar). $$$ **Rincón Chico** (✆ **54/2965/471-733;** www.rinconchico.com.ar).

# Shark Bay
## *Dolphins & Dugongs & Sharks, Oh My!*
### Northwest Cape, Western Australia

OFF SHORE, TOUGH FISHING LAWS HELP REVERSE THE DECIMATION OF PINK SNAPPER, POPULAR FOR commercial and recreational fishing. On shore, trampling and overgrazing of natural habitats by livestock have caused significant soil erosion and destroyed natural habitats.

You've gotta love that name. Shark Bay—how much more adventurous could a place sound? But the truth is, most visitors come here not to see bloodthirsty sharks but to ooh and aah over the bottlenose dolphins that cruise into the shallow water every morning. Rangers instruct visitors to stand still in the knee-deep water while the dolphins glide past; you're not even allowed to pet them, though they playfully nudge the tourists from time to time.

But there's so much more to Shark Bay. Its waters heave with fish, turtles, manta rays, sea snakes, the world's largest population of dugongs (aka manatees), and migrating humpback whales (June–Oct). You can see it all on a 2½-hour cruise on the sailing catamaran ***Shotover*** (✆ **61/8/9948 1481**), leaving from the Monkey Mia resort. Sometimes you see dozens of dugongs, though they leave the area mid-May through August.

On the harsh Peron Peninsula, which juts out into Shark Bay, even the beach is amazing—what looks like white sand turns out to be billions of tiny white seashells, along with stromatolites, foot-high rock formations that are really ancient fossils. On guided walks along the dunes and coastal cliffs of Francois Peron National Park, you'll probably encounter wallabies and emus (just to remind you that you're in Australia), and may even spot dolphins, dugongs, and whales out in the water.

So where are the sharks in all this? Up on the Northwest Cape. In Exmouth, 87km (54 miles) north of Monkey Mia, from late March to June tour boats take people out to snorkel with gentle whale sharks, the world's largest fish (true whales are bigger, but they're mammals). If manta rays are more your style, you can swim with them, too, in the deeper waters off the town of Coral Bay, on the other side of the cape. What's more, from November through late February, green and loggerhead turtles nest on the cape's beaches, which you can see on nighttime turtle-watch tours.

The Ningaloo Reef lies just a few steps off the beaches of the Northwest Cape, offering divers 250 species of coral and 450 kinds of fish to marvel at—grouper, manta rays, octopus, morays, potato cod, false killer whales, and large sharks. The seas seem to teem with life in this unspoiled setting, much less crowded than the Great Barrier Reef. The main drawbacks—and they're significant—are how long it takes to get anywhere, and how insufferably hot it gets between November and March. But plan your trip accordingly, and it may be the best ocean experience of your life.

---

(i) www.sharkbay.asn.au

✈ Shark Bay or Exmouth

🛏 $–$$ **Monkey Mia Dolphin Resort,** Monkey Mia Rd. ((© **61/8/9948 1320;** www.

monkeymia.com.au). $–$$ **Ningaloo Reef Resort,** Robinson St., Coral Bay ((© **61/8/9942 5934;** www.coralbay.org/resort.htm).

**TOUR Exmouth Diving Centre** ((© **61/8/9949 1201;** www.exmouthdiving.com.au). **Ningaloo Reef Diving Centre** ((© **61/8/9942 5824;** www.ningalooreefdive.com).

---

**At Water's Edge** **82**

# Mirror Lake
## *A Cloudy Mirror for Nature's Majesty*
### Yosemite National Park, California

EVERY SPRING, THE TENAYA CREEK WASHES TONS OF SILT AND MUD DOWN THE CANYON AND into Mirror Lake, and in summer the lake dries up. Until the early 1970s, the National Park Service dredged the lake periodically to preserve it as a popular tourist attraction, but since then the lake has been rapidly filling up with silt; it's destined to become what it once was—a small forest with a creek running through it.

Every American should visit Yosemite National Park at least once. But some summer weekends, it seems they've all decided to come at the same time. The park is only 3½ hours from San Francisco and 6 from Los Angeles, and that accessibility, coupled with the park's justly famous natural beauty, spells tourist crowds. There's no two ways about it.

Air pollution is the gravest environmental threat Yosemite faces (auto emissions on the crowded park roads are only one cause). Ozone damages the foliage of certain sensitive pine trees, and acid deposits in the snow or rain periodically overwhelm the lakes and rivers. Still, you can't blame pollution for what's happening to the postcard view at Mirror Lake.

The Yosemite Valley loop road visits several iconic vistas—Bridalveil Falls, the great Glacier Point overlook, the rounded summit of Half Dome, Yosemite Falls, and the awesome 7,549-foot-high (2,300m) sheer rock face called El Capitan, the world's tallest granite monolith. As snows melt from the surrounding peaks, the crystal-clear waters spill over the canyon walls in some of the most spectacular waterfalls on earth. (Upper Yosemite Falls is the tallest waterfall in North America; Ribbon Fall and Sentinel Falls join it on the list of the world's 10 tallest falls.) Among these, Mirror Lake is a particularly beloved sight. Like the name says, it offers up a near-perfect reflection of the surrounding mountain scenery, your classic Yosemite photo op. The trouble is, these days it's rapidly filling up with silt, and shrinking every year. Soon it may be more appropriate to call it Mirror Meadow.

To understand what's happening, remember that glaciers carved this valley out of the Sierra Nevada range, shearing vertical faces in the granite and scooping

Mirror Lake.

out lake beds. Formations like El Capitan and Half Dome are made of granite, a particular durable rock—that's why they thrust out so dramatically from the landscape. But as glacial ice moved through this valley eons ago, it also carried along rubble and debris, some of which still lies loosely scattered around the park. Carried off the peaks in snowmelt, this rubble and debris eventually ends up in the lakes. Ages ago, this already happened in many spots; Yosemite Valley itself used to be a lake. And in our lifetimes, Mirror Lake is doomed to follow this same fate.

You can't park a car at the trail head to Mirror Lake, so take the shuttle bus (Valley Stables stop) and follow the trail for 1 mile (1.6km) to the lake. From the shore you can still get a breathtaking view of Half Dome when spring snowmelt raises the water high enough. The sooner you get here, the better.

ⓘ **Yosemite National Park,** entrances on CA 41, CA 120, and CA 140 (✆ **209/372-0200;** www.nps.gov/yose)

✈ Fresno-Yosemite International

🛏 $$$ **The Ahwanee,** Yosemite Valley (✆ **559/252-4848**). $ **Tuolumne Meadows Campground** (✆ **800/436-7275;** http://reservations.nps.gov).

---

**83** At Water's Edge

# Mono Lake
## *Who Stole the Water?*
### Lee Vining, California

MONO LAKE WAS ON ITS WAY TO BECOMING A DRY SALT BED SURROUNDED BY A BARREN landscape after much of the water that once flowed into the lake was diverted to supply the growing population of Los Angeles. Fortunately, the alarm was raised in time, and today the state is managing the water supply and rebuilding the wetlands at Mono Lake.

Just east of Yosemite, another California lake has gone missing—and this time humans are to blame. Back in 1941, four of the five rivers that feed Mono Lake, California's largest natural body of water, were diverted to provide water for the population boom in Los Angeles. Not surprisingly, this desert salt lake's water level began to drop drastically. Visitors began to notice islands emerging in the center. A creepy complex of tufa towers, previously submerged, rose above the surface like the bleached bones of a skeleton.

Environmental protests and lawsuits throughout the 1970s and 1980s finally forced the state to reverse its water policy, and new, more efficient river dams now send regulated amounts of water back into Mono (pronounced Mow-no) Lake. Since their lowest point in 1982, the waters are slowly rising; the goal, set in a 1994 court decision, is to bring it up another 7 feet (2.1m), which may take 10 to 20 years. The 60-square-mile (155-sq.-km) lake was naturally twice as salty as ocean water, but at its worst it became three times saltier than the ocean. Recent saline levels are back to 79 grams per liter, about 10 grams per liter more than the eventual goal. The willows and cottonwood forests that once lined the lake's freshwater tributaries are on the rebound, now that water flows in those channels again. It's all great progress, but Mono Lake will never be what it was.

The ultimate irony is that those risen-from-the-dead tufa towers—limestone deposits formed by underground springs—have become an attraction in themselves. The Mono Basin Scenic Area Visitors Center runs guided tours of the area and has a terrific historical display telling the Mono Lake story. With its wetlands restored, Mono Lake is a major bird-watching area, with about 300 species either resident or migrating through; ospreys and rare California gulls nest on those accidental islands.

Since no native fish can survive in this alkaline lake, birds don't have to compete for food, especially their favorite treat, Mono's endemic brine shrimp. Thick swarms of alkali flies on the lakeshore (the name Mono actually means "flies" in the native Yokut language) may be annoying to humans but they're a feast for birds, especially for the tiny Wilson's phalarope, which gorges on them every August before migrating back to South America.

On summer weekends, **guided canoe tours** (✆ **760/647-6595**) explore the tufa towers, the wetlands of the creek delta, and the underground springs that fed the lake all those years when the streams were sent elsewhere. Thank God for those springs, which kept Mono Lake just barely alive, long enough for humans finally to do the right thing.

ⓘ **Mono Basin Scenic Area Visitors Center,** Hwy. 39 (✆ **760/647-3044**). Mono Lake (www.monolake.org).

✈ Reno-Tahoe or Fresno-Yosemite

🛏 $$ **Tamarack Lodge & Resort,** Twin Lakes Rd., Mammoth Lakes (✆ **800/ 626-6684** or 760/934-2442; www.tamaracklodge.com). $ **Fern Creek Lodge,** 4628 Hwy. 158, June Lake (✆ **800/621-9146** or 760/648-7722; www.ferncreeklodge.com).

**At Water's Edge**   84

# Lake Baikal

## *How Low Can You Go?*

### Southwestern Siberia

STILL CONSIDERED ONE OF THE WORLD'S MOST PRISTINE BODIES OF WATER, LAKE BAIKAL IS AT risk from pollution that threatens to despoil its clear waters and destroy its abundant plant and animal life, including some species found nowhere else in the world. Some conservation efforts have been taken—such as prohibiting logging operations on rivers leading into Lake Baikal—but risks from both air and water pollution remain high.

Lake Baikal.

Is Lake Baikal secretly an ocean in training? Sure, on the surface it's only the world's seventh-largest lake, but with depths of 1,500m (5,000 ft.) or more, it's by far the deepest—nothing else even comes close. A full 20% of the world's unfrozen fresh water is found here, as much water as in all the Great Lakes put together. Scientists also say it's probably the world's oldest lake, almost 25 million years old. And since it happens to be located on a widening continental rift, it's actually getting bigger every year, by about 2cm (³/₄ inch).

Set in a bowl of mountains and thick forests, Lake Baikal is aptly nicknamed "the Blue Eye of Siberia." Far from any ocean, it's fed by more than 330 rivers and streams, though only one, the Angara River, runs out, flowing 2,414km (1,500 miles) to the Arctic Ocean. The waters are so clear, you can see down hundreds of feet (it's said that some boaters get vertigo from looking over the side). Almost 1,800 species of flora and fauna live here, two-thirds of them

indigenous. Granted, many of those are microscopic invertebrates, including zillions of tiny crustaceans that filter and oxygenate the water, giving it its astonishing clarity. But the plump little Baikal seal—the world's only entirely freshwater seal—is cute enough to make up for that, and typically Siberian brown bear, elk, moose, and deer roam the woods on its shores.

Baikal contains such attractions as the Ushkaniye Islands, a preserve for the Baikal seals; Chivirkuisky Bay, a prime site for kayaking; the lakeside Circum-Baikal Railway, a former section of the Trans-Siberian Railway; and rugged Olkhon Island. Lake cruisers ply its waters, and it's a popular destination for Russian hikers, anglers, rock climbers, and skiers.

Until the Trans-Siberian Railway was built through here in the 1890s, Baikal lay relatively isolated, but in recent times pollution has become more and more of a threat. Since the early 1900s, lumber companies have been hauling out vast tracts of the trees that once anchored silt and sediment on the slopes. Heavy industry has created an even worse problem, particularly chlorine runoff from a pulp factory built in 1966 right on the lakeshore. Then there's air pollution from the nearest cities, Irkutsk and Ulan Ulde, and from coal-burning power plants near to the lake. With only one river flowing out, contaminated water can sit for a long time in Lake Baikal.

Anti-pollution laws are on the books, but customarily in Russia there's little enforcement if industry could be hampered. In 2006, however, President Putin vetoed a proposed East Siberian oil pipeline nearby, after environmentalists warned it could burst, given the area's seismic activity. It's a sign of hope for preserving this peerless, magical lake.

ⓘ www.irkutsk.org/baikal

✈ Irkutsk

🛏 $$ **Mayak Hotel,** 84A Gorkiy St., Listvyanka (✆ **7/395/4596910**). $$ **Hotel Angara,** 7 Suhe Bator, Irkutsk (✆ **7/395/2/255106**).

---

**At Water's Edge** **85**

# Chilka Lake Bird Sanctuary
## *Flaming with Flamingoes*
### Orissa, India

CHILKA LAKE IS A LARGE BRACKISH WATER ECOSYSTEM AND AN INTERNATIONALLY IMPORTANT wetlands area. In 2001, hoping to promote more tourism, the Indian government cut a passage for tour boats through a sandbar, altering the exchange of freshwater and saltwater that gave the lake its special quality, endangering fish habitat, and putting the entire lake at risk.

While there are many awe-inspiring temples in this east Indian province—the Sri Jagannath Temple in Puri, the Sun Temple of Konark—one of the most charming is the modest Kalijai temple, set on its own tiny island in the middle of a vast brackish lagoon. It's the setting that makes it so special: the impossible blue of the water, the craggy backdrop of mountains, and most of all, the number of colorful birds drawn to this rich feeding ground.

A seasonal push and pull rules the waters here in India's largest coastal lake. Fresh water pours in from the Mahanadi River in monsoon season, salt currents flush back from the Bay of Bengal during the dry season, and a long silted-up sandbar traps the waters in place. Some 225 species of fish have been counted in Chilka Lake, and where there's that many fish, there are bound to be loads of aquatic birds: white-bellied sea eagles, greyleg geese, purple moorhens, jacana, herons, and the world's largest breeding colonies of flamingoes, their vivid orange-pink flocks hard to miss. Migratory birds arrive October to March as well, from as far away as Siberia's Lake Baikal and the Himalayas. Though poaching has been a persistent problem—up to 20,000 birds a year may be killed—the government is now working hard to educate local villages in the importance of protecting the birds.

Reedy Nalaban Island is a sanctuary for migratory birds, especially dense flocks of all sorts of ducks and geese. You can visit Nalaban by boat, but it takes as long as 90 minutes, with no other land in sight for much of the trip. Guides know they have to cut their engines once they get near; they paddle closer, and you wade through the last stretch of 1.2m-deep (4-ft.) swampy water to get to an observation tower. Satapada Island is known for its rare Irrawaddy dolphins, but sightings are increasingly rare, as more and more dolphins have been fatally caught in fishing nets.

The local economy is based on fishing—it's quite a sight to see, as scores of small fishing craft steer out on the lake at sunrise in pursuit of mackerel, crabs, and prawn. The lake's so fertile, the fisherman and the birds have always shared in its bounty—until now. But with the traditional currents altered because of the new channel, weeds have begun to take over areas of the lake, and the fishermen are suffering. Kalijai, the goddess of the lake, must be weeping.

ⓘ www.tourismoforissa.com

✈ Bhubaneswar

🛏 $$$ **The Trident,** C.B.-1, Nayapalli, Bhubaneswar (📞 **91/674/230-1010;** www.oberoihotels.com). $$ **Mayfair Beach Resort,** Chakratirtha Rd., Puri (📞 **91/675/222**).

**86** At Water's Edge

# Lake Chapala
## *The Incredible Shrinking Lake*
### Southwestern Mexico

RUNAWAY DEVELOPMENT AND UPSTREAM POLLUTION HAVE NEARLY DESTROYED LAKE CHAPALA, which is an important wildlife habitat for native species and millions of migrating birds. Much of its water has been drained over the past 3 decades to supply Guadalajara, Mexico's second-largest city, as well as several nearby resort towns.

It seems like the ideal retirement spot—Mexico's largest freshwater lake, a serene alpine lake set amid gently rounded green mountains. Cool breezes, balmy winters, spectacular sunsets, and a cheap cost of living, yet only 45km (28 miles) south of the amenities of Guadalajara—how could you beat that?

The trouble was a lot of people got the same notion. Since 1975, the real estate boom in the Lake Chapala area, led by a flood of retirees from colder parts of North America, helped swell the population fivefold in the Guadalajara area. A string of resort towns along the north shore became known as the Chapala Riviera, an English-speaking haven for expatriate snowbirds in southwestern Mexico, land of mariachis and tequila.

Such unbridled growth could spoil any paradise. Guadalajara's mushrooming need for fresh water began to drain the lake, and it didn't help that faulty city water mains lose nearly half the water pumped out of the lake. Meanwhile, upstream communities built unauthorized dams to tap rivers flowing into the lake, and released sewage and chemical runoff to pollute the remaining water. By 2002, the lake had shrunk to one quarter of its original volume. Some lakeside villages now barely had water views, and coastal marshes became solid land that farmers promptly took over.

Though rainy seasons in 2003 and 2004 raised the water levels back to almost half of its capacity (reflooding the marshes in the process), Lake Chapala's fate still lies in the balance. The fish population is dwindling, and huge masses of water hyacinth coat the lake's shallow surface. To make matters worse, solutions get lost in political standoffs between the two states that verge on the lake, Jalisco and Michoacan. Jalisco has proposed an expensive dam just above the lake, which might artificially raise lake levels, but the root problems would remain.

Central Mexico needs Lake Chapala more than ever, and not just as a weekend getaway spot or a reservoir for drinking water. Many other local lakes and ponds have dried up in the past couple of decades, leaving Chapala a vital wildlife habitat. Some two million migratory birds have been counted here in recent years, including yellow robins, snowy egrets, great egrets, and a significant population of American white pelicans.

Too shallow for serious watersports, too polluted for fishing, Lake Chapala is the sort of destination where typical outdoor excursions may be a gentle shoreline hike or a boat tour to a midlake island. Despite an Anglo invasion, the Chapala Riviera has managed to preserve its old-fashioned Mexican quaintness, with cobblestoned streets, hand-carved wooden gates, and brilliant little gardens. If only the lake itself could preserve its old-fashioned health.

✈ Guadalajara

🛏 $$$ **Quinta Real,** Av. Mexico 2727, Guadalajara (© **800/445-4565** or 33/3669-0600; www.quintareal.com). $$ **La Villa del Ensueño,** Florida 305, Tlapeque (© **800/220-8689** or 33/3635-8792; www.villadelensueno.com).

---

**A River Runs Through It**  **87**

# Nassawango Creek Preserve
## *The Chocolate Bog*
### Snow Hill, Maryland

WHILE MUCH OF NASSAWANGO CREEK PRESERVE IS PROTECTED, AGRICULTURAL RUNOFF, INCREASED residential development, and wetland alterations continue to threaten this area. The Swainson's Warbler remains on the state endangered list, and bald cypress trees are protected because they are so rare in this part of the country.

Don't worry if Nassawango Creek's waters look chocolate brown—they've looked that way since Pocahontas's friend Captain John Smith first canoed up this stream in 1608. Naturally darkened by tannin from fallen leaves, Nassawango Creek is actually one of the most pristine tributaries of the equally dark Pokomoke River, which starts out in Delaware's Great Cypress Swamp and ends up in Chesapeake Bay. It's one of the Eastern Shore's most tranquil and unspoiled corridors, spooling its way through rare bald cypress swamp and forests of Atlantic white cedar, loblolly pines, and seaside elder, where a profusion of orchids bloom and warblers sing.

Captain John Smith had one thing right—canoeing is the best way to explore Nassawango Creek. This 18-mile (29km) stretch of water is part of a network of canoe routes called the **Bogiron Water Trail,** in honor of the iron-rich bogs around here, which gave rise to a thriving iron-smelting industry in the early 19th century. (The historic village of Furnace Town, center of that industry from 1828–50, lies inside the preserve boundary—information is available at the visitor center.) Rental canoes are available in Snow Hill. Turn off Route 12 onto Red House Road, drive 1 mile (1.6km) and turn right, where there's a designated parking area. Launch on the west side of the creek (look for yellow nature sanctuary signs); you can canoe all the way to the Pokomoke River.

As you paddle along the creek, keep an eye out for river otters and painted turtles, and for white-tailed deer and gray foxes in the woods around you; listen for the rat-tat-tat of the pileated woodpecker. In fall the marsh blazes red and gold with cardinal flowers and spotted jewelweed. You can also take a short, easy hike on the **Paul Leifer Trail** through those woods, where you'll see wildflowers like pink lady's slipper, mayapple, wild lupine, and jack-in-the-pulpit in spring.

Of course, when John Smith steered through here, there was nothing special about Nassawango Creek except its natural dark color. But these days, bald cypress forests rarely grow this far north, and many of those orchids and warblers are threatened species. Nassawango Creek shows us what the eastern shore was like, once upon a time. Nature can be hardy: Despite the years of iron smelting, the bog habitat replenished itself. But if this last sliver of the old woods goes, we'll never see its like again.

ⓘ **Nassawango Creek Nature Preserve,** Old Furnace Rd. (✆ **410/632-2032**)

✈ Baltimore/Washington International

🛏 $$$ **River House Inn,** 201 E. Market St., Snow Hill (✆ **410/632-2722;** www.riverhouseinn.com). $$ **Days Inn,** 1540 Ocean Hwy., Pocomoke City (✆ **410/957-3000;** www.daysinn.com).

---

88 A River Runs Through It

# The Walls of Jericho
## *The Grand Canyon of the East*
### Alabama/Tennessee

THIS RICH HABITAT SUPPORTS THE RARE LIMEROCK ARROWWOOD AND IS HOME TO THREE GLOBALLY imperiled fish species and 45 species of mussels, including the pale lilliput and the Alabama lampshell, which are found nowhere else in the world. The Walls of Jericho links other large tracts of forest in Tennessee and Alabama, and protects the headwaters of the Paint Rock River.

Once upon a time, famed woodsman Davy Crockett hunted in these rich woods. In the late 1800s, an awestruck traveling minister gave its cathedral-like limestone gorge the biblical nickname the Walls of Jericho. When it was owned by a family named Carter, they left the land open to cavers and hikers. But in 1977 a lumber company bought the area, closed it off, and began to hack down the forest that had kept the Paint Rock River headwaters so clean and clear.

Enter the Nature Conservancy and Forever Wild Alabama, two conservation organizations who finally purchased the Walls of Jericho in 2004. Now visitors can see this beautiful rock formation again, explore its intricate cave systems—a vital habitat for rare bats and even rarer salamanders—and hike or ride horses through its leafy upland forest and serene wooded ponds. Canoers know it as a fine wild whitewater run, one of the cleanest in Tennessee, with Category IV cascades and some portaging required to pass chattering waterfalls. Bird-watchers come in spring to hear a host of migratory warblers and other songbirds. Photographers come to discover a delicate wealth of Appalachian wildflowers—yellow and pink lady slippers, showy orchid, white fringeless orchids, white nodding trillium, Cumberland rosinweed, limerock arrowwood, bloodroot, and Dutchman's-breeches.

The purchase came just in time. The upper Paint Rock River—which is formed by the gorge's Hurricane Creek merging with the Estil Fork—is one of the largest watersheds in the southeast that is still intact and functional, home to 100 fish species (including the imperiled snail darter, sawfin shiner, and blotchside logperch) and an impressive 45 different species of mussels, including two (pale lilliput and Alabama lampshell) that occur nowhere else.

The trail to the Walls is about 3 miles (4.8km) each way, crossing lots of little streams that quickly swell in rainstorms, leaving the trail muddy for days. You'll be hiking through a variegated forest of maple, oak, hickory, beech, eastern red cedar, and tulip tree, passing rock outcroppings that may conceal caves, springs, or sinkholes. A separate access point down the road leads to an 8.3-mile (13km) horse trail. Farther up the narrow gorge (you'll be crossing the

state line into Tennessee), past beautiful waterfalls, you'll reach a large, bowl-shaped natural amphitheater, 150 feet (46m) wide with sheer 200-foot-high (61m) walls. As Turkey Creek cascades through the Walls, on its way to join Hurricane Creek, water spurts out of big holes and cracks in the canyon wall during heavy rains or the big spring flows. You'd almost swear the canyon was spouting for joy, so glad that it and its woods have been saved.

ⓘ **Walls of Jericho,** Hwy. 79, Hytop, AL (ⓒ **615/781-6622**)

✈ Huntsville, AL

⊨ $$ **Comfort Inn,** 23518 John T. Reid Pkwy., Scottsboro, AL (ⓒ **256/574-6740;** www.choicehotels.com). $$ **Jameson Inn Scottsboro,** 208 Micah Way, Scottsboro, AL (ⓒ **800/JAMESON** [526-3766] or 256/574-6666; www.jamesoninns.com).

---

**A River Runs Through It**  **89**

# Buffalo River
## *The National River That Started It All*
### Arkansas

POPULATION GROWTH IN THE OZARKS HAS INCREASED RESIDENTIAL, AGRICULTURAL, AND TIMBER development, along with the construction of additional water reservoirs, which reduce the number of natural caves. The resulting loss of foraging space and habitat threaten the Ozark big-eared bat, which plays a vital role in controlling moths and other insects.

In 1972, the early days of the environmental movement, Congress did a radical thing: It declared this backwoods Ozark waterway America's first national river. That meant that its 150 miles (241km) would never be dammed or dredged, simply allowed to flow as nature intended. It was a bold experiment—and it worked.

Beginning in the remote and rugged Ponca wilderness, the Buffalo cuts a winding descent through tall limestone bluffs forested with deciduous trees—oaks, locust, sweet gum trees—then meanders into the White River, leading to the Arkansas River, then the Mississippi, and finally the Gulf of Mexico. It's not totally unspoiled wilderness—evidence suggests that the ancient Rock Shelter People dwelt in caves in those bluffs, and 19th-century farmhouses scattered around the park recall an era of hardscrabble homesteading. In the 20th century, first mining and then logging companies set up operations for a time. But since 1972, the preserve has returned to its natural state, with clear water and healthy woodlands.

The prime way to enjoy the Buffalo River is on the water, whether you shoot the swift rapids in the upper river or take an easy float on the peaceful middle stretches, stopping off at sandbars and swimming holes or fishing for plentiful smallmouth bass or catfish. Check out river conditions before you go, since they vary widely from section to section (like rivers are supposed to). But don't overlook what's on shore, with over 100 miles (160km) of hiking trails and several disused roads converted to horse trails. Tucked around those riverside bluffs are caves, natural springs, waterfalls, and rock arches to explore, and you'll have a very good chance of spotting elk, with nearly 500 individuals living along the river. Elk this far east? Yes. The native elk disappeared as long ago as 1840, but a diligent restocking program in the early 1980s has restored them to the Ozarks. (Stop by the **Elk Education Center** in Ponca, ✆ **870/861-2432,** or the **Hilary Jones Wildlife Museum** on Hwy. 7 in Jasper, ✆ **870/446-6180.**) It's just too bad that the American bison for which the river was named are long gone.

But black bears still inhabit the woods, and great blue, little green, and white herons stalk along the banks. The woods are full of songbirds—finches, cardinals, mockingbirds, wrens, and thrushes. In spring, flowering trees—sarvis, redbud, dogwood—blossom in the woods, with wildflowers, ferns, and azalea bushes filling out the understory. Fall foliage is nothing short of spectacular.

Buffalo River.

Backcountry camping is allowed anywhere along the river, and rustic cabins built during the 1940s by the Civilian Conservation Corps are available for overnight stays. Waking up to a superb Ozark landscape—that's priceless.

ⓘ **Tyler Bend Visitor Center,** Hwy. 65, St. Joe, AR (✆ **870/439-2502;** www.nps.gov/buff)

✈ Harrison, AR

🛏 $$$ **River Wind Lodge,** Jct. Ark Hwy. 43 & Hwy. 74, Ponca, AR (✆ **800/221-5514;** www.buffaloriver.com). $ **Buffalo Point Lodge & Cabins,** Hwy. 268E, Yellville, AR (✆ **870/449-6206;** www.buffalopoint.com).

**TOUR Buffalo River Outfitters,** St. Joe, AR (✆ **800/582-2244** or 870/439-2244; www.buffaloriveroutfitters.com). **Buffalo Adventures Canoe Rental,** Jasper, AR (✆ **870/446-5406**). **Silver Hill Canoe Rental,** St. Joe, AR (✆ **870/439-2372**).

# San Miguel River Preserve
## *The River Nobody Messed With*
### Telluride, Colorado

THE SAN MIGUEL IS HOME TO ONE OF THE BEST KNOWN EXAMPLES OF THE GLOBALLY RARE narrowleaf cottonwood, Colorado blue spruce, and thinleaf alder riverfront plant communities. The Nature Conservancy protects more than 30 miles (48km) of the San Miguel River, keeping many parts of the waterway pristine.

There's been so much tinkering with the Colorado River Basin, it's a relief to find a river like the San Miguel. There are no dams along the San Miguel River; it hasn't been dredged or rerouted. It flows just as nature intended it, 72 miles (116km) from its source above Telluride, in the San Juan Mountains, down into the Dolores River, in the southwestern Colorado Desert.

Preserving rivers like the San Miguel not only protects the water supply system of the West, it also protects the wildlife that lives alongside rivers—which happens to be more than 80% of the wildlife in Rocky Mountain Colorado. Along the San Miguel—where there's been almost no human development—the riverside forests reflect the rising levels of the river's natural flood cycles. Walk the boardwalk trail through the **South Fork Preserve,** just northwest of Telluride. The interpretive signs point out a unique combination of trees living together: Colorado blue spruce, black twinberry, and narrowleaf cottonwood. (Upstream in the San Miguel River Canyon Preserve, northwest of Norwood, another unusual forest mix replaces the twinberry with thinleaf alder.)

Impressive stands of Ponderosa pines, aspen groves, and water birches occupy other stretches of the riverbank. These great forests attract so many species of birds—including the endangered peregrine falcon, Swainson's thrush, fox sparrow, and American dipper—that it's been designated as an Important Bird Area by the Audubon Society. You may not see the black bears and mountain lion that still prowl around here, but you'll see signs of beaver activity, and you'll probably spot river otters in the water—a species that had once nearly disappeared from the San Miguel, until conservationists successfully reintroduced them.

It's a rugged landscape, no question about it—look upward from the South Fork Preserve and you'll see 14,000-foot (4,267m) Wilson Peak of the western San Juan Mountains. Other nearby landmarks are Ophir Needles, a granite pillar topped with jagged outcroppings that's a designated National Natural Landmark, and Ames Wall, a shingled rock face composed of stratified rock types (granite, sandstone, and shale). In this untamed mountain wilderness, an untamed river flowing through it may hold the key to restoring the American West's rivers.

ⓘ **South Fork Preserve,** Ilium Valley Rd., Telluride, CO. San Miguel River Canyon Preserve, State Rd. 145, Norwood, CO.

✈ Telluride

🛏 $$$ **New Sheridan Inn,** 231 W. Colorado Ave., Telluride (ⓒ **800/200-1891** or 970/728-4351). $$ **The Victorian Inn,** 401 W. Pacific Ave., Telluride (ⓒ **800/611-9893** or 970/728-6601; www.tellurideinn.com).

# Swan River Oxbow Preserve
## *Vanishing Flower of the Marshes*
### Swan Lake, Montana

LOSS OF HABITAT DUE TO TIMBER HARVEST DEFORESTATION AND RUNOFF, DRAINAGE FOR RESIDENTIAL and agricultural development, removal of native vegetation, and the invasion of noxious weeds threaten the Swan River Oxbow Preserve. In addition, climate change (too many wet or dry seasons) prevents the natural recharging process that wetlands need.

Such a tiny, unassuming little flower, the Howellia Aquatilis. A delicate white-blossomed annual, it likes to be submerged in water, like the marshy ponds nestled inside the swan's neck curve of Montana's Swan River. But there's just one catch: The water howelia's seeds only germinate on dry land. In order to reproduce, it needs a marsh that dries up in summer—like the ones inside the curve of the Swan River. In California, Oregon, Idaho, and Washington, the water howelia's special wetlands are being drained or flooded; in other locations, it's being choked out by reed canary grass, a hardy intruder that likes exactly the same growing conditions. In order to save the water howelia, we need the Swan River Oxbow Preserve.

So who cares about one little aquatic flower? Well, the water howelia is an indicator of wetlands health; the same marshes that nurture it are ideal for many other flowers—round-leafed pondweed, small yellow lady's slipper—as well as water birds such as the common loon, ring-necked duck, mallard, cinnamon teal, spotted sandpiper, common goldeneye, and Canada goose. Marsh wrens, song sparrows, and yellow-headed blackbirds dabble at water's edge, and neotropical migrants like the western tanager, Swainson's thrush, red-eyed vireo, and Lincoln's sparrow have been known to visit. It's not only the wetlands, but the entire mosaic of habitats: It's an important grizzly bear corridor between mountain ranges (you may want to avoid peak grizzly season, mid-Apr to mid-June); elk, moose, and deer graze in adjoining sedge fens and meadows; and bald eagles, red-tailed hawks, and osprey roost in the cottonwood trees to the west. It's a quiet, undeveloped place, with no spectacular sights to see.

Yet the Swan River Oxbow is a paradigm of change—in a good, natural, untampered-with way. In this steep-sided glacial valley, the Swan River gradually shifted course over the years, forced by accumulations of silt to curve westward. The land inside the curve—the "oxbow"—floods in late spring, when the river is swollen with snowmelt, and hidden springs and water seeping up through the limestone till keep the water table high. In effect it's an inland delta, and one with remarkably pure water. As you walk through it on the nature trail (stay on the path—it passes through some very boggy patches), you may not notice the water howelia at all. But you're bound to see something else subtle and beautiful.

---

(i) **Swan River Oxbow Preserve,** off Porcupine Creek Rd., 2½ miles (4km) south of Swan Lake, MT ((C) **406/644-2211**)

✈ Kalispell

🛏 $$ **Bridge Street Cottages,** 300 Bridge St., Bigfork ((C) **888/264-4974** or 406/837-2785; www.bridgestreetcottages. com). $$ **La Quinta Inn and Suites Kalispell,** 255 Montclair Dr., Kalispell ((C) **406/ 257-5255;** www.lq.com).

# Kootenai River
## *Damming the Sacred River*
### Idaho/Montana/British Columbia

KOOTENAI WETLANDS IN IDAHO WERE ALMOST DECIMATED BY AGRICULTURAL DEVELOPMENT; PART of the wetlands is now being restored by environmental groups. In Montana, the endangered and aging white sturgeon population has stopped spawning due to loss of habitat caused by the Libby Dam; unless young fish live to spawning age the species is expected to be extinct in as few as 20 years.

The Kootenai River's other name is the Flat Bow River—perfectly apt, considering the wide loop it makes, an international arc from British Columbia, down the Rocky Mountain Trench into Montana, then swinging westward into Idaho and back north to Kootenay Lake in British Columbia. Eventually those waters make their way into the Columbia River, but they sure take their time getting there.

Humans just can't keep from messing around with the Kootenai, though. In the Idaho valley, its attendant wetlands were drained in the 1920s to create farmland, despite the fact that it's a significant migratory stopover for some 200,000 birds, including about 67,000 ducks and geese. It's only in the past few years that those migrating water birds have had a chunk of protected habitat to rest in, thanks to aggressive wetlands restoration by the Nature Conservancy and local partners.

In Montana, spectacular Kootenai Falls—a site sacred to the Kootenai Tribe—remains the last major waterfall on a northwest river where there's no hydroelectric plant. Despite protests by the tribe, several dam projects have been planned over the past century, with some still on the drawing boards. And only 31 miles (50km) upstream, Libby Dam was built in 1975, altering river flows and temperatures so significantly that the Kootenai's white sturgeon population—one of the few landlocked populations, and genetically

unique—may not survive another 30 years. The sturgeon are now confined to a sluggish, silty section of river below the falls, where spawning seems to have fallen off drastically.

Looking at Kootenai Falls, it makes perfect sense that the Kootenai consider it the center of the world, a vortex for spiritual forces. Its vivid green waters crash violently over boulders, dropping 300 feet (91m) in just a few hundred yards. No wonder the filmmakers of *The River Wild* used this location for the dreaded whitewater called the Gauntlet in the film (after complex negotiations with the tribe for permission to film this holy place).

Arriving on U.S. Highway 2, you can view them from picnic grounds at the county park above the falls, and even step out on a swinging bridge spanning the gorge. A narrow path leads through the woods down to the river, to those incredible falls. Be glad there's no power plant desecrating the rugged walls of this gorge—and hope that it stays that way.

---

✈ Kalispell

🛏 $ **Caboose Motel,** 714 W. 9th St., Libby, MT (✆ **800/627-0206** or 406/293-6201; www.mtwilderness.com). $ **The Ranch Motel,** 914 E. Missoula Ave., Troy, MT (✆ **406/295-4332**).

Kootenai River.

# Dunstan Homestead

## *A Spawning Odyssey*

### Middle Fork John Day River, Oregon

EFFORTS BY CONSERVATION GROUPS ARE UNDERWAY TO REVERSE DAMAGE FROM UNMANAGED gold mining in the 1940s, which turned part of the river into a rocky channel without the river bends and pools necessary for trout and salmon to spawn. Soil erosion in the meadows and along the riverbanks, also a result of mining, removed habitat and many of the nutrients and habitat necessary to support trees, shrubs, and fish.

First of all, you have to get the right river—there are two John Day Rivers in Oregon. And then you have to locate the proper fork, since the big John Day has four major tributaries: the mainstem John Day, the North Fork John Day, the South Fork John Day, and the Middle Fork John Day. They're all named after John Day, an early-19th-century explorer who wandered around this arid part of Oregon between the Blue Mountains and the Cascade range in the winter of 1811 to 1812. It's kind of a strange

choice, naming so many rivers after a guy who got lost.

Maybe Oregon has a lack of imagination when it comes to naming rivers, but they got everything else right. The John Day is the second-longest dam-free river in the United States, and it's never had fish hatcheries—which means it's like a paradise for Chinook salmon and steelhead. Unlike John Day, these magnificent fish don't need maps; they simply wrestle upstream for 484 miles (779km) from the

Pacific to get to the gravel shallows of the Middle Fork John Day River, where they spend their summers getting ready to spawn. It isn't easy—they have to get around three major Columbia River dams en route—but they persist, faithful to some age-old instinct.

Named for the homesteading family who owned the land, the Dunstan refuge is run by a collaboration of conservationists who've taken over 4¹/₂ miles (7.2km) of the river, on former ranch land. This stretch of the Middle Fork is a major breeding ground for redband trout, bull trout, and Pacific lamprey as well as the steelhead and salmon. The first challenge is to get the river back to its original meandering course, altered by gold miners in the early 1940s. The straightened river just doesn't have the shallows and pools in which fish spawn best, and it's not as good for growing the alders, cottonwoods, and willows that shade the river waters to keep them cool. Along with that rechanneling, ecologists are clearing the loose rock detritus that the miners left, which ruined several riverside meadows. They're also thinning the tangled upland forests of ponderosa pines and Douglas firs, where you may be able to spot Rocky Mountain elk, mule deer, white-tailed deer, grouse, sandhill cranes, Canada geese, and Columbia spotted frogs. Park your car anywhere along the highway and venture on foot into the woods, or find your way to the river's banks and peer into the teeming shallows.

There have been setbacks—a 1996 wildfire, a court fight over plans to allow cattle grazing in nearby national forests, and record-high summer temperatures in 2007, which killed many salmon. But encouraged by increasing numbers of redds (salmon spawning nests) every year, the conservationists fight on—it's the least they can do for the salmon and steelhead.

ⓘ C.R. 20, mileposts 13–17, near Austin, OR

✈ John Day

🛏 $$ **Dreamer's Lodge,** 144 N. Canyon Blvd., John Day (✆ **800/654-2849** or 541/575-0526). $ **Middle Fork Campground,** Malheur National Forest, C.R. 20, 9 miles (15km) west of Austin Junction (✆ **541/575-3000**).

---

**A River Runs Through It** 94

# Anavilhanas Ecological Station
## *Hiding Place of the Jungle Manatee*
### Novo Airão, Brazil

THE AMAZONIAN MANATEE, ENDEMIC TO THIS REGION, FACES A HIGH RATE OF EXTINCTION IN the wild. Anavilhanas is also home to other threatened species, including the giant arapaima fish, black caiman, and two species of river dolphin. While this area is protected by government decree, hunting and pollution from ships traveling the Rio Negro put the area at risk.

All manatees are not created equal. Take the Amazonian manatee, for example. It's the only freshwater manatee, and it's smaller than the other two species, on average only 3m (9 ft.) long and 450kg (992 lb.; granted, that's still big). A timid creature, it minds its own business in the backwaters of Amazon basin rivers. Since it only has molar teeth, its diet is limited to soft aquatic plants. Mothers only have one calf at a time, which they nurse for up to 2 years. So when the natives hunt them for meat and leather, invade their waterways with motorboats, and destroy their specialized habitat—well, it's hard for the manatees to hold their own.

The Amazonian manatee is just one species being studied and protected at the Anavilhanas Ecological Station, a Brazilian government nature reserve just northwest of Manaus (access is through the lodge of the same name). Set in the Rio Negro, a major Amazon tributary, it encompasses some 400 islands and hundreds of lakes, rivers, swamps, and sandbanks, the world's largest archipelago in a river. Since the reserve was created in 1981, it has relocated nearly all the inhabitants of the archipelago. And still, residents of Novo Airão and Manaus visit the islands to fish, hunt, and cut wood; Manaus building companies take sand and stones from the riverside, though rangers are monitoring this activity closely. Ships cruising the Rio Negro add pollution to the equation. And, of course, politics snarl up everything, with many locals increasingly resistant to international "interference" by conservation groups.

Though the islands of Anavilhanas are covered with forests, these are special forests, adapted to the fact that the islands are largely submerged during the high-water period, April to June. Notice, for example, the tree's aerial roots as you navigate around the islands in small boats—those come in handy when a tree is flooded for months at a time You'll see a lot of palm-trees, orchids, lichens, and on some islands, straggly shrublands; a lot of trees have curved, thin trunks and leathery leaves that can store water for the dry months. Animals are driven to higher ground, too, until the waters recede, revealing beaches and deeper channels. September and October may be your best months if you want to see wildlife.

Given the changing conditions of the river, the landscape is constantly shape-shifting, with islands relocating and channels altering their courses. A local guide, however, can help you keep your bearings, as well as identify the flora and fauna, most of which are unique to this one-of-a-kind environment. As you maneuver around its labyrinth of channels, lakes, and island, keep an eye peeled for those elusive manatees—or at least the playful river dolphins.

✈ Manaus

🛏 **Anavilhanas Jungle Lodge** (✆ **55/ 92/3622-8896;** www.anavilhanaslodge. com)

---

## 95

# The Okavanga Delta
## *Mokoro Cruising*
### Botswana

THE BOTSWANA GOVERNMENT HAS APPROVED SPRAYING INSECTICIDES TO CONTROL THE TSETSE fly population, and studies are underway to determine the effects of spraying on other insects, birds, and fish. As global temperatures rise, the delta's abundant water at certain times of the year makes this area vulnerable to pipeline drainage used to supply water to parched desert communities.

Okavango Delta.

Every winter—which in Botswana begins in July—the Okavango River flows south out of the uplands of Angola, its waters swollen to bursting by the rainy season. By the time it gets to this vast bowl in Botswana, it has overrun its banks, spreading out throughout the delta. Crystal-clear pools, channels, and lagoons spring up everywhere, playing host to a rich diversity of wildlife, who flock here in grateful escape from the adjacent Kalahari Desert.

Game lodges in the delta are classified as "wet" or "dry" according to whether or not they are surrounded by water during flood season, but it's not as if being surrounded is a problem—it just means you'll do all your traveling around by *mokoro*, a narrow canoelike boat propelled through the water by a human with a long pole. (Traditionally carved out of tree trunks, nowadays most are made from fiberglass.) These silent, shallow craft make it possible to get really close to birds and animals for wildlife viewing. As you glide along, the air is filled with the sounds of birds calling, frogs trilling, and antelope rustling in the reeds. Wildebeest, hartebeest, buffalo, and zebra roam the islands before you; elephants wade across channels guarded by hippos and crocs.

Game camps in the Okavango are generally tented affairs, since the operators are required to make no permanent marks on the land, but some of these are quite luxurious tents indeed. Most of the camps are set within the Moremi Game Reserve, in the northeastern segment of the delta, which is marketed as the "Predator Capital of Africa" for the number of lions and leopards you can sight. Given the complexities of travel within Botswana, it's best to book your lodgings as part of a package trip through a safari specialist company (see "Tour," below). They're pricey, yes, but the experience is once-in-a-lifetime special.

---

ⓘ **Moremi Game Reserve,** Botswana (http://moremi.botswana.co.za)

✈ Maun Airport

**TOUR Abercrombie & Kent** (✆ **800/554-7016** in the U.S., 27/11/781-0740 in South Africa; www.abercrombiekent.com). **Conservation Corporation Africa** (✆ **27/11/809-4300** in South Africa, 27/267/661-979 in Botswana; www.ccafrica.com). **Wilderness Safaris** (✆ **27/11/895-0862** in South Africa; www.wilderness-safaris.com).

# National Chambal Sanctuary
## *Bloody River in the Land of Taj Mahal*
### Uttar Pradesh, India

DESTROYED HABITATS AND THE INADVERTENT VICTIMS OF ILLEGAL NET FISHING, GHARIAL ALLIGATORS, called the monarchs of Indian rivers, are critically in danger of extinction. In the past few years, conservationists have stepped up efforts to stem the mass deaths of gharials, believed to be poisoned by lead and chromium in the water.

Ancient Indian myth gives the Chambal River some pretty bloody origins—created supposedly by the gushing blood of thousands of holy cows, cruelly slaughtered by the Aryan King Rantideva. But this unholy reputation turned out to be lucky for the Chambal River. Unlike the Ganges and other nearby rivers, it was left alone—and therefore unspoiled. Nowadays it's one of India's most pristine rivers, a crystal-clear waterway winding through Rajasthan, Mayar Pradesh, and Uttar Pradesh.

This long, narrow nature preserve lies only a couple hours' drive from the fabled Taj Mahal, but it seems a world unto itself. It's a toss-up as to which rare wildlife spottings are the most exciting along this calm, wide, shallow river. Is it the sight of enormous, narrow-snouted brown gharial alligators, basking on rocky islands? Or is it a flashing glimpse of Ganges River dolphins (practically vanished from the Ganges), arcing playfully from the shimmering blue-gray surface? Bird-watchers might claim it's the chance to see flocks of beautiful Indian skimmers hunting for fish, dipping their long curved orange bills into the water. Or maybe it's a brown hawk owl, roosting in the fig tree over your head, the marsh crocodiles lazing on the mud banks, or smooth-coated otters sliding into the water's edge.

The dry season (Oct–Apr) is the best time to visit, when the raging monsoon waters recede to leave dazzling white sand beaches and grassy spits along the river, and migratory birds settle in the shallows and marshes for the mild winter. Nature hikes, jeep tours, and even camel safaris are available, but the best way to explore the sanctuary is via motorboat, cruising through a mazy series of eroded sandy ravines thickly planted with acacias and other thorny tropical scrub thickets. Those forests are full of sambar, nilgiri, blackbuck, wolves, wild boars, and the dreaded dacoits (go with an armed guide for safety). You can also visit a nearby wetlands area that's an important breeding ground for the stately, elegant gray Sarus cranes. You won't see the blood of Rantideva's slaughtered cows, but you won't see pollution or overdevelopment, either.

(i) **National Chambal Sanctuary,** access points near Bah or Nandagaon, Uttar Pradesh

✈ Agra

🛏 $$ **Chambal Safari Lodge,** Jarar (Oct–Apr only; ✆ **91/94126 51921;** www. chambalsafari.com)

# Crystal River National Wildlife Refuge
## *Warm Winter Waters for Manatees*
### Crystal River, Florida

CRYSTAL RIVER NATIONAL WILDLIFE REFUGE PROVIDES CRITICAL WARM-WATER HABITAT FOR 15% to 20% of the entire U.S. manatee population. However, manatees, which breed infrequently and are often injured or killed in boating accidents, could be headed for extinction. Yet the tourist industry consistently resists proposals for further restrictions on recreational access and boating speeds that pose serious risks to these gentle giants.

It's an image out of *Miami Vice:* the cigarette boat slicing cleanly through Florida's warm coastal shallows. But the TV show never dealt with what happens when a speedboat collides with a nearsighted, 10-foot-long (3m), 1,200-pound (544kg) manatee. One thing is certain: It's a duel that the manatee never wins.

Between speedboat injuries and dwindling habitat, America's West Indian manatee population has shrunk to about 1,200

Manatee swimming in the Crystal River.

individuals, nearly a fourth of who winter in the same prime spot: the protected natural springs of King Bay in the **Crystal River National Wildlife Refuge.** Created specifically for manatees, the refuge features ideal manatee conditions: clear, warm, coastal shallows and spring-fed rivers where the temperature generally stays a steady 72°F (22°C; in warmer weather, manatees migrate north as far as Virginia or North Carolina). The refuge is only reachable by boat, usually on a guided excursion. Several approved local operators (see below) lead daily boat tours out into the manatees' favorite waters to let human swimmers and snorkelers interact with the manatees.

There are also manatee tours 7 miles (11km) south of Crystal River in the **Homosassa Springs Wildlife State Park,** where the waters are even shallower—only 4 feet (1.2m) deep. Manatees may even come close enough for you to pet their sleek gray-brown skin and feel the whiskers on their droopy snouts. Tours begin as early as 7am, when the manatees are around in greatest numbers; you'll be back at the dock by late morning.

After your face-to-face manatee encounter, you can go underwater in a floating observatory in Homosassa Springs Wildlife State Park to watch manatees in action, with thousands of fresh- and saltwater fish darting around them. As you'll notice through the observation glass, this is a rehabilitation facility that nurses manatees that have been injured by boat propellers.

The sight of their scarred bodies, missing fins, and truncated tails is a sad reminder of the threat of their extinction.

---

ⓘ **Crystal River National Wildlife Refuge** (ℂ **352/563-2088;** www.fws.gov/crystalriver). **Homosassa Springs Wildlife State Park,** 4150 S. Suncoast Blvd., Homosassa Springs, FL (ℂ **352/628-5343;** www.floridastateparks.org/homosassa springs).

✈ Tampa International

🛏 $$$ **Plantation Inn,** 9301 W. Fort Island Trail (ℂ **352/795-4211;** www.plantationinn.com). $$ **Best Western Crystal River Resort,** 614 NW U.S. 19 (ℂ **800/435-4409** or 352/795-3171; www.crystalriverresort.com).

**TOUR American Pro Dive,** 821 SE U.S. 19, Crystal River (ℂ **800/291-3483** or 352/563-0041; www.americanprodive.com). **Sunshine River Tours** (ℂ **800/645-5727** or 352/628-3450; www.sunshinerivertours.com).

 Denizens of the Deep

**98**

# Otter Island
## *Loggerhead Getaway*
### ACE Basin, South Carolina

COASTLINE DEVELOPMENT, FISHING, HUMAN DISTURBANCE OF NESTING AREAS, AND POLLUTION have hastened the decline of loggerhead populations. And because loggerheads range throughout the world's oceans during their long lives, they are a resource shared by many nations and owned by none. As a result, activities in one country may undermine conservation efforts in another.

Hear mention of the barrier islands of South Carolina, and what do you think of? Well-groomed golf courses, white beaches, million-dollar luxury homes—and loggerhead turtles?

Tucked in between the resort islands like Kiawah, Seabrook, and Hilton Head, there's another world, centered around the ACE Basin watershed, where the Ashepoo, Combahee, and Edisto rivers empty into St. Helena Sound. You'd never expect 140,000 acres (56,650 hectares) of undeveloped tidal marshes, upland forest, peat bogs, and barrier islands so close to Savannah and Charleston. The state runs it as a National Estuarine Research Reserve, protecting vital habitats for waterfowl and migratory birds along the Atlantic Flyway, that sky-high expressway for birds. Exhibits at the education center at Edisto Beach

State Park, at the south end of Edisto Island, will swiftly bring you up to speed on the ecology of this critical watershed.

There are no bridges or ferries to uninhabited Otter Island, a marshy 2,000-acre (809-hectare) barrier island just south of Edisto Island, but you can get there by boat from Bennett's Point, on Mosquito Creek at the end of Highway 26. (Head south from the boat landing into the Ashepoo River, then east about 6 miles/9.7km to Day Marker #2—Otter Island will be on your left.) Despite the name, otters aren't the main attraction here—it's loggerhead sea turtles, which swim in at night to deposit their eggs on its dark, protected beaches between May and September every year. With their big heads and powerful jaws, loggerheads munch on mollusks and crabs out in the ocean; their reddish-brown shells may measure as much as 3 feet (1m) long, and the turtles weigh up to 350 pounds (160kg). The hatchlings, however, are only about 2 inches (5cm) long when they emerge from the sand (again, usually at night) and, by the light of the moon, return to the water. Screens are put up to keep predators like raccoons away from the beaches when the eggs are incubating in the sand.

Isolated by open water, Otter Island has intentionally been left in a primitive state, but visitors are welcome; you can even camp overnight, with a permit, November to April. Fishing and bow-and-arrow hunting are also allowed with permits. The shoreline, with its narrow quartz-sand beaches, is fronted by a ridge of old sand dunes, now covered with forest scrub. Anchor your boat (a canoe or a motorboat less than 20 ft. long is ideal) along the shore and hike into its pine forests, following trickling creeks or the trails left by white-tailed deer (there are no formal trails). Raccoons, deer, feral hogs, and songbirds live in these woods, and you may even be able to spot a nesting pair of bald eagles, but watch out for ever-present rattlesnakes. Find your way to the fringe of a windswept marsh and, depending on the season, you may see wood storks and other wading birds. Chances are it'll be just you and the birds.

(i) **ACE Basin National Estuarine Research Reserve,** Bennett's Point, at the end of Hwy. 26, off Hwy. 17 (© **843/844-8822;** www.nerrs.noaa.gov/acebasin)

✈ Charleston

🛏 $$ **Andrew Pinckney Inn,** 40 Pinckney St., Charleston (© **800/505-8983** or 843/937-8800; www.andrewpinckneyinn.com). $$ **Wyndham Ocean Ridge Resort,** 1 King Cotton Rd., Edisto Beach (© **843/869-2561;** www.fairfieldresorts.com).

---

**Denizens of the Deep** **99**

# Ano Nuevo State Reserve
## *Love & Sex & the Elephant Seal*
### Half Moon Bay, California

ELEPHANT SEALS SPEND MOST OF THEIR LIVES AT SEA—THEY EVEN SLEEP UNDERWATER—BUT they mate and bear their young on land. Once hunted for their oil, by the late 1800s the world population of northern elephant seals numbered less than 100. Today, elephant seals are no longer on the brink of extinction, but they are still at risk from development and commercial fishing.

Surfers dig shooting the curls at crescent-curved Half Moon Bay, an hour south of San Francisco. Yet how many of them realize that there's a primal scene of sex, blood, and pain a stone's throw away on low, rocky Ano Nuevo Point?

It starts every November—the annual mating and birthing of the northern elephant seals. You can only witness this spectacle on a guided walk (daily Dec 15–Mar 15), which should be reserved months in advance. Nearly extinct until recently, these 3-ton (2,700kg) marine mammals (one look at their pendulous upper lips and you'll know why they're called elephant seals) live on the open sea for 10 months a year. When they start coming ashore in November, in such numbers that they carpet the beach, the

Elephant seals at Ano Nuevo.

females are already pregnant. From a distance (you really don't want to get too close to an elephant seal) you may see one bull seal protecting a harem of females as a few bachelors hang hopefully on the fringes. It's not a sight for the squeamish: Males clash in often-bloody mating battles, they mate frankly on the open sands, and females give birth on the dunes—all redeemed by the tender sight of mother seals cuddling their young.

The mating season runs from November until March, when the adults swim back to sea, leaving weaned pups to mature (by now, approximately 2,000 are born here each season). After April, the youngsters leave too, and the beaches are open to the public again. In spring and summer, however, adults occasionally return to the beach to molt; if you're lucky you'll see some then, but it's nothing like the massed bodies of winter.

Otherwise, you can enjoy the sight of smaller California seals sunning themselves year-round at Seal Cove Beach; in early spring and fall, look for migrating whales from the bluffs above Princeton-by-the-Sea. Birders know to hunt for rare loons, great blue herons, red-tailed hawks, and brown pelicans. Numerous hummingbirds carry out their own elaborate courtship ritual in the spring—but let's face it, that'll never be quite as big an attraction as the elephant seals mating.

ⓘ **Ano Nuevo State Reserve,** New Year's Creek Rd, Hwy. 1, Pescadero (ⓒ **800/ 444-4445,** 650/879-0227)

✈ San Francisco International

🛏 $$$ **Seal Cove Inn,** 221 Cypress Ave., Half Moon Bay (ⓒ **650/728-4114;** www.sealcoveinn.com). $$$ **Beach House Inn,** 4100 N. Cabrillo Hwy. (Hwy. 1), Half Moon Bay (ⓒ **800/315-9366** or 650/712-0220; www.beach-house.com).

# Mosquito Bay
## The Incredible Glowing Biobay
### Vieques, Puerto Rico

WHEN THE U.S. NAVY PULLED OUT IN 2003, 80% OF VIEQUES WAS SUDDENLY TRANSFORMED into the Caribbean's largest wildlife refuge. Today, development and tourism could endanger Vieques' natural wonders, including the magical bioluminescence in Mosquito Bay.

It's almost like something out of a horror movie—the eerie blue-green glow of the waters around you, responding to every flitting fish and swirling oar. But far from being a ghastly environmental freak, the phosphorescence of Vieques Bay is a 100% natural phenomenon, and one you have to see to believe.

In 2003, the U.S. Navy closed its installation on the island of Vieques, off the coast of Puerto Rico, and since then Vieques has begun to boom as an eco-friendly—and still charmingly scruffy—destination. With some 40 palm-lined white-sand beaches, and reefs of snorkel-worthy antler coral off shore, Vieques—7 miles (11km) off the big island's east coast, only an hour by ferry—has an obvious sand-and-sun appeal. But so have many other Puerto Rican beaches; what makes Vieques special is Mosquito Bay, just west of the main town, Isabel Segunda. It's nickname is Phosphorescent Bay for the way its waters glow in the dark, thanks to millions of tiny bioluminescent organisms called pyrodiniums (translation from science-speak: "whirling fire"). They're only about $1/500$ of an inch in size, but when these tiny swimming creatures are disturbed (by, for example, a hovering tour boat), they dart away and light up like fireflies, leaving eerie blue-white trails of phosphorescence.

These pyrodiniums exist elsewhere, but not in such amazing concentrations: A gallon of water in Mosquito Bay may contain upwards of three-quarters of a million such creatures. The local newspaper *Vieques Times* perhaps says it best: "By any name the bay can be a magical, psychedelic experience." You can even swim in these glowing waters, a sensation that's incredibly eerie and cool.

Don't make the mistake of coming here on a full moon, however—the glow of the pyrodiniums is only discernible on a cloudy, moonless night. If the moon's out, you can save your money, because you'll see almost nothing. (*Warning:* Some tour boats go out to the bay regardless of the full moon—and you won't get your money back if you're disappointed).

✈ Vieques

🛏 $$ **Wyndham Martineau Bay Resort,** Rte. 200 (© **787/741-4100;** www.wyndham.com). $$ **Hacienda Tamarindo,** Rte. 996, Barrio Puerto Real (© **787/741-8525;** www.enchanted-isle.com/tamarindo).

**TOUR Island Adventures** (© **787/741-0720**). **Blue Caribe Kayak** (© **787/741-2522**).

# Tortuguero
## *The Sea Turtles' Secret Getaway*
### Tortuguero, Costa Rica

SECLUDED TORTUGUERO IN COSTA RICA PROVIDES IDEAL NESTING CONDITIONS FOR FOUR endangered turtle species. Sea turtles are in constant danger of drowning after become tangled in commercial fishing nets or lines. Egg-laying females are extremely sensitive to light and sound, so any development near their nesting sites threatens to disrupt the turtles' reproductive cycle.

Tortuguero—the very name refers to sea turtles, or *tortugas* in Spanish, so it's an apt name indeed for this park, the top turtle-nesting site on Costa Rica's Caribbean coast. Luckily for the turtles, it's not easy for humans to get there; there are no roads, only a labyrinthine series of rivers and canals linking it to the port city of Limón, 80km (50 miles) away. Gliding on a boat through this dense green rainforest populated by howler and spider monkeys, three-toed sloths, toucans, and great green macaws is almost like a minicruise up the Amazon.

This undeveloped region's greatest resource is its wildlife, as nature lovers visit in ever greater numbers, putting a new stress on the fragile coastal ecosystem. A number of lodges perch on the hills around the tiny village of Tortuguero, all catering to the eco-tourist trade. Generally visitors book a package from one of those lodges that includes a bus from San José to Limón, the boat trip from Limón, rooms, and meals. Local guides are available to take you by dugout canoe up murky waterways into the rainforest, where you may see crocodiles, caimans, monkeys, herons, pygmy kingfishers, or river otters (jaguars and ocelots rarely come in view). Unfortunately, the native manatee population is nearly extinct, due to hunting and to chemical runoff from nearby banana plantations.

Packages also include the starring attraction: a guided 2-to-4-hour nighttime visit to the beach to watch sea turtles wade onto the volcanic black sand to lay their eggs. In fact, the only beach access at night is with an approved nature guide. Darkness and quiet are essential—if a female turtle detects any lights or movements, she will return to the sea without laying her eggs. (And given the increasing development of the Caribbean, there are fewer and fewer sufficiently dark, quiet coasts.) The mother crawls onto the beach, digs a huge pit, and then lays her eggs, as many as 100 at a time. Then she covers the pit in sand and crawls back into the ocean, never to see these offspring again.

Small sea turtles at Tortuguero.

Protected from local poachers, four species of turtles nest on this 35km-long (22-mile) stretch of black sand—the green turtle, the hawksbill, the loggerhead, and the world's largest turtle, the giant leatherback. Considering its great size (up to 2m/6 ft. long and weighing as much as 450kg/1,000 lb.), the giant leatherback is truly a spectacular turtle to see if you get the chance (Mar–May). From July through mid-October, it's more likely that you will spot green turtles. They are an endangered species all right, but that's hard to believe when you see massing by the thousands on Tortuguero beach.

---

(i) **Tortuguero National Park,** Tortuguero, Costa Rica ((C) **506/709-8091**)

✈ San José

🛏 $$$ **Tortuga Lodge,** Tortuguero ((C) **506/257-0766** in San José, 506/710-8016 in Tortuguero, www.costaricaexpeditions.com). $$ **Pachira Lodge,** Tortuguero ((C) **506/256-7080;** www.pachiralodge.com).

## Denizens of the Deep 102

# Turtle Islands Park
## *From Egg to Hatchling in the South China Sea*
### Sabah, Malaysia (Borneo)

VISITORS GET A FRONT-ROW SEAT HERE TO WATCH FEMALE TURTLES LAY THEIR EGGS IN THE SAND, and even take part in the action—helping park rangers gather eggs for incubation and releasing baby turtles into the sea. The turtles face the same dangers as other turtles worldwide. Many adult turtles are accidentally caught by fishing boats and drowned; and the survival rate of turtle hatchlings at most nesting sites is very low.

Like a marine version of Cirque Du Soleil, the sea turtles seem to have taken this extraordinary egg-laying act of theirs on the road. Halfway round the globe, the very same drama in Tortuguero is enacted every night on a tiny tropical island, off the coast of exotic Borneo.

Pulau Selligan is one of three islands in this state-run nature sanctuary in the Malaysian part of Borneo, that big island in the South China Sea. (Borneo itself is divvied up between Brunei, Malaysia, and Indonesia). Lying 40km (25 miles) offshore from the town of Sandakan, the sanctuary only accepts 50 tourists per night (book with a local tour company). Accommodations are extremely basic, and you have to stay overnight—because this spectacular show only plays nighttime performances.

After arriving by speedboat from Sandakan, you're free to laze around on the beach all afternoon, lulled by the tropical sun and the beautiful blue waters of the Sulu Sea. Here's the extent of your daytime entertainment options: study turtle exhibits in the park headquarters (two species nest here, green turtles and hawksbills), visit turtle hatchlings being raised in an outdoor nursery, or snorkel on the shallow coral reef that surrounds the island, busy with tropical fish. (Borneo in general is a fantastic scuba destination, though its most renowned site, Sipadan, has recently had resorts removed to prevent further degradation.) On the soft white-sand beaches, you may notice some curious tracks, evidence of last night's turtle invasion—deep round flipper scoops on either side of a wide shallow groove where the shell drags along.

As darkness falls, all visitors are confined to the park headquarters, waiting for a signal from a ranger. Curtain time could be anywhere from dusk until dawn, and you can't wait on the beach—if the turtles detect humans when they crawl ashore, they turn right around and swim away. Once the signal comes, guests go with a guide down to the beach to watch the female turtles deposit their ping-pong ball-shaped eggs into a hole they've scooped in the sand. They lay anywhere from 50 to 200 eggs at a time, trying to overcome with sheer numbers the vast odds against any one egg's surviving.

The next act is even more memorable— the audience-participation part of the show.

Rangers move the new-laid eggs to a nursery to incubate for the next 60 days— a measure that has dramatically increased the survival of these endangered creatures—and then a number of already-hatched baby turtles are brought down from the nursery for guests to release back into the sea. You actually get to hold a sturdy little hatchling, set it down on the beach, and watch it hustle back into the sea. It's completing the cycle of life—and you helped!

---

ⓘ www.malaysiasite.nl/turtle.htm

✈ Sandakan

**TOUR Discovery Tours,** Wisma Sabah, Lot G22, Jalan Haji Saman (✆ **60/88/221-244;** www.discoverytours.com.my)

---

**103** Denizens of the Deep

# Glacier Bay
## *Some Like It Cold*
Alaska

GLACIER BAY IS A SAFE HAVEN FOR MANY THREATENED AND ENDANGERED SPECIES. BUT THE protection offered by this famous fjord in southeast Alaska can't safeguard animals that migrate or wander beyond its borders, nor can it shield them from the damaging effects of disappearing habitat or depleted food supplies in other areas.

You can't blame global warming for what's been happening at Glacier Bay—this glacier's been receding for at least 2 centuries. When Captain George Vancouver visited this southeastern Alaska coast in 1794, he described the bay as a mere 5-mile (8km) notch in a massive 20-mile-wide (32km) glacier that reached more than 100 miles (160km) to the St. Elias Mountains. Fast-forward 85 years and you get naturalist John Muir's 1879 account of a bay more than 30 miles (48km) long. By 1916, it was 60 miles (97km) deep; it's now

a 65-mile-long (105km) fjord. At its mouth, mature spruce forests have been long established, but moving deeper into the fjord, you'll see the vegetation gradually become smaller and sparser, according to how many years that terrain has been exposed, until finally you reach a band of mosses, lichen, and loose rocky scree— and then a stark curtain of ice.

You can only stare at ice so long before you get distracted by the animals. Glacier Bay lies in one of the world's largest protected biosphere reserves. Humpback

Glacier Bay.

Retreating glaciers are good news for these animals, as well as mountain goats, coyotes, and wolves, whose territory just keeps growing. Arctic terns, jaegers, and puffins nest in the barren cliffs nearest to the glaciers, but as the hillsides become more vegetated, neotropical songbirds arrive in increasing numbers for their summer pilgrimage.

If you're like most visitors, you'll view the park from the water, either from the deck of a big cruise ship (park rangers come aboard to point out natural features) or on day cruises on a catamaran that can drop off hikers, kayakers, and campers at certain locations. Kayaking is a perfect way to get close to the park's wildlife, with surprisingly calm, sheltered waters for those who aren't experienced paddlers. For some serious bird-watching, come May through September—there's any number of great spots to hike to around Bartlett Cove, or you can kayak to the Beardslee Islands or Point Gustavus. The more you put into exploring, the more you'll see.

---

ⓘ **Glacier Bay National Park,** Bartlett Cove (✆ **907/697-2230;** www.nps.gov/glba)

✈ Juneau

🛏 $$$ **Glacier Bay Lodge,** Bartlett Cove, Glacier Bay National Park (✆ **888/BAY-TOUR** [229-8687] or 907/264-4600; www.visitglacierbay.com)

**TOUR Glacier Bay Tours** (✆ **888/BAY-TOUR** [229-8687] or 907/264-4600; www.visitglacierbay.com). **Glacier Bay Sea Kayaks** (✆ **907/697-2257;** www.glacierbayseakayaks.com). **Alaska Discovery Inc.** (✆ **800/780-6505;** www.akdiscovery.com).

whales make it their summer home, while minke whales, orcas, Dall's porpoises, and harbor porpoises feed in the icy waters offshore. It's easy to view the harbor seals raising their families on the ice floes of St. John's Inlet, and huge, tawny Steller sea lions and their pups on rocky islets at the mouth of the bay. The Steller sea lion population in Alaska is inexplicably declining, perhaps because their favorite food—walleye pollack and herring—have been overfished. It's heartening to see such a healthy community in these protected waters.

You may find moose and brown bears swimming across stretches of the bay, too.

# Cocos Island Marine Park
## *Cuckoo for Cocos Island*
### Costa Rica

WHILE ITS REMOTE LOCATION HAS PROTECTED COCOS ISLAND FROM HUMAN DEVELOPMENT, MANY rare and endemic plant species are endangered by feral pigs, deer, and rats. Pollution and climate change affect both land and marine habitats.

After a day-and-a-half boat ride, any spot of land would look good—but when Cocos Island rises out of the Pacific, a lush green tropical Eden with waterfalls spilling from its jungle cliffs, it's easy to think you've come to paradise.

Well, don't get carried away. This mountainous former pirate hideout, 482km (300 miles) southwest of the Costa Rican coast, has defeated settlers for centuries. (Though there are no native mammals on the isolated island, feral pigs, goats, rats, cats, and deer roam the wild interior, abandoned by residents who gave up years ago.) The rainfall is prodigious (600cm/240 in. a year), the high-altitude cloud forest is impenetrable; landslides carry off chunks of the coast when you least expect it. Today the only sign of civilization is a tin-roofed ranger station with a handful of rangers. The government forbids any land-based tourism at all, but that's okay—most people who come here are more interested in strapping on a tank and mask and heading under water.

To limit environmental damage, at present only three tour companies are regularly allowed to bring dive boats to Cocos Island, anchoring in one of its two large beach-fringed bays (Chatham and Wafer Bay) before heading for the offshore dive sites. Rather than exquisite coral reefs, the underwater terrain here is on an epic scale—huge jagged basaltic ridges, violent chasms, abrupt cliffs, boulders as big as a brontosaurus. The marine life is on an equally large scale: giant moray eels, whitetip reef sharks, droves of hammerhead sharks, dolphins, sailfish, hefty tuna and marlin, and occasionally the world's largest fish, the whale shark. A manta ray gliding overhead casts an immense shadow, momentarily blocking out the sun. Round a corner and you'll run into an octopus, lazily extending its fleshy tentacles.

With so many species crowding these fertile waters, it should come as no surprise that Cocos Island would also have a pack of its own homegrown endemic fish species, 27 at last count. Very few creatures in the sea look as weird as the red-lipped batfish, for example, with its pale triangular forehead, bulbous eyes, and scarlet kisser.

While you're anchored off Cocos Island, you may take a shore excursion to hike into the jungle, swim in a crystalline waterfall, or observe rare exotic birds like the Cocos Island cuckoo, the Cocos Island flycatcher, or the Cocos Island finch—a relative of Darwin's finch, from the nearby Galapagos Islands. Sure, the Galapagos are a few hundred miles away, but for Cocos Island, that qualifies as a next-door neighbor.

 San José

**TOUR Undersea Hunter** (✆ **800/203-2120;** www.underseahunter.com). **Okeanos Aggressor** (✆ **800/348-2628** or 985/385-2628; www.aggressor.com). **Dive Discovery** (✆ **800/886-7321** or 415/444-5100; www.divediscovery.com).

# Malpelo Fauna & Floral Sanctuary
## *Get a Piece of the Rock*
### Malpelo, Colombia

POLLUTION THREATENS TERRESTRIAL WILDLIFE ON THE ISLAND, AND ILLEGAL POACHING——ESPECIALLY by hunters seeking shark fins—threatens sharks and other marine life in this sanctuary for many rare and endangered species. The Sea Shepherd Conservation Society and other groups support underequipped park rangers in their efforts to enforce the fishing ban.

By itself, Malpelo Island is nothing—three naked stubs of gray volcanic rock sticking out of the Pacific Ocean. There isn't a single hotel or restaurant or even a beach shack, nothing but a crowd of masked boobies huddling on the lichened rocks and a half-deserted army base, 515km (320 miles) from the nearest mainland. If it weren't for the waters around the island, nobody would come here. Nobody would even have heard of it.

But those waters have been declared a 9.7km-wide (6-mile) no-fishing zone, a strictly patrolled sanctuary where all sorts of fish prosper. Here they can revert to natural patterns of behavior that have grown increasingly rare in Earth's over-fished oceans. The density of smaller fish draws astonishing numbers of sharks, giant grouper, and billfish, making this a site scuba divers speak of with awe. Frequently divers see groups of 300 hammerhead sharks at a time, and over 1,000 silky sharks at once. Hordes of angelfish, creole fish, and jacks flutter in formation, filtered sunlight glinting off their fins. Moray eels seem to be everywhere. Manta rays flutter gracefully around; dolphins skim deftly through the water. There have even been occasional sightings of the short-nosed ragged-toothed shark, a deepwater species so rare it wasn't even known to exist before Malpelo divers recorded it.

Malpelo is so far out in the ocean, so far from all development, that the waters are breathtakingly clear, and sunlight can penetrate much deeper than usual. Divers also love the steep underwater walls and beautiful caves around Malpelo. One favorite site, an outcropping of rocks called Three Musketeers, leads to an underwater labyrinth of caverns and tunnels fittingly named the Cathedral, where huge schools of fish dart about. The waters are warm, though often turbulent; because the currents are so tricky, every dive here is a drift dive. It's not for inexperienced divers.

Divers need government permission to visit the sanctuary, which tour organizers will arrange for you. You'll need to travel on a boat with sleeping accommodations, anyway, since no tourists are permitted on the island itself. The island is way too far from shore for a day trip; expeditions last at least a week, and some are done in conjunction with Cocos Island (above). But, hey, it seems only fair to put in some effort, if you want to have the diving trip of a lifetime.

✈ Buenaventura Airport

**TOUR Undersea Hunter** (© 800/203-2120; www.underseahunter.com). ***Doña Mariela,*** Wilfried Ellmer (www.imulead.com/tolimared/malpelo).

# Baja California
## *A Whale of a Time in Mexico*
### Bahía Magdalena & El Vizcaino, Mexico

AFTER BEING HUNTED TO NEAR EXTINCTION IN THE 1850S AND AGAIN IN THE EARLY 1900S, gray whales were the first whales put on the endangered species list. They made a remarkable comeback, but now numbers are dwindling again due to climate change that is warming the ocean and reducing their food supply. Oil exploration and seismic testing in the Bering Strait during calving season have placed the gray whale at further risk.

Seeing a gray whale close up can be a mystical, almost spiritual experience. It's not just that they're so big. It's not even their air of regal calm, or the effortless way their long mottled bodies slide through the water, mastering the sea. It's something more, something primordial in their meditative gaze and upcurved baleen smile, almost as if they possess some ancient secret wisdom.

At 14 to 15m (45–50 ft.) long and weighing 27,000 to 36,000kg (30–40 tons), gray whales are way too big for any aquarium—you've got to see them in their native habitat, the open sea. This eastern north Pacific population is by far the most numerous (they died out in the Atlantic a long time ago). As many as 3,000 to 5,000 individuals travel their long-haul migration route, from the Bering Strait where they spend summers to their winter home off of Mexico's Baja California peninsula. Down in Mexico, they'll spend January through March in warm protected bays, mating or giving birth.

Perhaps the best base for whale-watching is funky laid-back Loreto, an old colonial town on the Sea of Cortez that's popular with kayakers, sailors, and divers. From here, it's a couple hours' overland drive to Bahía Magdalena, where you can board a light skiff called a *panga* and spend about 3 hours in the coastal lagoon, getting close to the gray whales, and possibly a few humpbacks as well. If you're lucky, you'll encounter "friendlies"—whales who'll swim right up to your tour boat and hang out for a while, even letting people pet them. Just don't do anything that might look like you're menacing the calves—mother gray whales turn violent quickly when it comes to protecting their babies.

Up the coast from Bahía Magdalena, just off the Transpeninsular Highway in the El Vizcaino Biosphere Reserve, lie three other important gray whale refuges: Ojo de Liebre (aka Scammon's Lagoon, where nearly 1,000 whales may congregate at one time), Guerrero Negro, and Laguna San Ignacio. Inland, El Vizcaino is an arid, windswept desert, home to pronghorn

Gray whales breaching at Baja.

antelopes and bighorn sheep and spiny cacti, but its narrow strip of coastline is much more temperate. It's a popular wintering site for harbor seals, California sea lions, northern elephant seals, and blue whales, as well as osprey, brown pelicans, and terns. Bobbing around the lagoon in a panga, you can not only get close to the whales but you can also observe the shorebirds in their wetlands and the seals' rocky islands.

El Vizcaino's future is shaky, however, with expanding agriculture, oil drilling, highway construction, and boat traffic putting pressure on its already fragile environment.

So much has already been done to bring these whales back from the brink of extinction—if they lose these vital mating grounds, where can they turn next?

 Loreto

$$$ **Posada Las Flores,** Salvatierra and Francisco I. Madera, Loreto (© **877/245-2860** in the U.S., 613/135-1162 in Mexico; www.posadadelasflores.com). $$ **Plaza Loreto,** Hidalgo 2, Loreto (© **613/135-0280;** www.baja-web.com/loreto/loplaza.htm).

**TOUR Loreto Center** (© **613/135-0798**). **Las Parras Tours** (© **613/135-1010**).

**Denizens of the Deep**  107

# The Mekong River
## *King of the Golden Triangle*
### Chiang Saen/Chiang Khong, Thailand

SIX ADDITIONAL DAMS ON THE MEKONG RIVER, PROPOSED BY CHINA, THAILAND, AND VIETNAM to provide energy for their growing economies, could debilitate a river already stressed by earlier dams, pollution, and climate change. Many parts of the river would disappear during the dry season, and threaten many native species, including the critically endangered giant catfish and the Irrawaddy dolphin.

When it comes to growing huge fish, no waterway even comes close to the Mekong River. And among its monster fish, the prize-winner is the Mekong Giant Catfish, a sleek but toothless gray-and-white bottom feeder. How big is big? Would you believe nearly 2.7m long (9 ft.) and 293kg (646 lb.)? That's the size of a female caught near Chiang Khong in May 2005, officially the largest freshwater fish ever caught.

Along the course of the Mekong, people regard it as a sacred fish—this mystical vegetarian that seems to meditate like a Buddhist monk in the deep, stony pools of the river. It even appears in cave paintings in northeast Thailand dating over 3,500 years old. While Cambodians and some Thai people believe that eating its flesh brings bad luck, other Thais and the Chinese believe it's good luck. Some fishermen pray every April to be allowed to catch it, while others call in monks to lift the curse if they happen to catch one accidentally.

Mekong catfish.

Though you may not glimpse a giant catfish while you're here, the northern Thai border town of Chiang Khong will give you a good idea of what's happening to the Mekong. Chiang Khong is definitely a frontier town, popular with backpackers en route to Laos. Though it has no special attractions of its own, it's close to several waterfalls and rapids where various Mekong giant fish breed. (Khon Phi Laung are the rapids most linked with giant catfish.) Head upstream 70km (43 miles) from Chiang Khong and you'll reach the sleepy village of Chiang Saen, where you can take a longtail boat tour of the Golden Triangle, at the junction of the Mae Ruak River and the Mekong. (The Golden Triangle was reputedly once a hotbed of the international opium trade, which explains the Hall of Opium museum located here.) Stand at the crook of the river and you can see both Laos and Myanmar from the Mekong's Thai shore.

The Mekong laces together so many countries along its course—but given the rocky state of regional politics, this has only made conservation efforts harder. Visiting this rural province, you'll understand what a lifeline the Mekong River provides for the local population. What are they willing to sacrifice to save one fish—especially one fish that could feed an entire village?

But the number of these proud giants—"the king of fish," according to its Cambodian name—is falling, and falling fast. Scientists estimate that the giant catfish's numbers have declined 80% in the past 15 years, due to overfishing, destruction of habitat, river dredging, and the construction of dams upstream in China. Once prevalent in Laos, Cambodia, Thailand, Vietnam, and perhaps Myanmar and southwest China, the giant catfish now occurs only in the Golden Triangle, a small area where Thailand, Laos, and Myanmar meet. It's very likely that the giant catfish may become the first Mekong species in historic memory to go extinct.

✈ Chiang Rai

🛏 $ **Chiang Khong River View Hotel,** 141 Moo 12, Chiang Khong (📞 **66/53/791 375;** www.chiangkhong.com/riverview hotel.htm). $$ **Anantara Resort and Spa Golden Triangle,** 229 Moo 1, Chiang Saen (📞 **800/225-5843** in U.S., or 66/53/784 084; www.anantara.com).

# 3 From the Mountains to the Prairies

*Cedar tree in Lebanon.*

**108 Flowers**

# Kennebunk Plains Preserve
## *Where Blazing Star Still Blazes*
West Kennebunk, Maine

URBAN SPRAWL IS THE BIGGEST THREAT TO WILDLIFE AND NATIVE HABITATS IN MAINE, EVEN with more than 440,000 acres (17,000 hectares) of land already protected. As long as commercial and residential development can be controlled, the native habitats will be preserved.

Come here in late summer and you can't miss it: a wide expanse of grassland spangled with vivid purple wildflowers. It's known as the northern blazing star, and you won't find it anywhere else in Maine—or hardly anywhere else in the world. This one 135-acre (56-hectare) parcel of land holds a virtual monopoly on northern blazing star, with an estimated 90% of the world's specimens.

Kennebunk Plains is an oddball landscape for New England anyway. Such a classic prairie habitat hardly ever exists so close to the ocean—many of the plants that thrive here, such as little bluestem grass, are common out on the Great Plains but unknown in Maine. And though this protected parcel is open to the public to walk around in, you'll notice that the grasslands extend well beyond the preserve, occupying some 2,000 acres (800 hectares) of coastal plain with their deep deposits of sand, not washed up from the sea but dumped by ancient glaciers.

Working with the Maine Department of Inland Fisheries and Wildlife, the Nature Conservancy deliberately starts small fires—known as "prescribed burns"—on the preserve at periodic intervals, to scale back outlying patches of pitch pine and scrub oak forest. It's an ancient land-management strategy, the same used by Native Americans when they raised blueberries on this plain. By preserving the old ways, the Kennebunk Plains' 21st-century stewards hope to preserve this last remnant of what once was a common ecosystem.

Several rare or endangered bird species have found a haven on these unusual grasslands, including grasshopper sparrows, upland sandpipers, vesper sparrows, and horned larks. Black racer snakes thrive here too, one of only two known populations in the state. That's what happens when you get an oddball landscape—it enables entirely different species to thrive where they otherwise wouldn't. That's what diversity's all about.

ⓘ **Kennebunk Plains Preserve,** Hwy. 99, West Kennebunk, ME

✈ Portland

🛏 $$$ **The Tides Inn,** 252 King's Hwy., Goose Rocks Beach, Kennebunkport (✆ **207/967-3757;** www.tidesinnbythe sea.com). $$ **Yachtsman Lodge,** Ocean Ave., Kennebunkport (✆ **207/967-2511;** www.yachtsmanlodge.com).

# Eshqua Bog & Chickering Bog
## *Two Fantastic Fens*
### Central Vermont

WHILE THESE FRAGILE HABITATS ARE PROTECTED, COMMERCIAL AND RESIDENTIAL DEVELOPMENT and the pollution of groundwater by septic systems and other contaminates still threaten these preserves. In early 2008, for example, a gasoline storage tank in a central Vermont village rusted out, spilling 2,300 gallons of gasoline into the surrounding area.

Everybody knows about the brilliant colors Vermont puts on in autumn. Tour buses clog routes 4 and 12 every October, crammed with leaf-peeping tourists, and hotel rates shoot sky high. But fewer tourists know about Vermont's other show—in June, when its wildflowers finally burst into bloom.

Only an hour's drive apart (if you take I-89—much longer if you enjoy yourself on scenic Rte. 12), these two pocket preserves rival each other in the wildflower department. Though we usually think of orchids in terms of big, dramatic tropical rainforest blooms, New England has its own delicate orchids, mostly growing in wetlands like these. The first to show up every June all happen to be pink: dragon's mouth (also sometimes called swamp pink, for obvious reasons), grass pink, rose pogonia, and pink lady's slipper, which are more evident at Chickering Bog. Soon after, the headliner comes on stage: the showy lady's slipper, with its waxy white petals and curling purple underlip, standing up to a yard high. Showy lady's slippers are hard to miss at either Eshqua or Chickering when they erupt; Eshqua also has a few of the smaller and rarer yellow lady's slippers, and in July yet another lovely orchid blooms here, the white bog-candle.

Both preserves also feature the dramatic Northern pitcher plant, a purplish flower with inward-curved petals that collect water. It looks vaguely orchidlike, but it's got a deadly secret: Insects eventually drown inside this "pitcher" and are quietly digested by the plant. There's another insect-devourer in these fens, too: the innocent-looking sundew with its tiny white flowers—and sticky, bug-trapping leaves.

If you want to get technical, neither Eshqua Bog nor Chickering Bog is really a bog—bogs get their water from acidic sources, mostly rainwater, while fens are fed by calcium-rich groundwater. And because fens have more nutrients, you can expect to see more diverse plant communities there. There's no question about that at Eshqua Bog and Chickering Bog. A marshy depression at the base of a long hill, Eshqua has everything from blueberries and cranberries to larches, buckthorn, bunchberries, and cinquefoil; Chickering, which is slowly filling in (it's really wet at the north end), displays bog rosemary, rhodora, leatherleaf, red chokeberry, and blue flag iris. Just about every shrub and tree seems to have some sort of flower, and it's all wondrously fragrant and cool.

Both preserves have a single short walking trail, about a mile long, which is often elevated on a boardwalk so that visitors don't step on the fragile, peaty ground. It's not to protect your shoes, but to keep this exquisitely balanced habitat from damage. After all, you can't grow flowers like this in a flowerbed; you've got to have a bog. Or a fen.

---

ⓘ **Eshqua Bog Natural Area,** Garvin Hill Rd., Hartland, VT. **Chickering Bog Natural Area,** Lightening Ridge Rd., Calais, VT. **Nature Conservancy of Vermont** (✆ 802/229-4425).

Rutland

$$ **Kedron Valley Inn,** Rte. 106, South Woodstock, VT (© **800/836-1193**

or 802/457-1473; www.kedronvalleyinn.com). $$ **Three Church St.,** 3 Church St, Woodstock, VT (© **802/457-1925**).

# Grandfather Mountain
## *Heavenly Flowers*
### Blue Ridge Mountains, North Carolina

HUMAN ACTIVITY IS THE BIGGEST THREAT TO GRANDFATHER MOUNTAIN. NON-NATIVE PLANTS and animals have destroyed some native resources, and non-native insects and forest diseases have destroyed tree species.

"The face of all Heaven come to earth"— that's how naturalist John Muir described Grandfather Mountain when he first encountered it in 1898. Granted, Muir was prone to rhapsodizing over natural wonders, but in the case of Grandfather Mountain, he was right on the mark. One of the world's oldest peaks—geologists estimate its glittering quartzite rock is more than a billion years old—at 5,964 feet (1,818m), Grandfather towers above its neighbors, the patriarch of the Blue Ridge range.

Grandfather Mountain looks rugged and forbidding, that's for sure—winters can be harsh and snowy, and even in summer wind buffets the mountainside and

Flowers on Grandfather Mountain.

thick fog rolls in regularly. Upland trees and shrubs are stunted and hardy, creating a subalpine environment you'd never expect this far south. Watchful hawks soar on its updrafts—this is a significant site for Cooper's hawk, shark-shinned hawk, migrating broad-winged hawks, and peregrine falcons. But get closer and you'll find he has a softer side as well, sheltering more globally rare species than any other mountain east of the Rockies. Many are liverworts, lichens, and mosses; the cool, damp mountain climate is perfect for these to grow on the jumbled rocks that thrust out from Grandfather's acidic soils. Several others are delicate mountain flowers, like the spreading avens, bent avens, mountain bittercress, the roan mountain bluet, Gray's lily, Heller's blazing star, and late summer's dainty Blue Ridge goldenrod, which peep out of the crevices and rock niches of the upper elevations.

While some of the park's trails can be very strenuous—in a couple of places there are ladders built to scale steep spots—you can see a great cross-sampling of the preserve's astonishing variety of habitats on the 2.7-mile (4.3km) **Profile Trail** (trail head off Hwy. 105 near Banner Elk). This trail climbs gradually from streambed forests with thickets of dense rhododendron, up through hardwood and hemlock forest and bald heath, to the naked rock of high elevations where some of those rare mountain flowers hide out. **Black Rock Nature Trail,** just under 2 miles long (3km), offers a moderate walk through northern hardwood (lots of beautiful mountain ash and yellow birch) and spruce forests, where bird-watchers can hope to see some of the park's resident songbirds, like red-breasted nuthatches, winter wrens, hermit thrush, magnolia warbler, and chestnut-sided warblers, as well as the yellow-bellied sapsucker. The half-mile **Bridge Trail** climbs a series of switchbacks to the park's most popular site: the **Mile High Swinging Bridge,** the highest suspension footbridge in America, poised over an 80-foot-deep (24m) ravine. Along this trail in late spring you'll see brilliant pink Azalea vaseyi—not your garden-variety azaleas but an endangered variant, just another of Grandfather's very special flowers.

---

ⓘ **Grandfather Mountain,** north side of U.S. 221 between Blue Ridge Pkwy. and Linville, NC (ⓒ **800/468-7325** or 828/733-2013; www.grandfather.com)

✈ Asheville

🛏 $$ **Holiday Inn Express,** 1943 Blowing Rock Rd., Boone (ⓒ **800/HOLI-DAY** [465-4329] or 828/264-2451). $$ **Best Western Mountain Lodge,** 1615 Tynecastle Hwy., Banner Elk (ⓒ **828/898-4571;** www.bestwesternnorthcarolina.com).

Flowers  **111**

# The Grand Bay Savanna
## *Delicate Death Traps*
### Mississippi & Alabama

RAPID POPULATION GROWTH THREATENS THIS SENSITIVE COASTAL WETLAND, HOME TO SOME very unusual species, including several rare carnivorous plants. Fire suppression has altered its natural evolution and allowed the proliferation of non-native plants. Water quality continues to decline, although efforts are being made to restore savanna habitats and to protect native plants.

Insects, beware—you do not want to drink the water cupped so invitingly inside a pitcher plant's beautiful curved blossom. Once you get trapped inside those slippery petals, there's no way out. Sooner or later the deadly enzymes the flower secretes will digest you. It's a killer.

Down on the Gulf Coast, there used to be a lot of wet pine savannas where pitcher plants could lay their murderous traps. Unfortunately, as roads were built and land cleared for housing and/or industry, that coastal plain was irrevocably altered. Visit the Grand Bay Savanna, a huge swath of nature reserves straddling the border between lower Alabama and lower Mississippi, to see the last vestiges of what this land once looked like. Prime sites are the **Grand Bay National Wildlife Refuge** and the **Mississippi Sandhill Crane National Wildlife Refuge,** both on the Mississippi side of the reserve.

The funny thing is, when landowners developed this area, they thought they were doing the right thing by preventing forest fires in the pine plantations bordering their bayou-front homes. Wrong. Pitcher plants can only stand so much shade; when the pine woods get too thick, they die off. New shrubs invade, sucking moisture out of the boggy ground and turning it to solid land.

But pitcher plants do love bogs—and so do sundews, bladderworts, orchids, and snapdragons, all of which you'll see in abundance on portions of the pine savannas at Grand Bay. These wildflowers are uniquely adapted to live where water is close to the surface, there's a fair amount of sunlight, and the soil is nutrient poor. (Who needs nutrients from the soil when you can eat insects, anyway?) Periodic wildfires hold back invading trees and shrubs and keep the bog just the way the flowers like it. Now that this land has been set aside for conservation purposes, ecologists are doing prescribed burns to keep the ecosystems in balance.

Not only does Grand Bay Savanna have a pitcher plant bog, it has rare regional varieties of the sorts of flowers that inhabit pitcher plant bogs—Texas pipewort, Walter's sedge, myrtle-leaved St. Johnswort, coastal plain false-foxglove, thin-stemmed false-foxglove, stalked adders-tongue—plus a host of orchids: spreading pogonia, large white fringed orchids, yellow fringeless orchids, and giant spiral ladies'-tresses. While the beautiful, tall crimson pitcher plant is well known, it's accompanied by the much rarer yellow trumpet pitcher-plant, the parrot pitcher-plant with its odd hooked lips, the side-saddle pitcher-plant, and another rare carnivore called Chapman's butterwort. Bring your wildflower field guides with you to identify what you're seeing; some of these are so rare, you may not even find them listed.

ⓘ **Grand Bay National Wildlife Refuge,** 6005 Bayou Heron Rd., Moss Point, MS (📞 **228/475-7047;** www.fws.gov/grandbay). **Mississippi Sandhill Crane National Wildlife Refuge,** 7200 Crane Lane, Gautier, MS (📞 **228/497-6322;** www.fws.gov/mississippisandhillcrane).

✈ Mobile

🛏 $$ **Radisson Admiral Semmes,** 251 Government St., Mobile (📞 **888/201-1718** or 251/432-8000; www.radisson.com/mobileal)

# Willow Creek Preserve
## *The Butterfly Effect*
### West Eugene, Oregon

DEVELOPMENT IS THE BIGGEST THREAT TO WHAT'S LEFT OF THIS NORTHWEST PRAIRIE, HOME TO imperiled plant species like Bradshaw's lomatium, the Willamette daisy, and Kincaid's lupine. The Fender's blue butterfly, once considered extinct, is dependent on lupines for survival. Off-road activities disturb or destroy natural habitats, and introduced species threaten to choke out rare native plants.

Until 1989, entomologists had crossed the Fender's blue butterfly off their lists. As far as they could tell, it was gone. Kaput. Finito. Extinct.

And then they found them again, in this surviving sliver of native wet prairie on former farmland remarkably close to downtown Eugene, Oregon. Not surprisingly, the butterflies were found close to where the rare Kincaid's blue lupine grows. That makes perfect sense; the Kincaid's blue lupine is the only place where the Fender's blue will lay its eggs. Its larvae remain there, feeding on the bright purple flower spikes, for nearly a year. In late spring, the larvae hatch into adults, beautiful dark-blue butterflies about an inch long. As adults, they will feed on a wider variety of wildflowers. But that only lasts for 9 days before they lay their eggs—on the lupine, of course—and then die. The new larvae snuggle into the lupines, and the whole cycle begins again.

That's what happens when you preserve the old-time habitats. Spreading over 508 acres (206 hectares), Willow Creek Preserve is an intact remnant of the upland grasslands, ash woods, and perennial streams that used to cover this Northwest river valley. It's estimated that 99.8% of the native wet prairie has been lost to development since the 1940s. But here along Willow Creek, more than 200 native plant, 100 bird, and 25 butterfly species survive in healthy diversity. In late spring you'll find the starlike yellow clusters of the endangered Bradshaw's lomatium, while tall feathery blue camas perfectly complement snug yellow buttercups as they grow side by side in an open meadow. In midsummer, the endangered Willamette Valley daisy arrives, with its fat yellow center and pinkish ray petals. Lacy Oregon white-topped asters come along at the end of the summer.

In adjacent areas, trees and shrubs have taken over the native prairie; at Willow Creek, periodic burning holds them back, as nature intended, and lets the sun-loving flowers maintain their territory. (Bradshaw's lomatium, in fact, has increased by 50% in the areas where fire has been used to manage growth.) Non-native species like Scotch broom and Himalayan blackberry that have driven out the original species are regularly cleared out. Where the waist-high, fine-leaved tufted hairgrass should dominate, volunteers tear out the tough common teasel, an invasive thistle that's trying to take over. Sure, it takes a lot of work—but one glimpse of a Fender's blue butterfly makes it all worthwhile.

---

ⓘ **Willow Creek Preserve,** W. 18th Ave at Willow Creek, West Eugene, OR (✆ **503/228-9561**)

✈ Eugene

🛏 $$ **Valley River Inn,** 1000 Valley River Way, Eugene (✆ **800/543-8266** or 541/743-1000; www.valleyriverinn.com). $$ **The Secret Garden,** 1910 University St., Eugene (✆ **888/484-6755** or 541/484-6755; www.secretgardenbbinn.com).

# Santa Rosa Plateau
## *There's Gold in Them Thar Hills*
### Riverside County, California

HUMAN ACTIVITIES HAVE ELIMINATED MOST OF CALIFORNIA'S VERNAL POOLS—FOUND ALMOST nowhere else in the world. The state's remaining vernal pools provide habitats for a wide range of highly adapted organisms, including 27 species designated by the U.S. Fish and Wildlife Service as being of special concern. Pollution, fire, and invasive species continue to threaten this fragile habitat.

Halfway between the congested urban sprawl of Los Angeles and the congested urban sprawl of San Diego lies the only slightly less congested urban sprawl of inland Riverside County. And yet, astonishingly enough, in the middle of all this—right off of busy Interstate 15—lies an 8,000-acre (3,237-hectare) parcel of open California natureland, a habitat for mountain lions, mule deer, badgers, and bobcats tucked into the green and gold hills of the Santa Ana mountains.

This mosaic of chaparral, sage scrubland, and live-oak woodlands looks so typically Western, you'd almost expect the Lone Ranger to come galloping around the next hill. But it also includes one of the last holdouts of native prairie remaining in California. The Santa Rosa Plateau's prairie is the largest bunchgrass prairie in Southern California. Several trails lead through tall stands of deep-rooted, fire-resistant purple needlegrass, rippling in the wind. Fire resistance is key; using controlled burning, park rangers can stave off invasion by trees and shrubs, leaving the terrain to the hardy grass and to sun-loving spring wildflowers. You'll see everything from delicate little mariposa lilies, checkerblooms, and shooting stars to the vibrant Johnny jump-ups, lupines, and brilliant yellow California poppies. Look for the brown drooping blossoms of the chocolate lily, one of the world's few brown flowers, but sniff carefully—you'll see why it's also called the skunk lily.

Come in spring or early summer, especially if you want to appreciate the vernal pools—huge season pools that collect atop the plateau's flat-topped basaltic outcroppings in spring and vanish entirely by summer's end. When winter storms dump rain on these mesas in January and February, their hard surface won't absorb or drain the rainfall, so it just sits there in shallow declivities, waiting to evaporate. We're not talking mere puddles, either—the largest pool covers 39 acres (16 hectares) at its fullest. It's enough of a wetland to attract migrating water birds like green-winged teals and Canada geese. As spring warms up, though, the pools slowly begin to shrink, revealing successive rings of moist soil where flowers spring up from May on. The Vernal Pool Trail is raised on a boardwalk so you can closely observe the tiny blooms of some incredibly rare plants—California Orcutt grass, San Diego button-celery, thread-leaf brodiaea, Orcutt's brodiaea, and Parish's meadow foam—as well as vivid carpets of the more common yellow goldfields and purple downingia. You'll be out of luck by July or August—all that will be left is a naked scoop of dark rock, a ghost of the lake that used to be.

ⓘ **Santa Rosa Plateau Ecological Reserve,** 39400 Clinton Keith Rd., Murrieta, CA (ⓒ **951/677-6951;** www.santa rosaplateau.org)

✈ Riverside

# The Slopes of Mount Haleakala
## *An Isle of Ephemeral Flowers*
### Maui, Hawaii

HALEAKALA NATIONAL PARK IS HOME TO MORE THREATENED AND ENDANGERED SPECIES THAN any other U.S. national park. Invasive species are the biggest threat to the native plants and animals. Mount Haleakala is also the proposed site for the Advanced Technology Solar Telescope, a project that may cause irrevocable loss of its natural, cultural, and scenic resources.

Don't let the lush plantings of its luxury resorts fool you—Hawaii has more endangered species than any other state. Most of the frangipani and birds-of-paradise and other tropical flowers around the swimming pools are transplants from other countries that have displaced native species. Even worse, feral non-native pigs,

Mount Haleakala's yellow hibiscus.

goats, and axis deer have browsed unchecked for years, and, especially on Maui, resort development has destroyed habitat at a fearful rate. No wonder tourist leis are generally made of silk or plastic flowers these days.

Of course, with its isolated location in the middle of the Pacific Ocean, the Hawaiian Islands had more endemic species to lose in the first place. But the situation's so sad that even the state flower, the yellow hibiscus—or, in Hawaii, *pua aloalo*—is endangered. Growing on a shrub that can reach tree height, its blossoms are bright yellow with a maroon spot in the center. They're regarded by Hawaiians as symbols of the human soul, because they bloom pale yellow in the morning, darken in color throughout the day, and wither by nighttime, to be replaced next morning by new blooms. The yellow hibiscus now lives only in three enclosed sites on Maui, where the deer can't get to them, but slowly it's being restored in the wild. Meanwhile, you can view cultivated specimens, along with other hibiscus, passion flowers, plumeria, jade vine, trumpet vine, and orchids, at the **Kula Botanical Garden** in the upcountry town of Kula, Highway 377 (*C* **808/878-1715;** www.flowersofmaui.com).

In the wild, however, there are other rare native species to see. The most dramatic is the silversword, a tall spiky flower with spear-sharp silvery leaves and a sunflower-like head of tiny purple blooms. For years these curiosities were collected by the sackful to be sold for Chinese potions, specimen gardens, and amateur painters.

Unlike the here-today-gone-tomorrow hibiscus, silverswords take their time—a plant may wait 4 to 50 years before shooting up a 1- to 6-foot (.3–1.8m) stalk with a flowering purple head, usually between May and October. Rare as they are, they're fairly easy to spot in **Haleakala National Park,** which mantles the slopes of the world's largest dormant volcano. If you drive up zigzagging Haleakala Crater Road to the summit (it'll take at least an hour to get to the top), on the way back down, pull off at the Kalahaku Overlook to look for silverswords. If you have more time, a 10-mile lower loop of the Halemau'u Trail makes a round trip to Silversword Loop, through jagged flats of red and black lava rock.

For an even shorter hike, take the half-mile Hosmer Grove Nature Trail through a cool cloud forest. You won't see hibiscus or silverswords but you should see rare native silver geraniums—in Hawaiian, *nohoanu*—with their satiny white petals. Aloha!

ⓘ **Haleakala National Park,** Maui, Hwy. 378 (ⓒ **808/572-4400;** www.nps.gov/hale)

✈ Kahului

🚃 $$ **Banyan Tree House,** 3265 Baldwin Ave., Makawao (ⓒ **808/572-9021;** www.hawaiimauirentals.com). $$ **Olinda Country Cottages,** 2660 Olinda Rd., Makawao (ⓒ **800/932-3435** or 808/572-1453).

---

## 115 Flowers

# Bluebell Forests of East Anglia
## *The Essence of English Spring*
### Norfolk, England

THE DELICATE BLUEBELL'S ENORMOUS POPULARITY WAS ALMOST IT'S UNDOING, UNTIL LAWS were enacted to protect it from human destruction. Now this fragile flower faces a bigger threat from global warming, which makes spring arrive earlier each year. Without enough time to mature and set seeds, the bluebell can't survive. This deprives people of one of spring's greatest spectacles—the blue carpet of England's favorite wildflower.

Like a watercolor by Beatrix Potter, it's the quintessential English countryside—hollyhocks and larkspur by the garden gate and bluebells carpeting the woods. Imagine, then, the public outcry in the United Kingdom in 1981 when conservationists announced that they were putting the English bluebell on the protected list. Hybridization with the invasive alien Spanish bluebell has corrupted this woodland beauty, turning its deep-violet tightly curling bells on a sweetly drooping stem into flaccid, pale blue cones on a stiff stalk. Worst of all, the new hybrids barely have any scent. A true bluebell's perfume, though—that's like the essence of spring.

In 1998, when reporters caught vandals stealing 7,000 bluebell bulbs from the ancient Thursford Wood in East Anglia, a nationwide protest erupted. It's now against the law to remove bluebells from your land or to dig up its bulbs, and you get the feeling that if anybody tried it, the neighbors would be up in arms—that's how strongly the British feel about these iconic wild hyacinths.

In the Norfolk countryside, just a short drive from Norwich, lie a pair of ancient oak forests where you can still see old-fashioned bluebells carpeting the ground in April and May. Near Foxley Village, 24km (15 miles) northwest of Norwich on

Fakenham Road, the 121-hectare (300-acre) **Foxley Wood National Nature Reserve** is the largest remaining ancient woodland in Norfolk, so old that it was listed in the Domesday Book. Though it's principally oak, field maple, and birch, it also has such rare trees as wild service, small-leaved lime, and midland hawthorn. (Several conifers, introduced years ago as timber sources, are gradually being removed.) Along with the bluebells you'll find early purple orchid, dog's mercury, and meadowsweet; the lazy drone of butterflies fills the air in summer.

Drive another 10 miles or so to Fakenham and turn east 5km (3 miles) on A148 to find even older oaks at **Thursford Wood**, a 10-hectare (25-acre) remnant of original heath where some trees are 500 years old or more. The River Stiffkey runs through this nook of forest, pasture, and ponds. For centuries the oak trees have been pollarded—their main branches cut back to promote thicker foliage rather than height—and their lumpy trunks are covered with moss, lichens, and fungi. Ferns and rhododendrons flourish in the understory, heightening a distinctly Druidic atmosphere.

English botanists generally judge ancient woodlands by their profusion of bluebells—and Thursford lives up to that standard, for in May the ground here is completely hazed over with drooping violet bells. It would do Beatrix Potter's heart good.

---

ⓘ **Foxley Wood National Nature Reserve,** Fakenham Rd., Foxley (access off Tremelthorpe Rd. (© 44/1362/688706). **Thursford Wood Nature Reserve,** Holt Rd., Little Snoring.

🚂 Norwich

🛏 $$ **The Maid's Head Hotel,** Palace St., Norwich (© **44/870/609110;** www.corushotels.co.uk). $ **Pearl Continental Hotel,** 116 Thorpe Rd., Norwich (© **44/1603/620302;** www.pc-hotels.co.uk).

---

Flowers **116**

# Ben Lawers
## *Where the Wild Mountain Thyme Grows*
### Perthshire, Scotland

THE EFFECTS OF CLIMATE CHANGE IN SCOTLAND—MORE FREQUENT AND VIOLENT STORMS, dramatic temperature changes, winds of up to 80 mph, and rising sea levels—threaten the future of birds and rare alpine plants on the Ben Lawers reserve. Reduced snow cover and heavy rains are threatening fragile habitats and species, increasing the risk of erosion.

Ben Lawers isn't the tallest mountain in Scotland—in fact, it's not quite 1,220m (4,000 ft.), though some sneaky locals in the 19th century built a cairn on top to boost it over that mark. Nor is its lake, Loch Tay, the Highland's most romantic (that would be Loch Lomond), or most beautiful (Loch Rannoch, its northern neighbor). It doesn't even have a monster, like Loch Ness does.

But this rugged Perthshire peak has a lock on one claim to fame: Botanists say it has the U.K.'s richest display of alpine wildflowers, with 130 species identified so far. By a geologic fluke, Ben Lawers—the tallest peak in the seven-peak Munro range—has schist rocks at just the right altitude to support arctic and alpine flora. From June through August, as you scale the trail to the summit you may see pale blue alpine forget-me-not, frilly golden roseroot, snow pearlwort, blue alpine gentian, the daisylike alpine mouse-ear, and the five-petalled cups of various colored saxifrage, including the almost extinct Highland saxifrage. Fragrant flowering herbs like Alpine lady's mantle, blaeberry, moss campion, and wild mountain thyme cling to the rocks and perfume the air. Keep your eye out as well for Ben Lawers's rich bird life—ravens, ring ouzels, curlews, ptarmigans, dippers, and red grouse.

Even if you don't do the full climb from the visitor center (which can take 5 hr., leading first to a lower neighboring peak, Ben Ghlas), you can see much of the Alpine vegetation from a sign-posted nature trail; pick up an interpretive booklet at the visitor's center. You'll begin on a boardwalk over a bog, then climb a stile and follow Edramucky Burn (that's Scottish for stream); it should take at least an hour to do the full circuit. In July and August rangers lead weekly guided wildflower hikes; call in advance to book a place.

The protected plants lie within a fence; outside of the fence you can see how flocks of Highland sheep have trampled and overgrazed the mountain slopes that haven't been restored yet. It has taken a lot of work to bring the habitat back, and some species may still be lost in the end. Most of the trees and shrubs within the fence were planted within the past 10 or 20 years, but the flowers sprang back on their own—that's how ideal this terrain is for them.

ⓘ **Ben Lawers National Nature Reserve,** off the A827, 10km (6 miles) east from Killin (✆ **44/1567/820397**)

🚆 Dunkeld

🛏 $$$ **Kinnaird Estate,** Dunkeld (✆ **44/1796/482-440;** www.kinnairdestate. com). $ **Ben Lawers Hotel,** A827, Lawers (✆ **44/1567/820436;** www.benlawershotel. co.uk).

**117** **Flowers**

# Roundstone Bog
## *Magic Under Your Feet*
### County Galway, Ireland

CLIMATE CHANGE, WHICH BRINGS PERIODS OF HEAVY RAIN FOLLOWED BY UNSEASONABLY LONG spells of hot, dry weather, has taken a toll on this fragile bog. Thousands of visitors trample it each year, killing off the plants, while deforestation and development also threaten this ecosystem.

Once you pass Oughterard on the N59, all bets are off. The wooded green landscape of Galway suddenly turns into a flat, treeless, plum-colored plain of rippling sedge grasses. A cloud-curdled sky broods overhead; a line of steely blue mountains seems miles away. Park your car and just try to walk on that terrain—the ground shivers and quakes under your feet, and at any moment you may plunge knee-deep into water.

Once you find a solid track, though, you'll discover hidden gorges, streams, and even lakes tucked behind the grasses.

Roundstone bog.

Up close you'll see the harsh rock-strewn land is softened by gorse, lichens, mosses, and wildflowers. The strange reddish color you saw from the car is actually a tapestry of russets, golds, greens, blues, and peaty chocolate brown, a mix of all the heathers of Ireland. This is the famous Roundstone Bog of Connemara, and it's the crown jewel of Ireland's wild west.

Though much of Roundstone Bog falls within Connemara National Park, you don't have to go all the way to the park entrance in Letterfrack to explore it. Follow signs off N59 to the charming seaside village of Roundstone and then take minor roads between Roundstone and Clifden, the main town on the west coast. Look for gates that lead to walking tracks.

The bogs began to form 2,500 years ago, as heavy precipitation—it rains 2 out of 3 days around here—caused iron to leach down from the acidic soil and form a hard pan that trapped water. Dying vegetation rotted, sank into the waterlogged soil, and condensed into peat. Today one-third of Connemara is bog, and peat is an important local source of fuel. Although machine cutting is now illegal, folks still cut turf by hand; you'll notice stacks of turf bricks left by the roadside to air-dry.

Connemara is technically a blanket bog, lying flat across miles of terrain instead of snuggling into a hollow. Unlike scrubby mountain bogs, blanket bog supports grasses, sedges, and heathers. Here, purple moor grass dominates, but its overall color is variegated with ling heather, cross-leaved heath, Mackays heath, Irish heath, St. Dabeoc's heath, bell heather, and silky white tufts of bog-cotton. By ponds and marshy areas you'll find flowers such as tormentil, sundew, bog asphodel, louse-wort, and milkwort, many of them carnivorous plants that trap insects. In Connemara, the peat mattress is relatively shallow, so rock basins can catch enough rainwater to form small lakes; hummocks grow into small islands wooded with holly, yew, oak, or willow. Widespread flushes are dominated by bog myrtle, blowing a sweet scent across the bog.

In 1919 British aviators John Alcock and Alvin Whitten Brown completed the first North America–to-Europe airplane flight by crash-landing into the soft springy surface of Roundstone Bog. Ironically, 80 years later, in 1998 local residents fought off a proposed airstrip at nearby Derry-gimla. Progress is one thing, but don't mess around with our bog.

ⓘ **Connemara National Park,** N59, Letterfrack, County Galway (✆ **353/95/41054**)

✈/🚆 Galway City

🛏 $$ **Lough Inagh Lodge,** Recess (✆ **800/323-5463** or 353/95/34706; www.loughinaghlodgehotel.ie). $ **Errisbeg Lodge,** Clifden Rd., Roundstone (✆ **353/95/35807;** www.connemara.net/errisbeg-lodge).

**TOUR The Connemara Walking Center,** Market St., Clifden (✆ **353/95/21379**)

# Valley of Flowers National Park
## *The Fairies' Flowerpatch*
### Uttaranchal, India

INVASIVE PLANTS THREATEN THE RARE SUBALPINE FLORA HERE, INCLUDING MORE THAN 600 flower species—many of them so endemic, they don't even grow on Nanda Devi, the rugged peak 25km (16 miles) to the southeast. The park doesn't have many animal species, but all of them are nationally rare or threatened, including the endangered snow leopard (prized by poachers), the serow, and the rare Himalayan musk deer.

Ever since 1939, when British mountaineer Frank Smith sang its praises in his book *Valley of Flowers*, botanists have yearned to visit this remote Himalayan valley, a once-before-I-die sort of destination just across the border from Tibet. Local villagers refused to live here, though, convinced it was inhabited by fairies who would kidnap them (though they did graze sheep and goats here—no point in wasting good pastureland). Gazing upon its flower-filled meadows, you tend to agree with them—who else but fairies could be responsible for a place this beautiful?

Since it became a national park in 1982, grazing is forbidden in the valley, leaving its flowers to run riot. Unless you're a botanist specializing in Himalayan species, you may not be able to identify every flower you see. The park's closed November to May, when it's snowbound, but in June you'll find meadows carpeted with color. The display changes daily over the next 3 months, with the rosy June glow of pinks and reds gradually giving way to warm yellows later on in July.

Only 6km (3³/₄ miles) wide and 15km (9¹/₃ miles) long, the park lies in an east-west hanging valley at the head of the Bhyundar Ganga valley, fed by the Pushpawati river flowing off Tipra glacier. The valley's gentle slopes climb from forests of white birch, Himalayan maple, fir, yew, and rhododendron to lush alpine meadows where dwarf shrubs, cushion herbs, grasses, and sedges predominate. Here you'll find exquisite blue primulas, calendulas, trilliums, daisies, impatiens, geraniums, marsh marigolds, marsh orchids, lady's slippers, angelica, snow-white anemones, the rare blue Himalayan poppy, and the aptly named cobra lily, with its hooded bloom swaying on a tall stalk. In summer the place simply hums with wild bees and butterflies, and the fragrance is intoxicating (surely the work of fairies!). Above that lies a rocky moraine where stunted herbaceous shrubs like juniper cling to the rocks, with mosses, lichens, and delicate flowers tucked into crevices. Though there are signboards and marked paths through the valley, you'll be accompanied by local guides to make sure you don't trample or pick any flowers.

Westerners may be more familiar with the spiritual retreat of Rishikesh (where the Beatles communed with the Maharishi in 1968), several miles southeast of here, but nearby Govindghat has important Sikh and Hindu shrines too, and you'll see many pilgrims visiting this valley in conjunction with a temple visit. Whatever deities—or fairies—dwell in this hidden paradise, you'll feel like you're communing with something supernatural up here.

ⓘ **Valley of Flowers National Park,** Ghangrea, accessible via 13km (8-mile) path from Govingdghat

✈ Dehra Dun

🚃 Rishikesh

🛏 Various small guesthouses and rest houses are clustered at both Ghangrea and Govindghat.

**129**

**TOUR** **Garhwal Himalayan Explorations** (© **91/11/2794-8870** or 011/2794-7265; www.thegarhwalhimalayas.com). **GMVN**

**Treks** (© **91/13/6443-1793**; www.garhwal tourism.com).

**Flowers** **119**

# Mount Cook National Park
## *The Buttercup Masquerade*
### South Island, New Zealand

NON-NATIVE RED DEER, FALLOW DEER, GOAT, WAPITI, CHAMOIS, AND THAR THREATEN THE integrity of Mount Cook's alpine and forest ecosystems. Mustelids and rodents have devastated indigenous bird life, reducing most bird populations and driving several species to extinction. The area is further threatened by the logging industry and by roads for a large underground hydroelectric power station.

In the shadow of New Zealand's highest mountain—the awesome peak where Sir Edmund Hillary trained before tackling Mount Everest—who has time for a modest little white flower? Most visitors to Mount Cook National Park are in search of much bigger thrills—flight-seeing, downhill skiing, mountaineering, kayaking around glaciers, that sort of thing.

For naturalists, though, spotting a Mount Cook lily is a definite thrill because this rare white flower doesn't grow anywhere else but the Southern Alps of New Zealand's South Island. Yet here, on the sheltered slopes of Mount Cook (or Aoraki, to give it its Maori name), Mount Cook lillies grow by the thousands throughout the New Zealand summer, November through January.

Actually, the Mount Cook lily isn't a lily at all but a buttercup—and a giant buttercup at that, growing up to 1m (3 ft.) tall with flowers 5 to 8cm (2–4 in.) across, flaunting a double layer of dazzling white petals and conspicuous bright yellow stamens (though it's true that its glossy dark-green leaves do look like a waterlily). It's definitely a moisture-loving plant, which is good, because an awful lot of mist and rain rolls through these mountains, frustrating many a traveler who drove all the way here just to view a famous mountain peak and then move on.

It isn't just the Mount Cook lily, of course. There are 550 species of flora in this huge mountain park, and like the rest of New Zealand, an overwhelming number are endemic. Alongside that giant buttercup you'll see mountain daisies, snow gentians, mountain flax, fierce spikes of golden

A buttercup on Mount Cook.

Spaniard, loose clusters of the petite Alpine avens, and tiny-flowered South Island edelweiss. Although more than a third of the park lies under permanent snow and ice, the remaining two-thirds is mostly open to flowers, since there's very little forest on these steep, thin-soiled slopes. Unfortunately, a number of animals introduced to the area to provide hunters with game threaten to overrun the park, despite efforts by park rangers to keep them from overbrowsing the Alpine meadows.

From the park entrance at Mount Cook Village, a half-day ramble on the **Hooker Valley trail** offers plenty of flower viewing. And along the way, you'll cross two swinging bridges over gorges, pass two pristine lakes, cross a boardwalk over boggy tussocks, and wind up right at the frosty face of a glacier—probably encountering along the way at least a couple of keas, those nervy olive-green mountain parrots that are Mount Cook's unofficial mascots. Is that enough adventure for you?

ⓘ **Mount Cook National Park,** Bowen Dr., Mount Cook Village (✆ **64/3/435-1186;** www.doc.govt.nz)

✈ Mount Cook

⊨ $$$ **Hermitage Hotel,** Terrace Rd., Mount Cook Village (✆ **64/3/435-1809;** www.mount-cook.com). $$ **Glencoe Lodge,** Terrace Rd., Mount Cook Village (✆ **64/3/435-1809;** www.mount-cook.com).

---

**120** Into the Woods

# Ossipee Pine Barrens
## *The Woods Are Pitch Perfect*
### Ossippee/Madison/Freedom, New Hampshire

INVASIVE SPECIES THREATEN TO OVERRUN THE OSSIPEE PINE BARRENS, A GLOBALLY RARE ecosystem and one of the rarest types of forest in North America. Its survival—and the survival of the many rare wildlife species it supports—depends on careful management and strategic burning to reproduce the natural cycle of drought, fire, and regeneration that once enabled the pine barrens to flourish.

Forget all that stuff Smokey the Bear told us—sometimes fire is good for forests.

At least it is for some forests—like northern pitch pine/scrub oak pine barrens. But there are only about 20 such woodlands left. One of the largest is the Ossipee Pine Barrens, a patch of New Hampshire woods just east of Lake Winnipesaukee and south of the White Mountains. To keep it healthy, foresters have carried out a careful program of controlled fires.

This isn't just a question of tossing a live match into the woods and waiting for combustion. Once upon a time, fires swept through here periodically—say, every 25 or 50 years—but with increased settlement, fire prevention became the rule.

The woods are now full of dead branches and dense understory that could blaze out of control any minute. Before a fire is set, the woods must be thinned, and buffer belts created to contain the flames. Large white pines, which (unlike pitch pine) burn quickly, are removed as well and sold for timber, which helps to fund the project.

At last, a prepared parcel of land is set afire. Everything burns to the ground, or so it seems. But scrub oaks have very deep roots, and they recover quickly. Pitch pine seeds actually germinate better on burned ground, and their fresh shoots constitutes a whole new food for certain insects. Meanwhile, charred debris adds nutrients to the soil. Wild blueberry bushes—which the Ossipee pine barrens

Ossipee Pine Barrens.

Several endangered moths and butterflies that live here—like the frosted elfin butterfly—specifically feed on pitch pine rather than the red pines or white pines that have taken over many of New England's forests. And as a result, birds that feed on those moths and butterflies, such as whippoorwills, nighthawks, Eastern towhees, prairie warblers, vesper sparrows, and brown thrashers, are drawn to these woods, even as their numbers swiftly decline elsewhere. When was the last time you heard a whippoorwill's song?

A few parcels of the Ossippee Pine Barrens have already been burned; when you visit, take any of the various short walking trails and look at the differences between these "new" woods and the sections that haven't been burned. Some of the really mature pitch pines, best seen along **Hobbs Trail,** are 150 years old; others are mere saplings. Even Smokey the Bear would agree that a healthy forest needs both.

are full of—grow noticeably thicker and bushier after a fire. The temporarily leveled woodlands make room for the thickets and patches of meadow that rabbits and snakes love, types of growth that white pines often push out. It's a win-win situation: The forest becomes healthier and less prone to accidental wildfires that really could damage neighboring property.

(i) **Ossippee Pine Barrens,** Rte. 41, 2 miles (3km) north of Rte. 16, Ossipee, NH

✈ Laconia

🛏 $$ **Wolfeboro Inn,** 90 N. Main St., Wolfeboro, NH (📞 **800/451-2389** or 603/569-3016; www.wolfeboroinn.com). $$ **Stonehurst Manor,** Rte. 16, North Conway, NH (📞 **800/525-9100** or 603/356-3113; www.stonehurstmanor.com).

Into the Woods **121**

# Green Swamp Preserve
## *Nature Needs No Landfill*
### Supply, North Carolina

NEARBY COMMUNITIES HAVE DRAINED OR DIVERTED WATER FROM THE GREEN SWAMP TO supply new golf courses and resorts as well as local residents. Proposals for a landfill inside the preserve and a new interstate highway route through the swamp also threaten the survival of this rare ecosystem, which includes the endangered Venus' flytrap.

What do you see when you look at a swamp? Some people see a rich, diverse ecosystem that shelters unusual flora and fauna. But others, apparently, see a perfect site to dump trash.

That's what happened in 2000, when a giant landfill was quietly proposed for the grounds of North Carolina's Green Swamp Preserve. Talk about paving paradise to put up a parking lot! If local residents hadn't got wind of it, one of the country's last examples of a pocosin—an evergreen shrub bog—would right now be lying underneath a mountain of garbage taller than the Cape Hatteras Lighthouse. Fortunately, a grass-roots campaign was waged against the project, and for now at least, court rulings have blocked the landfill. In the process, local folks began to appreciate the swamp in their back yards as never before.

The word *pocosin* comes from an Algonquian term meaning "swamp on a hill." The pocosin doesn't look dark and murky like your classic swamp, but if you stepped off the boardwalk trail onto its spongy soil, you'd realize just how waterlogged it is. Gallberry, titi, and sweetbay are the dominant evergreen shrubs, and American alligators hang out here (if it's got an alligator, it must be a swamp). But longtime neighbors have nervously noted the swamp's gradual shrinking, as ditches have drained its waters to supply the area's growing population.

Along with the pocosin, you can also hike through one of the country's finest examples of a longleaf pine savanna, a once common regional habitat that elsewhere has converted to a monoculture of loblolly pine. In contrast, these savannas have a thriving, complex ecosystem. Within the dense undergrowth of wiregrass, growing in tall tawny tufts between slender, ramrod-straight pine trunks, you'll find the world's most diverse collections of orchids and carnivorous plants—four kinds of pitcher plants, two bladderworts, sundew, and a truly amazing number of the endangered Venus' flytrap, with its menacing toothed scarlet leaves.

Many of the plants in the Green Swamp benefit from the periodic burning they've been getting recently; not only are they fire tolerant, they've actually adapted to germinate better under fire conditions. The old-growth trees are often infected with red heart disease—but then, that's the absolute favorite spot for red-cockaded woodpeckers to nest, where they can easily drill a big hole in the softened trunk. (Look for holes surrounded with a shiny ring of sticky pine sap, which conveniently keeps out predators.) Once these woodpeckers have built these solid nests, they return to them year after year, making this woods one of the last strongholds of this highly endangered bird. If nothing else, that should have been reason to stop the landfill.

ⓘ **Green Swamp Preserve,** State Hwy. 211, 5½ miles (9km) north of Supply

✈ Wilmington

🛏 $$$ **Graystone Inn,** 100 S. 3rd St., Wilmington (✆ **888/763-4773** or 910/763-2000; www.graystoneinn.com). $$ **The Wilmingtonian,** 101 S. 2nd St., Wilmington (✆ **800/525-0909** or 910/343-1800; www.thewilmingtonian.com).

# Bad Branch Preserve
## *Colonel Boone's Wilderness*
### Cumberland Mountains, Kentucky

MANY RARE AND UNUSUAL PLANT AND WILDLIFE SPECIES THRIVE IN THE BAD BRANCH Preserve. Although the preserve is protected, environmental degradation such as water pollution, flooding, and erosion caused by mountaintop removal and surface mining threaten its intricate ecosystem. Rising temperatures and other climate changes caused by global warming can also upset its delicate ecological balance.

Daniel Boone would feel right at home in this Cumberland Mountain wilderness, where a river rages down the side of Pine Mountain, taking less than 3 miles (5km) to drop 1,000 feet (300m) in elevation. The sandstone cliffs of Bad Branch Gorge rise out of the dark-green forest with lots of crags and caves; sheer rock faces glisten with seeping water, and big boulders muscle up to the creek bank. One particularly gorgeous 60-foot (18m) cascade is beloved of photographers trying to capture the "perfect" wilderness waterfall. Bad Branch is officially one of Kentucky's Wild Rivers, and clearly deserves the title.

But get past the thunder and majesty of the falls and you'll find a delicate patchwork of habitats. A rare fish called the Arrow Darter populates highly aerated pools of clear water just below the falls. The endangered long-tailed shrew skitters around the hemlock forest, and snakes (some of them venomous, so beware) slither around the talus caves formed by piled-up boulders. Somewhere up in those magnificent cliffs lives a pair of nesting ravens, Kentucky's last two survivors of this once-common species.

Although this 2,400-acre (971-hectare) tract saw some logging in the 1940s, the diversity of plants growing here—especially the number of flowers—shows that it wasn't extensive. Some of those shaggy hemlocks may have been around long enough to have seen Daniel Boone himself explore these woods. Bring a field guidebook with you when you walk through the forest, because it's anything but a monoculture—along with the hemlocks stand sweet birch, yellow birch, basswood, tulip poplar, American beech, and buckeye trees (squirrels love the beechnuts and glossy brown buckeye nuts). But that's not all; smaller trees in the understory include flowering dogwood and umbrella magnolia, perfuming the air in spring along with sweet pepperbush and dense thickets of rosebay rhododendron. Several rare plants here, like matriciary grapefern, Fraser's sedge, and American burnet, are generally found farther north, and only in old-growth forests.

If you're an ambitious hiker, there's a steep, strenuous 7.5-mile (12km) trail to the top of Pine Mountain (actually a 21-mile-long/34km ridge), where the massive outcropping of High Rock provides an awesome panorama of the Cumberland Valley; you may be able to see into nearby Virginia or even farther south to Tennessee. Only a hardy handful make it to the top, though; the 2-mile (3km) trail to the falls is vigorous enough.

You have to drive a ways to get to this sort of wilderness, so make the most of it, taking the two-lane Daniel Boone Parkway through the densely green Boone National Forest. Officially it was renamed in 2003 after Congressman Hal Rogers, who wangled funding so it wouldn't be a toll road anymore, but locals defiantly use the old name anyway.

(i) **Bad Branch Nature Preserve,** 2½ miles (4km) east of U.S. 119 on KY 932, Whitesburg, KY

✈ London-Corbin, KY

🛏 $$ **Hampton Inn,** 70 Morton Blvd., Hazard, KY (📞 **606/439-0902;** www.hamptoninn.com). $$ **Holiday Inn Express & Suites,** 192 Corporate Dr., Hazard (📞 **606/487-0595;** www.ichotelsgroup.com).

---

**123** Into the Woods

# Cranesville Swamp Preserve
## *Frost Pocket*
### West Virginia & Maryland

LOGGING, FOREIGN INSECTS, AND AN EXCESSIVE DEER POPULATION HAVE DEPLETED THE FORESTS that shelter this swamp, allowing the sun and wind to dry and warm its cold, wet swampland. Environmental groups are working to preserve the swamp by replanting forests and managing wildlife to keep the fragile ecosystem in balance.

Be sure to bring an extra layer when you come to Cranesville Swamp. Even in the height of summer it can be chilly and damp, with traces of snow scattered about. But what else would you expect when you visit a frost pocket?

What biologists call "frost pockets" are rare freaks of nature, a combination of geologic, botanical, and historic factors. Back in the Ice Age, glaciers never got as far south as this neck of the Appalachians, but the coniferous forests they drove ahead of them did. When the glaciers receded, so did the conifers, to be replaced by deciduous forests—everywhere except for this tiny valley. It's as if a tiny fragment of Ice Age climate had been trapped in this crevice of the mountains. The Cranesville Swamp is chockfull of relict northern populations, extinct elsewhere in this region.

Situated on the border between the western bit of Maryland and West Virginia, the Cranesville Swamp Preserve has two habitats: a wet bog along tannin-dark Muddy Creek that drips with sphagnum moss, speckled alder, skunk cabbage, and rare sedges and grasses; and, where the ground has better drainage, an acidic conifer swamp forest full of northern species like tall eastern hemlock and red spruce, which you'd never expect around here. Even though this land was cleared from time to time—for logging, for farming, and most recently for power lines—the trees that grew back are still those relict species, which are best suited to this sliver of microclimate. You'll find tamarack (eastern larch) trees here, even though the next closest ones are 200 miles (320km) north. Dense patches of rhododendron, unusual ferns, and mossy ground cover make it feel as primordial as it is; there's even a species of ground cover called trilobite liverwort. Of course, where you get rare vegetation you get rare fauna as well—like the northern water shrew, the star-nosed mole, dark-eyed junco, Canada warbler, and the saw-whet owl.

Take a look upward and you'll see that Cranesville is snuggled inside a bowl—the uplands around it are 2,900 feet (85km) high, but the swamp itself is only 2,560 feet (780m) high. Not only does the swamp share the cool air and heavy snowfall of the surrounding mountains, the bowl actually pushes cold air down into the swamp, where it's not warmed by sunlight. No wonder those ancient conifers stay happy here—it sure feels like a little piece of Canada!

ⓘ **Cranesville Swamp Preserve,** WV C.R. 47-1, Cranesville, WV

✈ Morgantown, WV

🛏 $$ **Blackberry Blossom Farm,** Rte. 2, Albright, WV (📞 **304/379-8896;** www.blackberryblossomfarm.com). $$ **Clarion Hotel Morgan,** 127 High St., Morgantown, WV (📞 **304/292-8200;** www.clarionhotelmorgan.com).

---

## Into the Woods · 124

# Big Cypress National Preserve
## *Panther Party*
### South Florida

BIG CYPRESS NATIONAL PRESERVE IS A VAST WETLAND THAT IS HEAVILY USED FOR HIKING, hunting, and other forms of outdoor recreation. Managing this sensitive ecosystem is a challenge that has led officials at various times to close trails and ban airboats and off-road vehicles in an effort to protect wildlife, such as a small population of rare Florida panthers that live in the preserve.

Big Cypress National Preserve.

Don't let the name deceive you. You won't see giant cypresses here—most of them are mere upstarts, descendants of trees felled for timber in the 1950s. Still, it deserves to be called Big Cypress Forest because the tract itself is so big. Taken together with the contiguous Everglades National Park, they cover 2.7 million acres (1.1 million hectares)—that's a lot of south Florida to protect.

The Everglades gets all the press, but without the Big Cypress swamp, there would be no Everglades. Its cypress sloughs and marshes pour freshwater south into the Everglades, feeding the marine estuaries along Florida's southwest coast. Cypress trees just love water, and they anchor this swamp with tough roots and stout buttressed trunks that can withstand strong winds, a good thing in hurricane-prone Florida.

Big Cypress allows more recreational opportunities than the Everglades, though the popularity of off-road vehicles has caused concern lately, as it damages this sensitive drainage ecosystem, already impaired by misguided canal building and highway construction in the years past.

Backcountry camping and hiking can lead you deep into the wilderness, through dwarf cypress forest, slash pine forests, and saw-grass prairie. (Examine a blade of saw grass and you'll see the jagged edges that earn it its name). Perhaps you'll even go deep enough to surprise a Florida panther chasing down a deer—there are 30 to 35 of these elusive, endangered cats living here. More likely you'll see a bobcat, though, or a black bear; this is one of the last places in Florida with significant numbers of black bears.

If the trails look too wet (things get very squishy underfoot in summer), you can still see a lot of Big Cypress's wildlife by driving the 27-mile (43km) **Loop Road** or the 17-mile (27km) **Turner River/Wagonwheel/Birdon Roads Loop,** both accessible off of Highway 41. The latter follows two canals that attract wading birds, especially during the dry season, November to April. Graceful coastal plain willows trail their leaves into the canals, where you'll see herons stalking along the banks, an anhinga fishing with its long spearlike beak, or the double-crested cormorant (aka "snake bird") gliding surreptitiously with just its head above water. The dazzling white of egrets—cattle, snowy, and great egrets—makes them easy to spot from above, but for gullible fish looking upward, they appear like clouds in the sky. Past the saw-grass prairie to the north, tall cabbage palms—the Florida state tree—sway in the breeze. To the south, the prairie is edged by stands of slash pine, where the endangered red-cockaded woodpecker lives.

One species you're bound to see is dark alligators basking on the canal rims. Unlike crocodiles, alligators only live in freshwater—but that's what Big Cypress has. And if it wasn't here to keep the water fresh, who knows what would happen to the rest of south Florida?

ⓘ **Big Cypress National Preserve,** Oasis Visitors Center, Hwy. 41, Tamiami Trail (📞 **239/695-1201;** www.nps.gov/bicy)

✈ Miami International

🛏 $$$ **Ivey House B&B,** 107 Camellia St., Everglades City (📞 **239/695-3299;** www.iveyhouse.com). $$ **Rod & Gun Lodge,** 200 Riverside Dr., Everglades City (📞 **239/695-2101**).

---

**125** Into the Woods

# Pontotoc Ridge Preserve
## *Keeping the Cross Timbers Happy*
### Southeast Oklahoma

EXCESSIVE GROUNDWATER WITHDRAWAL, INVASIVE SPECIES, AND FIRE SUPPRESSION THREATEN the conservation in and around the Pontotoc Ridge Preserve. Eastern red cedar and other invasive species crowd out native plants and destroy wildlife habitat, and fire suppression leads to a loss of fire-dependent plants that are a critical part of this sensitive ecosystem.

To the first white explorers crossing the North American continent, the Cross Timbers seemed like the work of the devil. An impenetrable tangle of mixed oaks and undergrowth, it bristled all over a north-south limestone ridge, blocking the entrance to the Great Plains. The Plains Indians had only made it worse by their crafty custom of burning it down to increase forage land for bison—fire just made the Cross Timbers grow back thicker and wilder than ever. Limestone outcrops hid treacherous caves, and wild beasts lurked in its thickets.

Nowadays Oklahoma is a civilized place—so civilized that there's just about nothing left of the Cross Timbers. Its shallow, rocky soil didn't make good cropland, but over the years farmers hacked it down for pasture, let it be overrun by invaders like red cedar and sericia lespedeza, or, worst of all, kept it from burning down.

Nearly 3,000 acres (1,214 hectares) of the Cross Timbers are left, though, in one place: the Pontotoc Ridge Preserve. It's a vital mosaic of complementary habitats: As you hike through the preserve, you'll notice the landscape change from oak savannas on the uplands, then tall-grass prairie blending into mixed-grass prairie on rocky slopes, leading down to hardwood forest in the deeper soil along Delaware Creek.

The abutting edges of different ecosystems always encourage species diversity, as Pontotoc Ridge gloriously proves. With controlled burning by preserve managers, the savannas—a mix of post oak and blackjack oak—are thinned out enough to let a rich understory of sun-loving herbaceous plants flourish. That provides great food for wild turkey, deer, bobwhite, and quail, as well as migratory songbirds like painted buntings, summer tanagers, and black-billed cuckoos. Meanwhile, Bell's vireos and prairie warblers dart back and forth between the oaks and the nearby prairies, where prolific wildflowers attract a dizzying profusion of butterflies, over 90 documented species to date. (It's been identified by the Audubon Society as a regional hot spot of butterfly diversity.) Limestone outcrops support pincushion cactus, shooting star, and nodding ladies' tresses. One of the preserve's abundant springs is one of only four known sites where the Oklahoma cave amphipod lives. The bottomland forests—mostly American elm, slippery elm, sugarberry, and green ash—welcome bald eagles and pileated woodpeckers, both endangered.

Rich as this landscape looks, though, it's basically a semi-arid region. As the growing population of nearby Ada sucks more water from this limestone aquifer, the springs and streams of Poconoc Ridge are more important than ever. It's not just the endangered flora and fauna that need Poconoc Ridge; two-legged Oklahomans need it too, more than they realize.

---

(i) **Pontotoc Ridge Preserve,** Rte. 2, Stonewall, OK (© **580/777-2224**)

✈ Oklahoma City

🛏 $$ **Holiday Inn Express,** 1201 Lonnie Abbott Industrial Blvd, Ada (© **888/465-4329** or 580/310-9200; www.ichotels group.com). $ **Best Western Raintree Inn,** 1100 N. Mississippi Ave., Ada (© **580/332-6262;** www.bestwesternoklahoma. com).

---

Into the Woods **126**

# Big Thicket National Preserve
## *An American Ark*
### Southeast Texas

THE NATIONAL PARKS CONSERVATION ASSOCIATION IN 2003 IDENTIFIED BIG THICKET NATIONAL Preserve as the most endangered of all lands under National Park Service jurisdiction—but the preserve remains at risk from potential development and suburban sprawl.

Frankly, the National Park Service got here too late. While the name Big Thicket promises an intact tangle of woods, this national preserve, founded in 1974, lies scattered in various parcels around a well-settled East Texas area. The logging industry got a

Big Thicket National Preserve.

foothold here in the 1850s, decimating the great woods that baffled early-19th-century settlers; on many neighboring lands, cheap slash-pine forests replaced the ancient stands of pine and cypress. Then, around 1900, oil was discovered, and you know what that means in Texas. Though logging is now prohibited, oil and gas are still extracted from the preserve, which also allows hunting, trapping, and fishing.

But luckily, early timber baron John Henry Kirby set aside a portion of the old woods as hunting grounds, preserving enough of this unique biological crossroads—often called "an American ark"—to make it well worth visiting. It's like a naturalist's version of Disney's Epcot: An amazing confluence of species, driven south by Ice Age glaciers, coexist in one small area. A mere drive-through visit misses the point; you have to get out of your car and walk a couple of different short trails before you really get the point of Big Thicket. Its bogs and blackwater swamps resemble those of the southeast, rife with ferns, orchids, and insect-eating pitcher plants (follow the Pitcher Plant

Trail to see four out of five North American species, all in one place). Along the Kirby Nature Trail, bluebirds flit around eastern hardwood forests, yet nearby on the Sandhill Loop there are roadrunners roaming arid sandhills that look like they belong in New Mexico. Over at the Hickory Creek section, the Sundew Trail displays a riot of wildflowers on a prairie savanna more typical of the Central Plains. In fact, rangers have tallied nearly 1,000 different types of flowering plants around the preserve. You won't see them all, of course, but bring a field guidebook and it'll be well thumbed by the time you leave.

The American Bird Conservancy has named the preserve a Globally Important Bird Area, with nearly 186 resident or migratory species in one or another of its varied habitats. During migrations (late Mar to early May or Oct–Nov), patient birders can sight brown-headed nuthatch, Bachman's sparrow, and the red-cockaded woodpecker. The best locations are on the Hickory Creek savanna and along the short Kirby Nature Trail or the longer Turkey Creek Trail.

One long parcel added to the preserve follows the Neches River, great for white-water canoeing; another canoe trail on the Pine Island Bayou, down south close to Beaumont, lets you paddle through haunting stands of ancient bald cypress and tupelo, where you may even see an alligator or two. Sometimes it's hard to remember what state you're in—is this really Texas?

(i) **Big Thicket National Preserve,** 6102 FM 420, Kountze, TX (**℃ 409/951-6725;** www.nps.gov/bith)

✈ Beaumont or Houston

🛏 $$ **Pelt Farm B&B,** FM 421, Kountze (**℃ 409/287-3300;** www.peltfarm.com). $$ **La Quinta Inn,** 220 Interstate 10 N., Beaumont (**℃ 409/838-9991;** www.lq.com).

---

Into the Woods **127**

# Great Basin National Park
## *The Methusaleh Trees*
### Baker, Nevada

GREAT BASIN NATIONAL PARK FACES SEVERAL THREATS, SUCH AS GROUNDWATER DEPLETION, the invasion of cheatgrass and other foreign species that overwhelm native plants, and global climate change. A more immediate threat, a proposed coal-fired power plant, would pollute the air and deposit sulfur, nitrogen, and mercury in the lakes and rivers that many park animals depend on for water.

We all know what a desert looks like—hot and sandy, right? But the desert plateau of the American West isn't hot, and it isn't sandy: It's downright chilly on these mountain slopes, where specially drought-adapted plants like sagebrush, juniper, pinyon pine, manzanita, rabbitbrush, greasebrush, and Mormon tea cling to rocky soils and prevent erosion. Set along the Utah-Nevada border, Great Basin National Park isn't as well known as Yellowstone or Yosemite or even its Utah counterparts Bryce and Zion, but it offers great panoramas of surrounding desert and mountains—and groves of what may be the planet's longest-living trees.

The oldest tree ever recorded was a bristlecone pine called Prometheus, which was removed in 1964 from Great Basin and carbon-dated to 4,900 years old. There are other species of bristlecone pine over the West, but this one—Pinus longaeva, named the Great Basin bristlecone—appears to be the longest living.

The bristlecone is a true survivor. Because it's so slow growing, it has to compete by thriving at high elevations and exposed rocky sites, where other trees just can't grow. Notice how the trees have been bent and twisted by the wind and snow at these heights, often losing all branches on their windward sides, a condition called krumholtz. Ice crystals have polished their trunks, and the short dark-green needles are fire resistant as well as drought resistant. For bristlecones, slow growth is actually a virtue; it makes their wood so dense, it resists rot, fungi, insects, and even erosion. Take a look at its distinctive cones: The immature cones are purple to absorb heat, and mature brown cones have bristles at the end of their scales to aid with dispersal.

A hiking trail leads to the most accessible of the park's three bristlecone pine groves, beginning from the parking area at the base of Wheeler Peak, Nevada's second-highest mountain. In summer rangers often lead guided hikes here—check for times at the visitor center (where you can also buy tickets to visit the Lehman Caves, Great Basin's star attraction). The hike to the bristlecones is 4.6 miles (7.4km) round-trip and not steep, though at an elevation of 10,000 feet (3,000m), you may tire more easily than normal. The bristlecone grove lies 1.4 miles (2km) from the trail head, with a self-guided nature loop leading through the pines. This grove is unusual because it grows on glacial moraines of quartzite, not limestone, which bristlecones usually prefer. Hike another mile to the end of the trail to see an ice field and what is believed to be a rock glacier—a rock-covered permanent mass of ice moving very slowly downhill. A glacier in a desert—who'd have thought?

---

ⓘ **Great Basin National Park,** off NV 488, Baker, NV (✆ **775/234-7331;** www. nps.gov/grba)

✈ Salt Lake City

🛏 $$ **Silver Jack Motel,** downtown Baker (✆ **775/234-7323;** www.greatbasin park.com). $ **The Border Inn,** U.S. 50/6 at Nevada-Utah border (✆ **775/234-7300**).

## 128 Into the Woods

# Sherwood Forest
## *Ye Old Shire Wood*
### Nottingham, England

SHERWOOD FOREST IS DYING OF OLD AGE AND NEGLECT. LOGGING, AGRICULTURE, INDUSTRIAL development, and poor conservation practices have decimated this once vast woodland. Forest managers and conservation groups are seeking the millions of dollars required to plant 250,000 new trees and regenerate the legendary forest.

Even back in Robin Hood's day, Sherwood—meaning "shire wood"—Forest wasn't pure forest, but a mixed landscape of heath, pastureland, and wooded glades, with a few scattered hamlets. This royal hunting ground covered 40,500 hectares (100,000 acres), running 32km (20 miles) long and 13km (8 miles) wide. Only the king and his subjects could hunt here, but peasants could gather acorns, collect firewood, make charcoal, or graze sheep and cattle. It was truly the heart of Nottinghamshire.

Today, Sherwood Forest is a shadow of its former self, just a 182-hectare (450-acre) park surrounding the village of Edwin-stowe, squeezed between the urban areas of Nottingham and Sheffield. Around 1,000 stout oak trees survive, but recently they've been dying off fast from sheer old age. The most famous, the Major Oak—touted as Robin Hood's tree, though bark analysis suggests it may be younger than the 13th century—requires a lot of props and cables to stay standing.

Half a million tourists come here every year. Kitschy models of Robin Hood and his Merry Men are on display, and Robin Hood souvenirs sell like hotcakes in the gift shop. A weeklong summer Robin Hood festival features costumed jousters and jesters and troubadors aplenty.

But there's more to Sherwood Forest than the Robin Hood legend. The organization English Nature is fighting to keep Sherwood Forest vital, designating it as a National Nature Reserve in 2002. In 2007 the protected area was nearly doubled by adding the Budby South Forest, a stretch of gorse-covered heath previously used for military training. With the two areas combined, already the local populations of nightjars and woodlarks are increasing,

# 10 Places to See North American Prairie

Three kinds of prairies once covered an estimated 140 million acres (57 million hectares) of America: tallgrass prairie to the east, dominated by so-called sod grasses (bluestem, Indian grass, switch grass); short-grass prairies closer to the Rocky Mountains, where hardy buffalo grass and grama grass dominated; and a more varied mosaic of mixed-grass prairie in between. Prairie grasslands are perhaps the planet's most efficient ecosystem for removing carbon from the atmosphere—and yet 96% of these tough grasslands were lost. Against all odds, these parcels have survived:

**129 Edge of Appalachia Preserve, Ohio** Along Ohio Brush Creek, near Lynx, Ohio, a series of 10 adjacent preserves protect 13,500 acres (5,463 hectares) with pockets of rare Allegheny short-grass prairie along cliff edges, ridge tops, and forest openings. The limestone bedrock here is essential to the persistence of blue-stem grasses and wildflowers. The best hike is the 3-mile (5km) Buzzardroost Trail. *www.appalachiandiscovery.com.*

**130 Cressmoor Prairie Preserve, Hobart, Indiana** This 38-acre (15-hectare) parcel of land is a remarkable hunk of pure silt-loam prairie in the northwestern corner of Indiana. Walk its 2-mile (3km) mown trail and you'll soon be surrounded by prairie grass as high as 5 feet (8m), studded with brilliant flowers like prairie lily, sunflowers, blazing star, and a whole range of asters and goldenrod cycling through from summer through fall. *www.state.in.us/dnr/naturepr/npdirectory/preserves/cressmoor.html.*

**131 Nachusa Grasslands, Franklin Grove, Illinois** This preserve totals 3,000 acres (1,214 hectares), with a fair amount of that being tallgrass prairie and dry prairie, and on such a large-scale landscape, species diversity thrives. Many rare plants, including the threatened prairie bush clover, prosper here, as well as endangered butterflies and grassland birds like the dickcissel and grasshopper sparrow. *www.nature.org.*

**132 Terre Noir Blacklands, Arkadelphia, Arkansas** There used to be 12 million acres (5 million hectares) of blackland prairie, from Alabama to Texas. Only 10,000 acres (4,047 hectares) of this imperiled ecosystem have survived, mostly in Arkansas. There are no marked trails at this 240-acre (97-hectare) site along Highway 51 in southwestern Arkansas, but you can hike all over its rolling terrain, where wildflower-splashed prairie alternates with dense thickets of oak and pine. *www.nature.org.*

**133 Neal Smith National Wildlife Refuge, Prairie City, Iowa** With some 5,000 acres (2,023 hectares) of restored tall grass prairie—mostly seeded by plants rescued elsewhere by volunteers—the refuge is big enough to sustain larger prairie residents such as American bison,

Pawnee National Grasslands.

white-tailed deer, elk, pocket gophers, badgers, pheasants, red-tailed hawks, and Indiana bats. For a glimpse, check out the 2-mile (3km) Tallgrass Trail, which is paved, signposted, and handicapped accessible. *www.tallgrass.org.*

**⓭ Tallgrass Prairie National Preserve, Cottonwood Falls, Kansas** In the Flint Hills of northeastern Kansas, this 11,000-acre (4,452-hectare) preserve includes one area of quite rare prairie ecosystem: riparian bottomland tall-grass. The preserve's staff is replanting 500 acres (200 hectares) along Fox Creek to restore all the native plants of this rarely seen type of prairie. The Bottomland Trail has a 1-mile (1.6km) interpreted loop where you can watch the restoration in progress. *www.nps.gov/tapr.*

Tallgrass Prairie National Preserve.

Oglala National Grasslands.

**⓭ Tallgrass Prairie Preserve, Tolstoi, Manitoba** Here in the so-called Prairie Provinces, most prairieland was ploughed under for the vast wheat fields of Canada's bread-basket. Yet these 2,000 hectares (5,000 acres) in the Red River Valley were strewn with just enough boulders and swampy sloughs to make them untillable. Among the preserve's endangered flowers are the small white lady's slipper and nodding ladies tresses. The Prairie Shore self-guided trail loop is off Highway 209; the Agassiz Interpretive Trail is off Highway 201. *© 204/945-7775.*

**⓭ Buffalo Gap National Grassland, Kadoka, South Dakota** No less than 56 different species of grass grow here, the taller ones thriving in moist seasons, shorter grasses coming into their own in the height of summer. It's rife with prairie dogs, and the rare burrowing owls that take over their empty burrows. There's a 5¹⁄₂-mile (8.9km) loop trail with great badland vistas near Wall, South Dakota. *© 605/279-2125.*

**⓭ Oglala National Grasslands, Crawford, Nebraska** Rock hounds are drawn to this 95,000-acre (38,445-hectare) short-grass prairie preserve in northwestern Nebraska, a desolate-seeming badlands where fossils abound, stark rock formations are heaped around the Toadstool Geologic Park, and 10,000-year-old bison skeletons are excavated at the Hudson-Meng Bison Bonebed. *© 308/432-0300.*

**⓭ Pawnee National Grasslands, Briggsdale, Colorado** Lying in the rain shadow of the Rockies, this windswept 60-mile-wide (97km) plateau ripples with the distinctive dry green of short-grass prairie. Try the Birdwalk Trail starting out from the Crow Valley Campground to see lark buntings, Western meadowlarks, and mountain plovers; another wonderful hike takes you to the Pawnee Buttes, which thrust momentously upward from the plateau. *© 970/346-5000.*

not to mention the great-spotted woodpecker, green woodpecker, tawny owl, and redstart, which need old-growth forests to live. Over 1,000 types of spider and beetle infest the decaying wood of dead trees and fallen branches, deliberately left in place to feed them. Grazing cattle have been brought in to keep the woodlands open. Through these woodlands—a peculiarly English mix of oak, silver birch, rowan, holly, and hawthorn, with bracken ferns beneath—run footpaths and bridleways.

The tale of Sherwood Forest reads like a mini-history of Britain. Originally cleared by Roman legions, the Nottinghamshire countryside became fragmented in medieval times as great landowners enclosed their estates. (Scraps of the ancient forest persist on a set of private estates called the Dukeries, south of the town of Worksop.) In the Industrial Revolution towns and factories sprang up, destroying more woodland, which in the post-war era was replaced with quick-growing conifers planted for timber. But with several area coal mines recently closed down, there may be a window of opportunity to revert more of this East Midlands region to woodlands, planting new oaks and connecting existing parcels in a continuous corridor. The next chapter of Sherwood's story? It still remains to be written.

ⓘ **Sherwood Forest Park,** A614, Edwinstowe (ⓒ **44/1623/823202**). **Sherwood Forest Trust** (www.sherwoodforest.org.uk). **Sherwood: The Living Legend** (www.robinhood.co.uk).

✈ Nottingham East Midlands

🛏 $$$ **Strathdon Hotel,** 44 Derby Rd., Nottingham (ⓒ **44/1159/418501;** www.strathdon-hotel-nottingham.com). $$ **Nottingham Moat House,** 296 Mansfield Rd, Nottingham (ⓒ **44/1159/359988;** www.moathousehotels.com).

---

**Into the Woods**  **139**

# Newborough Forest
## *The Squirrel's Tale*
### Isle of Anglesey, Wales

NEWBOROUGH FOREST IS A CRITICAL HABITAT AND REFUGE FOR RED SQUIRRELS, A NATIVE BRITISH species forced to the brink of extinction by more aggressive non-native gray squirrels. If approved, a current plan to restore the original sand dune habitat by clear-cutting up to half the trees in Newborough Forest could also spell disaster for the red squirrels.

The gray squirrel is like a bad downstairs neighbor: He seems like a friendly guy when he moves in, but soon he's intruding on your space, borrowing your food, raising a pack of bratty kids, carrying in nasty germs, and playing loud music all night.

Okay, maybe they don't play music. But the North American gray squirrel—first introduced to England in 1876 as a novelty species, now numbering some 2.5 million throughout the U.K.—is running the native red squirrel off its home turf. Red squirrels are now almost extinct in Wales and England, though they're hanging on in parts of Cumbria, Northumberland, and Scotland. It's not that grays are attacking the smaller, tufted-ear red squirrels—they simply evolved in a more competitive econiche.

Newborough Forest.

Reds spend up to 70% of their time up in trees, preferably conifers, and hate to cross open ground; grays spend 85% of their time foraging on the ground, like either deciduous or conifer woods, and will travel up to 2km without tree cover. As Britain's old-growth spruce and pine forests were increasingly replaced with oak trees (grays love acorns; reds can't digest them), the red squirrel was doomed. Fences replaced the protective foliage of hedgerows, so reds no longer had corridors to move from one woods to another. Opportunistic grays, who survive the winter by beefing up in autumn, raided the precious food caches red squirrels needed to get through winter. And the final blow: Grays carry a squirrelpox virus, which they're immune to, but which will kill a red squirrel in 2 weeks.

Red squirrels are still common throughout continental Europe (though grays released in Italy are beginning to repeat the U.K. scenario). But they're a woodland species particularly dear to Britons, and their plight has been watched anxiously. It's been illegal to import gray squirrels since 1930, but the damage was already done. It's been illegal to kill red squirrels since 1981, but that's not enough. They need more conifer forest havens, which is what they've found in the Newborough Forest, in Wales's Isle of Anglesey.

Isolated from the mainland by the Menai Strait, Anglesey began with an aggressive gray-squirrel extirpation program, and in 2004 reintroduced red squirrels—brought from Yorkshire, Cumbria, and Scotland, for a healthy genetic mix—to this 750-hectare (1,853-acre) forest park, where they'd been extinct since 1996. Newborough is mostly thick stands of Corsican pines, planted in the 1940s and 1950s to protect the wide beaches and coastal dunes of adjacent Llanddwyn Island. A number of walking trails lead into the dusky woods; as you stroll around, listen for the rustle of squirrels in the branches and look for nest boxes, built to enhance breeding rates, and feeders put out to supplement winter food caches.

At present Anglesey's red squirrel population has boomed to over 200—nearly half of all the red squirrels in Wales may now be on this one small island. But in late 2007, a new deadly virus killed three squirrels. Animal lovers are holding their breaths—will this Cinderella story end in tragedy?

---

ⓘ **Newborough Forest Reserve,** Newborough, Anglesey, Wales. Save Our Squirrels (www.saveoursquirrels.org.uk). **The Friends of the Anglesey Red Squirrels** (www.redsquirrels.info).

✈ Liverpool

🛏 $$ **Gazelle,** Glyn Garth, Menai Bridge (✆ **44/1248/713364**). $$$ **Tre-Ysgawen Hall,** off B5111, Rhosmeirch (✆ **44/1248 750750;** www.treysgawen-hall.co.uk).

# Regional Nature Park of Corsica
## *Welcome Home, Deer*
### Corsica

PEOPLE ARE THE BIGGEST THREAT TO CORSICA'S REGIONAL NATURE PARK. THE RAPID EXPANSION of tourism has sparked plans to build new parking lots and allow more motorized vehicles in the park. Even more troubling, professional arsonists have been setting fire to large sections of the park, hoping to receive permission to build on land that will take many years to recover.

It may be called the Corsican red deer, but since 1970 there weren't any more left on Corsica. There were 300 Corsican red deer, however, in a sanctuary on neighboring Sardinia. And so in 1985, two breeding pairs were shipped across the strait between the two islands, launching a great experiment: to restore the Corsican red deer to Corsica.

Nowadays as many as 150 Corsican red deer live on this large Mediterranean island off the coast of Italy (though officially it has been part of France since 1768). Carefully bred in special reserves in the Parc Naturel Regional du Corse, which covers almost 40% of the island's rugged interior, they are then released into the wild in increasing numbers. Smaller than most types of European red deer, the Corsican deer has shorter legs—the better to scramble up mountains, perhaps—as well as shorter antlers and a longer tail. If you want to get technical, they are an introduced species, having been brought to the island 8,000 years ago from North Africa by seafaring Phoenicians. But having evolved as a separate species from North African red deer (who are practically extinct themselves), they qualify as natives by now—all the more reason to make sure they live here.

In Corsica's Mediterranean climate—hot, dry summers and mild, rainy winters—the characteristic local terrain is maquis, a low shrubby growth of juniper, gorse, myrtle, and oleander mixed with a dizzying profusion of scented herbs: rosemary, thyme, lavender, marjoram. It's an aroma that native Corsicans (like Napoleon Bonaparte) never forget. But Corsica's mountainous interior also has forests more typical of northern Europe, especially old-growth evergreen oak forest (mostly holm oak and cork oak), the Corsican deer's preferred habitat, where they browse on fresh buds and branch tips.

Corsica's coastal lowlands were cleared long ago, however, and more recently grazing and logging have eaten into the mountain forests. Tourism is an important industry here, but most holidaymakers head for the Riviera-like beaches, or take scenic drives around the spectacular rugged coast; the idea of protecting those inland forests for eco-tourism has only recently taken hold. But with a well-developed system of long-distance hiking trails crisscrossing the island, Corsica's interior makes a great hiking area. Hiking is the prime way to spot the island's many endemic species—a rare mountain sheep known as the mouflon, the little Corsican nuthatch, a rare woodland salamander, and several small orchids and ferns. And, of course, the red deer—if you see one when you're out walking, welcome him home.

ⓘ **Parc Naturel Regional du Corse,** information office in Corte (✆ **33/4-95-46-26-70;** www.parc-naturel-corse.com)

✈ Ajaccio

🛏 $$$ **Les Roches Rouges,** Piana (✆ **33/4-95-27-81-81;** www.lesrochesrouges.com). $$ **Hotel Restaurant Beau Sejour,** Quartier Vaita, Porto (✆ **33/20-71-08-11-33**).

# The Laurissilva
## *The Laurel Trees That Got Away*
### Madeira, Portugal

THE LAURISSILVA FOREST ON MADEIRA IS THE LARGEST IN THE WORLD, HOME TO MANY UNIQUE plant species. The primary threats here are population growth and increasing tourism. Goats and cattle that once roamed the forest, damaging soil, trees, and other vegetation, have been removed from the park.

Eons ago, the whole Mediterranean basin was covered with forests like these—tall evergreen hardwoods, with a rich tangled understory of ferns and flowering shrubs. The bay laurels that most people know were just one part of it; virtually unheard-of variants such as Laurus azorica and Laurus novocanariensis grew everywhere. But as the region became more arid, these subtropical species simply vanished, withered up, and died. The only place they remained were here, in the humid climate of Portugal's Atlantic Islands—Madiera, the Canary Islands, and the Azores.

Settled by Portuguese sailors in the 15th century, Madeira—the largest island in its own little archipelago—is a resort spot, known for Madeira wine, exotic flowers, and beaches full of holidaymakers. Two-thirds of the island is a conservation area, however, with a thick band of primary laurel forest cutting a swath across the mountainous spine of the island's cloud-weathed interior. Covering some 150,000 sq. km (58,000 sq. miles), they occupy almost 20% of the total island, a much bigger area than the surviving bits on the Canaries or Azores, which have been whittled down by grazing and farming. Some 66 species here don't even occur in the other island's laurel forests, including some beautiful rare brushes and orchids.

Growing on steep slopes and down into deep ravines, these dense silvery forests with their fine-cut leaves are a remarkable sight. Gnarled trunks tip dramatically downhill as if yearning toward the sea. Cascading waterfalls and tiny lakes punctuate the forests, and frequent fog and rain keep these uplands moist, just like the trees like it. Rare mosses and lichens drape tree trunks and trail from their branches. Among the unusual birds you may see here are buzzards, kestrels, chaffinches, the long-toed Madeiran laurel pigeon, and the firecrest.

Many walking paths into the forest follow levadas, hand-built raised stone aqueducts unique to Madeira; it's a good idea to go with a guide so you don't miss the most picturesque spots. Striding through this ancient landscape is like visiting another world, far from the beaches and bars on the coast. Don't miss it.

✈ Funchal

🛏 $$$ **Madeira Palácio,** Estrada Monumental 265, Funchal (✆ **351/291/70-27-02;** www.hotelmadeirapalacio.com). $$ **Quintinha São João,** Rua da Levada de São João, Funchal (✆ **351/291/74-09-20;** www.quintinhasaojoao.com).

**TOUR Nature Meetings** (✆ **351/291/52-44-82;** www.naturemeetings.com). **Madeira Wind Birds** (✆ **351/291/09-80-07;** www.madeirawindbirds.com).

# Daintree Rainforest
## *Time Warp on the Queensland Coast*
### Queensland, Australia

Before the Daintree rainforest was a protected area, several sections were sold to private landowners. Some landowners are concerned about conservation and appreciative of the rainforest's environmental importance, others are lobbying for power lines, bridges, and fences that will endanger wildlife and forever alter this rare ecosystem.

It's like someone stopped the clock—135 million years ago. This prehistoric landscape of bizarre plants like giant strangler figs, fan palms, cycads, and epiphytes like the basket fern, staghorn, and elkhorn is unlike anyplace else on earth. It has some of the weirdest plants you'd ever want to see, including poisonous species like the idiot fruit, burrawang palm, and towering wild ginger; be careful while hiking not to snag your skin on the prickly wait-a-while vine or stinging tree. Approximately 430 species of birds live among the trees, including 13 species found nowhere else on earth. And then there's the iridiscent blue Ulysses butterfly flickering through the giant ferns—spot one of those and you'll feel like a portal just opened to another world.

Daintree's status is much less shaky than most other endangered rainforests. Its battle was launched way back in the 1980s, with conservationists seeking to evict a long-established timber industry from the old-growth forest. Perhaps the last straw was the 1983 building of a road along the coastal fringe from the Daintree River to Cooktown; though it's only a rough four-wheel-drive track, it still provides access to formerly untouched sections of the rainforest, and several parcels of land along the corridor were sold to private owners. Luckily, conservation-minded politicians were voted into office and successfully pursued World Heritage Site status for the Daintree rainforest, which has halted logging and mining activities. But there still remains the issue of what landowners will do with their rainforest acreage.

Most visitors take a guided day trip into the park out of Port Douglas, including certain common features: a 1.1km (.7-mile) hike along the boardwalk of the Marrdja Botanical Trail, a stroll along an isolated beach, a picnic lunch in a secluded rainforest glade (each tour guide has a favorite spot), a 1-hour croc-spotting cruise on the Daintree river, and a stop off to see the churning rapids at Mossman Gorge.

If you want to get a little deeper, try a more specialized naturalist guide. Get into some nitty-gritty bushwalking with **Heritage & Interpretive Tours** (© **07/4098 7897;** www.nqhit.com.au), see crocodiles by night with **Dan Irby's Mangrove**

An azure kingfisher at Daintree.

**Adventures** (℃ **07/4090 7017;** www. mangroveadventures.com.au), or focus on bird-watching (the Wet Tropics have more than half the bird species in Australia, including beauties like the azure kingfisher) with **Fine Feather Tours** (℃ **07/ 4094 1199;** www.finefeathertours.com. au). You may also want to supplement your rainforest excursion with a visit to the **Rainforest Habitat wildlife sanctuary** (℃ **07/4099 3235;** www.rainforesthabitat. com.au), where you're guaranteed a close-up of elusive exotics like bandicoots and musky rat kangaroos and sugar gliders and giant tree frogs; its aviary is a special

treat, where some 70 Wet Tropics varieties of birds squawk, flutter, and preen all around you.

ⓘ Visitor centers at Cape Tribulation (℃ **61/7/4098 0052)** and Mossman Gorge (℃ **61/7/4098 2188).**

✈ Cairns

🛏 $$$ **Daintree Eco Lodge & Spa,** 20 Daintree Rd., Daintree (℃ **61/7/4098 6100;** www.daintree-ecolodge.com.au). $$ **Marae,** Lot 1, Chook's Ridge, Shannonvale (℃ **61/7/4098 4900;** www.marae. com.au).

---

### 143  Into the Woods

# Białowieża Forest
## *The Bison Will Abide*
### Poland/Belarus

AIR POLLUTION, INVASIVE SPECIES, A NEARBY RAILWAY LINE THAT CARRIES TOXIC CHEMICALS, and land reclamation projects that have upset the region's hydrological balance threaten this forest. Only about 8% of it lies within a strictly protected national park. Commercial logging is allowed in other parts of the forest, however, leading conservationists to fear that the remaining old-growth forest could be gone within 10 years.

It's all about the bison.

The big-shouldered European bison was a major game animal in this ancient forest, back when it was the royal hunting ground of the kings of Poland. (The name Białowieża, or "White Tower," refers to a hunting manor of 15th-century King Jagiello.) In 1541 the forest was made a hunting reserve to protect bison, although when Russia took over and the tsar divided the forest among his nobles, hunters overran it and cut the bison population to less than 200. But Tsar Alexander I declared it a reserve again in 1801, and the number of bison climbed to 700; in 1888, the Romanovs made it a royal retreat, sending bison as gifts to various European capitals while importing deer, elk, and other game animals for their hunting pleasure. Then came 1917 and the Russian Revolution; soon the tsars themselves were extinct.

German occupation in World War I ravaged the forest, and the last bison was killed in January 1919, 1 month before the Polish army swept back in.

Undaunted, in 1929 the Polish government bought four European bison from various zoos (the world population was down to about 54 individuals), bred them in captivity, and eventually reintroduced them to the forest, now a national park. Since then the bison have thrived, with over 300 today in the Polish section alone. The Poland-Belarus border runs through the forest, marked with a security fence that divides Poland's purebred bison from Belarus' hybrid bison and keeps them genetically isolated.

It's difficult for foreign tourists to visit the Belarus section, however, which requires permission from the ministry of interior in Brest. On the Polish side, though, the heart of the park is a strictly controlled area of 4,747 hectares (11,730 acres), viewable only by guided tour, though there are walking trails through an adjacent area that's only slightly less pristine. (There's also an adjacent reserve where you can see European bison, Polish tarpan ponies, elk, deer, roe-deer, wild boars, and wolves.) Thanks to 6 centuries of protection as a hunting preserve, the core zone contains relict habitats of the primeval forest that once covered Europe—sandy spruce-pine woods, peat bogs, lowmoor, oak-hornbeam-linden forest, alder and ash woods along the Howźna and Narewka rivers, and hollows of swampy alders. You'll see a number of massive ancient oak trees, each given its own name. Several of them are dead or dying, but that just makes them great

hosts for the hermit-beetle or the white-backed woodpecker.

It's only fitting that the remnant population of bison should live here. No tree in this area has ever been cut down by man; no tree was ever planted by man. It's not a restored forest, it's the original forest—how rare is that?

ⓘ **Białowieża National Park,** 17-230 Białowieża, Park Pałacowy 11 (✆ **48/85/ 682-9700;** www.bpn.com.pl)

✈ Warsaw

🚆 Bialystock

🛏 $$$ **Best Western Hotel Zubrowka,** 6 Olgi Gabiec St., Białowieża (✆ **48/85/681- 2303;** www.bestwestern.com). $$ **Hotel Bialowieski,** 218B Waszkiewicza, Białowieża (✆ **48/85/681-2022**).

---

Into the Woods **144**

# The Cedars of Lebanon
## *Grove of the Gods*
### Bsharre, Lebanon

FREQUENT ARMED CONFLICTS AND CONTINUING POLITICAL UNREST IN THE MIDDLE EAST threaten to place the remaining ancient Cedars of Lebanon squarely in the crossfire. Meanwhile, the most famous Lebanese cedars, those in the grove at Bsharre, are crowding each other, competing for sunlight, and achieving very little natural reproduction.

It takes ages to grow a cedar. But that's how long this grove has stood here, the last vestige of a primeval forest of cedar, cypress, pine, and oak that once covered Mount Lebanon. It was famous already in biblical times, a source of wood for Phoenician ships; Egyptians used cedar resin to embalm mummies, Moses directed Jewish priests to use its bark to cure leprosy, and both King Solomon and King David ordered cedar beams from here to build their famous temples in Jerusalem. In the Epic of Gilgamesh, this was the dwelling of the gods.

The Roman Emperor Hadrian had stone markers laid out to protect the forest, which has aided archaeologists in measuring its

original vastness. But as the Dark Ages and Middle Ages passed, villagers felled trees to fuel their kilns and cleared the land for farming. Nineteenth-century Ottoman troops removed a great deal of forest cover, and the occupying British army in World War II cut cedar railroad ties for a railway to Tripoli. All that's left is a few isolated patches in hard-to-reach mountain areas—and this grove, the oldest of them all, the famous Arz el Rab (Cedars of the Lord) in Bsharre, set above the dramatic Qadisha valley in a sheltered glacial pocket on Mount Makmel.

About 4km (2¹/₂ miles) up a twisting road from the village of Bsharre, Arz El Rab still has some aged 375 cedars, enclosed by a high stone wall built in 1876 by Queen Victoría to preserve the historic remnant. At least four of them are nearly 35m (115 ft.) high, which is tall for a cedar, with great spreading crowns of dark-green evergreen needles. Interspersed among them are several thousand young trees, planted over the past 30 years to revitalize the grove. But a cedar may not even produce fertile seed cones until it is 40 years old, and the wall is necessary to keep free-roaming goats from nibbling on young saplings. Even more beneficial is a new scheme to create a cedar plantation outside the wall, since the trees already grow so close together that the saplings don't get enough light. A healthy new stand of trees could be the first step in turning this little grove back into a full-fledged forest.

Since 1985, conservationists have been fertilizing, pruning, spraying pests, and eliminating widespread tree rot. They have laid out new walkways so that visitors don't wander at will, carving their initials on the trunks and trampling the vegetation under the trees. That vegetation is vital to protect new growth and to attract more birds (the grove is dangerously low in bird life), who could help kill tree-boring insects. They've even installed lightning rods so that no more trees are lost before those youngsters have time—oh, say, a century or two—to catch up.

ⓘ **Arz el Rab** (✆ **961/6/672 562,** May–Oct)

✈ Beirut

🛏 $$ **Hotel St. Bernard,** Arz el Rab (✆ **961/6/678 100**). $$ **Hotel Chbat,** Rue Gibran, Bsharre (✆ **961/6/672 672**; www. hotelchbat.com).

## 145 Into the Woods

# Michoacán Monarch Biosphere Reserve
### *Butterflies Are Free—and Homeless?*
#### Near Morelia, Mexico

MONARCH BUTTERFLIES FACE A VARIETY OF RISKS ALL ALONG THEIR 2,000-MILE (3,220KM) migration route between Canada and Mexico. Pesticides are a constant threat, and the monarchs' low tolerance for cold and wet conditions leave them vulnerable to winter storms, increased rainfall, and other climate changes. Meanwhile, deforestation of their winter habitat could be the fatal blow for the butterflies.

If anyone gave a prize for long-distance migration, monarch butterflies would clearly win. Their yearly autumn trek is over 2,000 miles (3,220-km)—pretty amazing considering that not a single individual in the immense swarm has ever flown the route before. (After all, they were hatched only a few weeks earlier.) And yet, without a GPS system, they head unerringly for the same nesting grounds high in the mountains of northeast Michoacán, Mexico, where their ancestors have overwintered since time immemorial.

But the fate of the species hangs on the fate of those nesting grounds—and right now, things are looking dismal. Relentless logging of the surrounding pine and oyamel (fir) forests is gobbling up the monarchs' habitat at a fearsome rate. Living close to the poverty line, the local loggers—*los ejidatarios*—use cheap methods that completely strip the mountainsides. With denuded mountain slopes surrounding the Michoacan Monarch Biosphere Reserve, 45% of the nearby forest canopy has degraded over the past 30 years. Without the protection of a healthy microclimate, a severe winter storm in January 2002 killed 75% to 80% of the monarch butterfly population. In 2001, the first steps were taken when Mexican President Vicente Fox established the Monarch Trust to protect the monarchs' winter home, but much still needs to be done. Without a long-term reforestation program, these glorious black-and-orange wonders could cease to exist forever.

The ancient Aztecs revered these poisonous butterflies, which they believed were the reborn spirits of fallen warriors, dressed in battle colors. (Note that the first butterflies tend to arrive on Nov 1, Los Dias de Los Muertos—the Day of the Dead.) Stepping into a grove of monarch-laden fir trees is like stepping into a kaleidoscope, with fragments of obsidian and gold flitting randomly around you. The branches on all sides actually sway under the weight of the butterflies, their gossamer wings whispering softly as the wind blows through the forest.

There are actually seven monarch nesting grounds in Michoacán (nesting season lasts from mid-Nov to Mar). Only two, however, are open to the public: **El Rosario** and **Chincua,** both reachable by day trip from the colonial-era city of Morelia, about halfway between Mexico City and Guadalajara. It is possible to visit the sanctuaries on your own, but a licensed English-speaking guide is a worthwhile investment—they can answer scientific questions, transport you reliably over the back roads to the sanctuary, and steer you right to the nucleus of the butterfly colony, which constantly shifts around the mountain throughout the season. Guided butterfly excursions take 10 to 12 hours, usually providing lunch. Several English-speaking guides can be contacted through a cooperative called **Mex Mich Guías** (www.mmg.com.mx).

---

ⓘ **Michoacán Monarch Biosphere Reserve,** near Angangueo and Ocampo, Mexico

✈ Morelia

🛏 $$$ **Villa Montaña** Patzimba 201, col. Vista Bella, Morelia (✆ **800/223-6510** or 443/314-0231; www.villamontana.com. mx). $$ **Best Western Hotel Casino,** Portal Hidalgo 229, Morelia (✆ **800/528-1234** or 443/313-1328; www.hotelcasino. com.mx).

## Into the Woods 146

# The Monteverde Cloud Forest
## *A Mountaintop Jungle*
### Monteverde, Costa Rica

THE MONTEVERDE CLOUD FOREST IS A BREATHTAKING NATURAL SETTING, AND HOME TO several rare and endangered species. Protecting and preserving the cloud forest is partly a matter of protecting the surrounding environment, and Costa Rica has made a strong commitment to that goal through careful land and water management and reforestation.

The steep, rutted dirt road passes through mile after mile of dry, brown pasturelands—a landscape that was once verdant forest, until humans entered the picture. All the more reason to appreciate what you find at the top of the mountain: a lush, tangled swath of greenery, where orchids and ferns trail from the treetops while monkeys chatter, tree frogs croak, and hummingbirds hum. Monteverde means "green mountain," and there couldn't be a better name for it. Walking here in the early morning mist with the whispering of leaves and disembodied bird calls all around can be an almost out-of-body experience.

Cloud forests are always on mountaintops, where moist warm air sweeping up the slopes from a nearby ocean condenses swiftly in the higher elevation, forming clouds around the summit. The clouds, in turn, condense moisture on the forest trees, giving rise to an incredible diversity of life forms—Monteverde boasts more than 2,500 plants species, 400 bird species, and 100 different mammal species. It's pretty hard to resist the option of a canopy tour, where you can zip around harnessed to an overhead cable, going from platform to platform high above the forest floor in the treetops, where two-thirds of the species live. Two good operations are **Sky Trek** (⟨✆⟩ **506/645-5238;** www.skytrek.com) and **Selvatura Park** (⟨✆⟩ **506/645-5929;** www.selvatura.com), both located outside the reserve near the town of Santa Elena.

Monteverde is no secret, and its main trails are often crowded with eco-tourists, all gaping (generally without any luck) to see rare and elusive species like the quetzal with its 2-foot-long (.6m) tail feathers. The density of the cloud forest, however, makes it possible to escape the crowds, once you branch off the central paths. Book a guided tour through your hotel, which will also reserve your admission (only 120 people at a time are allowed inside the reserve); the guide will be able to identify far more of the flora and fauna than you could spot on your own. Slightly less crowded than the Monteverde Reserve but with much the same flora and fauna, the **Santa Elena Cloud Forest Reserve** (⟨✆⟩ **506/645-5390**) may be a good alternative.

ⓘ **Monteverde Biological Cloud Forest Preserve** (⟨✆⟩ **506/645-5122;** www.cct.or.cr)

✈ Juan Santamaria International, San José

🛏 $$ **Monteverde Lodge** (⟨✆⟩ **506/257-0766** in San José or 506/645-5057 in Monteverde; www.costaricaexpeditions.com). $$ **Hotel El Establo** (⟨✆⟩ **506/645-5110;** www.elestablo.com).

**147** Into the Woods

# Gunung Leuser National Park
## *Paradise Lost*
### Sumatra, Indonesia

LOGGING, ROAD CONSTRUCTION, AND PALM-OIL PLANTATIONS EAT AWAY AT GUNUNG LEUSER National Park in Indonesia, one of the world's largest remaining tropical rainforests and most diverse wildlife habitats. Global warming is also a growing threat, because island nations like Indonesia will be among the first to feel the effects of rising sea levels.

It used to be the epitome of a tropical rainforest paradise—Sumatra, the large Indonesian island across the Strait of Malacca from Singapore. But in the last century, Sumatra went from 16 million hectares (40 million acres) of lowland rainforest to only 2.2 million hectares (5.5 million acres). Now it's down even further, to about 800,000 hectares (2 million acres). To be honest, mostly all that's left is Gunung Leuser National Park, which spreads like a pair of gasping lungs across the center of the island.

Formed in the mid-1990s out of several smaller reserves and parks, Gunung Leuser is truly a land of wonders. It's the only place in the world where viable populations of orangutans, tigers, rhinos, elephants, and clouded leopards live in the same region. The iconic rainforest bird, the helmeted hornbill, with its colorful long curved beak, builds its nests in the top of the tallest trees. The planet's largest flower—the Rafflesia arnoldi, a 1m-wide (3-ft.) red-brown bloom—as well as the planet's tallest flower, the weirdly phallic 1.9m-high (6-ft.) Amorphophallus titanium, both grow here naturally, sharing one memorable characteristic: They both smell so bad that they're nicknamed "the corpse flower."

Many visitors enter the park through the bustling tourist village of **Bukit Lawang,** where a fascinating orangutan rehabilitation sanctuary is open to the public. The Bohorek River flooded out this village in 2003, but it was quickly rebuilt; tubing on the river rapids is a popular activity. To trek into the park you must hire a guide, several of which tout in the streets of Bukit Lawang. Hikers with guides may also enter through **Ketembe.** Passing through the park, you may not see orangutans, elephants, or rhinos in the wild—and you probably don't want to meet a Sumatran tiger, though there are more than 100 of them here. But you'll certainly see lots of noisy gibbons, beautiful birds, chattering waterfalls, and bright tropical blooms amid lush green foliage.

Saving this rainforest is not going to be easy. The trees most often cut down are the big ones, the ones that don't produce seeds until they're 30 or 40 years old—many now are cut before they have a chance to leave seedlings behind. Such activities on the outskirts of the park whittle away habitats, disrupting animals' migratory patterns and mating grounds, and forcing them into the core of the park. Though the park was spared from the devastation of the 2004 tsunami, demand for Gunung Leuser's timber spiked when the tsunami-leveled town of Banda Aceh needed rebuilding.

It's not just about preserving land for rare animals and plants, or even because the rainforest ensures a clean water supply for the people of Sumatra. As one of the world's largest remaining rainforests, Gunung Leuser plays a vital role in counteracting greenhouse gases. Every hour, Indonesia loses another patch of jungle the size of 300 soccer fields. Our planet can't afford for it to go on like this.

✈ Medan

🛏 $$ **Jungle Inn,** Bukit Lawang. $$ **Back to Nature Guesthouse,** Bukit Lawang.

---

Into the Woods **148**

# Wollemi National Park
## *The World's Rarest Tree*
### Blue Mountains, Australia

THE WOLLEMI PINE HAS SURVIVED FOR 200 MILLION YEARS—BUT JUST BARELY. ONLY 23 trees still exist in the wild. To help ensure their preservation, private companies are now allowed to grow seedlings and sell them to gardeners and horticulturists all over the world. But the location of the wild trees is kept secret for their own protection.

Colored a hazy blue by sunlight glancing off of evaporating droplets of oil from the ever-present eucalyptus trees, the Blue Mountains are weird enough. But in the middle of it all is the ultimate weirdness: the world's rarest tree, a throwback to the Jurassic Age that exists only in one remote gorge in this rambling mountain park.

The Wollemi pine has been extinct for 30 million years—at least, that's what scientists thought until 1994, when three small stands were discovered in a hidden pocket of coachwood-sassafras rainforest. Soaring 35m (115 ft.) high, they have waxy leaves of a exotic lime-green color and pebbly cocoa-brown bark. Promptly nicknamed the "dinosaur tree," this species seems identical to trees recorded in Jurassic age fossils, but not in any later fossils. As a casual visitor you won't be able to see the Wollemi pines—access is strictly controlled, and the location of the canyon is kept secret by park management. Disappointing as this may be for tourists, it's all for the good of the trees. Botanists who are granted access for research purposes may one day be able to propagate new Wollemi pines for the rest of the world to enjoy.

Besides, a park that has Wollemi pines is bound to have other unusual and rare things to see. There's the *banksias conferta subsp. penicillata,* a rare endemic mountain shrub with a brushy cylindrical yellow flower. Along with koalas, wombats, and platypus, unusual-even-for-Australia species frolic about like the brush-tailed rock wallaby and the glossy black cockatoo. Near the old oil shale mine at Wolgan (the park contains a handful of such industrial ghost towns), an abandoned railway tunnel is eerily illuminated even in daytime by a population of glow-worms. Impressive geological formations like gorges, cliffs, caves, and steep sandstone escarpments make this one of the most rugged parks you'll ever see, with three rivers—the Wolgan, the Colo, the Capertee—carving through the wilderness. (Only the Colo is navigable by canoe or kayak, and then only in high water; canoeists can, however, paddle around atmospheric Dunns Swamp.) Most visitors venture only a short way into this huge park, but long-distance hikers and rock-climbers can really get into untrammeled wilderness.

Perhaps the most impressive experience of all is tramping through an unbroken stretch of forest dominated by eucalyptus trees, constituting almost 90% of the park. (No wonder koalas like to hang out here.) It's anything but monotonous, with 70 different eucalyptus species represented. Take time to note the differences in their barks and evergreen leaves and flowers as you walk around, and to inhale deeply their distinctive fragrance. No wonder the Blue Mountains look so blue!

✈ Sydney (129km/80 miles)

🛏 $$$ **Mercure Grand Hydro Majestic Hotel,** Medlow Bath (✆ **61/2/4788 1002;** www.hydromajestic.com.au). $$ **Jemby-Rinjah Lodge,** 336 Evans Lookout Rd., Blackheath (✆ **61/2/4787 7622;** www.jembyrinjahlodge.com.au).

**149** Into the Woods

# The Mabi Forest
## *Hang with the Tree Kangaroos*
### Yungaburra, Australia

LOGGING AND DEVELOPMENT OVER THE YEARS HAS LEFT THIS CRITICALLY ENDANGERED ECOSYSTEM severely fragmented, disrupting ecological processes such as seed dispersal and opening the door to invasive species that degrade wildlife habitat. An integrated government recovery program now offers the best opportunity to protect, rehabilitate, and, perhaps, expand the Mabi Forest.

Seen one Australian rainforest and you've seen them all, right? Think again. The Mabi forest is a whole other deal, a sun-filtered forest with a riot of exotic vines and shrubs and giant ferns covering the forest floor.

The leaves here grow so big and nutritious, it's a favored hangout for tree-hugging mammals like possums and tree kangaroos (*mabi* is the Aboriginal name for the local tree kangaroo). And birds? It has more different avian species than any other spot in the Wet Tropics, 114 different honeyeaters and kingfishers and bowerbirds and cuckoos, not to mention the chowchilla and the laughing kookaburra.

But soon—very soon—we may have to speak of the Mabi forest in the past tense. Only about 2% is left of the forest that once blanketed this tableland southeast of Cairns, and even that consists mostly of leafy fragments. Roads and clearings have sliced up the habitat and trapped its animals in tiny redoubts, threatened by invasive weeds and feral dogs from neighboring settlements. Two of its most typical residents, cassowary birds and musky rat kangaroos, have already fled elsewhere. The spectacled flying-fox and ring-tailed possum may be next.

The largest extant chunk of Mabi forest lies in 270-hectare (667-acre) Curtain Fig National Park. An elevated boardwalk leads visitors into the forest, so you can look down into the thick tangled understory and get close-up views of the canopy trees' buttress roots and woody lianas. Look up and you'll notice that the canopy in a Mabi forest isn't one impenetrable green ceiling but a varied skylight of evergreen and semi-deciduous treetops of different heights. White cedars and red cedars predominate (extensive logging of the red cedar was mainly responsible for this forest's destruction), but there's an astonishing variety of other unusual trees, including incensewood, candlenut, and black bean trees along with bollywood, satinash, and silky oak. If you're here in the dry season, you'll also notice a carpet of fallen leaves; the Mabi forest gets less moisture than other Wet Tropics rainforests and has adapted by including more deciduous trees.

It's only a 10-minute walk to the star attraction, a 500-year-old fig tree almost 50m (164 ft.) tall, skirted with an immense curtain of aerial roots that drop 15m (50 ft.) to the forest floor. This fig actually began life in the canopy, then grew vertical roots that over centuries strangled its host tree. The host tree rotted away and, voilá! a free-standing fig tree, with a thick trunk of interwoven roots.

The woods really begin to rustle and chatter after dark; come back at night armed with a special spotlight (get details at the information shelter) and you may be able to spot rare nocturnal creatures like the tree kangaroo or the large-eared Northern bat. After that, crocodiles may seem old-hat.

---

ⓘ **Curtain Fig National Park,** Atherton-Yungaburra Rd., Yungaburra (✆ **61/13/0013 0372;** www.treat.net.au)

✈ Cairns

🛏 $$ **Chambers Rainforest Lodge,** Lake Eacham, Atherton Tableland (✆ **61/7/4095 3754;** http://rainforest-australia.com). $ **Atherton Rainforest Motor Inn,** Kennedy Hwy. and Simms Rd., Atherton (✆ **61/7/4095 4141;** www.rainforestmotorinn.com.au).

**Mountain Dwellers** **150**

# Shenandoah National Park
## *The Bear Necessities*
### Skyline Drive, Virginia

AIR POLLUTION FROM FACTORIES AND POWER PLANTS IN THE MIDWEST AND MID-ATLANTIC states poses a serious threat to Shenandoah National Park, poisoning streams and killing or weakening trees, ferns, and other plants throughout the park, which are crucial to the black bears and other species that have returned to this park.

Black bear cubs at Shenandoah.

What's a North American forest without black bears? Some people fear them, others think they're cute and cuddly (a dangerous assumption). But however you picture them, these large furry trophy animals are part of our national mythology, as iconic as Davy Crockett and Teddy Roosevelt. There used to be two million black bears padding around North America before the Europeans came, but by the early 1900s, their numbers had dwindled to a tenth of that. They'd vanished completely from the eastern Blue Ridge, though a few still prowled around the Alleghany Mountains to the west.

But set aside a big enough chunk of land and even the large mammals, who need a fair amount of territory, will roam back. The American bison hasn't returned to Shenandoah National Park, but bobcats, black bears, and cougars have (not to mention the wily coyote, who isn't even native to Virginia). Along with them came the beaver, the river otter, and the white-tailed deer, happy to range again in a wide area of mixed forestland.

Black bears top the food chain in Shenandoah National Park, where they're the only bear species (no nasty grizzlies to compete with). The first bear returnees were sighted in 1937, right after Shenandoah was created, and once the restored hardwood forests were mature enough to produce acorns, the bears' numbers zoomed into the hundreds. You're likely to see one from May to October (they spend the winter in dens), concentrated on lower south-facing slopes in spring until things warm up. Bears are most active at dawn or dusk, but you might see them anytime. Bears are good for the environment: Though they eat smaller animals, they also like berries, acorns, and fruits, thereby dispersing seeds in their droppings; tearing apart decayed logs in search of insects, they speed the decomposition process that makes forest soil rich. Though cubs have a 20% mortality rate, carried off by hawks or coyotes mostly, adults tend to live for 30 years. Nobody preys on the adults, except for humans with guns—and hunting is forbidden in Shenandoah National Park.

Shenandoah is a long strip of park along the Skyline Drive, where many visitors come in cars, pull off at overlooks, and then drive on. A number of short, easy trails are accessible directly from the drive, like the 1.8-mile (3km) Story of the Forest Trail (a great hands-on seminar in forest succession), the 1.3-mile (2km) Limberlost Trail, with its profusion of mountain laurels in spring, or the 1.3-mile (2km) Frazier Discovery Trail. The 4-mile (6.4km) Rose River Loop gets you into more wilderness, and longer trails along Hawksbill Mountain and the Whiteoak Canyon are even more challenging. White-tailed deer, eastern cottontails, gray squirrels, and opossums are common sightings; even if you don't meet an actual bear, you may come across its droppings or tracks. Look for claw marks on tree trunks or ripped-open tree trunks.

---

ⓘ **Shenandoah National Park,** Dickey Ridge visitor center, Mile 4.6, Skyline Dr. **Harry F. Byrd visitor center,** Mile 51, Skyline Dr. (✆ **540/999-3500;** www.nps. gov/shen).

✈ Washington Dulles or Charlottesville

🛏 $$ **Big Meadow Lodge,** Mile 51.2, Skyline Dr.; $$ **Lewis Mountain Cabins,** Mile 57.5, Skyline Dr. (for both ✆ **800/ 999-4714** or 540/743-5108; www.visit shenandoah.com/lodging-dining/index. cfm, Apr–Oct)

**Mountain Dwellers** **151**

# Yellowstone National Park

## *A Grizzly Scene*

### Northwest Wyoming

YELLOWSTONE NATIONAL PARK HAS HAD REMARKABLE SUCCESS IN RESCUING ENDANGERED species from the brink of extinction—particularly grizzly bears and gray wolves—but many conservationists believe both species were taken off the endangered species list too soon and still face serious risks.

You'll want to bring a telephoto lens, or at least a pair of binoculars, because Yellowstone's signature endangered species—the grizzly bear, the bald eagle, the wolf—aren't necessarily animals you want to get too close to. In fact, it's against park regulations to get within 75 feet (23m) of any park animals, or within 300 feet (90m) of a bear. Don't even think of feeding them.

Most tourists make a beeline for the Lower Loop Road, where Old Faithful geyser spouts every 90 minutes, or for the spectacularly colored rocks of Mammoth Hot Springs just inside the north entrance. But the less traveled road east from Mammoth across the top of the park takes you through some prime wildlife viewing country—the Blacktail Plateau Drive loop, for example, or the road through the deep Lamar Valley. This northern range is full of hoofed grazing animals—elk, moose, bison,

pronghorn antelopes, deer, and bighorn sheep—perhaps 40,000 of them, who even migrate north out of the park as the summer progresses, searching for fresh pasture. Back in the 1960s, rangers culled the elk herd, worried that they were overgrazing this territory; one of the reasons for reintroducing the gray wolf to Yellowstone was to keep the population of grazers in check. New wildlife management policies, however, tend to let the herd's numbers adjust by natural processes. (Elk actually make the soil more fertile, tilling it with their sharp hooves and returning nutrients to the soil via feces and urine.) Another good area is the Hayden Valley, which lies west of the Tower-Yellowstone Lake road, south of Artist Point—it's prime grizzly habitat.

Put on your hiking boots and strike out away from the roads. Trails are well marked, and the hiking terrain tends to be

Bison at Yellowstone National Park.

**Washburn** rewards you with a 10,243-feet-high (3,122m) view over much of Yellowstone—and close-ups of bighorn sheep.

To go deeper into the woods, contact the **Yellowstone Backcountry Office** (✆ 307/344-2160) to get a permit; the backcountry season runs mid-June to the end of August. Trails around the backcountry's Shoshone Lake yield moose viewing, but the real treat is the 14-mile (23km) **Sportsman Lake Trail,** a day-long hike that passes through sagebrush plateaus full of elk and a meadow popular with moose. Early morning and dusk are the best times for spotting wildlife—a very good reason to camp in the park or stay at an in-park lodge, so you can snag those precious sightings.

moderate; it only takes a mile or so before you feel gloriously alone with the wildlife. Near Yellowstone Lake, 2-mile (3.2km) Storm Point trail is so popular with grizzlies, it's sometimes closed in spring, when they've just come out of hibernation. Off the Mammoth-Norris road near Liberty Cap, the 5-mile (8km) Beaver Ponds Loop offers views of moose as well as beavers. The 6-mile (9.6km) round-trip hike up **Mount**

ⓘ **Yellowstone National Park** (✆ 307/344-7381; www.nps.gov/yell)

✈ West Yellowstone Airport or Yellowstone Regional Airport, Cody, WY

🛏 $$ **Mammoth Hot Springs Hotel** (✆ 307/344-7311; www.travelyellowstone.com). $ **Madison Hotel,** 139 Yellowstone Ave., West Yellowstone (✆ 800/838-7745 or 406/646-7745).

**Mountain Dwellers**

**152**

# Great Sand Dunes National Park
## *The Colorado Dune Buggy*
### Southern Colorado

THESE REMARKABLE GIANT SAND DUNES CONTINUE TO BE RESHAPED AND REBUILT BY RESTLESS winds from the surrounding mountains. Home to several unique species found nowhere else, the Great Sand Dunes National Park is a harsh but fragile environment. Global warming and ongoing drought in the American West could push some species here beyond the breaking point.

It's right there on the map—Colorado, a landlocked state. So how can it have a park full of sand dunes?

These towering light brown dunes—the tallest in North America—were formed by southwesterly winds blowing across the San Luis Valley, where eroded glacial rock and silt were deposited by mountain streams onto a sandy valley floor. Reversing winds from the mountains piled the sand even higher, making them up to 750 feet (229m) high and unbelievably steep.

Such a bizarre isolated habitat is bound to attract an unusual species or two,

Great Sand Dunes National Park.

animals that aren't suited to the surrounding Rocky Mountain ecosystems and are too far away from the ocean to reach other sand dunes. There's the Ord's kangaroo rat, for instance, a long-tailed gerbil-sized rodent that never drinks water, getting its moisture instead from grasses and seeds that it stores in the moist sand below the dune surface. (It also has very efficient kidneys.) Somehow the kangaroo rat, usually found only in low deserts, can tolerate the huge range of temperatures up here, going from summer highs of 140°F (60°C) to 20 below zero (–29°C) on a winter night. Its long back feet enable it to leap like a kangaroo 5 feet (1.5m) in the air to escape any predators that wander onto the dunes.

The kangaroo rat is the dunes' only resident mammal, but several insects found nowhere else on earth also thrive. Some are so tiny you can't see them, but you should be able to spot the predatory Great Sand Dunes tiger beetle, a half-inch-long scavenger with a sharply marked brown-and-tan carapace, and an even larger omnivorous insect called the giant sand treader camel cricket, a brown-striped cricket an inch and a half long with special horny scoops on its hind legs that help it to push out of loose sliding sand. They are most active on the face of the sand dunes at night, illuminated by brilliant

desert moonlight. There are no designated trails on the dunes, so you can simply wander at will; you can even camp out in the dunes, outside of the day use area (ask rangers for directions). Be prepared for windy conditions, though—the winds that formed these sand dunes are still at work.

Bird-watchers head for the forested Montville or Mosca Pass trails, where you can see all sorts of colorful birds—black-headed grosbeaks, white-throated swifts, violet-green swallows, yellow-rumped warblers, and broad-tailed hummingbirds. There are even some wetland birds here, believe it or not—Medano Creek flows along the base of the dunes in spring and summer—and both bald and golden eagles have been sighted in the alpine highlands. To find everything from alpine peaks to sand dunes in one park—that in itself is pretty amazing.

ⓘ **Great Sand Dunes National Park,** Alamosa, CO (℃ **719/378-6399;** www. nps.gov/grsa)

✈ Alamosa San Luis Valley

🛏 $$ **Cottonwood Inn,** 123 San Juan Ave., Alamosa (℃ **800/955-2623** or 719/ 589-3882). $ **Best Western Alamosa Inn,** 1919 Main St. (℃ **800/459-5123** or 719/589-2567; www.bestwestern.com).

# Mount Rainier National Park
## *Flood Cascades Through the Cascades*
### Washington State

BETWEEN 1913 AND 1994, MOUNT RAINIER'S GLACIERS LOST NEARLY 25% OF THEIR VOLUME due to rising temperatures and decreasing snowfall. Massive flooding occurred in 2006 when the park received 18 inches (46cm) of rain in only 36 hours, forcing rangers to close the park for the first time since nearby Mount St. Helens erupted in 1980.

You can see Mount Rainier from the Puget Sound ferries, a snow-capped dormant volcano looming like a backdrop to the Seattle skyline, towering above the rest of the Cascades range. Landscapes just don't come more dramatic than this. Jagged basaltic lava rocks lie tumbled in the beds of mountain streams pouring crystal-clear waters off of Rainier's glaciers; elk march across high tableland meadows drenched with sunlight; down along the Ohanapecosh River, an awe-inspiring grove of immense ancient Douglas firs and western red cedars casts a serene cool shade.

It's a big park, so of course it has a lot of wildlife—mountain goats, black-tailed deer, elk, cougars, black bears, the whole mountain crew. Since hunting is prohibited, over the years since Rainier was made a national park, way back in 1899, the animals have largely lost their fear of humans. Pull out your binoculars to see mountain goats (which are, technically speaking, antelopes, not goats) scamper from rock to rock on Goat Island Mountain, on Mount Fremont, and at Skyscraper Pass, all reachable on trails leading from Sunrise Point. Hike through a flowered subalpine meadow and you'll see playful marmots—big, shaggy cousins to squirrels—loll on the rocks, catching some rays, seemingly oblivious to human observers. While you're up there, you may even be able to catch a glimpse of the somewhat shyer pikas, tiny rabbit relatives that inhabit rocky talus slopes. If you don't see them, you may at least hear their strange high-pitched beeping call.

There's always been the threat of Rainier erupting to worry about, though vulcanologists estimate it'll be another 500 years before Rainier's set to blow its top again. But disaster can strike at any time, as we were reminded in the fall of 2006, when a massive flood washed out several park roads, trails, campgrounds, power lines, service buildings, and one visitor center, especially in the flood-prone northwestern corner of the park. Creeks carved entirely new channels, sweeping boulders

Mount Rainier National Park.

in their path, mature trees were torn up by the roots, and mud and debris was littered everywhere.

Most of the damage was to man-made park features, however; the animals seemed to adjust and go on as always. The park completely closed down for 6 months for major repair work, but roads were all reopened within a year, though several backcountry trails and campsites remained closed as of spring 2008. (The 93-mile/150km **Wonderland Trail loop,** which circles the park and connects to many trail heads, reopened August 2007.) It was a sobering reminder that dramatic landscapes are often formed by dramatic natural events. These areas have flooded before; they'll flood again. It's nature's way.

---

(i) **Mount Rainier National Park,** Nisqually-Longmire Rd., Ashford, WA (© **360/568-2211;** www.nps.gov/mora)

✈ Seattle

🛏 $$$ **Paradise Inn,** near Paradise visitor center inside park (© **360/569-2275;** www.guestservices.com/rainier). $$ **Stone Creek Lodge,** 38624 Washington 706 E., Ashford (© **800/678-3942** or 360/569-2355).

## Mountain Dwellers 154

# Rocky Mountain National Park
## *The Saga of the Elk*
### Estes Park, Colorado

ROCKY MOUNTAIN NATIONAL PARK, DEFINED BY EXTREME COLD AND ABUNDANT SNOW, encloses the largest and most accessible expanse of alpine tundra in the lower 48 states. Global warming, which is creating warmer and drier conditions in the Rockies, could degrade the tundra and threaten cold-weather plants and animals.

First the elk were there, then they weren't. Then they were again.

In the old days, herds of North American elk happily roamed this part of the Colorado range, straddling the Continental Divide at altitudes of 8,000 feet (2,400m) and up. But intensive hunting had slashed their population so low by 1913 that the US Forest Service "borrowed" 49 elk from Yellowstone to release here. Meanwhile efforts were made to eliminate the elks' main predators, grizzly bears and gray wolves. The elk population rebounded—and how.

Drive along Rocky Mountain National Park's most spectacular route, the 48-mile (77km) Trail Ridge Road that bisects the park east to west, and you'll be cruising through gnarled alpine tundra, bare granite, and heathery slopes—you'll feel like you're at the top of the world. Nowadays, it's home to anywhere from 1,000 to 3,000 elk (also called wapiti, to distinguish them from the European elk, which is actually a moose—go figure). They drift in and out of the park seasonally in search of grazing land, but if you come here in late May or June you're very likely to see elk cows with their spotted calves, foraging along mountain creeks and gnawing on the bark of the slender aspen trees—look for the stripped patches they leave on tree trunks. In summer the Alpine Visitor Center, up at Fall River Pass, has a viewing platform where you can almost always see an elk or two.

Elk stay above the treeline in summer, but they descend to lower elevations in the fall, when mating season begins. The elk converge in montane meadows—prime spots are the Kawuneeche Valley,

Elk in Rocky Mountain National Park.

Horseshoe Park, Moraine Park, and Upper Beaver Meadows—near dawn and again at dusk. Be sure to stay by the roadside and remain as quiet as possible to watch this phenomenon, because the elk get very agitated. Bull elk do not physically fight over the females, but they put on quite a show, displaying their enormous antlers and powerful necks, and letting loose the most god-awful mating call you've ever heard—a series of low booming tones swooping up to a high-pitched whinny, followed by obscene chuffing and grunting. It's called bugling, and it's the trademark nighttime sound of the Rocky Mountain Park. Observing the elk courtship is such a popular activity, rangers send out alerts to let park visitors know where the biggest gathering is on any given autumn evening.

As more property along the park boundary gets developed, however, there's less open space for these wide-ranging animals, and their customary migratory routes are sometimes blocked off. But if it weren't for this park, they wouldn't be here at all.

ⓘ **Rocky Mountain National Park,** U.S. 36, Estes Park, CO (ℂ **970/586-1206;** www.nps.gov/romo)

✈ Denver

⊨ $$$ **Glacier Lodge,** 2166 CO 66, south of park entrance (ℂ **800/523-3920** or 970/586-4401; www.glacierlodge.com). $ **Moraine Park Campground,** Rocky Mountain National Park (ℂ **800/365-CAMP** [365-2269]; http://reservations.nps.gov).

# Denali National Park
## *Alaska's Big Five*
### Alaska

GLOBAL WARMING COULD ENDANGER MANY PLANT SPECIES AND DO SERIOUS DAMAGE TO critical wildlife habitat in Denali National Park's subarctic environment. Potential development also threatens Denali.

Africa has its Big Five, a checklist of important game animals to see on a safari. Well, Alaska has its own Big Five. Visitors to Denali National Park can check them off: Here's a big-antlered moose, browsing in a stand of willow; there's a stately caribou, its branching antlers outlined against the sky; there's a curly-horned Dall sheep clinging to a rocky hillside; there's a massive grizzly bear, raking open a salmon with its long claws; and finally, a gray wolf, restlessly surveying the tundra from a heathery knoll.

Since private cars are only allowed to drive to Mile 15 of the park's 90-mile (145km) main road, most visitors use the bus service to go deeper into the park on a dusty gravel track—either on regular shuttle buses or interpretive bus tours narrated by naturalists. The wildlife in Denali is so abundant, you actually do get major wildlife sightings right from the bus. Mile 9 is the best place to see moose, who prefer to be in forests close to lakes and marshes. At Mile 34, the rocky slopes and crags of Igloo Mountain are major Dall

Denali National Park.

sheep habitat. Miles 38 to 43 mark Sable Pass, where grizzlies tend to congregate. Mile 46 is the Polychrome Pass overlook, where you can spot caribou on the valley below. Mile 53 may be a good place to get out and hike around (you can reboard the shuttle bus at any point—they come by every half-hour); it's easy walking here along the glacier-fed Toklat River, where bears, caribou, and wolves frequent the rich bottomlands along the river.

All of these Big Five animals have healthy populations in Denali, although the caribou herd fluctuates—one harsh winter, like the winter of 1990 to 1991, can cut their numbers as much as a third. Denali's are just about the only Dall sheep population with such healthy numbers despite the close proximity of major predators. Wolves may be endangered in other parts of the country, but not in Alaska— rangers estimate that 14 wolf packs roam Denali, totaling around 90 wolves, a number finely calibrated to the amount of available prey. Grizzly bears, of course, aren't limited to eating meat—they'll eat anything from berries to caribou. In late July, in fact, they go into a feeding frenzy called hyperphagia, where they're so busy eating, they don't stop to worry about that

bus full of camera-snapping tourists pulling up nearby.

All of Denali's animals are well adapted to life in the subarctic. The big question is what will happen if global climate change warms the temperature, since the effect should be even more pronounced in high latitudes—and stronger still in mountainous regions like Denali. Everything from the food they eat to the way their coats grow has developed to deal with the harsh conditions of Alaskan winters. In a few years, could the Big Five become the Big Four . . . or the Big Three . . . or . . . .

---

ⓘ **Denali National Park,** Denali Park Rd., AK (✆ **907/683-1266;** www.nps.gov/dena)

✈ Fairbanks or Anchorage

🛏 $$$ **Earthsong Lodge** (✆ **907/683-2863;** www.earthsonglodge.com). $$ **Denali Bluffs Hotel,** Mile 238.4 Park Hwy. (✆ **866/683-8500** or 907/683-8500; www.denalialaska.com).

**TOUR** Reservations for bus rides essential: **Denali Park Resorts** (✆ **800/622-7275** or 907/272-7275; www.denaliparkresorts.com)

**Mountain Dwellers**

**156**

# Simien Mountains National Park
## *Trekking over the Roof of Africa*
### Ethiopia

THE ETHIOPIAN HIGHLANDS ARE AMONG THE MOST DENSELY POPULATED AGRICULTURAL regions in Africa. Even protected areas such as the Simien Mountains National Park are hemmed in by deforestation, crisscrossed by roads, and dotted with human settlements that endanger the survival of many native plant and animal species.

"The Roof of Africa"—what a perfect nickname for Ethiopia's Simien Mountains. Situated north of Lake Tana and the Tississat Falls, source of the Blue Nile, it rests high on a volcanic ridge, a majestic massif rising abruptly out of the hazy lowland plain.

Standing on its rim you can see for miles and miles and miles.

This isn't a place for a simple drive through, although roads cut across the park (road construction is controversial here, as it disturbs wildlife). By far the best way to see it is on foot. For many visitors, this includes climbing Ras Dejen, Ethiopia's highest mountain, but even if you don't scale the summit, shorter hikes are spellbinding, and totally unlike what you might have imagined North Africa would look like.

Ascending through the sere highland meadows, you'll see Ice Age relics such as the pineapple-like lobelia tree, which looks like a cactus but is really an evergreen, or the spiky flowers of the red-hot poker plant. Troops of gelada baboons crouch on gravelly hillsides, their long reddish hair visible against the dry scree. Once common throughout Africa, these shaggy baboons—they're nicknamed "lion monkeys" because of the males' flowing manes—now live only in Ethiopia. In fact, this is the largest intact population of them anywhere, for they have been exterminated as crop-raiding pests in agricultural regions. But up here where their natural habitat hasn't been disrupted, they get along with humans just fine. You can get quite close without upsetting them, perhaps even close enough to see the bare red patches on their chests that earn them their other nickname, "bleeding heart baboons."

Hike a little further north and you'll be negotiating around bare crags of dramatic purplish rock, interspersed with eroded gullies and narrow waterfalls. The resident mountain goats, a very rare ibex called the walia, hide out in the crevices, nibbling on lichens, herb grass, and heather. With their chestnut-brown backs, white underbellies, and long back-curved horns, they are beautiful indeed. There are nearly 1,000 of them in the park—it was originally created specifically to protect the last remaining walias—so your chances of seeing one are excellent. Rare Simien foxes live up here too, but they rarely reveal themselves to visitors.

At the gateway town of Debark, outside the park entrance, you can hire a local guide (required for park entrance), and perhaps rent a mule for your trek into the park. Several campgrounds are located throughout the park, as well as a few villages, though park officials have urged residents to relocate and turn the place over to the gelada and the walia.

---

✈ Addis Ababa

🛏 $$$ **Simien Eco-Lodge,** Buit Ras, Simien Mountain National Park

**TOUR Wild Frontiers** (✆ **44/20/7736 3968;** www.wildfrontiers.co.uk). **Dragoman Overland Adventure Travel** (✆ **44/ 1728/861-133;** www.dragoman.com). **Nature and Kind** (✆ **44/207/350-2240** or 0845/362-0300; www.natureandkind.com).

**Mountain Dwellers** 157

# Bwindi Impenetrable Mountain Forest
## *The Last of the Great Apes*
### Virunga Mountains, Uganda

ONLY A FEW HUNDRED MOUNTAIN GORILLAS STILL EXIST AND ALL ARE INCREASINGLY AT RISK FROM a variety of threats, including poaching, habitat destruction, and diseases transmitted by humans. One of the most serious threats to mountain gorillas is the ongoing political unrest and war in the region. Gorillas are sometimes caught in the crossfire between warring factions, and some have been killed deliberately.

Impenetrable as this mountain forest may be, there's one compelling reason to venture here: mountain gorillas. Gorilla safaris are an important tourist draw for Uganda, since nearly half the mountain gorillas in the world are found in one 330-sq.-km

(127-sq.-mile) preserve, in the southwestern corner's Virunga Mountains, where Rwanda, the Congo, and Uganda meet.

Considering only 700 or so of these magnificent primates are left (the other, smaller groups are near by in Rwanda's Volcanoes National Park and the Congo's Virunga National Park), it's impressive that Bwindi has so many. Bwindi now has four groups of gorillas to visit, each clan gathered around at least one silverback (adult male). You may not see all of them while you're here, though—the process involves tracking them through the densely verdant park. Slopes can be slippery, and the forest floor is matted with tangled vines, mouldering leaves, broken ferns, and fallen branches. But along the way you may also see chimpanzees, blue monkeys, or black-and-white colobus monkeys, with their flowing white tails and wizened faces. You might even surprise elephants, giant forest hogs, or small shy antelopes.

Once located, mountain gorillas provide spectacular viewing, because they are most active during the day, and spend more time on the ground than other primates, browsing and grooming and lolling about. Darker and larger than other gorillas, with longer hair (suitable for their cool high-altitude home), these apes have such humanlike feet and such intelligent dark brown eyes that it's easy to feel a spontaneous connection. They're endangered for the usual sad reasons—poaching, habitat destruction, diseases contracted from humans, and war (it's still unknown whether the Congo gorillas survived a September 2007 outbreak of violence).

You'll need a special government permit, obtainable either through your tour operator or by directly contacting the **Uganda Wildlife Authority,** Plot 7 Kira Rd., Kamwokya, P.O. Box 3530, Kampala, Uganda (*C* **256/ 414-346 287** or 256/414-355 000, fax 256/ 414-346 291; www.uwa.or.ug). Permits are strictly controlled and in great demand, so plan up to a year in advance. Only 12 tourists a day are allowed into Bwindi to track gorillas, though you may see some researchers as well, since it is a major international base for primate research. The dry seasons (Jan–Feb and June–Sept) are best for trekking through this damp, lush woodland.

They could just as well have called it the Bwindi Inaccessible Forest, because it's so hard to reach. Getting to Bwindi from Kampala requires a long drive on dusty roads across most of Uganda. But if it hadn't been so inaccessible, the ancient rainforest wouldn't have been left undisturbed—and the gorillas wouldn't still be here.

✈ Kampala

**TOUR Abacus Vacations Ltd.,** Kampala (*C* **256/312-261 930,** 256/752-827 492, or 256/772-331 332; www.abacusvacations. com). **Jewel Safaris,** Kampala (*C* **256/ 772-867 943;** www.jewelsafaris.com).

---

**158** Mountain Dwellers

# The Giant Pandas of Wolong
## *Saving the Chinese Giant*
Sichuan, China

FEWER THAN 1,600 GIANT PANDAS STILL LIVE IN THE WILD, AND THAT NUMBER IS DECREASING steadily. Poaching and habitat destruction are only part of the problem. Panda reproduction rates are low and infant mortality is high. The Wolong National Nature Reserve, with its breeding center and research facility, increases human understanding of how giant pandas reproduce and improves the odds of expanding the wild panda population.

# 10 Places to Sight Big Game

African hunters called them the Big Five: the **lion, leopard, rhinoceros, elephant,** and **Cape buffalo**—the five trophy animals that were hardest to find, most dangerous to stalk, and toughest to kill. Today, safari tours offer a different kind of shooting—with cameras, not guns—but the rare and elusive Big Five are still a thrill to spot. Except for Cape buffaloes, these species are all threatened or endangered in the wild. If you're heading for Asia instead, focus on the even more endangered **Bengal tiger, Asiatic lion, Asiatic elephant,** and **Indian rhinoceros.**

**159 Masai Mara, Kenya**   The Masai Mara is the northern end of the Greater Serengeti migration corridor, a land of lush grasses where Kenya's richest concentration of wild-life gathers. More than a million wildebeest pass through here, along with zebras and gazelles, and predators like lions, cheetahs, and hyenas lurk in the acacia trees. *Abercrombie & Kent:* ☏ *800/554-7016 or 630/954-2944. www.abercrombiekent.com. Micato Safaris:* ☏ *800/MICATO-1 [642-2861] or 212/545-7111. www.micato.com.*

**160 Serengeti National Park, Tanzania**   It's estimated that three million large animals live here, on either the arid plains to the south, where lions loll on rocky out-crops and Thomson's gazelle, buffalo, and elephant browse; or the open woodlands of the center, where leopards rest in the trees by day. *Tauck World Discovery: www.tauck.com. Micato Safaris:* ☏ *800/MICATO-1 [642-2861] or 212/545-7111. www.micato.com.*

**161 Ngorongoro Crater, Tanzania**   This ancient collapsed volcanic caldera in Tanzania is like a great fertile 19km (12-mile-deep) bowl, a self-contained 264-sq.-km

(102-sq.-mile) wilderness that's home to some 30,000 animals. Lion, black rhino, and elephant can be easily spotted in the relatively short grass. *Micato Safaris:* ☏ *800/ MICATO-1 [642-2861] or 212/545-7111. www.micato.com. Overseas Adventure Travel:* ☏ *800/493-6824. www.oattravel.com. Abercrombie & Kent:* ☏ *800/554-7016 or 630/954-2944. www. abercrombiekent.com.*

A lion overlooks the Serengeti.

**162 Lower Zambezi National Park, Zambia**   Elephants are the chief draw in this relatively undeveloped park across from Zimbabwe's Mana Pools. Canoeing along the Zambezi through a floodplain rich in acacia, winterthorn, and baobab trees, you'll see large herds of elephants, as well as buffalo, waterbuck, kudu, zebra, lions, and leopards. Swarms of hippos populate the river pools, and more than 300 bird species roost along its banks. *Wilderness Safaris: www.wilderness-safaris.com. Geographic Explorations:* ☏ *800/777-8183 or 415/922-0448. www.geoex.com. Abercrombie & Kent:* ☏ *800/554-7016 or 630/954-2944. www.abercrombiekent.com.*

A Rhinoceros at Ngorongoro.

**163 Palmwag Concession, Namibia**   Camelback expeditions into this private conservation area in the remote and rocky red hills of Damaraland focus on the last remaining free-ranging black rhinos, as well as desert-adapted Namibian elephants. Along the way you'll also view Hartman's mountain zebra, giraffe, oryx, springbok, kudu, and possibly lions, hyenas, and leopard. *Wilderness Safaris: www.wilderness-safaris.com. Geographic Explorations:* ℂ *800/777-8183 or 415/922-0448. www.geoex.com.*

**164 Chobe National Park, Botswana**   Botswana's oldest national park specializes in elephants—some 120,000 are drawn by Chobe's baobab trees, a vital water source in this semi-arid Kalahari Desert region. During the dry season the river is a vital watering spot for thousands of animals, including spectacular zebra migrations, large groups of giraffes, and plentiful wildebeest. *Odysseys Unlimited:* ℂ *888/370-6765 or 617/454-9100. www.odysseys-unlimited.com. Overseas Adventure Travel:* ℂ *800/493-6824. www.oattravel.com.*

**165 Hwange National Park, Zimbabwe**   Near Victoria Falls and along the edge of the Kalahari Desert, Hwange offers a mix of teak forests and arid savanna, where man-made waterholes have been placed to attract the grazing hordes: giraffes, sable antelope, buffaloes, and so many elephants that there's been talk of culling the herd, especially after recent droughts. Hwange has rare brown hyenas and one of the last populations of African Wild Dogs. *Overseas Adventure Travel.* ℂ *800/493-6824. www.oattravel.com.*

**166 Kruger National Park, South Africa**   Huge Kruger National Park has more mammal species than any other African game park, 147 in all. The large Sabi Sands Game Reserve, which includes the well-known bush camp Mala Mala, is one of the best places to view leopards in the wild. *Backroads:* ℂ *800/462-2848 or 510/527-1555. www.backroads.com. Abercrombie & Kent:* ℂ *800/554-7016 or 630/954-2944. www.abercrombiekent.com. Wilderness Safaris: www.wilderness-safaris.com.*

Elephant in Kruger National Park.

**167 Gir Wildlife Sanctuary, India**   The African lion has it easy compared to his Asiatic cousin. Somewhere around 300 Asiatic lions are left, and all live in this verdant region of Gujarat, part of Gir National Park. Other species in the park include king vultures, hyenas, leopards, nilgai, chinkara gazelles, and chowsingha. *Taj Gir Lodge.* ℂ *91/2877-85821. www.tajhotels.com.*

**168 India's Project Tiger Parks**   If you don't sight a Bengal tiger at Kanha National Park, you will at Ranthambore National Park or Bandhavgarh National Park, where the tiger population is even denser. Elephants and one-horned rhinos are the main attraction at the last stop, Kaziranga National Park. *Big Five Tours & Expeditions.* ℂ *800/ 244-3483 or 772/287-7995. www.bigfive.com.*

Sure, it would be the thrill of a lifetime to glimpse a giant panda in the wild—sighting one of these shy, highly endangered black-and-white bears in its native bamboo jungle would be an unbelievable coup. But just in case that never happens, you can be sure of seeing giant pandas, and lots of them, at this world-famous research and rehabilitation center in the humid mountain forest of Sichuan—and you'll be supporting panda preservation in the process.

There are only about 1,590 giant pandas left in the wild; maybe 10% of them live in Wolong, an area of densely forested mountains between the Sichuan Basin and Tibet. There are actually two separate entities here—Wolong National Nature Reserve (Wolong Ziran Baohu Qu), a 200,000-hectare (495,000-acre) protected area just east of Mount Qionglai; and the Giant Panda Breeding Center (Daxiongmao Siyang Chang) that is attached to it.

The center is a high-tech research facility, founded in 1963, where 60 or 70 pandas at a time are housed and fed in small naturalistic enclosures. Visitors press right up to the glass and gaze transfixed at panda after panda, from newborns to adults; you can even snap photos with tiny cameras disguised as panda babies. Many of the pandas here were taken from captivity or were injured; they may never be ready to be returned to the wild. But if they are, they move from the small enclosures into a large open forest area, where fences keep other animals out. The pandas in that transition area are still being fed, but they hone their other jungle-living skills.

While the breeding center's success rate on moving pandas back to the wild has been spotty, its real contribution lies in research on panda procreation. Pandas reproduce very slowly—often a female will bear only one child in her entire lifetime—and their young often die in infancy. These issues are the biggest factors in the shrinking panda population, more even than poaching or habitat destruction. Admission fees help to support this significant research.

Once you've finished your visit to the breeding center, you'll probably be drawn into the smaller but similar facility next door, devoted to lesser pandas (red pandas). Then head out into the surrounding reserve, an unspoiled beautiful landscape of yew, beech, and bamboo forests, with many excellent hiking trails. Panthers, macaques, golden monkeys, red pandas, white-lipped deer, wildebeest, takins, and—you guessed it—giant pandas all live here, though they are rarely seen by hikers.

To make your panda experience complete, wind up with a visit to the **Panda Museum** in the nearby town of Shawan, a good base for visiting the preserve.

---

ⓘ **Daxiongmao Siyang Chang** (Giant Panda Breeding Center), Hetao Ping (www.pandasinternational.org)

✈ Chengdu

🛏 $$ **Panda Inn** (Xiongmao Shanzhuang), Hetao Ping, next to the breeding station (✆ **86/837/624-3028**). $$ **Wolong Shanzhuang** (Wolong Hotel), in the Wolong Nature Reserve (✆ **86/837/624-6888**).

# Colca Valley
## *The Flight of the Condors*
### Southern Peru

THE ANDEAN CONDORS THAT GLIDE ABOVE PERU'S COLCA VALLEY ARE AN ENDANGERED species—only a few thousand still exist—but programs designed to reintroduce these enormous birds to the wild are working to increase their number. Because mating condors produce only one chick every 2 years and young condors stay with their parents for a full year before striking out on their own, reintroduction is slow and far from certain.

It's a simply stunning Andes panorama: the Rio Colca gorge, twice as deep as the Grand Canyon, set amid towering volcanic peaks. Now just imagine how it looks from the high-flying perspective of an Andean condor.

Colca Canyon was largely unexplored until the 1970s, but now it's a popular region for rafting, rock climbing, and mountain biking, organized through tours from the handsome colonial city of Arequipa. En route to the canyon, you'll drive through a string of traditional villages, isolated from modern times until roads were built in the 1980s. Local farmers have dealt with the mountain geography by building elaborate terraces for their crops; some of these terraces are 1,000 years old, surviving centuries of avalanches, landslides, earthquakes, and volcanic eruptions, which have always been a fact of life around here.

The road passes through the Salinas and Aguada Blanca Nature Reserve, where alpacas, guanacos, and vicuñas graze on the thin scrub of the altiplano plateau. While llamas and alpacas are common domestic animals, grazing near every village (llamas are raised as pack animals, alpacas for their wool), guanacos and vicuñas are wild endangered species, quicker and more delicate than their sturdy, shaggy cousins. Their tawny deerlike coats blend perfectly into the dry grasses. As you drive past, identify which is which—guanacos are larger than vicuñas, with black faces, while vicuñas have a slight camel-like hump. Peru still has more than any other country, but poaching is rapidly depleting the numbers of these graceful mountain camels.

The town of Chivay is most tours' overnight base, where you can adjust to the thin mountain air. Tours venture out next morning to the Cruz del Condor, an overlook 1,200km (3,960 ft.) high on the rim of the canyon, where you can witness a truly awesome natural spectacle: the world's largest birds in flight. Andean condors are so big (their wingspans average around 3.5m/12 ft.), they can't just take off from the ground like other birds—every morning they jump from a cliff and gradually ride upwards on thermal air currents rising from the canyon. From Cruz del Condor, you'll see these giant beauties circling the gorge below, rising higher with each circle, until eventually they are flying right above your heads.

An up-close view of these majestic birds is an unforgettable experience, and you'll wish it went on all day—but it doesn't. Once in the air, the condors go off in various directions searching for carrion, and the camera-clicking tourists leave. The birds return in the late afternoon—the homeward leg of their commute—but it's not as spectacular. June through September is the best time to witness large numbers of condors, but their numbers are dwindling every year. Don't put this one off.

✈ Arequipa

**TOUR Giardino Tours** (✆ **51/54/221-345;** www.giardinotours.com). **Ideal Tours** (✆ **51/19/883-5617;** idealtours@terra. com.pe). **Santa Catalina Tours** (✆ **51/54/ 216-994;** santacatalina@star.com.pe).

# Tasmania
## *God Save the Tasmanian Devil*
### Tasmania, Australia

MANY UNIQUE SPECIES THRIVE IN TASMANIA, ONE OF THE WORLD'S MOST UNUSUAL ECOSYSTEMS. However, increasing development, including logging, mining, and other industries, threaten many of the island's most beautiful places. The clash between wilderness and development—including the inevitable loss of habitat—is only one of the factors threatening Tasmanian devils.

What does a country do when its mascot is dying? Granted, there's nothing cuddly about the Tasmanian devil—these stocky, sharp-snouted little black beasts are vicious scavengers, not nearly as funny as Bugs Bunny's jabbering cartoon pal. But Tasmanians are perversely fond of those cranky doglike critters, and there's a passionate campaign afoot to save them from extinction. They may be the victims of their own bad habits—an appetite for roadkill on busy highways, and their habit of biting each other's faces while quarreling over carrion, thus spreading a rare facial cancer—but the loss of any species is a tragedy.

Dingoes wiped out the Tasmanian devils from Australia long ago, but dingoes never crossed Bass Strait to reach Tasmania, the big island that punctuates the Australian continent like the dot under an exclamation point. Island isolation gave Australia a menagerie of unique species, but Tasmania kicks it up another notch. While Australia's climate is mostly tropical, Tasmania lies in the temperate zone, which puts an entirely different spin on its ecosystem. Tasmania's got wallabies, bandicoots, wombats, and possums, but it's got different wallabies, bandicoots, wombats, and possums. It's also a land of unique tree frogs and parrots, a place of such ecological rarity that its wilderness has won World Heritage status.

Only a couple hours' drive from Hobart, Tasmania's capital, you'll find yourself in a rugged terrain of incredible beauty. Running through it like a spine is the 85km (53-mile) **Overland Track,** the best-known hiking trail in all of Australia. At one end the trail is anchored by Cradle Mountain, a spectacular jagged gray ridge face with four craggy peaks; at the other lies the long narrow glacier-carved Lake St. Clair, Australia's deepest freshwater lake. The trek between them traverses high alpine plateaus, marshy plains of rare button grass, springy heathland, fragrant eucalypt forest, dusky woods of myrtle beech (one of the few Australian native trees that isn't an evergreen), and one of the planet's last temperate rainforests. The path is well marked and improved, including stretches of boardwalk and a series of public sleeping huts. Tour companies run 5-to-10-day guided treks along its length; plenty of shorter hikes are available as well.

Along the way, you'll run into red-bellied pademelons (the kangaroo's Tasmanian cousins) and hordes of other scampering marsupials. As for the Tasmanian devil—well, they're shy little guys, despite that hideous screech they make. You may not see them in the wild, not if they can help it, unless there's a tasty dead possum to feed on.

Tasmanian Devil.

ⓘ **Tasmania Parks & Wildlife Service** (www.overlandtrack.com.au). **Save the Tasmanian Devil** (www.tassiedevil.com.au).

✈ Hobart

🛏 $$$ **Cradle Mountain Lodge,** Cradle Mountain Park (℃ **800/225-9849** in U.S., 44/20/7805-3875 in U.K., 61/3/6492 1303 in Australia; www.poresorts.com.au). **Waldheim Cabins,** Cradle Mountain Park (℃ **61/3/6492 1110;** cradle@dpiwe.tas.gov.au).

**TOUR Tasmanian Expeditions** (℃ **61/1800/030 230;** www.tas-ex.com). **Craclair Tours** (℃ **61/3/6424 7833;** www.craclairtasmania.com).

**171**  It's a Jungle

# Kamakou Preserve
### *Hawaii's Hidden Eden*
Molokai, Hawaii

KAMAKOU PRESERVE ON THE HAWAIIAN ISLAND OF MOLOKAI HOLDS MANY RARE PLANT SPECIES— some so rare that they can be found nowhere else. With so many unique species in such a small environment, one threat is that relatively few individual plants exist for each species, which makes them highly susceptible to hurricanes, disease, and other random events that could lead to serious depletion or extinction.

Tucked away on the highest mountain of Hawaii's least developed island—we're talking remote here—lies a remarkable bit of undiscovered Eden. Draped with mosses, sedges, and lichens, this misty humid habitat feels like a land lost in time.

Though you'd hardly believe it from the rugged, red-dirt appearance of most of Molokai, up in the mountains it rains more than 80 inches (200cm) a year—hence the rainforest, which supplies 60% of the island's water. An amazing 250 different plant species thrive here, 219 of them found nowhere else on earth. There's the alani, a citrus fruit cousin to oranges and lemons; the hapuu, or Hawaiian tree fern; and Hawaii's iconic ohia lehua, a knee-high tree with brilliant red, yellow, or orange blossoms.

It's not just thrills for botanists, either. Birders can train their binoculars on precious species such as the brilliant green amakihi, the nectar-sipping apahane, and the endangered Hawaiian owl. The last time anybody caught sight of a Molokai thrush, it was here in this lush rainforest. Same goes for the Molokai creeper bird (kakawahie).

Of course, you don't preserve rare species like this by letting just everybody tramp through. The Nature Conservancy carefully protects this nearly 3,000-acre (1,215-hectare) haven, which was ceded to them by the vast Molokai Ranch, that dominates Molokai's interior. The conservancy offers once-a-month guided walks along a 3-mile-long (5km) narrow boardwalk (the **Pepeopae Trail**) spanning the rainforest's boggy ground. The hike ends at a breathtaking vista over Molokai's inaccessible north coast, with its plunging emerald-green cliffs—truly a once-in-a-lifetime sight.

If the guided tour is full—reserve way in advance if you don't want to be disappointed—you can still visit on your own, though without a naturalist to guide you may miss the rarest species. It's still worth the effort, but getting here isn't easy. Go west from Kaunakakai 3½ miles (5.6km) on Highway 460, turn right onto an unmarked road that eventually turns to dirt, and drive 9 miles (15km) to the Waikolu Lookout, where you sign in. Drive another 2½ miles (4km) through the Molokai Forest, its

Kamakou Preserve.

stands of sandalwood trees still rebounding after being stripped for the shipbuilding industry. Go left at the fork to reach the trail head. The drive takes 45 minutes, the hike itself another 90 minutes (unless you dawdle—and of course you'll want to dawdle). But hey, if it were easy to get to, it wouldn't be so pristine, would it?

ⓘ **Kamakou Nature Preserve,** Molokai Forest Reserve Rd., Molokai, HI (𝄞 **808/** 537-4508 or 808/553-5236; www.nature. org/wherewework/northamerica/states/ hawaii/preserves/art2355.html)

✈ Hoolehua Airport

🛏 $$$ **The Lodge/Beach Village** at Molokai Ranch, Maunaloa (𝄞 **888/627-8082** or 808/660-2824). $ **Hotel Molokai,** Kamehameha V Hwy., Kaunakakai (𝄞 **800/535-0085** or 808/553-5347 in Hawaii; www.hotelmolokai.com).

It's a Jungle **172**

# Royal Chitwan National Park
## *The Royal Rhinos of Nepal*
### Nepal

CARVED OUT OF A SETTLED AREA, ROYAL CHITWAN NATIONAL PARK HAS A TROUBLING relationship with locals. Tigers from the park frequently kill livestock on nearby farms, while rhinos and other animals damage crops. Even worse, rhinos and tigers kill three to five local people every year, which is likely to escalate as settlements crowd closer to park boundaries.

Think of Nepal and you picture Himalayan peaks, right? Well, that's not all there is to Nepal. Along the Indian border in the southwest, Nepal spills into the flat Ganges floodplain, which used to make a supremely effective barrier—back in the days before DDT, nobody wanted to live in these swampy, malarial lowlands. And that was just fine with the one-horned Asian rhinoceros. As many as 2,000 browsed around here in relative peace and quiet.

Then between 1950 and 1960, new insecticides rid the Ganges plains of mosquitoes. The population tripled, the forest was slashed in half, and crops planted in its place. Habitat destruction wasn't the only problem—rhinos were also being poached out of existence, hunted for their horns, which are believed to have magical properties. Suddenly there were only 100 rhinos left.

That's when the government stepped in, taking 932 sq. km (360 sq. miles) of the former hunting grounds of the Nepali Ranas, expelling 22,000 residents, and turning it into Royal Chitwan National Park. Nobody dared poaching rhinos here—not with the Royal Nepalese Army patrolling its borders. Today there are about 400 Asian rhinos at Chitwan, a quarter of the world's total, as well as 50 breeding pairs of Bengal tigers.

Along the floodplain of the Rapti River are several lakes, where the rhinos hang out with storks and other marsh birds, otters, rare gharial crocodiles, and the even rarer freshwater Gangetic dolphins. The thick-skinned, huge gray rhinos cool off at water's edge, but then wander over to browse on the tall grasses a little farther from the river, where several kinds of deer and the mighty guar antelope also graze. The main body of the park is jungle, a dense forest of sal and teak trees with a curtain of vines and creepers and fragrant orchids blooming in the treetops.

Canoeing on the Rapti gives you a great view of the water birds. At Machans, observation towers allow you to watch wildlife with your binoculars from a distance without disturbing them. Right by the visitor center at Sauraha, you can visit an elephant breeding center; 1 km (half mile) down the road, there's a similar breeding center where you can get acquainted with the endangered gharial crocodile. Hikes into the jungle will score more wildlife sighting; it's a good idea to hire a guide, not only to identify species and prevent getting lost, but also to deal with any run-ins with rhinos, who can be extremely territorial.

Your last option may be touristy but it's irresistible—take an elephant ride into the

Royal Chitwan National Park.

jungle. Spring for the higher-priced ride to sit in a canopied howdah on the elephant's back.

---

ⓘ **Royal Chitwan National Park** visitor center, Sauraha (www.rhinos-irf.org)

✈ Bharatpur

🛏 $$$ **Tiger Tops Jungle Lodge,** Royal Chitwan National Park (✆ **977/1/436-1500;** www.tigermountain.com). $$ **Machan Wildlife Resort,** Royal Chitwan National Park (✆ **977/1/422-5001** or 977/56/20973; www.nepalinformation.com/machan).

---

It's a Jungle **173**

# Sepilok Orang Utan Rehabilitation Center
## *The Art of Being an Orangutan*
### Sandakan, Malaysia

ORANGUTANS ARE ONE OF THE MOST ENDANGERED SPECIES IN MALAYSIA. FOUND ONLY IN BORNEO and Sumatra, the orangutans' survival is constantly threatened by loss of habitat—due to logging, burning, or agriculture—and illegal hunting. The Sepilok Orang Utan Rehabilitation Center is a conservation facility that cares for orphaned young orangutans and teaches them the skills they will need not only to survive, but to thrive, in the wild.

It isn't easy being an orangutan.

First of all, their home territory is the rainforests of Borneo and Sumatra—where rainforest has been disappearing at an alarming rate over the past 50 years, hacked down for timber or cleared for palm oil plantations. Solitary, territorial creatures, orangutans don't thrive when they are crammed into increasingly small patches of habitat. These large vegetarians (males can be 1.5m/5 ft. tall and weigh 90kg/200 lb., though females are half that) need massive amounts of fruit to eat—but in the less fertile higher elevations they're being forced into, there are fewer fruit trees than in the lowlands. Ten years ago, there were perhaps 27,000 orangutans in these forests. Today, there may be less than 10,000, and fewer every day.

Exclusively tree dwellers—the world's largest arboreal mammals, who even find their drinking waters in the treetops—orangutans don't have a tail to swing from tree to tree like their neighbors, the proboscis monkeys. They use their arms instead to move around the rainforest canopy, which is probably why their arm span is up to 2.4m (8 ft.) wide. Baby orangutans are undeniably cute, but that's a problem too,

since poachers supplying the illegal pet market kill adults to steal their babies. Even their intelligence works against them—mothers need at least 6 years to pass on their complicated survival techniques to their young. When they lose their mothers as babies, they are deeply, deeply at risk.

That's where the Sepilok orangutan sanctuary comes in. Founded in 1964, this 43-sq.-km (17-sq.-mile) facility abutting the Kabili Sepilok Forest Reserve takes in orphaned young orangutans (many of them confiscated from poachers), feeds and nurses them—and teaches them all the skills their mothers would have taught. Today about 25 youngsters live at the sanctuary; another 60 to 80 have already been released into the reserve. Contact with humans is minimized to keep them from getting too dependent on humans, but from a walkway visitors can watch them being fed daily at 10am and 2:30pm. After that, you can hike through the reserve where you may spot more, swinging through the trees as nature intended. (**Hint:** Look for nests up in the canopy—an orangutan makes a fresh nest in a new spot every night.) A half-day walk on the Mangrove

Orangutan at Sepilok.

Forest Trail will take you past water holes through transitional forest, lowland rainforest, and on into the mangrove forest. In the forest, look for mouse deer, wild boars, gibbons, macaques, and fleshy-nosed proboscis monkeys; the mangrove swamp is home to dugongs and dolphins.

The sanctuary also houses a couple of endangered Sumatran rhinos, and occasionally other animals such as Malaysian sun bears, gibbons, or elephants. Sandakan is on the northwestern coast of Borneo, which is part of Malaysia; with dazzling beaches, preserved rainforest, and offshore coral reefs, it's a popular destination for those who love outdoor sports—and orangutans.

ⓘ **Sepilok Orang Utan Rehabilitation Centre,** 25km (16 miles) west of Sandakan (✆ **60/89/531180**). **Orangutan Appeal UK** (www.orangutan-appeal.org.uk).

✈ Kota Kinabalu

🛏 $$ **Sepilok Nature Resort** (✆ **60/89/765200;** http://sepilok.com). $ **Sepilok Jungle Resort,** Labuk Rd., Sandakan (✆ **60/89/533031;** www.sepilokjungle resort.com).

---

174  It's a Jungle

# Manu Biosphere Reserve
## *The Other Amazon*
### Peru

BEFORE GAINING THE PROTECTION OF THE PERUVIAN GOVERNMENT AND BEING NAMED A WORLD Heritage Site, the Manu Biosphere Reserve was kept pristine by its inaccessibility. The area is still remote, but the dangers of civilization are creeping closer and crowding the reserve on all sides. Logging, both legal and illegal, is taking place along park boundaries, and poaching is common.

As any schoolkid will tell you, the Amazon rainforest—the one ecologists are so desperate to save—is in Brazil. True enough, but it's not all in Brazil. The source of the Amazon lies in Peru, in the Andes mountains; in fact, fully half of Peru is covered with Amazonian rainforest. What's more, despite a period of rubber exploitation in the early 20th century, this large swath of it has been protected as a national park since 1968; it hasn't suffered the same degree of deforestation that the Brazil rainforest has. If virgin rainforest is what you're after, head for Peru's Manu Biosphere Reserve.

Biodiverse? Manu has been documented as the most biodiverse place on earth, with more than 15,000 species of plants, 1,000 types of birds, and 1,200 different butterflies. There are 13 various primates, not to mention tapirs, spectacled bears, ocelots, jaguars, and giant otters. In the thick jungle growth, you may not be able to see all of these elusive creatures, but a good guide will increase your chances. The butterflies, hummingbirds, howler monkeys, tamarins, capuchins, and macaws alone should make your trip satisfying.

Riverboats enable you to view the rainforest from one perspective, where black caimans bask on the sandy verges, agile giant otters fish in shallow ox-bow lakes, and thousands of brilliantly colored macaws and parrots gather at the Blanquillo Macaw Lick (Colpa de Guacamayos) to feed on a riverbank cliff of mineral salts. Trails have also been laid out to lead away from the river to various types of jungle habitat—bamboo, freshwater swamp, *tierra firme* forest, and floodplain, each with its different vegetation, birds, and animal life. Harpy eagles nest in the tops of Brazil nut trees, wide-branched cacao trees bear their large red fruits, and huge strangler figs grow down from the canopy around other trees until they take root and become trees themselves. Passion flowers blossom on thin trailing vines, and deadly nightshade perfumes the night air, as you're lulled to sleep by a murmurous chorus of frogs and insects.

Manu has remained unspoiled partly because it's so sparsely inhabited, and partly because it's so strictly controlled. There are two sections of reserve: the **Cultural Zone,** inhabited by several nomadic peoples and open to all visitors, and the much smaller **Reserve Zone,** which you can only visit with an authorized guide. Many tours come overland from Cusco, a 2-day journey through mountains and orchid-laden cloud forest before you come down into the lush lowland jungles. Flying to Boca Manu instead is expensive, but it'll get you into the heart of the reserve right away.

✈ Boca Manu

**TOUR Tropical Nature Travel** (✆ 877/827-8350; www.tropicalnaturetravel.com). **Manu Expeditions,** Peru (✆ 51/84/226-671; www.manuexpeditions.com). **Manu Nature Tours,** Peru (✆ 51/84/252-721; www.manuperu.com).

It's a Jungle 175

# Dja Faunal Reserve
## *Gorillas Going, Going, Gone . . .*
### South-Central Cameroon

POACHING IS A SERIOUS PROBLEM IN THE DJA FAUNAL RESERVE. WHEN TIMES ARE HARD, many low-income people in the region supplement their diets or their incomes with bushmeat. Logging roads give poachers access to the protected primates and other animals in the park. A plan to route the Trans-African highway along the southern boundary of the reserve could make things even easier for poachers.

Not so long ago, the mountain gorillas were the ones in real danger. These days, things look even grimmer for their lowland cousins.

It was bad enough that widespread logging and cocoa and coffee plantations were eliminating their rainforest habitat. Then falling prices for African coffee and cocoa drove more of the local population to poaching (an adult gorilla yields an awful lot of bushmeat). Now an epidemic of Ebola virus has swept like wildfire through central Africa, killing more than half of the lowland gorilla population, especially in the Congo and contiguous areas like Lobeke National Park.

The gorillas at Dja are still hanging in there, though. Ever since 1932, when Cameroon was still a French colony, this peaceful patch of jungle nestled into a great loop of the Dja River enjoyed protected status; 90% of it is still untouched evergreen rainforest, with a dense tree canopy nearly 60m (200 ft.) high. Though extensive logging and agriculture line its borders, there's never been any inside the reserve. All local residents were moved out in 1946—vines and creepers invade the shells of their abandoned villages. The only hunters permitted are local pygmies, using traditional methods, although the reserve has such limited staff (don't expect rangers or a visitor center), enforcement of the hunting ban is haphazard.

Dja is an unbelievable hot spot for primates—not only gorillas, but chimpanzees, black-and-white colobus, pottos, mangabeys, guenons, talapoin monkeys, and mandrill baboons with their colorful red-and-blue face masks also thrive. Between the jungle and the river, it's also a great birding area, with several species of finches, sunbirds, flycatchers, woodpeckers, turacaos, barbets, and hornbills; unusual birds here include Bates's weaver, Dja River warbler, and rare breeding colonies of gray-necked picathartes (rock-fowl). A few elephants wander through, scaly anteaters and wild boars root around, and leopards silently stalk smaller creatures like buffaloes, warthogs, striped bongos, and the odd marsh-dwelling antelopes called sitatungas.

No animals stalk the lowlands gorilla, though. The biggest and most powerful of all primates—males can be 1.8m (6 ft.) tall, females 1.5m (5 ft.)—they seem laid-back and sociable, plucking leaves and berries as they roam the jungle. Generally they're more slender and agile than the mountain species, colored gray or brown rather than black, with tufts of reddish hair on top of their skulls. But poachers have made them wary of humans—it's most likely you won't see one on a casual hike through the reserve. You'll have to become a gorilla detective, looking for their droppings, mats of flattened grass where they've rested, perhaps remnants of the sleeping platforms they build in trees every night as they migrate around the park.

Dja's future is uncertain. With increased tourism, Dja Faunal Reserve would inevitably add much-needed facilities, but floods of day-trippers might damage virgin habitat.

---

ⓘ **Dja Faunal Reserve,** east of Sangmélima (✆ **237/23-92-32**)

✈ Yaounde

🛏 $$$ **Hilton Yaounde,** Blvd. du 20 Mai, Yaounde (✆ **237/2-223-36 46;** www1. hilton.com). $$ **Mercure Yaounde Centre,** Av. El Hadj Ahmadou Ahidjo (✆ **237/ 2-222-21 31**).

# Okapi Wildlife Reserve
## *Held Hostage in the Congo*
### Northeastern Democratic Republic of the Congo

WAR IS AN ONGOING THREAT TO BOTH PEOPLE AND ANIMALS IN THE CONGO. MINING FOR COLTAN, a metallic element essential for cellphones and other high-tech devices to work, is also an ongoing threat. Miners ravage the forest and rivers in search of the precious metal. Ironically, coltan profits ultimately help finance the region's wars, prompting an international call to ban the use of coltan from the Congo.

In July 2002, war crashed into the Ituri Forest. This pristine stand of evergreen rainforest—traditional home to the Mbuti pygmies and a refuge for thousands of elephants, primates, and the endangered okapi—was invaded by two opposing insurgent groups in the Democratic Republic of the Congo's ongoing civil wars. They looted and plundered local villages, driving out the deeply traditional Mbutis for the first time in history. They set up camp in the forest, ruthlessly dining on chimpanzee.

The soldiers have left now, and thankfully not one okapi was lost. But it was a major setback to all the progress made by conservation officials since 1992, when one-fifth of the Ituri was set aside as the Okapi Wildlife Reserve. Nearly a third of the world's okapi population lives here, along with forest elephants, leopards, forest buffalo, pangolin, water chevrotain, and at least 13 different primates. Major threats to this forest habitat have been poaching for bush meat, deforestation, and small-scale gold mining. All of those illegal activities sprang back quickly when the staff was forced to leave in 2002, and since their return, it's been an uphill battle.

Even if you ventured into the war-torn DRC to visit the Ituri Forest, you might not be able to see any okapis—they are notoriously elusive, their striped legs providing ideal camouflage for moving silently through these dense green forestlands.

(Even the pygmies rarely spot any.) The only known relative of the giraffe, these tall creatures live nowhere else but the Congo basin; though it's hard to pin down their numbers, it's estimated that as many as 6,000 may live here in the Ituri Forest. You may be able to see some at the reserve's research center, which tends to injured okapis (often rescued from traps) and breeds some in captivity, sending a few of their offspring to zoos to keep the genetic pool varied (unlike the early days of this breeding center, established in 1952 to capture wild okapis and ship them off to American and European zoos.) Several Mbuti earn a living at the center by gathering leaves for the fussy okapi to eat, since these forest experts know exactly which trees these beautiful shy creatures favor.

It's not a place for the casual tourist—at least, not yet. But conservation efforts include converting local people from a dependence on poaching and destructive farming practices into sustainable agriculture and eco-tourism skills—convincing them to regard the rainforest's rich flora and fauna as a precious resource worth protecting. Eco-tourism could be the saving of the Ituri Forest—and of the okapis.

✈ Goma

**TOUR** **Go Congo Tours** (✆ **243/811-837010;** www.gocongo.com)

# Corbett National Park
## *Tiger, Tiger, Burning Bright*
### Northern India

INVASIVE SPECIES AND WEED INFESTATION CONTINUOUSLY THREATEN CORBETT NATIONAL PARK. Partly to blame is the Ramganga River Project, which changed the character of the park by replacing large tracts of grassland habitat with wetlands. Poaching is not a serious problem, but increasing population density near the park has led to more livestock killed by tigers and leopards, and retaliation by local farmers.

Of course you want to see a tiger. You're in India; you can't go home without seeing a Bengal tiger.

In 1973 the Indian government's Project Tiger was launched right here, at India's oldest national park, to protect the country's drastically dwindling tiger population. Tiger poaching is still a widespread underground industry, so Project Tiger has had to step up its efforts, adding 26 other sites. Still, sprawling Corbett, spread along the banks of the Ramganga River in the foothills of the Himalayas, remains a huge draw, not least because it's a lot more accessible than the other Project Tiger sites.

Streams feeding into the Ramganga furrow Corbett's terrain into wooded ridges and ravines, with sal and bamboo forests providing excellent cover for predators such as Bengal tigers (there are reportedly 150 in the park), leopards, and black bears. Wild boar snuffle around the trees, while a host of rhesus monkeys chatter overhead, warning of loitering pythons. Meanwhile herds of wild elephants, delicate spotted

Corbett National Park.

deer, sambar, and four-horned antelope (*chausingha*) roam the park's grassland savannas (*chaur*). Flocks of cormorants, marsh mugger crocodiles, and enormous golden mahseer carp share the river, and endangered gharial crocodiles lazily poke their long snouts up out of the Ramganga Reservoir. (A no-swimming sign on its shore warns SURVIVORS WILL BE PROSECUTED.)

Perhaps the best way to go looking for tigers is to take a 2-hour elephant ride from either Dhikala or Bijrani, tracking through the forests and across the plains, at either sunup or sunset when the tigers are most active. Book your place a day in advance if possible. If you do see a tiger, it's customary to give your elephant handler (*mahout*) an extra tip. Night safaris are another good option for spotting tigers and leopards, but you must book these with a tour operator—you're not allowed to drive your own car through the park at night.

Excursions of all kinds, from nature walks to bird-watching to jeep safaris to elephant rides, are usually booked through your hotel. Permits are required for entering the park—Corbett is divided into five tourist zones, and you're only allowed to visit one at a time (schedule a few days here if you want to see a range of habitats). March through June is the best season for wildlife viewing; the park is closed during the monsoon season, mid-June through mid-November, when the Ramganga floods its banks and park roads become impassable.

ⓘ **Corbett National Park,** Ramnagar (☏ **91/5947/25-1489**)

✈ Delhi

🚂 Ramnagar

🛏 **Claridges Corbett Hideaway,** Zero Garjia, Dhikuli (☏ **91/5947/28-4132;** www.corbetthideaway.com). **Infinity Resorts,** Dhikuli (☏ **91/5947/25-1279;** www.infinityresorts.com).

It's a Jungle

178

# Panna National Park
## *In the Shadow of the Rajahs*
### Madya Pradesh, India

POACHING IS A THREAT TO THE TIGERS OF PANNA NATIONAL PARK. HOWEVER, THE THREAT IS not as immediate or as great as indicated by reports in 2005, which claimed that the tigers at Panna had been virtually wiped out by poachers. A government re-census found a healthy population of tigers, and the false reports were traced to rumors started by local people who were unhappy with park officials.

Back in the days of the rajahs, this spread of jungle, forest, and grassland along the Ken River was a royal hunting ground, a *shikargah*, where tigers were protected only so that they could wind up as a trophy adorning some prince's palace. Today, the tigers can rest a little more easily. Panna is now a national park and Project Tiger reserve, close to the extraordinary ruined temples of Khajuraho and Asia's largest diamond mines.

At least 25 Bengal tigers prowl this protected valley, along with plenty of the sort of prey tigers have a taste for—nilgai, Indian gazelles, chital, sambar, and four-horned antelope. Though the park is relatively small, within that compact space the habitats are varied, which allows tigers (and the leopards, wild dogs, hyenas, and wolves who compete for the same prey) to venture onto the grasslands for hunting and then slip back into the jungle and deep ravines for safety. And because the park is small, tiger sightings are fairly frequent. Elephant rides are a popular way to track the tigers, and an exciting experience even if the tigers don't reveal themselves.

In this dry, hot region, the jungle you'll venture into looks much different than a rainforest jungle—deciduous trees like teak, Indian ebony, and flame-of-the-forest grow thickly here, along with several flowering species. Blossom-headed parakeets and paradise flycatchers dart around the jungle, with peacocks—India's national bird—strutting their stuff on the forest floor. Bar-headed geese and white-necked storks dabble around in the river, while the king vulture and honey buzzard patrol the tawny grasslands, looking for whatever carrion the hyenas haven't picked clean.

If you can stand the heat—and summers can be scorching here, until the monsoons begin in July—early summer is often the best time for wildlife sightings. Even animals who normally live outside the park wander in from the parched countryside, seeking the river's cool water. And when they come, the tigers will be lying in wait.

ⓘ **Panna National Park,** Madla Village (✆ **91/7732/252-134**)

✈ Khajuraho

🛏 $$ **Ken River Lodge,** Village Madla, District Panna (✆ **91/7732/27-5235**). $$$ **Jass Trident,** By-Pass Rd., Khajuraho (✆ **91/ 7686/27-2344;** www.oberoihotels.com).

---

**179** It's a Jungle

# Komodo National Park
## *Here Be Dragons*
### Indonesia

KOMODO NATIONAL PARK IS HOME TO THOUSANDS OF KOMODO DRAGONS—A TYPE OF monitor lizard whose large size and aggressive nature earned it a scary name—and protecting them is its principal purpose. The most serious threat to Komodo dragons is depletion of their prey by human poachers and the feral dogs that roam the island.

It takes a tough species to survive on a place like Komodo Island. This rugged volcanic island off the northwest tip of Flores, Indonesia, is wickedly hot and dry 8 months of the year—and then the monsoons drench it. Much of the island is rocky and barren, with patches of hardy savanna, bits of mossy bamboo cloud forest on higher ridges, and a tropical deciduous forest in the valleys, full of trees that are water-retention specialists.

Not many species can make it here, but the king of the island looks perfect for the job: the Komodo dragon, world's biggest lizard, a scaly monster 2.4 to 3m (8–10 ft.)

long that hasn't evolved much in 4 million years. This hefty reptile weighs anywhere from 45kg to 150kg (100–330 lb.), depending on how recently it has gorged on carrion. But it's no mere scavenger: The Komodo lies in wait in the grass, springs out and slashes its victim (Timor deer, wild pigs, buffalo) with powerful serrated teeth, and then lets them struggle off into the bush to die, poisoned by bacteria in the Komodo's saliva. Flicking its forked yellow tongue, the lizard "tastes the air" to detect the scent of rotting flesh, then ambles over to the corpse and feasts. Komodos are not only carnivores, they are cannibals; they'll even

Komodo dragon.

eat their young, who are forced to spend their first few months of life in the rainforest canopy to escape being eaten. (Luckily, they hatch just after the Jan–Feb rainy season, when there's plenty to eat up there.)

There are nearly 6,000 of these "dragons" (really a giant monitor lizard) on Komodo and a few neighboring islands, and most park visitors come here in hopes of sighting one. A Komodo station at Loho Liang is baited twice a week to draw Komodos for tourist viewing. You may also catch them basking in the sun in the early morning, raising their body temperatures (they are, after all, cold-blooded) before slinking off to hunt.

The park was initially established in 1980 to conserve the Komodo dragon, but as their population has stabilized, the real issue has become what's happening off shore, in the seagrass beds, mangrove forests, and coral reefs that make this a superb scuba diving destination. Tidal currents makes these interisland waters particularly rich, with more than 1,000 species of fish as well as dugong, sharks, manta rays, whales,

dolphins, and sea turtles. But several fishing villages remain within the park, all established before 1980, and their population has boomed to some 4,000 villagers. Intensive fishing is damaging the reefs and exhausting the waters—but can conservation officials deny the resident population their traditional livelihood, just to satisfy international environmental ideals? It's a hot issue, with no easy answer in sight.

---

ⓘ **Komodo National Park,** Loho Liang, Indonesia (www.komodo-gateway.org). **Komodo Foundation** (www.komodo foundation.org).

✈ Bima

**Boat** From Sape (Sumbawa Island) or Labuan Bajo (Flores Island)

**TOUR Flores Exotic Tours,** Labuan Bajo, Flores (✆ **62/385-21824;** www.komodo island-tours.com). **Floressa Bali Tours** (✆ **62/361-467625;** www.floressatours. com).

# Ujung Kulon National Park
## *Java Hideaway*
### Java, Indonesia

UJUNG KULON NATIONAL PARK IS ONE OF THE LAST EXTENSIVE AREAS OF LOWLAND RAINFOREST IN Java and the final refuge of the Java rhinoceros. Rhino poaching is still a serious threat to the small population of Java rhinos that inhabit the park, but anti-poaching patrols have been very successful at preventing illegal hunting inside the park.

The Indian rhinoceros has it easy, compared to Asia's other one-horned rhino, the Java rhinoceros. Less than 60 individuals remain, scrounging around this once remote peninsula of earthquake-prone Java, in the shadow of the feared volcano Krakatoa. (Another half-dozen cousins have been reported in Vietnam.) Slightly smaller than their Indian cousins, with different folds in their thick-skinned "armor," these Javans also have a long upper lip—and why not, since they're really pachyderms. Hiding out in the dense lowland forests of this protected park, they're safe at last from the widespread poaching that whittled their numbers so drastically; they're also far from the agricultural crops they used to raid, which gave them an unfair local reputation as pests.

This part of Java used to be farmland too—until August 1883, when the offshore volcano Krakatoa erupted, killing more than 36,000 people. Farmers fled and, with continued eruptions over the years—in 1952, 1972, 1992, 1994—they never moved back. The jungle reclaimed the land swiftly, especially fast-growing figs and palms. Protected by the sea on three sides and mountains on the other, the peninsula's like a Hollywood version of tropical beauty, with loads of orchids clambering over the trees—luminous white moon orchids, deep red pipit orchids, mauve dove orchids, and tiny white squirrel-tail orchids, which only open for 1 day—and large soft-petalled blossoms scattered over the beach every dawn.

The rhinos roam widely over these densely forested lowlands, especially active at night; they leave the tree cover to wallow in mud pools and venture onto beaches, but few park visitors actually spot one. Still, as you hike around Ujung Kulong trails, look for telltale rhino hoof prints and droppings on the trails. **Be careful:** Javan rhinos can run as fast as humans, and they're likely to charge fiercely if they see you.

The Javan tiger was driven out 40 years ago, but leopards, wild dogs, fishing cats, civets, and the Javan mongoose still thrive. Ujung Kulon also has five rare species of primates: the glossy black Javan silverleaf monkey and its slightly heavier gray relative the grizzled leaf monkey in the mountains; black-faced gray Java gibbons and nocturnal slow lorises in the forest; and long-tailed crab-eating macaques, who scamper around beaches and reefs at low tide. Over 250 species of birds live here, mostly hidden in the dense tree canopy (you'll hear their songs, all right), as well as a number of herons and storks and other water birds in the freshwater swamp and mangrove forest along the north coast.

The best way to get here is by boat from Labuan (5–6 hr.), where you can get entrance permits and make lodging reservations at the PHPA parks office; hire required local guides at Tamanjaya.

ⓘ **Ujung Kolon National Park,** visitor center at Tamanjaya. **International Rhino Foundation** (www.rhinos-irf.org).

✈ Jakarta

🛏 Several guesthouses in Tamanjaya and Peucang Island

**TOUR Wanawisata Alamhayati PT,** Jakarta (☎ **62/21-571-0392** or 21/570-1141). **Arthamara Wisata** (☎ **62/21-887-2924;** www.thousandisland.co.id). **Travelindo,** Yogyakarta (☎ **62/27-454-1409;** www.travelindo.com).

It's a Jungle **181**

# Khao Yai National Park
## *March of the Elephants*
### Thailand

LIKE MANY WILD PLACES, KHAO YAI NATIONAL PARK FACES THREATS FROM HUMAN DEVELOPMENT and encroachment. Agriculture is expanding to the east, luxury resorts and golf courses are springing up to the west, and the park is bisected in some places by highways that cross wildlife corridors and result in traffic accidents and animal fatalities.

Wild Asian elephants are the marquee attraction at Khao Yai, Thailand's oldest and largest national park. There are 120 of them still in the wild here—surely you ought to see some. After all, they are omnivorous vegetarians, eating grass, branches, leaves, and fruit as they ramble in the course of a day through many different vegetation zones. An elephant is an awfully big animal—how could you miss it?

So you hike through the jungle—mainland Asia's largest swath of monsoon forest, where towering moss-draped trees support a bewildering mass of creepers, climbers, lianas, strangler figs, orchids, lichens—and you spot your first evidence: birds pecking at a ball of elephant dung. In a bamboo forest on the lower slopes of the mountain, you spy gentle guars munching shreds of bamboo stalks left behind by choosy elephants, who only like the middle parts. You take a night safari in a jeep, using spotlights to catch nighttime wildlife activity—civets, sambars, a wild hog . . . but no elephant.

But then you get distracted. You cross the grasslands and hear the barking deer utter their distinctive cry. You hike up to a waterfall and surprise a waddling porcupine. You spend time in the observation towers, bird-watching for magnificent giant hornbills, or great flocks of Indian Pieds. A gibbon hoots in the trees above you; comical macaques loiter alongside the roads like furry little hitchhikers. At evening, your

Khao Yai National Park.

guide leads you to the bat cave on the edge of the park, where hundreds of thousands of tiny insect-eating bats swarm out to do their night's hunting. (Hiring a local guide is a very good idea, with over 50km/30 miles of trails to navigate, and so many different wildlife species to scout out.)

After all, Khao Yai is a big park, and only 20% is open to visitors, which is why really elusive species like tigers and clouded leopards can escape tourists completely. Khao Yai's size enables it to support large roaming species like elephants. Even better, a chain of parks across this region has almost completed a continuous wildlife corridor, so animals can range from park to park. Rangers and conservationists are joining forces to end the rampant poaching that endangers so many of Thailand's rare species.

Early next morning, as you head for the salt lick—the jungle equivalent of the village

green—you're not expecting elephants anymore. And then, you come around a bend in the trail and see the great gray pachyderm, placidly working at the salt with her pink tongue. You stand stock still, awed and overcome. She lifts her head, gazes at you, then swings her trunk and trots away.

Now you can go home.

ⓘ **Khao Yai National Park,** Pak Chong

✈ Bangkok

🛏 **$$$ Juldis Khao Yai Resort,** 54 Moo 4 Thanarat Rd., Pakchong. **$$ Garden Lodge,** Thanarat Rd. Km 7, Pak Chong (✆ **66/44-365 178;** www.khaoyai-garden-lodge.com).

**TOUR Contact Travel** (✆ **66/5327-7178** or 66/5320-4104; www.activethailand.com). **DTC Travel** (✆ **66/2-259-4535-6;** www.dtctravel.com).

---

**182** It's a Jungle

# Central Suriname Nature Reserve
## *Stalking the Cock-of-the-Rock*
### Suriname

THE CENTRAL SURINAME NATURE RESERVE IS SO LARGE AND INACCESSIBLE THAT MOST THREATS to the site are potential rather than immediate. The government has awarded several large-scale mining and logging concessions outside the boundaries of the reserve and its watershed, but as the surrounding areas continue to develop, it will become increasingly difficult to protect pristine ecosystems within the reserve.

Uninhabited is one thing; unexplored is something else. The Central Suriname Nature Reserve can't even publish a definitive catalog of its flora and fauna, because they just don't know what's there yet.

The CSNR was only created in 1998, combining three former nature reserves—two of them uninhabited, uncharted wilderness. Resorts? Visitor centers? Try a primitive airstrip with rudimentary guesthouses. If roughing it is right up your alley, this sprawling park could be the adventure of a lifetime.

Despite a number of gold and bauxite mines, the former Dutch colony of Suriname—which has less than 500,000 inhabitants—remains one of the most heavily forested nations on earth. Woodlands covers 90% of the colony. The creation of the CSNR—an area the size of New Jersey, 12% of Suriname's entire land area—was hailed by conservationists, for it protects the country's untrammeled interior just in time before logging and mining could move in. In the northern section of the reserve, Raleighvallen (Raleigh

Falls), you can see the country's characteristic moist highland forest, though here it's much richer and dense, featuring some 300 different species of trees, with a canopy that can be as high as 50m (165 ft.). Buttress roots and stilt roots help these towering trees maximize the nutrients they can suck from this thin soil. Palms dominate the understory, while ferns and fern mosses carpet the forest floor, and every inch of this complex web of vegetation seems crawling with life—butterflies, birds, snakes, lizards, you name it. No wonder they haven't logged it all in yet.

The best infrastructure is in the Raleighvallen area, which you can fly into from Paramaibo, or take the more gradual scenic route: Drive to Bitragon and then take a 4-to-5-hour boat trip up the Coppename River to Foengo Island, where the reserve's headquarters are. This area even has several hiking trails laid out, linking Foengoe Island to the airstrip and several natural landmarks—like the 250m-high (820-ft.) Voltzberg Dome, a bare granite inselberg rising abruptly high out of the forest. Raleighvallen is famous among ornithologists as a prime place to see superb jungle birds like red and green macaws and the

stunning crested orange-and-black Cock-of-the-Rock.

Jaguars live here (but good luck seeing one); giant armadillos lumber around; and giant river otters play in the various tributaries of the Coppename watershed. Sloths, tapirs, pumas, six kinds of monkeys—howler monkeys, tamarins, capuchins, saki, spider monkeys, squirrel monkeys—everything you'd expect from a South American jungle. It's not the Amazon basin, but even better—it's what the Amazon must have been like before rainforest destruction began.

---

(i) **Conservation International Suriname,** Paramaribo (② 597/421-305; cisgravn@sr.net)

✈ Paramaibo

⊨ Guesthouses on Foengoe Island, at Rudi Kappel airstrip in the Tafelberg area, and at the southern airstrip of Kayser

**TOUR METS Tours & Travel** (② 597/477-088; www.surinametourism.com). **The Foundation for Nature Preservation in Suriname (STINASU)** (② 597/476-597; www.stinasu.com).

**Run Wild, Run Free** · **183**

# Badlands National Park
## *Big News in Prairie Dog Town*
### South Dakota

HUNTED TO NEAR EXTINCTION, BIGHORN SHEEP HAVE BEEN REINTRODUCED TO THE BADLANDS, along with other endangered species, including black-faced ferrets and the swift fox. Considered endangered in Canada, swift foxes are not on the list in the United States, even though only 10% of the original population survives. Invasive plant species are a serious problem in the Badlands, but controlling them is a challenge.

The Badlands aren't so bad, really—just misunderstood. This windswept, treeless plain, carved by erosion into jagged spires and buttes and deep-gouged canyons, must have been hell for the early Sioux Indians and French-Canadian trappers to traverse; no wonder they slapped a disparaging moniker on it.

But those weird geological freaks are now this national park's biggest asset. In fact, these easily eroded sedimentary rocks preserved one of the richest caches of fossils ever—saber-toothed cats, three-toed horses, pygmy camels, you name it (during the summer, watch paleontologists unearth more at their worksite, nicknamed the Pig Dig). Not only that, but because the land was impossible to farm, today it's the country's largest remaining stand of mixed-grass prairie, a complex tapestry of nearly 50 different kinds of grasses, from the tall big bluestem to the short buffalo grass, along with a summertime profusion of wildflowers.

Where you've got prairie, you ought to have prairie dogs, of course, darting in and out of the tall grass along with the cottontail rabbits. To get up close, go 5 miles (8km) outside of the park, down Sage Creek Rim Road, to Roberts Prairie Dog Town, a 300-acre (196-hectare) complex of burrows set up for observation. Along with some 6,000 black-tailed prairie dogs, you may see another fascinating prairie dweller: the black-footed ferret, with its long weasel body and raccoonlike face. Said to be the most endangered mammal in North America, the black-footed ferret was actually ruled extinct in 1979, until a few survivors were discovered in Wyoming. Biologists bred the last 18 of them in captivity, then reintroduced 36 captive-bred ferrets here in 1995. It's now estimated that there are 250 in the park and surrounding areas. With so little prairie habitat left, this is one of the last places this native ferret can thrive—especially since its main food is prairie dogs, another rapidly waning species.

The 30-mile (48km) **Loop Road** follows the Badlands wall, a massed series of spires and ridges that rise abruptly from the prairie floor. As you drive, you may see pronghorn antelope and mule deer grazing, along with shaggy bison, another native species successfully reintroduced to the park. Look up at the rocky slopes to spot bighorn sheep, another reintroduced species. Of course, human intervention backfires sometimes; one of the biggest issues facing the Badlands park is the spread of non-native plants, such as Canada thistle, exotic grasses, and knapweed, inadvertently brought in by—you guessed it—humans.

There are a few bad things about the Badlands. You can't drink the water; it's too full of sediment. Those buttes are tricky to climb, with their loose, crumbly rocks. The parkland can be blistering hot in summer, prone to heavy rainstorms and lightning; punishing blizzards roll through in winter. And it is a long drive from almost everywhere. But remoteness has its virtues: So long as there's prairie, we'll still have bison, prairie dogs—and, once more, ferrets.

---

(i) **Badlands National Park,** SD 240 at Cedar Pass (✆ **605/433-5361;** www.nps.gov/badl)

✈ Rapid City

🛏 $ **Cedar Pass Lodge,** Badlands National Park (✆ **605/433-5460,** mid-Mar to mid-Oct). $$ **Badlands Ranch and Resort,** SD 44, Interior, SD (✆ **877/433-5599** or 605/433-5599; www.badlandsranchandresort.com).

# Custer State Park & Wind Cave National Park

## *A Home Where the Buffalo Roam*

### South Dakota

AFTER COMING BACK FROM NEAR EXTINCTION CAUSED BY MASS SLAUGHTER IN THE 1870s, American bison have been newly threatened by disease as well as loss of their natural habitat due to human population growth. Today, conservationists are increasingly concerned about protecting the genetic purity of American bison because of ranchers' efforts to cross-breed bison with cattle.

Once upon a time, herds of American bison were so huge, they filled the Great Plains, shaggy masses grazing as far as the eye could see, the most numerous species of large mammal on earth. It must have been quite a sight. Years of mass slaughter by Plains Indians decimated their numbers, and white commercial hunters in the late 1800s finished off the herds. In 1889, only 1,091 bison remained in all of North America.

The population is on the upswing again, but most of the half-million American bison today are raised as livestock on commercial ranches. Only about 30,000 are in conservation herds; fewer than 5,000 are free ranging and disease-free. And by a lucky coincidence, two of the most important herds are within a few miles of each other, on the plains of western South Dakota: Custer State Park and Wind Cave National Park.

Custer's herd is one of the world's largest, with 1,500 bison on the hoof, thanks to a patient breeding program using reintroduced individuals. Just west of the Wildlife Station visitor center in the southeast corner of the park stands a set of corrals where bison are held after the annual round-up in late September (the public is invited to watch the cowboys move 'em out) to thin the herd and keep it healthy. Calves are born in the spring; you can spot them easily in the herd, with their lighter tan coats. Exhibits at the wildlife center set forth other species you are likely to see here: white-tailed deer, pronghorn antelopes, elk, mule deer, mountain goats, burros, coyotes, prairie dogs, eagles, and hawks. The 18-mile (29km) **Wildlife Loop Road** circles through open grasslands and pine-clad hills, where those species roam, often coming close to the road early in the morning or at the end of the day.

Custer's herd, like most bison herds today, are hybrid animals, crossbred over the years with domestic cattle. **Wind Cave National Park,** however, deserves a special visit because its herd—though much smaller than Custer's, around 300 to 350 bison—is one of only four worldwide that is genetically pure. Thanks to a stringent inoculation program, it's also the only one that's free from brucellosis, a common bison infection. Driving through Wind Cave's extensive rangelands of mixed-grass prairie, you'll also see Rocky Mountain elk and pronghorn antelope, two other dwindling species this vital preserve protects—for now.

Bison at Custer State Park.

ⓘ **Custer State Park,** U.S. 16A, Custer, SD
(ℂ **605/255-4515;** www.sdgfp.info/Parks/
Regions/Custer). **Wind Cave National Park**
(ℂ **605/745-4600;** www.nps.gov/wica).
**American Bison Society** (www.american
bisonsocietyonline.org).

✈ Rapid City

⊨ $$ **Alex Johnson Hotel,** 523 6th St.,
Rapid City (ℂ **800/888-2539** or 605/342-
1210; www.alexjohnson.com). $$ **Sylvan
Lake Lodge,** SD 87 and SD 89 (ℂ **605/
255-4521;** www.custerresorts.com).

**185** **Run Wild, Run Free**

# Black Hills Wild Horse Sanctuary
## *Mustang Sally*
### South Dakota

DESPITE DESIGNATION AS PROTECTED ANIMALS BY THE U.S. GOVERNMENT, WILD HORSES ARE
threatened by habitat loss due to human encroachment and changes in forestry and land
management policies. Horse slaughter is illegal in the United States, but many wild
horses in the U.S. are rounded up and shipped to Mexico and Canada for slaughter.

Though horses are far from an endangered species, wild horses, the feral
descendants of the conquistadors' stal-
lions, are in dire straits indeed, driven
from their natural open range habitat by
ranchers and growing towns. The Forest
Service and Bureau of Land Management

just couldn't handle all the mustangs that
were captured and turned over to them.

But in 1988, an Oregon writer named
Dayton O. Hyde founded the Black Hills
Wild Horse Sanctuary, an 11,000-acre
(7,211-hectare) spread of canyon, pine forest, and most of all open prairie, where

# 10 Places Where the Bighorns Still Climb

Once there were two million bighorn sheep in North America. But by the beginning of the 20th century, they were down to a few thousand. Since the 1960s, hunting bans, habitat protection, and reintroductions are beginning to restore all three sub-species: Rocky Mountain bighorn sheep, desert (or Nelson's) bighorn sheep, and the most endangered of all, Sierra Nevada (or California) bighorns.

Bring your binoculars to spot them on their hillside ranges in the following parks:

**186 Anza-Borrego Desert State Park, California**   Anza-Borrega was specifically set aside as a habitat for desert bighorn sheep, which have lighter coats, longer legs, and smaller bodies than their Rocky Mountain cousins. The best viewing spots are the overlook on Montezuma Valley Road (S22) in summer, the summit of Yaqui Road (S3) in winter and spring, the entrance to Tamarisk Grove campground, and along the Borrega Palm Canyon Nature Trail. *© 760/767-4205. www.parks.ca.gov.*

**187 Joshua Tree National Park, California**   Considering all the human rock climbers in this stunning desert park on the edge of the Mojave, it's no surprise that four-legged rock climbers like the desert bighorn would thrive. When grass is scarce—and it usually is—the herd of about 250 bighorns simply browse on cacti. Most sightings occur around the jumbled granite formations of the Wonderland of Rocks, though larger herds live in the remote Eagle Mountains to the east and in the Little San Bernardino Mountains. *© 760/367-5500. www.nps.gov/jotr.*

**188 Canyonlands National Park, Moab, Utah**   One of the country's healthiest native herds of desert bighorn sheep roams the slopes of this dramatic high desert plateau, carved into intriguing shapes by the Colorado River. Their numbers have grown from around 100 in the 1960s to around 300 today. Hike into the side canyons to view them, foraging on the scrubby vegetation of the steep, rocky terrain. *© 435/719-2313. www.nps.gov/cany.*

**189 Mount Williamson Preserve, California**   The Bighorn Sheep Zoological Preserve protects one of only two native populations of Sierra Nevada bighorn sheep (herds were reintroduced in three other preserves in the 1980s). This 4-mile-wide (6.4km) preserve stretches north for miles along Mount Williamson, California's second-highest mountain. To protect the sheep, this area is only open December 15 to July 15; there are no roads but you can hike up the Shepherd's Pass trail. *www.sierranevadawild.gov/wild/john-muir.*

Mount Williamson Preserve.

**190 Rocky Mountain National Park, Colorado**   Thanks to reintroductions in 1978 and 1980, as many as 600 bighorn sheep now live in Rocky Mountain National Park. A prime place to see them in late spring and early summer is the "Bighorn

Crossing Zone" across Highway 34 at Horseshoe Park, where the sheep migrate to the meadows around Sheep Lakes for summer grazing. Or visit their alpine range: Take the short but strenuous trail near Milner Pass to the edge of the Crater (closed May to mid-July for lambing season). *© 970/586-1206. www.nps.gov/romo.*

**191 Yellowstone National Park, Wyoming** Rangers estimate 150 to 225 Rocky Mountain bighorn sheep roam on the northern ranges of Yellowstone. In winter, you can spot bighorns along the cliffs between Gardiner and Mammoth; watch for sheep crossing the road through the Gardner River Canyon. In summer there may even be traffic jams at Dunraven Pass, a section of the Grand Loop Road, where a band of ewes and lambs has become habituated to car traffic. *© 307/344-7381. www.nps.gov/yell.*

**192 Whiskey Mountain Habitat Area, Wyoming** The National Bighorn Sheep Center in Dubois, Wyoming, leads four-wheel-drive tours November to March through this windswept winter range filled with Rocky Mountain bighorns. After a worrisome die-off in 1991, this herd declined to less than 700, but lamb survival seems on the upswing again, thanks to control of the predator coyote population. *© 888/209-2795 or 307/455-3429. www.bighorn.org.*

**193 Glacier National Park, Montana** It's not just the grizzly bears that threaten the Rocky Mountain bighorns in Glacier, it's the dwindling patches of alpine meadows. Though this park still has 400 to 600 sheep, glacier melt and lack of wildfires have allowed forests to overtake the meadows. You can often spot bighorns from your car at Logan's Pass along the Going-to-the-Sun Road, but you'll increase your chances by hiking upper mountain trails, like the Highline Trail or the Iceberg Ptarmigan Trail. *© 406/888-7800. www.nps.gov/glac.*

Glacier National Park.

**194 Banff National Park, Alberta** The Rocky Mountain bighorn sheep population is in healthier shape in the wilds of western Canada, where habitat loss is not as significant as in other parks. You can often see them grazing right by the roadside of Highway 93, the Icefields Parkway from Banff to Jasper (keep a watch out when passing through steep rocky road cuts), or the quieter parallel route Highway 1A, the Bow Valley Parkway. *© 403/762-1550. www.pc.gc.ca.*

**195 Vaseaux Bighorn National Wildlife Area, British Columbia** After the last Ice Age, a few Sierra Madre bighorn sheep migrated north into southeastern British Columbia. The largest surviving herd of them lives here, on the rocky bluffs and roadside fields around mountain-ringed Vaseaux Lake. Follow old logging access roads into the protected area, then follow hiking trails to explore along Vaseaux Creek and McIntyre Canyon. *www.env.gov.bc.ca/bcparks.*

rescued mustangs can be let loose to live out their lives without ever wearing a saddle or being led into a stall. With about 500 horses on the preserve these days, this is America's largest wild horse herd.

The Black Hills was one of the few places in the country where Hyde could find this much free grassland for relatively little money, since his nonprofit enterprise was on a shoestring budget. Today the sanctuary supports its work by charging for tours, which range from a 2-hour guided bus ride around the core of the sanctuary to a full-day excursion via 4-wheel-drive to more remote areas. (The tours aren't cheap, but most visitors report that they were worth the price, especially considering that the money goes to fund further wild horse rescue.) Reservations are essential. Besides rolling past grazing mustangs, tour participants view new foals in their enclosure—you may even be able to pet the older colts, for although these horses have never been broken to saddle, they have been well treated by humans and haven't developed any fear of them. (Some of the older mustangs on the range may not be so trusting, however.)

Tours also drive out to Native American petroglyphs, homestead sites, and the remains of a movie set—the movies *Crazy Horse* and *Hidalgo* were both filmed here.

There's a short nature trail to walk on, with interpretive information on the ecology of the prairie. The sanctuary also sells several foals every year, both to raise money and to keep the herd at a sustainable size, and has a brisk gift-shop trade.

The Cheyenne River flows through this prairie preserve, providing an essential water source in this arid region. Though fences keep the horses on this rambling property, other animals have wandered in to make it their home as well—white-tail and mule deer, the occasional elk, wild turkeys, and the inevitable coyotes and cougars. Eagles and falcons soar overhead, and prairie dogs have moved in to build their burrows. And why not? It's a prairie—which is all these horses ever needed.

---

(i) **Black Hills Wild Horse Sanctuary,** 12163 Highland Rd. (off Hwy. 71), Hot Springs (© **800/252-6652** or 605/745-5955; www.wildmustangs.com)

✈ Rapid City

⌦ $$ **Black Hills Wild Horse Sanctuary Cabin,** on sanctuary grounds (© **800/252-6652** or 605/745-5955; www.wildmustangs.com). $ **Rodeway Inn,** 402 Battle Mountain Ave., Hot Springs (© **605/745-3182;** www.choicehotels.com).

---

**Run Wild, Run Free** **196**

# Wild Horse Sanctuary
## *Phantom & Friends*
### Shingletown, California

HORSE MEAT IS A GOURMET MEAL IN SOME PARTS OF THE WORLD, WHICH IS WHY AMERICAN wild and domestic horses end up on dining tables in Europe and Asia. Slaughtering horses is illegal in the United States. In the meantime, dwindling habitat and lack of protection put sanctuaries like this among the few remaining places where wild horses are safe.

Who says that wild mustangs vanished along with the Wild West? Don't tell that to the Phantom Stallion, who defiantly roamed the hills near Dayton, Nevada, as recently as 2006. When this beautiful, untamable white mustang—made famous by a series of children's books—was finally captured, there was one logical place to send him to spend the rest of his days: The Wild Horse Sanctuary in Shingletown, California.

Though it's a smaller operation than the Black Hills sanctuary—only 5,000 acres (3,287 hectares), with a herd of around 300—this California preserve got into the business of rescuing wild horses 10 years earlier, in 1978, and was the first to bring media attention to the Bureau of Land Management's quiet practice of slaughtering wild horses found on public lands, which nobody wanted to adopt. It's a beautiful site, near Lassen National Park (which accounts of the volcanic rock cropping out of these mountain meadows), with lusher pastureland than the South Dakota preserve. Extensive pine and oak forests provide winter cover for the horses, as well as a number of tough, ornery little burros who have joined their ranks. Naturally, other animals live here as well—deer, raccoon, badgers, black bear, gray fox, quails, and wild turkeys, as well as less friendly neighbors such as coyote, bobcats, and mountain lions. Within the shelter of the herd, the horses are safe from those natural predators, as they never would be if they were maverick mustangs fending for themselves.

Saving wild horses is an expensive business, and the sanctuary—which, like the Black Hills sanctuary, sells a few foals every year to raise money, making room for older horses who are unadoptable—hasn't yet completed visitor facilities, although they do offer wild horse viewing on foot on Saturdays and Wednesdays. Even better are the 2- and 3-day weekend pack trips they offer in spring and summer, and a 4-to-6-day cattle drive in the fall. (Overnights are spent in a set of frontier-style sleeping cabins on the verge of a pristine vernal lake). Volunteers are also welcome to come help feed the wild horses in winter, when grazing is scarce, and build visitor facilities. Hey, every bit helps.

ⓘ **Wild Horse Sanctuary,** 5796 Wilson Hill Rd., Shingletown, CA (✆ **530/335-2241;** www.wildhorsesanctuary.org)

✈ Redding

🛏 $$$ **The Weston House,** Red Rock Rd., Shingletown (✆ **530/474-3738;** www.westonhouse.com). $$ **Hat Creek Resort,** CA 44/89, Old Station, CA (✆ **530/335-7121;** hatcreekresort@juno.com).

---

**197** Run Wild, Run Free

# Red Deer Range
## *The Great Stags of Scotland*
### Galloway, Scotland

ONCE NEARLY EXTINCT, THE RED DEER OF SCOTLAND HAVE ADAPTED SO WELL THAT THEY ARE now considered a nuisance. With no natural predators except for hunters, red deer have proliferated and are being blamed for devouring vegetation that feeds and shelters smaller animals and birds.

Raising its majestic antlers to the Highlands sky, the red deer is a rugged Scottish icon, as much a fixture of the national image as kilts and whiskey. It's hard to believe that at one time these great beasts were nearly extinct in Scotland.

Looking uncannily like North American elk (though scientists declare they're two different species), the red deer is U.K.'s largest wild mammal. Once common through England, Wales, and Scotland, its traditional stronghold was Scotland's great Caledonian Forest. But as forests across the British Isles—including the Caledonian Forest—were cut down in the 18th century, the red deer began to vanish as well. By the mid–19th century, they seemed well on their way to extinction in the wild.

And yet somehow the red deer have survived, by adapting to different landscapes—pushed north to the cooler, more thinly vegetated mountains and moors of the Highlands, where they browse on heather and blaeberry, rowan, aspen, and willows. The modern red deer is considerably smaller than its ancestors, though, and this may not just be a function of altered diet. Today's red deer are descended not from wild deer but from game herds that British aristocrats traditionally kept on their estates in Scotland, which were eventually released into the wild. Over the years these sportsmen tended to kill the largest and most magnificent stags, thus weakening the genetic pool, whereas natural predators like the wolf, the lynx, and the brown bear (all now extirpated from Britain) helped strengthen the genetic stock by culling the old and the weak. Another size factor may be hybridization with the smaller sika deer, imported as game animals from Japan.

Whatever they've done to survive, as many as 350,000 red deer now roam in Scotland—quite a comeback. In fact, some farmers are beginning to complain about too many red deer, overgrazing sparse pastureland. One proposal to control deer numbers is to reintroduce the wolf to the Highlands. It's as if nature has come full circle.

A reliable place to observe red deer in the wild is not in the Highlands, but down in the Lowlands, in Galloway Forest Park. From A712, halfway between New Galloway and Newton Stewart, a .8km (half-mile) trail leads to a viewing area where a number of red deer are protected in their own woodland range. (Nearby is a similar range for wild goats.) This area is ancient farmland that's been allowed to go back to forest, and the deer have happily returned—you can even observe their rutting rituals in the autumn, with stags proudly clashing antlers. One can only imagine how bonnie they were once, in their Caledonian prime.

ⓘ **Galloway Forest Park,** Clatteringshaws, A712 (℡ **44/1671/402420;** www.forestry.gov.uk/gallowayforestpark)

✈ Prestwick

🚌 Dumfries

🛏 $$ **Longacre Manor,** Ernespie Rd., Castle Douglas (℡ **44/1556/503-576;** www.kayukay.co.uk/dumfrieshotels/longacrecastledouglas.html). $$ **Urr Valley Country House Hotel,** Ernespie Rd., Castle Douglas (℡ **44/1556/502-188;** www.scottish-inns.co.uk/urrvalley).

---

Run Wild, Run Free **198**

# Wild Horses of the Camargue
## Allez, Allez, *Little Dogies*
### Southern France

POLLUTION AND CLIMATE CHANGE THREATEN THE FRAGILE HABITATS OF THE CAMARGUE. HIGH levels of copper, cadmium, lead, mercury, and zinc have been found in the local eel population, an important food source for wintering birds like herons and egrets. Rising water levels from climate change threaten the fragile delta, home to more than 640 plant species, of which 105 are considered rare and endangered.

Camargue Horse.

France's cattle country doesn't look at all like the American West—instead of rolling scrub-covered plains, it's a marshy delta where two arms of the Rhone river empty into the Mediterranean. But the black bulls raised in the Camargue are prized beasts, raised for the bullfights held in nearby Arles and Nimes, and they are herded by a distinctive crew of French cowboys called *gardians*, who wear large felt hats and prod the cattle with a long three-pronged stick. (It's thought, in fact, that the first American cowboys were gardians who emigrated on French ships to the port of New Orleans, then hired themselves out to herd cattle in East Texas.) The gardians ride the range on small white horses said to have been brought here by the Saracens, whose wild cousins can still be seen running free through the salt marshlands.

Descended long ago from Arabian horses, these sturdy little steeds have distinctive long manes and bushy tails, which evolved over the centuries to slap the pesky, gluttonous mosquitoes who thrive in these wetlands. (Spend much time here and you may wish you had a tail, too.) Their hoofs are so tough, they don't need even horseshoes. You may spot black or dark brown foals scampering beside their mothers in the herd, but they all turn white by the time they're adults.

It's an exotic corner of France, with whitewashed houses, plaited-straw roofs, roaming Gypsies, and pink flamingoes. Two to three dozen stables (depending on the time of year) along the highway from Arles to Stes-Maries offer expeditions on horseback into the park. Given the easy temperament and sure-footedness of Camargue ponies, these rides are recommended even for those who have never been on a horse before. On horseback, you can ford the waters to penetrate deep into the interior where black bulls graze, wild ponies gallop, and water birds nest.

With the most fragile ecosystem in France, the alluvial plain of the Camargue has been a national park since 1970, and exotic flora and fauna abound. The bird life here is the most luxuriant in Europe—not only colonies of pink flamingos but some

400 other bird species, including ibises, egrets, kingfishers, owls, wild ducks, swans, and ferocious birds of prey. The best place to see flamingo colonies is the area around Ginès, a hamlet on N570, 5km (3 miles) north of Camargue's capital, Stes-Maries-de-la-Mer—a perfectly preserved medieval walled town set amidst swamps and lagoons, long ago an embarkation point for the crusades and well worth a visit.

(i) **Camargue National Park,** D570 near Stes-Maries-de-la-Mer, France

🚌 Arles

🛏 $$$ **Hotel Les Templiers,** 23 rue de la République, Aigues-Mortes (ⓒ **33/4-66-53-66-56**). $$ **Hotel Jules Cesar,** 9 bd. des Lices, Arles (ⓒ **33/4-90-52-52-52;** www.hotel-julescesar.fr).

**Run Wild, Run Free** 199

# Wild Ass Wildlife Sanctuary
## *Salty Tales in the Indian Desert*
### Gujarat, India

SALT-MINING OPERATIONS NEARBY DESTROY NATIVE HABITAT AND CREATE AIR AND NOISE pollution that threaten endangered wild asses. In addition, heavy commercial traffic has driven these animals away from their former breeding areas. Gujarat is also home to most of India's highly polluting textile, pesticide, and chemical plants.

In the Little Rann of Kutch, the animals don't need a calendar to know what the season is. When the monsoons sweep through this low-lying desertland (*rann* means desert in Gujarati), only a few humps of land rise above the flood. Some 2,000 animals cluster on the islands, or *bets,* waiting out the rains. Once the waters recede, though, the lower land becomes a vast salt flat, and the animals spread out to browse on the dry thorny scrub. Up the slopes from the flats, animals can also graze on less salty intermediate areas known as *kala-lana.* Toward the end of the dry season, they drift back towards those bets, where the last thick stands of grass still grow.

This is the largest wildlife sanctuary in India, nearly 5,000 sq. km (1,930 sq. miles), originally founded in 1972 to protect India's rare wild asses, one of the last three species of wild ass in the world (the other two are in Central Asia and Tibet). Less than 2,000 of these Indian wild asses survive today, all here in the Rann of Kutch. The blazing heat of summer and long weeks of drought conditions are nothing to these hardy little creatures. With their tawny backs and white underbellies, they blend perfectly into the desert salt flat landscape. They're just about impossible to catch, because they can reach a speed of 70km (45 mph), and can sustain a 24kmph (15 mph) pace for a good 2 hours at a time; tracking them on an open jeep safari is your only hope of getting a sustained up-close sighting.

Along with the asses, the sanctuary harbors blackbuck, chinkara, hedgehog, wolf, jackal, fox, striped hyena, caracal, jungle cat, and desert cat. There are birds here, too—cranes, flamingoes, larks, pelicans, falcons, even the rare Houbara bustard—although they tend to settle in during the monsoons, where the land is one vast marsh, and migrate elsewhere when things get dry. Watchtowers have been set up for panoramic wildlife observation; sunrise or sunset are prime viewing times.

Looking at this bleak desert landscape, you'd think there would be no competition to threaten the wild asses, but there is. Since this is a saline desert, salt mining is a major local industry, yielding 25% of India's salt supply, and illegal operations steal into the park continually. There's also an Indian army firing range within the sanctuary. Still, it takes a lot to shake the Indian wild ass from its native ground. So far, nobody has.

ⓘ **Wild Ass Sanctuary,** Zainabad, India

✈ Ahmedabad or Bhuj

🚆 Viramgam

🛏 $$ **Rann Resorts,** near Dasad Village (www.wildlife-india-tours.com). $$ **Desert Coursers,** east of Hwy. 10 (www.wildlife-india-tours.com).

# 4 Big Skies

*Acadia National Park.*

# Acadia National Park
## *The Falcons Are Back, Baby*
### Mount Desert Island, Maine

ACADIA CONTAINS MANY DIFFERENT ECOSYSTEMS—FROM FRESHWATER WETLANDS AND coastal tide pools to alpine forests—and rare or endangered plant and animal species. Threats to the park include invasive plant and insect species—purple loosestrife now threatens 20% of the park's wetlands—and rising sea levels, which harm coastal ecosystems with flooding and saltwater intrusion.

There's a bunch of hackers loose in Acadia National Park. But among ornithologists, hackers are the good guys—the ones who hand-rear chicks and reintroduce them into the wild. At Acadia National Park, those hackers are proud to say that they got peregrine falcons nesting in the wild again for the first time in 35 years.

Acadia is a glacier-chiseled mound of rugged cliffs, picturesque coves, and quiet woods connected by causeway to the coast of Maine—a perfect habitat for these beautiful soaring raptors. But peregrines are endangered these days, due to nest robbing, hunting, and toxic pesticides (even though these are banned in the U.S., peregrines may eat migrant songbirds from countries where the use of DDT is still common). By the mid-1960s, researchers said peregrines were no longer breeding anywhere in the eastern United States.

In response, in 1984 specialists at Acadia started breeding peregrines in captivity in a strictly controlled program to prepare them for the wild. The first 22 chicks were hacked into a cliff face overlooking Jordan Pond each spring from 1984 to 1986. In 1991 the first hacked birds finally bred, nested, and hatched their own chicks, raising them in the cliffs of Champlain Mountain.

Park resource managers monitor peregrines' comings and goings carefully, so don't be surprised if trails are temporarily closed to protect mating and nesting spots. Even if the trail's closed, the **Precipice Trail parking area** offers prime viewing of their nesting cliff on Champlain Mountain (daily from mid-May to mid-Aug, rangers lead a program describing peregrine activity). During mating, the birds feed each other in midair and show off with elaborate swoops, tumbles, and dives. In April and May, they take turns nest sitting; in June you may spot the tiny white balls of fluff that are baby falcons. In July and August, watch fledgling falcons try out their wings with ever-longer forays from the cliffs.

Your best introduction to Acadia is a circuit on the 20-mile (32km) **Park Loop Road,** a spectacular drive that follows the island's rocky shore past picturesque coves, looping back inland along Jordan Pond and Eagle Lake with a detour up Cadillac Mountain, the highest point on the East Coast north of Rio de Janeiro. But don't stop there. Go kayaking around Frenchman's Bay, populated by seals and osprey; bike around the forested interior on crushed-rock carriageways laid out for Gilded Age tycoons; visit a series of geological formations using a GPS system to track down EarthCache clues; or take a catamaran cruise to the offshore feeding grounds of humpback, finback, minke, and (occasionally) right whales. And never forget to look up in the sky—the peregrines could be there, watching you.

🛏 $ **Bar Harbor Campground,** Rte. 3, Salisbury Cove (ⓒ **207/288-5185**). $$ **Harborside Hotel & Marina,** 55 West St., Bar Harbor (ⓒ **800/328-5033** or 207/288-5033; www.theharborsidehotel.com).

Flying High **201**

# Adirondack State Park
## *Loon-ey Tunes*
### Northern New York State

ADIRONDACK STATE PARK FACES A RECURRING THREAT OF POTENTIAL DEVELOPMENT AND logging on tracts of private land in and around the park. Acid rain is an increasing problem throughout the Adirondacks, and the loon population is threatened by mercury in the thousands of lakes, ponds, and rivers that flow through the park.

Their official name is the common loon, but there's nothing common at all about these striking black-and-white water birds with the red eyes and the haunting call. Congregating on the forest-fringed Adirondack lakes of northern New York State, they're such an essential part of a North Woods summer, they're the region's de facto trademark. It's hard to imagine the place without them—but someday we may have to.

This 6-million-acre (2.4-million-hectare) wilderness park enfolds a complex web of some 3,000 lakes and ponds, strung along 6,000 miles (9,656km) of rivers and streams. Despite scattered pockets of settlement—the biggest town is Lake Placid, home to two Winter Olympics—it's a huge intact ecosystem, with plenty of corridors where wildlife can roam freely, either on land (white-tailed deer, moose, red foxes) or on the water (beavers, perch, trout, ducks, geese, and loons).

Because loons live a long time and are very high on the food chain, they are what ecologists call "sentinels"—when they're healthy, it's an indicator that the whole ecosystem is in good shape. But these days, studies of the loon population reveal

many environmental threats, including mercury runoff in the water, acid rain, and disrupted shoreline. We humans can choose to eat something else if the local fish have high mercury counts; loons can't. When their fish diet is contaminated, neurotoxins build up in their bodies, breeding rates plummet, and their behavior becomes erratic.

To sight loons, head for the water—they only go ashore to mate or to tend their eggs. With legs set far back on their bodies, these big birds (wingspans up to 2 ft./.6m) are clumsy walkers but fantastic swimmers, able to dive up to 90 feet (27m) to spear fish with their daggerlike black beaks. Silent in winter, in summer they're outright noisy, with a distinctive shivering hoot—even if you don't see them you'll know they're around.

To sample the mosaic of Adirondack habitats, walk the nature trails around the Adirondack Park Visitor Center at Paul Smiths (12 miles/19km north of Saranac Lake). A boardwalk crosses a boreal fog, with an overlook tower on Barnum Pond for sighting loons, ducks, and herons; the 0.8-mile (1.3km) Barnum Brook Trail skirts Heron Marsh, where you can see a nest box used by common goldeneye (another "common" species that has become uncommon). Head south on Route 30, through Lake Clear, to **Floodwood Road,** a 5-mile (8km) drive with several turnouts for ponds, streams, bog pockets, and forest that yield excellent birding in late spring and summer. Stop at Polliwog, Middle, or Floodwood ponds and listen quietly—the loons are there.

ⓘ **Adirondack Regional Tourism Council** (✆ **518/846-8016;** www. adirondacks.org)

✈ Saranac Lake

🛏 $$ **Hilton Lake Placid Resort,** 1 Mirror Lake Dr., Lake Placid (✆ **800/755-5598** or 518/523-4411; www.lphilton.com). $$ **Best Western Golden Arrow Hotel,** 150 Main St., Lake Placid (✆ **518/523-3353;** www.golden-arrow.com).

---

**202** Flying High

# Cape May Migratory Bird Refuge
## *Where the Birds Are*
### West Cape May, New Jersey

LOSS OF HABITAT IS ONE OF THE MAJOR THREATS TO THE MANY BIRD SPECIES THAT FLOCK HERE. Swimming, sunbathing, and other recreational uses on the beaches pose a threat to beach-nesting birds and disrupt the feeding habits of migratory shore birds. Destruction of unprotected upland habitat by dredging, ditching, groundwater pumping, and off-road vehicles is also a serious threat.

It's been said that there are two kinds of birders: those who have birded Cape May and those who aspire to bird Cape May. Tens of thousands of raptors swarm here every fall—peregrine falcons, northern harriers, sharp-shinned hawks, just for starters—along with over a million seabirds, including rare beauties like black skimmers. You almost can't avoid spectacular sightings. Spring brings thousands of migrating shorebirds, songbirds, and waterfowl. On an April morning, it's possible to see ibis, egrets, plovers, and dowitchers strolling along the beach, or at least bitterns dabbling around in the reeds. It's outstanding in terms of quantity and quality; the rare is the norm.

Cape May lies on the Atlantic Flyway, a major pathway for migrating birds; many water birds extend their stay here because of the availability of horseshoe crabs in Delaware Bay. And that's not even mentioning the many species that reside year-round here on the tip of the Cape May peninsula, a natural haven on the otherwise heavily developed Jersey shore. Set at a transitional latitude, where southern loblolly pines and swamp oaks meet northern pitch pine forests, it's also got dunes, fresh- and saltwater marshes, ponds, a pristine beachfront—a range of habitats to suit every bird's taste.

When they tire of birds (as if!), visitors to Cape May can train their binoculars on more than 100 species of butterflies and over 75 species of dragonflies and damselflies. Flurries of monarchs fill the sky in October in a dazzling show of autumn color.

Known as "the meadows" by locals, the refuge (owned and operated by the Nature Conservancy) provides a nesting place for least terns and piping plovers, protecting them from the feral cats and rats and recreational vehicles that have driven them to endangered status. You can't disturb their nesting area, but you can observe them on the refuge's beach in June and July. Just off the beach lie the remains of the former Victorian resort town of South Beach, which was destroyed by a storm and claimed by the ocean in the 1950s. The land remained an open meadow until 1981; it now spans 229 acres (93 hectares) with trails winding through marsh edges, offering a close view of its inhabitants. The refuge offers daily nature walks and a handicapped-accessible observation platform.

Cape May itself is America's oldest seaside resort town, dotted with Victorian hotels, houses, and mansions. There are loads of quaint B&Bs in town, where you're bound to run into fellow birders, all enjoying the best bird-watching of their lives.

---

ⓘ **William D. and Jane C. Blair Jr. Cape May Migratory Bird Refuge,** Sunset Blvd., Cape May (✆ **609/861-0660**)

✈ Newark or Baltimore

🛏 $$$ **The Star Inn,** 22 Perry St. (✆ **800/297-3779**; www.thestarinn.net). $$ **The Montreal Inn,** Beach at Madison Ave. (✆ **800/525-7011** or 609/884-7011; www.montreal-inn.com).

## Flying High 203

# Sandy Island
## *Red-Cockaded Homebodies*
### South Carolina

THOUGH SAFE FROM THE KIND OF COMMERCIAL DEVELOPMENT THAT WOULD DESTROY ITS fragile ecosystem, Sandy Island serves as a safe haven for the rare and endangered species, including the red-cockaded woodpeckers that have taken refuge here. However, loss of habitat from such causes as hurricanes and other natural disasters continues to pose a serious threat.

The red-cockaded woodpecker is a handsome bird, but very picky: It will nest only in live pines in large open stands. And how many of those are left these days?

These beautiful woodpeckers were once abundant; now they may be reduced to only 4,500 family groups, their preferred habitats eliminated by logging and agriculture. To make matters worse, in 1989 Hurricane Hugo destroyed many of the trees that give them shelter and sustenance. Fortunately, they have found a haven in Sandy Island, South Carolina, a pristine coastal ecosystem sandwiched between two rivers and reachable only by boat. It's a rich mix of cypress swamps, longleaf-pine and oak forests, salt marshes,

and sand hills rising as high as 78 feet (23m). Those longleaf pines are perfect for red-cockaded woodpeckers, who feed on the beetles, ants, roaches, wood-boring insects, and spiders that live in pines. Pecking vigorously at the pine trunks, they also release sticky resin that flows down the trees, thus setting up a handy barrier to thwart predators like snakes. Other trees just don't offer that feature.

Once the red-cockaded woodpeckers find those perfect pines, they're real homebodies. They don't migrate, keep the same mates for several years, and raise their young in communal groups of five to nine birds, on savannas and open pine forests. Within a group, only one pair breeds each year, the female laying two to four eggs in a cavity in a mature pine tree; other group members help incubate eggs and raise the young. After fledging, the young commonly stay with the group—another generation of homebodies.

It's scary to think that not so long ago, in 1993, developers planned to build a bridge to connect this isolated community to the mainland. Once a rice plantation, now inhabited only by a few descendants of former plantation slaves, peaceful Sandy Island is less than an hour's drive from the frenetic attractions of Myrtle Beach; on its northeast border lies Brookfield Gardens, a popular historic-home attraction. The 3-year legal battle to block bridge construction centered on protecting Sandy Island's endangered species. This time, the environmentalists won.

You still have to catch a boat to visit Sandy Island, and when you get here, you won't find visitor facilities—just forest, wetlands, and wildlife. Bring your binoculars so you can pick out the red-cockaded woodpecker that saved this island: He'll be the one with the black-and-white barred back, large white eye patches, black cap, and the small red streak on each side of the head, like an ornament on a hat. Chances are good he'll be in a pine tree.

ⓘ **Sandy Island,** near Murrell's Inlet, SC (www.nature.org)

✈ Myrtle Beach International Airport

**BOAT LANDINGS** Sandy Island, Wacca Wache, Samworth Wildlife Management Area, Yauhanna.

🛏 $ **Holiday Inn Express,** 11445 Hwy. 17 S, Pawley's Island (✆ **888/465-4329** or 843/235-0808; www.ichotelsgroup. com). $$ **Hampton Inn,** 150 Willbrook Blvd., Pawley's Island (✆ **800/426-7866** or 843/235-2000; www.pawleysisland hamptoninn.com).

**204** Flying High

# The Agassiz Dunes Preserves
## *Dances with Prairie Chickens*
### Fertile, Minnesota

INVASION BY FOREIGN AND EXOTIC PLANT SPECIES THAT CAN OVERWHELM NATIVE SPECIES AND reduce critical habitat threatens the rare ecosystem here. And with so little grassland left, the last prairie chickens are stuck in small isolated populations, without a chance for healthy genetic mixing.

Once upon a time, a great glacial lake shimmered across the upper Midwest, west of today's Great Lakes. When the waters receded, a vast flat prairieland remained, where bison grazed, prairie dogs burrowed, and hawks circled overhead. Then the settlers came to plow it all under. But what could they do with the ridges and dunes that had once been Lake Agassiz's shoreline? That hilly, dry, infertile terrain wouldn't support much except tough grasses and gnarled bur oaks. Useless.

Ecologists finally noticed the Sand Hills, and realized they had a treasure on their hands. Beauty is only part of it: In early spring, pasque flowers run wild over the rippling terrain; in late summer, blazing star, purple coneflower, and sunflower add vibrant color. But even more important, patches of rare habitat inevitably become havens for rare species—like the Powesheik skipper butterfly, vesper sparrows, upland sandpipers, red-headed woodpeckers, ruffed grouse, or the plains pocket gopher.

# 10 Places Where the Sky's Still Dark at Night

"Dark sky" is like a Holy Grail for stargazers. But on this increasingly populated planet, areas with no light pollution from nearby human settlements have become increasingly rare. Just imagine what sky events like the Northern Lights or Perseid meteor showers could look like in a truly dark sky. The following sites not only offer dark skies, they also have stargazing programs with local night-sky experts.

Mauna Kea.

**205 Mauna Kea, Hawaii**   Many native Hawaiians felt that building this international cluster of powerful telescopes on the summit of Mauna Kea, the world's tallest mountain (measured from the sea floor), violated its spiritual significance to the Hawaiian people. But determined to capitalize on this unique unpolluted site so close to the equator, the astronomers prevailed. You can only visit the summit's 11 telescopes (one of which is the world's largest) by 4WD vehicles or on a guided tour. ✆ *808/961-2180. www.ifa.hawaii.edu/info/vis.*

**206 Natural Bridges National Monument, Lake Powell, Utah**   Set on a sandstone mesa in the middle of Utah's high-desert plateau, Natural Bridges is not only beautiful by day but it also offers some of the darkest, clearest night skies in the nation—in fact, the International Dark-Sky Association named it the world's first International Dark Sky Park in 2007. ✆ *435/692-1234. www.nps.gov/nabr.*

**207 Great Basin National Park, Twin Falls, Idaho**   The low humidity, clean air, and high elevation of this remote national park all contribute to its supremely dark night skies. Unless the sky is cloudy, or the moon is too full, head for prime stargazing spots at the Wheeler Peak/Bristlecone Trail parking lot, Mather Overlook, and the Baker Archeological Site. ✆ *775/234-7331, ext. 212. www.nps.gov/grba.*

**208 Cherry Springs State Park, Coudersport, Pennsylvania**   Surrounded by farmland and state forest, with a mountain range blocking the nearest large city, and far inland from the cloud effect that sometimes gathers over the Great Lakes, this 48-acre (19-hectare) park is renowned for its dark skies (and local anti-light-pollution ordinances). An official Pennsylvania State dark sky preserve, the park holds regular public stargazing nights. ✆ *814/435-5010. www.dcnr.state.pa.us/stateparks/parks/cherrysprings.aspx.*

**209 Torrance Barrens, Bala, Ontario**   Set on a flat shelf of bedrock, where the only trees are too stunted to block the horizons, Torrance Barrens is surrounded by other parklands and conservation areas, so it has remarkably little sky glow and 360-degree views. *www.muskokaheritage.org/natural/torrancebarrens.asp.*

**210 Gordon's Park, Manitoulin Island, Ontario**  Set on Manitoulin Island in northern Lake Huron, this eco-campground takes advantage of its remote location by setting aside a portion of the resort, with both tent sites and cabins, as a dark-sky preserve. The skies here are the darkest in Ontario. ℭ *705/859-2470*. *www.gordon spark.com.*

**211 McDonald Park Dark Sky Preserve, Abbotsford, British Columbia**  Named a dark sky preserve in 2000, this western Canada park near the U.S. border is shielded by a mountain from the light pollution of the only nearby towns; its views are limited to the southern and western skies, but they are extraordinarily dark, despite the park's proximity to Vancouver. *www.fvas.net/dsp.html.*

**212 Cypress Hills Dark-Sky Preserve, Alberta/Saskatchewan**  This 40,000-hectare (98,900-acre) expanse of forest-fringed prairie is Canada's fourth designated dark-sky preserve—and the country's largest. Stargazers recommend camping at the Meadows campground, which has unobstructed sky views. ℭ *306/662-5411. www. cypresshills.com.*

**213 Yorkshire Dales National Park, Yorkshire, England**  The U.K.'s prime stargazing territory is this 1,812-sq.-km (700-sq.-mile) park in the north, where relatively treeless moors leave 360-degree views, elevations are high (the park straddles the Pennines mountain range), and air pollution and light pollution are minimal. A vast network of public footpaths cross the moors, so you can choose your stargazing spot. ℭ *44/969 666210. www.yorkshiredales.org.uk.*

Yorkshire Dales National Park.

**214 Warrumbungle National Park, New South Wales, Australia**  The night sky looks completely different in the Southern Hemisphere—don't miss it if you're down here. While rock climbers love this park for its volcanic rock spires, flat areas near Camp Blackman offer the most panoramic skies. Nearby Coonabarabran is known as the astronomy capital of Australia, with a planetarium at the Skywatch Observatory on Timor Road (ℭ *61/2/6842 3303;* www.skywatchobservatory.com) and the country's largest observatory, Siding Springs (www.aao.gov.au). ℭ *61/2/6825 4364. www2.nationalparks. nsw.gov.au/parks.nsf.*

And where you've got ancient prairie, you just may get the greater prairie chicken. This endangered bird was made to live in mixed-grass plains, with its intricately barred plumage for camouflage, and its ground forager's diet of insects, seeds, and fruits. They move back and forth from the tall, dense grass, where they hide their nests in late spring, to more open short-grass prairie, where hatchlings peck around in summer. The most fascinating sight, though, comes in April or May on the short grass, as adult males perform a fascinating courtship dance—drumming their feet, ballooning out their orange neck patches, and letting loose a booming call you can hear a mile away.

The greater prairie chicken is in trouble (though not so bad as its cousins, the now-extinct heath hen and Attwater's prairie hen, which survives only in southeast Texas). With little grassland left, the last prairie chickens are stuck in small isolated populations, without a chance for healthy genetic mixing. That's why ecologists are studying the population that roosts around Fertile, Minnesota, on two closely related

sites: the 640-acre (259-hectare) Agassiz Environmental Learning Center on the edge of this small town, and the 417-acre (169-hectare) Agassiz Dunes Natural and Scientific Area a couple miles outside of town. The AELC is easier to explore, with interpretive displays at its Nature Center, 10 miles (16km) of trails, panoramic bluff overlooks, unique "blow-outs" where sand dunes persist, and a botanical garden of native plants. You can hike, ride horses, or cross-country ski on these trails. It's a little quieter out at the Agassiz Dunes NSA, though, where the greater prairie chickens are more in evidence. If you're lucky, you may even catch that spring mating dance.

(i) **Agassiz Environmental Learning Center,** 400 Summit Ave. SW, Fertile, MN (© **218/945-3129;** http://aelcfertile.org). **Agassiz Dunes Natural and Scientific Area,** off Hwy. 32, Fertile, MN (www. nature.org).

✈ Bemidji

⊨ **Sand Hill Motel,** 605 S. Mill St, Fertile (© **218/945-6114**)

---

# Sandy Island Bald Eagle Preserve
## *Unlikely Looking Love Birds*
### Missouri

A COUPLE DECADES AGO, THE BALD EAGLE WAS NEARLY EXTINCT, DUE TO DDT CONTAMINATION of their prey and habitat. Since the United States banned DDT in the 1960s, bald eagles have made an impressive comeback, but DDT is regaining popularity worldwide as a weapon against mosquitoes that spread diseases, which could threaten bald eagles again.

Just a few miles from metropolitan St. Louis is an astonishing spectacle, better than any nature special on TV: nesting American bald eagles, roosting by the hundreds in the tall silver maples and cottonwood trees. It's like a cross between Alfred Hitchcock's The Birds and a Fourth of July patriotic film montage: You can

almost hear "God Bless America" playing in the background.

It happens every January and February at the Sandy Island Bald Eagle Sanctuary, on the banks of the Mississippi River. Though the sanctuary is technically closed November through February, to protect the eagles' nesting grounds, visitors can watch these magnificent birds from an observation platform, provided with a powerful viewing scope. During warmer months, you won't get the eagle display, but you can enjoy 28 acres (11 hectares) of wilderness here, along with plenty of other prime bird-watching. A couple decades ago, the bald eagle was nearly extinct. But the species has made such a strong comeback, it's been promoted from "endangered" to merely "threatened" on the Endangered Species List. Currently, there are approximately 65,000 bald eagles in North America.

Few other wintering spots are quite as impressive—and as accessible—as Sandy Island. These majestic birds, who live an average of 25 years, are known for mating for life. The female lays one to three eggs per year, and chicks remain in the nest for 10 to 11 weeks. The term "bald" is, of course, a misnomer; they earned that name at a time when the word "bald" meant "white." Bald eagles do have distinctive white heads, but they don't get those until they're adults—don't expect to see white-headed chicks peeping out of those nests.

While most schoolchildren can tell you that Benjamin Franklin objected to making the bald eagle our national bird, they probably don't know why he objected to them: He didn't think it seemly that a bird that ate carrion should represent the United States. In nature, of course, eating carrion qualifies as a public service. But while the bald eagle will eat carrion and small mammals, its preferred diet is fish. You can see the eagles soaring over water at the sanctuary, casting wide shadows as they hunt for fish. (Some adult birds have wingspans that stretch up to 8 ft./2.4m). The sanctuary's location is no accident: It's just downstream from Lock and Dam No. 25, listed on the National Register of Historic Places, and the birds take advantage of the open water created by the dam. It's very handy for the birds—and even handier for us bird-watchers.

(i) **Sandy Island Bald Eagle Preserve,** Hwy. N, Winfield, MO (www.nature.org)

✈ St. Louis

🚌 $$ **Adams Mark,** 315 Chestnut St., St. Louis (© **800/444-2326** or 314/241-1102). $$ **Drury Inn Union Station,** 201 S. 20th St., St. Louis (© **800/378-7946** or 314/231-3900; www.druryhotels.com/properties/unionstation.cfm).

## 216 Flying High

# Eckert James River Bat Cave Preserve
## *Sunset at the Bat Cave*
### Mason, Texas

DESPITE THEIR UNDESERVED REPUTATION AS PORTENTS OF EVIL AND CARRIERS OF DISEASE, BATS are beneficial to humans, preying on insects that damage crops and producing guano that is used as fertilizer. But bats are also remarkably vulnerable to humans; one act of vandalism at a roost site can wipe out a whole colony or cause the bats to evacuate.

The scene is right out of a vampire movie: At dusk, millions of bats rise from their cave and darken the sky as they rise upward, looking for prey. The swarm keeps growing, swirling like a tornado, the high-pitched chirps and screeches rising to deafening levels. Their prey, of course, is not human blood but insects—each of these little brown bats must eat nearly its own weight in insects each night, including thousands of mosquitoes, moths, and

Bats take flight at Eckert James.

cutworms. It's nature's method of pest control, and a whole lot better than DDT.

The Eckert James River Bat Cave Preserve, home to the Mexican free-tailed bats, is one of the largest bat nurseries in the country. The 8-acre (3.2-hectare) preserve's immense cave provides a habitat for some four million pregnant bats between May and September, where each bat mom gives birth to a single pup sometime in June or July. It's one of the few places on earth where you can still observe this fragile species. Because Mexican freetails live in such huge colonies, human interference with just one roosting site can wipe out a significant percentage of the species, and they reproduce so slowly that they can't catch up—their numbers keep declining dramatically every year.

A century ago, ranch owner W. Phillip Eckert saw this cave as a productive source of bat guano, which he mined and sold as crop fertilizer. In 1990, his grandson saw the cave in an entirely different light: He and his wife donated it to the Nature Conservancy as a bat refuge. The conservancy now runs interpretive tours of the site from mid-May through early October, Thursday to Sunday from 6 to 9pm. (Some sunrise tours, where you can watch bats returning to the cave, are also available.) Of course, the exact time of day when the bats emerge varies throughout the season, according to when sunset falls; call the center for estimated emergence times for your visit. Just remember that the bats aren't here October through April—that's when they migrate south to Mexico. (They are, after all, Mexican freetailed bats.)

Besides protecting this specific site, this refuge aims to educate the public about bats in general, an often misunderstood and underappreciated group of species. Bats not only perform a vital role in insect control, they also disperse seeds and cross-pollinate many plant species. If those bats ever disappeared, farmers would discover in a hurry how much they needed them—but by then it might be too late.

(i) **Eckert James River Bat Cave Reserve,** James River Rd., Mason, TX (© **325/347-5970;** www.nature.org)

✈ San Antonio

✉ $ **Hill Country Inn,** 454 Fort McKavitt St (Hwy. 87 N), Mason (© **325/347-6317**). $$ **Fredericksburg Inn & Suites,** 201 S. Washington, Fredericksburg (© **800/446-0202** or 830/997-0202; www.fredericksburg-inn.com).

**217** Flying High

# Ramsay Canyon Preserve
## *Hummingbird Capital USA*
### Hereford, Arizona

Aᴛ ᴏɴᴇ ᴛɪᴍᴇ, ʜᴜᴍᴍɪɴɢʙɪʀᴅs ᴡᴇʀᴇ ʜᴜɴᴛᴇᴅ ꜰᴏʀ ᴛʜᴇɪʀ ʙʀɪɢʜᴛ ꜰᴇᴀᴛʜᴇʀs, ʙᴜᴛ ᴛᴏᴅᴀʏ ᴛʜᴇ biggest threat they face is loss of habitat. Hummingbirds are found only in the Western Hemisphere, and most of the 320 hummingbird species remain in the Tropics. Of the few hummingbird species that summer in North America, a surprising number find their way to Ramsay Canyon.

Each spring, a frantic buzz begins to spill out of the wooded gorge of Ramsay Canyon, in Arizona's Huachuca Mountains. An infestation of killer bees? No, it's just the busy whirring of hummingbird wings, as those tiny speed freaks zip around the canyon's multitude of wildflowers.

With 15 recorded species of these tiny jewel-like birds, Ramsay Canyon deserves its status as a National Natural Landmark. Of course, much more than hummingbirds inhabit this ecological crossroads, where the Rocky Mountains and Mexico's Sierra Madre run into the Sonoran and Chihuahuan deserts; this sheltered mountain gorge with its year-round stream (a rarity here in the arid Southwest) is a virtual "sky island," protecting all sorts of rare species from the lemon lily to the ridge-nosed rattlesnake.

When it comes to birds, though, Hereford, Arizona, is a birding hot spot, with nearly 200 species to be seen throughout the year. (Other excellent birding spots in the area include network of trails around the **San Pedro House,** © **520/508-4445,** on Ariz 90 east of Sierra Vista, and the **Southeastern Arizona Bird Observatory,** © **520/432-1388,** www.sabo.org,

on Ariz. 80 north of Bisbee.) The bird-watching season starts with a rush of songbird migration in April; just as the last of the hummingbirds leave in September, there's a glorious burst of butterfly appearances, the perfect coda to the birding season.

Though it covers only 380 acres (152 hectares), the Ramsey Canyon preserve encloses quite a number of diverse habitats. Follow the Hamburg Trail along Ramsey Creek and you'll see water-loving sycamores, cottonwoods, and willows, often within a few feet of cacti, yucca, and agaves. A steep series of switchbacks takes you to a scenic overlook amid towering pines. It's the mix of habitats that makes birding here so particularly rich. While golden eagles, Arizona woodpeckers, and Mexican jays live here year-round, rare neotropical birds such as the painted redstart, hepatic tanager, and dusky-capped flycatcher are common in the spring and fall migration seasons. And the hummingbirds hang out from late April all the way through September, with peaks in mid-May and late August. Several of the hummingbird species that arrive every season are colorful Mexican types who rarely show up anywhere else in the United States, like the berylline, white-eared, magnificent, blue-throated, broad-billed, and violet-crowned hummingbirds.

Wear bright-red clothing when you visit, the better to attract the darting little birds towards you. If the scent of the canyon's wildflowers doesn't overwhelm your senses, the swoony sensation of being circled by hummingbirds certainly will.

(i) **Ramsay Canyon Preserve,** 27 Ramsay Canyon Rd., Hereford, AZ (🕿 **520/378-2785;** www.nature.org)

✈ Tucson

🛏 $$$ **Ramsey Canyon Inn Bed & Breakfast,** 29 Ramsey Canyon Rd., Hereford (🕿 **520/378-3010;** www.ramsey canyoninn.com). $$ **San Pedro River Inn,** 8326 S. Hereford Rd., Hereford (🕿 **877/366-5532** or 520/366-5532; www.san pedroriverinn.com).

## Flying High 218

# Yellowstone National Park
## *The Big Park's Big Birds*
### Northwest Wyoming

Outdated and inadequate sewage systems in and around the park threaten Yellowstone's rivers, streams, and wetlands, an important source of food for the trumpeter swans and bald eagles. The native cutthroat trout, a food source for eagles, has declined dramatically due to invasive species and disease.

Yellowstone National Park is a majestic chunk of Rocky Mountain wilderness, where geysers spout, wide-antlered elk roam high meadows, and the rivers teem with trout. It's only natural that such a park should also have majestic birds, and so it does: America's great raptor, the bald eagle, and the world's largest waterfowl, the trumpeter swan. Both of these endangered birds gravitate to water—trumpeter swans dunk for aquatic vegetation in slow shallow water, and keen-sighted bald eagles cruise over lakes and streams, ready to dive after succulent trout. If sighting these birds is your Yellowstone priority, head for the rivers, and for Yellowstone Lake at the very heart of the park.

From the west entrance, drive along the Riverside turnout to trace the Madison River, where swans dabble in the shallows, or hike the 0.6-mile (1km) Harlequin Lake Trail to a small lake populated with all sorts of waterfowl, including trumpeters. Bald eagles patrol this neighborhood because the Madison's two tributaries, are the Gibbon and Firehole rivers, are renowned trout streams; from the lookout at Gibbon Falls you may spot them circling overhead.

Deeper into the park, the road from Canyon Village to Fishing Bridge follows the Yellowstone River, where trumpeter

Trumpeter swans float in Yellowstone.

swans mingle with pelicans and Canada geese. Two trails lead to panoramic views of one of the bald eagles' favorite summer fishing spots, Yellowstone Lake: the 4-mile (6.4km) Elephant Back Loop (near the Lake Yellowstone Hotel turnoff) or the 2-mile (3.2km) Storm Point Trail (3¹/₂ miles/5.6km west of Fishing Bridge).

There are a couple dozen resident trumpeter swans in Yellowstone, although their numbers quadruple in winter when migrating trumpeters arrive from Canada (Montana qualifies as a winter resort for these northerners). The resident swans build their nests in cattails and bulrushes at water's edge in May and hatch their chicks in June. Bald eagles, on the other hand, nest up high, on large tree platforms, from late February to mid-March; Yellowstone has perhaps 26 nesting pairs these days. Younger eagles migrate from the park in winter, but the nesting pairs (bald eagles mate for life) stay put, feeding on carrion and waterfowl when their fishing waters freeze up.

Once upon a time, Yellowstone could also boast the world's tallest bird, the whooping crane—but the last of Yellowstone's whooping cranes died in 2000, after colliding with some power lines. Trumpeter swans have been known to meet the same fate. For the bald eagles, now that their fish are free of DDT, the main threats are harsh winters and scarce food. But Yellowstone has proven a safe refuge for these magnificent birds—may it be so forever.

ⓘ **Yellowstone National Park** (✆ **307/ 344-7381;** www.nps.gov/yell)

✈ West Yellowstone Airport or Yellowstone Regional Airport, Cody, WY

🛏 $$ **Mammoth Hot Springs Hotel** (✆ **307/344-7311;** www.travelyellowstone. com). $ **Madison Hotel,** 139 Yellowstone Ave., West Yellowstone (✆ **800/838-7745** or 406/646-7745).

---

**219** Flying High

# Yosemite National Park
## *Hearing the Dawn Chorus*
### Yosemite, California

YOSEMITE NATIONAL PARK IS HOME TO 150 DIFFERENT BIRD SPECIES AND CONTAINS NEARLY all of the different ecosystems that occur in the Sierra Nevada. Invasive plant species pose risks to native habitat while invasive bird species, such as wild turkeys and white-tailed ptarmigan, compete with native species for food and nesting sites.

At midday, it's a zoo. Crowds of cars and RVs inch along the Yosemite Valley road, passengers gaping at 3,000-foot-high (900m) glacier-carved granite walls and the waterfalls that drop down them. But show up at dawn and you'll find another zoo, the kind with real animals. It's then that Yosemite National Park reveals its other face: an open-air aviary with a truly awesome bird display.

Those towering cliffs? A perfect place for peregrine falcons to nest. Recently

removed from the endangered list, peregrines returned to Yosemite a few years ago, and there are now at least four nesting pairs. Climbers know they're there only because certain prime rock faces are closed off in nesting season, but in the morning you may even see these dark-hooded raptors in the central valley, soaring around near the massive granite outcrops of El Capitan or Glacier Point.

Those great old-growth forests? A welcome refuge for forest birds like the

**213**

pileated woodpecker, blue grouse, Williamson's sapsucker, Nashville warbler, golden-crowned kinglet, dusky flycatcher, mountain chickadee, spotted owl, or, high overhead, the endangered northern goshawk. You don't even have to head to the backcountry to see them; just drive down Glacier Point Road, south of the Yosemite Valley loop. An early morning stroll along the road to the Bridalveil campground should yield several sightings.

Hike up to a meadow—McGurk or Peregoy, also along Glacier Point Road, are good ones—to find mountain quail, mountain bluebirds, and calliope or rufus hummingbirds; the red-breasted sapsucker may be working an aspen tree at meadow's edge, and if you're really lucky you may even see a great gray owl perched watchfully, waiting for meadow prey. These beautiful owls don't generally live this far south—the next closest population is hundreds of miles away, in northern California—but Yosemite apparently keeps the great grays quite happy.

Those signature waterfalls? Where else would a black swift build its nest? Even famous Bridalveil Falls, off the Yosemite Valley loop, may attract this rare high flier, though you'll have to get there at dawn, before the daily tourist influx, to see one.

One bird that may reveal itself even in midday is the Steller's jay, a mischievous creature nicknamed the "camp robber" because he'll swoop down to grab bits of food right off a picnic table.

Many of the species John Muir recorded here a century ago are sadly gone. But his general description still stands true: "The whole range, from foothills to snowy summits, is shaken into song every summer; and though low and thin in winter, the music never ceases." Just get here early if you want to hear it.

---

ⓘ **Yosemite National Park,** entrances on CA 41, CA 120, and CA 140, Yosemite, CA (ⓒ **209/372-0200;** www.nps.gov/yose)

✈ Fresno-Yosemite International

🛏 $$$ **The Ahwanee,** Yosemite Valley (ⓒ **559/252-4848**). $ **Tuolumne Meadows Campground** (ⓒ **800/436-7275;** http://reservations.nps.gov).

Flying High **220**

# Klamath Basin Wildlife Refuges
## *The Eagle Has Landed*
### Oregon & California

THE BIGGEST CHALLENGE FACING THE KLAMATH BASIN REFUGES IS TO KEEP ENOUGH WATER TO preserve the wetlands, which support thousands of migrating birds. But because of shrinking wetlands, salmon are dying, crops are thirsting, and the migrating bird population is dwindling. With farmers pitted against wildlife experts, and water managers against both, this tenuous patchwork of habitats is once again at risk.

It seemed like a bright idea in 1905: build dams along the Klamath River and turn its wetlands—approximately 185,000 acres (74,000 hectares) of shallow lakes and freshwater marshes in southern Oregon and northern California—into agricultural land. Trouble was those wetlands sat right on the Pacific Flyway. They were a major migration stopover for over six million waterfowl, as well as a year-round home for American white pelican, double-crested cormorant, and several types of heron.

Today less than a quarter of those original wetlands remain, mostly in six national wildlife refuges. President Theodore Roosevelt created the Lower Klamath Refuge in 1908, followed in 1911 by the Clear Lake Refuge; two more were added in the 1920s, Tule Lake Refuge and Upper Klamath Refuge. In 1958, the Klamath Marsh Refuge was acquired from the Klamath Indians. In 1978, the last piece fell in place: Bear Valley Refuge, which despite the name is really all about bald eagles.

With 4,200 acres (1,680 hectares) of old-growth ponderosa pine, incense cedar, and white and Douglas firs set on a sheltered northeast slope, Bear Valley is exactly the sort of place where wintering bald eagles want to roost—tall trees with stout wide-branching limbs, easily accommodating these big raptors. From December to mid-March, as many as 300 eagles a night may roost here (several mating pairs stay on through spring and build their treetop nests in Bear Valley as well). Though visitors can't enter the Bear Valley refuge, on early winter mornings birders plant themselves on Highway 97 at the base of the refuge to watch hundreds of eagles fly out to their hunting grounds. By day, the predatory eagles pick off dead and dying ducks and geese in the rich marshes nearby, culling the struggling winter flock. You can watch them from 10-mile (16km) auto-drive routes in Tule Lake and Lower Klamath—dozens of eagles at a time, circling overhead or perched expectantly on clogs of ice near open water. Snatching their prey in their talons, they'll pluck its feathers in mid-air

before feasting on it. It's gruesome, and utterly fascinating.

The driving routes in Lower Klamath and Tule Lake refuges also offer excellent views of the massive spring and fall waterfowl migrations; you'll need a canoe to visit Upper Klamath and Klamath Marsh, summer hot spots for nesting pelicans, egrets, heron, ducks, and grebes.

A century later, the Klamath River project continues to backfire. And in the next round of critical decisions, everyone seems to have an opinion, a vested interest, and a vote—except for the birds.

---

ⓘ **Klamath Basin National Wildlife Refuges** (📞 **530/667-2231;** www.fws. gov/klamathbasinrefuges). **Bear Valley National Wildlife Refuge,** off Hwy. 97, near Worden, OR. **Tule Lake National Wildlife Refuge,** Hill Rd., Tulelake, CA. **Lower Klamath National Wildlife Refuge,** Stateline Hwy. 161, Tulelake, CA. **Upper Klamath National Wildlife Refuge,** West Side Rd. (Hwy. 140), south of Fort Klamath, OR. **Klamath Marsh National Wildlife Refuge,** Silver Lake Rd., Sand Creek OR.

✈ Klamath Falls

🛏 $$$ **Shilo Inn,** 2500 Almond St., Klamath Falls (📞 **541/885-7980;** www. shiloinns.com). $$ **Best Western Olympic Inn,** 2627 S. 6th St., Klamath Falls (📞 **541/882-9665;** www.bestwestern. com).

---

**221**  Flying High

# The Eagles of Skagit River
## *Baldy Bed & Breakfast*
### North Cascades Mountains, Washington

RISING AIR AND WATER TEMPERATURES COULD HAVE A PROFOUND EFFECT ON FISH, BIRD, AND animal species and the intricate ecosystem that supports them. Melting glaciers in the mountains could alter the flow of rivers and streams, lead to flooding that would damage critical habitat, and disrupt the reproductive cycle of several species.

Bald eagles know a good thing when they find one. Escaping the frigid Canadian winter, they cruise down to the North Cascades of Washington State, to a cozy little spot on the Skagit River. They know what happens here every December through February: Millions of exhausted chum salmon, coming to the tail end of their spawning runs, are going to wash up dead on the gravel bars of the Skagit. As far as the eagles are concerned, it's an all-you-can-eat buffet.

The accommodations can't be beat, either: old-growth forests of hemlock, cottonwood, and Pacific silver fir, perfect roosting trees for bald eagles. No wonder this is one of the best bald-eagle wintering grounds in North America—by mid-January, as many as 300 baldies may be hanging out here. The premium suites are Barnaby Slough's thick stands of mature cottonwood, alder, and bigleaf maple, set right by the shallows where those tasty dead salmon pile up, ripe for the plucking—it's nature's version of room service. If that hotel's sold out, there are plenty of other trees elsewhere, thanks to a cooperative effort by various state, federal, and private entities, which have combined parcels of land along this Skagit corridor to protect the eagles.

Humans can't go into the eagle refuges, but with so many birds around, it's easy viewing right from the roadside. Stop in first at the Skagit River Interpretive Center to get maps and other information. Three special eagle observation sites have been set up, all along State Road 20: at **Howard Miller Steelhead Park,** at the **Mile Post 100 rest area,** and at the **Marblemount Fish Hatchery,** where you may also enjoy a weekend tour of their salmon spawning operations. Trained eagle guides are on hand to help you get the best sightings. Best times of day are dawn until about 11am, at which point the eagles are satiated and head back to their roosts to nap and digest. Cloudy days are actually better for viewing, because on sunny days the eagles tend to soar farther afield after their meal, joyriding on the updrafts rising from the Skagit River Valley.

For a really exciting up-close view, take a guided 10-mile (16km) raft trip down the Skagit from Marblemount to Rockport. You're not allowed to enter the river until after 11am, so the eagles' brunch won't be disturbed, but there's still plenty to see along the river, including the beavers, river otters, and black bears who work this river, too—that is, once the eagles have finished bellying up to the buffet.

(i) **Skagit River Interpretive Area,** Howard Miller Steelhead Country Park, 52809 Rockport Park Rd., Rockport (© **360/853-7626;** www.skagiteagle.org, Fri–Mon)

✈ Seattle/Tacoma

⊨ $$ **Buffalo Run Inn,** 60117 State Rd. 20, Marblemount (© **877/828-6652** or 360/873-2103; www.buffaloruninn.com). $$ **Grace Haven,** 9303 Dandy Place, Rockport (© **360/873-4106;** www.wordof graceministries.homestead.com/grace haven.html).

TOUR **Blue Sky Outfitters** (© **206/938-4030;** www.blueskyoutfitters.com). **Wildwater River Tours** (© **800/522-9453** or 253/939-2151; www.wildwater-river.com).

# Hakalau National Wildlife Refuge
## *Under the Volcano*
### Upcountry Hawaii

SEVENTY-FIVE PERCENT OF ALL U.S. SPECIES THAT HAVE BECOME EXTINCT ARE HAWAIIAN, including half of the islands' native bird species, and many more are threatened or endangered. Disease and habitat loss both play a role in the destruction of native species, but the biggest conservation problem Hawaii faces is the continuing flow of new non-native species into the islands.

You need to call ahead to get the combination to unlock the refuge gates—that's how carefully this sanctuary for forest birds is guarded. Even so, you can only visit on weekends. But the Big Island of Hawaii has a right to be protective of its native birds; there aren't many, and they're disappearing fast.

Driving on the Saddle Road across Hawaii's rugged interior, you'd hardly expect to find a rainforest—not on the volcanic slopes of Mauna Kea, the world's

tallest mountain (if you count the fact that it starts thousands of feet under the ocean surface). But the eastern slopes of Mauna Kea get a lot of rain—250 inches (635cm) annually at the lower elevations—and lush tropical greenery will flourish here, given half a chance. While the upper reaches of this 33,000-acre (13,200-hectare) refuge are still rebounding from years as a cattle ranch (ongoing work is replacing overgrazed pastures of alien grasses back to native vegetation), the lower elevations

Hakalau National Wildlife Refuge.

feature beautiful stands of tall koa trees and red-blossomed ohia; there are two lobelia trees, of a species so endangered that only five are still known to exist in the wild.

The name *hakalau* means "many perches," and there couldn't be a better description of this bird-rich habitat. Flitting through the closed-canopy forest, these endemic birds are bright with tropical color; with patience and a good pair of binoculars, you should spot several. Three kinds of honeycreepers live here: the yellow amakihi and the tiny scarlet iwi and apapanes, with their sharply curved beaks to dig deep for nectar in ohia blossoms. (**Note:** The iwi's the one with the red beak; the apapane's is black). Then there's the dusky yellow chickadee-like Hawaii creeper; the plump little blue elepaio, a flycatcher who snags its prey in midair; the yellow akiapolaau with its bright black eye and a curved beak to dig caterpillars out of trees; the finchlike orange honeycreeper known as the akepa; and the omao, which looks like a robin only with a soft blue breast.

Soaring above the canopy, you may even spot the endangered Io, the buff-and-brown Hawaiian hawk that many traditional Hawaiians claim as their *aumakua,* or guardian spirit. The hawks do what they can to get rid of the feral cats, rats, and mongeese that prey on small forest birds, but the refuge's rangers still need to be vigilant as well.

You'll need a four-wheel drive vehicle to get up here, what with bumpy Saddle Road (Hwy. 200), a 2-mile (3km) climb north up steep Mauna Kea Summit Road, then 17 miles (27km) east on gravel-surfaced Keanakolu Road to that locked gate. But to see birds like this, it's worth it.

ⓘ **Hakalau Forest Refuge,** Keanakolu Rd., Hawaii (② **808/443-2300;** www.fws. gov/pacificislands/wnwr/bhakalaunwr. html)

✈ Hilo

🛏 $$$ **The Palms Cliff House Inn,** Honomu (② **866/963-6076;** www.palmscliffhouse.com). $ **Dolphin Bay Hotel,** 333 Iliahi St., Hilo (② **808/935-1466;** www. dolphinbayhilo.com).

**TOUR Hawaii Forest & Trail** (② **800/464-1993** or 808/331-8505; www.hawaiiforest.com)

**Flying High 223**

# Balranald
## *The Corncrake in the Crofts*
### North Uist, the Hebrides, Scotland

RISING SEA LEVELS DUE TO GLOBAL WARMING ARE THE LEADING THREAT TO THE UNUSUAL coastal ecosystems. Balranald is home to machair, a rare type of habitat that occurs mostly in Scotland and Ireland. Dropping sea levels created this habitat, but rising sea levels could wipe them out.

The Western Isles aren't exactly the most far-flung of Scotland's islands—that honor goes to the Shetlands—but stand on the rocky headlands of Balranald, looking west onto the cold, gray North Atlantic, and you feel like you're hanging onto the rim of the continent. This windswept landscape is the last stop before Newfoundland, which is why so many birds end their westward flights here.

It's an extraordinary refuge for waders and seabirds, its marshes and sandy bays hosting dunlins, sanderlings, terns, sandpipers, and lapwings aplenty. If that were all North Uist had to offer, birders would still have a reason to come here. But a few steps inland, you'll find what makes this island really special: the machair.

With its rich tapestry of summer flowers—wild pansies, poppies, marigolds, marsh orchids, eyebrights, silverweed, daisies, purple clover—the machair is a unique sort of grassland, a sort of peaty low-lying pasture that takes over a beach after a drop in sea level creates a new beach. Because its soil is mostly crushed seashells, it's tremendously fertile.

The machair's birdlife is amazing: Being so close to the sea, it attracts both meadow species—twites, skylarks, meadow pipets, and corn buntings—and shorebirds like ringed plovers, redshanks, oystercatchers, greylag geese, and barnacle geese. But the real star attraction here is one of Europe's most endangered species, the corncrake. On the U.K. mainland, the corncrake has been driven out of its natural habitat by industry and intensive farming practices; the Outer Hebrides now have two-thirds of the U.K. corncrake population. Yet here it's quite common from mid-April to early August. You can hear its spooky rasping call everywhere, especially

at night, but sighting one of these secretive birds is a different matter. Once the machair grows tall in mid-June, the bird is much harder to spot, with its barred brown-and-white back for camouflage. Looking like a slimmer sort of partridge, it steps deftly through the grasses, but the bright chestnut of its wings and legs make it instantly recognizable when it rises in flight.

A 4.8km (3-mile) nature trail winds through the croft land, traversing the machair and leading to the headlands. There's a visitor center open in summer, at Goulat, near Hougharry, and guided tours are led twice a week.

---

(i) **Balranald Nature Reserve,** Hougharry, 4.8km (3 miles) northwest of Bayhead, North Uist (✆ **44/1463 715000**)

✈ Benbecula

**FERRY** Lochboisdale (from Oban), Lochmaddy (from Skye)

🛏 $$ **Langass Lodge,** Locheport (✆ **01876/580-385;** www.langasslodge. co.uk). $ **Lochmaddy Hotel,** Lochmaddy (✆ **01876/500-331;** www.lochmaddy hotel.co.uk).

---

**224** **Flying High**

# Veracruz River of Raptors
## *Raptor Rapture*
### Veracruz, Mexico

EVERY YEAR, MILLIONS OF NORTH AMERICAN RAPTORS COME TO VERACRUZ, STOPPING TO rest en route to their winter habitats in Latin America. Threats to this vital link in the raptor flyway include habitat loss due to agriculture, ranching, and development. Conservation groups work to monitor the migrating birds, educate the public about their value, and preserve critical habitat in the forested foothills.

It's not a real river at all, not in the watery sense—but when you see the stream of huge birds soaring overhead, you'll know why this migration route is traditionally referred to as the River of Raptors.

It's a bird-watching miracle you'll never forget. Each fall, large predatory birds funnel into the state of Veracruz, Mexico, soaring in from every major North American flyway en route to their winter grounds in Central and South America. Some five to six million cruise through, including just about all the broad-tailed hawks, Swainson's hawks, and Mississippi kites in existence. There are a million-and-a-half turkey vultures, not to mention sharp-shinned hawks, American kestrels, merlins, northern harriers—just about any swooping avian predator you can think of.

It's a sort of geographic fluke, a bottleneck created where Mexico's eastern Sierra Madre converges with the east end of the central volcanic belt, pouring into a narrow lowland passage in east-central Mexico. Add to that the effect of abundant thermal updrafts in this warm coastal plain, and you've got ideal flying conditions for big birds like these raptors, who are already tired from their long migrational flights.

And so they arrive, between late September and mid-October. One great base for viewing them is **Cardel,** a coastal town surrounded by lowland thorn forest and lagoons that provide prey for those hungry raptors. Set up in the afternoons with your binoculars and telephoto camera lenses (find a spot in the shade—it can be very warm here) and you'll be astonished at the number and variety of raptors you may identify. Note how they converge toward a useful thermal, swirling one after another into an upward spiraling vortex, known as a "kettle." Coming out of the kettle into a long straight glide, they tend to settle into layers according to body weight, with heavier birds like turkey vultures riding at the bottom, streamlined broadwings cruising at the top.

Another prime raptor-viewing site is right where the bottleneck occurs: up in the mountains at **Xalapa,** a handsome colonial-era city that's the capital of Veracruz. This stunning highland landscape (you may recognize its wooded gorges and tumbling waterfalls from the movie *Romancing the Stone*) has cloud forests, shade-coffee plantations, and pine-oak forests that harbor many other interesting bird species to watch when you get tired of the raptors. As if you could ever get tired of the raptors.

✈ Veracruz

🛏 $$$ **Hotel Mocambo,** Boca del Rio, Veracruz (© **229/932-0205;** www.hotel mocambo.com.mx). $$ **Mesón del Alférez,** Sebastián Camacho 2, Xalapa (© **228/ 818-0113;** www.pradodelrio.com).

**TOUR Pronatura/HawkWatch International** (© **800/726-4295** or 801/484-6808; www.hawkwatch.org). **Borderland Tours** (© **800/525-7753** or 520/882-7650; www. borderland-tours.com).

Flying High 225

# Cousin Island Special Reserve
## *Where the Birds Watch You Back*
### The Seychelles

SINCE IT WAS ESTABLISHED IN 1968, THE WORLD'S FIRST INTERNATIONALLY OWNED BIRD RESERVE has preserved habitats that support many rare species, from forest wetlands to seashores. However, beach erosion threatens nesting areas of the endangered hawksbill turtle.

Such a cheeky bird, the magpie robin. With bold black-and-white plumage similar to the European magpie, and a friendly, curious personality like the tame European robin, it's fearless toward humans—especially when the humans in question have food. They'll follow you as you walk down the beach, and even seek out dinner on your

Cousin Island.

kitchen table, if you've been careless enough to leave an open window or door.

One of the few places in the world to see this big-personality bird is Cousin Island, a tiny granite speck of an island in the Indian Ocean. Small as it is, this former coconut plantation has been restored to its original cover of lush tropical forest, and it's become known as an amazing haven for birds. Cousin Island—the world's first internationally owned bird reserve—was established in 1968 to protect the endangered Seychelles warbler, a melodious bird whose call is similar to the human whistle. Today this island sanctuary supports many rare species. In addition to the magpie robin and Seychelles warbler, it hosts the Seychelles fody, a small yellowish bird that was once hunted to the verge of extinction because it competed with humans for the eggs of seabirds. There's the Seychelles blue pigeon with its bright red cap, the Seychelles sunbird with its curved black beak, and a host of terns, noddies, and shearwaters hanging out along the shore.

It's not all birds, though: Cousin Island is also the area's most important nesting site for hawksbill turtles. Up to 100 turtles come ashore to bask in the daylight, where you can easily observe them. On other beaches on the island, they nest and lay their eggs under cover of dark. Cousin Island has its own giant tortoises, which at one time were nearly eradicated from the Seychelles; a plethora of geckos, skinks, and other lizards also call it home.

Though the Royal Society for Nature Conservation owns the island, it is administered by the International Council for Bird Preservation, now known as BirdLife International. Thanks to the efforts of the ICBP, magpie robins were brought here from Fregate Island, and fodies were transferred from Cousin to Aride Island, establishing new populations to ensure species viability.

Over 10,000 nature lovers visit Cousin Island each year, binoculars in tow, and many educational groups also make the trek. There is no lodging on the island—apart from bird nests, of course—but the Cousin boat only takes about 90 minutes from Praslin, an island well stocked with hotels, fabulous beaches, and breathtaking mountain views. Plan your trip to coordinate with the sanctuary's hours, Monday to Friday between 10am and midafternoon.

(i) **Cousin Island Special Reserve** (© **248/718-816;** www.natureseychelles. org)

✈ Seychelles Airport

🛏 $$ **Indian Ocean Lodge,** Grand Anse Beach (© **248/233-324**). $$$ **Berjaya Praslin Beach Resort** (© **248/286-286;** www.berjayaresorts.com/beachresort_praslin.htm).

Flying High **226**

# Coiba Island
## *Take a Walk on the Wild Side*
### Panama

HOME TO 147 SPECIES OF BIRDS AND 36 SPECIES OF MAMMALS, COIBA ISLAND IS AN EXOTIC habitat. Offshore lies the second-largest coral reef in the eastern Pacific. However, high value of native timber puts the island at risk from logging, tourism disrupts habitats and native species, and illegal fishing remains a threat to marine life around this island.

You're walking through an uninhabited tropical island. Overhead a flock of scarlet macaws takes flight, their distinctive squawks and screams filling the air. But don't spend too much time taking in the spectacle—you might miss the howler monkeys on the tree next to you.

After hiking for hours, you've seen more exotic birds and animals than you could ever imagine, and you are falling under the breathtaking spell of Coiba Island, an untamed mosaic of forests, beaches, mangroves, and the second-largest coral reef in the eastern Pacific, far off the coast of Central America.

Coiba stayed in this wild state almost by accident: Ever since 1912 it had been a penal colony, and a very effective one, too. Far from the mainland, covered with wild jungle, surrounded by shark-infested waters, who would even try to escape from such a place? As a result, settlers who might have harvested Coiba's magnificent hardwood forests or cleared the land for housing never moved here. The prison closed in 2004, but Panama's National Authority of the Environment still has a strong presence on the island, protecting this natural treasure, which draws visitors from all over the globe. The entire 495-sq.-km (191-sq.-mile) island is open to hikers, with trails that even amateurs can walk with ease, as well as so-called "machete" trails which require—well, you get the picture.

Along with the scarlet macaw, Coiba is a haven for the crested eagle, which can be seen soaring overhead looking for prey. Easily identified by the frill of upstanding feathers on top of its black head, the crested eagle loves to fish, but it also has a special fondness for snakes—and Coiba has many snakes, some of them extremely poisonous. (Another deterrent to prison escapes.) There's plenty of prey on Coiba for the crested eagle, and it plays an important role in the habitat, keeping down the numbers of certain species that might overrun this little slice of Eden. With 147 species of birds, along with 36 species of mammals, it's incredibly biodiverse. Four whale and dolphin species can also be spotted in offshore waters, including killer whales (orcas), humpback whales, and the rare pantropical spotted dolphin. The flora is so lush and abundant, botanists have yet to finish categorizing it.

Coiba Island also contains remnants of pre-Columbian settlements, which disappeared when the Spanish arrived in the 15th century. Except for the penal colony, it has remained uninhabited since then. Only an hour's flight from Panama City, it can be visited as a day trip, an escape from civilization you won't soon forget.

✈ Marcos A. Gelbart Airport

🛏 $$ **Avalon Grand Panama,** Panama City (☎ **800/804-6835;** www.smartstays. com/avalon-grand-panama-panama-city).

$$ **Country Inn & Suites by Carlson,** Panama City (☎ **888/201-1746;** www. countryinns.com/panamacitypan).

**Flying High**

## 227

# Mamirauá Nature Reserve
### *Flying High in the Floods*
#### Upper Amazon Basin, Brazil

AS A DESIGNATED "SUSTAINABLE DEVELOPMENT RESERVE"—THE FIRST OF ITS KIND IN LATIN America—Mamirauá helps to protect rare bird and animal species and threatened habitats. As long as Mamirauá continues to be protected, it will avoid the fate of many other areas in the Amazon basin, which have been destroyed by burning, logging, mining, and poaching.

When the rainy season hits this part of the Amazon Basin, it really hits. Waters can rise as much as 12m (39 ft.), covering many treetops, and most of the forest floor lies submerged for up to 4 months. The only animals who survive are those who live in the trees—monkeys, sloths—and water dwellers such as the rare Amazon manatee, pink dolphins, and black caimans. But it doesn't bother the birds—birds never need ground anyway, do they?

An astonishing total of some 400 different bird species have been recorded in the Mamirauá Nature Reserve, a 57,000-sq.-km (22,000-sq.-mile) protected varzea, or seasonally flooded forest. Follow trails through the lush rainforest (the same trails you can hike on in the dry season will require a canoe in flood season) and you'll see—and hear—a host of tropical birds such as parrots, toucans, and scarlet macaws living their lives in the treetop canopy. You may even see the harpy eagle, the world's biggest raptor, who dives down into the canopy with talons as big as a grizzly bear's claws to snatch up canopy-dwelling sloths, monkeys, and opossums for his dinner.

Take a boat along the narrow channels that connect the reserve's many lakes, and a host of water birds can be spotted—snowy egrets, herons, cormorants, kites, grullas, tinamous, bitterns, ospreys, curassows. You may even see a couple of very strange creatures, like the hoatzin, a pheasantlike marsh bird with a wild spiky feathered crest, which is quite common around here—mostly because its horrible manurelike smell (it's nicknamed the "stink bird," and rightly so) means that only the most desperate creatures would ever eat it. And talk about showy head crests—there's none showier than the cotinga, otherwise known as the umbrella bird for the elaborate fan of headfeathers it spreads during courtship.

A constant flow of botanists and biologists come to Mamirauá to do scientific research, but it's a social experiment as well. Dozens of villages remain within the area, home to some 20,000 people—*ribeirinhos*—who, instead of earning a living by slash-and-burn agriculture, logging, mining, or poaching, are being taught sustainable farming methods and given eco-tourism jobs. The Pousada Uacari Lodge, for example—a hotel built on floating rafts to accommodate the waters' rise and fall—is staffed as much as possible by local people, many of them guiding lodge guests into the rainforest. Now that they've been given a vested interest in keeping the rainforest healthy, they've become proactive in protecting the amazing flora and fauna here, even helping to patrol the reserve. It's an important model for saving the rainforest—no doubt the birds would approve.

 Tefé

🛏 $$ **Pousada Uacari Lodge** (© 55/97/3343-4160;** www.uakarilodge.com.br), 564km/350 miles west of Manaus

**TOUR Amazon Adventures** (© **800/232-5658** or 512/443-5393; www.amazon adventures.com)

---

Flying High **228**

# Stewart Island
## *Last Stop for Kiwis*
### New Zealand

KAKAPOS, THE LARGEST PARROTS BY WEIGHT IN THE WORLD, ONCE THRIVED ON STEWART ISLAND. Habitat destruction and predators such as cats, rats, and stoats that swam to the island from the mainland drove the kakapo to near extinction. Without protection, the kiwi may face the same fate, as the numbers of kiwi are declining every year.

New Zealanders love their national bird, the kiwi; they even proudly refer to themselves as "kiwis" from time to time. But these days it's well-nigh impossible to see one of these funny little flightless brown birds in the wild—that is, except on Stewart Island.

New Zealand's third island is also the farthest south, just across a narrow strait from the South Island, with a wonderful temperate climate and so much wildlife you won't believe it. (Only 1% of the island is inhabited.) Hiking, kayaking, and diving are the main forms of entertainment on this rough-and-ready island, and there's plenty of wildlife to enjoy here, including outstanding bird-watching. With so much natural habitat, you can easily view uniquely New Zealand species like the kaka, tui, weka, kereru, and korimako, though you probably won't be able to see the nearly extinct kakapo and kokako.

Frequent sightings of the famously shy kiwi are the icing on the cake. All it takes is a little luck—or a little extra effort, like booking a nighttime kiwi-spotting boat tour with Bravo Adventure Cruises (see "Tour," below). (Though kiwis are not always a nocturnal species, they have often become so in order to avoid predators.) Taking only 15 passengers at a time so as not to spook the kiwis, these 3-hour tours involve prowling the length of remote Ocean Beach with flashlights. The plump, spiky-feathered kiwis can be found poking around the washed-up kelp, sniffing out food like sand hopper with the nostrils located at the end of their long pointed beaks. Darting and skittering about in their ungainly, comical way, the kiwis take a little patience to see, but they're worth it.

Stewart Island.

Technically, Stewart Island's kiwi is its own species, slightly different from the spotted kiwis and brown kiwis found on the North and South islands; the Stewart Island kiwi has larger legs, a longer beak, and slightly lighter-colored plumage. But on the mainland, kiwi populations are declining at alarming rates. Dogs and ferrets prey on adult birds, while feral cats and stoats raid nests to devour chicks. At the same time, the native forest and scrub that are the kiwis' natural habitats are being devoured for pastureland and human settlement, driving the remaining kiwis into ever-smaller areas—a real problem for highly territorial creatures like kiwis.

Stoats and ferrets haven't made it over to Stewart Island yet, though, and human settlement is still sparse. For now, the Stewart Island kiwis still have a stable population. Their cousins on the mainland should have it so good.

ⓘ **Stewart Island** (www.stewartisland. co.nz). **Save the Kiwi** (www.savethekiwi. org.nz).

✈ Stewart Island (service from Invercargill, South Island)

🛏 $$$ **Port of Call,** Leask Bay Rd. (✆ **64/ 3/219-1394;** www.portofcall.co.nz). $ **South Sea Hotel,** Elgin Terrace, Oban (✆ **64/3/219-1059;** www.stewart-island. co.nz).

**TOUR Bravo Adventure Cruises** (✆ **64/ 3/219-1144**)

# Mission Beach
## *Make Way for Cassowaries*
### Queensland, Australia

KEEPING THE CASSOWARY ALIVE DEPENDS ON COOPERATION BETWEEN CONSERVATIONISTS, government agencies, developers, and local residents. Regulating private and public land use, and maintaining and protecting habitat and food supplies, will help to keep this region a safe environment for a highly endangered species.

Somehow the folks of Mission Beach, Australia, have managed to keep their town off the tourist radar—quite a feat, considering they're only an hour's boat ride from the Great Barrier Reef. When you take the Mission Beach turnoff from the Bruce Highway, at first you seem to be in the middle of nowhere. Dense tangled vine forests almost hide the town from view until you round the corner to Mission Beach proper, an appealing cluster of shops, restaurants, and hotels. You know you're finally here when you see the sign: DANGER—CASSOWARY CROSSING.

If Mission Beach weren't so laid back, the cassowaries wouldn't have stayed here. After all, these highly endangered 1.8m-tall (6-ft.) birds abandoned areas like the Mabi Forest inland—a significant loss for those forests, since roaming cassowaries disperse an extraordinary number of seeds in their excrement. Scientists reckon only about 900 southern cassowaries remain in the Wet Tropics, but about 100 of these ostrichlike black birds live in the last patches of rainforest around Mission Beach, which is actually a cluster of four small towns strung along an 18km-long (11-mile) beach. It's a surprisingly diverse habitat, with half of the world's remaining licuala fan palms, six ancient flowering plant families, and 60% of all Australia's butterflies.

Though they mostly keep to the forest, cassowaries have been known to stroll right through town, cruising for the fallen fruit and low-hanging fruit that's the staple of their diet. (Being flightless, they can't forage any higher than that.) They're certainly spectacular to look at, with a peacock blue neck, long red wattles, and a stiff blue casque like an Aztec headdress. Despite their stately walk, however, they're aggressive creatures, with enormous claws that can swiftly disembowel an enemy. Never approach one, and if you do accidentally disturb one, back off slowly and hide behind a tree.

Even in conservation-minded Mission Beach, cassowaries have lost about 50% of their critical habitat in the past decade. And living around humans really isn't healthy for them, between dog attacks, car accidents, and the temptations of unsuitable snacks stolen from humans. (Never hand-feed a cassowary.) Still, Mission Beach promotes itself as the cassowary capital of the world, and great local efforts have been made to protect these spectacular rare birds, Australia's largest land creatures. Check out the wildlife displays at the C4 Environment Centre in town, then explore cassowary territory on the 8km (5-mile) Licuala Fan Palm trail, which starts at a parking lot on the Mission Beach–Tully Road. There's even a "follow the cassowary footprints" trail for kids.

ⓘ **C4 Environment Centre**, Porters Promenade, Mission Beach (✆ **61/7/4068 7197;** www.cassowaryconservation.asn.au)

✈ Cairns

🛏 $$$ **The Horizon,** Explorer Dr., Mission Beach (✆ **1800/079 090** or 61/7/4068 8154; www.thehorizon.com.au). $ **Mackays,** 7 Porter Promenade, Mission Beach (✆ **61/7/4068 7212;** www.mackaysmission beach.com).

**230** Flying High

# Lord Howe Island
## *The Lords of Lord Howe Island*
### Australia

MORE THAN HALF OF THE ORIGINAL RECORDED SPECIES OF BIRDS ON THIS ISLAND ARE EXTINCT, DUE to hunting; non-native predators such as black rats, cats, and owls; and overgrazing by farm animals. Now that the island is protected and managed, the most serious threats are oil and chemical water pollution, and groundwater pollution from sewage management.

There are a lot of outdoor things to do on a Lord Howe Island holiday—swim in a crystal-clear lagoon, marvel at tropical fish in a coral reef, hike trails through palm and banyan forests—but sooner or later the place turns every visitor into a bird-watcher. Not only does it have a lot of birds, it has rare birds—and, best of all, they aren't shy of people.

Possibly Australia's best birding site, Lord Howe Island is a carefully preserved nature sanctuary, where only 400 tourists are allowed at a time. Seventy-five percent of the island, including much of the southern mountains and northern hills, is a permanent protected nature reserve. Many of its 350 residents are ancestors of the island's first 18th-century settlers. Life here is slow paced; people get around on bikes instead of cars and just about everybody diligently recycles.

Lord Howe Island is home to over 130 bird species, between residents and migratory visitors. There are 14 species of

seabird alone, which roost and nest here in huge numbers. Walking trails along the island's ragged east coast provide great views of seabirds such as terns, boobies, noddies, and shearwaters. Star among them is one of the world's rarest birds, the Providence petrel, which nests near the summit of Mount Gower. This sturdy-looking seabird is so trustful of humans that it can even be called out of the air—and might even decide to rest in your lap.

The rarest resident of all is the Lord Howe Island woodhen, found nowhere else but Lord Howe Island. This flightless brown bird, about the size of a bantam rooster, is listed as an endangered species, but the combined efforts of Australia's national wildlife service, the Lord Howe Island Board, and the Foundation for National Parks and Wildlife have resulted in a successful breeding program, and they now populate many parts of the island—some have even nested in residents' back yards. The best place to see

**227**

Lord Howe Island.

them is on the 3km (2-mile) Little Island trail, where you can also see some beautiful emerald ground doves.

For impressive aerial feats, look to the skies, especially over the tropical forests of the northern hills, and you'll see the beautiful red-tailed tropic bird, with its elegant red tail streamers. When courting, it will fly backwards, in circles, and, for good measure, throw in some vertical displays. It's a splendid sight, and one few birders ever get to see.

A speck off of Australia's east coast, equidistant from Sydney or Brisbane, Lord Howe Island is only a 2-hour plane ride from the mainland. Conveniently, there are just enough hotels on the island to handle all 400 visitors.

---

ⓘ **Lord Howe Island** visitor center (✆ **1800/240 937** or 61/2/6563 2114; www. lordhoweisland.info)

✈ Lord Howe Island

🛏 **Blue Lagoon Lodge** (✆ **61/2/6563 2006**). **Pinetrees Resort Hotel** (✆ **61/ 2/6563 2177;** www.pinetrees.com.au).

**TOUR Lord Howe Nature Tours** (✆ **61/ 2/6563 2447**)

# Karera Wildlife Sanctuary
## *The Flight of the Bustard*
### Madya Pradesh, India

ANGRY LOCALS, FEELING CONSTRAINED BY CONSERVATION EFFORTS THAT LIMIT THEIR USE OF LAND and resources, are being blamed for hostile actions that have killed off Karera's population of the endangered great Indian bustard, which the sanctuary was developed to save.

It's easy to get hung up on your species count. Bird-watchers are guiltier than anybody when it comes to obsessing over that life list—and if you've come all the way to India determined to find the last of the great Indian bustards, well, that's what you need to see.

Karera Wildlife Sanctuary should be your best bet—after all, it was founded in 1981 specifically to protect the great Indian bustard. For this leggy long-necked bird, similar in size to a young ostrich, the thorny open grassland of Karera is an ideal habitat, and a dozen or so were supposed to live in Karera—but there have been no actual sightings in the past couple of years, despite the offer of a reward for reports of any nest site or adults in the wild. (Park officials have glossed over the situation, insisting that the birds are still there, but it is, after all, in their interests to do so—this sanctuary's very existence is supposed to hinge on the GIB.) It's a reality that must be faced: Sometimes we lose the race to preserve endangered species.

Once you accept that you may have missed the great Indian bustard—a wary and elusive bird that was never easy to see here—you can focus on the sanctuary's other considerable charms. Between migrants and residents, more than 245 other bird species live in the Karera reserve.

Park yourself on the shores of Dihaila Jheel, the monsoon-fed lake that is the park's sole water source, soon after the rains stop in mid-September and you'll see a host of water birds—herons, egrets, spoonbills, teals, pintails, and black-bellied river terns. Impressive numbers of dragonflies and damselflies hover over the lake, while butterflies and Indian robins seem to be everywhere in the acacia forest and grasslands.

And you may end up being charmed instead by the blackbuck, the sanctuary's other celebrity species. These handsome antelopes, with their spectacularly ringed spiral horns, thunder around those very same open grasslands that were preserved for the bustard, in herds of 15 or 20, each headed by one dominant male. Back in 1981 when the preserve was founded, only 100 blackbucks were here; now their numbers are up to 2,000, although they are still considered a threatened species elsewhere. Forget the great Indian bustard—here's the real success story at Karera Wildlife Sanctuary.

✈ Gwalior Airport

🛏 $$ **Tourist Village or Chinkara Motel,** Shivpuri (☎ **91/755-2554340;** http://shivpuri.mp.gov.in/hotels.htm)

# 10 Places to See Piping Plovers Nest

It's not hard to drum up support for the piping plover. Anybody who's encountered these bright-eyed little puffs of sand-colored feathers scurrying along a beach knows how adorable they are. In 1985, their East Coast population had sunk to 722 breeding pairs, but by 2007 they had rebounded to 1,743, thanks to aggressive efforts to protect their traditional nesting areas. However, matters are riskier for the Great Lakes population, which had declined to only 11 to 14 pairs; the count's back up to 60 pairs, but they're still seriously endangered.

A piping plover.

These birds like the same kinds of beaches we do—open sands close to the tide line, preferably with some sparse dune vegetation nearby. Check out the following protected beaches, where, with binoculars, you can observe plovers foraging and raising their downy chicks.

**232 Wells Beach, Wells, Maine** Along Maine's southern coast, here's a model of private-public cooperation: Beachfront homeowners notify Maine Audubon when they spot a piping plover nest, and Audubon volunteers build mesh enclosures, designed so plovers can fly out but predators can't get in. Walking trails at the Wells National Estuarine Research Reserve let you explore the mosaic of salt marsh, tidal mud flats, and beach that attracts more plovers every year. *342 Laudholm Farm Rd. ℂ 207/646-1555. www.wellsreserve.org.*

**233 Cape Cod National Seashore, Massachusetts** Along the Outer Cape's north-south arm of barrier beach, since 1961 this National Seashore has preserved a plover-friendly habitat with 30 miles (48km) of wide white beach, backed by dunes, tidal marshes, and freshwater kettle ponds. Nesting areas are fenced off along the six swimming beaches, but controversy still swirls over how much off-road vehicle use should be permitted during the April to September breeding season. *ℂ 508/255-3421. www.nps.gov/caco.*

**234 Goosewing Beach, Little Compton, Rhode Island** This narrow Rhode Island Sound beach provides piping plovers with an ideal setup—level sands for nesting, with the muddy flats of a salt pond behind it supplying food. The Nature Conservancy has hired an on-site plover warden to monitor the beach, where piping plovers and least terns nest side by side, mid-April to early September. *ℂ 401/635-4400. www.nature.org.*

**235 Griswold Point, Old Lyme, Connecticut** At the mouth of the Connecticut River, this mile-long sand spit between the river's marshy estuary and Long Island Sound is fenced off from Memorial Day to Labor Day, but you can view nesting piping plovers and least terns from adjacent White Sands Beach (where plovers often visit). *www.nature.org.*

**㉛ Mashomack Preserve, Shelter Island, New York**   Between the North and South forks of heavily populated Long Island, residential Shelter Island has set aside a third of its land for this 2,039-acre (825-hectare) preserve off of Route 114. Although piping plover nesting areas on the beaches are fenced off in season, several trails allow you to explore the surrounding mosaic of tidal creeks and salt marshes. ℂ *631/749-1001. www.nature.org.*

**㉗ Sea Bright, New Jersey**   Along New Jersey's crowded coastline, the piping plover population isn't making much progress—except along Route 36 in northern Monmouth County, particularly Sea Bright and Northern Monmouth Beach. Since 2002, when the Army Corps of Engineers renourished the beaches, significantly widening the sands and rebuilding dunes, the piping plovers have come back in force. *Borough of Sea Bright: ℂ 732/842-0215. www.sea-bright.com. Borough of Monmouth Beach: ℂ 732/229-2204. www.monmouthbeach.us.*

**㉘ Sleeping Bear Dunes National Lakeshore, Empire, Michigan**   The dune-lined shore of Lake Michigan is the last stronghold of the Great Lakes piping plover population. They're present from late April through August, with new chicks hatching in June. Prime spots to see them (from afar, of course—you may need to do some wading) are on the mainland near the mouth of the Platte River, in the Sleeping Bear Point area, and on North Manitou Island. ℂ *231/326-5134. www.nps.gov/slbe.*

**㉙ John E. Williams Preserve, Turtle Lake, North Dakota**   One of the world's largest concentrations of breeding piping plovers settles every spring into this treeless landscape in central North Dakota, on the gravelly, salt-crusted fringes of shallow alkali lakes, which teem with the tiny crustaceans that plovers love. Nesting beaches are closed off in season, so bring your binoculars to view the plovers from other spots on the lake. ℂ *701/794-8741. www.nature.org.*

**㉚ Lake McConaughy, Lemoyne, Nebraska**   As much of the North Platte River's sandbars became overgrown, the piping plovers had to move on. In the 1980s they discovered the wide white beaches of 12-mile-long (19km) Lake McConaughy, created in the Depression by the construction of Kingsley Dam. Despite heavy recreational use and recent droughts, its beaches now support nearly 200 piping plover nests every year—lower lake levels just mean wider beaches for plover nests. ℂ *308/284-8800. www.ngpc.state.ne.us.*

**㉛ Quill Lakes, Wynard, Saskatchewan**   This set of three shallow, saline lakes in east-central Saskatchewan are full of mud and gravel, surrounded by freshwater marsh—perfect for piping plovers. Westernmost Big Quill Lake (the other two are Middle Quill and Little Quill) gets an average of 284 birds flying in to breed every summer. At the Wadena Wildlife Wetlands, on the shore of Little Quill Lake, you can spot the plovers from the Plover's Path trail, along the lakeshore beside the Jesmer Marsh. ℂ *306/338-3454. www.wadena.ca/ecotourism.*

# Desert National Park
## *When You Least Expect It . . .*
### Rajasthan, India

ONE OF THE SMALLEST DESERT AREAS IN THE WORLD, DESERT NATIONAL PARK IS HOME TO MORE than 300 bird species and hundreds of animal species. Limestone mining, oil exploration, poaching, and potential conflicts in the adjacent military zone make this an especially fragile and vulnerable ecosystem.

You have to be a tough bird to make it in the Desert National Park. One of India's largest national parks, it comes by its name fairly—this arid scrubland in the west Indian state of Rajasthan looks god-forsaken indeed, 3,000 sq. km (1,160 sq. miles) of craggy rocks and salt flats and sand dunes. Yet, despite this fragile eco-system, it's surprisingly hospitable to birds. Predators like eagles, harriers, falcons, and kestrels haunt these Thar Desert plains, as well as the usual crew of scavengers, like buzzards and vultures.

But one resident bird is a surprise indeed—the critically endangered great Indian bustard, a beautiful cranelike bird that stands about a meter (3 ft.) high, with a sinuous white neck and slim black-crested head. Having disappeared from so many of its other sanctuaries, why does the GIB—the largest of India's four species of bustard—seem to thrive here? And yet it does, in relatively high numbers—it's estimated that only 500 of these magnificent birds still exist, but there may be as many as 50 here in Rajasthan.

Set in a military zone near the Pakistan border, Desert National Park is difficult to visit—you'll need to obtain a permit in Jaisalmer, not an easy process, which is why it's best to visit with an experienced tour operator who can make all arrangements. Park wardens can arrange a hike into the desert to areas where the wide-ranging bustard is known to appear.

The grasslands where the GIB used to live are fast disappearing, and even protected grassland preserves tend to favor larger endangered animals like tigers, antelopes, and rhinoceros. The GIB has also been a victim of poaching over the years, and may be killed by outraged farmers who still view it as a crop pest. It's not a bird that can quickly replenish its numbers, either. The female lays only one egg a year, which may be destroyed or eaten by other animals. Unlike other species, where both members of the nesting pair cooperate in guarding the nest and feeding their chicks, the male bustard mates with several females and doesn't participate in raising the young—the female's pretty much on her own for the full year it takes to bring her child from egg to fledgling. Without a sanctuary to protect the nesting environment, survival rates of young bustards would be low indeed.

Still, it's baffling why the great Indian bustard has succeeded here, when it has become extinct so many other places. The political instability of the region may, in the short term, help the GIB by limiting human settlement and tourism—but if war breaks out, would these last few bustards survive?

 Jaisalmer

**TOUR Exotic Journeys** (© **800/554-6342;** www.exoticjourneys.com). **Indian Nature Tours** (© **91/11/6596 99433;** www.wildlifeindia.co.uk).

# Metompkin Island
## *A Red-Knotty Problem*
### Eastern Shore, Virginia

EXCESSIVE HARVESTING OF HORSESHOE CRABS HAS CREATED A PERILOUS SITUATION FOR RED knots, the migratory shorebirds that depend on a ready supply of horseshoe crab eggs during their annual spring stop in Delaware Bay. To help give the little birds a fighting chance, the state of New Jersey has imposed a moratorium on harvesting horseshoe crabs, with stiff fines for violators.

It's hard not to love the jaunty little red knot. Though it's only 10 inches tall, weighing less than 5 ounces, that's big for a sandpiper. Just watch this robust little shore bird strut along the tidal mudflats on short, stout black legs, poking its straight beak into the sand. All it wants is to gorge itself on horseshoe crab eggs, double its body weight in 2 weeks, and then fly on north. Way north.

Don't let its size fool you: The red knot is one of the world's most prodigious long-distance fliers, breeding every summer in northern Canada, Alaska, and Siberia, then heading some 10,000 to 15,000 miles (16,100–24,150km) south—as far as Tierra del Fuego in South America—for the winter. That makes its springtime stop-off on the Delaware Bay all the more important: If it doesn't fatten up then, what will it live on when it gets to the tundra, where the ground's still too frozen to peck for insects?

As many as 90% of the American red knot subspecies arrives all at the same time on Delaware Bay every spring; on just two barrier islands, Parramore and Metompkin, some 3,000 red knots were counted during one recent May. Once heavily hunted in North America, the red knot is now a protected species; its feeding grounds on Parramore and Metompkin islands are refuges. But if it's not one thing, it's another: A recent drastic decline of horseshoe crabs in the Chesapeake waters spells serious trouble for the red knot, which is so dependent on its traditional staging grounds.

Parramore Island can only be visited for research purposes, but Metompkin is open to the public for hiking, bird-watching, and fishing (its north end is part of the Chincoteague National Wildlife Refuge; its south end is in the Nature Conservancy's Virginia Coast Reserve). You'll need a boat to get here—one nearby boat ramp is at Gargathy Neck in Accomac, Virginia. Though the beaches may not be accessible during migration, on this flat marshy island it's easy to view the red knots when they descend en masse. Notice how, below their mottled gray backs, the red knots' dull-white underbelly is beginning to turn pink; by breeding season, the breast and head will be robin red, the most colorful sandpipers around.

The Audubon Society currently estimates the red knot population at 1.1 million, but some counts show a 50% annual decline recently. American policy alone can't protect this long-distance flier—it's still hunted in large numbers in South America. Canada has listed it as endangered, Audubon has it on its special concern list, but despite several petitions, the U.S. federal government still hasn't declared the red knot endangered. In 2003, however, scientists warned that the American subspecies could be extinct as soon as 2010. Time is running out.

ⓘ **Chincoteague National Wildlife Refuge** (📞 757/336-6122; www.nps.gov/asis). **Virginia Coast Reserve** (📞 757/442-3049; www.nature.org).

✈ Norfolk

🛏 $$$ **Island Motor Inn Resort,** 4391 N. Main St., Chincoteague (📞 757/336-3141; www.islandmotorinn.com). $$ **Refuge Inn,** 7058 Maddox Blvd., Chincoteague (📞 888/257-0038 or 757/336-5511; www.refugeinn.com).

---

Waterfowl **244**

# Cumberland Island National Seashore
## *Tern to the Left, Plover to the Right*
### Southeastern Georgia

OVER 335 SPECIES OF BIRDS SHOW UP HERE AT SOME POINT DURING THE YEAR, DRAWN BY empty dunes, whispering marshes, and—yes—the blessed absence of pesky humans. Only 300 people are allowed on the island at any given time.

It takes 45 minutes by ferry to chug over to Cumberland Island, an undeveloped barrier isle at the southern end of the Georgia coast, practically into Florida. Considering that it's a National Seashore, its gleaming sands are often surprisingly deserted—that is, from a human perspective. Only 300 people are allowed on the island at any given time. But from a bird's point of view, it's a veritable Las Vegas, a major destination on the Atlantic flyway.

"Undeveloped" isn't quite accurate: Cumberland Island was once a sea cotton plantation and then a summer retreat for the Carnegies, and a handful of buildings are still scattered around the island, one of them being the island's only lodging, the Greyfield Inn (see "Lodging," below). But Cumberland's been basically uninhabited for a long time, and the wilderness has closed in. The island's roadways seem mere tunnels through a vine-draped canopy of live oaks, cabbage palms, magnolia, holly, red cedar, and pine, a maritime

forest that covers 15,000 acres (6,000 hectares). An even larger portion of the island on the western side is fertile salt marsh. The abundant wildlife includes alligators, armadillos, raccoons, deer, and wild turkeys, as well as a herd of nearly 300 wild horses, who graze (some ecologists say overgraze) on the marsh grasses. Loggerhead turtles nest on its sands, as do several birds—please respect cordoned-off beach areas in season.

Cumberland's 16-mile-long (26km) beach isn't just a bland strip of powdery sand, like some manufactured oceanfront resort: Little meadows nestle between the dunes, creeks cut their way to the sea from freshwater ponds, and tidal mudflats glisten. All of this makes it inviting for birds. Hike or bike down to Pelican Banks, the southernmost point of the island, and you'll be able to view black skimmers, numerous ducks, and the endangered American oystercatcher, a sleek black-and-white bird with a bright-red bill that

Cumberland Island National Seashore.

lives here year-round. Another threatened species, the least tern, arrives on the tidal flats in late April, where it courts, breeds, and nests, hatching chicks by mid-June. Further north, along the main beach, the Roller Coaster Trail leads past dunes where gray-and-white Wilson's plovers—endangered gray shorebirds with black-banded necks and thick black bills—build their nests. Freshwater ponds behind the dunes provide perfect nesting terrain for white ibis, herons, egrets, and the endangered wood stork, a magnificent white wader with a dark head and black-tipped wings.

In late spring and summer, birds far outnumber humans on Cumberland Island. It's their resort—trespass with care.

---

ⓘ **Cumberland Island National Seashore,** St. Mary's, GA (ⓒ **912/882-4336,** ext. 254; www.nps.gov/cuis)

✈ Jacksonville

**FERRY** 45 min. from St. Mary's, reservations (ⓒ **912/882-4335** or 877/860-6787)

🛏 $$$ **Greyfield Inn,** Cumberland Island (ⓒ **904/261-6408;** www.greyfield inn.com). $$ **Emma's Bed & Breakfast,** 300 W. Conyers St., St. Mary's (ⓒ **877/749-5974** or 912/882-4199; www.emmasbed andbreakfast.com).

# Cypress Island Preserve
## *The Year of the Empty Nests*
### Lafayette, Louisiana

DREDGING IN SOME OF THE NEARBY BAYOUS, PLUS FLOOD CONTROL MEASURES AND STREAM alterations to improve navigation on the Mississippi River, have changed the natural water flow. Fragmentation of the woods and wetlands on Cypress Island disrupts the ability of native birds to breed successfully and threaten their survival.

The bird-watchers were there, same as every year. So what happened to the birds?

The south end of Louisiana's Lake Martin is perhaps North America's most renowned rookery for wading birds, named by the Audubon Society as one of the country's top 10 bird-watching sites. As many as 20,000 birds—herons, egrets, ibises, roseate spoonbills, and other long-legged beauties—nest in among the cypress trees and buttonwood bushes every spring.

But in the spring of 2006, something ruffled their feathers. Thousands of nesting pairs suddenly flew away, abandoning eggs they had already laid, never to be hatched. Though trespassing is prohibited in the rookery's waters during nesting season, from February 1 through July 31, rangers speculate boat traffic commotion may have been what scared off the birds in 2006. The Nature Conservancy has installed cameras to monitor the area and cordoned off the rookery during nesting season with thick metal cables.

Ornithologists let out a sigh of relief in 2007, then, when breeding season proceeded as normal. They were all back again—the white ibis, the American anhingas, the black crowned night herons, the great egrets, the cormorants, the roseate spoonbills, the little blue and the great blue herons. And beginning in the spring of 2009, bird-watchers should have a new boardwalk walking trail and 20-foot (6m) viewing tower hidden among the cypress trees, so they can get an even closer glimpse of them without disturbing the nesting areas. (Formerly bird-watchers had to watch from the road and nearby shore.)

The preserve covers 9,500 acres (3,845 hectares), 2,800 acres (1,113 hectares) of which covers Lake Martin, a picturesque cypress-tupelo swamp hung with curtains of trailing Spanish moss. A levee has been built here to ensure that water levels stay high enough to support wildlife and recreation (it's a very popular fishing lake). The rest is bottomland hardwood forest and live-oak forest, where songbirds like vireos and thrushes can be heard.

Lake Martin also has its share of alligators, up to 1,800 individuals, some as big as 10 feet (3m) long—in fact, it may be the best spot in Louisiana to see big alligators. They're so prevalent, the 2.5-mile (4km) walking trail along the top of the levee is closed during alligator nesting season, June to October. The alligators lurk right around where the birds build their nests, hoping to snap up a drowned chick or two. But they actually improve matters for the birds, scaring off raccoons and beavers and opossums that might otherwise raid the nests. Whatever happened in 2006, you can't blame the gators.

---

ⓘ **Cypress Island Preserve,** Rookery Rd., Beaux Bridge, LA

✈ Lafayette

🛏 $$ **Maison Des Amis,** 111 Washington St., Beaux Bridge (📞 **337/507-3399;** www.maisondesamis.com). $$ **Bois des Chênes Inn,** 338 N. Sterling, Lafayette (📞 **337/233-7816;** www.members.aol.com/boisdchene/bois.htm).

# Caddo Lake State Park
## *Down on the Texas Bayou*
### East Texas

THE MOST SERIOUS THREAT TO CADDO LAKE—THE ONLY NATURAL LAKE IN TEXAS—IS AN invasive species of aquatic fern called Salvinia molesta, or giant salvinia, a noxious weed that doubles in size every 2 to 4 days and quickly suffocates life below the water's surface. Efforts to eradicate it—using herbicides and weed-eating beetles—have met with limited success.

An ivory-billed woodpecker is the Holy Grail of bird-watching—rumors of its appearance in deep Louisiana, and then in Arkansas's Big Woods, set American birders atwitter. But there's a good chance that this mysterious, not-after-all-extinct bird could reappear at its old home by Caddo Lake.

Why not? Caddo Lake's the sort of mysterious swampy place that even has its very own Bigfoot, aka the Caddo Critter. Canoeing through this East Texas wildlife haven, following murky moss-hung backwaters between immense bald cypress trees, you get the feeling that anything could happen down here.

Though Caddo Lake is in Texas, it's actually the western half of one big bayou that stretches over into Louisiana. The South's largest natural freshwater lake, and the largest intact cypress forest left in the world, it has endured many threats—dammed in 1911, dotted with oil derricks in the early 20th century, polluted by an ammunition factory until the 1990s—but since 1993, Caddo has been a protected refuge. Even so, a new threat has arisen lately: giant salvinia, an invasive aquatic fern brought into the lake by boaters that has already killed off sections on the Louisiana side.

Fishermen love this maze of overgrown sloughs, ponds, and waterways, its 42 miles (68km) of boat roads teeming with largemouth bass, catfish, and crappie. But it's equally a hot spot for bird-watchers, with about 240 species to look for, from red-tailed hawks to pileated woodpeckers

and more waterfowl than you could shake a stick at.

Local birders recommend hanging out along Big Cypress Bayou and Mill Pond; in the summer sky you may spot anhingas and Mississippi kites sailing overhead. In the nearby town of Uncertain, a shallow slough called Goose Prairie (right in front of Crip's Camp) is generally full of wading

Caddo Lake State Park.

birds, wood ducks, and the occasional shorebird. In winter you may even see a migrating bald eagle. Half a mile (1km) west of the park entrance, the intersection of TX 43 and FM 2198 has a handy hill for observing the fall migration: White ibis, wood stork, osprey, Mississippi kite, bald eagle, chimney swift, and purple martin are just some of the many birds recorded here.

A swampy area where Harrison Bayou crosses Plant Road (C.R. 2607) on the southern boundary of Caddo Lake Wildlife Management Area is prime habitat for wood duck, great egrets, cattle egrets, green herons, little blue herons, and great blue heron. If it's more heron action you want, go south of the park on TX 43, turn east on FM 805, and near Pine Needle Lodge you can often find yellow- and black-crowned night herons, as well as fish crows, brown nuthatches, and a ton of warblers in summer.

As for where the ivory-billed woodpecker will show up—well, that's anybody's guess.

(i) **Caddo Lake State Park,** FM 2198, Karnack, TX

✈ Shreveport

🛏 $$ **Caddo Lake Cabins,** 131 Bois D'Arc Dr., Uncertain, TX (✆ **903/789-2063**). $ **Pine Needle Lodge,** 400 PR 7805, Jefferson, TX (✆ **903/665-2911;** www.pine needlelodge.com).

## Waterfowl 247

# Aransas National Wildlife Refuge
## *The Story of the Gulf Survivors*
### Austwell, Texas

RISING SEA LEVELS AT THE ARANSAS NATIONAL WILDLIFE REFUGE THREATEN TO DROWN OUT beaches where sea turtles nest and wetlands that provide critical habitat for many bird species. Altering rainfall patterns, due to climate change, may also lead to extended periods of drought that would disrupt the breeding habits of whooping cranes, once again threatening their survival.

It's a story environmentalists like to tell over and over again, to lift their hearts when they get discouraged: how North America's largest bird, the whooping crane, was brought back from the brink of extinction. By 1941, there were only 15 of these beautiful giants left—an entire species, reduced to just 15 birds. Yet today, thanks to a dedicated team of conservationists, their numbers are back up to 200 individuals in the wild, and still growing.

To look at a whooping crane, you wouldn't call it fragile or vulnerable—an adult male stands a full 5 feet (1.5m) high, with a commanding 7-foot (2m) wingspan.

But cranes are not rapid reproducers. Females don't begin to lay eggs until they are 4 years old, and when they do, they lay two eggs but hatch only one chick. To save the species, wildlife biologists decided to steal the second egg (the mother's going to abandon it anyway) and hatch it elsewhere. Using those extra hatched chicks, the scientists have been able to establish a few new flocks elsewhere and get the whooping cranes back on the road to survival.

The descendants of those 1941 survivors still winter down on Texas's gulf shore in the Aransas National Wildlife Refuge; technically, they are the only natural population in the world. Though these cranes migrate some 2,400 miles (3,900km) up to the Northwest Territories of Canada in summer, they faithfully return here every year from November through April, where they feed on blue crabs, crayfish, frogs, and wolfberries. Beginning in late winter, you can observe them from a 16-mile (26km) paved road that loops through several habitats; the best views are from the 40-foot (12m) observation tower or on a boardwalk trail through a salt marsh to the coast. To be certain of seeing whooping cranes, however, you can book a half-day guided tour along the shoreline in a shallow-draft boat past the birds' most popular waters,

With the luxurious long legs and throat typical of shore birds, whooping cranes have an especially elegant plumage—solid white, with just a touch of black on the wing tips and around the eyes, like an artful touch of mascara, and a dashing red cap on the top of the head. If you're lucky, you may see their distinctive courtship ritual, a dance that includes wing flapping, head bowing, acrobatic leaps into the air, and—yes, you guessed it—loud whooping.

(i) **Aransas National Wildlife Refuge,** FM 2040, Austwell, TX (✆ **361/286-3559;** http://southwest.fws.gov/refuges)

✈ Corpus Christi

🛏 $$$ **The Lighthouse Inn,** 200 S. Fulton Beach Rd., Rockport (✆ **866/790-8439** or 361/790-8439; www.lighthouse texas.com). $$ **Village Inn Motel,** 503 N. Austin St., Rockport (✆ **800/338-7539** or 361/729-6370).

**TOUR Rockport Chamber of Commerce** (✆ **800/826-6441** or 361/729-6445; www. rockport-fulton.org)

---

**248** Waterfowl

# The Cape Town Colony
## *March of the African Penguins*
### Cape Town, South Africa

FROM A POPULATION OF TWO MILLION AT THE START OF THE 20TH CENTURY, THE NUMBER OF African penguins has declined more than 90%, and the species continues to slide toward extinction at the rate of 15% per decade. Oil pollution, overfishing of their food supply, and poaching are ongoing threats.

It was the world's worst coastal bird disaster—an oil spill off the shores of South Africa in 2000 that coated the feathers of some 20,000 African penguins, 40% of the world's population, living on Robben and Dassen islands. Thanks to hundreds of devoted volunteers, the birds were rescued, hand-cleaned, and transferred to a sanctuary, from which they were eventually rereleased into the wild.

Despite that heroic effort, though, the African penguin is still endangered. Its numbers have been depleted by egg and guano poaching (the African penguin prefers to lay its eggs in guano deposits). Overfishing has robbed the ocean of the anchovies, sardines, and squid that they feed upon. Fur seals and feral cats prey upon them. With commercial shipping on the rise, oil spills have become more and more frequent. Even conservation efforts may be harming them, as controversy still swirls around the practice of clipping metal

African penguins return year after year to this haven, where they breed and nest from fall through winter (that's Mar–Aug in South Africa). You can view them from a raised boardwalk overlooking Foxy Beach—look for eggs in nests, tucked beneath beach vegetation or buried in the sand, or newly hatched chicks covered with fluffy gray down. Older penguin babies have blue-gray backs and white stomachs, in contrast to the adults' black and white with a black stripe across their chests. Even the tallest adults are only about 50cm (20 in.) tall. The species is also called blackfoot penguins because of their webbed black feet, or jackass penguins because of their braying calls.

Come in the late afternoon, when the seabirds have finished their day of ocean-fish catching and return home to disgorge partially digested fish into the mouths of their chicks. If you're out in the water, you can feel them whiz right past you, swimming at speeds up to 24kmph (15 mph). Technically, they're flightless birds—but underwater, they fly just fine.

Penguins in Boulder Coastal Park.

tags on their flippers for scientific monitoring purposes.

All the more reason, then, for the penguin reserve at Boulder Coastal Park. Surprisingly close to Cape Town, near popular Foxy Beach, a thriving population of some 2,500 African penguins nests among large granite boulders, where they can dig a protected burrow in the sand and lay their eggs. With commercial fishing banned from False Bay, the nearby waters have plentiful fish for the penguins to feed upon. Unfazed by the presence of humans, the penguins often waddle right onto Foxy Beach.

ⓘ **Boulder Coastal Park,** in Table Mountain National Park, Cape Town, South Africa (✆ **021/701-8692;** www.cpnp.co.za)

✈ Cape Town International

🛏 $$ **De Waterkant Village,** 1 Loader St., De Waterkant (✆ **021/409-2500;** www.dewaterkant.com). $$ **British Hotel Apartments,** 90 St. George's St., Simon's Town (✆ **021/786-2213;** www.britishhotelapartments.co.za).

# Kawainui Marsh
## *Marsh Madness*
### Oahu, Hawaii

KAWAINUI MARSH, THE LARGEST REMAINING WETLAND IN HAWAII, IS HOME TO A NUMBER OF rare and endangered species—but the marsh itself is at risk. Trash disposal and sewage have polluted the waters of the marsh and degraded wildlife habitats, and invasive species pose additional threats to native birds and plants that depend on the marsh.

Viewed from up high, from the Pali walking trail, you wonder how such a broad green meadow escaped the development that has eaten up most of Oahu. Nearly 1,000 acres (400 hectares) of open land, Kawainui is a stone's throw from Kailua. But go down and step on it: It jiggles underfoot, like walking on a waterbed. That's not grass at all; it's a dense mat of floating vegetation.

Early Polynesian settlers used this marsh (an ancient bay that silted in—hence the name, which means "big water" in Hawaiian) to plant taro and coconut trees and set up a fish farm; later Chinese settlers made it a rice paddy. Ecologists fought to preserve it from development in the 1960s, but not until 2007 was government funding finally allocated to build a visitor center and walking trails, and restore more open water for birds. Until that work's finished, the best place to see the marsh is from an overlook on Kapaa Quarry Road, off the Kalanianaole Highway.

You'll actually see two different kinds of floating green stuff: bulrushes underlaid with peat, and California grass, a seasonally flooded bog meadow growing on mineral soil. Slopes above the marsh are anchored with exotic trees and shrubs like koa haole, guava, Chinese banyan, and monkeypod. On the inner edges, you'll see some open water, with waterlilies, water hyacinth, and water lettuce floating on the surface. And it's this habitat—which is dramatically shrinking—that shelters four endangered native birds.

First there's the black-headed **Hawaiian moorhen** (gallinule), or *alaeula*, recognized by its red frontal shield and beak; legend says the moorhen scorched its beak bringing fire from the gods to the Hawaiian people. Aalaeulas build nests of reeds among the vegetation at water's edge, and roost at dusk in low trees or bushes to hide from predators. The **Hawaiian coot,** or *alae keokeo*—which looks like a slightly larger moorhen, but with a white frontal shield and beak—builds its nest right on top of the floating mat of grass. Standing 16 inches (40cm) tall on long pink legs, **Hawaiian stilts,** or *aeos,* are black on top and white underneath, with a long skinny black bill; they nest on mudflats and feed in nearby marshy shallows. The mottled brown **Hawaiian duck,** or *koloa maoli,* is an adaptable bird—so adaptable that it breeds freely with common mallards, thus driving itself into extinction. (The koloa maolis here are mostly hybrids; the only true Hawaiian ducks left are on Kauai.)

Rare black-crowned herons and great frigate birds also reside here, in one of Hawaii's last wetlands. For the sake of all these birds, that long-awaited restoration plan had better stay on track.

---

ⓘ **Kawainui Marsh,** off the Kalanianaole Hwy, east of Kailua (www.kawainuimarsh.com)

✈ Honolulu

🛏 $$ **Shrader's Windward Country Inn,** 47-039 Lihikai Dr., Kaneohe, Oahu (✆ **800/735-5071** or 808/239-5711; www.hawaiiscene.com/schrader)

# Booby Pond Nature Reserve

## *Safety in Numbers*

### Little Cayman Island

COMMERCIAL FISHING IS DEPLETING THE RED-FOOTED BOOBIES' FOOD SUPPLY WHILE COASTAL development is eliminating many of the trees and shrubs where the birds nest. Meanwhile, climate scientists are predicting more frequent and severe hurricanes in the years ahead, which could have a devastating effect on red-footed boobies and other species throughout the Caribbean.

If this scene had a soundtrack, you'd hear ominous drum rolls and deep bassoons: Cue up a massed horde of red-footed boobies, thousands of them, hovering tensely at twilight above the Caribbean Sea. Now enter, stage left, a circling crew of magnificent frigate birds, marauders famous for stealing other birds' food, stretching their 2.4m-wide (8-ft.) pointed black wings. The boobies draw a breath; then suddenly they spiral upward in a column, wheel swiftly, and dive like torpedoes toward shore. The magnificent frigate birds dart in to attack. Who will win this battle for survival?

Booby Pond Nature Reserve.

This drama is played out every evening in nesting season on Little Cayman Island, an isolated, sparsely inhabited scrap of coral and sand in the Caribbean Sea, due south of Cuba. About 5,000 nesting pairs of red-footed boobies—the largest colony of this species in the Western Hemisphere, a third of all the red-footed boobies in the entire Caribbean—hatch their chicks each February in the land-locked saltwater lagoon of Little Cayman's 82-hectare (204-acre) Booby Pond Nature Reserve. By day, the red-footed boobies roam long distances from Little Cayman, flying as far as Cuba or Jamaica, to fill their crops with squid and small fish to take back to their chicks. Back at the lagoon, they disgorge that food into the chicks' waiting beaks—that is, if they can get past the frigate birds first.

The smallest species of booby, the red-footed boobies are still good-size birds, with a wingspan of nearly 5 feet (1.5m). Adults are either buff-colored or white with dark wingtips, blue bills, and, of course, unmistakably bright red feet. Their wetland nesting grounds are strictly off limits to visitors, but lookout platforms have been built around the edges of the pond so you can witness this twilight battle; there are also telescopes on the veranda of the visitor center, a traditional Caymanian gingerbread bungalow.

During the day, other rare water birds visit the pond as well, including the shy West Indian whistling duck and a lot of snowy egrets, pure-white long-necked birds with a distinctive shaggy plume at the back of their heads. Instead of red feet like the boobies, they have yellow feet at the end of long black legs—they almost look as if they have stepped in paint.

While the boobies' daily struggle with the frigate birds is dramatic, a more serious drama here is Cayman's susceptibility to hurricanes. When 2004's Hurricane Ivan devastated Little Cayman, ornithologists waited nervously for news of the boobies nesting grounds. Luckily, the mangroves survived, and the colony's numbers have held steady. Will they be so lucky next time?

ⓘ **Booby Pond Nature Reserve,** near Blossom Village, Little Cayman (www.nationaltrust.org.ky/info/rfboobies.html)

✈ Grand Cayman

🛏 $$ **Pirates Point Resort,** Preston Bay, Little Cayman (✆ **345/948-1010;** www.piratespointresort.com). $$ **The Anchorage,** Seven Mile Beach, Grand Cayman (✆ **813/333-6532** or 345/945-4088; www.theanchoragecayman.com).

---

**251** Waterfowl

# Bharatpur Bird Sanctuary
## *Jewel in the Crown*
### Rajasthan, India

EARLY IN 2008, UNESCO THREATENED TO REMOVE THE BHARATPUR BIRD SANCTUARY FROM its list of World Heritage Sites because a severe water crisis has led to a sharp reduction in the number of birds using the park. As few as 100 migratory birds visited the sanctuary in 2007, compared to the usual 10,000.

Flash back to the days of the Raj, when privileged members of the British ruling class amused themselves at this duck-hunting preserve, not far from the Taj Mahal. Imagine the champagne corks popping as Lord Linlithgow, viceroy of India, strode in from a record-setting day of shooting—an incredible 4,273 birds downed in just 1 day.

There's no shooting anymore in the Bharatpur park, a wildlife sanctuary since 1956. With over 375 species of birds, today it's the number-one bird-watching destination in India—some would even say the world. Sure, it started out as a maharaja's hunting ground, when Maharaja Suraj Mal in 1726 flooded a natural depression of land to attract swarms of

ducks (some 20 duck species are still found here). But that history of protection kept this compact chunk of wetlands, woods, and grassland an inviting mosaic of habitats.

Winter is the best season, when migrants from the north join year-round residents around Bharatpur's shallow, marshy lakes. From perky little shorebirds like the greater painted snipe and the solitary lapwing, to long-legged waders like the black bittern and Sarus crane, there's a rich community at water's edge. Paved walkways make it easy to get about the park, either on foot, on bicycle (rent them at local lodges and hotels), or, easiest of all, by hiring a rickshaw-wallah, a trained guide who will transport you in his cycle-rickshaw.

With a million visitors a year in a relatively small (2,600-hectare/6,400-acre) area, Bharatpur hardly feels like a wilderness. Some visitors complain about the heavy traffic on its main road, feral cattle grazing on the grassland, and noisy water pumps. The sheer volume of birds, however, is astounding, and they seem unfazed by all those gawking humans. A group of rare Dalmatian pelicans gathers their crudely built nests; elegant common and demoiselle cranes soar in for the winter. Some of the park's most stunning residents are its storks—black-necked, painted, Asian openbills—stepping in their stately, deliberate manner through the shallows. In the woods near the water, you may see dusky eagle owls and all sorts of spotted eagles (imperial, white-tailed, greater, and Indian spotted eagles). In the grasslands, one must-see bird is the iconic Indian courser, a speedy little ground bird with beautiful black-and-white stripes like an eyemask on its russet-colored head.

After all this, it would be greedy to feel disappointed that Bharatpur's marquee attraction, a pair of critically endangered Siberian cranes, seems to have stopped migrating into the park. All the more reason to appreciate the rare species that still come here—and remember that they, too, grow more vulnerable every day.

Bharatpur Bird Sanctuary.

ⓘ **Bharatpur-Keoladeo Ghana National Park,** National Hwy. 11, Bharatpur (✆ **91/5644/22777**)

✈ Delhi

🚆 Bharatpur

🛏 $$ **Laxmi Vilas Palace,** Kakaji Ki Kothi, Bharatpur (✆ **91/5644/223523;** www.laxmivilas.com). $$ **Bharatpur Forest Lodge,** inside Bharatpur National Park (✆ **91/5644/22722**).

---

Waterfowl **252**

# Sultanpur National Park
## *Sunday in the Park with Storks*
### Gurgaon, India

DROUGHT IN INDIA IS FORCING MIGRATORY BIRDS AND OTHER SPECIES TO COMPETE WITH FARMERS for life-giving water. Lack of sufficient rain is shrinking the marshy wetlands around Sultanpur Jheel, the lake in Sultanpur National Park, and sending many bird species in search of other places to nest and feed.

On weekends, picnickers drive from Delhi to Sultanpur Jheel for the day, just to lounge near small Sultanpur Lake and stroll the raised brick walkway that circles its marshy shores. It's a 3.5km (2-mile) circuit that can take as long as 2 hours, never taking you too close to the water. How many of those day-trippers are aware how rare those birds in the lake might be?

But serious birders—the kind who come here at dawn, bring powerful binoculars and telephoto lenses, and time their visit to coincide with the winter migration—know what they're seeing. They can distinguish between the long-necked great flamingoes and bald-headed painted storks, or between the pouch-beaked rosy pelican, the flat-beaked spoonbill, and the white ibis with its sharp black curved beak. The elegant bluish-gray demoiselle crane, the striking black-winged stilt, the soft brown pond heron—they're all here, browsing the shallows, flapping low over the water, or weighing down the branches of the acacia trees. And that's just the exotic big waders, for a start. For a dedicated birder, spotting the feathered reddish crest of a hoopoe, the iridescent green of a rose-winged parakeet, or the blue-and-scarlet plumage of a white-throated kingfisher in the trees is a thrill that's hard to top.

In many ways, the caretakers of Sultanpur did things right. Originally a seasonal pool of monsoon overflow, brackish Sultanpur Jheel (lake) held enough crustaceans, fish, and insects to attract birds, but then dried up in the dry season. It was drained and made a "proper" year-round lake after the sanctuary was declared a national park in 1991; a couple artificial islands were built where birds could roost, and mounds built in the surrounding tawny grasslands. Besides the birds, blackbuck and nilgai were encouraged to graze here, as well as sambar and four-horned antelope. Additional trees were planted around the lake, largely acacias and neem, which are known to attract birds. The shores were landscaped with lawns, shrubs, and bougainvilleas, shrewdly placed so as not to block views of the lake. Four watchtowers were set up at key sites, and a small interpretive museum assembled. Some local ornithologists protested that the natural wild feel of the place was lost in favor of making an attractive picnic site, but so long as the birds kept coming, it seemed irrelevant.

But now that a series of droughts has hit India, Sultanpur Lake—which used to disappear completely—has been tapped to irrigate nearby farmers' fields. Birds that had come to depend upon that year-round habitat have abandoned the shrinking wetlands; some of its most treasured species are already gone, including the purple heron and the possibly-extinct Siberian crane. When the drought cycle ends, will they ever come back?

(i) **Sultanpur National Park,** NH-15A, Gurgaon-Jhajjar Rd.

✈ Delhi

🛏 $$$ **Oberoi Maidens,** 7 Sham Nath Marg, Delhi (✆ **91/11/2397-5464;** www.oberoihotels.com). $ **Master Paying Guest House,** R-500 New Rajinder Nagar, New Delhi (✆ **91/11/2574-1089** or 91/11/2585-0914; www.master-guesthouse.com).

Sultanpur National Park.

# 5 Going to Ruins

*Machu Picchu.*

# The Hill of Tara
## *Gone with the M3*
### County Meath, Ireland

IN AN EFFORT TO STOP OR AT LEAST SLOW THE DESTRUCTION OF THE HILL OF TARA, CONSERVATIONISTS and government supporters are working to make the hill a designated World Heritage Site. This would help to preserve the Gabhra Valley, between the Hill of Tara and the Hill of Skryne, and protect the surrounding landscape by preventing commercial development along the path of the new motorway.

Ireland is a nation of storytellers, where seemingly every mossy stone and country crossroads has a tale spun about it. But even so, there's no disputing the legendary significance of the Hill of Tara, traditional seat of the High Kings of Ireland. No wonder a plan to run a new superhighway past it has generated storms of outrage.

On first glance, Tara today doesn't look like much—a 90m-high (300-ft.) hill dotted with grassy mounds, some ancient pillar stones, and depressions that show where the Iron Age ring fort, Ráith na Ríogh, encircled the brow of the hill. But audiovisuals at the visitor center deconstruct just what those mounds represent, as if peeling away the centuries from this time-hallowed ridge. Prominent on the hilltop are the ring barrow called Teach Chormaic (Cormac's House) and the Forradh, or royal seat, with a granite coronation stone known as the Lia Fáil (Stone of Destiny), standing erect at its center. The trenches of three other smaller ring forts are nearby, as well as an excavated passage tomb just to the north, the astronomically aligned **Mound of the Hostages,** which dates to 2000 B.C.

The wood timbers of the old royal halls rotted long ago; the last great *feis*—a triennial banquet of princes, poets, priests, and politicians—was held in A.D. 560, after which the rise of Christianity forced ancient Celtic traditions into hiding. But Tara was always more than just one hill—it was the epicenter of Ireland's foremost kingdom, and several other important prehistoric sites are in the same valley. From the Hill of Tara, in the distance you can spot the great burial mound of Newgrange and the Hill of Slane, where St. Patrick readied himself to take on the Irish pagans— which, of course, he needed to do at Tara, Ireland's symbolic heart.

The N3 highway, heading northeast out of Dublin toward the town of Kells, already ran close enough to Tara to shake its foundations; now a larger limited-access motorway, the M3, is being built even closer, 2.2km (1⅓ miles) away, with a major interchange right near the sacred hill. During construction, a number of megalithic souterrains—underground buildings—some dating from the 7th century, have been bulldozed, probably the homes of important nobles and courtiers living near the king's fort. When a 2,000-year-old henge named Lismullin with megalithic decorations on its stone was unearthed in March 2007, construction was temporarily halted—but work proceeds on other sections of the road, despite vociferous citizen protests. Alternate routes have been proposed, but to no avail. The ghosts of the High Kings must be weeping.

The great burial mound of Newgrange.

ⓘ **Hill of Tara,** off the N3, Navan, County Meath (ⓒ **353/46/902-5903;** www.savetara.com)

✈ Dublin

🚂 Navan

🛏 $$ **Conyngham Arms Hotel,** Main St., Slane (ⓒ **800/44-UTELL** [448-8455] in the U.S. or 353/41/988-4444; www.cmvhotels.com). $ **Lennoxbrook Country House,** Kells (ⓒ **353/46/45902**).

**Ancient Mysteries** **254**

# Ggantija
## *Going Back to Mother Earth*
### Gozo, Malta

VANDALISM, A SEVERE STORM, AND WORK IN NEARBY STONE QUARRIES DAMAGED THIS ANCIENT temple, leading to a renovation that was completed in 2005. A recent steep increase in fees has helped to reduce the number of visitors, while new interpretive centers seek to instill more respect. Buffer zones around the temples are also improving the situation.

The temple of Ggantija.

Legend has it that Ggantija was built, like the name suggests, by a giant—not only that, but a female giant, who made the whole thing in 1 night while holding a baby in her other arm. Being a woman, she built this sanctuary in the rounded curves of the female form; worshippers entered and left the temple through the birth canal, as if reliving their own birth experience.

This stupendous fertility goddess relic was constructed between 3600 and 3000 B.C., which makes it the world's oldest man-made free-standing building—although these days it isn't entirely free-standing, but propped up with unsightly metal scaffolding. Still, you can't deny the elemental power of these pitted limestone blocks—stern gray on the outer walls, warm yellow for the inner walls—which weigh up to 60 tons and cover an area of 1,000 sq. m (10,764 sq. ft.); there are two adjacent temples, like a mother and daughter. The rear wall alone rises 6m (20 ft.). Delicately incised geometrical designs ornament the

stone, lovely curling shapes that seem hardly possible from artists working with just simple flint knives. A faint blush of red here or there reminds us of the bold red ocher paint that once decorated the megaliths. Imagine being inside these oval chambers when they were roofed over and painted a dark, warm red—it must truly have felt like entering a womb.

Older than the Pyramids of Giza, older than Stonehenge, Ggantija has stubbornly weathered the centuries, along with 50 other megalithic temples on the islands of Malta. No one knows why this Mediterranean people went through an explosion of temple building in this period, or why their culture swiftly declined around 2300 B.C.—it may have been famine, deforestation, or overpopulation. Today, however, the temples are one of Malta's chief tourist attractions, and busloads of tourists tramp through ancient sites that were only built to admit a select few worshippers.

Ggantija is the largest and most intact of all these temples, partly because it's off the beaten track on the small island of Gozo (a 20-min. ferry ride from Malta). But it was the first to be dug up, back in the 1820s, when the art of excavation was in its infancy; many carvings and sculptures apparently disappeared, and stones were disturbed and/or damaged.

ⓘ **Ggantija,** Temples St., Xaghra (𝒞 **356/ 21/553 194**)

✈ Malta

🛏 $$$ **Westin Dragonara,** 5 Dragonara Rd., St. Julian's (𝒞 **356/21/381 000;** www. starwoodhotels.com). $$ **San Andrea Hotel,** Xlendi Promenade, Gozo (𝒞 **356/21/ 565 555;** www.hotelsanandrea.com).

**Ancient Mysteries** **255**

# The Caves of Lascaux
## *Rock of Ages*
### Le Dordogne, France

AFTER SURVIVING FOR 15,000 YEARS OR MORE, THESE ANCIENT CAVE PAINTINGS HAVE BEEN seriously damaged over the past 60 years by artificial light and carbon dioxide—both byproducts of tourism. Efforts are also under way to halt the spread of a fungus, possibly caused by a climate control system installed in 2001.

Scientists called it the "green sickness"— the atmospheric changes that were destroying the world's most famous cave paintings. It should have been no surprise, though, considering that several million tourists had crowded through Lascaux's underground chambers to gawk at this astonishing cache of prehistoric artwork— bulls, wild boars, stags, horses, and deer, rendered in dynamic, lifelike tableaux.

Lascaux has been closed to the public since 1964, although qualified archaeologists can still apply to visit. (Write to the Direction Régionale des Affaires culturelles, Service Régionale de l'Archéologie, 54 rue Magendie, 33074 Bordeaux, 𝒞 **33/5/ 57-95-02-02**). It's a paradox that rises again and again in archaeology. What are we preserving ancient sites for, if not to look upon them?

Who knew, back in 1940 when the caves were first discovered, what a big deal they would turn out to be? Four French boys stumbled upon these caves by accident, hunting for their dog one afternoon; they crawled into a cave (the Dordogne region is honeycombed with such caves) and saw its walls daubed with hundreds of figures in vivid ochers, yellows, browns, and reds. Archaeologists soon followed, and dated the art—a mix of some 600 engravings, detailed line drawings, and paintings—back to the Stone Age, some 15,000 to 20,000 years ago.

Opened to the public in 1948, the caves became one of France's hottest tourist sites, just as the post–World War II travel boom was taking off. Naturally cool, still, and dark, the caves offered ideal artifact storage conditions, which is why these drawings were so well preserved in the first place. But with artificial light installed, increased air circulation, and—worst of all—the carbon dioxide exhaled by over 1,000 visitors a day, the limestone walls began to corrode, and tiny mosses and lichens bloomed. But even banning the general public wasn't enough; soon after a climate-control system was installed, there was a major outbreak of white fungus in

2001, and spots of mold were detected in late 2007, spurring officials to shut the caves temporarily to all but the most essential visitors.

Nowadays, you'll have to be content with the nearby Lascaux II, an above-ground concrete replica that contains faithful copies of some 200 paintings. Even Lascaux II is carefully controlled, with only 200 visitors allowed per day; from April to October, you can buy tickets outside the Montignac tourist office (place Bertrand-de-Born, ✆ **33/5/53-51-82-60;** www.bienvenue-montignac.com). We've all seen pictures of these artworks, but seeing them in context is something else—even in this fake setting, the sheer number and variety of images is mind-boggling. Still, one big thing is missing: the sensation of connecting with those prehistoric artists through the actual paintings themselves.

ⓘ **The Caves of Lascaux,** off D706, 2km (1¼ miles) from Montignac, France (✆ **33/5/53-51-95-03**), closed Jan

🚂 Condat-Le-Lardin

🛏 $$ **Hotel Le Relais du Soleil d'Or,** 16 rue du 4-Septembre, Montignac (✆ **33/5/53-51-80-22;** www.le-soleil-dor.com), closed Feb

# Valley of the Vizérè
## *Stone Age Hangouts*
### Le Dordogne, France

ALTHOUGH THE GROTTE DE FONT-DE GAUME, THE GROTTE DES COMBARELLES, AND THE CAVE at Cap Blanc have so far escaped some of the problems that plague the caves of Lascaux, they are not immune from those threats. Care must be taken to manage tourism and population growth in the area, and to mitigate the effects of pollution and climate change on local habitats.

Frustrated that you can't enter the Lascaux Caves to see those world-famous cave paintings? Don't write off a trip to the Dordogne so fast. This region has been on archaeologists' map since 1868, when prehistoric skeletons were first unearthed in a cave at Les Eyzies-de-Tayac. It's a hotbed of Stone Age relics, inscribed as a UNESCO World Heritage Site called the Valley of the Vizérè.

Three authentic caves are still open to visitors here. Having learned a lesson from what happened at Lascaux, they all strictly limit the number of visitors per day, so call in advance for reservations, up to a year ahead if possible. The **Grotte de Font-de-Gaume** (on D47, 1.5km/1 mile outside Les Eyzies, ✆ **33/5/53-06-86-00**) is decorated with skilled Stone Age paintings of bison, reindeer, horses, and other animals, juxtaposed with graffiti from 18th-century British schoolboys—a fascinating palimpsest of different layers of civilization. More recently unearthed, **Grotte des Combarelles** (D47, 17km/11 miles north of Bergerac, ✆ **33/5/53-06-86-00**) has carved figures dating back to the Stone Age, depicting musk oxen, horses, bison, and aurochs (wild oxen) in surprisingly naturalistic detail. Perhaps the most impressive of all is the **Cap Blanc** cave (Marquay, Sireuil, ✆ **33/5/53-06-86-00**), which was first discovered in 1909; it's the world's only prehistoric sculpted frieze open to the public, featuring immense figures of bison, horses, and reindeer sculpted in relief out of the limestone 15,000 years ago by Cro-Magnon artists.

Complementing these sites is **Roque St. Christophe** (Peyzac-le Moustier, ✆ **33/5/53-50-70-45**), a sheer 80m-high (262-ft.) limestone cliff over a kilometer-long (¹/₂-mile) stretch of the Vezere River, where frost and water have gouged out long shelves of rock and about 100 declivities. These rock balconies—handy as lookouts as well as shelters—have been inhabited almost continuously for 55,000 years, beginning in Paleolithic times; in the Middle Ages, they were enlarged so that an entire town and fort could be housed here. Similar dwellings were hewn in the base of cliffs by Cro-Magnon residents at **Laugerie Basse** (just north of Les Eyzies on D47 ✆ **33/5/53-06-92-70**).

On their own, any of these sites is well worth visiting, but the concentration of sites in this one river valley—as many as 147 excavations and 25 decorated caves—gives you a remarkable sense of just how vital these prehistoric communities were. The **Musée National de la Préhistoire** in Les Eyzies (✆ **33/5/53-06-45-45**) displays a hoard of artifacts excavated from many other sites in the area. These tantalizing fragments are all we have left of these people—they're like a time machine to a very different world.

---

ⓘ **Les Eyzies** tourist office, 19 rue de la Préhistoire (✆ **33/5/53-06-97-05;** www.leseyzies.com)

🚆 Les Eyzies

🛏 $$$ **Hotel Les Glycines,** Rte. De Périgueux, Les Eyzies-Tayac-Sireuil (✆ **33/5/53-06-97-07;** www.les-glycines-dordogne.com)

# Altamira Cave
## *Picassos of Prehistory*
### Cantabria, Spain

BACTERIA FROM THOUSANDS OF TOURISTS HAVE IRREPARABLY DAMAGED THESE CAVE PAINTINGS that date back to the Ice Age. Preservation efforts have also created damage by altering the natural atmosphere inside the cave. Speculation exists that the Altamira Cave may collapse sometime in the future, which makes visits to this ancient site (when allowed) especially meaningful.

Michelangelo's painting the ceiling of the Sistine Chapel was nothing new—a bunch of nameless artists did the same thing 15,000 years ago, at the end of the Ice Age. In an S-shaped set of caves at Altamira, Spain, instead of the Creation they depicted bison, boars, and horses, leaping and plunging across the cave ceiling. Whoever these artists were, they created perhaps the most beautiful cave paintings anywhere.

The paintings are almost all in one main room of the cave system, called the Polychrome Chambers. Bison are the star players here, with the most stunning section featuring 21 red bison stampeding across the ceiling—you can practically hear them stamp and snort. Using only three colors—ocher, red, and black—these are large-scale pictures, practically life-size, and executed in meticulous realistic detail, rippling muscles, bristling manes, and all. The paintings were ingeniously positioned to take advantages of natural bulges and furrows in the rock, giving a three-dimensional realism to the animals. Another unusual feature is eight engraved anthropomorphic figures, various handprints, and hand outlines, almost as if the artists were determined to leave their own signatures.

Although the cave was discovered in 1868, it wasn't until 1879 that a little girl—daughter of the nobleman who owned the land—noticed paintings on the ceilings of the dark cave. Because they were so well preserved, archaeologists insisted they were forgeries; not until 1902 were they authenticated. Over the course of the 20th century, the Altamira cave became so popular with visitors that, inevitably, harmful bacteria were tracked in and damaged these masterpieces. Even more damaging were the walls built in the 1950s to prop up the ceiling of this karst cave, which seemed on the verge of natural collapse: The walls cut off the main chamber, thus irrevocably altering the atmospheric conditions that were responsible for its perfect preservation in the first place. The cave has been repeatedly closed to the public ever since

the 1970s; currently no visitors are allowed, but cave officials hope to grant limited access again eventually, so keep checking for updates.

In the 1960s, anticipating such closures—or even total collapse of the cave—a couple of exact replicas were built, one for the Deutsches Museum, another to be displayed in Madrid. In 2001 an even more precise replica was opened a few hundred feet away from the original cave. Called the Altamira Center, it's much more convincing than Lascaux's replica: the ceiling paintings were copied using sophisticated computerized digital-transfer technology that captured every crack, stain, and hollow of the original. Who needs to damage the real thing any further, when all of the incredible artistry lives on here?

ⓘ **Cuevas de Altamira,** Santillana del Mar (✆ **34/94/281-80-05**)

✈ Santander

🛏 $$ **Casa del Marqués,** Cantón 26, Santillana del Mar (✆ **34/94/281-88-88**). $ **Hotel Siglo XVIII,** Revolgo 38, Santillana del Mar (✆ **34/94/284-02-10**).

---

**258** Ancient Mysteries

# Dun Aengus
## *A Ruin & a Riddle*
### Aran Islands, Ireland

EROSION IS THE NATURAL RESULT WHEN SANDY BEACHES AND ROCKY CLIFFS ARE EXPOSED TO THE elements over time, but increasingly violent seas, acid rain, and higher winds brought on by climate change all increase the damage—and that's what's facing Dun Aengus.

Set broodingly on a 90m-high (300-ft.) western cliff, Dun Aengus looks ready to crash into the sea at any moment. And it's true, geologists tell us; battered by the elements, that limestone karst is already in the process of crumbling. But this mysterious Iron Age fort is hanging tough.

The weathered look of this rough-piled mass of dark gray stones is part of its aura. Walking around Dun Aengus (or to give it its proper Gaelic name, Dún Aonghasa), at times you'll come perilously close to the edge of the cliff, with no guard rail between you and certain death on the rocks below.

Dun Aengus.

the ground, and its walls are certainly defensive—3m (8 ft.) high in some places, and the thickest 4.3m (14 ft.) thick. Yet the design of the structure—three concentric semicircles opening to the sea—looks more like a theater than a fortress. If it was a fort, why are there no dwellings inside, or any provision for bringing in water in case of siege? And within the centermost horseshoe, what is the purpose of that large table rock, almost like a sacrificial altar?

The Aran Islanders are a hardy lot, living in stone cottages, speaking only Gaelic among themselves, and casting out to sea every day in small round currachs made of tarred canvas. In many ways life here hasn't changed much for centuries—it's a time-warp experience to ferry over from modern Galway City to Kilronan, the main town on the island of Inishmore (Inis Mór). At the docks you can rent bikes or hail a minivan or, even better, an old-fashioned jaunting cart to get around the island; it's only 7km (4½ miles) west to Dun Aengus.

There are several similar structures nearby: Dun Dubhchathair, 2.5km (1½ miles) southwest; Dun Eochla the same distance northwest; and Dun Eoghanacht, 7.2km (4½ miles) west-northwest. Though smaller than Dun Aengus, they have the same primitive power, the same sense of mystery. If only these stones could speak!

Though it's closer to the edge than it used to be, this sea-cliff location was undoubtedly always an important element of its defense, not to mention its vantage point for spotting the ships of any invader.

Who built Dun Aengus? Scholars disagree: it could have been an ancient Celtic tribe called the Fir Bolgs, a few centuries B.C., or it could have been 8th- or 9th-century Danes. Nor can scholars agree on what the fort was used for. When you walk up the hill (a 20-minute hike from the visitor center), you pass a chevaux-de-frise zone, where sharp stones jut defensively out of

---

ⓘ **Dun Aengus** (✆ **353/99/61008**)

✈ Inis Mór; Galway City

**FERRY** Kilronan

🛏 $$ **Galway Harbour Hotel,** New Dock Rd., Galway (✆ **353/91/569466;** www.galwayharbourhotel.com). $$ **Kilmurvey House,** coast road, Inis Mór (✆ **353/99/61218**).

# Rock Shelters of Bhimbetka
## *Human Timeline*
### Madhya Pradesh, India

WITHOUT PROTECTION FROM THE NATIVE TREES THAT USED TO SHELTER THE AREA, THE BHIMBETKA site is battered by scorching heat, hail, and heavy rains, and invasive fig-tree roots are breaking up the rocks. Not a minute too soon, an intensive conservation project will address soil, water, and forestry issues.

You can't ignore it; the very name Bhopal is synonymous with environmental disaster. It almost doesn't matter that these ancient caves have sheltered their artworks for 12,000 years—who comes to Bhopal anymore to see them?

It's a pity. Tourism to Bhopal died abruptly in 1984, after the deadly gas leak at a Union Carbide pesticide plant, but the area has two amazing historical sites: the Buddhist complex at Sanchi (p. 420) and the caves of Bhimbetka, which contain the earliest record of human life in India. Since they were first discovered in 1957, some 700 rock shelters have been identified around here; you can tour 15 of the most spectacular ones, which have been developed with walkways, lighting, and guides.

And what extraordinary art they contain. Unlike the older European caves, where most of the art depicts animals, the figures in Bhimbetka's rock shelters are mostly human—and they're not just hunting but dancing, feasting, worshipping, harvesting, waging war, giving birth, and burying their dead. Studying them, you can see the range of weapons they used, from bow-and-arrow and swords to barbed spears and pointed sticks. Because they were painted in different eras (the most recent date only back to medieval times), you can trace changes in religious rites, artistic styles, and even fashion, from loincloths to tattooed bodies to tunics. The range of animals portrayed is specifically Indian:

alongside bison and horses you'll find rhinoceros, tigers, lions, elephants, crocodiles, and peacocks. (Check out "Zoo Rock," nicknamed for the number of animals it depicts.) The best paintings are arrestingly dramatic, showing the terror of a hunter cornered by an angry bison, or the panic of a mother elephant whose child is being taken by trappers.

Notice how generations of cave dwellers used and reused their walls as a canvas, covering faded Paleolithic hunting scenes with bolder depictions of a warlike later era. The paints they used were chiefly colored earth, vegetable dyes, and animal fats, which were "fixed" chemically by the oxide in the rocks. That fluke enabled them to survive for centuries, even though they're not in sealed caves, but in open chambers within massive sandstone outcrops. Heaped high on wooded hills where the inhabitants could keep watch on the plains below, they're a stunning feature of the landscape—but just wait until you go inside.

---

ⓘ **Bhimbetka,** in Ratapani Wildlife Sanctuary, Hwy. 69 southwest of Bhopal (✆ **91/748/022-4478**)

✈ Bhopal

🛏 $$ **Jehan Numa Palace,** 157 Shamla Hill, Bhopal (✆ **91/755/266-1100;** www.hoteljehanumapalace.com)

# Pulemelei Mound
## *Lost in the Jungle*
### Savaii, Western Samoa

WITHOUT EFFORTS TO PROTECT IT, PULEMELEI MOUND COULD FALL VICTIM TO THE ECOLOGICAL stressors that affect other parts of Savaii, including pollution, population growth, mining, logging, and agriculture, which have destroyed native forests and habitats.

Researchers agree upon two points: The Pulemelei Mound is important, and it is big. After that, the arguments start to fly.

The biggest ancient structure in Polynesia (65×60m/213×197 ft. at its base, and 12m/39 ft. high), the stepped pyramid of Pulemelei—or Tia Seu, as some call it—may have been a chieftain's residence, a ritual site for pigeon snaring, a sentry tower, a celestial observatory, or a place of worship. Stone pedestals at the corners of its leveled-off top may have been ceremonial thrones for worthies, or receptacles for conch-shell trumpets that were blown every night to call holy spirits back to this resting place. Some Polynesians believe it was built by the great god Togaloa, or that it was the launching point for the great West Polynesian Diaspora—which makes this place equally significant to Tahitians, Hawaiians, and New Zealand Maoris. Some even believe Pulemelei is the gateway to the afterlife, which explains the neatly aligned entryways scooped out of the earthen slopes on its east and west side, a feature found on no other such mound. Sitting silently, overgrown and crumbling, in the middle of the jungle, it still has a curious aura and power.

Pulemelei's island, Savaii, is the largest in this volcanic South Sea archipelago, but it's much more rugged than its neighbors. As South Pacific hideaways go, this is it: lush inland jungles and waterfalls, desolate-looking lava fields, a beach-edged lagoon or two, and very few other tourists, though it's only an hour's ferry ride or a 10-minute flight from the Samoan capital of Apia on Upolu Island. Many historians consider Savaii the cradle of Polynesian civilization—it was a major political capital, and any chieftain who lived here would have been powerful indeed. Archaeologists think the mound was built about A.D. 1100 to 1400, but the settlement that surrounds it seems to have been mysteriously abandoned between 1700 and 1800 and was swallowed up by jungle—until anthropologists started poking around in the 1950s.

Left alone, this pile of packed earth and basalt stones will soon be swallowed by jungle again. But that's another thing no one can agree on—what is to be done with Pulemelei. Located on an old copra plantation, it's still privately owned, though the landowners would like to develop the site for tourism. Local villagers have taken them to court to stop excavations, which they believe desecrate the holy site. When a team of archaeologists a team of archaeologists carrying on the work of Thor Heyerdahl finally began to dig here in 2003, here in 2003, ritual fires were lit to purify the area, in case human remains were disturbed (Heyerdahl's people discovered none), but it's still a politically sensitive issue. Hire a local guide to lead you through the jungle to Pulemelei, and imagine what this site could look like, when—and if—it's ever properly preserved.

ⓘ **Pulemelei,** Lesolo Plantation

✈ Savaii

🛏 \$\$ **Kitano Hotel Tusitala,** Beach Walk St., Apia (🕾 **685/21122;** www.kitano. ws). \$\$\$ **Vacations Beach Resort,** Manase Village, Savaii (🕾 **685/54001** or 685/54024; www.vacationsbeachfales.com).

# Cueva de las Manos
## *A Show of Hands*
### Patagonia, Argentina

CUEVA DE LAS MANOS HAS ESCAPED THE EFFECTS OF RAMPANT TOURISM THAT PLAGUE OTHER cave painting sites. There's no buildup, no state-of-the-art visitor center, no bus-tour hordes straggling through—at least not yet.

At first you'd swear a bunch of first-graders had been let loose in this rock niche in the Rio Pintura canyon: A flurry of stenciled handprints, in red and yellow and white, cover the walls by the hundreds, like a bunch of eager pupils waving to get the teacher's attention.

These handprints are perhaps 600 years old. No one knows why they're there. From the size of the hands, it seems they would have belonged to 13-year-old boys—it's possible that stamping your handprint in this sacred cave was a coming-of-age ritual among the native Tehuelches. You'll also notice that they're nearly all left hands; presumably the boys used their right hands to hold blowpipes for the paint, several of which have been found lying around the cave. And if you look hard, you may be able to find one startling handprint with six fingers—freaky.

Long before the Tehuelches started painting hands here—as long as 8,000 or 9,000 years ago—Cueva de las Manos (Cave of the Hands) was already decorated with prehistoric rock art, particularly detailed hunting murals. As befits a site on the Patagonian steppes, of course, the animals in those hunting scenes are guanacos; among the handprints at one spot you can also see the three-toed footprint of a rhea, South America's equivalent of an ostrich. Notice also the big red splotches on the ceiling—anthropologists guess those were made by tossing up a *boleadora,* or leashed hunting ball, that had been dipped in ink.

The Rio Pinturas canyon is rugged, scenic, and remote—remote even for Patagonia—which is why the cave wasn't really discovered until the 1970s. As a result, it's still in good shape, even though it's relatively exposed to the elements. The entrance to this alero, or rock overhang (it isn't a true cave), is quite large, 15m (49 ft.) wide and 10m (33 ft.) high, but it does slope upward and becomes more protected back by the paintings. Railings have been erected to prevent visitors from touching the paintings, but otherwise it's undeveloped; it's actually on private land, and open to the public only by permission of the owner.

Cueva de los Manos certainly is off the beaten track; it still isn't included on most tour itineraries, being so far from Patagonia's other attractions. But that makes it all the more impressive, wild and lonely and as yet unspoiled.

(i) **Cueva de los Manos,** in Francisco P. Moreno National Park, RP 97, south of Baja Caracoles

✈ Perito Moreno

🛏 $$ **Belgrano,** Av. San Martín, Perito Moreno ((C) **54/43/2019**). $ **Estancia Los Toldos,** Hostería Cueva de las Manos, RN 40 ((C) **54/4901-0436,** cuevadelasmanos@ hotmail.com).

**TOUR Patagonian Travel Adventures** ((C) **831/336-0167;** www.patagonia adventures.com). **Footloose Adventure Travel** ((C) **800/873-5872** in the U.S. or 44/845/330-6094 in the U.K.; www.foot loose.com).

# 10 Places to See Petroglyphs

From the dawn of time, humans have felt compelled to interpret their environment with art—and by carving it in stone, they ensured it would last through the centuries. Etched into the surface of caves, canyon walls, and hillsides, these petroglyphs (as opposed to "pictographs," or paintings on rock) are more than just graffiti from the ancients—anthropologists see them as cultural history and, most often, sites of religious importance to their makers. Most are still considered sacred sites by their descendants, which makes it even more imperative to protect them.

Here are 10 outstanding petroglyph sites that have survived—so far:

**262 Nine Mile Canyon, North of Price, Utah** Actually 40 miles (64km) long, this eastern Utah canyon is like a drive-through gallery of over 10,000 petroglyphs, carved into its black rock face around A.D. 1000 to 1200 by the long-vanished Fremont Indians. Hunters, shamans, horses, elk, snakes, turkeys, bighorn sheep, owls, and even centipedes are depicted; the best is a large hunting scene in Cottonwood Canyon. *www.byways.org/explore/byways/15780. www.ninemilecanyoncoalition.org.*

**263 Petroglyph National Monument, Albuquerque, New Mexico** On the outskirts of Albuquerque, Pueblos and other prehistoric Native Americans carved some 25,000 pictures into the dark basaltic boulders of this volcanic escarpment along the Rio Grande. Despite a number of lawsuits, the city is enlarging two highways through the monument, close to the Boca Negra Canyon, the most visited section of the park. ✆ *505/899-0205. www.nps.gov/petr.*

Petroglyph National Monument.

**264 Three Rivers Petroglyph National Recreation Area, New Mexico** Around 20,000 pale images are carved into the dark rocks of this basalt ridge in the northern Chihuahuan Desert of south-central New Mexico. From scorpions and jackrabbits to hawks, humans, and geometric designs, these etchings are relics of the Mogollon peoples who lived here between A.D. 1000 and 1400. ✆ *505/525-4300.*

**265 Valley of Fire, Overton, Nevada** Only 55 miles (89km) from Las Vegas, this dramatically eroded Mojave rockscape preserves a set of stunning 3,000-year-old rock carvings by Pueblos and prehistoric basket makers. A mere .5-mile (.8km) loop trail through Petroglyph Canyon reveals panel after panel of slick dark rock etched with astoundingly expressive figures—bighorned sheep, dancers, birds, suns. ✆ *702/397-2088.*

Valley of Fire.

**266 Puako Petroglyphs, Holoholokai Beach Park, Hawaii** On a shelf of pahoehoe lava rock the size of a football field, some 3,000 intricate figures carved by ancient Hawaiian artists make up the largest rock art site in the Pacific, a site full of *mana*, or spiritual power, for the Hawaiian people. *Mauna Lani Resort.* © *808/885-1064.*

Puako Petroglyphs.

**267 Cerros Pintados, Tarapaca, Chile** In the barren Atacama Desert of northern Chile, the Cerros Pintados— or "Painted Hills"—displays over 350 figures of humans, animals (mostly alpacas and llamas), and intricate abstract symbols on some 66 panels carved, sculpted, or painted onto 3.2km (2 miles) of bare hillsides. The scale is often titanic—one human figure is 100m (328 ft.) high. Dated between A.D. 500 and 1450, the geoglyphs have been damaged by illegal mining, erosion, and unsupervised tourism. *www.turismochile.com.*

**268 Coa Valley, Portugal** The first carvings here were made in Paleolithic times (40,000–10,000 B.C.); the most recent were chiseled at the beginning of the 20th century. In the 1990s, a dam project nearly submerged these long-hidden carved boulders and canyon faces along 17km (11 miles) of the river Coa, in northeast Portugal, but it was prevented by an international protest campaign. Carvings are still being excavated in this little-known archaeological gem. © *351/279/768 260. www.ipa.min-cultura.pt/coa.*

**269 Twyfelfontein Uibasen Conservancy, Namibia** In the stark red Namibian desert, these 6,000-year-old rock engravings created by the San bushmen of the Kalihari almost seem to glow under the desert sun. Whereas most bushman art in Africa (at Tsodilo in Botswana, and several sites in South Africa) are painted, here nearly 2,000 figures are carved onto open rock faces, including elephants, rhinoceroses, ostriches, and giraffes.

**270 Ku-ring-gai Chase National Park, New South Wales, Australia** Just northeast of Sydney, this park full of gum trees and rainforest also has several panels of Aboriginal rock art carved into the relatively soft Sydney basin sandstone. A 2.5km (1.5-mile) trail to the basin leads you past the best-known ones, featuring kangaroos, emus, and wallabies (note the hunters' boomerangs). © *61/2/9457 9322.*

**271 Dampier Rock Art Complex, Murujuga, Western Australia** It's the world's largest collection of petroglyphs—and neighboring industrial developments are killing it. Pollution generated by local petrochemical plants on the Burrup Peninsula is dissolving the natural varnish of the rock faces, into which ancient Aboriginals chiseled some 250,000-plus figures, more than 10,000 years ago. You can find these engravings— many of them extraordinarily beautiful—incised on boulders and rock outcrops all over the peninsula. Go early in the morning, before the rocks get too hot. *www.burrup.org.au.*

# Easter Island
## *Mute Witnesses*
### Rapa Nui, Chile

CONSERVATIONISTS WARN THAT CONTINUED CLEAR-CUTTING OF FORESTS, WHICH DESTROYS NATIVE habitats and contributes to soil erosion, could ultimately turn the remaining fertile lands of Easter Island into barren rock. Without conservation management, the island will be unable to sustain its growing population and will be less attractive for tourists, who come to see the giant, enigmatic sculptures.

Though it may be the most remote inhabited place on earth—4,000km (2,485 miles) off the coast of Chile—Easter Island lives on tourism. And just about every visitor comes here to see the same thing: an enigmatic horde of some 600 immense stone figures hewn from dark volcanic tufa rock.

Some of Easter Island's 600 *moais*.

You can't deny the power of these sculptures. The faces are huge, with jutting brows and square jaws and startling white coral eyeballs. Every statue is strikingly individual, which suggests that they represented specific ancestors rather than gods. They were designed to be mounted grandly on ceremonial stone platforms, ringed around the edge of the island.

But these big statues are shrouded in mystery. Fossil evidence suggests that Rapa Nui (the native name, which means "Navel of the World") was once covered with palm trees, which the original islanders may have razed during a frenzy of statue building—an act that spelled environmental doom for this isolated population. (Trees are being replanted, but it's still a shadeless place.) Because that first population died out, no oral tradition has been passed down to explain why the statues, or *moais*, were built; many were found lying half-finished in an inland quarry, tumbled carelessly on their sides, or abandoned midroute to their pedestals. When the first Europeans visited the islands in 1722, the moais were upright; 50 years later, the next visitors found them knocked over, whether by desperate islanders or by hostile neighbors we'll never know.

Even more baffling, how were such massive sculptures built by such primitive people? Experts assume that the moais were hauled from the quarry to the coast on a wooden sledge atop log rollers—hence the need for cutting down trees.

Apparently the eyes weren't added until they were levered upright onto the platforms. Perhaps the islanders thought the eyes gave the moais spiritual power—when the statues were knocked from their platforms, most were toppled face forward, as if to hide the eyes in shame.

Some statues have been reerected; they stand in an inscrutable row, staring wordlessly over this volcanic blip in the middle of the Pacific. Cruise ships pull up, disgorging 800 to 900 passengers at a time; private island-hopping charter planes pop in, letting privileged travelers tramp around, snap a few shots of the moais, and then jet off somewhere else. In an already damaged environment, the level of tourism in summer (Nov–Mar) is reaching critical levels—and most of it is short-term visitors who

contribute little to the local economy. Dependent on tourist dollars, modern-day Easter Islanders are exploiting their last precious resource, as carelessly as their ancestors exploited those now-vanished forests. Will they be able to safeguard these mysterious sites before it's too late?

ⓘ **Easter Island** (Isla de Pascua), 5¹/₂ hr. from Santiago (www.netaxs.com/trance/rapanui.html)

✈ Mataveri (on Easter Island)

🛏 $$$ **Hotel Iorana,** Ana Magoro (📞 **32/100312;** www.hoteliorana.cl/english.htm). $$ **Hotel Hanga Roa,** Av. Pont (📞 **32/100299;** www.hotelhangaroa.cl).

(273) **Ancient Mysteries**

# The Nazca Lines
## *Designing the Desert*
### Nazca, Peru

THE NAZCA LINES, ONE OF THE MOST INTRIGUING AND MYSTIFYING ANCIENT SITES IN THE world, faces many threats—from a major highway that already cuts through the site, to flooding and mudslides due to global warming and deforestation. The Nazca Lines are so vast they can only be seen and appreciated from the air, which may be one reason so many people have treated them carelessly: out of sight, out of mind.

Sure, you can see the Nazca Lines from ground level, but why not see these ancient geoglyphs as they were meant to be seen—from the air? Sprawling over nearly 1,050 sq. km (400 sq. miles) of the San Jose desert in southern Peru, the Nazca Lines may be the most mysterious of ancient wonders: at least 10,000 rocky lines forming gargantuan designs—not only trapezoids, zigzags, and spirals, but also plant and animal shapes, carved out of the barren earth.

The Nazca Lines were built by pre-Inca peoples between 300 B.C. and A.D. 700, experts believe; they've lasted a long time. But in just a few decades, this awesome sight has been dealt a series of deadly blows. In 1934 the Pan-American Highway

was built right across the Nazca Valley, rudely bisecting one lizard figure; nowadays drivers cut cross-country to avoid paying tolls, their wheels jolting right across some of the lines. Farms and residences creep ever closer; new factories blow in pollution; global climate change and deforestation trigger severe flooding and mudslides. Tomb raiders dig for ancient artifacts, potholing the terrain, and recently squatters have set up illegal camps dangerously close to the lines.

Even tourism is a threat. The more people who walk here, the more damage is caused to this delicate terrain, a thin crust of rocky scree on top of spongy soil. That peculiar composition made these unique figures possible in the first place: Its ancient builders removed dark surface stones to expose the pale soil beneath, laying the darker stones along the edge to sharpen the contrast.

No one knows why the Nazca Lines were built, but there's no shortage of theories: that they were an astronomical calendar; that they marked underground sources of water; that they were pointers to direct divine spirits to bring rains; even that they were landing strips for alien spacecraft. The animal shapes do match age-old Andean fertility symbols, particularly those associated with water. But it's still mind-boggling to imagine these ancient people going to all the trouble of designing a pattern they'd never be able to view in its entirety—let alone doing it so accurately.

This is one site where flyovers really are the best way to go. Several operators in

Nazca offer sightseeing flights; you can even book a day trip from Lima through **Aero-Condor** (✆ **51/1/422-4214;** www.aero condor.com). From the window of an airplane, you can easily identify specific shapes—a parrot, a hummingbird, a spider, a condor, a dog, a whale, a monkey—and they're huge: the spider is 55m (180 ft.) long, the monkey 100m (328 ft.) wide. The eeriest of all is one humanlike figure with his hand raised in greeting—an ancient astronaut, perhaps?

✈ Lima

🛏 $$ **Hotel Nazca Lines,** Jr. Bolognesi s/n Nazca (✆ **51/56/522-293**). $ **Hotel Alegria,** Calle Lima 166, Nazca (✆ **51/56/ 522-702;** www.nazcaperu.com).

**Ancient Mysteries** 274

# Kuelap Fort
## *Fortress of the Cloud People*
### Chachapoyas, Peru

KUELAP'S ISOLATION HIGH IN THE ANDES HAS KEPT IT WELL PRESERVED THROUGH THE CENTURIES. However, the Peruvian government's plan to make it easier for tourists to explore Kuelap threatens this ancient city. Plans include a new airport, improved roads, and a cable car to sweep tourists up and down the mountain. The resulting vibration, pollution, foot traffic, and souvenir hunting could damage Kuelap.

If Kuelap had been easy to get to, it might have beaten out Machu Picchu as Peru's most famous archaeological site. After all, this ruined prehistoric fort is at least twice as old as Machu Picchu, and quite a bit bigger—with its massive limestone walls and hundreds of buildings, it's the largest ancient building in the Americas. Some archaeologists estimate that Kuelap, which took 200 years to build, contains three times more stone than the Great Pyramid at Giza.

But it always took grit and persistence to get here: a jolting 12-hour bus ride from Chiclayo, an overnight stay in the provincial town of Chachapoyas, and then another

bone-rattling 3-hour journey with a local guide up the mountain to the fortress. (That is, unless you were mad enough to hike or ride a horse up the final climb from the village of Nuevo Tingo.)

Perched high and lonely on this Andes peak, Kuelap was built by the Chachapoya, a warrior race who thrived in Amazonian cloud forests from the 9th to the 15th century A.D., when they finally were conquered by the Incas. Mummies found in the area suggest that the Chachapoyans were unusually tall, light skinned, and fair haired, another reason for their nickname, "cloud people." The Incas occupied the

Kuelap Fort.

fort themselves several years later, after the Chachapoyans had abandoned it, and then abandoned it themselves when the Spanish destroyed their empire.

Kuelap seems stark and forbidding at first, with its bristling golden walls and tricky narrow entrance passages. Having been so isolated, though, the fort is in a remarkable state of preservation, with hundreds of buildings used for everything from ritual sacrifice to lookout towers to communal kitchens; its decorative carvings are still sharply incised. Yet it doesn't feel all scrubbed up; the lush cloud forest vegetation creeps over the stones, and llamas graze placidly outside the walls. There are still so few visitors, you might be rambling about by yourself, communing with the spirits of these enigmatic pre-Incans.

Though it was discovered in 1843—60 years before Machu Picchu—Kuelap wasn't really opened to tourism until the 1970s. But there's been a lot of interest in this ancient mountain stronghold lately, especially since the 2007 discovery of 80 human skeletons. Kuelap's on the verge of being the next "hot" destination—who knows what that will do to spoil its sense of mystery?

---

ⓘ **Los Tambos Chachapoyanos** (www.kuelap.org)

✈ Chiclayo

🛏 $$ **Choctomal Lodge,** Choctomal Village (✆ **866/396-9582** in the U.S. or 51/41/478-838; www.marvelousspatuletail.com)

**TOUR Kuoda Tours** (✆ **51/84/263-010 in Peru;** www.inturkuoda.com). **Peruvian Secrets** (✆ **44/1248/430 621** in the U.K.; www.peruviansecrets.co.uk). **Chachapoyas Tours** (✆ **866/396-9582** in the U.S., or 407/583-6786; www.kuelapperu.com).

# El Fuerte de Samaipata
## *The Fort That Wasn't*
### Bolivia

NEGLECT AND POPULARITY EQUALLY THREATEN EL FUERTE DE SAMAIPATA. WHILE THE BOLIVIAN government has done little to preserve or protect the site, this unique sculptured rock is a popular destination for tourists and Bolivians alike. Erosion and foot traffic have gradually damaged many of the mysterious sandstone ruins. Now, with the government showing more interest, the site may finally be preserved, but will it ever be understood?

They may call it El Fuerte, but there's no way this was meant to be a fort. What military purpose could ever have been served by those fanciful animal shapes, the jaguars, snakes, and cats carved into this immense reddish sandstone? And that stone water tank looks utilitarian enough, until you examine the two long parallel stone troughs that run downhill to the town, with zigzag channels radiating away from it. No wonder some folks think this was a landing strip for alien spacecraft.

When the Spanish conquistadors first stumbled on these enigmatic ruins in the mountains of central Bolivia, they were baffled, too. But, being conquistadors, they called it a fort and used it as such. Later, they too abandoned it and let the weeds take it over. Only in modern times have archaeologists tried to solve the riddle of Samaipata. Why, for instance, were those stone seats on this hillside arranged in just that way—a circle of 12 seats facing inward, and another three inside the circle facing out? Was it a religious ceremony, a court of judgment, or what? And even stranger, once you follow the two parallel water troughs, you notice that their lines converge at a certain point in the sky—the point where Venus and Jupiter had a parallel rising at sunrise on August 20, 1066. Or was it the flyover of Halley's Comet in March 1066 that the lines commemorate?

A 2-hour drive from Santa Cruz, Bolivia's largest city, El Fuerte de Samaipata is a popular day's outing, and with the spectacular views from this high Andes hilltop, you can see why. But as a set of ruins, it's not developed much—the city downhill from the carvings is only half excavated, and remnants of several temples around the hill are badly overgrown. With its jumbled Inca, pre-Inca, and Spanish elements, the site is a little confusing—hire a guide from Santa Cruz if you really want to get some insight. Locals who come here seem less interested in interpreting the culture than in simply roaming around the carvings. As a result, the inner area has finally been cordoned off—so much foot traffic has damaged these ancient sandstone forms, already seriously eroded by the elements.

It remains to be seen how the authorities will develop this site. Nowhere else in the Americas did any culture develop a huge sculptured rock like this—you get the sense that there must be a great story behind it. But can that story be unlocked before the carvings and buildings crumble irretrievably?

---

ⓘ www.samaipata.info

✈ Santa Cruz

🛏 $$$ **Hotel Los Tajibos,** Av. San Martin 455 (✆ **591/3/3421-000;** www.los tajiboshotel.com).

**TOUR Rosario Tours** (✆ **591/3/369-656;** www.welcomeargentina.com/rosario/ outings.html). **Michael Blendinger** (✆ **591/ 33/9446-816,** mblendinger@cotas.com.bo).

# Teotihuacán
## *Ghost Town of the Gods*
### Mexico

TEOTIHUACÁN—AT ONE TIME THE LARGEST CITY IN THE WORLD—TODAY IS THREATENED BY TWO modern urban problems emanating from nearby Mexico City: smog and suburban sprawl. Air pollution corrodes the pyramids and damages the murals, frescoes, and other irreplaceable features at this historic site while rampant development—anchored by a Wal-Mart store that can be seen from the top of the Pyramid of the Sun—threatens to overrun the ancient city.

Once upon a time, some 200,000 people lived here, the absolute epicenter of ancient Mesoamerica society. In A.D. 500, it had more people than Rome and sprawled over 31 sq. km (12 sq. miles). Yet we know precious little about the people of Teotihuacán, least of all why they abandoned this great metropolis so abruptly around A.D. 750. Were they invaded by enemies? Was there an epidemic? Were there just too many people for the region's food and water supply to support?

While historians ponder these mysteries, Teotihuacán is under siege again today—from the polluted air of overpopulated Mexico City, from hordes of daytrippers, and from encroaching sprawl.

When the site was discovered early in the 20th century, the temple had disappeared and the pyramid— the third-largest pyramid in the world, after the Great Pyramid of Cholula (near Puebla) and Egypt's Great Pyramid (p. 275)—was an overgrown mass of rubble. As excavation and restoration proceeded, the beauties of this city were rediscovered. One amazing aspect of Teotihuacán is how it was laid out in accordance with celestial observations. Climb 248 steps to the top of the Pyramid of the Sun to see its precision: The front wall of the pyramid is exactly perpendicular to the point on the horizon where the sun sets at the equinoxes, and the rest of the grand buildings lie at right angles to it.

Walking up the main north-south street, the Calzada de los Muertos (Avenue of the Dead), look for a bit of wall sheltered by a modern corrugated roof: the fragment of a jaguar painting suggests what this street looked like when all its original paintings were intact. Proceed to the Pyramid of the Moon; upon its plaza sits the Palace of Quetzalpapalotl, where lavish figures of Quetzal-Mariposa (a mythical bird-butterfly) are painted on walls or carved in pillars; behind it, the Palace of the Jaguars has murals and frescoes of jaguars. At the south end of the Avenue of the Dead, in the immense sunken square named the Ciudadela (Citadel), there's the Feathered Serpent Pyramid and the Temple of Quetzalcoatl, with large serpents' heads jutting out from collars of feathers carved in the stone walls.

Whatever its original name was, the Aztecs named it Teotihuacán when they discovered these ruins, a name meaning "Place Where Gods Were Born." Doesn't a divine birthplace deserve a little more respect?

---

ⓘ **San Juan Teotihuacán,** Mexico

✈ Mexico City

🛏 $$$ **Hotel Four Seasons,** Reforma 500, Mexico City (✆ **800/332-3442** in the U.S., 800/268-6282 in Canada, or 55/5230-1818; www.fourseasons.com). $$ **Hotel Imperial,** Paseo de la Reforma 64, Mexico City (✆ **55/5705-4911;** www.hotelimperial.com.mx).

**265**

# Tiwanaku
## *Building Blocks in Bolivia*
### Bolivia

TIWANAKU, THE ANCIENT SITE OF A COMPLEX COMMUNITY AND THE FORMER CENTER OF A VAST empire, has repeatedly suffered damage in the centuries since its people vanished. Many of its archaeological sites are now in poor condition. Damage from hopeful looters continues to be a risk, and the site is also threatened by erosion.

We don't know how the ancient Tiwanaku people built this city, with its massive stone blocks, complex plumbing, ingenious farming methods, and haunting monoliths. For all their technological sophistication, the Tiwanaku had no written language—we can only piece together the riddle, from crumbling evidence.

What we do know is that this site has been plundered ever since the Incas discovered it in the 14th century, a hundred years after the Tiwanaku vanished. The Spanish conquistadors rummaged here for gold; 18th- and 19th-century builders quarried the site for stone; in the early 20th century the military used it for target practice. Then came that botched restoration in the 1960s, where major landmarks were moved and clumsy walls thrown up where they didn't belong.

But perhaps Tiwanaku's advanced state of decay is part of the story this site has to tell visitors—the story of a once-great culture that collapsed after the water levels dropped in nearby Lake Titicaca, which eventually receded many miles away. The Tiwanaku culture lasted 28 centuries, from 1600 B.C. to A.D. 1200, and for 5 of those centuries they dominated South America, ruling a vast region from southern Peru down to northern Argentina and Chile—and then the drought did them in.

This city was founded in approximately 200 B.C., but between A.D. 600 and 800 its population boomed to somewhere between a quarter-million and 1.5 million people. To sustain such a population in this high plateau was nearly impossible, if it hadn't been for their raised-field agriculture, an amazing terraced irrigation system that scientists are still studying with awe. But what really impresses visitors to this Tiwanaku capital is the bold scale of its architecture, based on massive ashlar blocks transported from quarries 40km (25 miles) or more away—even though the Tiwanaku had not developed the wheel.

Highlights of the site, which have been excavated and at least partially restored, include the Kalassaya, the main temple area, dominated by the stone-carved Sun Gate that could accurately gauge the position of the sun; the Semi-Underground Temple, decorated with stones representing different leaders from around the world; and the Akapana pyramid, believed to be an observatory and temple to worship the sky. Take time to appreciate the stylized geometric decorations carved so precisely onto the surviving stones. An on-site museum displays several ceramics, monoliths, and figurines unearthed here—when you think

Tiwanaku's Sun Gate.

how much was carried away, it's amazing this much was left.

Many plundered pieces ended up in La Paz, at the **Museo Nacional de Arqueologia,** Tiwanaku 93, La Paz (*©* **591/2/2311-621**). Who knows where the rest ended up?

ⓘ **Tiwanaku,** La Paz-Puno Rd.

✈ La Paz

🛏 $$ **Hotel Rosario del Lago,** Rigoberto Paredes and Av. Costanera, Copacabana, Bolivia (*©* **591/102/862-2141;** www.hotelrosario.com/lago)

**TOUR Diana Tours,** in La Paz (*©* **591/2/2350-252**). **Crillon Tours,** in La Paz (*©* **591/2/2337-533**).

---

**278** Ancient Mysteries

# San Agustín Archeological Park
## *Cult of the Dead, Land of Danger*
### San Agustín, Colombia

LOOTING CONTINUES TO THREATEN THE SAN AGUSTÍN ARCHEOLOGICAL PARK, WHICH CONTAINS hundreds of pre-Columbian stone statues. During the 1980s and 1990s, at least 17 carvings were stolen, including one that weighed more than 544kg (1,200 lb.) and was later found at a California gallery and returned to Colombia.

Mysterious, haunting, enigmatic, eerie— all these adjectives and more apply to the San Agustín Archeological Park. It's a vast city of the dead, with 14 separate sites scattered over nearly 650 sq. km (250 sq. miles). More than 500 massive stone statues stand here, perfectly preserved on groomed lawns, set off with awesome mountain views.

What a pity that nobody gets to see them.

Well, some hardy souls do travel here— mostly Colombians, anthropologists, and backpackers with a yen for on-the-edge travel. But given the political situation in Colombia—between a long, vicious civil war and the violent drug trade—it's one of the most dangerous countries in the world to visit. Kidnappings and bombings happen with alarming frequency. At the time of writing, the U.S., U.K., Canadian, and Australian governments still issue warnings against travel to Colombia, particularly rural areas. Coastal Cartagena gets a fair amount of tourism, but not San Agustín, which is deep in the tropical

Andes—a 10-hour bus ride from Bogota (backpackers do it overnight to save a night's hotel cost) or a 4-hour ride from the regional airport of Neiva.

Apparently created to serve as guardians of the dead, these statues range in size from tiny (20cm/8 in. high) to gargantuan (7m/23 ft.). Carved from dark, craggy volcanic rocks, they depict gods and mythical animals, grouped in ceremonial arrangements, often around burial chambers. The heads are large and the faces bold, expressive, and challenging. The pre-Inca culture that produced them may have ruled this region from as early as the 6th century B.C. to as late as A.D. 1200, but they seem to have vanished without a trace—even the local indigenous people have no legends to explain the death cult that apparently thrived here.

The main collection is at Parque Arqueologico, about 3km (2 miles) west of the town of San Agustín; two other outstanding sites are Chaquira, just northeast of the town, with its massive figure etched into the face of a cliff overlooking the

Magdalena River; and Alto los Idolos, 27km (17 miles) northeast of town, a complex necropolis with stark imposing monoliths on a high Andean hillside. Because so many different sites exist, walking around to all of them would require a few days; horseback excursions and jeep tours are better options (hotels in the area can help arrange these). English-speaking guides can be hired at the Parque Arqueologico.

Though violence is rarely directed specifically at tourists, it is possible to get caught in the crossfire, so to speak. Yet Colombia needs tourism revenues to develop alternatives to the drug trade. San Agustín could be key in drawing tourists—if the government could only make it safe to visit.

---

ⓘ www.sanagustin.com.co

✈ Neiva

🛏 **Finca El Maco,** Maco, San Agustín (✆ **57/8/837 34 37;** www.elmaco.ch)

**TOUR Nueva Lengua International** (✆ **202/470-2555** in the U.S., 57/1/753 24 51 in Colombia; www.travelsanagustin.com)

# Tutuveni Petroglyphs
## *The Writing's on the Wall*
### Northeast Arizona

TUTUVENI, A SACRED SITE OF UNPARALLELED CULTURAL IMPORTANCE TO THE HOPI PEOPLE AND A vital resource for archaeologists, has suffered much damage by vandals and souvenir hunters. Spray-painted graffiti has destroyed approximately 10% of the symbols that are carved into the stones at Tutuveni, which record more than 1,000 years of Hopi history and culture.

At first it looks like just a pile of rubble, this flat-topped mound of jumbled sandstone boulders on an arid stretch of Arizona's Navajo reservation. Get a little closer to the blocks at the base of the slope, however, and you'll see a bewildering variety of symbols carved onto the top and sides of those stones. Graffiti? Well, yes, unfortunately some of it is graffiti—but the rest are ancient hieroglyphics, the definitive record of ancient Hopi tribal history.

Tutuveni—the name is the Hopi word for "writings"—is more than just another petroglyph: This mass of boulders represents a virtual Rosetta stone for deciphering the Hopi language. Another 100 boulders scattered along a 500-foot (150m) stretch carry additional petroglyphic symbols, adding up to the largest concentration of such images in the American Southwest. It's like the Hopi version of the Great Library at Alexandria, a sacred pilgrimage site that preserves a record of their culture over 1,000 years. Yet, though it's been listed on the National Register of Historic Places since 1986, Tutuveni sits on an unprotected site by the side of U.S. Highway 89, easy prey for vandals and souvenir hunters.

More than 5,000 Hopi-clan symbols are incised into the stones of Tutuveni Petroglyph Site, recording the family trees of generations. Oral tradition in nearby villages dates the stones from A.D. 1200, a date supported by scientific analysis of the rock surfaces. In Hopi tradition, leaving such visible and concrete evidence of their past is an important tradition, signifying their stewardship of the ancestral landscape; specific places are as important as the history they commemorate, suffused with a life essence that can't be transplanted to another place. Even though this location is technically on a Navajo reservation, it's sacred to the Hopi people, a shrine on the Hopi Salt Trail, the traditional pilgrimage route to Ongtupqa (the Grand Canyon). As recently as the 1950s, Hopis were still making this pilgrimage to their venerated salt mine in the Grand Canyon, and stopping here to record their passage.

More than three-quarters of the vandalism has happened in the past 25 years. Historians have recently photographed as much of the stones as possible and made line drawings of some of its symbols, hoping to preserve as much as possible before they disappear—which they may in the next 10 years, if nothing is done. As far as the Hopi are concerned, though, a faithful copy is beside the point. It has to be these stones, and this place, or all the sacred power is lost.

---

ⓘ **Hopi Cultural Preservation Office** (✆ **928/734-3612**)

✈ Tuba City, AZ

🛏 $$$ **Quality Inn Navajo Nation,** Main St. and Moenave Ave., Tuba City (✆ **800/644-8383** or 928/283-4545; www. qualityinntubacity.com). $$ **Hopi Cultural Center Restaurant & Inn,** Second Mesa (✆ **928/734-2401;** www.hopiculturalcenter.com).

**280** Ancient Mysteries

# Mesa Verde National Park
## *Fire in the Canyon*
### Southwestern Colorado

WILDFIRES ARE THE MAJOR THREAT TO MESA VERDE NATIONAL PARK AND THE ANCIENT CLIFF dwellings left behind by the Anasazi people. Decades of fire suppression have allowed brush and scrub vegetation to build up, and increasing drought conditions have turned it into miles of kindling, which can burst into flame at the first lightning strike and quickly burn out of control.

Wildfires have been a fact of life in the American Southwest since time immemorial—and time immemorial is what Mesa Verde is all about. Over 1,500 years ago, the Ancestral Puebloans (also called the Anasazi) first began to settle in these canyons and mesas, giving up their nomadic hunter-gatherer lifestyle for permanent agricultural settlements. Safe in their cliff-faced dwellings, with a water supply seeping down through the sandstone, they could ride out the inevitable fires.

But in the 20th century, fire suppression was the name of the game. As a result, this Southwest landscape now carries an increased fire load of dense vegetation that turns tinder-dry in droughts—which, in this era of climate change, are becoming more and more frequent. In the summers of 2000 and 2002, the park was closed for several weeks, with more than half its land blackened by lightning-caused fires. It's the biggest challenge facing park management at Mesa Verde National Park, the largest archaeological preserve in the United States.

With over 4,000 sites, Mesa Verde is an astounding place to visit. A long drive with many overlook points leads through a stunning canyon to the mesas where the Ancestral Puebloans built their vertical cities. Stop at the **Far View Visitor Center** to book ranger-led tours of its three most awesome sites—**Cliff Palace, Balcony House,** and **Long House.** Cliff Palace is just what its name promises—a 151-room, four-story apartment house set under the rim of a cliff, with stepped-back roofs forming penthouse courtyards for the next level up. The 45-room Balcony House

# 10 Prehistoric Mounds to Visit

Barrows, tumuli, cairns, dolmens—whatever you call them, symmetrical earthen mounds (often heaped over a stone structure) were independently developed by ancient cultures around the world. Today their gentle rounded shapes bear mute, mysterious witness to the lives of another era. Perhaps because they were usually built as graves—a honor reserved for warriors or rulers and their families—a spooky, spiritual aura often surrounds them.

Here are a few that have been excavated and preserved:

**281 Newark Earthworks, Newark, Ohio**   These gentle grassy humps, 3 to 14 feet (1–4.3m) high, enclose a space big enough to hold four Roman Colosseums and are aligned for lunar observations twice as accurately as Stonehenge—it's only when seen from the air that their geometric precision becomes evident, a 40-acre (16-hectare) octagon enclosing a 20-acre (20-hectare) circle. The Hopewell Indians built the mounds around A.D. 250, but in 1933, the property's owners built a golf course over them. A truce between the club and anthropologists resulted in a viewing platform near the parking lot. © **800/600-7178** or 740/344-1919. www.ohiohistory.org/places/newarkearthworks.

**282 Serpent Mound, Locust Grove, Ohio**   Built by the prehistoric Fort Ancient tribe around A.D. 1000, this earthwork in rural southern Ohio isn't a simple circular mound but a sinuous 1,330-foot-long (405m) shape that, seen from the air, perfectly represents a serpent swallowing an egg. Scholars aren't sure whether it was built to tell a myth or to commemorate an astronomical event like an eclipse or a comet; its head is aligned with the summer solstice. © **937/587-2796.** http://ohsweb.ohiohistory.org/places/sw16/index.shtml.

**283 Cahokia Mounds, Cahokia, Illinois**   The biggest mound in the Western Hemisphere sits on this 2,200-acre (890-hectare) site across the Mississippi River from St. Louis, in what was once (A.D. 1100–1200) the biggest city north of Mexico. Its builders, the mysterious Mississippian people, erected 67 other immense earthen structures here, evidently for public ceremonies (there are remains of human sacrifice); the big one, Monk's Mound, was a royal residence. © **618/346-5160.** www.cahokiamounds.com.

Cahokia Mounds.

**284 Ocmulgee Old Fields, Macon, Georgia**   Until the 1930s, when archaeologists finally excavated these ceremonial Mississippean mounds, they were encroached upon by farmland. Although it was declared a national monument in 1936, the government only acquired 702 acres (284 hectares); many mounds are still on private property. © **478/752-8257.** www.nps.gov/ocmu.

**285 Effigy Mounds, Harper's Ferry, Iowa**   Built around A.D. 600 by a tribe of ancient nomads, these are not only mounds but mounds in the shape of tribal totems—bison, deer, turtles, lizards, and especially bears, eagles, and falcons. This 2,500-acre (1,011-hectare) park on the bluffs of the upper Mississippi River has over 200 of these mounds, some of which bear traces of fire pits, suggesting that their purpose was highly ceremonial. *© 563/873-3491. www.nps.gov/efmo.*

**286 Manitou Mounds, Stratton, Ontario**   The Ojibway name is Kay-Nah-Chi-Wah-Nung, "Place of the Long Rapids," and this site on the north bank of the Rainy River has been held sacred by the Ojibway for over 8,000 years. Near the Kay-Nah-Chi-Wah-Nung Historical Centre, the remains of villages, campsites, and as many as 25 burial mounds have been found. The mounds are a 3km (2-mile) hike from the visitor center, through prairie-oak savanna with some stirring panoramic views. *© 807/483-1163. www.fort franceschamber.com.*

**287 Newgrange, Slane, Ireland**   Older than Stonehenge, older even than the pyramids of Giza, this massive 5,000-year-old burial mound—actually a megalithic passage tomb, 11m (36 ft.) tall and 79m (260 ft.) in diameter—presides serenely atop a hill near the Boyne River, not far from the Hill of Tara. Its white quartz facade has been rebuilt, but using authentic stones found at the site. The elaborately carved walls of the internal passage are aligned with sunrise at the winter solstice. *© 041/ 988-0300. www.knowth.com/newgrange.htm.*

**288 Gamla Uppsala, Uppsala, Sweden**   Three large 6th-century burial mounds of Viking royalty surmount a ridge by a temple grove used for religious sacrifice (both animal and human) in what was once the capital of the Svea kingdom, and traditionally regarded as the residence of Odin, the chief Norse god. There are 250 other surviving grassed-over mounds in the area (there were once 2,000). *© 46/18/16-91-00.*

**289 Sammallahdenmäki, Kivikylä, Finland**   Dating from the Bronze Age (1500–500 B.C.), this remote hillside site in an unspoiled forest of gnarled pines in southeast Finland features 33 burial cairns (excavations have found cremated human bones), covered not with soil but with heaped granite rocks, now weathered and mossed over. *www.nba.fi/en/sammallahdenmakieng.*

**290 Bin Tepeler, Salihli, Turkey**   Along the Izmir-Ankara highway, near the ruins of ancient Sardis, you'll pass a dramatic necropolis with hundreds of tumulus graves heaped in the arid landscape, close to Lake Marmara. Named Bin Tepeler—or "thousand hills"—at least 90 of these mounds were the tombs of Lydian aristocracy and royalty; look for the 69m-high (226-ft.) mound of King Alyattes, father of the legendarily rich King Croesus.

Anybody home? Exploring Mesa Verde.

hangs above Soda Canyon, with stone stairs, log ladders, and narrow crawl spaces for the agile residents to scramble about from level to level. The Long House stretches across a long alcove in Rock Canyon, with 150 rooms and 21 kivas (subterranean chambers used for ceremonies and meetings) and a large public plaza for community gatherings.

You can't enter those protected ruins on your own, but there's plenty else to see. Behind the Chapin Mesa Museum, a paved .25-mile (.4km) trail leads to **Spruce Tree House**, a 130-room dwelling set inside an 89-foot-deep (27m) alcove; another 3-mile (5km) trail from Chapin Mesa runs along a canyon rim to an impressive panel of petroglyph rock art. A 6-mile (10km) drive along the Mesa Top Loop Road alone has 10 stops where you can either overlook dwellings or take a short walk to dwellings. A .5-mile (.8km) hike from Wetherill Mesa allows you to compare a 13th-century Step House with three 7th-century pit houses made by earlier Puebloans. It's as if you're watching these ancient people gradually perfect their idea of how to use the land for protection from the elements—wind, rain, and fire.

ⓘ **Mesa Verde National Park,** off U.S. 160, Cortez, CO (ⓒ **970/529-4465;** www.nps.gov/meve)

✈ Cortez

🛏 $$ **Holiday Inn Express,** 2121 E. Main, Cortez (ⓒ **800/626-5652** or 970/565-6000; www.coloradoholiday.com). $ **Anasazi Motor Inn,** 640 S. Broadway, Cortez (ⓒ **800/972-6232** or 970/565-3773; www.anasazimotorinn.com).

# Hovenweep National Monument
## *The Towers They Left Behind*
### Southern Utah & Colorado

EROSION AND FLASH FLOODS THREATEN THE UNIQUE SANDSTONE TOWERS AND OTHER STRUCTURES built by the ancient Anasazi people at Hovenweep. As the surrounding landscape has become more arid, fewer plants can anchor the soil and slow the wind that blows across the mesas and through the canyons.

At Mesa Verde and Canyon de Chelly you'll see Ancestral Puebloans dwellings—but in this isolated valley, straddling the Colorado-Utah border, it's anybody's guess why they built these 20-foot-high (6m) sandstone towers, pierced with tiny windows. Were they sentry towers? Grain silos? Ceremonial chambers? Town halls? Celestial observatories?

Many fewer visitors find their way here, and yet in some ways it's the most intriguing Ancestral Puebloan site of all. At the visitor center—located by the best preserved of the towers, Square Tower, in the Utah half of the monument—you can get directions on how to reach five other sections (Cajon, Cutthroat Castle, Goodman Point, Holly, and Hackberry/Horseshoe) spread over a 20-mile (32km) stretch of high desert plateau. They're remote and difficult to find, along poorly maintained dirt roads—but that solitude and isolation makes these mysterious ruins even more compelling.

By the late 1200s, as many as 2,500 people lived in this canyon-carved plateau. Instead of hollowing out cliff faces, the Hovenweep builders created multistory free-standing buildings—some square, some round—plastering together large fitted sandstone blocks with a mortar of clay, sand, and ash. These centuries-old shells are surprisingly solid, testament to the extraordinary engineering techniques the Ancestral Puebloans had developed by this late period of their civilization. Set ingeniously on top of great boulders, the towers were built apparently from the inside out, one floor at a time, using no outside scaffolding.

You'll notice that almost all of these settlements were placed at the heads of canyons, usually near springs of water. While some towers have features that suggest a defensive role, as if to guard their canyons, others incorporate features of the ceremonial kivas found at other Anasazi sites—perhaps those springs were considered sacred. Protecting water sources must have been crucially important in this arid terrain; you'll see examples of the small stone dams the resourceful Hovenweep people built on mesa tops to capture rainfall to irrigate their crops. In the end, it was a 23-year drought that finally drove these people from their exquisitely built towers, to resettle farther south, where their descendants are modern-day Pueblo and Hopi Indians.

Although the Ancestral Puebloans found this area rich farmland, it's only sparsely vegetated today—and without plants to anchor the soil, landslides and flash floods are an ever-present risk. What's more, there's much more seismic activity here—no matter how well those Anasazi built these towers, an earthquake could topple them tomorrow.

(i) **Hovenweep National Monument,** McElmo Route, Cortez, CO ((C) **970/562-4282** or 435/719-2100; www.nps.gov/hove)

✈ Cortez

🛏 $$ **Holiday Inn Express,** 2121 E. Main, Cortez ((C) **800/626-5652** or 970/565-6000; www.coloradoholiday.com). $ **Anasazi Motor Inn,** 640 S. Broadway, Cortez ((C) **800/972-6232** or 970/565-3773; www.anasazimotorinn.com).

# Canyon de Chelly
## *Hanging Out with the Anasazi*
### Northeastern Arizona

SCIENTISTS, ARCHAEOLOGISTS, AND SOME ENVIRONMENTALISTS FEAR THAT AGRICULTURAL AND business activities by the Navajo tribe are damaging fragile ecosystems and ancient dwellings and artifacts in Canyon de Chelly. The area is also threatened by invasive species that destroy native habitat, cause erosion, and increase the risk of fire.

Though Canyon de Chelly is a national monument, it's on Navajo reservation land—and that's where the problem begins. The National Park Service is anxious to preserve this major archaeological site, with its 5,000-year-old dwellings and rock art from the Ancestral Puebloans (also known as the Anasazi). But for the Navajos, these sandstone canyons are also a place to grow corn, graze their livestock, and lead visitors around on lucrative horseback and four-wheel-drive tours. What that's doing to the canyon's delicate ecosystem is a source of running debate.

Granted, it's not just the animals. Invasive species, especially tamarisk and Russian olive trees, have gained a foothold and are altering streambeds, causing erosion, and creating a fire hazard. But expensive eradication projects get hung up in negotiations between the land's Navajo owners and the parks system.

When this remote section of northeastern Arizona was made a Navajo reservation, archaeologists hadn't yet discovered the value of its Ancestral Puebloan remains. Ancestral Puebloan civilization reached its zenith between A.D. 1100 and 1300, but evidence suggests that these particular canyons were occupied as long ago as A.D. 300. In the nooks and crannies of the canyons you'll see more than 100 ancient dwellings hollowed into the rock walls, including several circular sacred rooms, or kivas. The most recent, and most impressive, ruins are the ghostly pale White House Ruins in Canyon de Chelly, but visit adjacent Canyon del Muerto as well to see its ancient tombs—

Canyon de Chelly.

the Tomb of the Weaver, near the Ante-lope House ruins, and the Mummy Caves.

Two scenic drives lead you through the park: the 15-mile (24km) North Rim drive, which overlooks Canyon del Muerto, and the 16-mile (25km) South Rim drive, which overlooks Canyon de Chelly (pronounced "duh Shay"). Hiking trails lead down to the Antelope House and White House ruins, but to really explore the canyon floor, you'll have to hire an authorized Navajo guide. Along the way, don't get so hung up on the relics that you forget to notice the scenery—at several spots the canyons open up to breathtaking rugged vistas of glowing red-and-yellow stone.

It's a sacred ground for the Navajos as well; you can see their ancient picto-graphs, designed in colorful paint on dark patches of where seeping water oxidized on the sandstone walls (known as "desert varnish"). In contrast, the Ancestral Puebloans's designs were petroglyphs, created by chipping away the desert var-nish to expose lighter-colored rock

beneath. Commemorating important tribal events, both kinds of rock pictures are windows into an ancient way of life. The Navajo have been guardians of this land for a long time—can we question the wis-dom of how they choose to care for it?

(i) **Canyon De Chelly National Monu-ment,** off Rte. 191, Chinle, AZ (© **928/674-5500;** www.nps.gov/cach)

✈ Flagstaff

🛏 $$ **Holiday Inn Canyon de Chelly,** Indian Rte. 7, Chinle (© **800/HOLIDAY** [465-4329] or 928/674-5000; www.ic hotelsgroup.com). $$ **Thunderbird Lodge,** Chinle (© **800/679-2473** or 928/674-5841; www.tbirdlodge.com).

**TOUR De Chelly Tours** (© **928/674-3772;** www.dechellytours.com). **Canyon de Chelly Tours** (© **928/674-5433;** www. canyondechellytours.com). **Justin's Horse Rental** (© **928/380-4617**). **Tot-sonii Ranch** (© **928/755-6209;** www. totsoniiranch.com).

**293** Crumbling Classics

# The Pyramids of Giza
## *Desert Scandal*
### Cairo, Egypt

UNRESTRICTED DEVELOPMENT AND URBAN SPRAWL FROM NEARBY CAIRO THREATEN THE ancient pyramids and the Great Sphinx. Air pollution eats away at the magnificent struc-tures, and sewage from adjacent slums weakens the plateau upon which they stand. Ongoing efforts to complete a multilane beltway around Cairo pose additional risks to these irreplaceable wonders.

Of all the original Seven Wonders of the Ancient World, only one is still standing: the Great Pyramid of Cheops. Granted, its pinnacle was lopped off, and the polished white limestone that once faced its slop-ing sides was scavenged ages ago. But there it is in the Egyptian desert, the larg-est in a trio of stupendous royal tombs, with a quirky monument called the Sphinx

alongside. It's quite a sight to see—if only you could see it.

Today, aggressive throngs of souvenir vendors, tour touts, and taxi drivers crowd the entrance to the pyramids. Though camel rides and horseback tours are now banned from the monument area, visitors still clamber unchecked over the ancient landmarks. The haphazard sprawl and

The Second Pyramid of Chephren.

Chephren, and the much smaller red-granite Third Pyramid of Mycerinus—and designed to imitate the rays of the sun shining down from its zenith, so that the buried king might ascend to heaven using his pyramid as a ramp. The great mystery is how they were erected at all, given the primitive technology available. Obviously it took a lot of manpower, or rather slave power: The construction of the Great Pyramid was like a gigantic 20-year public works project, giving the workers extra income during the annual flooding of the Nile.

The Great Sphinx wasn't part of the original plan, but was improvised to get rid of a limestone knoll that blocked King Chephren's view of his pyramid—a brilliant bit of serendipity, as it turned out. It's a gargantuan likeness of Chephren himself, dressed up as Harmachis, god of the rising sun. Fragments of orange-red paint still cling to the battered face, which was vandalized by medieval Muslims. Its soft limestone, however, has required continual restoration; in the late 1980s, the paws (and the left shoulder, which fell off in 1989) got a makeover, though there was no way to repair the broken-off royal "artificial beard."

Most tourists expect a visit to the famed pyramids to be a once-in-a-lifetime thrill, not a tawdry letdown. It's the only Ancient Wonder we have left—what a pity it's come to this.

pollution of Cairo comes right to the edge of the archaeological zone, yet Egyptian officials seem unconcerned about protecting the site.

It's difficult now to get that iconic long-distance view of the three pyramids looming in the desert; you can't really see them until you're so close, you're staggered by their size—an estimated 2,300,000 stones compose the Great Pyramid alone, weighing on average 2.5 tons apiece (some are even 9 tons). Oriented precisely to the points of the compass, they were built for three Pharaohs of the 4th Dynasty (about 27th c. B.C.)—the Great Pyramid of Cheops, the slightly smaller Second Pyramid of

---

ⓘ **Giza (Al-Jizah),** Arab Republic of Egypt

✈ Cairo International

🛏 $$$ **Semiramis InterContinental,** Corniche El-Nil, Cairo (ⓒ **888/424-6835** or 20/2/2795-7171; www.ichotelsgroup.com). $$ **The Nile Hilton,** 1113 Corniche El-Nil (ⓒ **800/HILTONS** [445-8667] or 20/2/2578-0444; www.hilton.com).

# The Valley of the Kings
## *Danger Under the Desert Sands*
### Luxor, Egypt

DECADES OF BAD URBAN WATER DISPOSAL AND FAULTY IRRIGATION SYSTEMS ARE THE MOST serious threats to the ancient underground tombs in the Valley of the Kings. In addition, an underground reservoir has begun to overflow, undermining the ground beneath the tombs and eroding their stone foundations.

After all, this is Egypt—a desert country where 90% of the population crowds onto 5% of the land, along the banks of the Nile. The problem has always been a lack of water. So who'd have expected that this world-famous necropolis may be destroyed by too much water?

But that's what's happening beneath the famed Valley of the Kings, where a critically backed-up natural underground reservoir is beginning to erode the stone foundations. It's a particular problem because the pharaohs of Thebes (now Luxor)—unlike their Lower Nile predecessors at Memphis (now Giza)—built their royal tombs underground, a cunning strategy to foil the sort of tomb robbers who'd pillaged the pyramids. The pharaohs deliberately chose high, dry ground for their tombs—but apparently it wasn't high or dry enough. Since the construction of the Luxor Bridge, 7km (4¹/₃ miles) north of the Valley of Kings, was completed in 1997, the clay substratum of the ground beneath the monuments had already been compromised; the pooling water was an accident waiting to happen.

Over 60 personages (mostly royalty) in the 18th, 19th, and 20th dynasties built their mazelike subterreanean crypts here, brilliantly decorated and stuffed with treasure. In the end, of course, they were no more thief-proof than the pyramids—only Tutankhamun's treasure survived intact up to modern times—but the stunning artistry on their walls makes a visit here well worth the long trip up the Nile from

Cairo. A number of tombs are open to the public on a rotating basis, though the rules for touring them are strict: photography is forbidden (most paintings are widely reproduced anyway), visitors must be quiet and file in one by one, and nothing must be touched. With thousands of tourists visiting the valley each day, that's still a lot of extra humidity and dirt for the ancient walls to be exposed to. If you're lucky, on the day you visit you may be able to see the burial chamber of the tomb of Ramesses VI (12th C. B.C.), where magnificent ceiling paintings depict the stars and other heavenly bodies; or the dazzling quartzite sarcophagus in the tomb of King Tutankhamun (though most of Tut's treasures were moved long ago to the Egyptian Museum in Cairo).

North of Luxor, the picturesquely jumbled ruin of the Temple of Karnak faces the same underground threat, and its elaborately incised round columns could collapse any day now. Engineers at both sites are hard at work, digging trenches and repairing irrigation systems, trying to solve the problem before it's too late. Will they succeed?

---

ⓘ Nile St., Luxor (*℡ 20/95/382 215*)

✈ Luxor International

🛏 $$$ **Le Meridien Luxor,** Khaled Ben El Walid St. (*℡ 20/95/2366-999*). $$ **Luxor Hilton,** next to the Temple of Karnak (*℡ 800/HILTONS* [445-8667] or 20/95/237-4933; www.hilton.com).

# Petra

## *Red Rock Wonder*

### Southern Jordan

ALTHOUGH AIR POLLUTION, EARTHQUAKES, AND EROSION FROM WIND AND RAIN PUT THIS ancient city carved out of rock at risk, Petra's most serious threat may be from uncontrolled tourism. Some 80% of the original carvings and decorated facades are believed to be lost, and more damage is done each year as a growing number of tourists scramble over the site looking for souvenirs.

You twist and turn through the Siq, a narrow mile-long sandstone gorge through the Jordanian desert. You come to the last bend—and there before you, just visible in the gap, is a dramatic columned temple cut right out of a cliff face. The fierce desert sun flashes on its columns and pediments and mythological figures; you catch your breath in wonder.

Half a million tourists squeezed through that narrow entrance in 2007, a new record for Petra, Jordan's premier ancient landmark. With no areas railed off, they were free to scale its sheer walls, scrawl on the rocks, break off bits of stone for souvenirs. Already threatened by seismic activity, air pollution, and erosion from the winter rains, how much longer can Petra safely host such crowds?

Petra sprang up between 400 B.C. and A.D. 100, a natural stopping-point on important trade routes. Camel caravans paid heavy duties to Petra's tax collectors, whose wealth gave rise to a grand cityscape chiseled out of the rose-colored living rock. Deep in this natural stronghold, this Arab tribe was conquered by no one, though many tried; not until Red Sea shipping bypassed caravan routes did a diminished Petra finally fall under control of Rome. Its ancient buildings have been eroded by desert sand and wind, but because they were gouged out of the cliffs rather than free-standing rocks, they haven't toppled like many buildings of

similar eras. Their original plaster and paint has worn off, but the city still glows with the natural color of the rose-red rock.

Emerging from the Siq, the first wonder you see is the Khazneh, a site featured in *Indiana Jones and the Last Crusade*. Legend had it that a wicked pharoah buried a sumptuous treasure here, and in later centuries Bedouins aimed random bullets at the urnlike round tholos centered in the Khazneh's broken pediment, hoping it would burst open and spill forth the

The desert fortress of Petra.

pharoah's riches. Beyond lie the spectacular royal tombs, which became more than just burial places—they were 1st-century architectural fantasies, picking up an eclectic mix of elements from cities like Alexandria and Rome, their ornate facades completely out of proportion to the small chambers within.

The citizens of Petra were quite the cultural chameleons: temples built to Nabataean deities were later adapted to Roman gods, and possibly to Christian saints in the Byzantine era. On a summit behind the yellow-sandstone Temple of Dushara, you'll even see the remains of a fort built by 12th-century crusaders. Another climb to the clifftop will take you to the High Place of Sacrifice, a circular ceremonial arena set up explicitly for gruesome acts of blood sacrifice—and also killer views of the surrounding desert.

---

ⓘ www.petranationalfoundation.org

✈ Amman or Aqaba

🛏 $$$ **Mariott Petra,** Queen Raina Al Abdullah St., Wadi Mousa (ⓒ **962/3/215-6407;** www.marriott.com). $$$ **Golden Tulip,** King's Way, Wadi Mousa (ⓒ **962/3/215-6799;** www.goldentulip.com).

---

**296** Crumbling Classics

# Abu Mena
## *Guided by Camels*
### Alexandria, Egypt

DESTRUCTION FROM BELOW THREATENS THE RUINS OF THE FABLED CITY OF ABU MENA, considered one of the five most important historic sites in Egypt. Irrigation for crops in nearby fields, part of a land reclamation project started some years ago, has caused the water table to rise. As a result, the water has eroded the soft, clay soil beneath the ancient city and several buildings have collapsed.

If you want to see what Luxor's fate could be, behold what has already happened at Abu Mena. Once the greatest Christian holy city of the east, a bustling pilgrimage site that sparkled with marble and glittered with mosaics, its carefully excavated foundations are now caving in.

Long ago, Abu Mena was a forlorn spot in the Libyan desert, where Menas—a Libyan-born Roman legionary who converted to Christianity and died a martyr's death in Phrygia—was buried when the camel bearing his corpse home stopped in the desert and refused to budge. Ninety springs of water were said to flow miraculously from the grave, creating an oasis of vineyard and olive groves. A few years later, a shepherd who found Menas's grave gained mystical healing powers. After he cured Roman emperor Constantine's daughter, Constantine ordered a church to Menas built on the site.

By the late 4th century the little desert church was so overwhelmed with pilgrims, seeking healing miracles from St. Menas, a large basilica was built in its stead, soon joined by an even grander basilica with 56 marble columns and rounded niches of polychrome marble—distinctively Coptic touches found nowhere else in early Christian architecture. By A.D. 600, Abu Mena had become a substantial city of churches, monasteries, houses, and artisans' workshops, an ancient version of Lourdes with its own thriving culture. Wandering the mazelike streets of the ruined city, you can clearly distinguish the great basilica and the bath complex where pilgrims took the curative waters. Pottery flasks containing the holy water were much-sought-after relics, decorated with an image of St. Menas with two camels.

Conquering Muslims razed the city repeatedly from the mid–7th century onward, until eventually it disappeared beneath the shifting sands. It was rediscovered by German archaeologists in 1905; more recent excavations in the 1990s uncovered such fascinating features as a dormitory for poor pilgrims, an abbot's palace, a cemetery, and a complex of wine presses and cellars.

The main buildings of Abu Mena—the basilica, baths, baptistery, and church—are still intact, but in the northwest precincts of the city you can already see caved-in areas. The crypt under the church—the holy tomb that gave rise to this entire city—has been closed to the public and filled with sand to stave off collapse. Meanwhile, antiquities officials battle to have old-fashioned irrigation stopped immediately, and replaced with modern methods that don't flood the soil. With no buffer zone established, Abu Mena has crops growing right up to its borders, part of a World Bank–funded land-reclamation project that was the agriculture officials' pride and joy a decade ago. Nowadays, it's more like Egypt's shame.

(i) www.stmina-monastery.org/abu_mena.htm

✈ Alexandria

🛏 $ **Union Hotel,** 164 26th July Rd., Alexandria (✆ **20/3/480-7537**). $$$ **El Salamlek Palace,** Montazah Gardens, Alexandria (✆ **20/3/547-7999**).

**Crumbling Classics**  297

# Masada
## *After the Flood*
### Israel

THE AREA AROUND MASADA IS USUALLY SO ARID THAT FOR CENTURIES EROSION WAS NOT A serious problem. However, when torrential rains pelted the ancient fortress 2 years in a row, water seeped into the walls of Masada, weakening them so much that Israeli officials believe the historic site will collapse unless it is thoroughly reinforced.

It wasn't 40 days and 40 nights, but it was enough of a deluge—massive cloudbursts right over this normally arid hilltop on the Dead Sea. It happened in 2003, and again in 2004, weakening the mortar between the huge stone blocks of King Herod's fortress. Masada was the greatest of Hebrew strongholds—is it on the brink of falling at last?

King Herod first built this stout fortress atop its inaccessible desert plateau around 30 B.C.; after Herod's death, with Israel under Roman control, a small Roman garrison occupied the mount. But during the Jewish revolt in A.D. 66, Masada was seized by a tenacious (and well-armed) band of Jewish zealots, who lived off of vast stores of food left by Herod. Finally, in A.D. 73, 3 years after Jerusalem had fallen, the Romans got fed up with this last pocket of resistance. They built a ramp to scale the rock—in itself a remarkable piece of engineering—and attacked Masada with 10,000 troops, pulling out all the stops: siege engines, flaming torches, rock bombardments, battering rams. It seemed only a question of time until the 900 defenders surrendered. After one brutal night attack,

Masada.

the Romans, seeing Masada now defenseless, decided to storm the fort at dawn. Expecting to fight their way in, the Romans were astonished in the morning by the Jews' lack of resistance—then awed when they discovered why: The 900 Jewish men, women, and children inside had committed mass suicide rather than succumb.

Excavations over the years have unearthed the most exciting relics in all of Israel: the original palace, synagogue, casement walls, houses, straw bags, plaits of hair, pottery shards, stone vessels, cosmetics, cooking utensils, and scroll fragments marked with Hebrew names—perhaps the very lots cast by the defenders as they decided who would kill the others rather than let them fall into Roman hands.

Yet as you explore the site, you'll see signs everywhere of the water damage. A corner of the Roman siege encampment at the base has collapsed; parts of the ritual baths (mikvehs) used by the Jewish defenders have crumbled to pieces. Some flaking ancient frescoes have already been removed for preservation, and the

gorgeous floor mosaics may be next. (A museum is soon to open at the foot of the fortress to house such items.) But what worries Masada's staff most is the structural damage; several hundred meters of the supporting wall could go at any moment.

Masada has for generations been practically synonymous with Israeli pride; half a million visitors a year come here. Closing Masada down completely for major structural repairs would be controversial indeed. But what if there's no other choice?

---

ⓘ **Masada National Park,** Dead Sea Highway (✆ **972/7/658-4207**)

✈ Jerusalem

🛏 $$$ **Golden Tulip Dead Sea Hotel,** Ein Bokek (✆ **972/8/6684646;** www.tulip inndeadsea.com). $$ **Kibbutz Ein Gedi Resort Hotel,** Ein Gedi (✆ **800/844-4007** or 972/8/659-4222; www.ngedi.com/guest_house.htm).

# Old Acre
## *Leading the Crusade*
### Akko, Israel

RELIGIOUS AND POLITICAL STRIFE IN THE MIDDLE EAST IS AN ONGOING CRISIS, AND HISTORIC sites like Old Acre can easily be caught in the crossfire. The ancient walled city is also still occupied, and without proper maintenance and renovation, it will eventually crumble—if it isn't blown up before then.

Holy wars? They used to be good news for Acre. In its time, Acre has been ruled by the Phoenicians, by King David, by Alexander the Great, by the Ptolemaic kings of Egypt, but the crusades was what really made them famous. Throughout the crusades, armies of Christian knights from Europe, heading east to "free" the Holy Land from Muslim rule, made this ancient seaport their home away from home.

Today, however, Acre lies in a section of Israel embroiled in new holy wars. Given that most of the inhabitants of the old walled city are Palestinian Israeli, there's something telling about how those historic areas have been left to crumble and collapse by Israel's government.

This is a city with many layers of history—literally. Rising above industrial modern Acre, the walled Old City has an Arab profile, with romantic minarets and palm trees against the sky. During the Ottoman Empire, the Turks held sway, and Acre's green domed Al-Jazzar Mosque,

The Hospitallers' Fortress at Acre.

with the Turkish Bazaar tucked in behind it, and the nearby Hamman al-Pasha (Turkish Bath) testify to the glory of those years. But the base of old Acre's walls date from 1104, when the knights of the First Crusade renamed Acre "Saint Jean d'Acre" and built a great sandstone fortress here. Since the 1950s the knights' city has been gradually excavated from underneath the 38m-high (125-ft.) walls of Acre Citadel, the Turks' prison. (Today the citadel houses the **Museum of Heroism,** ℂ **972/4/991-8264,** honoring Jewish underground fighters imprisoned by the British who staged a mass escape in May 1947, as seen in the movie *Exodus*.) A replica of the crusaders' Enchanted Garden blooms beside the visitor center for the Knights Halls, headquarters of the powerful crusader order the Knights Hospitallers. In the first hall off its central courtyard is a graphic example of the layered architecture—the bottom shows the crusaders' arches, the top the Ottomans'. You can just picture these vaulted Gothic ceremonial halls hung with crusaders' banners and coats of arms. Nearby you can also peek into barracks and storerooms—a medieval toilet was even uncovered. The Templars' Tunnel, in the southeastern part of the Old City, on Haganah Street, is another crusader relic, a 320m-long (1,050-ft.) tunnel carved out of rock as a secret passage from the fortress to the port.

Set above the sparkling turquoise sea, all these layers of history have their stories to tell. Unfortunately, today's sectarian strife makes it increasingly hard to hear them. Having been named a World Heritage Site by the United Nations in 2001, Acre is required to keep historic sites in good repair—but what good is that when their neighborhoods are falling apart?

ⓘ 1 Weitzman St., Old City (ℂ **700/70-80-20;** www.akko.org.il)

✈ Haifa

🛏 $$$ **Le Meridien Haifa,** 10 David Elazar St. (ℂ **972/4/850-8888;** www.fattalhotels-israel.com). $$$ **Palm Beach Hotel and Country Club,** Acre Beach (ℂ **972/4/987-7777**).

**299** **Crumbling Classics**

# Ancient Byblos
## *Oil on the Water*
### Jbeil, Lebanon

IN JULY 2006, AN ISRAELI BOMBING ATTACK ON LEBANON RIPPED OPEN OIL TANKS, UNLEASHING 15,000 gallons of oil along Lebanon's Mediterranean coast. Horrendous masses of sludge filled the once-scenic harbor at the ancient city of Byblos, now renamed Jbeil, a port that's welcomed seafarers for 700 centuries.

Most historians regard Byblos as the oldest continuously inhabited city in the world; some consider it the first real city ever built. There are so many ruins here, you'll find ancient columns carelessly toppled by the roadside. It has gone by many names: the Phoenicians called it Gebal, the Greeks Byblos, the crusaders Gibelet. Legend says it was founded by the god Chronos himself, and that Thoth invented the linear alphabet here.

Set high on a cliff just above Jbeil's harbor, the archaeological zone is a fascinating juxtaposition of ruins from many eras. You enter through a castle the crusaders built in the 12th century, when it was an important military base for them. Within the zone, several huts and building foundations date back to Neolithic times, around 5000 B.C., when it first began to take on the shape of a town. Byblos's most impressive ruins date from its Phoenician era: the Great Temple of Resheph, the Temple of Baalat Gebal, and the Temple of the Obelisks. Jumping forward in time, there's also a fine historic house from the days when the Ottoman Turks ruled. Near the cliff edge, a beautiful Roman theater offers panoramic sea views that remind you why this city was such a prize to myriad rulers—it was the greatest seaport in the eastern Mediterranean, back when the eastern Mediterranean was the center of the civilized world.

Notice the conglomeration of different architectural styles: as Byblos was absorbed into one empire after another, successive occupiers—Assyrians, Persians, Greeks, Romans, Muslims, Turks—kept rebuilding these temples instead of razing them. The Temple of Resheph, for instance, was rebuilt during the Greco-Roman period as a temple of Adonis, the city's patron god in that era; you can also see remains of a Roman colonnade just outside the Temple of Balaat Gebal. Near the archaeological zone, on Rue du Port, check out the Church of St. John the Baptist, the crusaders' 12th-century cathedral, which looks as Arab as it does Romanesque, with Byzantine mosaics scattered all around.

With Lebanon in the grips of an Israeli blockade, an international team of rescuers had to be flown in to hand-clean the oil from the foundation stones of the port's two medieval towers. The oil spill may have been cleaned up, but the warfare that caused it rages on. Very few tourists these days get to Byblos, and the town's economy is drying up. It's the oldest city in the world—who will care for it now?

✈ Beirut

🛏 $$ **Byblos Sur Mer,** Rue du Port (© **961/9/548 000;** www.byblossurmer. com). $$$ **Riviera Hotel,** the Corniche, Manara, Beirut (© **961/1/373 210;** www. rivierahotel.com.lb).

**Crumbling Classics**  **300**

# Arg-É-Bam
## *Rising from the Rubble*
### Bam, Iran

ARG-É-BAM, A HISTORIC CITY BUILT ENTIRELY OF MUD, WAS LEVELED IN A SINGLE MORNING IN 2003 when a powerful earthquake reduced it to rubble. UNESCO and Iranian experts are working together to rebuild and restore the site, but with a potential lack of political and financial support needed to sustain the restoration project, it could take decades to complete, and the threat of another earthquake could undo the work once it is done.

If it wasn't a ruin before, it is now.

The ancient Parthian citadel of Arg-é-Bam was one of the world's best-preserved historic sites, a remarkably intact mud-brick walled city of some 400 houses surrounding a hilltop fort in the Dasht-é-Lūt desert. Sometimes called the Emerald of the Desert—a major stopping point on the Silk Road to China—most of its buildings dated from around A.D. 200 to 250. After an Afghan invasion in 1722, the city went into a long decline, existing only as a military barracks until the 1970s, when archaeologists restored it as a historic attraction: the world's largest adobe structure, an open-air museum of 2,000 years of Middle East history.

Only a 10-minute walk from the booming modern city of Bam, a total cityscape still stood—houses, bazaars, gymnasiums, stables, schools, observatories, bathhouses, a Jewish quarter, even a couple of mosques which still held services. Though the tawny adobe looked slightly crumbled and worn, this many-towered city was a place where you could stroll around narrow cobbled streets and mysterious arched alleyways and easily imagine the daily life of the ancients. Despite Iran's troubled political relations, Arg-é-Bam attracted a growing number of international tourists.

Then disaster struck. On the morning of December 26, 2003, an earthquake of 6.6 intensity shook both the citadel and adjacent modern Bam. In a city of 90,000, more than 25,000 were killed and another 30,000 injured; 70% of the modern city was destroyed, and the ancient citadel was levelled.

The adobe architecture that had served both Bam and Arg-é-Bam so well for centuries was actually part of the problem; instead of toppling in chunks, as concrete or marble buildings might have, the adobe—a mix of clay, palm trunks, straw, and stones—simply collapsed in heaps. The high death toll in the modern city was caused by the fact that people were smothered in mounds of fine rubble, rather than being trapped under slabs of solid rock that might have left air pockets for them to breathe.

International rescue organizations leaped into action, bringing emergency food rations and medical supplies. Modern Bam has been rebuilt, though it's much smaller these days, having lost nearly a third of its population. But the citadel? The slow process of restoring Arg-é-Bam's rubble, which may take as long as 40 years to complete, has begun. The quake exposed some underground finds which must be excavated first; then selected major buildings will be rebuilt, using as much of the original earthen materials as possible. It's still open for visitors, though, and in time, the restored site may be fascinating indeed—but it will never again be the intact original.

✈ Bam

🛏 $$ **Azadi Hotel,** Janbazan Blvd. Dasht Bagh, Bam (*©* **98/344/90091-7**)

**301** **Crumbling Classics**

# The Roman Ruins of Baalbek
## *Spoils of War*
### Bekaa Valley, Lebanon

THE ANCIENT TEMPLES OF BAALBEK ARE ALREADY FRAGMENTS OF WHAT THEY ONCE WERE, BUT continuing strife in the Middle East threatens to reduce the ruins to rubble. A sacred place of worship since before recorded history, Baalbek has more recently become a target in the recurring conflicts between Israel and Lebanon.

Even in Rome, they never had temples like these—the immense Jupiter temple at Heliopolis was the largest ever built in the Roman Empire, and the adjacent Temple of Bacchus is the most completely preserved Roman temple anywhere. Baalbek also features a lovely round Temple to Venus, and a staircase of a Mercury temple, all set on a platform of enigmatic prehistoric rocks. This is what was left after the "pagan" temples were ransacked by later Christians and waves of Islamic invaders—we can only imagine how magnificent it was in its heyday.

The ruins of Baalbek.

Baalbek is Lebanon's number-one tourist destination—but unfortunately, this largely Shiite city is a major Hezbollah stronghold, and in the tinderbox of Mideast politics, anything could happen. When Israeli soldiers attacked in the summer of 2006, their bullets and bombs shook the ruins badly. One block of stone fell, cracks on the Jupiter and Bacchus temples opened, and the city's *souk* (bazaar) was directly damaged.

For some 5,000 years, this has been a sacred site: The Phoenicians worshipped Baal here, well before the Romans showed up in 15 B.C., and it may have been a Bronze Age sanctuary before then, judging by how weathered that stone base is. The Romans called it Heliopolis and made it a major pilgrimage site, though the version of Jupiter worshipped here was suspiciously similar to Baal, just as Bacchus resembled their old Dionysus and Venus their old Astarte. (Customizing Roman culture to local traditions was a key strategy in holding together that far-flung empire.)

In the Great Court outside the Jupiter temple, only six rose-granite columns remain (there once were 128), but the Bacchus temple has 42 columns left, as well as several exquisite sculptured reliefs. One reason why they've stood so long—despite all the earthquakes that have hit this town—is the solid foundation they rest upon, a base of 400-ton monoliths; in the western retaining wall alone, three stones weigh over 1,000 tons. But that's nothing compared to the immense Stone of the Pregnant Woman (Hajar el Hibla), 21m (69 ft.) long, 4.8m (16 ft.) high, and nearly 4.2m (14 ft.) deep, still lying in the nearby quarry; it's the largest piece of stonework ever crafted.

Scientists can't explain how those ancient people cut stones this big, let alone moved them uphill to the temple site or inserted them so snugly in place. Roman accounts of the building of Heliopolis are strangely silent about the titanic stones, suggesting they were already here long before those upstart Romans arrived. After all that, to be shattered by our modern political stalemates would be a shame indeed.

ⓘ **Baalbek ruins,** Rue Abdel Halim Hajjar (✆ **961/8/370 645**)

✈ Beirut

🛏 $$ **Palmyra Hotel,** Rue Abdel Halim Hajjar (✆ **961/8/376 011**)

# Nineveh
## *Black Market History*
Mosul, Iraq

LOOTING AND DEVELOPMENT HAVE DONE GREAT DAMAGE TO THE ANCIENT CITY OF NINEVEH, once the capital of the Assyrian empire. Today, the biggest threat to the city, its remaining artifacts, and other antiquities is the war between the United States and Iraqi insurgents. Until the war ends and Iraq is politically stable, nothing can be done to protect or preserve any of its ancient treasures.

The looting began in 1991 and it hasn't stopped. With the Iraqi government enmeshed in war, desperate citizens are stripping the country's ancient ruins for quick cash. Who knows if Iraq's heritage will ever be fully reassembled?

A prime example is the fabled ancient Assyrian capital of Nineveh. Razed by Babylonians in 612, it lay buried under rubble until the mid–19th century, when archaeologists swooped in to carry off artifacts to the great museums of Europe. (Call them the first wave of looters.) But in the 20th century, the Iraqi people had developed great pride in protecting their antiquities. With the Gulf Wars, all that has gone by the wayside.

On the east bank of the Tigris, two mounds represent what was once Nineveh, both of them overlaid with suburbs of the modern city of Mosul. One mound, Nabī Yūnus—thought to be the burial place of the biblical prophet Jonah—can't be excavated because it's a sacred site with a mosque, but the other, Kouyunjik, has been extensively explored. First, French archaeologists found the royal palace of Sargon II; then a British explorer named Austin Henry Layard unearthed the 80-room palace of Sennacherib, who ruled around 700 B.C. and made Nineveh a world-class capital of over 100,000 people. Nineveh's heyday lasted only a century—705 to 612 B.C.—but in that short time it became a gorgeous city

of boulevards, open squares, and gardens, with an elaborate system of canals and aqueducts and 15 lavish sculptured gates punctuating its heavy mud-brick walls. (Three of those gates have been at least partially reconstructed around town.)

The remains of Sennacherib's palace—known in its day as the "palace without a rival"—is one of only two Assyrian palaces remaining (the other is at nearby Nimrud, 40km/26 miles south). Over the years, the Sennacherib palace's entry court and throne-room chambers were restored and roofed over into a museum, to display its stunning series of sculptured relief panels and cuneiform inscriptions, depicting the king's victories and other historical events. Starting in 1991, however, recognizable fragments of these tablets have been spotted in world art auctions—generally prime center sections, not just broken-off corner pieces. Experts assume that most of the palace's artwork has been looted by now. Illegal as these relics would be, it's unlikely that Iraq authorities will ever manage to reclaim them—and even so, if the rest of the panel has been reduced to rubble, these vivid storytelling friezes will have lost all continuity.

Across the river, Mosul is a major oil-processing center, and a diverse city full of Sunnis, Kurds, Arabs, and Assyrian Christians—which means it's a hotbed of insurgency. Until the war has ended, it would be foolish to come here just to see antiquities. After the war, maybe . . . if there's anything left.

✈ Mardin, Turkey or Baghdad, Iraq

🛏 It is not advisable to travel to Iraq at this time.

# Babylon
## *One Sacrilege After Another*
### Al Hillah, Iraq

BABYLON, A CITY OF BOTH HISTORY AND LEGEND, HAS BEEN SERIOUSLY DAMAGED BY WAR AND development, and those remain the two major threats to the ancient city. The U.S. war in Iraq continues to endanger Babylon and other ancient sites in Iraq, and Iraqi officials' own plans for post-war Babylon could be just as destructive.

Desperate Iraqi citizens aren't the only ones destroying their country's patrimony. In 2003, American troops committed even greater sacrilege: building a helipad atop a mound of mud-brick debris in the ruins of ancient Babylon. Heavy vehicles rumbled over centuries-old pavements, trenches were dug into artifact-filled soil, and carved figures in the Ishtar Gate were destroyed by soldiers prying out bricks for souvenirs.

The most fabled of ancient cities, Babylon has occupied this prime Mesopotamian site on the Euphrates river since the 3rd millennium B.C. In the 18th century B.C. it was the capital of Hammurabi's empire, where the world's first code of law was written. Under Nebuchadnezzar II (605–562 B.C.), the city was transformed into a brilliant capital, with such landmarks as the Etemenanki ziggurat, the Ishtar Gate, and the Hanging Gardens, named one of the Seven Wonders of the Ancient World (though some historians believe those were actually in Nineveh). Even under Persian rule, Babylon was an administrative capital and center of learning, especially astronomy and mathematics. Twice it was the largest city in the world—from 1770 to 1670 B.C. and from 612 to 320 B.C., with a population that may have topped 200,000.

In the ancient world, that would have been huge.

Babylon had lain abandoned for centuries, its sunbaked bricks carted away until only foundations remained. Then in 1985, Saddam Hussein started rebuilding on top of the old ruins, ordering a combination of restoration and new construction to duplicate the city of Nebuchadnezzar—a copy, granted, but with that special Hussein flair. He erected an immense picture of himself and Nebuchadnezzar at the entrance to the ruins, and had his own name inscribed on building bricks, just as that ancient ruler had done, horrifying many archaeologists. The Ishtar Gate was recreated, and the ceremonial stone boulevard leading from it, Processional Way, was restored. Hussein built a ziggurat-style palace for himself over some old ruins, and was just about to string a cable car over Babylon when war broke out (since the downfall of Hussein, the work has ground to a halt).

At first the presence of U.S. troops protected Babylon from looters, but soon the protectors were causing more trouble than they were preventing. U.S. Marines lived in Saddam's palace, and the rest of the city was turned into a military depot, which was transferred to Polish forces in September 2003. World outrage, however, prompted the occupying forces to return the site to Iraq's antiquities officials in January 2005.

Iraqi leaders have spun ideas for continuing Hussein's rebuilding project once the war is over, creating a new cultural center with shopping malls, hotels, and perhaps a theme park—why not? Archaeologists are already shaking their heads.

✈ Baghdad

🛏 It is not advisable to travel to Iraq at the present time.

**Crumbling Classics**

**304**

# Legendary Urkesh
## *Sifting Through the Tell*
Tell Mozan, Syria

BURIED AND LOST FOR CENTURIES, THE ANCIENT CITY OF URKESH WAS FINALLY UNEARTHED BY archaeologists in the past 20 years. Built of adobe, the walls and buildings of Urkesh are now vulnerable to wind and rain and must be protected if they are to be preserved. Development also poses a serious threat to the archaeological site where Urkesh was discovered, as local communities continue to expand.

For years, the legendary city of Urkesh taunted archaeologists like a cruel mirage. Agatha Christie and her husband, archaeologist Max Mallowan, searched for it in the 1920s and 1930s, but they ruled out the Tell Mozan area. When a UCLA team began their dig here in 1984, they had no guarantee that this 150-hectare (370-acre) mound in the middle of a stark flat plain in northeast Syria held anything at all.

As they began to dig, they found the remains of mud-brick city walls and several houses, along with what seemed a royal palace, a monumental temple terrace, and an enigmatic underground pit, buildings that dated from the right period—5000 to 1500 B.C. But not until 1995, when they unearthed several seal impressions in the palace, could they definitively say that, yes, they had finally solved the mystery of Urkesh. For archaeologists, the thrill of discovering a whole new culture would be like an astronomer discovering a new planet.

Around 3000 B.C., the writings of Mesopotamian peoples like the Hittites and Akkadians frequently mentioned Urkesh as the great holy city of the Hurrians, a nation with its own unique language and mythology, and with great wealth based on copper mining in the Anatolian mountains to the north. Still, no trace of the Hurrians themselves existed anywhere—a baffling riddle for archaeologists. This mound didn't look too promising at first, for it had been plowed extensively and quarried for building stone. Generations had built their houses on top of the collapsed ruins of earlier houses, building up the mound century by century, so there was a lot of debris to plumb.

Today, the excavated ruins at Tell Mozan seem sharply gouged out of the flat, windswept top of the tawny mound, which rises 28m (92 ft.) above the surrounding plain. Excavators have reconstructed the foundations of the temple—now known to be a temple to Kumarbi, the Hurrians' chief god. Work continues on the royal palace, slowly and meticulously. Cagelike scaffolding covered with weatherproof fabric is used to protect

# 10 Magical Stone Circles

Everybody can picture the world's most famous circle of prehistoric standing stones, England's Stonehenge. But while Stonehenge is one of the most complete stone circles still standing, many others around the world are equally compelling. It isn't just their age—a spiritual aura lingers around these sites, some confluence of cosmic energy or electromagnetic pull . . . or just plain magic.

Here are some of the most impressive remnants:

Mysterious Stonehenge.

**305 Stonehenge, Salisbury Plain, England** Originally built around 2500 B.C., it was replaced around 2300 B.C. with even bigger stones, the 45-ton Sarsen sandstone blocks you see today. The circle is perfectly aligned with the sun on the summer solstice. Unfortunately, immediate access has been cut off to tourists—you'll have to circle around it on a walkway that never gets closer than 15m (50 ft.). ✆ *44/1980/623108. www. stonehenge.co.uk.*

Avebury.

**306 Avebury, Wiltshire, England** The largest megalithic site in England, built from 3000 to 2400 B.C., Avebury could have fit the entire Stonehenge site inside the smallest of its three concentric circles. Despite centuries of depredation, more than 100 pitted and worn stones survive, some of them once nearly 60 tons in size. Gentle grassy slopes mark its once-immense ditch and bank. ✆ *44/1672/539250. www.avebury-web.co.uk.*

**307 Stanton Drew, Somerset, England** Only 13km (8 miles) south of Bristol, a peaceful set of open fields outside the village of Stanton Drew holds a well-kept secret: Britain's second largest stone circle, 113m (371 ft.) in diameter, with 27 of its original 36 stones, though many are broken and/or toppled. Two other smaller circles stand nearby; it's on private land, but open to the public. *www.englishheritage.org.uk.*

**308 Boscawen-Un, Near St Buryan, Cornwall, England** The completeness of this small ellipse, along with its untamed setting, gives it an especially Druidical flavor. Lichened and overgrown with gorse, the 19 neatly spaced granite stones rise toward the west, as if angling the face of the circle; the distinctively slanted center stone points toward the point of midsummer sunrise. *www.into-cornwall.com.*

**309 The Rollright Stones, Long Compton, Oxfordshire, England** Cut from the same golden limestone as the colleges at nearby Oxford, the ragged stones known as the King's Men stand shoulder to shoulder in a near-perfect circle, 32m

(104 ft.)—or 38 Druid cubits—in diameter. Legend says a king and his followers were turned to stone by witches from Long Compton (known as a center of witchcraft). A solitary monolith nearby is called the King's Stone; another set of gnarled rocks, called the Whispering Knights, form a gateway to the site. *www.rollrightstones.co.uk.*

**310 Ring of Brodgar, Near Stromness, Orkney Islands** This sparsely populated archipelago 10km (6 miles) north of the Scottish mainland is dotted with Pict and Norse cairns, but the oldest and most impressive monument is the Ring of Brodgar (1560 B.C.), on the island called Mainland. Brodgar still has nearly half of its original 60 stones, surrounded by a deep ditch carved out of solid bedrock. (*) *44/1856/872856. www.visitorkney. com.*

Ring of Brodgar.

**311 Callanish, Isle of Lewis, Scotland** On this northernmost island of the Hebrides, a remarkably intact Neolithic temple, built around 1800 B.C., is laid out in the unusual shape of a Celtic cross. At its center is a circle of 13 standing stones, hewn from the rugged local gneiss, around a burial cairn. Legend says the stones were an ancient race of giants, turned to stone by St. Kiernan when they refused to convert to Christianity. (*) *44/851/703088. www.isle-of-lewis.com.*

The stones of Callanish.

**312 Beltany, Raphoe, County Donegal, Ireland** Built around 2000 B.C., this large hilltop circle still has 64 closely set 1.8m-tall (6-ft.) stones (originally there may have been 80), though many stones are broken and tipping. Lumpy turf inside the circle suggests it was a burial site, though one triangular cup-marked stone aligns mysteriously with sunrise on May 1—the pagan holiday known as Beltane. *www.beltany-circle.com.*

**313 Almendres Menhir, Near Evora, Portugal** One of Europe's oldest circles (some of it dates to 5000 B.C.), Almendres is actually two overlapping circles on an east-facing hilltop, built at different times and oriented to the two different equinoxes. Don't miss the solitary huge stone (menhir) a short walk away, and ponder the riddle of how it's connected to the circle.

**314 Carnac, Brittany, France** Carnac's Field of Megaliths takes the prize for most megaliths at one site—nearly 3,000 monumental stones, some up to 20m (60 ft.) tall, stand lined up enigmatically in three different groupings, each with a circle at the end. Erected around 4500 to 3300 B.C., these great pre-Celtic megaliths may represent some form of ancestor worship. (*) *33/2/97-52-89-99.*

the mud-brick structures once they're uncovered. (The scaffolding also helps visitors imagine what the buildings might have looked like.) It's a fascinating opportunity to watch state-of-the-art excavation in progress.

But adobe is such a vulnerable material, more needs to be done to strengthen the walls now that they are exposed to the elements. Recently, local settlements have expanded toward the site, and a power line and a new road are planned to run right into the archaeological zone. There is so much left to do at Tell Mozan—can they peel back all the layers of the past before the present catches up with them?

✈ Al Qamishli

🛏 $$ **Al Qamishli Hotel,** Al Saied Al Reas St., Al Qamishli (© **963/52/443355**). $$ **Al Sufara'a Hotel,** Al Saied Al Reas St., Al Qamishli (© **963/52/432993**).

**Crumbling Classics** **315**

# Amrit
## *The Ancient Global Village*
### Tartus, Syria

EVEN IN RUINS, THE ANCIENT PORT CITY OF AMRIT ON THE SYRIAN COAST IS STILL BEAUTIFUL and full of archaeological treasures. But as the nearby city of Tartus continues to expand, the coastline where Amrit once stood becomes increasingly valuable as a possible site for resort hotels and other development.

Among Syria's ancient sites, Amrit is one of the most beautiful—and one of the least protected. That's part of its charm, but charm won't be enough to save it if the real estate becomes valuable enough. Over the past 25 years, various developers have launched projects to build hotels here, extending the sprawl of the popular Syrian beach resort of Tartus. In some cases, they were stopped only at the last minute, usually because construction crews had dug up valuable artifacts—an easy thing to do in a locale that's been settled since the Bronze Age.

Looking at the ruins of ancient Amrit, it's hard to figure out whether these people were Phoenicians, Egyptians, Persians, or Greeks. The answer is, a little of each—they were confident citizens of a global village, long before humans knew they even lived on a globe. There's no harbor here now, but evidence shows one existed

that later silted up. Amrit became prominent around 3000 B.C. as a mainland extension of the island nation of Arwad, just offshore from Tartus. Amrit's chief ruins today date back to the era of Persian rule (6th c. B.C.), but the central temple is shrewdly dedicated to Melqart, a god of the original Phoenician inhabitants, and Eshmun, a god of the Egyptians, with whom the Phoenicians had always traded extensively. Less than a kilometer (¹/₂ mile) south of the temple, two funeral towers nicknamed the Spindles *(al maghazil)* stand atop burial chambers, where distinctly Egyptian-like sarcophagi were excavated. In 333 B.C. when Alexander the Great took over the city (by then it was going by the Greek name Marathus), the temple was adapted to the worship of Hercules. What's more, another excavation on the other side of the river reveals an ancient stadium, dating from 1500

Amrit's funeral towers.

B.C.—a stadium 225m (738 ft.) long and 30m (98 ft.) wide, whose design is exactly like the famous Greek stadium at Olympia, but built several centuries earlier.

Back and forth Amrit went—independent for a while, then defeated again by Arwad, then part of the Roman Empire, and then abandoned by the Romans for Tartus, which had a larger harbor. In the Byzantine era, Amrit rebounded, but by the time of the crusades, it had declined so much that the crusaders raided it for stone to build their island stronghold on Arwad.

From the 18th century on, Amrit was protected as a romantic set of ruins, which is exactly what it remains today—overgrown with soft green grass where sheep graze freely, favored by locals as a peaceful picnic site. Edged by a graceful colonnade, the grass-choked artificial lake surrounding the temple is still rumored to have healing powers. A concrete-slab resort here? Sacrilege.

---

ⓘ www.amrit-syria.com

✈ Lattakia

🛏 $$ **Daniel Hotel,** Sharia al-Wahda, Tartus (ⓒ **963/43/220 581**). $$ **Bilbars Hotel,** Sharia Okbah Ben Nafee, Crac des Chevaliers (ⓒ **963/31/741 201**).

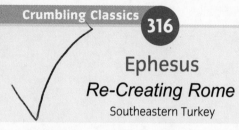

# Ephesus
## *Re-Creating Rome*
### Southeastern Turkey

MANY TOURISTS ARE DRAWN TO THE EXTENSIVE ROMAN RUINS IN EPHESUS, AND MANY OTHERS come because Ephesus was such an important site to the early Christians. However, an aggressive plan to make the Ephesian ruins appeal to tourists by reconstructing ancient sites to re-create the look and feel of the Roman city that once stood here, threatens the integrity this historic city.

Ephesus has been great many times in its history. In the Greek era, its Temple of Artemis was one of the Seven Wonders of the Ancient World (though all that's left today is one forlorn column in Selçuk, off the road to Kuşadası). It was a major Roman colony in Asia Minor, and in the early Christian era, Ephesus was where Jesus' mother Mary settled after the Cruci-fixion (her house, now a church, is nearby in Meryemana) and where St. Paul preached his most famous sermons. But when the crusaders came through in the 1300s, they found only a small Turkish village, its harbor silted up and its temples toppled by an earthquake in 614.

Today Ephesus is great again—the larg-est collection of Roman ruins east of the Mediterranean, it's one of Turkey's must-see tourist stops. But how many of those ruins are genuine? The Turkish govern-ment reconstructed much of what has been excavated here, moving statues and friezes indoors to the **Ephesus Museum** in Selçuk (on the park at Aatür Caddesi) and patching together ancient buildings and colonnades to re-create the sense of a bustling Roman town. At what point will ancient Ephesus no longer feel ancient?

The archaeological zone requires only a mile of walking, but it'll take 2 or 3 hours to do it justice. Entering at the top of the hill, walk first through the **Upper Agora,** the official part of town, which is full of tem-ples, monuments, fountains, a town hall, and the Odeon, where the government council met. Sloping away from it is

**Curettes Way** (curettes were a class of priests dedicated to Artemis, Ephesus's patron goddess)—notice the pockmarks on the pavement made by thousands of horses' hoofs over the centuries. Across from the Gate of Hercules (that's Hercules wearing the skin of the Nemean Lion), you'll see how the Ephesians curried favor with Roman emperors, building the two-story Trajan's Fountain and the **Temple of Hadrian,** with its glorious Corinthian-col-umned porch. Behind the temple are a grand set of Roman baths, the **Baths of Scholastika.**

Across Curettes Way, pass up a colon-naded shopping street to the **Terraced Houses,** where the richest citizens lived. It's a great window into the sophisticated lifestyle of the Roman Empire—running water, heating systems, private inner courtyards, and a rich decor of mosaics and frescoes. Just past there, the **Library of Celsus** was built to impress, with its outsized two-tiered facade and three levels of niches for storing scrolls or books; the **Marble Way** (paved in real marble) leads from there to the **Great Theatre,** a hillside amphitheater that could seat 44,000. It's impressive indeed—just don't look too close.

✈ İzmir

 $$ **Hitit Hotel,** Tariş Yani-Şarapçı Kuyu Mevki P.K. 66, Selçuk (© **90/232/892-6920;** www.kusadasihotels.com). $$ **Hotel Kalehan,** İzmir Cad., Selçuk (© **90/232/892-6154;** www.kalehan.com).

# Aphrodisias
## *A Marvel in Marble*
### Southeastern Turkey

AFTER A CENTURY OF EXCAVATIONS, THE FAMED MARBLE OF APHRODISIAS IS IN SORRY SHAPE. Some of the earlier excavators didn't properly prepare the ancient stones, which are now exposed to the elements. While excavation is still ongoing, many previously revealed areas are already beginning to crumble; some have had to be closed to visitors.

If you want to build a beautiful city, it helps to start out next to a marble quarry. With all that exquisite white and blue-gray marble on hand, it's not surprising that Aphrodisias attracted the finest sculptors of its day. What sculptor wouldn't want to try his hand at depicting the city's patron goddess, Aphrodite, goddess of love?

While Ephesus may be Turkey's best-known archaeological site, the more remote Aphrodisias is just as large and valuable—and much less crowded. It's still easy to picture the town as it was laid out in Greco-Roman times—temple, agora, council house, baths, theater, and huge stadium. The builders of Aphrodisias filled these buildings with statues, sculpted decorations, and carved inscriptions, taking advantage of the local talent pool. One fine example is the Tetrapylon, a beautifully preserved ornamental gate with fluted Corinthian columns and a triangular lintel full of mythological figures. Several statues around the site have been moved for safekeeping, most of them to the on-site museum.

Later generations were great recyclers—when chunks of stones fell from earlier monuments, they simply used them again, inserting many early inscriptions in walls of later buildings. More than 2,000 inscriptions are visible, mostly from the days of the Roman Empire. Notice, though, that the names Aphrodite and Aphrodisias were often struck out—once this became a Byzantine Christian city, renamed Stavropolis ("City of the Cross"), its leaders wanted to erase its pagan past. These Christians also converted the Temple of Aphrodite into a basilica, another great adaptive reuse project.

Though there was continuous settlement here from the Bronze Age on, Aphrodisias was hard hit by earthquakes in the 4th and 7th centuries A.D., when many of the classical-era buildings were toppled and laid under rubble. What's left of the Sebastion, for example, is nothing but a tumbled collection of huge marble chunks, parts of a unique temple built to worship the emperor Augustus. The modern village of Geyre covered the site until the 20th century, when cottages were moved to allow archaeologists to plumb the classical city beneath.

From a distance, the ruined columns and massive building blocks of Aphrodisias still gleam on their grassy site, surrounded with slim cypress trees. It's only when you get closer that you see what dire condition some sections have fallen into. The damage could still be reversed—will the Turkish government invest in Aphrodisias before it's too late?

(i) Aphrodisias (**© 90/256/448-8003**)

✈ İzmir

🛏 $$ **Richmond Hotel,** Karahayit Koyu, Karahayit (**© 90/258/271 4078;** www.richmondhotels.com.tr). $$ **Pamuksu Boutique Hotel,** Gölyeri Mevkii Stad Caddesi 52, Pamukkale (**© 90/258/272 2109;** www.pamuksuhotel.com).

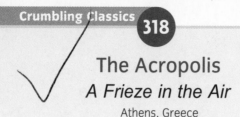

# The Acropolis
## *A Frieze in the Air*
Athens, Greece

RISING HIGH ABOVE ATHENS, THE ACROPOLIS AND ITS SACRED TEMPLES AND MONUMENTS have survived wars, earthquakes, and the enthusiasm of early archaeologists who carried away many precious artifacts. Today smog from Athens is gradually destroying many of the Acropolis's remaining sculptures and structures, including the famous Parthenon.

For 25 centuries, these marble columns and pediments have floated above the rat race of Athens, glowing beige at dawn, golden at high noon, rose at sunset, ethereal white in the moonlight. Successive waves of invaders took over this sheer rocky outcrop—the Romans made it a brothel, the Christians an orthodox church, the Turks a mosque and arsenal—and earthquakes and explosions did their part as well. Still, nothing could erase the serene, sacred beauty of the Acropolis.

In 2007, the Acropolis Museum was opened at the base of the sacred mount to display indoors as much of the world-famous statuary as could safely be removed from the site. Set on architectural pylons so as not to disturb ongoing excavations of the 3th-, 4th-, and 7th-century ruins beneath the site (a view of the excavations is an exhibit in itself), the modern museum incorporates as much natural light as possible for viewing the artifacts, arranged in chronological order. The climax is a majestic glass gallery displaying the few Parthenon friezes the Greeks still possess, since 19th-century British diplomat Lord Elgin carted off most of them to the British Museum.

The Acropolis.

Though you may begin your visit in the museum, walking up onto the sacred mount itself is essential. Though we've all seen it a hundred times on posters and postcards, to actually be here, to walk around its crumbling stones, can be the experience of a lifetime. Ignore the tourist crowds: Find a place to sit, and gaze out over modern Athens sprawling below.

People lived on the Acropolis as early as 5000 B.C., for this hilltop was an ideal defense against invaders. In classical times, as Athens's population grew, citizens moved down from the Acropolis, but it remained a sacred site. Still, the Acropolis's height couldn't protect it in 480 B.C., when Persian invaders destroyed most of its monuments. Athenian statesman Pericles ordered the Acropolis rebuilt; almost all of what you see today comes from that era.

Though you enter through the Roman-era Beulé Gate, that's merely an entrance to the real entrance: the monumental Propylaia arch. Just above the Propylaia, to the right, is the beautifully proportioned Temple of Athena Nike; to the left, the Erechtheion, tomb of an Athenian king

named Erechtheus, its pediments lifted by a supporting cast of female figures, or caryatids. But the real star of the show is the Parthenon, the great temple dedicated to Athena. Only in person can you truly appreciate its optical illusion: big as it is, this temple seems light and graceful, with 46 slender columns (17 on each side, 8 at each end) ranged along the outsides. Its columns and stairs appear straight, yet all are minutely curved, with each exterior column thicker in the middle.

The airy look of the Parthenon is also due to the fact that it has no roof—in 1687, the Venetians, trying to capture Turkish-occupied Athens, blew it to smithereens. The Parthenon survived even that—surely it can survive smog.

ⓘ **The Acropolis,** Dionissiou Areopagitou (✆ **30/210/321-0219**)

✈ Athens International, Spata

🛏 $$$ **Hilton,** 46 Leoforos Vas. Sofias (✆ **800/445-8667** in the U.S. or 30/210/728-1000; www.hilton.com). $$ **Athens Cypria,** 5 Diomias (✆ **30/210/323-8034**).

# The Olympic Stadium
## *Summer of the Torch*

### Olympia, Greece

THE WILDFIRES THAT THREATENED THE ANCIENT OLYMPIC STADIUM IN 2007 SERVED AS A stark reminder than no place on earth can ever be completely safe from the forces of nature. Because the stadium at Olympia is still so important to the Olympic Games, along with being a site of great cultural significance to the Greek people, it is protected from the dangers that threaten many other ancient sites—but nature can't be tamed.

For days in the summer of 2007, the world watched the news with bated breath. Consuming vast areas of the Greek mainland, fires swept down from the forests, gobbling villages and farmland. Hundreds of

people evacuated their homes, and at least 60 people were killed. Even the skies over Athens turned black.

While fires elsewhere were quenched, a wall of flame rampaged toward the gates of the ancient stadium in Olympia, home of the Olympic Games. Helicopters flew overhead, spraying the ruins with foam and water and preemptively reducing nearby pine and cypress groves to charred stumps. Volunteers on the ground grabbed buckets to douse the site.

Eventually this Herculean effort saved Olympia. It's an apt comparison, since legend claims that Hercules himself founded the Olympic Games. After completing the last of his 12 labors, the stories say, to celebrate he paced off 192m (600 Olympic ft.) and ran the distance without taking a single breath. That distance became the length of the stadium at the religious sanctuary of Olympia, and for over a millennium, from 776 B.C. to A.D. 393, athletic contests were held here every 4 years. Contestants came from as far away as Asia Minor and Italy; the entire Greek world called a truce so athletes and spectators could journey safely to Olympia—that's how important the games were to ancient Greece.

Thousands poured into Olympia to see the games; the surrounding countryside became a tent city. Events included footraces, short and long jumps, wrestling and boxing contests, chariot races, the arduous pentathlon (discus, javelin, jumping, running, and wrestling), and the vicious pankration (which combined wrestling and boxing techniques). The most prestigious event was the stade, or short footrace, from which we get the word "stadium."

The site itself is a jumble of foundation stones and toppled columns, marking various buildings around the ancient sanctuary. You'll see the ruins of Roman baths where athletes and spectators took hot and cold plunges; slender columns mark the site of the gymnasium and palestra, where athletes practiced footracing and boxing. Olympia was devoted to the worship of Zeus, so there's one temple devoted to Hera (Zeus's wife) and an even bigger one for Zeus, which once contained an enormous gold-and-ivory statue of Zeus, one of the Seven Wonders of the Ancient World. Passing through a vaulted archway to walk onto the pavement of the old stadium, which could accommodate 45,000 on its sloped sides, you can just imagine the roar of the ancient crowd.

Every 2 years, the Olympic flame is kindled here by sunlight and then relayed by torch to the site of that year's games. In 2008, there was a sort of bitter irony as the flame was lit again, with the blackened hillsides in the background. It was a grim reminder that natural disaster could strike any heritage site without warning—no place is safe from that.

(i) **Tourist office** (✆ **30/26240/23-100**)

🚃 Olympia

🛏 $$$ **Grecotel Lakopetra Beach,** Kato Achaia, Achaia (✆ **30/26930/51-713**). $ **Hotel Praxitelous,** 7 Spilliopoulou, Ancient Olympia (✆ **30/26240/225-92**).

**Crumbling Classics**

**320**

# The Colosseum
## *Call in the Lions*
### Rome, Italy

OVER THE YEARS THE COLOSSEUM HAS BEEN DAMAGED BY EARTHQUAKES, STRIPPED OF ITS marble facing, begrimed by exhaust from cars whipping around the vicious traffic circle outside, and shaken by subway trains rumbling below. However, Rome has started work on a multimillion-dollar project to restore its best-known symbol.

The Colosseum.

Perhaps no classical Roman ruin evokes the excesses of the late Empire like the Colosseum. In A.D. 80, the opening event was a weeks-long bloody combat between gladiators and wild beasts. Later shows kept upping the ante: Vestal virgins from the temple screamed for blood, ever-more exotic animals were shipped in to satisfy jaded curiosities, and the arena floor was flooded for not-so-mock naval battles. (Really big events like chariot races were held at the Circus Maximus, on the other side of the Palatine hill, today a formless heap of ruins.) As you standing on the walkways, gazing through the arches into the bowl of the arena, the cries of those ancient spectators still seem to echo through the ages.

To modern eyes, however, it's the damaged profile of this time-ravaged elliptical shell that we recognize from pizza boxes and movies—reconstructed models in movies like *Gladiator* seem weirdly off-kilter. As it stands today, only one side still sports the original four-tiered design (each level has a different style of column, like a textbook illustration of Doric, Ionic, and Corinthian). The wooden arena floor itself, where gladiators had their bloody face-offs, has rotted away, revealing honeycombed lower levels where elephants, lions, and other wild animals waited to be hoisted up in cages to the arena floor. The seats that once accommodated 50,000 spectators are gone, leaving only tiered ledges of crumbling stone.

Unlike the Pantheon across town, which was spared demolition because it was converted in the Christian era to a church, the Colosseum moldered for years, quarried for building materials. The adjacent Roman Forum, too, is a jumble of fallen stones, ringed with dusty paths and weeds. The ruined state of these landmarks is picturesque in itself, an integral part of their appeal—who'd stand in line for hours (literally hours in summer, unless you spring for a private guide) if all there was to see was Disney-esque reconstruction? But that's no excuse for letting environmental stresses damage these ancient stones any further. In future, be prepared for more areas to be closed to visitors as essential repairs are carried out, not only in the Colosseum but all over Rome.

---

(i) **Piazzale del Colosseo,** Via dei Fori Imperiali (© **39/6/7004261**)

✈ Leonardo da Vinci International Airport

🛏 **$$$ Hotel de Russie,** Via del Babuino 9 (© **800/323-7500** in North America, or 39/6/328881; www.roccoforte hotels.com). $ **Hotel Grifo,** Via del Boschetto 144 (© **39/6/4871395;** www. hotelgrifo.com).

**Crumbling Classics** **321**

# Herculaneum

## . . . *Dust to Dust*

### Outside Naples, Italy

LIKE ITS NEIGHBOR POMPEII, HERCULANEUM WAS BOTH DESTROYED AND PRESERVED WHEN Mount Vesuvius erupted in A.D. 79. However, uncontrolled exposure to light, wind, and rain has damaged many artifacts and buildings unearthed at Herculaneum. The site also has suffered from theft and vandalism, and from tourists who carry away souvenirs and damage delicate structures as they walk through the site.

Though they both were destroyed in that same fateful day in A.D. 79, Herculaneum was always smaller than its more celebrated neighbor Pompeii; even today, its archaeological zone is only one-fourth the size of Pompeii's. The good news for serious travelers is that Herculaneum doesn't get nearly the same volume of tourist traffic. Come here in the mornings, when the day-trippers are still herding like sheep around Pompeii, and you can have its ghostly precincts nearly to yourself.

But Herculaneum also doesn't make enough money to fund the conservation work necessary to protect its stones. Too much exposure to the elements, vandalism, water damage from the adjacent town, and damage from inappropriate excavation carried out years ago, the ruins here are deteriorating at an even faster rate than Pompeii's.

Herculaneum was first discovered long before Pompeii, in 1709, sheerly by accident, while workers were digging a well. It still hasn't been completely excavated by any means. It was more heavily buried than Pompeii, for one thing, and mostly under hardened mud and lava flow rather than ash. Whereas the weight of ash collapsed buildings at Pompeii, more large complex structures survived at Herculaneum, which are harder to unearth. Matters are further complicated by the fact that nearby slums cover yet-unexplored sections of the buried town. Excavation work has been halted for the time being, given the need to focus on conservation of existing ruins.

Most visitors make Herculaneum a hurried add-on to Pompeii, often dropping it entirely from the itinerary when they discover how absorbing Pompeii can be. But Herculaneum deserves a visit on its own merits. For one thing, it was an entirely different sort of town from workaday Pompeii—an upper-class resort where aristocrats lived in luxury. A window into their elite lifestyle is offered at the Casa dei Cervi (House of the Stags), where a fair amount of sculpture was preserved. There are several other fine houses as well: **Casa** del Bicentario (House of the Bicentenary), **Casa a Graticcio** (House of the Wooden Cabinet), **Case del Tremezzo di Legno** (House of the Wooden Partition), and the **Casa di Poseidon** (House of Poseidon), most of which are named after their most intriguing architectural features.

You'll get an idea of how these patricians spent their leisure time at the **Amphitheater** (don't miss the exquisite mosaic here), the **Palestra** sports arena, and the lavishly adorned baths (Terme Suburbane). Best of all may be the **Villa of the Papyri,** where an amazing trove of

charred ancient scrolls was found. Herculaneum's fascinations are endless—you'll just have to dig a little deeper to find them.

---

ⓘ **Ufficio Scavi di Ercolano,** Corso Resina, Ercolano (ℂ **39/81-7390963**)

✈ Naples's Aeroporto Capodochino

🛏 $$$ **Hotel Excelsior,** Via Partenope 48, Naples (ℂ **39/81-7640111;** www.excelsior.it). $$ **Hotel Britannique,** Corso Vittorio Emanuele 133 (ℂ **39/81-7614145;** www.hotelbritannique.it).

---

# Paestum
## *Italy's Piece of Ancient Greece*
### Campania, Italy

THE ANCIENT CITY OF PAESTUM, SITE OF THREE WELL-PRESERVED GREEK TEMPLES AND MANY other archaeological treasures, is threatened by rapid and seemingly chaotic development extending outward from nearby cities and towns, which could damage this magnificent site and as-yet-undiscovered antiquities.

Who would have thought that, so near the luxe resorts of the Amalfi Coast, you could wander around a Greek colony founded in 600 B.C.? Even the ancients wrote about the roses of Paestum, which bloom twice a year, splashes of scarlet perfectly complementing the salmon-colored stones of its Greek temples.

Abandoned for centuries, the ruins of Paestum began to attract archaeologists in the mid–18th century, shortly after Pompeii was discovered up the coast and became all the rage. The malarial swamps that drove out its residents in the Middle Ages were finally drained in the 20th century; the water buffalos who grazed here were corralled onto farms. It's a much less complete ruin than Pompeii, though. Much of the ancient town lies beneath private property and has not been excavated; farmland and modern houses run right up

to the edge of the archaeological zone, and a major highway borders the site. A road built through the ruins in the 1700s destroyed half of its Roman amphitheater. And after all these centuries, those crumbling ruins have in some spots been thoughtlessly patched with modern concrete. Its off-the-beaten-track quality was always part of its charm, but nearby beach resorts creep closer every year.

What's fascinating about Paestum is that it's really two ruined cities atop each other. The first was the Greek city of Poseidonia, a vigorous trading center that was the northernmost Greek colony in Italy. Poseidonia was renamed Paestum when the Romans took over in 273 B.C. Though they settled right on top of the Greek town, the Romans could not bring themselves to knock down its three mighty temples, and so, curiously enough, Paestum's Greek ruins are more completely preserved than the Roman remains.

The largest is the 5th-century **Temple of Neptune** (Neptune being the Roman name for Poseidon), although archaeologists think it really was devoted to Zeus's wife Hera. Much of it is still standing—six columns in front, crowned by a massive entablature, and 14 columns on each side. Both the Temple of Hera and the Temple of Athena are even older, dating back to the 6th century B.C. The Temple of Hera, Italy's oldest Greek temple, is surprisingly intact, with 9 chunky Doric pillars in front and 18 on the sides. The Temple of Athena (also called the Temple of Ceres) has 34 stout Doric columns, along with ragged bits of its triangular pediment and a large altar.

Across from the Temple of Athena, the on-site museum displays some metopes removed from the Temple of Hera and some fine tomb paintings from the 4th and 5th century B.C.; don't miss the beautiful paintings of the Diver's Tomb. Hundreds of Greek tombs were recently discovered at Paestum, yielding a trove of paintings and clay figures. There is so much more to be uncovered here—if only the ruins could get a little respect.

(i) **National Archaeological Museum of Paestum,** Via Magna Grecia 917 (✆ **39/ 828-811023**).

✈ Naples

🚆 Paestum

🛏 $$ **Strand Hotel Schuhmann,** Via Marittima (✆ **39/828-851151;** www.hotel schuhmann.com)

---

**Crumbling Classics** **323**

# Pompeii

## *Ashes to Ashes . . .*

### Outside Naples, Italy

EARTHQUAKES AND VOLCANIC ERUPTIONS STILL THREATEN POMPEII, JUST AS IT DID 2,000 years ago, but today it is also in danger crumbling under the feet of its many admirers. Every year, two million tourists walk the ancient streets of Pompeii, awestruck by this Roman city that was perfectly preserved in a moment of unexpected tragedy when Mount Vesuvius erupted and buried Pompeii and its citizens in mud and ash.

Pompeii has already endured one natural disaster, buried in volcanic ash and mud after Mount Vesuvius erupted in A.D. 79. There's a melancholy aura about this ghost city, yet somehow Pompeii is exciting not because it was destroyed, but because it was saved—preserved by the very same volcanic debris, like a fly caught in amber, as it was 2,000 years ago.

Mount Etna still rumbles above the town—the last time it erupted was 1944, and it could go again any day. In this seismic area, earthquakes are another ever-present threat (among the ruins you can tell that Pompeii was still rebuilding from an A.D. 62 earthquake when the eruption hit). But these days the biggest threat to Pompeii may be its own popularity. It's such a convenient day trip from Naples that two million tourists a year shuffle through these fragile streets, and the pavements are getting worn, the relics crumbling from so much traffic. The situation's become so dire, in July 2008 the Italian government appointed a special commissioner to direct an emergency rescue effort for the deteriorating antiquities.

In other cities, a few large and important classical buildings survived; in Pompeii it was a whole town, and there's no

The ruins of Pompeii.

better place to imagine the daily life of the ancient Roman Empire. Not every artifact of ancient Pompeii remains on-site: The Pompeiians themselves (those who escaped alive) returned once the ashes had cooled to grab a few treasures before abandoning the town. The buried city was discovered again in 1599, and serious excavation began in the mid–18th century. Several of the most precious mosaics and frescoes were taken up to the National Archaeological Museum in Naples (Piazza Museo Nazionale 18–19, *C* **39/81-440166**). Still, plenty is left to see, including some surprisingly erotic frescoes and mosaics.

Highlights include the House of the Vettii's black-and-red dining room with its frescoes of delicate cupids; the spectacular frescoes in the House of the Mysteries, outside the city walls; and the imposing House of the Faun, with no less than four dining rooms and two spacious peristyle gardens. In the center of town is the forum, the heart of Pompeiian life, surrounded by a basilica, the Temple of

Apollo, the Temple of Jupiter, and the Stabian Thermae (baths), where you'll even see some skeletons. The open-air Great Theater could hold 5,000 spectators at its bloodthirsty battles between wild animals and gladiators.

The main thing, though, is to walk these paved streets between largely intact buildings and visualize the citizens going about their daily routines on that August day, just before the exploding cloud blotted out the sun. Pompeii is not just about Pompeii—it's a paradigm of what could happen to any community struck suddenly by natural disaster.

---

ℹ️ **Ufficio Scavi di Pompeii,** Via Villa dei Misteri 1, Pompeii (*C* **39/81-8610744**)

✈ Naples's Aeroporto Capodochino

🛏 $$$ **Hotel Excelsior,** Via Partenope 48, Naples (*C* **39/81-7640111;** www. excelsior.it). $$ **Hotel Britannique,** Corso Vittorio Emanuele 133 (*C* **39/81-7614145;** www.hotelbritannique.it).

# Hadrian's Wall
## *The End of Civilization*
### Northern England

OVER THE PAST 2 MILLENNIA, NATURE BROKE DOWN SOME SECTIONS OF HADRIAN'S WALL, and many stones from the wall were removed and used to build other structures, but much of the wall is still intact. Besides nature itself, the biggest threat to Hadrian's Wall are the tourists who flock to the site each year and walk on the wall.

The wild and forbidding Cheviot Hills make an effective buffer between England and Scotland—but surveying the site in A.D. 122, Roman emperor Hadrian wasn't convinced that was enough to protect this farthest-flung frontier of his sprawling empire. He ordered his legionnaires to reinforce the border with a great defensive wall, 117km (73 miles) long, from the North Sea to the Irish Sea. In Romans' eyes, it marked where civilization ended and the barbarian world began.

With great fanfare, a footpath was completed in 2003 along the length of the wall, from Wallsend on the east coast to Bowness-on-Solway on the west, even plunging through urban areas of Carlisle and Newcastle. What a great idea it seemed, and it quickly become one of Great Britain's most popular treks—to the point of endangering these fragile old stones. U.K. heritage officials now urgently warn hikers to stick to the signed path, not to tread on the wall's ramparts (tempting as they may look), and to avoid the winter months, when the ground beside the wall is wet and artifacts underground could be damaged. The best time to visit is May through September, when a special bus service from Hexham visits major sights along the wall.

Though Hadrian's Wall was originally made of turf, eventually the whole wall was done in stone, with a fortified "castle" every 1.6km (1 mile), sentry turrets in between, and full-fledged forts every 8 or 16km (5–10 miles). The Romans built well; though stones were pilfered from the wall for centuries, many fragments still stand, some on private property (these are often the sections in worst condition) and a significant part in Northumberland National Park. The 45km (28 miles) of wall between Chollerford and Walton is one of the best-preserved sections, where the wall is quite visible and runs through high wild moorland with wonderful views to the north. Near Housesteads, the **Housesteads Fort and Museum** (✆ **01434/344363**) displays a partially excavated Roman fort, Vercovicium, though the most impressive remnant of a fort is nearby at Chollerford: **Chesters Roman Fort and Museum** (✆ **01434/681379**), a Roman cavalry fort originally built astride Hadrian's Wall.

If walking's not your thing, the B6318 road more or less traces the wall, with signposts to major sights along the route. At the **Roman Army Museum** (B6318 at A69, ✆ **01697/747485**), you can visit a barracks room outfitted to depict living conditions in the Roman army; a short walk from here you can scale Walltown Crags, one of the most imposing and high-standing sections of the wall. Visit indeed—but treat the wall with the respect it deserves.

ⓘ www.hadrians-wall.org

🚊 Hexham or Haltwhistle

🛏 **George Hotel,** Chollerford, Humshaugh, near Hexham (✆ **44/1434/681611**)

# Angkor Wat
## *Glory in the Jungle*
### Siem Reep, Cambodia

MORE THAN A MILLION TOURISTS VISIT THE ANCIENT CITY OF ANGKOR WAT EVERY YEAR, PUTTING tremendous stress on the sandstone temples, stairs, and walkways. Hotels and resorts that have sprung up to serve the tourists are using so much groundwater that some of the temples at Angkor Wat are beginning to sink into the ground as underground aquifers are depleted.

In 1861, it was just a mysterious hulk in the Cambodian jungle, a pile of jumbled laterite and sandstone blocks shrouded in roots and vines. Today, however, the ancient city of Angkor Wat—capital of the Khmer kingdom from 802 until 1295—is Cambodia's chief tourism attraction, a breathtaking sprawl of temples and shrines that covers 98 sq. km (38 sq. miles).

Benefiting from a boom in exotic travel since 1993, Angkor Wat's annual visitor totals have shot from 7,500 to over a million. Foot traffic is wearing ruts on sandstone stairs and walkways, and the faces of poorly conserved sculptural panels are crumbling away. Several of the site's more than 40 temples are sinking into the sandy ground as area hotels and resorts drain

Angkor Wat.

underground water sources. It's one of the world's most endangered classical sites, and the Cambodian government—which has already hiked up entrance fees to limit the number of visitors—may have to impose stricter quotas or even close certain buildings in the very near future.

The resplendent main temple, also called Angkor Wat, is the star attraction—its four-spired profile has virtually become the symbol of Cambodia. Dating from the 12th century, it stands 213m (700 ft.) high from its base to the tip of its highest lotus-shaped tower, the largest religious monument ever built. Scholars believe that this sandstone temple's symmetry mirrors the timeline of the Hindu ages, like a map or calendar of the universe. Approaching from the main road over a *baray*, or reservoir, you climb up three steep levels to the inner sanctum; you'll be high up for an inspiring view.

Of course, the most famous—some would say clichéd—view is not from Angkor Wat but of Angkor Wat: from the five-tiered Phnom Bakheng, topping a hill just past the entrance to Angkor Wat. Its narrow staircases get packed with up to 3,000 tourists some evenings at sunset, putting incredible wear and tear on the ancient Khmer temple.

Another large temple complex called Angkor Thom—or "great city" in Khmer—is dotted with many temples; don't miss the bas-reliefs on the Terrace of the Leper King and the Terrace of Elephants. One of the most imperiled temples here is the center-piece of this complex, a fantastical Buddhist temple called Bayon, with four huge enigmatic stone faces, each cosmologically aligned with a compass point (the same is true of each of its 51 small towers).

One temple—Ta Prohm—has been deliberately left overgrown in foliage, the roots of fig, banyan, and kapok trees cleaving its massive stones. It's an intriguing notion—what if Angkor Wat had been left in the jungle forever? Would it be better off today?

---

✈ Siem Reap

🛏 $$$ **Sofitel Royal Angkor,** Vithei Charles de Gaulle (© **855/63/964-6000;** www.accor.com). $ **La Noria,** off Rte. 6 northeast of Siem Reap (© **855/63/964-242**).

**Crumbling Classics** 326

# The Temples of Khajuraho
## *The Sacred & the Profane*
### Madya Pradesh, India

NEW BUSINESSES AND HOMES ARE CROWDING INTO THE BUFFER ZONE AROUND THE TEMPLES of Khajuraho, while a nearby airstrip shakes the foundation of these fragile structures. Officials are growing concerned that the temples and the erotic art they contain could become targets of religious fundamentalists in India, who have protested depicting Hindu gods and goddesses and sexual beings.

The naughty frescoes of Pompeii are nothing compared to the X-rated sculptures decorating these 10th- and 11th-century temples, found in 1838 in the jungles of Madya Pradesh. Built by the Chandela kings, a robust clan of Rajput warriors, 25 exuberant many-spired sandstone temples stand in a cluster (there were originally 85), full of artwork frankly celebrating the pleasures of the human body.

Sexy art aside, these temples are astonishingly beautiful, as increasing numbers of tourists can testify. The only real sin here is how the modern world is encroaching on the site, desecrating what really should feel like a spiritual site.

In these richly sculpted temples, you make a ritual clockwise circuit around the inner sanctum past beautifully rendered friezes of gods, nymphs, animals, warfare, and various bodies twined together in hot-blooded passion. The most spectacular—and most erotically charged—temples are within the Western Group, including the large Lakshmana Temple, the elegantly proportioned Kandariya Mahadev Temple with its 872 statues, Devi Jagadambi Temple (devoted to Kali), Chitragupta Temple (devoted to Surya, the sun god), and the Temple of Vishvanatha. Take your time strolling through, for every sculptured panel has a story to tell. Not all are erotic; many narrate the exploits of the Hindu gods, particularly Shiva and Vishnu in various incarnations. It's all part of the parade of life that these temples extol.

The Eastern Group consists of both Hindu and Jain temples—you can tell them apart because the ascetic Jain philosophy ruled out sculpture that was too graphic (though voluptuous nudity was apparently okay, as you'll see in the Parsvanatha Temple). One of the most fun temples here is the 11th-century Hindu temple honoring Vamana, a plump dwarf incarnation of Vishnu; also check out the sculpted bells on the pillars of the Ghantai Temple. In the Southern Group, notice the dizzying ornamentation of the Duladeo Temple, one of the last temples built before the Sultans of Delhi squeezed out the Chandela kings.

Across the road from the entrance to the Western Group, the Archaeological Museum displays a modest selection of sculptures collected from various Khajuraho sites—it's a good way to see close-up details of carved figures that usually occur high on the temple walls and spires. To get the most out of your temple tour, rent an audio guide or hire an official guide through the Raja Café, tourist office, or your hotel. Avoid all those unofficial touts and guides, no matter how much they pester you—and they will.

✈ Khajuraho

🛏 $$$ **Radisson Jass,** By-Pass Rd. (✆ **91/7686/27-2344**). $$ **Ken River Lodge,** Village Madla (✆ **91/7732/27-5235;** www.kenriverlodge.com).

---

**Crumbling Classics**

### 327

# Buddhas of Bamiyan
## *Gone, but Not Forgotten*
### Bamiyan, Afghanistan

THE BUDDHAS OF BAMIYAN ARE NOT THREATENED, THEY'RE GONE. THEY WERE BLASTED INTO rubble in 2001 by Taliban forces bent on destroying what they considered religious idols. Except for a few broken pieces of stone, all that remains of the two giant statues carved into a sandstone cliff overlooking the Silk Road—an ancient trade route that linked Asia and Europe—are the two shallow caves where they once stood.

If the Taliban had been trying to outrage world opinion, they couldn't have done it better. In March 2001, Taliban soldiers willfully blew up two monumental statues of standing Buddhas in Afghanistan's Bamyan valley. Tanks, cannons, rockets—they turned the whole artillery loose on these silent ancient figures, rooted in the face of a sandstone cliff. No one could mistake it for an accident of war.

As fundamentalist Wasabi Muslims, of course, the soldiers claimed they were only following Muslim practice, which forbids worshipping idols. In reality, the destruction may have had more to do with the fact that this oasis city of Bamiyan served as a base of Taliban opponents. Since taking over the city, the Taliban had been shelling the faces of the Buddhas for at least 4 years before they finally smashed them.

Dating from the 3rd and 5th centuries A.D., these magnificent figures were carved right out of the cliff face, though details were then modeled onto the sandstone in an adobelike mixture of mud and straw. Originally they were then coated with stucco, painted in bright colors (long since worn away) and bedecked with jewels (also long gone). By all accounts they were dramatic indeed, the world's tallest standing Buddhas. The older one was 36m (120 ft.) high, the later one a gigantic 53m (175 ft.) tall. Their arms, apparently sheathed in copper, reached outward; their expressive faces were great wooden masks, possibly also sheathed in copper.

Interestingly enough, the Buddhas wore Greek togas, a cultural touch that Alexander the Great had brought with him into India, living proof of the interchange between cultures in the ancient world. Set at a stopping place along the Silk Road, the two statues became a pilgrimage site for monks and merchants, and the cliffs around them were pocked with austere little caves where Buddhist monks lived. While Buddhist religion doesn't consider statues themselves as holy, they were cherished by Bamiyan residents—most of whom are now Muslims themselves—as cultural relics.

Nowadays, all we have left of the Buddhas are photographs, and a pair of yawning silhouettes gouged deeply into the pale hewn cliff face. An international effort to rebuild them is underway—the local residents saved as many pieces as possible, to be incorporated into the reconstruction—but given the political instability in Afghanistan, it may be some time before reconstruction begins, if ever. And no matter how faithful the copies of those great figures might be, they still won't be the originals.

✈ Kabul

🚌 It is not advisable to travel to Afghanistan at the present time.

# The Great Wall
## *A Great Fall for the Great Wall?*
### China

FIERCE SANDSTORMS SWIRL OUT OF THE ARID LANDSCAPE, SCOURING, CRACKING, AND ERODING some sections of the Great Wall of China, reducing them to mounds of dirt. Tourism, neglect, and willful destruction by developers have also taken its toll.

They don't call it the Great Wall of China for nothing—it stands 6m (20 ft.) wide at the base and between 6 and 9m (20–30 ft.) high, wide enough for five horses to ride abreast along its ramparts. It used to cover a distance of some 6,200km (3,800 miles) long when you connected all the fragments—but nowadays, perhaps only 2,500km (1,500 miles) still stands.

The Great Wall of China.

The part most tourists visit—the part familiar to all of us from TV and tourist posters—is clearly medieval, reconstructed of stout stone and brick during the Ming dynasty (1368–1644). However, the Great Wall really begins east of Beijing at Shānhâiguān, on the coast of the Bó Hâi Sea, and runs west all the way to the Gobi Desert. That's a lot of wall, and the older sections are built not of stone but of rammed earth—which is crumbling at a terrible rate. Years of destructive agricultural practices have turned the region surrounding the wall in remote Gansu province into an arid desert, where sandstorms brutally whip its packed-earth surface, seriously eroding a 40km (25-mile) stretch. Vandalism and pilfering have been epidemic for years; in Shaanxi province in 2003, parts of the wall were even dismantled to get materials for building a road.

Of course, no emperor ever purposely set out to build a Great Wall—it evolved more gradually, over the years. Back in the Warring States Period (453–221 B.C.), rival kingdoms built defensive walls against their enemies, and subsequent emperors connected the various bits, adding more as necessary to keep out Huns and Mongols and other invaders. The most developed section is at **Bādálîng,** only 70km (43 miles) northwest of Beijing, where you'll find a museum, theater, restaurants, souvenir stands, even a cable car. Restoration has left the pale gray stones of its high slotted battlements *(duo kou)* looking suspiciously crisp and new; tourists huddle on its stout stone watchtowers every 70m (230 ft.) and snap photos of themselves with the wall visibly zigzagging up the green mountains behind them. Even closer to Beijing is the recently restored section at **Jūyōngguân,** 55km (34 miles) northwest of the city.

To see a more authentic patch of wall without going all the way out to the remote provinces, visit **Jīnshānlîng (𝄃 010/8402-4647).** The hike along the wall from here to the Miyún Reservoir is roughly 10km (6 miles) and takes 3 to 4 hours. As the number of fellow hikers begins to dwindle and you reach authentically crumbling parts of the wall, at last you begin to sense what the Great Wall really was all about.

---

ⓘ **The Great Wall of China** (www. greatwall-of-china.com.cn)

✈ Capital Airport, Beijing

🛏 $$$ **Grand Hyatt,** Dōng Chāng'ān Jiē 1, Dōngchéng District (✆ **86/10/8518-1234;** http://beijing.grand.hyatt.com). $$ **Lusōng Yuán Bīnguan,** Banchang Hútòng 22, Dōngchéng District (✆ **86/10/6404-0436;** www.the-silk-road.com).

## Crumbling Classics 329

# Chichén Itzá
## *Marvel of the Ancient Mayan*
### Yucatan, Mexico

AT CHICHÉN ITZÁ, THE CORROSIVE CHEMICALS IN ACID RAIN ARE GRADUALLY DESTROYING THE Mayan art and monuments for which the site is internationally famous. Acid rain—sulfuric acid and nitric acid particles and debris—damages stone and metal as well as plant life.

Chichén Itzá.

As Mexico's most popular Mayan ruin, Chichén Itzá (Chee-chen Eet'-zah) gets more than its share of tour groups, and being named one of the Seven Wonders of the Modern World in 2007 will no doubt accelerate matters. But while hordes of visitors may spoil the charm of this immense ruined 9th-century city, the real threat comes from the sky—in the form of acid rain. With so much heavy industry around the Gulf of Mexico, the hot, humid Yucatan peninsula is particularly prone to polluted rainfall. Given the climate and the softness of local building materials, these ancient ruins are suffering.

Actually, it's not the entire Chichén Itzá site that was named to the Seven Wonders list, but one magnificent building: **El Caracol (The Observatory),** a grand white stepped pyramid where astronomers peered through slits in a circular tower to chart the approach of the all-important equinoxes and summer solstice. Even its design reflects the Mayans' celestial obsessions: Four stairways leading up to the central platform each have 91 steps, making a total of 364; add the central platform and you've got 365, equal to the days of the solar year. On either side of each stairway are 9 terraces, equaling 18 on each pyramid face, the same as the number of months in the Mayan calendar. The pyramid is precisely aligned to cast a moving shadow—said to be the spirit of the feathered serpent—on its northern stairway at sunset on the spring and fall equinox, an awesome twice-a-year event to witness.

One of the things that makes Chichén so memorable is the artwork chronicling so many aspects of Mayan culture—and this is where acid rain is wreaking the most damage. In the **Juego de Pelota,** Chichén's main ball court, the black mold is quickly obscuring scenes carved on both walls of figures playing a jai-alai–like game in heavy protective padding—spot the kneeling headless player, blood spurting from his neck, while another player calmly holds his head (legend has it that losing players paid with their lives). In the **Temple of Jaguars,** a flaking mural chronicles a battle in a Mayan village. In the **Temple of the Skulls,** where sacrificial victims' heads were displayed on poles, are pictures of eagles tearing hearts from human victims, carved into the leaching stone; the **Platform of the Eagles'** carved reliefs show eagles and jaguars clutching human hearts in their talons and claws. Most impressive of all is the **Temple of the Warriors,** named for the carvings of warriors marching along its walls; a figure of the god Chaac-Mool sits at the top of the temple, surrounded by columns carved to look like enormous feathered serpents—more like molting feathered serpents, these days.

ⓘ **Chichén Itzá,** near Pisté (www.maya yucatan.com)

✈ Merida

🛏 **$$ Hotel Mayaland,** Zona Arqueológica (✆ **800/235-4079** or 52/985/851-0127; www.mayaland.com). $$ **Villas Arqueológicas Chichén Itzá,** Zona Arqueológica (✆ **800/258-2633** or 52/985/851-0034).

**330** Crumbling Classics

# Machu Picchu
## *Lost City of the Incas*
### Near Aguas Caliente, Peru

HALF A MILLION PEOPLE COME TO MACHU PICCHU EVERY YEAR, DOING SERIOUS DAMAGE TO the unmortared stone buildings, weakening the ground that supports them, and increasing the risk of landslides.

South America's most popular tourist sight, Machu Picchu gets 500,000 visitors a year, all funneling in by the same few routes. Individual travelers no longer can approach the traditional way, on the Inca Trail, a 4-day, 43km (27-mile) hike from Qorihuayrachina (there's also a 2-day version from Wiñay Wayna; both routes are still open to guided tours). It's clear that the old Inca citadel is beginning to reach maximum capacity—yet in 2007 a new bridge was opened 16km (10 miles) away to improve bus access, an alternative to the excursion trains from Cusco, and the idea of installing a cable car to bring more tourists up the mountain still floats around.

How different this is from the 16th century, when Spanish conquistadors hunted in vain for Machu Picchu, rumored to be full of Inca gold. No one else could find it either; abandoned by its own citizens, Machu Picchu lay hidden 2,450m (8,000 ft.) high among the clouds in the Andes, swallowed by jungle for 4 centuries. Scholars can't agree whether this 15th-century city was mainly a fortress, a temple complex, a market town, or an astronomical observatory. What they could tell, however, was how skillfully its stonemasons fitted its unmortared walls together. Lately, though, those stones have begun to show telltale gaps.

Some geologists predict that with so much tourist traffic, a major landslide is due at Machu Picchu, sending the whole glorious city tumbling down into the Urubamba River. There have already been smaller slides downhill, apparently aggravated by tour buses rumbling up the steep highway; fault lines have been spotted in the granite shelf upon which Machu Picchu was built. Uncontrolled development in the base town of Aguas Calientes is also polluting the cloud-forest ecosystem that sets off Machu Picchu like a jewel.

The Incans sought to build in harmony with nature, as you can appreciate from the breathtaking panorama by **Funerary Rock,** just inside the entrance: Steep terraces, gardens, granite and limestone temples, staircases, and aqueducts all are integrated gracefully into hillsides, and forms of buildings seem to echo the very shape of the mountains. Celestial observations were important to the Incas, too; at the famous **Temple of the Sun,** windows are perfectly aligned to catch the sun's rays at the winter solstice (in June down here) and focus them on the stone at the center of the temple. The baffling **Inntihuatana,** or "hitching post of the sun," is a ritualistic carved rock that seems to have functioned as some sort of sundial or calendar. The religious role Machu Picchu played is evident, especially around the Sacred Plaza, with its two masterfully decorated temples; across a smooth green central lawn lies the residential section, which is also fascinating to explore.

Stricter supervision of visitors is in the offing, which may include timed-entry tickets and a cap on how many can enter each day. But will that be enough?

---

 Cusco

🛏 $$$ **Machu Pichu Sanctuary Lodge,** next to the ruins (✆ **51/84/246-419;** www.orient-express.com). $ **Hostal Machupicchu,** Av. Imperio de Los Incas, Aguas Calientes (✆ **51/84/211-065**).

**TOUR Andean Life** (✆ **51/84/249-410;** www.andeanlife.com). **Big Foot Tours** (✆ **51/84/238-568;** www.bigfootcusco.com). **Explorandes** (✆ **51/84/244-308;** www.explorandes.com).

**Crumbling Classics** 331

# Chan Chan Archaeological Zone
## *Urban Planning, Chimu-Style*
### Moche Valley, Peru

ONGOING EROSION THREATENS CHAN CHAN'S ADOBE RUINS, ESPECIALLY DURING YEARS WHEN El Niño weather patterns cause severe flooding and heavy rainfall along the Peruvian coast. Global climate change, which is expected to intensify the cycle of drought, rain, and flood, will only accelerate the damage.

Excessive tourist traffic? That's the least of Chan Chan's problems. This enormous pre-Incan city in northern Peru is still off the beaten track, and likely to remain so. It's a pity that half the tourists who presently throng Machu Picchu couldn't be diverted to this crumbling adobe metropolis, one of the most important archaeological sites in Peru—and one of the most endangered.

There are nine walled palace complexes here, each with its own tombs and temples and throne rooms and reservoirs, but their riches were ransacked long ago by the Spaniards and subsequent *huaqueros* (grave robbers, or treasure hunters). Excavation began at Chan Chan in the mid-1960s, and the site is still being plundered—on top of that, now that the fragile adobe has been exposed, it's eroding at a fearsome rate.

Until defeated by the Incas in 1470, the capital of the once-vast Chimú Empire was the largest settlement in pre-Columbian America. Begun around 1300, it reached all the way from Huanchaco port to Campana Mountain, an area covering more than 25 sq. km (9¾ sq. miles) of desert floor, which unfortunately means you may need a taxi to travel between the four main excavated areas (taking a taxi is also a good idea for avoiding the muggers who occasionally lurk around the quiet ruins). Once you get the hang of its urban layout, you'll see how architecture defined social class in this highly stratified society. The principal complex to visit is the Tschudi Palace, which has been partially restored. Note the aquatic-theme friezes in its ceremonial courtyard and the walls of the Sanctuary, which are textured like fishing nets. (The abundance of ocean motifs here is not surprising, considering how close the residents were to the Pacific Ocean.)

The **Museo de Sitio de Chan Chan,** along the road back toward Trujillo, displays ceramics excavated from Chan Chan and explains the layout of the city and its history. Two smaller pyramid temples, Huaca Esmeralda and Huaca Arco Iris, much closer to Trujillo, are also well worth visiting. **Huaca Arco Iris (Rainbow Temple,** also called **Huaca El Dragón**) has some dazzling rainbow-shaped friezes and bas-reliefs with snake, lizard, and dragon motifs. At **Huaca Esmeralda** you can see some friezes that have not yet been restored, an interesting contrast to the crisply restored ones elsewhere.

---

ⓘ **Museo de Sitio de Chan Chan,** Jr. Independencia cuadra 5, Trujillo (✆ **51/44/ 807210**)

✈ Trujillo

🛏 $$$ **Hotel Libertado Trujillo,** Jr. Independencia 48 (✆ **51/44/232-741** or 51/1/442-995 for reservations; www. libertador.com.pe). $ **La Casa Suiza,** Los Pinos 451 (✆ **51/044/461-285;** www. huanchaco.net/casasuiza).

# Tikal

## *Temples of the Jaguar Clan*

### El Peten, Guatemala

THE MAYAN PYRAMIDS AND OTHER STRUCTURES AT TIKAL ARE MADE OF SOFT LIMESTONE, which is particularly vulnerable to erosion by wind, rain, and the relentless humidity of the surrounding jungle. Although Tikal awes many of its visitors, some can't seem to resist scrawling graffiti on the exposed walls or breaking off pieces of stone to carry home as souvenirs.

One of the many pyramids of Tikal.

Nestled in lush subtropical jungle, where parrots and toucans and monkeys chatter in the canopy overhead, the Mayan ruins of Tikal are the ace in Guatemala's tourist deck. Once ruled by a dynasty known as the Jaguar Clan lords, this immense temple complex is a fascinating look into the heart of an ancient culture.

Perhaps Guatemala has been too eager to exploit Tikal's popularity, however: Tourist masses are beginning to deteriorate these pre-Hispanic monuments, already eroded by exposure to the humid rainforest climate. With very few guards to monitor them, vandalism and graffiti are common. Day-trippers leave litter around the site, which has attracted vultures, and formerly wild animals are becoming dependent on being fed by tourists.

Tikal is a huge site, covering 10 sq. km (6 sq. miles), although only about 5% of the ruins have been excavated so far. It was once the ceremonial heart of a city of 100,000 people, who gathered on its plazas for everything from religious rites (often including human sacrifices) to ball games (where the losers sometimes became human sacrifices). The chief sights are half a dozen rectangular pyramids of gray limestone; notice how precisely cut and mortared the stones are, even though the Mayans had no iron tools. These pyramids go by intriguing names like the Temple of the Masks, the Temple of the Jaguar Priest, and the Temple of the Double-Headed Serpent, which at 63m (212 ft.) was the tallest building in North America until the late 1800s—it could be called the first skyscraper. It's quite a climb to its top plateau, but as you look out over the rainforest, try to imagine the ancient city as it was during Tikal's heyday, from about 600 B.C. to A.D. 900.

For the Mayans, pyramid building was an act of devotion, to exalt their god/kings by setting them on man-made mountains. The exteriors are huge, with broad, steep ceremonial stairways leading solemnly to their peaks, but inside are only small chambers for ceremonial purposes. At public events, kings and nobles were seated grandly atop the pyramids; the acoustics are so perfect that you can speak at a normal volume from Temple I and be heard clearly on Temple II, all the way across the Grand Plaza.

Hundreds of standing stones dotting the grounds minutely record historic events and long-dead kings, with either carved pictures or glyph symbols. Jaguars do still prowl the surrounding jungle, though they're too wary to let you spot them. Who knows? Maybe the ghosts of the ancient Mayan kings aren't so far away.

ⓘ **Tikal Parque Nacional,** near Flores, Guatemala

✈ Flores

🛏 $$$ **Jungle Lodge,** Tikal National Park (no phone; www.enjoyguatemala. com). $$ **Jaguar Inn,** Tikal National Park (ⓒ **502/926-0002;** www.jaguartikal.com).

333

# Naranjo
## *Tikal's Unlucky Rival*
### El Peten, Guatemala

OVER THE YEARS, NARANJO HAS SUFFERED DAMAGED BY EROSION, FOREST FIRES, CIVIL WAR, and a steady parade of looters, who have stolen many of its most valuable artifacts and severely damaged the ancient site in the process. Today, along with recurring risk of development, continued looting still threatens this former Mayan city.

In the thick rainforests of Guatemala's Peten province, any number of archaeological treasures are hidden. Tikal is by far the best known, and best developed; in stark contrast stands nearby Naranjo, once Tikal's chief Mayan rival and now a mysterious pile of stones collapsing in the rainforest.

Why isn't Naranjo better known? Well, if anything could go wrong at the Naranjo site, it did. Even though it's situated within the tropical jungle of the Maya Biosphere Reserve, Naranjo has suffered from deforestation, forest fires, erosion, and encroaching human settlements, damaging the foundations of its plazas and pyramids and tombs. Highway construction projects are frequently proposed that would slice right across the reserve—bringing more visitors to Naranjo, but also damaging the ecosystem. But the biggest problem has always been looting, ever since the site was discovered a century ago. Looters have pilfered thousands of valuable artifacts, meanwhile damaging the buildings that remain. By now, some 150 looter's trenches and tunnels have gutted almost every building in Naranjo's urban core.

Capital of the Mayan kingdom of Saal, Naranjo was a power to reckon with from A.D. 546 until its mysterious decline in the mid–9th century. The central part of the site, which covers a square kilometer (¹/₃ sq. mile), has more than 112 structures, organized in six acropolises, as well as two palace compounds and two ball courts, their foundations cleared away from the creeping jungle vegetation. Perhaps most distinctive are the many stelae around the site, upright columns of basalt stone with carved inscriptions chronicling Naranjo's history in detail. Even if you can't decipher those dense inscriptions, they're still powerful evidence of these people's pride in their culture.

Many classic pieces of sculpture and polychromed ceramics came from Naranjo—in fact, some of the finest Mayan relics ever were removed from the tombs here, now found in collections around the world rather than at the site itself. For years, international antiquities collectors actually approved of removing art from Naranjo, where damage was almost certain, especially during Guatemala's civil war in the 1960s and 1970s. Since the late 1990s, archaeologists working at Naranjo have repeatedly been driven off by armed and dangerous looters, many of them "retired" guerrilla fighters. The scientists are racing against time to record what is left.

With Guatemala striving to protect its archaeological heritage, Naranjo was incorporated into the Yaxhá National Park in 2004, which hopefully can provide a little more protection—if it's not too late. In 2007, the American TV series *Survivor* was filmed in this park, giving Guatemala's Mayan ruins a big shot of media exposure. Maybe international attention will finally expose the shame of what's happened to Naranjo.

ⓘ **Naranjo,** Route El Caobo, Yaxhá Nakún-Naranjo National Park

✈ Flores

🛏 $$$ **Jungle Lodge,** Tikal National Park (no phone; www.enjoyguatemala. com). $ **El Sombrero Eco Campground,** Yaxha NaKun Naranjo National Park (✆ **502/7783-3923;** www.ecosombrero. com).

# 6 City & Town

*New Orleans.*

# New Orleans
## *The Uncertain Road Back from Disaster*
### Louisiana

IN AUGUST 2005, HURRICANE KATRINA NEARLY WIPED THE CITY OF NEW ORLEANS OFF THE FACE of the earth—a sobering reminder of just how fragile our bubble of civilization can be. Though some pockets have revived, this national treasure is still in critical condition. More than ever, New Orleans depends on tourism revenues to rebuild hospitals, schools, and residential neighborhoods.

The news footage shocked the world—an American city drowning, all power blacked out, bodies floating face down in eddying floodwaters, highways jammed with refugees.

New Orleans has always been a true original among American cities, a quirky town where people dance with parasols at funerals; believe in voodoo and vampires; eat exotic foods like beignets, po-boys, and gator-on-a-stick; and throw plastic beads off of Mardi Gras floats. And in some respects, the Katrina disaster was also a special case—a man-made tragedy more than a natural one. Decades of misguided engineering destroyed the delta's natural wetland drainage system in favor of shoddy, crumbling levees; on top of that came the one-two punch of inadequate federal disaster aid and corrupt, inefficient local government. But as our seas rise, we may see more Katrina-style disasters—who knows what other city may be saved by the lessons we learn from New Orleans today?

The greatest devastation was wrought on the city's poorest neighborhoods. One of the few areas originally built above river level was its prime tourist sector, the French Quarter, a Spanish-flavored fantasy of wrought-iron balconies and flower-filled courtyards and mysterious louvered windows. Major attractions that have reopened include the Aquarium of the Americas, 1 Canal St. (© **504/581-4629**);

the touristy-but-fun Historic Voodoo Museum, 724 Dumaine St.; the Old U.S. Mint, 400 Esplanade Ave., now a museum of New Orleans jazz and Mardi Gras; and the charming open-air French Market, Decatur Street, from Jackson Square to Esplanade Avenue. You can also visit the art galleries of the Warehouse District or the antebellum mansions of the Garden District; ride the St. Charles Street streetcar to the Audubon Zoo, 6500 Magazine St. (© **504/581-4629**); or tour the city's atmospheric cemeteries, where the above-ground graves prove that New Orleans always suspected a flood was imminent.

New Orleans is also one of the few American cities with an indigenous cuisine, a spicy, alluring mix of Spanish and French and Acadian influences. The restaurant industry has fought valiantly to recover, with landmarks like Commander's Palace, 1403 Washington Ave. (© 504/899-8221); Antoine's, 713 St. Louis St. (© 504/581-4422); Galatoire's, 209 Bourbon St. (© 504/525-2021); K-Paul's, 416 Chartres St. (© 504/524-7394); and Emeril's, 800 Tchoupitoulas St. (© 504/528-9393), all reopened. And speaking of indigenous, there's the city's signature jazz—the return of the late-spring New Orleans JazzFest (www.nojazzfest.com) was heralded as eagerly as the first post-Katrina Mardi Gras, another milestone on New Orleans's rocky road to recovery.

(i) (C) **800/672-6124** or 504/566-5011; www.neworleanscvb.com

✈ Louis Armstrong New Orleans International

🛏 $$$ **Omni Royal Orleans,** 621 St. Louis St. ((C) **800/THE-OMNI** [843-6664] or 504/529-5333; www.omniroyalorleans.com). $$ **Hotel Monteleone** ((C) **800/535-9595** or 504/523-3341; www.hotelmonteleone.com).

**335** Cityscapes in Peril

# Downtown Detroit
## *The Derelict Heart of Motor City*
### Detroit, Michigan

PLACED ON THE NATIONAL TRUST'S 11 MOST ENDANGERED PLACES LIST IN 2005, THE DOWNTOWN hub of Detroit—the eighth-largest metropolitan area in the United States and home to some stunning, iconic architecture—is still fighting for its life.

While many American cities reinvigorated their downtown area at the end of the 20th century, in Detroit the problems seemed insurmountable. Plagued with racial tension since 1967 riots, Detroit experienced not only "white flight" to the suburbs, but middle-class black flight as well. The swift decline of the American motor industry crippled the city's long-time economic base. What had once been a jewel of a downtown, graced with classic ornamented skyscrapers and classy hotels, became a mere shell, with hundreds of architectural gems standing derelict.

Detroit's much-heralded rebirth is fraught with controversy. The mirrored towers of the Renaissance Center, built as General Motors headquarters in the 1970s, spearheaded some new construction, especially along the Detroit River riverfront. An elevated PeopleMover train was installed to loop around downtown, and recently state-of-the-art new stadiums were built for the resurging Detroit Tigers baseball team and the Lions football team. Farther out from the downtown core, the Cultural Center was expanded with a new science museum and museum of African American History (an appropriate institution for a city that's now 80% black). In 1999, three big casinos were opened: the MGM Grand at U.S. 10 and

Bagley Avenue, the MotorCity on Grand River Avenue, and the Greektown Casino on Lafayette.

But preservationists argue that the city should restore its historic buildings rather than raze them for new construction. There are some promising signs—the long-awaited renovation of the Book Cadillac, once the city's premier hotel; the restoration of the Wayne County Building, with its iconic clock tower over downtown; the reopening of several theaters in the arts district around Grand Circus Park (the Music Hall Theater on Madison Ave., the Fox Theater on Woodward Ave.). Classic skyscrapers like the Penobscot Building and the Guardian Building lure new tenants with their historic beauty. When the baseball stadium was being built, two historic buildings, the Gem Theater and the Century Club, were moved and restored rather than being razed.

Yet downtown landmarks such as Hudson's department store and the Madison Lenox and Statler hotels were recently demolished; the city knocked down several just to "clean house" before hosting Super Bowl XL in 2005. Other icons like the Michigan Central railroad station, the National Theater, the Fine Arts Building, the Wurlitzer Building, the Lafayette Building, and the old

**319**

Tiger Stadium stand empty, some of them with trees sprouting out of their roofs. The exquisitely ornate Michigan Theater was converted, grotesquely, to a parking lot. The empty United Artists Building skyscraper was colonized by graffiti artists who painted colorful designs on hundreds of windows. Several proposed rehabs, many of them for loft conversions, fell through. Vacant lots of rubble crater downtown, creating an urban prairie of desolation.

The glory that was mid-century Detroit will never be completely restored; the question is how many vestiges can yet be preserved. It's a case study of decay, loss, and, one hopes, reinvention.

---

ⓘ **Preservation Wayne** (✆**313/577-3559;** www.preservationwayne.org)

✈ Detroit Metropolitan Airport

🛏 $$$ **Detroit Marriott at the Renaissance Center,** 400 Renaissance Center (✆ **888/228-9290** or 313/568-8000; www. marriott.com). $$ **The Inn on Ferry Street,** 84 E. Ferry St. (✆ **313/871-6000;** www. theinnonferrystreet.com).

---

**Cityscapes in Peril** **336**

# Mexico City
## *On Shaky Ground*
### Mexico

IN THE AFTERMATH OF THE DEVASTATING EARTHQUAKE OF 1985, INTERNATIONAL ATTENTION WAS drawn to restoring the city's 680-block historic district, with some of the finest colonial architecture in the Western Hemisphere. However, the earthquake drew attention to deeper, and more intractable, problems—the city's seismic instability and its location on a depleted aquifer that's sunk at least 10m (33 ft.) in the past century.

In hindsight, the 8.1 earthquake that hit Mexico City on September 19, 1985, was a turning point. Thousands were left homeless, water mains burst, disease ran rampant; in the end, some 10,000 were dead and an estimated $5 billion of property was damaged.

As renovations ensued, the community became aware of the treasures in their midst. For example, although the Hotel Prado was destroyed, Diego Rivera's famous mural *Dream of a Sunday Afternoon in Alameda Park* was saved and a new museum built for it on Plaza de la Solidaridad. The remnants of the Rule Building (a neoclassical early-20th-century movie palace shattered in the earthquake) and the former site of the cloister of San Francisco are being converted into a state-of-the-art visitor center.

While tourist activity had shifted over the years out to neighborhoods like Chapultepec Park, Zona Rosa, and Xochimilco with its canals and Floating Gardens, a new emphasis was placed on the Centro Histórico.

Given the nature of Mexican politics, the government has been slow to address two perennial Mexico City problems—its reputation for violent street crime (including abductions) and the brown mantle of smog that hangs over the city. Mexico City sits in a bowl, surrounded by a ring of mountains that trap the belching output of three million cars and 35,000 industrial sites. Recent public safety measures seem to have reduced crime, and measures like lead-free fuels and tougher emission controls have lowered ozone levels—but visitors still need to be wary.

Despite structural repairs, two of the Centro Histórico's architectural gems, the glorious Art Nouveau/Art Deco **Palacio de Bellas Artes** (Calle López Peralta) and Latin America's largest church, the baroque 17th-century **Catedral Metropolitana** (on the *zocalo*, or central plaza), are noticeably sinking into the soft bottom of what was once Lake Texcoco. When the Spanish conquistadors built their capital, they based it on the ruins of the Aztec capital Tenochtitlan—the 17th-century **Palacio Nacional** (on the zocalo) is set atop the former palace of Moctezuma II, and the ruins of five Aztec temples have been unearthed in the past couple of decades (check out the **Museo del Templo Mayor** on the zocalo). The foundations of this great crowded metropolis are anything but stable.

Whether the government will invest what's needed to shore up the buildings—and address the aquifer issue—is still in doubt. Luckily, population growth seems to have slowed; perhaps the pollution, crime, and overcrowding can now be addressed. The historic center is looking better these days, but it's a long climb back.

---

ⓘ **The Mexico File** (📞 52/55/5592-2665; www.mexicofile.com)

✈ Benito Juárez International Airport

🛏 $$ **Best Western Hotel Majestic,** Av. Madero 73 (📞 **52/55/5521-8600;** www. majestic.com.mx). $ **Hotel Catedral,** Calle Donceles 95 (📞 **52/55/5521-6183;** www. hotelcatedral.com).

---

**337** Cityscapes in Peril

# Venice
## *The Lagoon's Sinking Jewel*
Italy

SCIENTISTS ESTIMATE THAT THIS WORLD TREASURE IS SINKING ABOUT 6.4CM (2½ IN.) PER decade. Flooding is the most urgent problem. A plan to hold back the rising Adriatic with a system of mobile underwater barriers has met with controversy, and at any rate won't be completed until at least 2011.

Set on 118 separate islands, dredged out of a marshy lagoon and shored up on wooden pylons, Venice floats upon the Adriatic Sea like a mirage. Amsterdam and Bruges and a few other European cities may have a network of canals draining their cityscape, but in Venice the canals are the cityscape—creating land to go with it was an engineering triumph over nature.

Nature, however, has a way of striking back. In the first decade of the 20th century, the city's central piazza, St. Mark's Square, flooded less than 10 times a year, but by the 1980s it generally was underwater 40 times

a year. In recent years, the problem has grown even more acute, with as many as 40 floods between September and March alone.

Unlike other canal cities, Venice has no streets at all, only canals (more than 150 of them) and paved walkways. Motor launches and anachronistic black gondolas are the way to get around town—that and walking, which usually means getting lost in a maze of narrow stone lanes and high-arched bridges. Perplexing as it is, that layout was a matter of necessity—buildings were erected wherever land seemed solid

One of Venice's canals.

enough, while winding channels between the islands became the major canals, like the sinuous Grand Canal, or the unbridged (cross it by ferry) Giudecca channel.

Most tourists simply mill around the colonnaded Piazza San Marco—arguably the loveliest public space in the world— and file through the guidebook must-sees: St. Mark's Basilica, a glorious Byzantine church with glittering gold mosaics; the iconic Campanile bell-tower; and next to it the exotic Doge's Palace, with its Arabian Nights facade. But getting beyond San Marco is essential to understand Venice. Cruise the Grand Canal, lined with Venetian Gothic *pallazzi;* stroll around the city, popping into obscure churches and browsing street markets. Hop on a vaporetto and visit the outlying islands—Murano, home of exquisite glass makers; Burano, the island of lace makers; or the Lido, Venice's local beachfront.

Every time I visit Venice, I'm struck by its unique sensory impact, all of it expressing the watery essence of the city. There's a constant murmur of water lapping against stone; the very air feels magically moist against your skin. Then there's that faint scent of decay, a blend of rotting foundations, crumbling plaster, and sediment slushing around the canal floors. Somehow it manages to be intensely evocative, even magical. It's the sheer Venice-ness of Venice—and it can never be reproduced.

ⓘ ℂ **39/41/5298711;** www.savevenice. org or www.veniceinperil.org

✈ Venice's Aeroporto Marco Polo

🛏 $$$ **Locanda Ai Santi Apostoli,** Strada Nuova, Cannaregio (ℂ **39/41/ 5212612;** www.locandasantiapostoli.com). $$ **Pensione Accademia**, Fondamenta Bollani, Dorsoduro (ℂ **39/41/5237846;** www.pensioneaccademia.it).

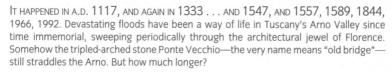

# Florence
## *Bridging the Centuries*
### Italy

IT HAPPENED IN A.D. 1117, AND AGAIN IN 1333 . . . AND 1547, AND 1557, 1589, 1844, 1966, 1992. Devastating floods have been a way of life in Tuscany's Arno Valley since time immemorial, sweeping periodically through the architectural jewel of Florence. Somehow the tripled-arched stone Ponte Vecchio—the very name means "old bridge"— still straddles the Arno. But how much longer?

Standing at the arched opening halfway over, you can gaze out at this beautiful Italian city and imagine all the history this bridge has seen. The original Roman-era wooden bridge, straddling the Arno at a vital crossing point, was washed away in 1117 and replaced in 1220 by a more durable stone version, lined with shops in the medieval custom. The Ponte Vecchio became the heart of 13th-century Florence; the crenellated stone **Palazzo Vecchio** was built by its north end (today housing the famous **Uffizi**

**Gallery**), and Florence's cathedral, the **Duomo,** was erected near by, distinctively striped in white, green, and pink marble and topped by a huge red-tiled dome. When the 1333 flood wiped out that bridge, a new and improved version was built; what we see today is this 1345 version.

In 1540, with the Renaissance in high gear—Michelangelo had sculpted his *David,* Leonardo had painted the *Mona Lisa*—the second Cosimo de Medici moved into the Palazzo Vecchio and decided to

Ponte Vecchio.

spiff up the bridge connecting his new digs with the Medicis' **Pitti Palace** across the Arno; he hired Giorgio Vasari to add a private bypass, a windowed corridor over the shops (today it's the Uffizi's portrait gallery annex). Half a century later, Ferdinand de Medici, still not satisfied, banned the butchers who'd traditionally conducted business from the Ponte Vecchio, replacing them with ritzy goldsmiths and jewelers. (Crossing the bridge, look for a bust of Benvenuto Cellini, the most famous goldsmith ever.) It remains a jewelry district to this day; in the 1966 deluge, a fortune in gems and precious metals washed downriver.

A third level of shops was gradually tacked on, which coincidentally made the bridge stronger, able to withstand repeated floods. A new threat arose, however, in 1944, when the Nazis, beating a desperate retreat through Italy, planted explosives to blow up Florence's bridges and cut off their Allied pursuers. At the 11th hour, some art lover in command (allegedly Hitler himself) decreed that the Ponte Vecchio be spared.

After the 1966 flood, the restored Ponte Vecchio was closed to vehicular traffic. River management has improved, banning the deforestation and sediment mining that contributed to the 1966 tragedy. But despite those measures, another flood in 1992 overwhelmed the banks of the Arno, caused by the same climate change conditions that have raised river levels across Europe. Can this Renaissance landmark survive? Only time will tell.

---

ⓘ ✆ **39/55/290-832;** www.firenze turismo.it

✈ Amerigo Vespucci Airport

🚆 Florence

🛏 $$$ **Grand Hotel Villa Medici,** Via il Prato 42 (✆ **39/55/2381331;** www.villa medicihotel.com). $ **Hotel Casci,** Via Cavour 13 (✆ **39/55/211686;** www.hotelcasci.com).

---

**Cityscapes in Peril** **339**

# Salzburg
## *Mozart's Hometown*
### Austria

THE SALZACH HAS ALWAYS BEEN FLOOD-PRONE, AND AS CLIMATE CHANGE, DEFORESTATION, and melting Alpine glaciers make rivers throughout Europe flood more frequently, Salzburg is increasingly at risk. What's more, its pedestrianized historic center—known as a stage-set perfect collection of 17th- and 18th-century baroque architecture—sits right on the lower-lying left bank of the Salzach.

Every August, the picturesque Austrian town of Salzburg is flooded with music lovers, paying tribute to Salzburg's most famous son, Wolfgang Amadeus Mozart. In 2002, however, tourists weren't the only thing flooding Salzburg's cobbled streets. Swollen by several days of extraordinary rainfall, the Salzach River burst its banks just south of the city. Bridges and roads were closed for hours, and 1,000 buildings were partly or totally submerged. For several tense hours, it appeared the flood would wash the old town away.

Salzburg has always been a little unusual. Though it was never a royal capital, its medieval power and prestige were based on a

Mozart's tombstone, Salzburg.

bishops weren't above spritzing a visiting dignitary in the eye to get a good laugh). Their home church, **Salzburg Cathedral,** has been praised as the finest Renaissance Italian church ever built north of the Alps.

Mozart, as it happens, couldn't wait to leave his provincial hometown and get to Vienna, but today he's Salzburg's main tourism draw. A statue of Mozart was erected in 1842 in the center of town, in a cafe-lined plaza renamed, naturally, Mozart-platz; the town's premier music hall is named the Mozarteum. Head through the narrow shop-lined streets of the historic district to the composer's birthplace, the **Mozart Geburthaus,** Getreidegasse 9, the cramped apartment where the Mozart family lived until he was 17; his boyhood violin, his concert violin, and his viola, fortepiano, and clavichord are on display. In 1773 the family moved across the river to the roomier **Mozart Wohnhaus,** Makartplatz 8, bombed in World War II but rebuilt as a Mozart museum in 1996. While Mozart's music is performed all year round, the summer Salzburg Festival is the premier event: For tickets, contact the box office at Hofstallgasse 1, A-5020 Salzburg (© **0662/ 8045;** www.salzburgfestival.at).

succession of prince-archbishops, who were urbane power brokers rather than dour monks. Compare the gloomy **Hohensalzburg Fortress,** their first stronghold on the rocky heights of the Mönchberg, to the luxuriously decorated **Residenz** down by the river where they moved later; across the river you can also see the French-style confection of **Schloss Mirabell,** built for one of the prince-archbishop's mistresses (you may recognize the splendid gardens from *The Sound of Music*). The archbishops' summer retreat at **Schloss Hellbrunn,** 20 minutes southeast of the city, is positively light-hearted, especially its elaborate gardens, full of exotic grottoes, water-powered *automata,* and so-called "water jokes" (apparently the

ⓘ **Tourismus Salzburg GmbH** (© **43/ 662/889870;** www.salzburginfo.at)

✈ Salzburg-Mozart Regional

🛏 $$ **Hotel Mozart,** Franz-Josef-Strasse 27 (© **43/662/872274;** www.hotel-mozart. at). $ **Altstadthotel Wolf-Dietrich,** Wolf-Dietrich-Strasse 7 (© **43/662/871275;** www. salzburg-hotel.at).

# Prague
## *River Rage*
### The Czech Republic

IN 2002, WITH THE CZECH REPUBLIC INUNDATED BY THE WORST RAINS SINCE 1890, THE VLTAVA River—which flows through the heart of Prague—swelled to freakish heights, its fierce brown waters churning through the sandstone arches of the landmark 14th-century Charles Bridge. Though new dikes and barriers are in place, rising rivers still threaten this historic city.

What happened to Salzburg in August 2002 was nothing compared to what happened in Prague. Several historic areas disappeared under water, including the baroque palaces of Kampa Island and the atmospheric Mala Strana neighborhood at the foot of Prague Castle. The gold-crowned Renaissance-style National Theater was nearly destroyed, and a beloved elephant and several other animals were drowned at the Prague Zoo. Fifty thousand residents were evacuated from their homes, the subway (designed, ironically, to double as a flood system) filled with water, and power was lost for days. Estimates put the damage at $3 billion.

In the much-visited Jewish quarter, Josefov, two important sites were submerged: Europe's oldest Jewish house of worship, the vaulted Gothic sanctuary of **Staronová synagoga;** and the 15th-century **Pinkas Synagogue,** an affecting memorial to the 77,297 Czech Jews killed by the Nazis. Luckily, both synagogues survived intact, and the 20,000 jumbled gray tombstones of the **Old Jewish Cemetery,** U Starého hřbitova 3A, were high enough to escape the floodwaters.

When the waters receded, there was endless muck and debris to clear away, but most landmarks survived. High embankments protected much of the narrow cobbled streets of Staré Mêsto (Old Town), which filmmakers have often used as a stand-in for turn-of-the-century London or Paris; the hilltop **Prague Castle** complex remained above the waters, too. The several locations of the **National Gallery** art

museum suffered no damage. The iconic baroque set piece of **Staromêstské námêstí (Old Town Square),** with its famous glockenspiel, was unharmed.

When the Communist regime fell in 1989—the so-called "Velvet Revolution"—beautiful Prague was one of the first eastern European cities to draw western tourists, but the transition to free-market capitalism has not been without a few rough patches. Restaurants and taxis often gouge tourists, hotel rooms are hard to come by, traffic clogs the streets, and in high season visitors shuffle shoulder to shoulder through the picturesque narrow alleys of Old Town. There are some who say that Prague has already lost the aura that made it special.

But this city of golden spires is still a magnificent, one-of-a-kind sight, and renovations necessitated by the flood have left some areas spruced up better than ever. True, the disaster revealed flaws in the city's flood-control system, many of them the legacy of shortsighted planning under Communist rule. Since 2002, new dikes and barriers have been put in place, which withstood high waters in March 2006. But with rivers everywhere rising to new heights, will that system be enough?

ⓘ **Prague Information Service** (www.pis.cz or www.prague-info.cz)

✈ Ruzynê Airport, Prague

🛏 $$$ **Hotel Pariz,** U Obecního domu 1 (✆ **420/222-195-195;** www.hotel-pariz.cz). $ **Hotel Cloister Inn,** Konviktská 14 (✆ **420/224-211-020;** www.cloister-inn.cz).

The tightly packed gravestones in Prague's Old Jewish Cemetery.

**341** Cityscapes in Peril

# St. Petersburg
## *Venice of the North*
### Russia

FLOODS HAVE CONTINUALLY THREATENED ST. PETERSBURG. ENVIRONMENTALISTS SAY THAT NEW dams to manage the flood will back up pollution in St. Petersburg's already-compromised water supply. Which would be worse—catastrophic floods, or living on a cesspool?

Unlike Moscow, St. Petersburg was built all at once, conceived whole by Peter the Great. Eager to establish a seaport for mostly landlocked Russia, he set his glittering new capital on Baltic marshes, with a network of canals for drainage. The first flood hit in August 1703, 3 months after the city was founded.

Since then, more than 300 floods have hit the city; the worst were in 1824 and 1924, but lately, with global warming, they've been getting more severe—and more frequent.

To manage the flood threat, a series of dams across the Gulf of Finland were begun in 1980, halted during the 1990s financial crisis, and resumed in 2003.

St. Petersburg didn't develop exactly as Peter planned; today it is centered on the south bank of the Neva River, but he envisioned its center being the **Peter & Paul Fortress (Petropavlovskaya Krepost)**, on Hare's Island (Zaichy Ostrov) across from the Winter Palace. The complex includes the **Peter and Paul Cathedral,** the city's tallest building from 1723 until the 20th century, which holds the tombs of all Russian czars and their families from Peter's day through the last of the Romanovs (assassinated Czar Nicholas II and his family were reburied here in 1997). Also at the fortress, the **Trubetskoi Bastion** housed such political prisoners as Fyodor Dostoyevsky, Leon Trotsky, and Vladimir Lenin's brother.

The ghosts of the czars still seem to linger at elegant **Palace Square (Dvortsovaya Ploshchad).** Standing under the Alexander Column—a 600-ton monolith topped by a cross-carrying angel, commemorating the Russian victory over Napoleon—imagine all that this asymmetrical plaza has seen, from royal coaches pulling up to the baroque **Winter Palace** on one side, to Communist solidarity marches in front of the long curved **General Staff Building.** Through the grand courtyard of the Winter Palace today, you enter the state **Hermitage Museum** (www.hermitagemuseum.org), which houses the peerless art collection of the czars. The Hermitage's extravagantly decorated salons, with their marble columns and parquet

floors and dazzling chandeliers, display an incredible catalog of Renaissance Italian art, including two rare DaVinci Madonnas, and loads of Dutch and Flemish masters; it has more French artworks than any museum outside of France.

You may also want to stroll around the formal gardens of the Summer Palace; glean literary insights at the Dostoyevsky House and Nabokov House museums; walk along Nevsky Prospect, St. Petersburg's greatest boulevard; and photograph the blindingly bright beveled domes of the Cathedral of the Saviour on the Spilled Blood, commemorating the spot where Czar Alexander II (who freed Russia's serfs in 1861) was assassinated in 1881.

ⓘ www.petersburg-russia.com

✈ Pulkovo-2 International Airport

🛏 $$$ **Corinthia Nevsky Palace,** 57 Nevsky Prospekt (✆ **7/812/380-2001;** www.corinthia.ru). $$ **Pulford Apartments,** 6 Moika Embankment (✆ **7/812/325-6277;** www.pulford.com).

Cityscapes in Peril

342

# Dubrovnik
## *The Unstrung Pearl of the Adriatic*
### Croatia

OCTOBER 1991 MAY SEEM LIKE A LONG TIME AGO, BUT REMINDERS OF THE SIEGE OF DUBROVNIK are still evident—in the unnatural orange of new terra-cotta roof tiles, in bullet holes pocking the surface of old stone facades. It took years for tourism to rebound, even after the city's infrastructure and buildings were restored.

The so-called "pearl of the Adriatic" faced a peril worse than anything since its devastating 1667 earthquake. For 10 months, Serb forces surrounded Dubrovnik, cutting off supplies and services while shelling its UNESCO-protected monuments.

Since medieval times this key Adriatic seaport has been tussled over by Venice,

Hungary, Turkey, and other powers. Rebuilt in the baroque style after the 1667 quake, its Old Town is now a pedestrianized zone of churches, palaces, squares, and monuments, nestled inside a nearly intact set of medieval walls. You can walk the entire circuit of the walls in about an hour. The Western Gate (Pile) and the Eastern Gate

(Ploce) are connected by the wide quarter-mile-long boulevard Stradun, its glossy limestone pavement worn by years of footsteps; its tiny side streets are full of atmospheric cafes and shops.

Inside both the Pile Gate and the Ploce Gate are ornamented stone Onofrio fountains, built in the 15th century so that entering visitors could wash away plague germs. Centuries later, during the 1991 siege, their ancient hydrosystems provided precious drinking water for cut-off city residents. Facing the fountain inside the Pile Gate is the Renaissance-Gothic facade of St. Saviour Church, one of the few churches to survive the 1667 earthquake. Beside it is a 14th-century Franciscan monastery, whose lovely library, cloisters, and bell tower were damaged in 1991 shelling.

Inside the Ploce Gate, the other Onofrio fountain sits in busy Luza Square, whose centerpiece is the 15th-century Orlando column, a rallying point in 1990 for Dubrovnik's freedom fighters. Also on Luza Square is the church of St. Blaise, the city's patron saint. Though it was built post-earthquake, in the early 18th century, inside is a silver-plated state of St. Blaise holding a 15th-century model of Dubrovnik as it looked before 1667. Also on the square, the 15th-century Sponza Palace arts complex has a special Memorial Room commemorating Croatian patriots who died during the 1991 to 1992 siege. Near the southern city walls, the largest church in town is the Jesuit Church of St. Ignatius of Loyola, whose long flight of baroque stairs—reminiscent of Rome's Spanish Steps—were badly damaged in the siege but have since been restored.

---

ⓘ **Dubrovnik Tourist Board** (☎ **385/20/ 323-887;** www.tzdubrovnik.hr)

✈ Dubrovnik International

🛏 $$$ **Hilton Imperial,** Marijana Blazica 2 (☎ **385/20/320-320;** www.hilton.com). $$ **Hotel Zagreb,** Setaliste Kralja Zvonimira 27 (☎ **385/20/436-146**).

Dubrovnik.

# Istanbul
## *Big Boom in the Bosphorus*
### Turkey

POLLUTION, A GROWING POPULATION, AND THE CONTINUED THREAT OF ANOTHER DEVASTATING earthquake put Istanbul at risk. Seismologists predict another earthquake before 2025. Will Istanbul be ready to cope?

Population explosion is too mild a term for what's happened in Istanbul. Ever since the 1970s, enormous numbers of Turks flooded into the capital, lured by jobs in new factories on the city's fringes; cheap new housing sprang up, much of it substandard. Between the factories and greater numbers of cars on traffic-choked roads, air pollution rapidly worsened; the water supply and sewage systems just can't keep up. (Pollution concerns probably cost Istanbul its bid for the 2008 Olympics.) It was all brought to a head in August 1999, when a major earthquake hit those crowded jerry-built suburbs, leaving 18,000 dead and many more homeless.

Istanbul has long teetered between Europe and Asia, between Islam and Christianity, between its historic past and the demands of a modern city. Those paradoxes are part of why it's so fascinating to visit, of course. A prime example is **Ayasofya,** which for almost a thousand years was the largest Christian church in the world; converted to a mosque in 1453, when Mehmet II took over the city, it became a museum in 1935 under Atatürk, at which point its dazzling frescoes and mosaics were restored, though the minarets remained. Compare it to the **Blue Mosque,** which was built as a mosque by Ahmet I in 1609; outside it's a riot of domes and minidomes and six gold minarets, while the lofty interior glows with exquisite decorative tiles, mostly in blues and greens (hence the name). Perhaps the most magnificent mosaics in the city are at **St. Savior in Chora,** where a wealth of 14th-century treasures was restored in the 1940s after many years under plaster.

Mehmet II also erected a suitable palace for 4 centuries of Ottoman rulers: **Topkapi Palace,** an exotic marvel of ceramic tiles, inlaid ivory, and ornate friezes and mosaics set at the tip of a peninsula commanding the Bosporus Strait. You can see the swords of Mehmet the Conqueror and Süleyman the Magnificent in the Imperial Armoury, as well as the loot they collected in the Treasury (the Holy Relics Section contains the first copy of the Koran). With a separate admission ticket you can tour the Harem, where up to 800 concubines lived in cramped cubicles—except for the sultan's favorites, who occupied his lavish sea-view apartments.

There are any number of other Byzantine churches and mosques to visit, but to grasp the paradox of Istanbul, roam through the **Grand Bazaar (Kapalı Çarşısı),** a labyrinth of over 2,600 shops and several individual marketplaces. The exuberant free-for-all of the bazaar—prices can be insane and haggling over merchandise is an age-old custom—could stand as a metaphor for Istanbul itself.

---

✈ Atatürk International, Istanbul

🛏 $$$ **Çirağan Palace Hotel Kempinski Istanbul,** Çirağan Cad. 84 (© **800/ 426-3135** in the U.S., 90/212/258-3377 in Istanbul; www.ciraganpalace.com). $$ **Mavi Ev (Blue House),** Dalbastı Sok. 14 (© **90/212/638-9010;** www.bluehouse. com.tr).

# Old Jerusalem
## *Sacrilege in the Holy City*
### Israel

THE BIGGEST FACE-OFF THESE DAYS IN OLD JERUSALEM MAY BE BETWEEN ARCHAEOLOGISTS, who want to preserve the city's priceless antiquities, and modern developers. How far can they go before the essential character of Jerusalem is destroyed forever?

Everybody wants a piece of Jerusalem. Not only is this "City on the Hill" a holy city to much of the world—Judaism, Islam, and Christianity all have major shrines here—it's also deeply embroiled in the Israeli-Palestinian conflict, with every new development weighed for its political implications. A major highway system sits just 9m (30 ft.) from the walls of the Old City, so that visitors have to climb a pedestrian overpass in order to enter the Jaffa Gate. Eccentric, small-scale 19th-century neighborhoods in the New City, with their quaint networks of pedestrian streets, courtyards, and Ottoman-era mansions, are being demolished and replaced with office blocks. A new wave of 30 skyscrapers is planned for the previously low-rise center of West Jerusalem.

For centuries this city has been tugged to and fro. King Solomon erected the first great Jewish temple here in 957 B.C.; Nebuchadnezzar destroyed it 4 centuries later. In 34 B.C. King Herod built the greatest religious complex in the eastern Roman Empire—which the Romans leveled in A.D. 70. (At Temple Mount's foot, a surviving fragment of Herod's wall is known as the **Wailing Wall** because for centuries Jews have crowded here to mourn the loss of their temple.) After the Muslim conquest of A.D. 638, Temple Mount was rebuilt with Islamic holy places. **El Aksa Mosque** here is the third holiest Muslim place of prayer after Mecca and Medina, and the dazzling **Dome of the Rock** protects a rock revered by Muslims as the spot where Prophet Muhammad viewed paradise. To Jews, however, it's the rock where Abraham proved his faith by nearly sacrificing his son Isaac.

As a political compromise, the walled Old City was divided into five sections: Temple Mount, the Muslim Quarter, the Jewish Quarter, the Christian Quarter, and the Armenian Quarter. But even there, factions compete: The dour sandstone **Church of the Holy Sepulchre** in the Christian quarter is a site so holy that Roman Catholics, Armenian Orthodox, Greek Orthodox, Egyptian Coptics, Ethiopians, and Syrian Orthodox all claim it. Founded by Constantine, the first Christian emperor of Rome, it enshrines what tradition claims is the tomb of Jesus Christ (it once also held the Cross that Jesus was crucified on, but the Persians stole that centuries ago).

Outside of the Old City, the **Mount of Olives** contains one of the oldest, perhaps the holiest, Jewish cemeteries in the world, as well as the spot where Jesus ascended to heaven, the spot where Jesus taught his disciples the Lord's Prayer, and the courtyard where Jesus supposedly prayed the night before his arrest, each sanctified with its own church. With a legacy this rich, no wonder everybody's fighting over Jerusalem.

✈ Jerusalem

🛏 $$$ **Jerusalem Sheraton Plaza,** 47 King George St. ((🕐 **800/325-3535** or 02/629-8666; www.sheraton.com). $$ **King Solomon Hotel,** 32 King David St. ((🕐 **02/569-5555**).

Old Jerusalem.

## Cityscapes in Peril 345

# Hong Kong
### *The Big Land Grab*
#### Hong Kong S.A.R., China

A CENTURY OF LAND RECLAMATION HAS WHITTLED HONG KONG'S ICONIC HARBOR DOWN TO MORE than half of its original size, and with more big projects on the boards, Hong Kong may have reached a tipping point.

That postcard view of Hong Kong's Victoria Harbour, bristling with skyscrapers—what glittering urban romance it promises.

This former Crown Colony once seemed a magic portal into the Far East, one with English spoken everywhere and modern creature comforts at hand. Wooden boats bobbed in the harbor beside ocean liners, crumbling tenements leaned against modern high-rises, and rickshaws trundled past gleaming Rolls-Royces. But commercial interests increasingly outweigh the charming and picturesque, and the new Chinese governors show no signs of reversing that trend. Not only is the harbor being nibbled away, the few parks and gardens around the island—its green lungs—are under pressure. Right on the waterfront, a huge new government headquarters will fill in what was once a British Royal Navy base; two other major harborfront sites are planned across the harbor in West Kowloon and where Kai Tak airport used to stand.

On this crowded urban island with its steep interior, vistas have always been a significant asset. The classic views are from the decks of the green-and-white **Star Ferry,** a 5-minute ride between Kowloon and Hong Kong Island's Central District across the ever-shrinking Victoria Harbour. On Hong Kong Island, an 8-minute ride on the **Peak tram**—the world's steepest funicular railway—takes you to the top of Victoria Peak, where there are spectacular views of the city below. The modern **Peak Tower** has a viewing terrace, but many visitors prefer to get their views from the older cliffside footpaths, where you can feel the expat British vibe of this exclusive residential enclave.

For more exotic Asian atmosphere, ride the rickety old double-decker trams around the northern end of Hong Kong Island. From your upper-deck seats, you'll see laundry hanging from second-story windows, signs swinging over the street, and markets twisting down side alleys. Jump off at Des Vouex Street and Morrison Road to browse the still-colorful shopping streets of the Western District—Hillier Street, Bonham Strand, Man Wa Lane. At Des Vouex Road and Queen Victoria Street, a zig-zagging series of escalators takes you up to the Mid-Levels of Victoria Peak; it takes 20 minutes to go up, but be prepared to walk back down.

What's happened to Hong Kong Island may be prefigured by the development of nearby Lantau Island for Hong Kong Disneyland, and the explosive growth of Macau—a former Portuguese colony 64km (40 miles) west of Hong Kong, across the pearl River estuary—into the Las Vegas of the Far East. Where will the growth end?

ⓘ **Hong Kong Tourism Board** (✆ 852/2508 1234;** www.discoverhongkong.com)

✈ Hong Kong International

🛏 $$ **BP International House,** 8 Austin Rd., Kowloon (✆ **800/223-5652** or 852/2376 1111; www.bpih.com.hk). $ **The Salisbury YMCA,** Salisbury Rd., Kowloon (✆ **800/537-8483** or 852/2268 7000; www.ymcahk.org.hk).

---

**346** Cityscapes in Peril

# Kathmandu
## *Shangri-La in Crisis*
### Nepal

TO THE MOUNTAIN TREKKERS AND HIPPIES WHO FIRST FLOCKED HERE IN THE 1960S, THIS Himalayan capital seemed like an isolated Shangri-La. But Kathmandu is now a city of around 700,000 people, with rapidly worsening pollution—diesel fumes fill the air, and the sacred Bagmati River has become a jet-black stagnant mess.

In this mountain region, earthquakes, landslides, and floods pose a continual threat; to make things worse, a decade of conflict between the government and Maoist rebels drained the resources needed to protect its wildlife and historic monuments. A peace agreement was signed in late 2006, but the truce is still precarious.

And the cultural heritage of the Kathmandu Valley is so worth saving. This

Kathmandu.

temple. But don't stop there; wander around the city's maze of narrow streets, finding smaller temples, open-air markets, and miniature shrines tucked around the bustling city, a jumbled juxtaposition of the new and the old.

The most ancient site in the valley is the 1,600-year-old Hindu shrine of Changu Narayan, devoted to Vishnu, 12km (7½ miles) east of the city; elaborate stone carving, woodwork, and silvercrafting are festooned over seemingly every surface of this temple. Set amid jungle only 5km (3 miles) east of the city, the gold-roofed temple of Pashupatinath, sacred to Lord Shiva, is one of the holiest of Hindu shrines, drawing pilgrims from all over Asia. Its stairsteps ripple down to the Bagmati River, which despite its pollution remains a revered cremation site.

In Nepal, Hinduism interwines harmoniously with Buddhism, especially at Syambhunath and Bouddhanath, two famous stupas, or circular monuments built for meditation. Tibetan monks, Brahmin priests, and Newar nuns all worship at the hilltop Syambhunath complex, 3km (2 miles) west of the city; notice the watchful eyes of all-seeing Buddha painted on all sides of the stupa. Tibetan Buddhists predominate at the monastery complex of Bouddhanath, 6km (3¾ miles) west of the city, with its immense 36m-high (118-ft.) stupa decorated with prayer wheels and 108 tiny images of Buddha, as well as another set of those watchful painted eyes.

compact mountain valley has not one but three historic towns—Patan, Bhaktapur, and Kathmandu itself, each with a beautiful, if crumbling, collection of buildings around a central square. Kathmandu city gets its modern name from the two-story wooden pagoda on Durbar Square named Kaasthamandap (or Maru Sattal), built in 1596, supposedly from the timber of a single tree, without a single nail or external support. The rest of the Durbar Square complex—the seat of the Malla dynasty who built much of the city—includes nearly 50 temples, shrines, and palaces, including the former royal Hanumandhoka Palace, Kumari Ghar (Abode of the Living Goddess), and the vermilion-walled Taleju

✈ Tribhuvan International Airport

🛏 $$$ **Dwarikas Hotel,** Battisputali, Kathmandu (© **977/1/447 3725;** www.dwarikas.com). $$$ **Hyatt Regency Kathmandu,** Taragaon, Boudha (© **977/1/449 1234;** http://kathmandu.regency.hyatt.com/hyatt/hotels/index.jsp).

# Little Italy
## *Ghosts of the Godfathers*
### New York City, New York

ONE OF NEW YORK'S MOST ICONIC ETHNIC NEIGHBORHOODS, CELEBRATED IN FILMS FROM *THE Godfather* to *Mean Streets*, has nearly vanished. Though a vestige of Little Italy is still preserved, burgeoning Chinatown threatens to engulf Mulberry Street from the south and east and trendy SoHo and "NoLIta" (short for "North of Little Italy") nip at its heels from the north and west.

From a 3-block stretch of Mulberry Street just north of Canal Street, imagine what Little Italy once was like, when it covered 17 city blocks. In the late 19th century, a wave of Italian immigrants, mostly from Sicily and Naples, moved into this tenement neighborhood, which the upwardly mobile Irish had begun to vacate. Note the red-brick tenement architecture, narrow but deep, designed to squeeze in as many small rooms as possible; their street faces are hung with a maze of iron fire escapes.

The Church of the Most Precious Blood, 109 Mulberry St., still operates the traditional Feast of St. Gennaro, which is held here with arcade lights and food stalls every September. Several stores remain on Mulberry and intersecting Grand Street: There's DiPalo's Fine Foods on the northeast corner of Mott and Grand, the Alleva Dairy cheese shop at 108 Grand St., and E. Rossi & Co. music store at 191 Grand St. At the intersection of Mulberry and Broome streets, Caffé Roma is an old-fashioned tile-floored pastry shop where you can stop for cannoli and espresso; Caffé Ferrara at 195 Grand St. is larger and brighter, though a bit less atmospheric. The Italian restaurants that line Mulberry Street thrive on tourist trade, offering traditional Italian meals at anything but bargain prices.

Above Grand Street, Mulberry gets a little quieter. You'll pass a few unmarked street-level entrances that belonged to the old Italian social clubs; at Spring Street, leafy little DeSalvio Park still retains some of the old neighborhood's feel. Just east on Spring Street, Lombardi's Pizza is the resurrection of a 1905 coal oven pizzeria.

The smaller Italian-American enclave in west Greenwich Village—near Father Demo Square, on Bleecker Street west of Sixth Avenue—seems more robust than Little Italy these days. But like the Irish before them, as younger generations of Italians improved their economic status, most of them moved out to the suburbs, especially Staten Island. Although Manhattan's Little Italy has withered, its spirit lives on at Arthur Avenue, just south of Fordham Road in the Bronx, where several thriving food stores supply Italian specialties to Italian-American suburbanites. The only thing missing is the tenements.

---

ⓘ **NYC & Company** (ⓒ **800/NYC-VISIT** [692-8474]; www.nycvisit.com)

✈ John F. Kennedy International, Newark Liberty International, LaGuardia

🛏 $$ **Washington Square Hotel,** 103 Waverly Place (ⓒ **800/222-0418** or 212/777-9515; www.washingtonsquarehotel. com). $ **Best Western Seaport Inn,** 33 Peck Slip (ⓒ **800/HOTEL-NY** [468-3569] or 212/766-6600; www.bestwestern.com).

# Baltimore's Row Houses

## *Getting the Scoop on the Stoop*

Baltimore, Maryland

BALTIMORE'S POPULATION HAD DECLINED SO SHARPLY, BY 2000 IT WAS ONLY TWO-THIRDS OF what it had been in 1950. With the city's population again rising, architectural historians hope to see many of the remaining row house neighborhoods restored.

Think Baltimore, and what do you picture? Most probably, if you've seen the movies *Tin Men, The Accidental Tourist,* or *Hairspray,* you'll immediately envision a long straight street lined with a continuous front of matching row houses. It's Baltimore's quintessential urban feature, where famed Baltimoreans from Betsy Ross and Edgar Allan Poe to critic H.L. Mencken have lived. Ever since the 1790s, the vast street grid of this working-class port city has been lined with terraces of small single houses. Wave after wave of new immigrants settled into these tightly packed house fronts, where they could ride streetcars or walk to their jobs and grab a piece of the American dream.

But in the second half of the 20th century, the American dream decamped to the suburbs—and in Baltimore, the defection was particularly severe. Though the Inner Harbor rejuvenation of the 1980s spurred some gentrification—mostly burnishing historic row houses close to the waterfront, in Federal Hill, Fells Point, and Canton—block after block of row houses stood derelict throughout the rest of this dwindling city. From the late 1990s on, the city government's solution was to send out wrecking crews and knock them down by the thousands, leaving gaping holes in already decrepit inner-city neighborhoods.

Granted, the term "row house" covers an extremely wide range of housing stock. They can be three or four stories high in some posh areas, simple two-story structures in others. The front doors may open onto small porches, petite front yards, or, more often, a low bare stoop with a railing. (A surprising number of these humble stoops, though, are made from the fine local white marble, which housewives traditionally scrubbed to a shine with Bon-Ami scouring powder.) While most houses are built of brick, in some neighborhoods each house in the row features its own stylish stone pediment or cornice to set it apart; in others, the brick has been covered with a stuccolike protective veneer called Formstone, popular in the 1950s.

Visit the Patterson Park/Highlandtown Historic District in East Baltimore to see a still-intact streetscape of middle-class row houses, where various owners added their own touches, from Formstone to picture windows to porch seating. Mount Vernon's and Bolton Hill's row houses are more upscale, with brownstone exteriors and iron fences. It's the overall profile, though, that lingers in the eye—the low, orderly, harmonious silhouette of these city blocks, and how they express the personality of Baltimore, nicknamed "City of Neighborhoods."

---

✈ Baltimore-Washington International

🛏 **$$$ Baltimore Marriott Waterfront Hotel,** 700 Aliceanna St., Inner Harbor East (© **410/385-3000;** www.baltimoremarriott waterfront.com). **$$ Brookshire Suites,** 120 E. Lombard St. (© **866/583-4162** or 410/625-1300; www.harbormagic.com).

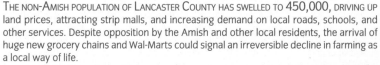

# Lancaster County
## *Sprawl Meets the Plain Folk*
### Pennsylvania

THE NON-AMISH POPULATION OF LANCASTER COUNTY HAS SWELLED TO 450,000, DRIVING UP land prices, attracting strip malls, and increasing demand on local roads, schools, and other services. Despite opposition by the Amish and other local residents, the arrival of huge new grocery chains and Wal-Marts could signal an irreversible decline in farming as a local way of life.

Sure, Lancaster County looks bucolic—all those rolling hills, winding creeks, neatly cultivated farms, and covered bridges, not to mention the presence of Amish farmers, dressed in their old-fashioned black clothes and driving buggies at a slow clip-clop along country roads.

But in 1998, suburban sprawl was identified as Pennsylvania's number-one environmental problem, and Lancaster County—only 50 miles west of Philadelphia along Route 30—was singled out as the most endangered area in reports by the Sierra Club and the World Monuments Fund. Since then, the county has embarked an aggressive program to conserve farmland, mostly by locking in easements on existing farms. Even so, observers estimate that Lancaster County is losing 1,000 farm acres a year.

In Lancaster County, farmland is valuable not only because it produces food, but because it attracts tourism—which adds $1 billion a year to the county's economy. Tourists support wonderful farmer's markets (try the Central Market in Lancaster, the Bird-in-Hand Market on Route 340 in Bird-in-Hand, or the Meadowbrook Market in Leola), as well as outlets for traditional handicrafts like pie baking, quilt making, furniture making, and basketry. Individual farmers can and often do cash in on tourism with everything from hayrides and petting farms to roadside stands and bed-and-breakfasts. The challenge is to strike the right balance between tourist infrastructure and the pastoral landscape that draws the tourists.

In summer, the main roads around Lancaster can be clogged with traffic, and horse-drawn vehicles can cause bottlenecks; get a good area map so you can venture onto quiet back roads, where you have a better chance of seeing Amish farmers in their daily rounds. (Just remember: Photographing them seriously violates their beliefs.) Stop at local farm stands to buy their excellent produce, and you'll have a natural opportunity to exchange a few words. In quaintly named Intercourse, Pennsylvania, **The People's Place,** 3513 Old Philadelphia Pike (© **717/768-7171;** closed Sun) has displays explaining the subtle distinctions between three local sects: the Amish, the Mennonites, and the Brethern, who settled here in the early 18th century. Stop east of Lancaster for a guided tour of the 10-room **Amish Farm and House,** 2395 Lincoln Hwy. (© **717/394-6185**). The **Landis Valley Museum,** 5 miles (8km) north of Lancaster at 2451 Kissel Hill Rd. (© **717/569-0401**), is a 21-building "living arts" complex where costumed interpreters demonstrate Pennsylvania German culture and folk traditions.

---

ⓘ **Pennsylvania Dutch Convention & Visitors Bureau** (© **800/PA-DUTCH** [723-8824]; www.padutchcountry.com)

✈ Philadelphia

🛏 $$$ **Willow Valley Family Resort,** 2416 Willow St. Pike, Lancaster (© **800/444-1714** or 717/464-2711; www.willowvalley. com). $$ **Country Inn of Lancaster,** 2133 Lincoln Hwy. E., Lancaster (© **717/393-3413;** www.countryinnoflancaster.com).

# 10 Last-of-Their-Kind Towns

Lost in the forward-hurtling rush of civilization, by some quirk of fate each of these 10 small towns managed to escape modernization. They're not just architectural stage sets, but intact embodiments of their own distinct cultures—the way things used to be before our global village got so homogenized.

Civita di Bagnoregio.

**350 Civita di Bagnoregio, Lazio, Italy** Founded by ancient Etruscans on a tufa-rock plateau overlooking the Tiber valley, in the late 1600s this walled medieval hill town was severed from the rest of Bagnoregio by erosion and land-slides (a single pedestrian bridge connects them today). Plans to shore up the crumbling outcrop are underway, as tourists have discovered the frozen-in-time beauty of these golden stone buildings. ✆ *39/761/793231.* www.civitadibagnoregio.it.

**351 Jimingyi Post Town, Huailai, China** Scarcely changed since its Ming dynasty heyday, Jimingyi (Cock Crow) was a vital component in the Chinese imperial transportation network—a walled town along the post road where couriers could change horses. The compact, fortified medieval town (145km/90 miles northwest of Beijing) is remarkably intact, including the 800-year-old Ningyong Temple, several aristocratic courtyard houses, and an imposing dou-ble-roofed gate tower. *www.china.org.cn/english/travel/108995.htm.*

**352 Gammelstads Kyrkstad, Luleå, Sweden** Sweden once had 71 such "towns"—clusters of snug one-room wooden cottages where country parishioners could stay over-night to attend Sunday church services. Only 16 have survived, the largest of which is this 424-cottage settlement that sprang up around the white-washed belfry of Nederluleå church, the largest medieval church in Norrland. ✆ *46/920/29 35 81.* www.lulea.se/gammelstad.

**353 Vlkolínec, Ružomberok, Slovakia** Straggling up the Carpathian slopes, half of this mountain village's traditional deep-gabled log houses are year-round resi-dences, the other half vacation homes (another part of the village burned down during a Slovak revolt in World War II). There's little difference between 16th-century and 19th-century houses—none have running water or sewers, and chickens and goats roam free outside. ✆ *421/44/432 10 23.* www.vlkolinec.sk.

**354 Amana Colonies, Iowa** Settled by a German religious sect in 1855, these seven hamlets along the Iowa River maintained a strict communal lifestyle until 1932, with members working, eating, and worshipping together in what's now a landmarked district of some 500 historical buildings. Every village has its own store, school, bakery, dairy, and church; assigned homes stand in the middle, ringed by barns, craft workshops, and factories (as in Amana refrigerators). ✆ *319/622-7622.* www.amanacolonies.com.

**355 Oak Bluffs, Martha's Vineyard, Massachusetts** In 1889, there were as many as 140 of these "cottage camps" built for summer religious retreats, a phenomenon of the late-19th-century religious revival in the United States. Most have since been razed or redeveloped; not so the Campground in Oak Bluffs, with its assemblage of doll-like Victorian gingerbread cottages set closely on narrow streets surrounding the open-sided Tabernacle, where Methodist preachers once declaimed. *© 508/693-0525. www.mvcma.org.*

**356 Crespi d'Adda, Lombardy, Italy** From 1878 to 1928, this model industrial town was built by the enlightened Crespi cotton-mill owners—a handsomely decorated factory accompanied by 50 roomy stucco houses, each allotted to two or three families and surrounded by its own garden. Despite Depression-era bankruptcy and fascist management in the Mussolini era, the village still looks much the same, with most houses owned by descendants of Crespi workers; the factory only ceased production in 2004. *www.villaggiocrespi.it.*

**357 Letchworth Garden City, Hertfordshire, England** Letchworth was developed in 1903 to exemplify the ideals of social reformer Ebenezer Howard. As an experiment in urban planning, it pioneered many features still used today— separate zoning for industry and residences, the preservation of trees and open spaces, affordable housing (the so-called Cheap Cottages), traffic roundabouts, and a surrounding Green Belt. The architecture is still charmingly rural and small scale. *© 44/1462/487868. www.letchworthgc.com.*

Oak Bluff's "cottage camp."

**358 Portmeirion, Wales** This Mediterranean-style vacation village is a breathtaking surprise on the rugged coast of northern Wales. Constructed from 1925 to 1973, it embodied founder Clough Williams-Ellis's utopian theories on harmonizing architecture with nature; its guests included many artists, writers, and social thinkers. Pastel Palladian villas, Arts and Crafts cottages, and an Art Deco hotel are set amid flower-filled terraces, sloping lawns, and mature woods of yew, oaks, and rhododendrons. *© 44/1766/770000. www.portmeirion-village.com.*

Crespi d'Adda.

**359 Arcosanti, Arizona** "Arcology"—the marriage of architecture and ecology—is the philosophy of Italian architect Paolo Soleri, who launched this prototype community in the high Arizona desert (70 miles/113km north of Phoenix) in 1970. The antithesis of urban sprawl, its compact, solar-powered buildings are designed to use as little acreage and energy as possible; its futuristic-looking cluster of domes, vaults, and greenhouses is largely cast from concrete made of local desert silt. *© 928/632-6217 or 602/254-5309. www.arcosanti.org.*

# Sweet Auburn

## *Odd Twist of Civil Rights History*

### Atlanta, Georgia

IT'S A WEIRD PARADOX OF MODERN HISTORY: CIVIL RIGHTS PIONEER MARTIN LUTHER KING, JR., helped usher in a new era of racial equality, but in doing so, he may have dealt a death blow to the hometown-within-a-town that nurtured him—Sweet Auburn, Atlanta, Georgia.

From the 1890s to the 1960s, the 10-block area around Auburn Avenue was the center of African-American enterprise in Atlanta, forced by racially restrictive "Jim Crow laws" to become a self-sufficient community. Landmarks in this historic neighborhood include the Beaux-Arts headquarters of the Atlanta Life Insurance Company, founded in 1905 by former slave Alonzo Herndon and eventually the second-largest black-owned insurance company in the United States; the Rucker Building, Atlanta's first black-owned office building; and the offices of the *Atlanta Daily World*, the first black-owned daily newspaper, founded in 1928. A significant element of the neighborhood was its churches, including the Big Bethel AME, First Congregational, and Ebenezer Baptist Church, where King, his father, and his grandfather were all ministers. The Royal Peacock Club (originally the Top Hat Club) hosted black musicians such as B. B. King, the Four Tops, the Tams, and Atlanta's own Gladys Knight.

But after the civil rights struggles of the 1960s, those segregation laws were repealed. With new opportunities finally available, blacks moved out of Sweet Auburn; they no longer had to patronize its blacks-only enterprises. Suddenly it was just another inner-city neighborhood, and the construction of a new highway, I-75/85, slashed right through its heart.

Starting in 1992, however, concerted efforts were made to restore its luster. The first element was to restore King's birthplace, a modest Queen Anne–style house at 501 Auburn Ave., to its appearance when young Martin lived here—even the linoleum is an authentic reproduction. The Gothic Revival–style Ebenezer Baptist Church at 407 Auburn, where his father and, later, King himself were pastors, is now operated as a living museum, with guided weekday tours. Determined to make Sweet Auburn a vital neighborhood again, the Historic District Development Corporation (HDDC) has built or rehabilitated more than 110 single-family homes and over 50 affordable rental units, deliberately avoiding free-market gentrification, which usually prices low-income residents out of a neighborhood. HDDC is now rehabbing Sweet Auburn's commercial streetscape as well.

Somewhat less in character is the hulking modern **King Center,** 449 Auburn Ave. (© 404/524-1956; www.thekingcenter. org), a memorial and educational center now directed by King's son. In its exhibition hall, you can see King's Bible and clerical robe and a handwritten sermon; on a grim note, there's the key to his room at the Lorraine Motel in Memphis, Tennessee, where he was assassinated. In nearby **Freedom Plaza** rests Dr. King's white marble crypt, surrounded by a five-tiered reflecting pool.

(i) **Martin Luther King, Jr., National Historic Site,** 449 Auburn Ave. (www.nps.gov/malu). **The Friends of Sweet Auburn** (www.sweetauburn.com).

✈ Atlanta

🛏 $$$ **The Georgian Terrace Hotel,** 659 Peachtree St. (© **800/651-2316** or 404/897-1991; www.thegeorgianterrace.com). $$ **Marriott Stone Mountain Park Inn,** 1058 Robert E. Lee Dr., Stone Mountain (© **770/469-3311;** www.marriott.com).

**TOUR Atlanta Preservation Center** (© **404/876-2041;** www.preserveatlanta.com)

---

**361** **Neighborhoods in Transition**

# Kenilworth Village
## *Tear Downs in Utopia*
### Illinois

KENILWORTH, LIKE MANY OF CHICAGO'S NORTH SHORE SUBURBS, IS AT THE EPICENTER OF AMERICA'S "tear-down" trend. The 19th-century community is losing its original housing to make way for bigger houses, minicastles geared to a 21st-century lifestyle.

There's a whole string of posh suburbs along the Lake Michigan shoreline north of Chicago, but even in that elite company, Kenilworth stands out. Though it's only ⁶/₁₀ of a square mile (1.5 sq. km) in area, with a population well under 3,000, Kenilworth is known as one of America's richest zip codes. The village only has about 850 houses, yet 47 were demolished between 1993 and 2006—not because they were decrepit, but because their owners hungered for bigger, modern houses.

But the "tear-down" trend is particularly controversial in Kenilworth, which is the only one that was a planned community. It was developed by Joseph Sears starting in 1889, named after a town he'd recently visited in England's Lake District. Sears laid out amenities like paved streets, sidewalks, uniform street lamps, plantations of shade trees, and buried utilities; he dictated lot sizes, prohibited alleys and fences, and set high-quality construction standards. Insisting on designs that harmonized with their neighbors, he attracted some of the Chicago area's finest architects to design distinctive homes (no cookie-cutter repetition here). Commercial establishments were limited to Green Bay Road, parallel to the railroad lines, and blacks could only live in Kenilworth if they were live-in servants.

During the 1893 Columbian Exposition in Chicago, many famous visitors made a side trip to admire Sears's grand experiment. Drive along the refined, leafy streets of Kenilworth and you'll still see house after house of prime Queen Anne, Arts and Crafts, and Prairie Style architecture, full of art glass and ingenious carpentry. Though Frank Lloyd Wright's only entry was the Hiram-Baldwin House at 205 Essex Rd., contemporaries like Daniel Burnham and George W. Maher designed several houses here (Maher even did the graceful Italianate fountain that is the village's centerpiece), including one Maher house that's open to the public: Pleasant Home, 127 S. Home St. (© **708/383-2654;** www.pleasanthome.org).

But by today's standards, you'll notice those lots seem small, many less than a quarter acre. The houses have fewer bathrooms, smaller kitchens, and smaller garages than today's lifestyles demand.

Rather than undertake a costly historic restoration, some new buyers hope to simply knock down and start over. The affluent citizens of Kenilworth are squaring off, some seeking to get their town listed on the National Register of Historic Places to increase its protected status, others fighting to keep restoration a purely voluntary affair. Zoning ordinances are a hot topic on the commuter train into downtown Chicago, on the sidelines of weekend soccer games, and on summer afternoons at the town beach on Lake Michigan. After all, a man's home is his castle . . . isn't it?

ⓘ **Village of Kenilworth** (ℂ **847/251-1666;** www.villageofkenilworth.org)

✈ O'Hare International

🛏 $$ **Homewood Suites,** 40 E. Grand St., Chicago (ℂ **800/CALL-HOME** [225-5466] or 312/644-2222; www.homewood suiteschicago.com). $$ **Hotel Allegro Chicago,** 171 N. Randolph St., Chicago (ℂ **800/643-1500** or 312/236-0123; www.allegro chicago.com).

---

**Neighborhoods in Transition** **362**

# Harry S Truman Historic District
## *Where the Buck Stops*
### Independence, Missouri

THE TRUMAN NEIGHBORHOOD IS A PERFECT TIME CAPSULE OF MID-20TH-CENTURY SMALL-TOWN AMERICA, but its survival is tenuous. Threatened by encroachment from Kansas City, it was listed an endangered place by the National Trust. However, thanks to the efforts of local preservationists, the Truman district was removed from the list in 2003.

To understand George Washington or Thomas Jefferson, you visit grand manor houses on Tidewater Virginia estates. But to understand Harry S Truman, you have to go to a tidy little frame house on a side street of a small Missouri town.

Thrust into the presidency by Franklin Roosevelt's death, Harry S Truman—who'd only been vice president for 10 weeks—was a plain-spoken Missourian, fond of mottoes like "If you can't stand the heat, get out of the kitchen" and "the buck stops here." You can see a desk sign with that saying, along with a host of other Truman memorabilia, at the Harry S Truman Library in Independence (off U.S. 24 at Delaware St.), along with his doughboy uniform from World War I, the natty walking canes and straw hats that were his trademarks, the upright piano his wife, Bess, played at White House parties, and the safety plug that was pulled to detonate the Nagasaki bomb. Truman's grave lies in the courtyard.

The place that really conveys Truman's common-man qualities, though, is the Truman home at 219 N. Delaware St. Both Harry and Bess were small-town folks, and their summer White House was simply Bess's family home, a gabled white Victorian house with a scrollwork corner porch, where the Trumans lived from 1918 on. (Before then, Harry ran a farm out in Grandview, Missouri, also part of the historic site.) Bess's brothers lived in adjacent houses, and one of Harry's favorite aunts lived across the street, all of which you can visit on a guided tour. Get tickets early in the day, because they do sell out—tours are limited to eight people because the rooms are small. Inside the house, virtually untouched since Bess Truman died, you'll see the red kitchen table where Harry and Bess ate breakfast, the book-lined study that was Truman's favorite retreat, and the wide back porch where they played cards and ate meals during hot Missouri summers.

With the sprawl of Kansas City edging closer, by the 1990s the simple frame houses of this neighborhood began to lose value; many were subdivided into apartments. The neighborhood had grown so shabby—the facade of a house across the street even collapsed—that the National

Trust put it on its list of Most Endangered Places. Thanks to a group of local preservationists, who campaigned to give tax abatements to homeowners for home renovations, the Truman district was removed from the list in 2003. Chalk up one victory for preserving small-town values.

✈ Kansas City International

🚇 $$$ **Westin Crown Center,** One Pershing Rd., Kansas City, MO (© **800/WESTIN-1** [937-8461] or 816/474-4400; www.westin.com/crowncenter). **$$ Embassy Suites**, 220 W. 43rd St., Kansas City, MO (© **800/EMBASSY** [362-2779] or 816/756-1720; www.embassysuites.com).

**TOUR** Truman tour tickets, 223 N. Main St. (© **816/254-9929;** www.nps.gov/hstr)

---

**363** Neighborhoods in Transition

# The Fourth Ward
## *The Death of Freedman's Town*
### Houston, Texas

LIKE MANY INNER-CITY NEIGHBORHOODS, IN THE 20TH CENTURY THE POVERTY-STRICKEN FOURTH Ward was considered fair game for urban renewal. New townhouses and lofts threaten to take over the neighborhood's last remaining "shotgun shacks."

They called them "shotgun shacks" because you could fire a gun in the front door and have it whistle clean out the back—that is, if your bullet didn't interrupt a card party or prayer meeting along the way. These one-room-wide, single-story houses, lined up along narrow brick-paved streets, were the signature housing stock of the Fourth Ward, back when it was known as "Freedman's Town," a magnet area for recently freed

slaves after the Civil War. During nearly a century of Jim Crow segregation laws, the Fourth Ward became a self-contained community with its own churches, schools, stores, doctors, and lawyers; it held the city's only black public library and black hospital. Houston's equivalent of Harlem centered on Dallas Street, lined with jazz clubs and restaurants, hopping till all hours of the morning.

The Antioch Missionary Baptist Church.

In the 1940s, to make way for the North Central Expressway, some 1,500 homes were knocked down, and much of the Freedman's Cemetery was paved over (it was finally exhumed in the 1980s). In the 1960s the Fourth Ward was again bisected by a traffic artery, in this case the Pierce Elevated, an elevated stretch of I-45 arrowing into downtown. Split in two by that concrete hulk, the neighborhood further degenerated. The downtown chunk of it was razed for skyscrapers (the historic Antioch Missionary Baptist Church still stands on Clay St., surrounded by the big glass boxes). What had been a 40-block area shrank to about 16 blocks.

The Midtown part, southwest of I-45, is currently being redeveloped, but mostly in the form of new construction—trendy post-modern townhouses and lofts for young professionals on one side, characterless two-story houses and apartment blocks built as "affordable housing" on the other. Despite the attempt to make some units affordable, longtime residents are being driven out by rising rents. A ragtag community of home-less people periodically camp out in the dank shadows under the Pierce Elevated. Between 1910 and 2000, this historically black neighborhood's black population fell from 17,000 to around 600; nowadays only about one-third of the neighborhood is black, while over half is Hispanic.

And what about the shotgun shacks? Many have fallen into such disrepair, the city's only recourse was to knock them down. Small as they were, they wouldn't have attracted yuppie rehabbers anyway. Weeds poke around the remaining brick streets of the Fourth Ward, which have been haphazardly patched with concrete. It's just another slice of American history petering out.

✈ George Bush Intercontinental

🛏 $$$ **Hilton University of Houston,** 4800 Calhoun Rd. (© **800/HOTELUH** [468-3584] or 713/741-2447; www.hilton.com). $$ **Best Western Downtown Inn and Suites,** 915 W. Dallas St. (© **800/780-7234** or 713/571-7733; www.best western.com).

# Alhambra
## *California Cottage Culture*
San Gabriel Valley, California

ONCE AN ARCHITECTURALLY RICH CITY, ALHAMBRA IS LOSING THAT HERITAGE DUE TO MODERNIZATION. The shade trees and palms that once lined the sidewalks have been uprooted for new construction, and never replaced. The once-quiet streets bear an increased traffic load, with more multifamily dwellings and an expanded commercial district.

Quaint old-fashioned brochures tempting people to move to this California town in 1903 touted it as a "City of Homes," its palm-shaded streets lined with charming Craftsman cottages and Spanish Mediterranean bungalows. For East Coast natives lured west by California's mild year-round climate, it seemed a vision of paradise.

Unlike many real-estate promises, this one turned out to be entirely true. Up through the 1930s, Alhambra was a magnet for tasteful middle-class housing. In the late teens and early '20s, houses of an even grander scale began to appear, castlelike Spanish-style stucco villas and Moorish fantasies, alongside a good number of gingerbready Victorian manses. Like neighboring Pasadena, Alhambra maintained a refined, conservative image, at least in contrast to other parts of booming Los Angeles.

Where did Alhambra lose its way? Like many communities throughout the United States, in the second half of the 20th century Alhambra seemed seduced by the idea of modernization. With its population swelled by successive waves of immigrants—Italians in the 1950s, Mexicans in the 1960s, and Chinese in the 1980s—the town's hunger for new development seemed insatiable. From the 1960s on, a succession of those historic homes were razed, to be replaced either with larger, more "up-to-date" houses, apartment blocks, or commercial buildings. The historic pre-1940 homes are still there— mostly the more modest properties, the classic Spanish and Arts and Crafts bungalows—but you'll have to look harder to find them.

With larger buildings occupying the same small lots, Alhambra has also lost a significant amount of its green space in the past 20 years. Despite pressure from some preservation activists, the town government has been slow to enact zoning— which might, for example, promote single-family housing, control add-ons, mandate landscaping, or limit population density.

Perhaps most baffling of all, there's been little effort to gain historic preservation status for the last few well-preserved neighborhoods like Ramona Park, Mayfair, Emery Park, and Midwick. Modest as some of these frame and stucco cottages may seem, they are stellar examples of their architectural styles; even from the outside you can see the remarkable craftsmanship that went into them. Compared to the featureless boxes with which they've been replaced, it's no contest.

ⓘ **Alhambra Preservation Group** (✆ **626/755-3467;** www.alhambrapreservation.org)

✈ Los Angeles International

🛏 **$$ Artists' Inn & Cottage Bed & Breakfast,** 1038 Magnolia St,. South Pasadena (✆ **888/799-5668** or 626/799-5668; www.artistsinns.com). **$ Saga Motor Hotel,** 1633 E. Colorado Blvd., Pasadena (✆ **800/793-7242** or 626/795-0431; www.thesagamotorhotel.com).

**Neighborhoods in Transition**  **365**

# Over-the-Rhine
## *Reversing the Tide*
### Cincinnati, Ohio

URBAN NEGLECT AND FLIGHT HAS LEFT THIS HISTORIC 19TH-CENTURY NEIGHBORHOOD, FILLED with Italianate row houses, vacant and deteriorating. A listing on the National Register of Historic Places helped focus the attention of urban historians, but much work remains to be done to save this community.

It wasn't really the Rhine that 19th-century German immigrants crossed, trooping home from work in downtown Cincinnati—it was just the Miami and Erie Canal. Still, once they had crossed it they felt at home, in a vibrant German-speaking community with their own churches, shops, and newspaper (and some 50 breweries). They built solid homes in the then-popular architectural styles, especially Italianate row houses. It was one of the most densely populated neighborhoods in the Midwest—the sort of working-class urban neighborhood that made America great.

The 20th century, however, did not treat Over-the-Rhine kindly. To begin with, the disused and stagnant canal was replaced by a failed streetcar line, then a failed subway, and eventually was paved over into the traffic-heavy Central Parkway. As German-Americans moved up the economic ladder and out of the neighborhood, they were replaced by day laborers, mostly black, from the South. The decline of Cincinnati's prominent machine-tool

industry, then white flight to the suburbs, hit hard. By the 1970s, Over-the-Rhine had become just another inner-city neighborhood plagued with drugs, crime, and racial unrest.

Still, some 1,200 historic buildings remained, though many stand vacant and deteriorating. To jump-start investment, developers spruced up the area around 12th and Vine streets to attract young professionals looking to live close to downtown. At the same time, Over-the-Rhine Community Housing is focusing on developing affordable housing so that current residents won't be priced out of the neighborhood. With a population that's now 80% black, 20% white, Over-the-Rhine must steer a careful course between yuppification and urban renewal.

Despite decades of neglect, Over-the-Rhine still has several attractions, including the Cincinnati Music Hall, 1241 Elm St., where both the Cincinnati Opera and Cincinnati Symphony perform, a marvel of

Cincinnati Music Hall.

eclectic red-brick architecture that some have dubbed Sauerbraten Byzantine. Across the street, 6-acre (2.4-hectare) Washington Park is a peaceable green space with lots of benches and statues. The Findlay Street Market, built in 1852, attracts a wide ranging clientele to its busy collection of food vendors, Ohio's largest indoor market. Cincinnati's oldest church, Old St. Mary's Catholic Church, 123 E. 13th St., still holds Mass in German and Latin every Sunday in a tall-steepled Greek Revival building. The historic Romanesque St. Paul Church at 12th and Spring streets is now a bell and clock museum showcasing the products of the Verdin Company.

But the main thing remains the housing—block after sloping block of neat three- and four-story brick Italianate beauties, most with their ornate cornices, window pediments, and door lintels intact. Many are in a shocking state of neglect; gaping holes in several blocks show what has been lost already. Can Over-the-Rhine cross back over?

---

ⓘ www.irhine.com

✈ Cincinnati/Northern Kentucky International

🛏 $$ **Millennium Hotel Cincinnati,** 150 W. 5th St. (ⓒ **800/876-2100** or 513/352-2100; www.millennium-hotels.com). $$ **Symphony Hotel,** 210 W. 14th St. (ⓒ **513/721-3353;** www.symphonyhotel.com).

# Lima Centro
## *Crumbling Colonials*
### Lima, Peru

LIMA IS STRUGGLING TO REMAKE ITSELF. NOTORIOUS FOR ITS STREET VIOLENCE IN THE CHAOTIC 1980s and 1990s, this once iconic city became a place tourists simply bypassed. Today, though, preservations are uncovering and restoring its architectural treasures.

Ah, the glory that was Lima, once the absolute power center for Spain's South American empire. But after a devastating earthquake in 1746, Lima slid into a rapid decline; today it's a sprawling, most unlovely metropolis, with depressing shantytowns *(pueblos jóvenes)* ringing the city. However, its many classic colonial buildings in the old *centro* (named a UNESCO World Heritage Site) are finally getting a long-deserved makeover.

The place to start exploring it is the Plaza de Armas, which has witnessed everything from bullfights to some of the worst excesses of the Spanish inquisition. Despite a surface layer of grime and bustle (note how the twin yellow towers of the baroque cathedral have been dulled by smog and mist), it's still a harmonious architectural piece set around a central bronze fountain. Go inside the cathedral to see the mosaic-encrusted chapel containing the tomb of Francisco Pizarro, the conquistador who founded Lima in 1535 (and killed the Inca's emperor to seal the deal).

Directly south of La Catedral, the Jesuit church of San Pedro (Azángaro at Ucayali), is the city's best-preserved early colonial church, austere on the outside but a riot of gilded altars and baroque balconies inside. The Convento y Museo de San Francisco (Plaza de San Francisco) is a strikingly restored, yellow-and-white 17th-century complex with some fabulous Moorish ceilings, beautiful cloisters, and a bone-crammed set of catacombs. Other fine colonial churches nearby include the handsome baroque facades of Iglesia de La Merced (Jr. de la Unión at Miró Quesada) and San Agustín (Jr. Ica and Jr. Camaná).

Probably the best reason to prowl around the Centro, however, is to scout out its opulent colonial palaces; home over the years to Lima's ruling elite and power brokers. Few houses are open to the public—only Casa Riva-Agüero (Camaná 459), with its beautiful green-and-red courtyard, and Casa Aliaga (Jr. de la Unión 224), the oldest surviving house in Lima—but you can gawk at the restored exteriors of Casa de Osambela Oquendo (Conde de Superunda 298), the tallest house in colonial Lima; Palacio Torre Tagle (Ucayali 363), with its gorgeous baroque stone doorway and carved dark-wood balconies; Casa Negreiros (Jr. Azángaro 532), Casa de las Trece Monedas (Jr. Ancash 536), Casa Barbieri (Jr. Callao at Rufino Torrico), Casa de Pilatos (Jr. Ancash 390), and Casa la Riva (Jr. Ica 426). As you go from mansion to mansion, though, notice how many other buildings on these streets are still run-down, some of them even occupied by squatters. Can this neglected jewel of a historic district find its way back?

ⓘ iPerú (✆ **51/1/427-6080;** www.peru. org.pe)

✈ Jorge Chávez International

🛏 $$ **Hotel Colonial Inn,** Comandante Espinar 310, Miraflores, Lima (✆ **51/1/ 241-7471;** www.hotelcolonialinn.com). $ **La Posada del Parque Hostal,** Parque Hernán Velarde 60, Santa Beatriz, Lima (✆ **51/1/433-2412;** www.incacountry.com).

**TOUR** Lima Tours (✆ **51/1/424-5110)**

# Little Green Street
## *A Narrow Slice of the Past*
### London, England

LITTLE GREEN STREET ISN'T IN THE CENTER OF LONDON, BUT MAYBE THAT'S WHY IT SURVIVED so long—it's one of only a few intact Georgian streets left in the whole metropolis. These two-story brick houses may have survived the Blitz in World War II, but the inexorable march of gentrification is another thing altogether.

It's not even a full neighborhood, just a 1-block-long street, a narrow cobblestoned lane lined on both sides with perhaps a dozen modest 18th-century terraced houses.

What's especially ironic is that the houses of Little Green Street, just off Highgate Road in Kentish Town, aren't themselves being knocked down. They are listed as Grade II historic properties, which in British parlance means they're entitled to a certain degree of landmark protection. No, it's the street itself that lies in danger, by an accident of urban geography. The land behind Little Green Street now stands derelict, and a developer won initial approval to build an underground parking garage, 20 new houses, and a block of flats there. Just north of trendy Camden Town and east of posh Hampstead, Kentish Town is no doubt ripe for gentrification. There's only one catch: To build those new structures, trucks and heavy construction equipment would have to be routed up and down Little Green Street.

The street comes honestly by its name: Little Green Street is only 2.5m (8 ft.) wide. Lorries and backhoes would barely scrape through this lane, coming within inches of the terrace's neatly painted front doors and bow windows. What's more, no studies had been done to test how much the constant rumbling and vibrations of that traffic would affect the foundations of these 225-year-old buildings, given a projected construction period of 4 years.

Little Green Street looks like a perfect slice of Regency London; it's been celebrated in the poetry of that quintessentially British poet John Betjeman, and used as the setting for music videos and photo shoots. The campaign to save Little Green Street has not only knit together the dozen families who live there, it has attracted actors, writers, musicians, and others concerned with preserving London's historic character. In February 2008, the Camden Town Council denied the developers construction access to Little Green Street, but the appeals process continues. Little Green Street's safety is by no means certain. Stay tuned.

---

ⓘ **Little Green Street Blog** (www.little greenstreet.com)

✈ Heathrow International

🛏 $$ **Hart House Hotel,** 51 Gloucester Place, Marylebone (✆ **44/20/7935-2288;** www.harthouse.co.uk). $$ **Vicarage Private Hotel,** 10 Vicarage Gate, South Kensington (✆ **44/20/7229-4030;** www. londonvicaragehotel.com).

# Spitalfields
## *To Market, to Market*
### London, England

FOR MORE THAN 300 YEARS, SPITALFIELDS HAS SURVIVED MYRIAD CHANGES IN LONDON'S EAST End. But as urban renewal changes the dynamic of this area, so to will it alter this historic institution.

Through centuries of British history, persecuted refugees and racial outcasts found a haven in London's East End. In the 18th century, it was Huguenot silk weavers driven out of France; in the 19th century, it was Jews fleeing pogroms in eastern Europe; in the 20th century, it was Bangladeshi immigrants. Check out the mosque in Brick Lane: Originally a Huguenot church, it became a synagogue in the 19th century, then was converted to a mosque for Bangladeshi Muslims in the mid–20th century. Each group brought their own flavor to the neighborhood; each, in turn, moved out of these crowded, unfashionable streets as soon as they could.

A focal point since the 17th century was the Spitalfields meat and produce market, held at first in an open field, which was replaced by a handsome covered market building in 1875. By then, however, the old merchant dwellings surrounding the market had been sliced up into crowded, dilapidated slums, huddled around narrow lanes and alleys. This was the grimy side of Dickensian London, where criminals like Fagin and Bill Sykes dealt in thievery and prostitution—the haunt of Jack the Ripper in 1888 (he's said to have met some of his victims at the Ten Bells pub on Commercial St.).

In the 1960s, well-meaning preservationists focused on saving those old merchant terraces from the wrecking ball. Of course, as one after another of those Georgian relics were refurbished, squatters were evacuated and house prices skyrocketed. And trendy rehabs haven't been the only face of urban renewal around Spitalfields—large modern office blocks have sprouted on the western edge, spilling over from the City of London. The produce market was moved out to Leyton in 1991. Although landmark status saved the remaining third of the old Spitalfields Market building from demolition, it was soon converted to an upscale retail mall for crafts, antiques, and organic and gourmet foods. Other street markets in the area include the Brick Lane Market (fruit and vegetables, clothes, and household goods); the Sunday-only Petticoat Lane Market (bargain-priced clothing and leather goods), and Columbia Road Market (potted plants and garden items), but their customer base is dwindling.

It's not as if anybody wanted to revive the Victorian squalor of the district, but to some, the smartness of the "new" Spitalfields seems a betrayal of the East End's colorful past. Case in point: the baroque Nicholas Hawksmoor gem, Christ Church Spitalfields, which has been turned into a posh concert venue on Fournier Street between Brick Lane and Commercial Street. Yes, the buildings have been preserved—but if the vitality of the East End lives on anywhere, it's in the string of curry restaurants along Brick Lane.

---

ⓘ **Spitalfields** (www.spitalfields.org.uk)

✈ Heathrow International

🛏 $$ **Hart House Hotel,** 51 Gloucester Place, Marylebone (✆ **44/20/7935-2288;** www.harthouse.co.uk). $$ **Vicarage Private Hotel,** 10 Vicarage Gate, South Kensington (✆ **44/20/7229-4030;** www.london vicaragehotel.com).

# Prenzlauerberg
## *In Search of a* Kiez
### Berlin, Germany

CITIES ARE DYNAMIC ENTITIES, ALWAYS EVOLVING, BUT GERMAN REUNIFICATION WAS TRULY A shock to the system for long-divided Berlin. What happened in Prenzlauerberg was normal urban evolution, but it was played out at dizzying speed.

Built as housing for factory workers in the 1860s, the cramped tenements of East Berlin's Prenzlauerberg became a magnet for artists, thinkers, students, and orange-haired punks in the days of the Soviet-controlled German Democratic Republic. It was the sort of radical quarter where you'd expect political activity, like the government resistance that emanated from the Protestant Gethsemane church on Gethsemanestrasse. For a cheap meal, you could always have a grilled sausage at Konnopkes Imbiss, under the U-Bahn tracks between Schönhauser Allee and Danziger Strasse. This northern suburb had a definite character, a real *kiez* (German for a neighborhood you feel connected to).

But with reunification, those historic tenements with their trees and courtyards seemed pretty attractive to young professionals eager to renovate prime real estate. Unlike other districts of East Berlin, they hadn't been bombed in World War II and had somehow escaped being replaced with the GDR era's typical boxy concrete apartment blocks. It still had a few atmospheric landmarks, like the handsome 19th-century brick water tower that rises over Kollwitzplatz, the Prater Beer Garden (Berlin's oldest) on Kastanienalee, and a handful of disused breweries ripe for redevelopment. (One of them, the Kulturbrauerei on Sredzkistrasse, now houses a warren of bars, restaurants, a cinema, and the district's tourist information center beneath its brick towers and chimneystacks.) Remnants of the days when this was a Jewish neighborhood are found in an old synagogue on Rykestraße and a Jewish cemetery on Schönhauser Allee.

And so in the early 1990s free-market forces took hold and the yuppies moved in, repainting the dull facades in bright colors and designs. Nightlife exploded, particularly around Kollwitzplatz and Kastanienallee, with a fairly active gay scene; a constant rotation of hip boutiques, galleries, and sidewalk cafes attract the leisured classes by day. Weekly street markets at Kollwitzplatz and Helmholtzplatz add to the lively atmosphere. Students and punks—those perennial urban colonizers—were quickly priced out of the area.

Prenzlauerberg.

**351**

In the hyperactive post-reunification climate, nothing in Berlin stays the same for long. Already the really hot nightlife has moved elsewhere (to the east), and the first wave of yuppies are starting families—there's a surprising number of baby strollers around. It's anybody's guess what the character of Prenzl'berg will be in the end—but at least those classic old buildings have been restored.

ⓘ **TIC** (✆ **49/30/4435 2170;** www.tic-in-prenzlauerberg.de)

✈ Berlin-Tagel

🛏 $$ **Hotel Hackescher Markt,** Grosse Präsidentenstrasse 8 (✆ **49/30/ 280030;** www.loock-hotels.com). $$ **Myers Hotel Berlin,** Betzer Strasse 26 (✆ **49/30/440140;** www.myershotel.de).

## Neighborhoods in Transition 370

# Inner Town
## *Watching the River Flow*
### Ceský Krumlov, Czech Republic

AFTER THE RAGING WATERS OF THE VLTAVA WREAKED HAVOC ON PRAGUE IN 2002, THEY gushed through a snaky series of bends around the town of Ceský Krumlov. The town's historic castle sat safe on its dramatic rocky hill, but that didn't help the low-lying Inner Town. Czech officials watched in horror as their Bohemian tourism jewel threatened to wash away.

Since the fall of communism in 1989, the Czech government has invested heavily in sprucing up historic Krumlov, a near-perfect assemblage of medieval and Renaissance-era town houses. Under Communism this area had little money to spare for "development," which turned out to be a boon—no glass-and-steel monstrosities to spoil the architectural beauty. Tourism is now a mainstay of the town economy; it's jam-packed every summer, especially at the summer solstice for the *Slavnost petilisté ruze* (Festival of the Five-Petaled Rose), when townfolk dress up in Renaissance costume and the streets are full of living chess games, music, plays, and staged duels.

Most of the flooded buildings were speedily reconstructed, but this picturesque town center remains seriously at risk. Dominating the town from across the river, **Ceský Krumlov Château** (Apr–Oct, by guided tour only) is a suitably grand gray stone castle packed with ancestral portraits and heavy tapestries where the powerful Rozmbeck family presided over the town's medieval heyday. Later, the prominent Schwarzenberg family ruled this roost (along with the brown bears that traditionally live in the moat). Though it was founded in the 13th century, a 16th-century makeover is responsible for the present exterior; inside are some stunning baroque and rococo interiors.

But cross the wooden bridge to Krumlov's low-lying Inner Town and you'll discover what tourists really fall in love with—the harmony of its red roofs, gabled house fronts in a range of colors, and narrow medieval streets (check out the town model at the **Okresni Muzeum,** Horni ulice 152). The cobblestoned, traffic-free Inner Town contains many charming buildings, such as the late Gothic **St. Vitus Cathedral** (great views from its tower), the **Radnice (Town Hall),** at námestí Svornosti 1, with Gothic arcades and Renaissance vaulting, and the **Hotel Ruze,** Horni 154, a 16th-century amalgamation of Gothic, Renaissance, and rococo influences.

But as you wander closer to the river, notice the high-water marks on some of the quirky bank-side houses. Scientists gloomily predict that deforestation and climate change will make the Vltava flood again, and again, in future years. If floods wipe out the Inner Town, will the tourists still pour into Ceský Krumlov?

(i) **Tourist Information Centre** (© 420/380/704-622; www.ckrumlov.cz)

✈ Prague

🛏 $$$ **Hotel Ruze,** Horní 154 (© 420/380/772-100; www.hotelruze.cz). $ **Pension Na louzi,** Kájovská 66 (© 420/380/711-28; www.nalouzi.cz).

---

## 371 Neighborhoods in Transition

# The Paris of the North
## *Art Nouveau Riga*
### Riga, Latvia

NEWLY INDEPENDENT AGAIN, RIGA'S IN THE GRIP OF AN ECONOMIC BOOM, AND IT'S BECOME notorious for the worst traffic congestion in Europe. Those beautiful streetscapes are now choked with cars and rife with air pollution. However, a new construction project will route traffic around the city center.

Yes, Latvia was a Russian possession from 1710 to 1918, and part of the Soviet Union for another half century, from 1940 to 1991, but Riga always felt more German than Russian. This bustling Baltic port may have been the Russian empire's third-largest city (after Moscow and St. Petersburg), but German was still the official language until the late 19th century. It's not surprising that, despite some fine medieval city walls and guildhalls, Riga's real claim to fame would be a spectacular flowering of a German architectural style: Jugendstil.

Though it's often called the Paris of the North, Riga's Art Nouveau architecture is much more akin to Vienna's, though it's even more concentrated here—more than a third of the central district's buildings. As in Barcelona, Riga's turn-of-the-century building boom coincided with the rise of several talented young local architects, notably Mikhail Eisenstein (father of the Russian film director Sergei Eisenstein). Even more importantly, the sheer exuberance of Jugendstil dovetailed with a burst of Latvian nationalism.

Walk along Alberta Street, where a flurry of construction from 1901 to 1908 composed a magnificent ensemble of

Riga, Latvia.

**353**

buildings, many by Eisenstein. You'll want binoculars or a telephoto lens to pick out all the ornamental details, from stone sculptural reliefs to wrought-iron gates and balconies, colorful stencils, and brilliant touches of stained glass. Elizabetes, Strelnieku, Kr. Barona, Chaka, and Gertrudes streets are also particularly rich; notice how the clean lines of the architecture sweep your eyes upward to ornate steeples, clocks, cornices, and rooftop decorations. The imaginative detail is incredible—from amazingly expressive human faces to droll pelicans, chubby squirrels, sleek greyhounds, and majestic lions. In Esplanade Park, you can see the evolution of the style in the Academy of Arts, which imposes Jugendstil elements on a Neo-Gothic base, and the State Museum of Fine Arts, eclectic on the outside but with classic Jugendstil touches like the entrance staircase and sculptured figures over the front doors.

But gaping at those early-20th-century marvels isn't so easy these days, given the explosion of traffic in Riga's city center. Riga has taken steps to address the problem at last: In 2008, the first stage of a new Southern Bridge route across the Daugava will be completed, the biggest construction project in the Baltic states in 20 years, to route traffic around the city center. Paris itself has recently made great strides in reducing urban congestion; why not the Paris of the North?

ⓘ www.riga.com

✈ Riga

🛏 $$$ **Grand Palace Hotel,** Pils 12 (✆ **371/7044000;** www.grandpalacehotel riga.com). $$ **Laine Hotel,** Skolas Iela 11 (✆ **371/67289823;** www.laine.lv).

## Neighborhoods in Transition  372

# Old Jewish Ghetto
## *Under the Wrecking Ball*
### Budapest, Hungary

THE WAR IS ON FOR THE SOUL OF JEWISH BUDAPEST. IT'S BEEN DESCRIBED AS "COWBOY capitalism," with no city planning to guide the process of restoring this historic neighborhood, while grass-roots activists scramble to offer alternative visions for commemorating the ghetto's unique history.

The battleground is the 19th-century Jewish quarter in Budapest's seventh district. The first shots were fired in mid-2004, when more than a dozen abandoned buildings in this run-down neighborhood were snapped up by condo developers. Suddenly, even landmarked buildings were being torn down and new projects going up everywhere.

Once home to the strongest Jewish community in Europe, Budapest still has about 100,000 Jewish citizens. During World War II, Hungary's Jews weren't exterminated to the extent that they were in other countries, and many continued to live here after the Soviets "liberated" Budapest. But after decades of Communist government, their religious identity and cultural cohesion were seriously weakened (although Hungarian Jews were granted more freedoms than Jews in many Soviet-controlled regimes—Budapest kept its rabbinical school and had the only matzoh factory behind the Iron Curtain).

Just compare that number to the second half of the 19th century, when some 200,000 Jews were packed into this district on the Pest side of the Danube. You can get

Budapest's Jewish Quarter.

commemorate his Hungarian forebears. Among other sites nearby are the Jewish Museum, next to the Synagogue at Dohány 2; the Rumbach Street Synagogue, the center of the orthodox Jewish community at the Kazinczy Street Synagogue; or the Mikveh on Kazinczy Street, the only Jewish ritual bath left in Pest.

In 2006, in the backyard of Király 15, construction workers razing an old building for new construction knocked down the last fragment of the stone wall the Nazis built in 1944 to enclose the Jews in their ghetto. The developers forge ahead. But as the district is transformed, among the trendy new bars, restaurants, and nightclubs springing up, several have become gathering places for hip young Jews. Check out the bars Siraly, Kiraly 50; Kuplung, Kiraly 46; Szoda, Wesselenyi 18; or the dinner club Spinoza, Dob 15—their Jewish roots aren't obvious, but a core group of patrons certainly feel the connection.

a glimpse of that past in Gozsdu Court, a series of seven small courtyards between Kiraly and Dob streets, just behind the Great Synagogue (Dohány 2–8). Back in the late 19th and early 20th centuries, this was a hot spot of small stores and tradesmen's workshops, a buzzing center of the community. The synagogue itself is well worth a visit; still an active house of worship, it's the second-largest synagogue in Europe, a 19th-century fantasy of Byzantine and Moorish motifs. Interestingly, its restoration was funded by actor Tony Curtis, to

(i) **Budapest Tourism Office** (www.budapestinfo.hu)

✈ Budapest

🛏 **$$ Hotel Erzsébet,** V. Károlyi Mihály u. 11–15, Budapest (✆ **36/1/889-3700;** www.danubiusgroup.com). $$ **Hotel Papillon,** II. Rózsahegy u. 3/b (✆ **36/1/212-4750**).

**TOURS Cityrama** (✆ **36/1/302-4382;** www.cityrama.hu)

---

**373** Neighborhoods in Transition

# Hutong Neighborhoods
## *Hiding Out in the Alley*
### Beijing, China

TO MAKE ROOM FOR THE 2008 OLYMPICS, HUTONGS—COMPLEXES OF LOW-BUILT RESIDENTIAL quadrangles (or *siheyuans*), connected by narrow alleyways—began to be razed. In the early 1980s, Beijing had over 3,000 such hutongs; by early 2008, only 500 were left, with over a third of the central city recently revamped.

Hutong house.

Chinese officials were determined to remake Beijing into a modern showcase city for the 2008 Olympics—the hutongs simply had to go. What did it matter that they'd been the basis of Beijing's urban fabric since the 14th century? Hutongs made Chinese society look backward, and with the world's eyes on China, that simply would not do.

Granted, this wholesale destruction began in the 1950s during Mao Tse-Tung's Cultural Revolution, with old hutongs sacrificed in order to erect high-rises and wide boulevards; hutong dwellers were resettled in apartment buildings with amenities like central heating and indoor plumbing that were rare in the hutongs. But in the new era of Chinese capitalism—the Second Industrial Revolution, some call it—the Beijing Municipal Construction Committee in 2004 announced that it would demolish more of the old housing, displacing 20,000 households. Given the

lack of property rights in China, there wasn't much those citizens could do.

But dissent was boiling to a head. In 2003, suicide attempts by displaced hutong residents highlighted the crisis. In 2002, the government promised to give landmark protection to several hutongs, but in 2007 it finally committed 1 billion yuan to refurbishing 44 dilapidated hutongs in downtown Dongcheng, Xicheng, Chongwen, and Xuanwu. Chinese Tour now includes hutong excursions on its city tours, using cycle rickshaws to navigate the narrow lanes.

The hutong lifestyle is a perfect expression of traditional Chinese culture. Within its shady courtyards, communal social networks—especially extended families—became the basic building blocks of Beijing cultural life. While some hutongs were built for aristocrats, humbler merchants and craftsmen and laborers huddled together in much smaller courtyards. The name "hutong" comes from the Mongolian word for "well," reflecting the idea of a community's central meeting point. With their upturned eaves, wooden doors and windows, decorative brickwork, and garden plantings (traditionally, pomegranate trees) or fishponds in the central courtyard, these hutong complexes have a distinctly Chinese flavor—presumably, the very thing the Olympics were meant to showcase.

In Beijing, well-preserved upper-class hutongs around the Drum Tower and Shichahai Lake are worth visiting. You may also want to check out Beixinqiao Hutong, near Beixinqiao station on the no. 5 subway, which has the most twisty alleys. Near Qián Mén at the south end of Tiananmen Square, you'll find Qianshi Hutong on ZhuBaoshi Street, where the narrowest alley is only 40cm (16 in.) wide, and the longest hutong, 6.5km-long (4-mile) Dongjiaomin Hutong, between Chang'an Avenue and East Street and West Street.

✈ Capital Airport, Beijing

🛏 $$$ **Grand Hyatt,** Dōng Chāng'ān Jiē 1, Dōngchéng District (✆ **86/10/8518-1234;** http://beijing.grand.hyatt.com). $$ **Lǔsōng Yuán Bǎnguân,** Bânchâng Hútòng 22, Dōngchéng District (✆ **86/10/6404-0436;** www.the-silk-road.com).

**TOUR Beijing Hutong Tourist Agency** (✆ **86/10/6615-9097**)

# 7 Where History Was Made

*The Alhambra.*

# The Tower of London
## *Where the Ravens Stand Guard*
London, England

AS CLIMATE CHANGE RAISES OCEAN LEVELS, ONE OF THE RIVERS WATCHED MOST NERVOUSLY is the Thames. With frequent flooding from spring overflows upriver and North Sea storm surges, the iconic Tower of London, on its banks, is among the national treasures at risk.

In the 20th and 21st centuries alone, there were major floods in 1928, 1947, 1953, 1959, 1968, 1993, 1998, 2000, 2003, 2006, and 2007—several of them occurring even after 1984, when the massive flood-control gates of the Thames Barrier were supposed to have solved the problem.

And when the Thames does overwhelm its banks, several of Britain's most revered landmarks are at risk. First and foremost is the Tower of London, a sprawling fortified compound begun by William the Conqueror in 1078 to keep the recently conquered Saxons in check. Originally a royal residence, it was set right on the river, handy in the days when river barges were the speediest means of transport. The section fronting on the river has been furnished to recreate the era of Edward I, with guides in period costume and a copy of Edward's throne.

When James I took over from Elizabeth I in 1608, however, the royal family moved out—understandably, for over the years the Tower had come to be the realm's most important prison. On the walls of the Beauchamp Tower, you can read the last messages scratched by despairing prisoners; according to legend, two little princes (the sons and heirs of Edward IV) were murdered by henchmen of Richard III in the so-called Bloody Tower. Sir Walter Raleigh languished here for 13 years, and Sir Thomas More spent the last 14 months of his life in a whitewashed prison cell in the Bell Tower. Many of these prisoners arrived by boat through the spiked iron portcullis of Traitor's Gate, before being publicly executed in the central courtyard on Tower Green (including two of King Henry VIII's wives, Anne Boleyn and Catharine Howard).

As a fortress, the Tower also made a safe place to store weapons and treasures. The Jewel House contains the Tower's greatest attraction, the Crown Jewels, some of the world's most precious stones set into robes, swords, scepters, and crowns. Prepare to stand in long lines to catch glittering glimpses of the jewels as you scroll by on moving sidewalks.

The Tower of London.

Guided tours of the compound are led by the Yeoman Warders (aka "Beefeaters") in their distinctive red-and-gold uniforms. And don't forget to look for the pack of glossy black ravens fluttering around. According to legend, the Tower of London will stand as long as the ravens remain—so just to be safe, one wing of each raven is clipped.

ⓘ **The Tower of London,** Tower Hill (✆ **0870/756-6060;** www.hrp.org.uk/toweroflondon)

✈ Heathrow International

🛏 $$ **Hart House Hotel,** 51 Glouces- ter Place, Marylebone (✆ **44/20/7935- 2288;** www.harthouse.co.uk). $$ **Vicarage Private Hotel,** 10 Vicarage Gate, South Kensington (✆ **44/20/7229-4030;** www. londonvicaragehotel.com).

## Historic Haunts **375**

# Greenwich Maritime Center
## *When Britain Ruled the Seas*
### Greenwich, England

So what if Greenwich isn't a seaport? This Thameside village 6.4km (4 miles) east of today's London was the epicenter from which England once ruled the seven seas. But with all its historic sites clustered along the river, Greenwich is threatened by the fluctuations of the Thames.

From its hilltop red-brick Royal Observatory, designed in 1675 by Christopher Wren, British astronomers gave England an edge in navigation and timekeeping that kept a vast empire in line. Its Royal Naval College, a Wren-designed complex on the former site of Henry VIII's favorite palace, trained the officers that protected England's shipping lanes. And moored here is the swiftest clipper ship of its day, the 19th-century *Cutty Sark*.

Today's Greenwich, however, wears a distinct sense of having lost its luster. The decade-old Greenwich Foundation is trying to turn that situation around, but it's an uphill battle. The actual Royal Observatory moved out of town (too much light pollution) in the 1950s, leaving that lovely Wren building a mere museum in Greenwich Park. In fact, the hilltop site was useless for observation from the very start—it wasn't properly aligned with celestial meridians, a fact no one bothered to tell its patron, King Charles (the telescopes

were surreptitiously installed in a shed in the garden instead). Still, that imaginary line running through Greenwich remains 0° longitude, the point from which each new day officially begins, as per world agreement in 1884. There's a classic photo op here, as you stand astride the brass inlay representing the Greenwich Line.

As for the Royal Naval College (King William Walk), the school was moved to Shrivenham in 1998. In fact, the college was only here since 1869; before that this handsome baroque campus was a retirement home for seamen (such quality digs, though, do indicate Britain's respect for seafarers). At least you can visit the magnificent Painted Hall, where naval hero Lord Nelson lay in state in 1805.

The *Cutty Sark*? It's closed for restoration, a project complicated by a mysterious 2007 fire that damaged 80% of the iron frame. Fortunately, some of the most important parts of the ship—including its 46m-high (152-ft.) mainmast and half the planking—were already in storage because of restoration, and workers salvaged its ornate figurehead from the blaze. While curators scramble for additional funds to rebuild the ship, many items are displayed at the conservation site visitor center. Even when it's restored, however, the *Cutty Sark* will still be in dry dock, never again to sail the seas.

Mementos of England's seafaring might are displayed at the **National Maritime Museum,** Park Row (© **020/8312-6608;** www.nmm.ac.uk): cannon, ship models, and all sorts of relics, from the dreaded

cat-o'-nine-tails used to flog sailors, to Nelson's coat from the Battle of Trafalgar, showing the fatal bullet hole in his left shoulder.

---

ⓘ **Greenwich Foundation** (www.old royalnavalcollege.org)

✈ Heathrow International

🛏 $$ **Hart House Hotel,** 51 Gloucester Place, Marylebone (© **44/20/7935-2288;** www.harthouse.co.uk). $$ **Vicarage Private Hotel,** 10 Vicarage Gate, South Kensington (© **44/20/7229-4030;** www. londonvicaragehotel.com).

# Leiden Pilgrim Museum
## *Before Plymouth Rock*
### Leiden, the Netherlands

MODERN COMMERCIAL DEVELOPMENT HAS THREATENED WHAT LITTLE IS LEFT OF THIS ESSENTIAL bit of Pilgrim history. The Pilgrim Museum may be the last place to see period relics from America's founding fathers.

Perhaps the only visitors to this tiny brick house in Leiden are Americans—after all, why should the Dutch care about a vagrant crew of religious dissidents from the 17th century? But those dissidents happened to be the Pilgrim Fathers, who lived in this tolerant Dutch university town for 11 long years before sailing to a fresh beginning in the New World. To Americans, it's a remarkable piece of history.

Granted, there's no record of any Pilgrim family lodging in this particular house, but the last verifiable Pilgrim residence—the home of William Bradford, later governor of New Plymouth—was razed in 1985 to make way for a housing project. This museum opened on Thanksgiving Day 1997, displaying furnishings and documents from the period (1609–20) when some 400 families of English Pilgrims found refuge in Leiden, along with other

exiled Protestant sects from around Europe.

At the museum, you can pick up a brochure for an hour-long self-guided walking tour of Pilgrim sites in Leiden. There's the **Lodewijkskerk (Louis Church),** where William Bradford attended meetings of the city's cloth guild. The **Groenehuis (Green House)** on William Brewstersteeg was attached to a printing shop where William Brewster and Thomas Brewer published religious pamphlets that infuriated King James and the Church of England. Plaques at the great Gothic **Sint-Pieterskerk (St. Peter's Church),** in a small square off Kloksteeg, memorialize the Pilgrims, who worshiped here and who lived in its shadow.

An almshouse, the **Jean Pesijnhofje,** now occupies the restored **Groene Port (Green Door)** house on Kloksteeg, where

Inside the Leiden Pilgrim Museum.

Reverend John Robinson and 21 Pilgrim families lived. Though Robinson never made it to the New World, Philip de la Noye—stepson of the Belgian Protestant for whom the almshouse is named—eventually did; his surname would eventually contract to Delano (one of his descendants was Franklin Delano Roosevelt). At **Rapenburg Quay,** you can see where on July 21, 1620, 66 Pilgrims set off on canal barges for the harbor of Delft, where the Speedwell would take them back to England—and a waiting ship named the *Mayflower.*

But two other significant Pilgrim landmarks have been threatened with demolition—the remains of St. Catherine's Hospital, where a wounded Dutch army volunteer named Miles Standish was treated (off Aalmarkt at Mandenmarkerssteeg), and the last mossy stone wall of the Vrouwekerk (Vrouwekerksteeg), where Pilgrims and French Huguenots worshipped together, including ancestors of Ulysses S. Grant and both presidents Bush. These two landmarks stand in the way of modern commercial developments proposed for Leiden's center. International protests staved off the demolition for a while, but the developers have deliberately let them deteriorate further. The Pilgrims' imprint upon Leiden grows fainter every day.

ⓘ **Leiden American Pilgrim Museum,** Beschuitsteeg 9 (ℂ **31/71/512-2413;** www. pilgrimhall.org/leidenmuseum.htm)

✈ Amsterdam

🚄 Leiden

🛏 **$$ Hotel de Doelen,** Rapenburg 2 (ℂ **31/71/512-0527**)

# Alhambra
## *Moorish Pleasure Palace*
### Granada, Spain

AS EUROPE'S HISTORIC MONUMENTS FACE UNSUSTAINABLE CROWDS, THE ISSUE OF HOW TO control visitation levels becomes critical. Drawing over two million visitors a year, this great Spanish castle in 2005 instituted a new policy: timed admission tickets to spread each day's crowd of 7,500-plus visitors more evenly through the day.

The *Calat Alhambra*—the name means Red Castle—looks forbiddingly somber, looming on a rocky outcropping above the city of Granada in southern Andalusia. But get within and you'll discover a Moorish fantasy, a perfect expression of Spain's Muslim past. While a portion of the original rugged 9th-century fort still exists at the core, the castle was transformed starting in 1238 by the Nasrid princes. (Of course, after the Reconquest, in 1526 Holy Roman Emperor Charles V inserted a new Renaissance palace in the middle of this Moorish stronghold.)

The extravagance and sensuality of the Nasrid lifestyle seems diametrically opposite to the fortresslike exterior. Around the arcaded Patio de los Leonares (Court of the Lions), with its immense fountain resting on 12 marble lions, every room tells a story; and now that the press of tourists has been reduced, you can actually view these rooms at leisure. In the Sala de los Abencerrajes, with its richly adorned honeycombed ceiling, the last emir, Boabdil, staged a banquet for his most powerful rivals, only to have his guards massacre them in mid-dinner. In the Sala de los Reyes (Hall of Kings), a great banqueting hall with an exquisitely painted leather ceiling, one sultan beheaded 36 Moorish princes because he suspected one had

seduced his favorite wife. The Hall of the Mexuar was once the sultan's main council chamber; Spanish rulers converted it into a Catholic chapel in the 1600s.

There's even more outside the Alhambra's walls: The Generalife, the sultans' summer retreat, where they used to spend their summers locked away with their harems. Look for the Escalera del Agua (Water Staircase); an enclosed Asian garden, Patio de la Acequía, with water jets arching over its long central pool; and Patio de la Sultana, the secret rendezvous point for Zoraxda, wife of Sultan Abu Hasan, and her lover.

Book your ticket in advance through any branch of BBVA (Banca Bilbao & Vizcaya; © **34/90/222-44-60;** www.alhambra-patronato.es). Come here at night, when floodlights bathe the exotic gardens and palaces—it's a sight you'll never forget.

(i) **The Alhambra,** Palacio de Carlos V (© **34/95/822-09-12**)

✈ Granada

🛏 $$$ **Parador de Granada,** at the Alhambra (© **34/95/822-14-40;** www. parador.es). $$ **Hotel Palacio Santa Inés,** Cuesta de Santa Inés 9 (© **34/95/ 822-23-62;** www.palaciosantaines.com).

# Versailles
## *Ruined Retreat of the Sun King*
### Versailles, France

THE FIERCE WINTER STORMS THAT PUMMELED EUROPE IN DECEMBER 1999 WERE BOUND TO take down some property—but did it have to be Louis XIV's showplace?

Known (for good reason) as the Sun King, this French monarch devoted 50 years to remaking his father's hunting lodge into a royal residence so fabulous, its very name betokens luxury living. Here, he typically hosted some 3,000 courtiers and their retinues at a time. Given the constant entertainment and lavish banquets, few turned down the chance to join the glittering throng—to gossip, dance, plot, and flirt away while the peasants on their estates sowed the seeds of the Revolution. It all caught up with later monarchs Louis XVI and Marie Antoinette, who were eating cake at Versailles on October 6, 1789, when they learned that citizen mobs were converging on the palace. Versailles became a museum under Louis-Philippe (1830–48) and has remained so ever since.

When the 1999 storm hit, hurricane-force winds peeled layers of lead from the roof and blasted out thousands of windowpanes—but those were quickly repaired before the rain could get at the priceless interiors. Today, visitors can tour the State Apartments, loaded with ornate furniture, paintings, tapestries, vases, chandeliers, and sculpture. The most dazzling room—a long arcade called the Hall of Mirrors, with windows along one wall and 357 beveled mirrors along the other—is where the Treaty of Versailles, officially ending World War I, was signed in 1919.

Versailles.

The gardens, though—that's another story. The Gardens of Versailles were the ultimate in French formal garden design, with geometrical flower beds, terraces, pools, topiary, statuary, lakes, and some 50 fountains. An estimated 10,000 beeches, cedars, junipers, and firs were flattened in the storms, 90% of them over 200 years old. Among the trees lost were a Corsican pine tree planted by Napoleon and a tulip tree from Virginia given to Marie Antoinette. Although new seedlings were planted, it will take years—centuries—before those leafy avenues look the way they did.

Most of the trees were not only old, they were too tall for their root systems—Versailles was built over a swamp, and the water table is so high, trees never sink deep roots. Versailles' gardeners see the replanting as a long-overdue chance to restore the park's original design. However, since the days of the Sun King, Paris's suburbs have overtaken his country hideaway. With the trees gone, you can now see apartment towers from the royal terraces—hardly the effect Louis intended.

---

ⓘ **Château De Versailles** (✆ **33/1/30-83-78-00;** www.chateauversailles.fr)

✈ Orly or Charles de Gaulle

🚆 Versailles

🛏 $$$ **Hotel de Fleurie,** 32–34 rue Grégoire-de-Tours (✆ **33/1/53-73-70-00;** www.hotel-de-fleurie.tm.fr). $$ **Hotel Lord Byron,** 5 rue de Chateaubriand (✆ **33/1/43-59-89-98;** www.escapade-paris.com). $ **Timhotel Le Louvre,** 4 rue Croix des Petits-Champs (✆ **33/1/42-60-34-86;** www.timhotel.fr).

379 Historic Haunts

# Lutherstadt Wittenberg

## *Nailed to the Door*

Wittenberg, Germany

Wittenberg has survived a lot of tumult—during the Protestant Reformation, the Thirty Years' War, World War II, the Iron Curtain years—but climate change presents a whole new challenge. Though repairs and renovations were promptly carried out after 2002's major flood, the probability of another inundation looms on the horizon.

There's a reason why they call it a flood plain. Swollen by heavy rains and excessive snowmelt in the Czech mountains, in August 2002 the Elbe river raged through Saxony, looking for a place to spread out. When it reached Wittenberg, the Elbe was already 7.5m (25 ft.) higher than usual, ready to burst its banks. While the church spires of the old town center, set on higher ground north of the river, escaped the worst of it, the waters simply gushed into the flatter working-class suburb of Pratau, turning it into one big lagoon.

As the waters rose, the infrastructure of this former East German region was strained to the utmost. Wittenberg's flood defenses were simply overwhelmed; the main road and railway connections were washed out for days. Residents were evacuated, and when they returned, they found their abandoned homes sodden and thick mud slopped everywhere.

Most of the sights of Wittenberg—officially renamed Lutherstadt Wittenberg, to honor its connection with the great religious reformer Martin Luther—are clustered mainly in the historic center, away from the industrial clutter of the modern town. Look for the round, crown-topped tower of the Schlosskirche at Friedrichstrasse 1A, where Martin Luther nailed his radical *95 Theses* to the door in 1517 (the brass doors there today are a 19th-century addition, engraved with his theses—in church Latin, of course). Luther's affectingly simple tomb is inside. Luther preached most of his dangerously dissident sermons, however, at the twin-towered Gothic parish church of Stadtkirche St. Marien, Judenstr. 35., where he's even depicted in the great altarpiece painted by Lucas Cranach the Elder (you can see Cranach's house on Marksplatz). After splitting from the Catholic faith, Luther—no longer bound by priestly celibacy—also married his wife, a former nun, in the Stadtkirche. Their family home, the Lutherhalle, Collegienstr. 54—a former Augustinian monastery disbanded at the start of the Reformation—has been turned into a

museum displaying Luther's desk, his pulpit, first editions of his books, and the wood-paneled lecture hall where he taught students. The towering Luthereiche (Luther's Oak) at the end of Collegienstrasse outside the Elster gate commemorates the spot where Luther in 1520 defiantly burned the papal edict that excommunicated him. Statues of Luther and his humanist scholar friend, Philip Melancthon, have been erected in the cobbled central square, in front of the big white City Hall (Rathaus).

---

✈ Berlin

🚌 Wittenberg

🛏 $$ **Grüne Tanne,** Am Teich 1 (📞 **49/ 3491/6290;** www.gruenetanne.de)

# Gu Gong (The Forbidden City)
## *Outliving the Emperors*
### Beijing, China

NOWADAYS NEARLY SEVEN MILLION VISITORS A YEAR CROSS THE THRESHOLD OF THIS 500-YEAR-old imperial palace, home to an unbroken line of 24 Chinese emperors. Between Beijing's air pollution and so much foot traffic, the ancient pavements and buildings are wearing down at an unprecedented rate.

It may have been forbidden once, but since the last emperor left in 1923, this vast complex where Chinese emperors lived from 1420 to 1923—beginning long before Columbus sailed to the Americas and ending right before Lindbergh flew across the Atlantic—now belongs to the people. Limiting tourist access would be a ticklish proposition for the Chinese government, since most of the visitors are Chinese citizens, getting in touch with their heritage. Many sections may be closed when you visit, due to a massive renovation lasting through 2020.

Still, there's no one must-see section—it's the scale and harmony of the whole that's so impressive, an irrefutable statement of Chinese imperial might. It's truly the most spectacular palace in China, an immense layout of red-walled buildings

topped with glazed vermilion tile and ringed by a wide moat. It was originally built by an army of workers in only 14 years, although after various ransackings and fires, most of what you see today was built in the 17th century under the Qīng dynasty. Notice the blue and green tiles trimming several of the up-curled roofs—the Qīngs were Manchus, and this color reminded them of their native grasslands.

You enter through the Meridian Gate, but before you go farther, check out the largest gate, the Gate of Heavenly Peace, where Mao Zedong made his dramatic announcement founding the People's Republic in October 1949. (You can't miss it—look for the giant portrait of Mao hanging above the central door.) The Gate of Supreme Harmony leads into the perfectly

The Forbidden City.

symmetrical outer court, with its three grand ceremonial halls, where the emperor conducted official business.

Then comes the inner court—the emperor's private residence—which was truly the Forbidden City; only the imperial family (plus a host of concubines and eunuchs) were allowed here. Three elegant palaces face onto the inner court, and at its rear is a marvelous garden of ancient conifers, rockeries, and pavilions.

If you can, venture beyond the central axis, where all the tourists mass, to the quiet maze of pavilions, gardens, courtyards, and theaters on the eastern side—it's well worth paying this section's extra admission fee. Look for the Hall of Clocks (Zhōngbiǎo Guǎn) and the Zhēnfēi Jǐng (Well of the Pearl Concubine), a narrow hole covered by a large circle of stone. Here, a 25-year-old favorite was stuffed down the well as the imperial family fled during the Boxer Rebellion; she'd dared to suggest that the emperor stay to face the mobs. Defying the emperor? Not a good idea.

ⓘ North side of Tiananmen Square, across Cháng'ān Dàjiē, Běijīng (© **86/10/ 6513-2255,** ext.615)

✈ Capital Airport, Beijing

🛏 $$$ **Grand Hyatt,** Dōng Chāng'ān Jiē 1, Dōngchéng District (© **86/10/8518- 1234,** http://beijing.grand.hyatt.com). $$ **Lǚsōng Yuán Bīnguǎn,** Bānchǎng Hútòng 22, Dōngchéng District (© **86/10/6404- 0436;** www.the-silk-road.com).

**Historic Haunts**

## 381

# Shackleton's Hut
## *Outpost in the Polar Night*
### Cape Royds, Antarctica

AFTER WEATHERING A CENTURY OF ANTARCTIC BLIZZARDS, IT'S NOT SURPRISING THAT THIS modest wooden building, built in 1908, would need a little TLC. Still, it isn't easy to renovate a house that lies in darkness several months at a time, with constant freezing temperatures and hurricane-force winds.

The race to be the first explorer to reach the South Pole engrossed public attention at the beginning of the 20th century. Both the leading British contenders, Sir Robert Scott and Sir Ernest Shackleton, left base huts behind in Antarctica, and the sight of these lone, fragile dwellings on the Antarctic ice still inspires awe.

Making his second Antarctic expedition, Shackleton anchored his ship the *Nimrod* at McMurdo Bay in February 1908. He and his men set up this prefabricated wood hut under a protective ridge of volcanic rock at Cape Royds on Ross Island, where they waited to attempt their trek to the South Pole. In these cramped quarters—10×5.7m (33×19 ft.), with a 2.4m (8-ft.) ceiling—15 men slept, ate, and studied through the cold, dark winter. (They conducted a number of scientific investigations while in Antarctica, mainly to underwrite the race to the pole.) Their clothing, equipment, books, and even their food still lie scattered around the musty hut as if they'd just walked out the door. In fact, when a member of Scott's expedition stopped in 2 years later, he found tins of butter, jam, and gingerbread biscuits, all perfectly fresh. Of course, he took them.

Shackleton's hut was first restored in 1961, and the extreme cold of its surroundings have helped to preserve it. But in recent years more and more visitors have been allowed in—about 700 a year—and even though only eight people go in at a time, brushing their shoes off first and not touching anything inside, inevitably there's been wear and tear. The condition of the hut became so urgent that in 2008 a team of conservators stayed in Antarctica throughout the astral winter to carry out their work in 24-hour darkness. The urgency of this restoration effort testifies to the enduring appeal of this heroic era of Antarctic exploration.

Shackleton and his team got within 161km (100 miles) of the South Pole—the furthest south any human had yet gone—but he never made it to the pole itself. Scott did, in 1911, but only days earlier Roald Amundsen had already planted the Norwegian flag there. Tragically, Scott and his men died returning to base. Shackleton returned 3 years later on the *Endurance* and became the first to cross the Antarctic over land. A heroic era indeed—preserving its last few monuments is the least we can do.

---

**TOUR Polar Cruises** (© **888/484-2244** or 541/330-2454; www.polarcruises.com). **Quark Expeditions** (© **800/356-5699** or 203/656-0499; www.quarkexpeditions. com). **Escorted Antarctica Tours** (© **847/ 306-5595;** www.escortedantarcticatours. com).

# Berlin Wall
## *Shadow Across the City*
### Berlin, Germany

THROUGHOUT THE CITY OF BERLIN, LINES OF COBBLESTONES, BRASS MARKERS, OR GREEN PARKS delineate where the Berlin Wall once stood. With Berlin undergoing a frenzy of real-estate development, who knows how long they'll be left in place?

History is notoriously slippery, but it's treacherously so in Berlin, the once-divided capital of reunified Germany. Berlin still hasn't figured out how to deal with the scar across its heart—the shadow of the Berlin Wall.

A little historical schizophrenia would only be natural. After World War II, Berlin

A segment of the Berlin Wall.

was neatly divided into four sectors, to be administered by the four Allies that had won the war. That didn't last long. Soon the Soviet Union sealed off the western sectors from the surrounding territory of East Germany, which it controlled; the Allies responded with the 1948 to 1949 Berlin Airlift, to get supplies into blockaded West Berlin. After that, some 2.5 million East Germans defected to the West—until August 13, 1961, when overnight the Soviets surrounded West Berlin with barbed wire. That was replaced with a hulking wall of concrete, stretching east and north from Potsdamer Platz—absorbing one of Berlin's loveliest landmarks, the neoclassical **Brandenburger Tor (Unter den Linden).** The final version of the Berlin Wall was two parallel walls with a booby-trapped no-man's-land between, searchlit at night so armed Soviet guards could shoot escapees.

And yet East Germans kept risking death to get to freedom. False passports got some through the heavily guarded crossing point from East to West Berlin—nicknamed Checkpoint Charlie—and others tunneled underneath; yet others tried everything from chairlifts to hot-air balloons to get over the wall. Some 5,000 succeeded, but Soviet guards fatally shot nearly 200 East Germans in mid-escape. Then the Soviet Union fell apart—almost overnight, it seemed—and on November 9, 1989, the wall came tumbling down,

with jubilant Germans on both sides cheering the bulldozers.

Lest we forget, a 70m (230-ft.) stretch of the wall has been reconstructed as part of the **Berlin Wall Memorial,** on Ackerstrasse at Bernauer Strasse, where two stainless-steel walls hold fragments of the original wall. The memorial also incorporates a Chapel of Reconciliation and a ponderous-sounding Documentation Room.

In 2005, however, a grass-roots memorial—incorporating chunks of the original wall, along with some 1,200 crosses commemorating escapees who died—was thrown up on either side of Friedrichstrasse, only to be torn down by the government 2 months later. Its builders didn't own the land, but protesters accused the government of trying to suppress their version of history. In its stead, there's the **Museum Haus am Checkpoint Charlie,** Friedrichstrasse 44 (© **49/30/2537250**), a small museum soberly chronicling those daring escapes, along with a restored watchtower. There are still other watchtowers and bits of wall around the city; follow the walking tours outlined at www. berlin-mauer.de to scout them out.

---

✈ Berlin-Tagel

🛏 $$ **Hotel Hackescher Markt,** Grosse Präsidentenstrasse 8 (© **49/30/280030;** www.loock-hotels.com). $$ **Myers Hotel Berlin,** Betzer Strasse 26 (© **49/30/ 440140;** www.myershotel.de).

# Salt River Bay
## *Columbus's American Landing*
### St. Croix, U.S. Virgin Islands

SIMPLE CARELESSNESS AND NEGLECT THREATENS THIS COASTAL AREA ON SALT RIVER BAY, THE site of Columbus's first landing on what is now U.S. soil. Though it's a national park, many visitors have damaged archeological sites and spoiled the sensitive natural environment, including one of the last stands of mature hardwood trees left on St. Croix.

It must have looked inviting—the lush north coast of this 28-mile-long (45km) Antilles Caribbean island, the largest of its neighbors. Christopher Columbus promptly christened it Santa Cruz (Holy Cross), anchored his fleet of 17 ships, and sent some men ashore to the village to find fresh water. Naturally, along the way the crewmen decided to pick up a couple of the native Tainos for slaves. But they didn't expect the Carib Indians—themselves aggressive invaders who'd only recently taken over the island—to come at them with spears and arrows. By the time the Europeans sailed away, one Carib and one Spaniard lay dead. And so began the history of European settlement in the United States.

The site of Columbus's first landing on what is now U.S. soil—recorded as November 14, 1493, in the log book from his second New World expedition—could be a significant cultural attraction, if only St. Croix could get its act together. This coastal area on Salt River Bay was declared a national park in 1993, to coincide with the 500th anniversary of Columbus's landing, but for many St. Croix locals, the Salt River Bay refuge remained just a handy place to camp out and dump loads of trash (including burned-out cars).

In 2004, however, a crucial parcel of land was acquired with a hilltop white estate house that could be converted into a visitor center, a permanent presence at the site. Now that the site is completed, this park may finally be ready to take off. Salt River Bay has a remarkable set of archaeological sites—including vestiges of a prehistoric settlement, the remains of a ceremonial Taino ballcourt, and the ruins of a 17th-century Dutch colonial fort—but many of the excavators who investigated this site since the 1880s hauled whatever artifacts they found off to various museums around the world. Park managers hope that they can retrieve them for display in the new visitor center.

At present most of the park's visitors are more interested in its ecological features, which are admittedly outstanding. Salt River Bay contains the largest remaining mangrove forest in the Virgin Islands and a submarine coral canyon that attracts divers from around the world. Caribbean Adventure Tours (© **340/778-1522;** www. stcroixkayak.com) runs kayaking trips out of Salt River Marina; the nighttime ones are particularly intriguing, where you can explore the bioluminescent waters of the bay glowing at night.

---

ⓘ **Salt River Bay National Historical Park and Ecological Preserve,** Rte. 75 to Rte. 80, Christiansted (© **340/773-1460;** www.nps. gov/sari, Nov–June). **St. Croix Chamber of Commerce** (© 340/733-1435).

✈ Henry E. Rohlsen Airport

🛏 $$$ **The Buccaneer,** Gallows Bay, North Shore (© **800/255-3881** or 340/ 773-2100; www.thebuccaneer.com). $$ **Inn at Pelican Heights,** 4201 Estate St. John, off Rte. 751 (© **888/445-9458** or 340/713-8022; www.innatpelicanheights. com).

# Pompeys Pillar
## *Captain Clark's Panorama*
### Billings, Montana

GENERATIONS OF TOURISTS HAVE CLIMBED THE ROCK TO SEE THE SWEEPING YELLOWSTONE Valley panorama that so stirred explorers Lewis and Clark in 1806. Hulking grain elevators now stand right across the road from this rock, called Pompeys Pillar, spewing dust into the air and disrupting the natural vista.

Traveling down the 670-mile-long (1,080-km) Yellowstone River, it would be hard to miss Pompeys Pillar—a great bulging outcrop of golden sandstone, standing more than 100 feet (30m) high on the south bank of the river, the tallest elevation for miles in any direction. The local Crow Indians revered it as "the place where the mountain lion lies" and carved animal figures into the rock face. When the white explorers came along in 1806, something about the butte's mysterious power compelled them to add their mark as well.

It's a simple autograph incised in the rock face—*Wm Clark, July 25, 1806*—in some ways no different from the thousands of

Pompeys Pillar.

other carvings added by fur trappers, soldiers, gold prospectors, railroad workers, and homesteaders over the past 2 centuries. But Clark's graffiti is the only physical evidence the Lewis and Clark expedition left behind them as they charted the United States' newly acquired western wilderness for President Jefferson. Do they really want to look down on a complex of high-speed grain elevators?

Outraged protesters temporarily stopped United Harvest from building a 100-acre (40-hectare) grain-loading plant on neighboring land in September 2000, but in the end, a handful of history buffs weren't enough to stop the multinational conglomerate.

Pompeys Pillar has been a landmark for a long time. In 1873, Custer's troops camped here before facing the Sioux at Little Big Horn. The Northern Pacific Railroad built a protective iron grill over Clark's signature in the 1880s because so many passengers got off at the nearby station to view it. It was officially named a National Historic Landmark in 1965, and a national monument in January 2001 (after the grain plant uproar underlined the need to protect the site). A new visitor center with extensive exhibits was opened in 2006 to mark the bicentennial of Clark's visit. You can climb the butte on a protective boardwalk (1,000 ft./300m long, with 200 steps) to view Clark's signature, now encased under glass. Other trails on the site lead to a replica of the expedition's canoes and to a scenic overlook.

In his journal, Clark named the rock formation "Pomp's Tower" after the toddler son of their Shoshoni guide, Sacagawea (the baby's real name was Jean Baptiste Charbonneau, but Clark nicknamed him Pompy, or "Little Chief" in Shoshoni). The pillar isn't Pompy's only claim to fame, either—he even appears on the U.S. gold dollar, being carried by his famous mother.

ⓘ **Pompeys Pillar National Historic Monument,** off I-94 at exit 23 (✆ **406/875-2400;** www.pompeyspillar.org, May to mid-Oct)

✈ Billings

🛏 $$ **Historic Northern Hotel,** 19 N. Broadway, Billings (✆ **406/245-5121**). $$ **The Josephine Bed & Breakfast,** 514 N. 29th St., Billings (✆ **800/552-5898** or 406/248-5898; www.thejosephine.com).

**Making America** **385**

# White House of the Confederacy
## *Under Siege Again*
### Richmond, Virginia

ONGOING EXPANSION OF THE VIRGINIA COMMONWEALTH MEDICAL CENTER THREATENS TO engulf this site, home to Confederate President Jefferson Davis. The museum's board has had to weigh the idea of uprooting the house and carting it off to another spot altogether, although in 2006 it was decided the house should stay put—for now.

Just in case the South rises again, this exquisite neoclassical mansion with its grand white-columned portico lies ready and waiting. Many authentic furnishings remain, the very ones used by Jefferson Davis; his wife, Varina; and their children in the 1860s when Davis served as president of the Confederate States of America.

But while Davis would feel right at home inside, the outside view of this gray stucco mansion would disturb him indeed. The skyscrapers of modern downtown Richmond tower over this three-story home and its attached museum, a far cry from the gracious Court End residential neighborhood in which the house was built in 1818. The modern buildings of the Virginia

Commonwealth Medical Center surround it now on three sides; if the Davis home's site were cleared, the center would no doubt fill the vacuum at once.

During Davis's tenure as president of the Confederacy from 1861 to 1865, this stately home at 12th and Clay streets hosted political conferences, military strategy sessions, and, most of all, elegant luncheons and receptions designed to lift the sagging spirits of the South's leaders as the war dragged on. General Robert E. Lee received his commission as commander of the Confederate Army here. The public areas downstairs have a fussy, formal Victorian elegance—the entrance hall with its classical statues of Comedy and Tragedy holding gas lamps, the dining room with its ornate ceiling decoration, the center parlor presided over by a fine oil portrait of Davis. On the second floor, however, you get a better sense of the Davis family—where the president, often in poor health, worked from his home office, close to the bedrooms and nursery where his five young children (two born in this house) played. Tragically, in 1864 his 5-year-old son Joseph died from an accidental fall from the east portico.

Being so close to the North, Richmond was under constant threat of invasion; the city overflowed with wounded soldiers and prisoners of war. Davis and his family fled Richmond in April 1865 as Union troops bore closer; a few days later Abraham Lincoln toured the abandoned mansion. After the war it became a public school, and in 1890 it was nearly demolished—until a group of Richmond society ladies rallied to save it and turn it into a museum. Floods of mementoes and artifacts were donated by veterans' families all over the South. While some are on display today in the White House itself, many more are in the attached museum, where displays include clothing, weapons, Confederate memorabilia, and even a replica of Lee's headquarters.

ⓘ **Museum of the Confederacy,** 1201 E. Clay St. (✆ **804/649-1861;** www.moc.org)

✈ Richmond

🛏 $$$ **The Jefferson Hotel,** 101 W. Franklin St. (✆ **800/424-8014** or 804/788-8000; www.jeffersonhotel.com). $$ **Linden Row Inn,** 100 E. Franklin St. (✆ **800/348-7424** or 804/783-7000; www.lindenrowinn.com).

**386** Making America

# Beauvoir
## *Jefferson Davis's Last Stand*
### Biloxi, Mississippi

PRESERVATIONISTS RALLIED TO RESCUE WHAT WAS LEFT OF BEAUVOIR AFTER SUFFERING THE wrath of Hurricane Katrina in 2005, which devastated much of Mississippi's coast as well as New Orleans. But how many hurricanes can this historic structure withstand?

After the tumult of the Civil War, former Confederate President Jefferson Davis seemed like a lost soul—barred from politics, stripped of his beloved Mississippi plantation Brierfield, traveling restlessly around the world. At last he found a haven in this serene white cottage on the Mississippi Sound, where in 1877 he settled down to write his memoirs, raise a few

crops (oranges and grapes, mostly), and enjoy his final years with his wife, Varina.

Among the many Gulf Coast sites pummeled by Hurricane Katrina in 2005, Beauvoir seemed one of the most tragic scenes. Submerged under a 24-foot (8m) storm surge, its green storm shutters were battered, lacy lattices crumpled, the roof ripped off, its gracious wraparound verandas torn

# 10 American Battlefields to Fight For

The United States has a very short history, compared to Asian and European nations. And yet we seem to have a mania for enshrining our battlefields—a mania that can lead to modern-day battles between preservationists and real-estate developers, between historians and naturalists. Here are 10 American battle sites where those dramas are being played out today:

**387 Minute Man National Historic Park, Lexington & Concord, Massachusetts** The first shots of the American Revolution were fired here on April 19, 1775, beginning with a dawn skirmish on Lexington's village green and ending amid the farms of Concord later that day. The battle corridor between the towns, along Route 2A, has been declared a Scenic Byway, but it's been a struggle to protect it from Boston's suburban sprawl. The protected confines of the park itself highlight stirring postcard sights like the North Bridge and the Minuteman Statue. ✆ *978/369-6993. www.nps.gov/mima.*

**388 Valley Forge, Pennsylvania** Though it's not technically a battlefield, Valley Forge—where General George Washington nursed his ragtag Continental Army through the bitter winter of 1777 to 1778—represents a significant chapter in Revolutionary War history. You'll see replicas of the ramshackle huts the troops built, the grassy mounds of old defenses, and the hard-packed parade ground where Baron Von Steuben sharpened their battle skills. ✆ *610/783-1077. www.nps.gov/vafo.*

**389 Okeechobee Battlefield, Florida** Just in time, the state of Florida in 2006 purchased a crucial 145-acre (58-hectare) parcel of saw-grass swamp and pineland to preserve from residential development this major battle site from the 1837 Second Seminole War. Col. Zachary Taylor made his name by quelling an uprising by Seminole and Miccosukee warriors. An annual reenactment takes place every winter; musket balls are still buried in the marsh's cypress trees. ✆ *863/634-9587.*

Harpers Ferry.

**390 Harpers Ferry, West Virginia** The beautiful valley where the Shenandoah and Potomac rivers meet was a strategic spot even before the Civil War—a major railroad depot and site of the U.S. Arsenal, which radical abolitionist John Brown raided in 1859. The war wreaked havoc on the town, which changed hands eight times, most notably with Stonewall Jackson's victory at the 1862 Battle of Harpers Ferry. ✆ *304/535-6029. www.nps.gov/hafe.*

**391 Antietam, Maryland** One of the nation's best preserved battlefields, the picturesque valley of Antietam commemorates September 17, 1862—often called the bloodiest single day in American history (23,000 casualties)—where the Confederacy's first attempt to invade th e North ended in defeat. General Lee's farmhouse headquarters at Antietam, however, may soon have a view of a cell tower thrusting 30 feet (9m) above the tree line. ℭ *301/432-5124.* *www.nps.gov/anti.*

**392 Gettysburg, Pennsylvania** This rolling swath of farmland saw the Civil War's most decisive battle; Abraham Lincoln delivered his famous speech here a year later. Walking around this historic landscape can be a spine-tingling experience, especially with a tour guide to narrate tragic events at the very places they transpired. ℭ *866/889-1243.* *www.nps.gov/gett.*

**393 Vicksburg National Battlefield Park, Mississippi** Set on 1,800 acres (720 hectares) of riverside bluffs, this military park commemorates the 47-day-long Siege of Vicksburg in 1863, which the Union won the same day as Gettysburg. Thickly scattered with monuments, the park has many deteriorating markers and historic sites; vandalism, soil erosion, and rampant kudzu persist, and forests have overgrown battlefields, obscuring any sense of what the fighting was like. ℭ *601/636-0583.* *www.nps.gov/vick.*

Vicksburg National Battlefield Park.

**394 Fredericksburg and Spotsylvania County National Park, Virginia** Not one but four major Civil War battles were waged on this wooded patch of Virginia countryside: Robert E. Lee's early victories at Fredericksburg and Chancellorsville, balanced by Confederate defeats in 1864 at the Wilderness and Spotsylvania Courthouse. It's the second largest military park on the planet, with two visitor centers, four historic structures, and miles of driving and walking trails. ℭ *540/373-6122.* *www.nps.gov/frsp.*

**395 Monocacy, Maryland** Confederate troops would have captured Washington in July 1864 if an outnumbered force of Union soldiers hadn't delayed them at this patch of farmland just outside Frederick, Maryland. An oasis amid the modern Washington metro sprawl, Monocacy is at risk of being spoiled by three developments: the smokestack of a proposed waste facility, the possible erection of high-voltage transmission towers, and the widening of a busy commuter highway. ℭ *301/662-3515.* *www.nps.gov/mono.*

**396 Pearl Harbor, Honolulu, Hawaii** A date that will live in infamy, FDR called it—December 7, 1941, when Japanese bombers attacked U.S. ships at Pearl Harbor, Honolulu, the first attack on American soil since the War of 1812. The centerpiece is the USS Arizona Memorial, where just 6 feet (1.8m) below the water's surface, you can see the deck of the 608-foot battleship that sank that day, killing 1,177 sailors. ℭ *808/422-0561.* *www.nps.gov/usar.*

Pearl Harbor.

from the raised foundation. The Jefferson Davis Presidential Library that opened here in 1998 was also badly damaged, losing nearly a third of its collection, and several outlying buildings were leveled. But a determined crew of conservators went to work at once, supported by a combination of FEMA grants and private donations. Considering the general devastation of the Gulf Coast, hiring workers and getting building materials was often a challenge, but Beauvoir's saviors persevered. As of March 2008, the repairs on the main house were nearly completed, though much work remained to be done on the 51-acre site. The Library Pavilion where Davis worked on his books was demolished by the storm and is to be replaced with a replica.

Surrounded with cedars, oaks, and magnolia trees—many of them dripping with Spanish moss—with wide Gulf views from the front porch and a quiet little bayou tucked behind the house, Beauvoir's Deep South charm must have been balm to Jefferson Davis's soul. As opposed to the stately formality of the Confederate White House in Richmond, this one-story house had a much more relaxed aura. Working in the book-lined library pavilion across the lawn, he wrote two books in a burst of literary energy—*The Rise and Fall of the Confederate Government* (1881) and *A Short History of the Confederate States of America* (1889).

Sadly, he had only a few years to enjoy it—he died in New Orleans in 1889 (he was eventually reinterred in Richmond's Hollywood Cemetery). After Varina's death, the estate became the site of a retirement home for Confederate veterans; a cemetery on the property contains the graves of several Beauvoir residents, including the Tomb of the Unknown Confederate Soldier.

ⓘ **Beauvoir,** 2244 Beach Blvd., Biloxi (✆ **228/388-4400;** www.beauvoir.org)

✈ Gulfport-Biloxi International Airport

🛏 $$ **Best Western Cypress Creek,** 7921 Lamar Poole Rd. (✆ **800/466-8941** or 228/875-7111; www.bestwestern.com). $$ **Star Inn,** 1716 Beach Blvd., Biloxi (✆ **228/374-8888;** www.starinnbiloxi.net).

---

Making America 397

# Erie Canal National Historic Corridor
## *Clinton's Ditch Redux*
### Albany to Buffalo, New York

IN 2001, THE ERIE CANAL WAS NAMED A NATIONAL HERITAGE CORRIDOR. HOWEVER, THERE'S NO single source of funding, and projects may fall between the cracks. Whether they'll succeed to resurrect this historic waterway remains to be seen.

Perhaps it was inevitable—once New York City no longer needed the Erie Canal, the Erie Canal was left to die. Superseded by the St. Lawrence Seaway, the interstate highways, and air freight, this monumental artificial waterway simply withered away. Old towpaths are deserted, and moss and weeds sprout along its stone walls. Once-prosperous upstate New York—with 80% of its population living along the canal's corridor—continues to falter.

New York Governor DeWitt Clinton was derided in 1817 for his plan to build a canal linking the Hudson River to the Great Lakes, but "Clinton's Ditch" soon transformed New York State into a commercial powerhouse, making New York City the nation's most important port and giving rise to several industrial cities along its

The Erie Canal.

course—Albany, Schenectady, Utica, Syracuse, Rochester, Buffalo. Within 9 years after it opened in 1825, enough tolls were collected to pay off its $10-million construction cost (a whopping sum at the time). An engineering marvel of its age, the original canal was 363 miles (584km) long, 40 feet (12m) wide, and 4 feet (1.2m) deep; flat-bottomed barges were pulled along it by horses and mules plodding on a waterside towpath. Quaint as it seems, this revolutionary (and nonpolluting) method of transport cost one-tenth of the price of hauling goods on land.

The most significant feature so far is the Old Erie Canal State Historic Park, a 36-mile stretch of original canal just east of Syracuse, where you can view the old canal towpath and ruined stone aqueducts. Its highlight is the recreated 1840s townscape at **Erie Canal Village,** at the intersection of routes 46 and 49 in Rome,

which offers costumed interpreters, mule-boat rides, and narrow-gauge train excursions. For an in-depth look at the boats that plied the canal, you can also visit the nearby **Chittenango Landing Canal Boat Museum,** 7010 Lakeport Rd., Chittenango. Twelve miles (19km) north of Albany in Waterford, where the Mohawk River merges with the Hudson, there's an Erie Canal Historic Corridor visitor center at **Peebles Island State Park**. Nearby, you can see a long-abandoned aqueduct at the **Schoharie Crossing State Historic Site,** in Fort Hunter, which also includes a 3.5-mile-long (5.6km) section of the original canal.

Meanwhile, sections of towpath have been developed as bike trails, connecting with existing roadways to create a 260-mile-long (419km) trail along the course of the canal. The longest section is the 100-mile (161km) stretch from Lockport to Fairport in western New York (for a map contact Parks and Trails New York at www.ptny.org). The Erie-Champlain Canal Boat Company (© **518/577-6363;** www.eccboating.com) also offers canal boat tours from Waterford, where you can have the experience of being lifted 169 feet (51m) around Cohoes Falls through a series of five locks, the highest canal lift in the world.

ⓘ **Erie Canalway National Heritage Corridor Commission** (www.eriecanal way.org)

✈ Albany, Syracuse, Buffalo

🛏 $$ **The Morgan State House,** 393 State St., Albany (© **888/427-6063** or 518/427-6063; www.statehouse.com). $$ **The Craftsman Inn,** 7300 E. Genesee St., Syracuse (© **800/797-4464** or 315/637-8000; www.craftsmaninn.com).

**Making America** 398

# Eleutherian College
## *An Education in Freedom*
### Lancaster, Indiana

HAVING STOOD EMPTY FOR YEARS, THE DILAPIDATED BUILDINGS OF ELEUTHERIAN COLLEGE— a long-abandoned campus that pioneered racial integration—are finally getting a well-deserved restoration.

Sometimes the most progressive ideas are found in unlikely places. This bustling village in the farmland of southern Indiana, for example—who'd expect to find traces here of an antislavery hotbed?

Lancaster—a small town 10 miles (16km) north of Madison—was at the very epicenter of the Midwest's abolitionist movement. Beginning in the 1830s, the Neil's Creek Anti-Slavery Regular Baptist Church flourished in Lancaster. When a visiting minister from Ohio, Reverend Thomas Craven, preached about his dream of a school educating whites and blacks, men and women, together—a radical idea in those days—the congregation declared themselves ready to make his dream a reality. Thus did Eleutherian College come into being, a secondary school that was not only coed, but racially integrated—a bold experiment indeed.

Classes began in 1848 in an old meeting house near the village sawmill on Middle Fork Creek. Not everyone in the community welcomed the new black students; though Indiana was officially a northern state, sentiments in this part of the state were generally pro-slavery (they were just across the Ohio River from Kentucky, after all), and there were plenty of hostile confrontations. Yet the college's supporters pushed on, and by 1856 they'd built a simple yet imposing three-story Greek Revival building of local field stone on a nearby hilltop, topped by a square white-frame bell tower. Along with seven classrooms, the building featured a two-story-high chapel, proof of the religious conviction that infused the school's political stance.

By 1856, Eleutherian—which was chiefly a teacher training college—had 18 black students enrolled, 10 of them former slaves. In 1860 the college had 200 students, 50 of them black. Both teachers and students helped to hide fugitive slaves at the college on their way north to freedom. Once the Civil War broke out, the college's grounds housed soldiers training to join the Indiana Sixth Regiment. Male Eleutherian students, black and white, flocked to join the Union Army; many would lose their lives, fighting for a cause close to their hearts.

But as the years passed, the need for a school like Eleutherian dwindled; it finally shut down in 1887. A grade school occupied the building until 1937. For years after that it stood empty, and increasingly derelict. Finally Historic Eleutherian College Inc. was formed to buy the site in 1990; the nonprofit organization also purchased the nearby Lyman Hoyt House, home of a local abolitionist who was an active Underground Railroad conductor. Restoration work continues on the badly dilapidated main college hall, but a visitor center with historic displays was recently opened; tours of the Hoyt House are available by appointment.

ⓘ **Historic Eleutherian College,** 6927 W. State Rd. 250 (*©* **812/273-9434;** www. eleutherian.us)

✈ Louisville

🛏 $$$ **Whitehall Bed & Breakfast,** 1229 W. Main St., Madison (*©* **812/273-3024;** www.whitehallbb.com). $$ **Riverboat Inn Hotel,** 901 E. 1st St., Madison (*©* **812/265-2361;** www.riverboatinn.net).

---

**399** **Making America**

# Little Rock Central High School
## *Following the Steps of the Nine*
### Little Rock, Arkansas

THE LITTLE ROCK CENTRAL HIGH SCHOOL PLAYED A VITAL PART IN THE CIVIL RIGHTS DEVELOPMENTS of the mid–20th century. Yet because it remained a working high school, its development as a historic site has been a challenge.

Imagine the courage it took for nine African-American teenagers to walk into Central High School in September 1957, ready to enroll for the new school year. Central was an all-white school, and a prestigious one at that—an imposing collegiate Gothic beauty with a turreted roofline and sweeping front staircase. It had 100 classrooms, a field house, a football stadium, and many other luxuries unheard of at Dunbar High, the black school a few blocks away.

The ink was still fresh on the Supreme Court's pro-integration ruling in *Brown v. Board of Education*—now all that was needed was a test case, and civil rights leaders were prepared to give the nation one. It was a tense chapter in American history, played out daily in newspapers and television newscasts.

Visiting this landmark of recent history has always been complicated—not because the building is old or dilapidated, but because it's still a fully functioning school, in top condition. For years, visitors to the site had to make do with the displays at an old Mobil gas station across the street, converted into a visitor center, and tours were only available outside of the school term.

On the 50th anniversary of the Little Rock crisis, however, a dedicated visitor center was finally opened in September 2007, with all nine of the original Little Rock Nine present. Ranger-led tours are now permitted inside the school building, although only six per week, limited to 10 people (reserve well in advance).

At the center, videos, taped oral histories, and photographic displays tell the story of that fateful September. Arkansas's governor was all ready for the black students: Defying federal desegregation orders, he had the Arkansas National Guard turn them away. Three weeks later, the Nine finally entered the building to start classes, but an incensed crowd of protesters outside made the scene so dangerous, Little Rock police had to escort the kids out

Little Rock Central High School.

again. Next morning, the 101st Airborne showed up, on orders from President Eisenhower, to usher the black students safely inside, while TV news cameras whirred.

As the school year wore on, the troops and TV cameras stopped hovering outside, but opponents of integration kept tempers at a boiling point inside Central—"If parents would just go home and let us alone, we'll be all right," one white student remarked. One of the Nine, tired of continual harassment, quit school and moved to New York City. Another, Ernest Green, graduated in spring, commenting wryly,

"It's been an interesting year." Yes, but a year that changed history.

ⓘ **Little Rock Central High School National Historic Site,** 2125 W. Daisy L. Gatson Bates Dr. (✆ **501/374-1957;** www.nps.gov/chsc)

✈ Little Rock National

🛏 $$$ **The Peabody Little Rock,** 3 Statehouse Plaza (✆ **501/906-4000;** www.peabodylittlerock.com). $$ **Doubletree Hotel Little Rock,** 424 W. Markham (✆ **501/372-4371;** www.doubletreelr.com).

Making America  400

# Rivers of Steel
## *Heritage Lost*
### Greater Pittsburgh, Pennsylvania

THE FOOTBALL TEAM IS STILL NAMED THE STEELERS, BUT THE HULKING MILLS THAT ONCE LINED the Allegheny and Monagahela rivers have disappeared, razed in the 1970s and 1980s rather than retooled to compete with foreign steel. Preservationists are now scrambling to resurrect the vestiges of this historic era.

Steel town? Not Pittsburgh—not any more. Once upon a time, Pittsburgh steel was used everywhere—in the Brooklyn Bridge, the Panama Canal, the Empire State Building, the Oakland Bay Bridge, the United Nations headquarters. Today, high-tech industries and medical centers now support Pittsburgh's substantially shrunken population. With those belching smokestacks gone, Pittsburgh's skyline looks completely different.

Perhaps Pittsburgh was too hasty in erasing the gritty evidence of its former industrial might. Preservationists are now working to mold what's left in outlying towns into the Rivers of Steel Heritage area. The most substantial element so far is the U.S. Steel works in Homestead, east of Pittsburgh, built in 1879. Once covering nearly 400 acres (160 hectares), this was the world's largest producer of steel in World War II. Though the works were shut in 1987 and demolished, a row of brick smokestacks along the Monongahela River anchors the Waterfront retail center, which also displays quaint relics like a huge gantry crane and a 1900-era heavy steel forging press.

Other attractions in Homestead are being proposed as the nucleus of an urban national park: the rusted hulk of the Carrie Furnaces, the valley's oldest and last remaining blast furnace; the Pump House, scene of a bloody 1892 face-off between 10,000 striking workers and 300 Pinkerton detectives hired by industrialist Henry Clay Frick; and the Bost Building, a Victorian-era hotel that served as union headquarters during the Homestead Strike, which is now a visitor center for the heritage area. Plans are to build walkways around the 92-foot-high (28m) Carrie Furnaces towers, along with more kitschy ideas such as a monorail, cafes, decorative lighting, and other amusements to "spice up" the disused 38-acre (15-hectare) industrial site.

Other area towns have preserved vestiges of Big Steel's associated industries. In Braddock, the Edgar Thomson Works, one of Andrew Carnegie's original century-old mills, still produces hot iron to be made into steel; in Tarentum, the Tour-Ed Mine lets you explore a former coal mine, which produced fuel to power those factories; in Scottdale, the Shoaf's Mine

and Coke Works has been preserved with more than 300 block and beehive ovens; and in Brownsville, the restored W.A. Young & Son's Foundry and Machine Shop shows the craftsmanship required to keep factory machinery operative.

In Pittsburgh itself, however, the chief reminder of Big Steel is the cultural institutions founded by the steel barons: the **Carnegie Museum of Art,** 4400 Forbes Ave., Oakland; the **Carnegie Museum of Natural History,** 4400 Forbes Ave., Oakland; the **Carnegie Science Center,** 1 Allegheny Ave.; and the **Frick Art & Historical Center,** 7227 Reynolds St. As for the immigrants who actually made the steel, they're commemorated by the **Nationality Rooms** in the Cathedral of Learning at the University of Pittsburgh, 24 classrooms decorated in the architectural styles of Pittsburgh's major immigrant groups.

---

ⓘ **Rivers of Steel Heritage Area visitor center,** 623 E. Eighth Ave., Homestead (📞 **412/464-4020;** www.riversofsteel.com)

✈ Pittsburgh

🛏 $$$ **Omni William Penn,** 530 William Penn Place (📞 **888/444-6664** or 421/281-7100; www.omniwilliampenn.com). $$ **Holiday Inn Pittsburgh at University Center,** 100 Lytton Ave. (📞 **888/465-4329** or 412/682-6200; www.ichotelsgroup.com).

**401** Making America

# Bethlehem Steel Works
## *Reinventing a Steel Town*
### Bethlehem, Pennsylvania

THE SKELETONS OF EMPTY STEEL MILLS HAUNT THE SKYLINE OF BETHLEHEM, PENNSYLVANIA—a Big Steel company town if there ever was one. City fathers have struggled with whether to replace them with new industry, turn them into a museum, or allow the controversial introduction of a casino.

Pittsburgh may be denying its Rust Belt roots, but at the other end of the state, Bethlehem, Pennsylvania, has had to take a different tack. Founded in 1861 in this quiet

Moravian town, the Bethlehem Steel Corporation became the nation's second-largest steel producer, at its peak sustaining a 5-mile-long (8km) steel works that covered thousands of acres and accounted for one-fifth of the town's revenue; 165,000 workers were employed here in 1957, many of them immigrants from Eastern and Southern Europe.

Today, Bethlehem Steel Corporation is still in business elsewhere, but the hometown works in Bethlehem ground to a halt in November 1995. The great steel mills on the south bank of the Lehigh River stood silent and rusting, their black smokestacks cold. Train tracks that shuttled freight trains continually in and out of the plants lay weed-choked and empty. It was a haunting scene, with a certain decaying majesty.

While some buildings have been cleared away, much of the brown field still stands deserted. Bethlehem Steel announced in 2000 that they were redeveloping the plants into a commerce center called Bethlehem Works, but only a few small firms opened offices. The next great hope was the National Museum of Industrial History, an affiliate of the Smithsonian, originally planned to open in 2003.

But as that project stalled, a whole new approach began to take shape. In December 2006 the state awarded a gaming license to Las Vegas Sands Corporation to open a slot-machine casino and attached hotel on another section of the property. Restaurants, shops, and a concert hall are envisioned as part of this Sands Bethworks development as well. With this commercial anchor in place, the industrial history museum moved ahead, with a somewhat scaled-down design. Some heavy machinery from the Bethlehem plant was salvaged to be displayed in the new museum, but much of it will feature historic artifacts from the Smithsonian's collection, with no specific Bethlehem connection.

The developers soon discovered how well built those old factories were; they stubbornly resisted demolition, causing significant delays in the project. The design is intended to honor the legacy of the site, with exposed steel trusses and brick walls, a massive ore crane incorporated into the casino entrance, and lighting that imitates the red night-time glow of blast furnaces.

As a prop to the area's flagging economy, the Sands Bethworks was welcomed—but many in town wonder whether the flash and glitter of a casino belong in a town founded by a religious sect, whose tidy fieldstone buildings still line the leafy streets of the historic district across the river. The poetic desolation of the abandoned mills looks pretty good in contrast.

---

ⓘ www.sandsbethworks.com. www.nmih.org.

✈ Lehigh Valley International

🛏 $$$ **Hotel Bethlehem,** 437 Main St. (✆ **800/607-BETH** [607-2384] or 610/625-5000; www.hotelbethlehem.com). $$$ **Sayre Mansion Inn,** 250 Wyandotte St. (✆ **877/345-9019** or 610/882-2100).

---

Making America 402

# Cook County Hospital
## *The Real ER*
### Chicago, Illinois

NAMED ONE OF THE NATION'S 11 MOST ENDANGERED PLACES BY THE NATIONAL TRUST FOR Historic Preservation, stately Cook County Hospital managed to stave off demolition from knee-jerk urban renewal—until 2008, when four wings of the Beaux Arts structure were demolished.

When it comes to hospitals, shiny and new always seems better. Even a venerable institution like Chicago's Cook County Hospital, purposely built to treat the urban poor, eventually came to seem outdated. In 2002, an entirely new Cook County Hospital was opened, equipped to provide the latest in 21st-century health care. Its nearly-century-old predecessor was slated for demolition, to be replaced with a large park—a welcome amenity in this Near West Side neighborhood with its jumble of medical buildings.

But then the public outcry began.

When Cook County Hospital opened in 1914, it was a product of the Beautiful City movement, which sought to make every public building an impressive monument. Architects Paul Gerhardt and Richard Schmidt created a Beaux Arts showplace, its facade adored with fluted Ionic columns and sculptured pediments, bands of gray granite alternating with yellow brick and glazed terra-cotta tile in gray, yellow, and cream colors. Massive as it was—2 blocks long, eight stories high—it was so superbly proportioned, it seemed elegant rather than heavy. Details were applied lavishly, from baroque cartouches and ornate cornices to delicate heads of lions and cherubs. The poorest patient could feel proud to be treated in such a majestic edifice.

The campaign to save County from the wrecking ball was only partly about its architectural grandeur, however. For many other supporters, the hospital's historic importance mattered equally. As the nation's largest public hospital, in its early years it admitted so many immigrants, it was nicknamed Chicago's Statue of Liberty. Then, as Chicago's demographics changed, County served an entirely black patient base, joined in its last years by more Hispanics and Asians. Yet it maintained its stature as one of the world's great teaching hospitals; it housed the nation's first blood bank (1937), first trauma center (1966), and first AIDS clinic (1983). Its doctors made breakthrough advances in treating sickle cell anemia, and its emergency room was legendary for its excellence (the TV show *ER* was modeled on County).

A flurry of public protests stopped the demolition in 2003; since then, Cook County Hospital has sat in limbo, as several redevelopment plans have been batted back and forth. In 2004, it was named one of the nation's 11 Most Endangered Places by the National Trust for Historic Preservation. In January 2008, the bulldozers finally moved in—but only to demolish four wings jutting from the south side of the building, later additions that weren't architecturally distinguished. That's a hopeful sign—chances are getting better and better that this exquisite gem of a public building will be preserved after all.

---

ⓘ **Old Cook County Hospital,** 1835 W. Harrison St.

✈ O'Hare International

🛏 $$ **Hotel Allegro Chicago,** 171 N. Randolph St. (ⓒ **800/643-1500** or 312/236-0123; www.allegrochicago.com). $$ **Homewood Suites,** 40 E. Grand St. (ⓒ **800/ CALL-HOME** [225-5466] or 312/644-2222; www.homewoodsuiteschicago.com).

---

403 **Making America**

# The Survivors' Staircase
## *Flight to Safety*
### New York, New York

FOR YEARS AFTER SEPTEMBER 11, 2001, VISITORS CAME TO GAZE UPON GROUND ZERO IN LOWER Manhattan—even though it was just a huge rectangular crater where the World Trade Center buildings used to stand. Only one haunting feature remained above ground: a 37-step flight of granite-clad stairs, torn from its travertine plaza, leading nowhere.

The World Trade Center's Survivors' Staircase.

But on September 11, that stairway led somewhere—it led from the World Trade Center's aboveground plaza to Vesey Street, and safety. Untold hundreds of office workers stampeded down them, fleeing the 110-story towers before they collapsed. It was the only way out of the smoke, flames, and falling debris.

Even after the North and South towers collapsed, fatally damaged by the terror attacks of that morning, this stairway somehow remained in place. Over the next several months, rubble was cleared from all around it, but still the stairs stood. Already damaged badly by the disaster, they were further shaken by the vibrations of construction all around, as new buildings began to rise—a station for the PATH commuter train to New Jersey, a World Trade Center memorial, and a new skyscraper named Freedom Tower. But this stairway, already known as the Survivors' Staircase, outlasted it all, a survivor itself.

The stairway's location, however, was right in the middle of the footprint of a new building to be erected on the 16-acre (6.4-hectare) site. Though preservationists and survivors fought to have the stairs preserved in situ, it became clear that the stairs would have to be moved. The Port Authority of New York and New Jersey, which owns the site, claimed that the staircase was too large (175 tons) to be moved intact, given the concrete bulkhead that supported them, but in late 2007 a compromise was reached: the flight of steps would be pried out of their concrete base and installed at the September 11 memorial.

In March 2008, a crane lifted the stairs, their granite risers protectively encased in plywood, and put them on a truck, which hauled them off to a storage site nearby. Eventually, they will be moved again in the memorial, where they'll be installed near the original footprints of the twin towers, along with several other World Trade Center relics.

Granted, there's one last piece of the towers remaining in place—a foundation wall below the ground—but with the stairs gone, nothing visible remains of the old World Trade Center. To some survivors and victims' families, the loss of this last vestige is poignant. But when you consider that these lifesaving stairs might have been razed a long time ago, having them preserved at all counts as a victory.

---

ⓘ **NYC & Company** (☏ **800/NYC-VISIT** [692-8474]; www.nycvisit.com)

✈ John F. Kennedy International, Newark Liberty International, LaGuardia

🛏 $$ **Washington Square Hotel,** 103 Waverly Place (☏ **800/222-0418** or 212/777-9515; www.washingtonsquarehotel.com). $ **Best Western Seaport Inn,** 33 Peck Slip (☏ **800/HOTEL-NY** [468-3569] or 212/766-6600; www.bestwestern.com).

# The Mount
## *Edith Wharton's Country Cottage*
Lenox, Massachusetts

AFTER AN AWARD-WINNING REFURBISHMENT THAT RESTORED THE MOUNT'S ORIGINAL ELEGANCE in 2006, the foundation that operates Wharton's home discovered that it faced foreclosure—the bank loans that had underwritten that massive rehabilitation were coming due, and there wasn't money enough to pay them.

Upper-class society was Edith Wharton's literary turf—nobody, except perhaps her friend Henry James, could more minutely dissect the lives of late-19th-century American aristocrats. Wharton knew those people's manners and mores because she herself had been born into that privileged class in 1862. Naturally, her country estate in the Berkshire mountains befit her social position—a splendid white Palladian villa, redolent of wealth and refinement.

This house wasn't just a piece of real estate for Wharton—she designed it herself, based on principles she outlined in her influential 1897 book, *The Decoration of Houses,* co-authored with architect Ogden Codman, Jr. The intricate formal gardens, too, were designed according to the tenets of her *Italian Villas and Their Gardens* (1904). She described the Mount in her autobiography as a "spacious and dignified house" and "my first real home." Set on stone terraces above its formal garden, this three-story mansion offered a wide veranda, loads of large black-shuttered windows to let sunlight pour in, and neoclassical touches throughout the gracious interior. Her luxurious bedroom suite shows where she wrote her first best-selling novels, *The House of Mirth, Madame des Treynes,* and *Ethan Frome,* often writing for hours propped up in bed.

Wharton lived here from 1902 until 1911, just as her literary career was taking off; she sold the Mount after her first marriage ended (a society match to an unstable, unfaithful husband) and lived in Europe for the rest of her life. Though it was a showplace in Wharton's own time, by 1997 the estate showed the wear and tear of years of heavy visitation and inadequate upkeep. The mansion and its outbuildings—stable, gatehouse, greenhouse—looked shabby and dilapidated. The gardens had lapsed into an overgrown mess.

Nine years of intense restoration brought the house and gardens back to their former glory by 2006. In 2005, another significant investment was made: acquiring Wharton's personal 2,600-volume book collection, now proudly displayed at the Mount. Unfortunately, this most recent chapter of the Mount's history reads like something out of one of her novels. With its foundation facing foreclosure, an urgent fundraising campaign was immediately launched to raise the $3 million necessary to save this literary and architectural landmark. After all that has been done to revive the spirit of Edith Wharton's beloved estate, to have it shut down by bankers would be the ultimate blow.

ⓘ 2 Plunkett St. (✆ **413/551-5111;** www.edithwharton.org, May–Dec only)

✈ Pittsfield

🛏 $$$ **Gateways Inn,** 51 Walker St., Lenox (✆ **800/492-9466** or 413/637-2532; www.gatewaysinn.com). $ **Lenox Inn,** 525 Pittsfield Rd., Lenox (✆ **413/499-0324**).

# Walden Pond
## *Thoroughly Thoreau*
### Concord, Massachusetts

IN THE MID-1980s, A CONDO DEVELOPMENT AND AN OFFICE BUILDING WERE NEARLY BUILT ON two adjoining tracts of land of Walden Woods; the Walden Woods Project conservation group bought those tracts of land, but at least 30% of the woods are still not officially protected and vulnerable to development.

Even back in 1859, Walden Woods were threatened, in danger of being leveled for farmland. "All Walden wood might have been preserved for our park forever," Henry David Thoreau noted sadly in his journal, nostalgic already for the way Walden Pond looked when he lived there in a simple cabin from July 1845 to September 1847.

Today, Thoreau's 1854 book about that sojourn, *Walden: Or Life in the Woods,* is revered as a bible of the conservation movement. But when Thoreau lived beside this deep kettle-hole pond in the Massachusetts farmlands, Concord was a separate village, not the unit of Boston suburban sprawl that it has since become. Although 2,700 acres (1,080 hectares) of woods have been protected surrounding Walden Pond (designated a National Historic Landmark), development presses right up to its margins. In the mid-1980s, a condo development and an office building were nearly built on two adjoining tracts of land; the Walden Woods Project conservation group bought those tracts of land, but at least 30% of the woods are still not officially protected and are vulnerable to development.

Within the park, recreational use has taken its toll. The pond is popular for swimming and boating in summer; folks

Walden Pond.

wandering off the hiking trails trample the vegetation at water's edge, causing the shoreline to erode. To many visitors, these woods aren't a literary shrine, they're a state park, and the rangers have had to ban dogs, bicycles, and outdoor grills, and limit visitors to 1,000 a day. The pond's fish have died out; it's artificially stocked now. It's been hard to keep the water clear, with a nearby landfill and septic systems leaching into the aquifer that feeds the pond; acid rain is another problem. Visitors unwittingly bring in exotic species, and swimming inevitably leads to clouds of algae.

Still, it's better than it was—from 1866 to 1902 there were cafes, swings, a baseball diamond, and a dining pavilion on the shore. Most of the woods had been cut down in 1922 when the state acquired the property (a 1938 hurricane mowed down many more trees, including some Thoreau himself planted). Named a National Historic Landmark in 1965, Walden Pond and its woods were restored to a more natural state in the '60s and '70s, as the burgeoning environmental movement fostered deeper admiration for Thoreau's "experiment in simplicity." The woods have grown back, the same native mix of pine, hickory, and oak Thoreau knew. A replica has been built of Thoreau's one-room cabin, but it's across the road from the pond, next to a parking lot (a marker indicates the original site overlooking the pond). Nowadays you'll have to come on a weekday, or in spring or fall, to experience the solitude Thoreau enjoyed.

---

ⓘ **Walden Pond State Reservation,** Rte. 126, Concord (✆ **978/369-3254**)

✈ Logan International

⊨ $$ **Doubletree Guest Suites,** 400 Soldiers Field Rd. (✆ **800/222-TREE** [8733] or 617/783-0090; www.doubletree.com). $ **The MidTown Hotel,** 220 Huntington Ave. (✆ **800/343-1177** or 617/262-1000).

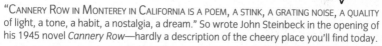

**406** **Literary Landmarks**

# Cannery Row
## *Sanitized Steinbeck*
### Monterey, California

"CANNERY ROW IN MONTEREY IN CALIFORNIA IS A POEM, A STINK, A GRATING NOISE, A QUALITY of light, a tone, a habit, a nostalgia, a dream." So wrote John Steinbeck in the opening of his 1945 novel *Cannery Row*—hardly a description of the cheery place you'll find today.

And yet Monterey does promote Steinbeck's gritty image of Cannery Row, this harborside strip where a dozen sardine-canning operations operated through the first half of the 20th century. A fleet of sardine boats once nosed up to these wharves and unloaded their catch directly onto conveyor belts; noisy rattling machines stuffed the little fish into tins before they came out the other side, to be packed straight onto Southern Pacific freight trains. During the two World Wars especially, America's appetite for canned sardines seemed limitless, and the canneries boomed. Given the odors and the noise, Ocean View Avenue—a street once known for its seaside resort hotels—was fit only for bordellos and flophouses. No wonder Steinbeck, fresh off the success of his Dust-Bowl epic *The Grapes of Wrath*, reveled in such a pungent milieu.

If you come to Cannery Row today expecting to see Steinbeck's "whores, pimps, gamblers, and sons of bitches," you'll be sorely disappointed. The so-called Silver Tide of sardines—funneled into Monterey Bay by an upwelling of cold, nutrient-rich waters through the underwater Monterey

Canyon—abruptly gave out in the early 1950s, fished to death by specialized boats called purse-seiners introduced in the 1930s. By the time Ocean View Avenue's name was officially changed to Cannery Row in 1958, the industry was already dead.

In the 1960s, restaurants moved in, building on the fame of Steinbeck's bestseller. The final stroke came in 1984 when the disused Hovden Cannery was gutted and transformed into the Monterey Bay Aquarium, a state-of-the-art facility devoted to the ecology of this rich bay. In one respect at least, the Monterey Bay Aquarium *is* true to Steinbeck's book: Its approach is based on the work of marine biologist Ed Ricketts, Steinbeck's close friend and the model for *Cannery Row*'s main character. Working out of a weather-beaten laboratory (800 Cannery Row) sandwiched between two canneries, Ricketts's work on tide pools and ecology was groundbreaking.

Cannery Row today is packed with family restaurants, midpriced hotels, and souvenir shops; the corrugated iron walls of old cannery buildings are painted bright cheery colors—and the stench has disappeared. The train tracks behind the canneries have become a paved trail for cyclists, joggers, and in-line skaters. A short distance away, fishing operations continue at a few nondescript piers, but the so-called historic district is distinctly flavorless. Steinbeck would probably have nothing but scathing remarks to make about it.

On the other hand, he'd love that aquarium.

---

✈ Monterey Peninsula Airport or San Francisco International

🛏 $$ **Casa Munras Garden Hotel,** 700 Munras Ave. (℃ **800/222-2558,** 800/222-2446 in CA, 831/375-2411; www.casamunras-hotel.com)

---

**Literary Landmarks** **407**

# Strawberry Hill
## *Walpole's Gothick Folly*
### Twickenham, London

FLAGRANTLY REJECTING THE 18TH CENTURY'S NEOCLASSICAL STYLE, WALPOLE'S MEDIEVAL "folly" sparked the Gothic Revival craze that dominated early-19th-century architecture. Folly it may be, but this long-neglected historic property is an architectural treasure—or will be, once the original design is restored.

Sir Horace Walpole isn't read much anymore—the dilettante son of a famous prime minister, he was more a "man of letters" than a serious author, best known for the trashy (for its time) thriller *The Castle of Otranto* (1764), which ignited the so-called Gothic novel craze. But Walpole's Gothic obsession did have a lasting impact on architecture, thanks to his 35-year-long remodeling project, Strawberry Hill, in the London suburb of Twickenham.

Occupied since 1923 by St. Mary's College, Strawberry Hill bounced from owner to owner after Walpole died childless in 1797 (apparently fussing over his house

interested him more than marrying and begetting heirs). One relative, a dissipated rake, sold off the original contents of the house in 1842; others made renovations, some tasteful, some not. An ambitious renovation is finally underway, but its cost is estimated at £8 million. While English Heritage has donated several thousand pounds, urgent fundraising continues (it helped that the house was featured on the popular BBC series *Restoration* in 2004).

Walpole took a modest existing house and just kept adding turrets and towers and battlements until he'd doubled the place in size. He and his various architects spent

Inside Strawberry Hill.

years on historical research, gathering ideas for decorative treatments—then threw authenticity out the window, creating a fanciful mélange that was part castle, part cathedral, part quirky country house. Using their "modern" technology, they often substituted papier-mâché for plaster, and custom-made wallpaper for stone tracery—long-gone elements that require painstaking work to replicate. The sheer exuberance of the design is what makes it so marvelous. Everywhere you look there are Gothic arches, trefoil windows, or painted designs on glass.

Take the library, for example, with its intricately fretted cream-colored arched bookcases and a lofty ceiling encrusted with coats of arms. A monumental fireplace dominates the Holbein Room, looking like a minicathedral in its own right. A riot of white-and-gold fan vaulting covers the ceiling of the Long Gallery, its walls hung in crimson damask and gilded mirrors. The painted lead-paned glass in the Round Room's window embrasure is a marvel, as is its ceiling, which took advantage of the room's shape to imitate a rose window from St. Paul's Cathedral—the old St. Paul's Cathedral, Walpole insisted, before Christopher Wren mucked around with it.

Because of college activities and ongoing restoration, Strawberry Hill is only open for public tours on Sundays, though private group tours can be arranged. It can also be rented for special events (hey, any cash is welcome).

ⓘ www.friendsofstrawberryhill.org

✈ Heathrow International

🛏 $$ **Hart House Hotel,** 51 Gloucester Place, Marylebone (🕐 **44/20/7935-2288;** www.harthouse.co.uk). $$ **Vicarage Private Hotel,** 10 Vicarage Gate, South Kensington (🕐 **44/20/7229-4030;** www.london vicaragehotel.com).

# Cimitero Acattolico per gli Stranieri
## *A Romantic Resting Place*
### Rome, Italy

OSCAR WILDE IN 1877 CALLED THIS "THE HOLIEST PLACE IN ROME"; HENRY JAMES BURIED his fictional heroine Daisy Miller here. Today, though, the gravestones of this garden are begrimed and deteriorating from Rome's polluted air; some areas are sinking so badly that gravestones are collapsing.

The name's a mouthful—the Non-Catholic Cemetery for Foreigners, an outsiders' refuge if there ever was one. There are plenty of places in the Eternal City for Catholic Italians to be buried, but the Church wouldn't allow Protestants to be buried in consecrated ground. This rambling walled garden on the outskirts of town was the only option for Americans and other Europeans who happened to be living in Rome when they died.

Unsupported by the Church, the graveyard depends on modest voluntary entry fees, charitable donations, and money from plot owners to maintain its landscaping. With so many other sites to see in Rome—classical ruins, Renaissance palaces, baroque churches, the Vatican, not to mention those *La Dolce Vita* streetscapes and trendy shopping streets—very few visitors make their way out here. And yet an extraordinary number of famous people are interred in this cypress-shaded spot. For lovers of English literature, the most compelling are the graves of the Romantic poets Keats and Shelley.

John Keats—author of some of English literature's finest odes and sonnets— moved to Italy in 1820, seeking a mild climate to ease his tuberculosis. Living in rented rooms near the Spanish Steps (now operated as the Keats-Shelley House, Piazza di Spagna 26), attended by a friend, the painter Joseph Severn, he declined swiftly and died in February 1821, aged 25. His simple gray tombstone says "Here lies one whose name is writ in water"—though of course Keats's fame after his death grew far beyond the limited success of his lifetime.

Severn, who remained in Rome for years afterward, asked to be buried next to him, a testament to Keats's friendship.

Upon Keats's death, the far more successful poet Percy Bysshe Shelley wrote one of the world's great elegies, "Adonais," mourning Keats's tragic early death. By a cruel twist of irony, Shelley himself died a year later, drowned off the coast of Tuscany in a sailing accident—with a volume of Keats's poetry in his coat pocket. Shelley—himself only 29 when he died— was buried here next to the grave of his infant son William, who'd died of fever in Rome 3 years earlier. The writer Edward Trelawny, a friend of Shelley and Byron's, was buried nearby 30 years later.

Browse around the graves and you'll see inscriptions in more than 15 languages; the various faiths represented include Eastern Orthodox, Islam, Zoroastrianism, Buddhism, and Confucianism as well as Protestants. Funded by the French government, the similar Père Lachaise cemetery outside Paris draws streams of tourists to the tomb of rock star Jim Morrison; meanwhile, the Protestant Cemetery languishes in neglect and obscurity.

(i) **The Non-Catholic Cemetery in Rome,** Via Caio Cestio 6 (© **39/6/5741900;** www.protestantcemetery.it)

✈ Leonardo da Vinci International Airport

🛏 $$$ **Hotel de Russie,** Via del Babuino 9 (© **800/323-7500** in North America, or 39/6/328881; www.roccofortehotels.com). $ **Hotel Grifo,** Via del Boschetto 144 (© **39/6/4871395;** www.hotelgrifo.com).

# Anne Frank's Chestnut Tree
## *A Dying Symbol of Hope*
### Amsterdam, the Netherlands

ANNE FRANK WATCHED THIS TREE OUTSIDE HER WINDOW WHILE CONFINED TO THE TINY SPACE she shared with her family. In the fall of 2007, due to trunk rot, local officials condemned the tree to be felled. Whether or not they will succeed is still up in the air.

It's a tragedy that these secret rooms were ever needed in the first place. It's an even worse tragedy that they were finally discovered by the Nazi police, along with the eight Jewish *onderduikers*—divers or hiders—holed up here.

The sad story of the Frank family became emblematic of all Holocaust victims when, after World War II, Otto Frank—the only member of his family to survive the death camps—published his daughter Anne's wartime diary. Today, thanks to the millions of people who've read Anne's poignant memoir, their hideout is one of Amsterdam's top tourist draws. But one element of it may soon be lost forever.

From July 1942 to August 1944, Anne's world was abruptly shrunk to these four rooms and a tiny damp attic, secretly connected to her father's office and warehouse. For more than 2 years, her only contact with nature was the chestnut tree she could glimpse from her window. She eagerly drank in the sight of it, noting in her diary when it bloomed, how many leaves it bore, how it glistened in the moonlight. It consoled her, and yet reminded her that freedom lay outside these walls.

This immense tree has dominated the backyard of this outwardly typical Amsterdam canal house for some 150 years. When an oil spill threatened it more than a decade ago, the government paid to have its massive roots laboriously hand-cleaned.

But its problems now are more serious: infestation by the horse chestnut miner moth, and an aggressive case of trunk rot brought on by tinder polypore and honey mushroom fungi. In the fall of 2007, local officials condemned the tree to be felled—until an outpouring of protests from around the world convinced them to try more radical measures to save the tree instead.

In summer you may have to queue for an hour or more to enter the house. After climbing its steep interior stairs, which were hidden by a moveable bookcase, you'll reach the barely furnished, cramped rooms. (All the Franks' furniture was confiscated after the arrest.) You can see a map upon which Otto Frank hopefully charted the progress of the war; even more touching are the photos Anne pinned up of Deanna Durbin and the young English princesses Elizabeth and Margaret. And with luck, you may still be able to gaze, as she did, out the back window and see the branching crown of the chestnut tree, reaching hopefully toward the sky.

---

ⓘ **Anne Frankhuis,** Prinsengracht 263 (ⓒ **020/556-7105;** www.annefrank.nl)

✈ Amsterdam Schipohl

🛏 $$ **Estheréa,** Single 305 (ⓒ **020/624-5146;** www.estherea.nl). $ **Amstel Botel,** Oosterdokskade 2–4 (ⓒ **020/626-4247;** www.amstelbotel.com).

# 8 Tarnished Gems of Architecture

*La Sagrada Familia.*

# Leaning Tower of Pisa
## *Tilting Just So*
### Pisa, Italy

THE GOOD CITIZENS OF PISA STAUNCHLY BELIEVE THAT THE LEANING TOWER WILL NEVER FALL. Originally built on poor foundations, the tower has withstood several mild earthquakes and extensive bombing in World War II. The Tuscan sun pouring daily onto the Piazza del Miracoli makes the stonework continually expand and contract, aggravating the tilt—and still it stands.

For years, however, anxious city fathers measured the tower—and found it leaning a fraction of an inch further every year. A decade-long restoration in the 1990s arrested the tilt, removing tons of soil from under the foundation and placing lead counterweights at the monument's base; open again to the public (in small groups), it has nearly stabilized now, restored to the same angle it had reached in 1838. It's judged to be good for the next 300 years at least.

The Tower of Pisa may be the most instantly recognizable building in the Western world, with the possible exception of the Eiffel Tower. A grayish-white stack of colonnaded marble rings with a neat top hat, it has a certain architectural élan, but what really makes it famous is that rakish tilt, 14 feet (4m) off the perpendicular. Ironically, Benito Mussolini tried to have it straightened entirely in the 1930s, but the concrete poured into its foundation only made it sink further, thus perpetuating Pisa's claim to tourist fame.

Begun in 1173, this eight-story freestanding bell tower, or campanile, was designed as an addition to the cathedral at Pisa. But as the third story was completed, in 1198, it became obvious that the tower was leaning. The builders discovered that the site they'd chosen wasn't solid rock, as they'd thought, but water-soaked clay, and the tower had been designed with a shallow foundation that couldn't compensate. The architect, Bonnano Pisano, skipped town. Work was halted for decades while Pisa fought an on-again-off-again war with Florence. When the tower was finally completed in 1319, Pisa was a much less powerful city-state than it had been (in 1392 it was annexed by Florence). The bells were finally installed in the top in 1350, but they are no longer rung, for fear the vibrations might rattle the tower.

Visitors can climb the 294 steps to the top and imagine standing beside Galileo Galilei, the Pisa-born physicist and astronomer, when he dropped objects of different weights from the top to prove his theory of bodies in motion (though historians dispute whether he actually conducted that experiment). In World War II, when it was a Nazi observation post, the Allies considered knocking it out with an artillery strike. A U.S. Army sergeant cancelled the strike, thus saving the tower for generations of tourists and pizza-box designs.

ⓘ Piazza del Duomo 17 (✆ **39/050-560547;** www.duomo.pisa.it)

✈ Galileo Galilei Airport

🚂 Pisa

🛏 **$$ Royal Victoria,** Lungarno Pacinotti 12 (✆ **39/050-940111;** www.royal victoria.it)

# Taj Mahal
## *A Love Story in Stone*
### Agra, India

POLLUTION, FLOODING, AND EXCESSIVE TOURISM THREATEN THIS OVER-THE-TOP MAUSOLEUM. If the plan to close the Taj Mahal—built by Shah Jahan (fifth emperor of the Mughal dynasty) to mourn his favorite wife, Mumtaz Mahal—goes into effect, it would reduce it to a mere postcard silhouette instead of the spiritual experience it can be.

Even a recent rise in admission prices doesn't deter floods of tourists from shuffling through the Taj Mahal—three to four million tourists every year. Between the crowds and the air pollution that's eating away its white stone facade, tourism officials are considering closing this 17th-century landmark to the public, leaving its fabulous domed symmetry—that graceful center onion dome, the four smaller surrounding domes, the slender punctuating minarets, the serene reflecting pool—visible only from afar.

When you pass through the red-sandstone gatehouse, you enter tranquil Persian-style hanging gardens, a welcome respite from the hectic city outside. When you get up close, you can see that what seemed like a sugar-cube white building is in fact marvelously ornate, with exquisite detailing covering the marble inside and out—a technique called *pietra dura,* which came from either Italy or Persia, depending on which scholar you read. Islamic crescent moons, Persian lotus motifs, and Hindu symbols are gracefully combined.

The Taj Mahal.

Past the central pool rises the arched octagonal building containing the tomb of Mumtaz, its white dome ringed by four minidomes. Two red mosques flank the mausoleum on either side, one required by the Muslim faith, the other a "dummy" built for the sheer love of symmetry.

Only when you enter the buildings can you view the interiors' stunning lapidary decoration, inlaid with precious stones—agate, jasper, malachite, turquoise, tiger's eye, lapis lazuli, coral, carnelian. Notice how the panels of calligraphy, inlaid with black marble, are designed to get bigger the higher they are placed, so the letters appear the same size to a beholder on the ground level. When Shah Jahan himself died, his tomb was placed beside Mumtaz's, the only asymmetrical note in the mausoleum chamber. The two tombs (oriented, of course, toward Mecca) are surrounded by delicate filigreed screens, ingeniously carved from a single piece of marble.

Shah Jahan placed this memorial beside the Yamuna River, despite the constant risk of flooding, because it was next to the bustling market of the Tajganj, where it is said he first saw Mumtaz selling jewels in a market stall. Work started in 1641, and it took 20,000 laborers (not to mention oxen and elephants) 22 years to complete; its marble came from Rajasthan, the precious stones from all over Asia. In the late 19th century, the badly deteriorated Taj Mahal was extensively restored by British viceroy Lord Curzon; what will today's Indian government do to preserve this treasure?

ⓘ Tajganj, Agra (✆ **91/562/233-0496**)

✈ Agra

🛏 $$$ **Welcomgroup Mughal Sheraton,** 194 Fatehaabad Rd., Taj Ganj, Agra (✆ **91/562/233-1701;** www.welcom group.com). $$ **Jaypee Palace Hotel,** Fatehabad Rd. (✆ **91/562/233-0800;** www.jaypeehotels.com).

### 412 Iconic Designs

# Melnikov House
## *A Rebel's Moscow Masterpiece*
### Moscow, Russia

CONSIDERING HOW FEW MELNIKOV BUILDINGS EXIST, SURELY THE RUSSIAN GOVERNMENT COULD find a way to protect his one undisputed masterpiece. The current cowboy atmosphere of Moscow's real-estate situation and nearby development threatens its very existence.

After all, it was the government's fault that Melnikov didn't produce more. Back in 1933, Josef Stalin forbid avant-garde architect Konstantin Melnikov to practice his craft, just as he was reaching the height of his powers. Melnikov was allowed, however, to go on living in the house he'd designed in the late 1920s—his home and studio—on Krivoarbatsky Lane in Moscow's exclusive Arbat neighborhood. Experimental as it was, the design was approved by city commissioners who saw it as a notable work of art, not just a house.

The design still looks bold: two connected three-story cylindrical towers punctuated with large hexagonal windows, arranged in a geometrical pattern that cast shifting patterns of light throughout the day. Except for the straight glass wall at the front of one tower, beneath the plaster facade the underlying structure was built of intersecting hexagons as well—a honeycomb lattice of brick, an ingenious solution to the era's strict rationing of construction materials (it's built only of brick and wood, with no steel girders). The largest room inside is Melnikov's workshop on the third floor, where light pours in through 38 hexagonal windows. The idiosyncratic layout includes only one large bedroom, where the whole family slept.

Though excommunicated from architecture, Melnikov became a portrait painter and art teacher and lived in the Arbat house until his death in 1974, when his son Viktor—also a painter—took it over. Despite mounting family squabbles over its ownership, Viktor lived in increasing poverty in order to preserve his father's house, paintings, and archive of architectural drawings until he, too, died in February 2006.

That's when the circling buzzards moved in. A half-cousin who had inherited a half-share in the house had sold it to a real-estate developer. Viktor's will left his half-share to the Russian government, on the condition that it be turned into a Konstantin Melnikov museum. But murky negotiations between the heirs and Moscow's anti-preservationist mayor have

held up that plan; it still isn't open to the public, and sections of the floor and walls have collapsed, due to Viktor's lack of funds for structural repair. (Recent construction of condo high-rises nearby have only made the structural instability worse.)

Still, you can view it from the outside, where its round towers and honeycomb glazed windows make as dramatic a statement as they did in 1929. Look above the glass wall to see the sign proclaiming Konstantin Melnikov's name—a gutsy advertisement for a man who'd soon be in disgrace. It's about time he got the honor he deserved.

ⓘ 10 Krivoarbatsky Pereulok, off of Arbat, Moscow

✈ Moscow

🛏 $$$ **Sheraton Palace,** 19 1st Tverskaya-Yamskaya Ulitsa (𝄐 **7/95/931-9700;** www.sheratonpalace.ru). $$ **Cosmos,** 150 Prospekt Mira (𝄐 **7/95/234-1000;** www.hotelcosmos.ru).

---

Iconic Designs **413**

# Battersea Power Station
## *Power in a Beautiful Package*
### London, England

BATTERSEA POWER STATION'S TAPERING WHITE CONCRETE CHIMNEYS—ONE AT EACH CORNER of the red-brick Art Deco masterpiece—have been cold since the plant closed in 1983; they're crumbling badly. While government and private investors and local community boards wrangle over its future, the building becomes more derelict every day.

Dominating the south bank of the Thames, the Battersea Power Station has been a London landmark ever since it was built in 1933. Designed by Sir Giles Gilbert Scott— who also designed Britain's beloved red telephone booths—it's been featured on a Pink Floyd album cover and in movies from Alfred Hitchcock's *Sabotage* to the Beatles' *Help!* It's even been a setting for a Monty Python sketch.

When the London Power Company first proposed this massive coal-fired Thameside plant, the public was skittish about such a large-scale power grid—much larger than anything existing—so the company strove to make it aesthetically pleasing as well as functional. It's still one of Europe's largest brick structures, but its stately proportions and exterior decorative detail lend it confident majesty. Inside,

Battersea Power Station.

the Art Deco control room features parquet floors and wrought-iron stairways, not to mention Italian marble in the turbine hall.

New technology eventually made Battersea's turbines obsolete, and in 1975 the older half was shut down. Historic preservationists acted quickly to secure landmark protection before the second half was also shut down. (It now has a Grade II listing, meaning it can't be demolished or altered without government approval.) In 1984, a plan was approved to convert Battersea into a theme park, but after some initial construction, financial problems stopped the project in 1989. By 2003 new owners were ready to proceed with a mixed-use development incorporating shops, restaurants, and cinemas, complemented by new buildings that would include hotels, offices, and residences. Then in 2005 the project hit a snag, as the owners tried to remove the four decaying chimneys; a wave of protests halted the

demolition. In November 2006 new owners bought the property, and dropped the mixed-used plan. One proposal is to make the plant the home of the government's new United Kingdom Energy Technologies Institute, which is studying solutions to climate change—a fitting use indeed.

Battersea's sister power station, Bankside—also designed by Sir Giles Gilbert Scott—was also decommissioned in the 1980s, but it has since found new life as the Tate Modern Gallery. Many believe that Battersea was the more beautiful of the two, but it currently sits as a molding, desolate hulk, waiting for those pie-in-the-sky renovation plans to become a reality.

✈ Heathrow International

🛏 $$ **Hart House Hotel,** 51 Gloucester Place, Marylebone (✆ **44/20/7935-2288;** www.harthouse.co.uk). $$ **Vicarage Private Hotel,** 10 Vicarage Gate, South Kensington (✆ **44/20/7229-4030;** www.londonvicaragehotel.com).

# Taliesin
## *The Wright Idea*
### Spring Lake, Wisconsin

OPERATED BY A PRIVATE, NONPROFIT ORGANIZATION, TALIESIN STANDS IN DESPERATE NEED OF funds for proper upkeep. Crashing branches have caved in roofs, poor drainage has weakened foundations, and the hill bearing Wright's home had to be shored up before it slid into the lake below.

Ask most Americans to name a famous architect and they'll probably say Frank Lloyd Wright. More than a third of his buildings are on the National Register of Historic Places; 24 are full-fledged National Historic Landmarks. But if you really want to understand what made Wright tick, visit his Wisconsin home, Taliesin.

Here, on a rolling 600-acre (240-hectare) campus with his students living around him, many ideas Wright later translated into blueprints were tried out and tested. Most of this took place during the Depression, however, when commissions were few and far between, and much of the construction was on a shoestring budget. Now those buildings are falling apart.

Though Wright (1867–1959) grew up in Madison, Wisconsin, he spent his boyhood summers in this Wisconsin River valley on his uncle's farm, exploring the natural world, which would later play a large part in his architecture. Naturally he returned here in 1911 after making his mark as an architect in the Chicago area. There's a juicy story attached; he originally built it as a refuge for himself and his mistress, Mamah Borthwick Cheney. Tragically, in 1914 Mamah was killed in an arson fire at Taliesin. A grieving Wright rebuilt the house. Ten years later, Wright was living here with his third wife, Olgivanna, when the living quarters burned down again and had to be rebuilt a third time. After Wright's death in 1959, Olgivanna lived here until she died in 1985.

Tours of the campus are offered May to October. The house itself is quintessential Wright design, with cunningly interlocked horizontal planes of fieldstone, wood, and gray concrete seeming to grow right out of a hillside. Several other buildings are scattered around the property, some of which—the Shingle-style Unity Chapel, the Hillside School, and a residence called Tan-y-deri—were among his first designs, long before he bought this property. Set in a rich agricultural area, Taliesin was also a working farm, and Wright created a set of low-slung barns—the Midway Barns—for that purpose. In 1932, Wright started up the Taliesin Fellowship, a sort of architectural commune (it has since evolved into the Frank Lloyd Wright School of Architecture) living and working at Taliesin. You can still see residential fellows working in its many nooks, stone terraces, and Japanese-style courtyards every summer. They're keeping Wright's legacy alive in one respect—but keeping the house itself intact is an equally essential task.

---

ⓘ 5607 Co. Hwy. C, Spring Green (✆ **877/598-7900;** www.taliesinpreservation.org)

✈ Madison

🛏 $$$ **House on the Rock Resort,** 400 Springs Dr. (✆ **800/822-7774** or 608/588-7000; www.thehouseontherock.com). $$ **Silver Star Inn,** 3852 Limmex Hill Rd. (✆ **608/935-7297;** www.silverstarinn.com).

# Ennis House
## *A Concrete Vision*
### Los Angeles, California

DAMAGE SUSTAINED FROM A 1994 EARTHQUAKE AND RECENT HEAVY RAINS RENDERED THIS rare Frank Lloyd Wright gem unsafe. In August 2005, the Ennis House Foundation began to rescue this architectural masterpiece, embarking on what's estimated to be a $20-million restoration.

At first glance, this house in Los Angeles's Los Feliz neighborhood, just south of Griffith Park, doesn't seem even remotely similar to the Prairie Style architecture for which Frank Lloyd Wright became famous. It almost looks like a Mayan temple, with its soaring vertical masses decorated with a repeating geometric design, incised onto 16-inch-square concrete blocks.

But a Frank Lloyd Wright design it is, the last—and greatest—of four Southern California houses Wright designed in the 1920s. In this brief phase of his career, Wright focused on what he called textile block architecture, a response to the dry, rugged landscape of Southern California, so different from his native Wisconsin prairie. Built for Mabel and Charles Ennis in 1924, the Ennis House suffered neglect at the hands of a series of owners, though it appeared in several movies including the futuristic *Blade Runner* and dark Hollywood fable *The Day of the Locust*. Severely shaken in the 1994 Northridge earthquake, the house's retaining wall was further damaged by heavy rains in the winter of 2004, and in March 2005 was tagged by the city's building department as unsafe to enter.

Intrigued by the challenge of transforming lowly concrete into a noble building material, Wright designed these houses using 3-inch-thick (7.6cm) precast concrete blocks, stacking them in neatly aligned columns and rows, attached not with mortar but with cunningly concealed thin steel rods. The blocks' surface designs added warmth and tactile depth, especially effective under the light and shadow cast by the Southern California sun. The houses were further enlivened with huge art glass windows and doors, including in the Ennis House a wisteria-patterned glass mosaic mural over the living room fireplace that is one of the loveliest decorative features Wright ever designed.

Set on the southern foothills of the Santa Monica Mountains, the Ennis House almost seems a continuation of the mountain ridge behind it—in its own way, the house is an expression of Wright's lifelong credo of harmony with nature. There was always something about building a house on a hillside that fascinated Frank Lloyd Wright, but hillsides are notoriously unstable building sites. With that crucial retaining wall replaced, the Ennis House restoration has moved onto more aesthetic interior work. You can still drive past and admire the composition of its textured masses; hopefully this Wright beauty will be open to the public again someday.

---

ⓘ 2607 Glendower Ave., Los Angeles (📞 **323/660-0607;** www.ennishouse.org)

✈ Los Angeles International

🛏 $$ **Roosevelt Hotel,** 7000 Hollywood Blvd., Hollywood (📞 **800/950-7667** or 323/466-7000; www.hollywoodroosevelt.com). $$ **Beverly Garland's Holiday Inn,** 4222 Vineland Ave., North Hollywood (📞 **800/ BEVERLY** [238-3759] or 818/980-8000; www.beverlygarland.com).

# Fallingwater
## *A River Runs Through It*
### Fallingwater, Pennsylvania

MAJOR REPAIRS, WHICH WERE COMPLETED IN 2002, PREVENTED FALLINGWATER, THE ONLY Frank Lloyd Wright house with its original furnishings intact, from collapsing into the stream that runs through it.

Frank Lloyd Wright was 67 years old—considered well past his prime—when a wealthy Pittsburgh department store magnate named Edgar Kaufmann commissioned him in 1935 to design a weekend house in western Pennsylvania. Looking at Wright's initial plans, most engineers said it wouldn't stand. Even Kaufmann was taken aback when Wright first showed him the plans. What a crazy idea, cantilevering three levels of the house out from the side of a hill, letting a waterfall tumble right beneath the terraces! The old man must really have lost it, his doubters muttered.

Yet it turned out to be one of the most famous and influential house designs of the 20th century; recently the American Institute of Architects voted it the "best all-time work of American architecture." It sparked not only a late-in-life resurgence in Wright's career, but a whole new Modernist style of architecture. The house—appropriately

Fallingwater.

named Fallingwater—seems a flat-roofed series of sandstone ledges magically carved out of the hillside rather than appended to it, with extensive windows and terraces everywhere to dapple the interior with light from the surrounding woods. Wright's principle of harmony with nature never was more perfectly expressed than in this house.

Those engineers were partly right, though. After more than 60 years, this national architectural treasure required a major effort to stabilize the main cantilever, reinforce the poured concrete foundation, and strengthen the flagstone and redwood floors with steel girders. Without those repairs, which were completed in 2002, Fallingwater might have collapsed into Bear Run, the cascading stream that runs through it.

Fallingwater is the only major Wright residence available for tours which still has all the original furnishings intact. This is important because Wright's vision included furniture (both built-in and free-standing) that he designed specifically for the house, right down to lamps, hassocks, and rugs. The stone hearth in the living room was built from boulders found on the site, some of them simply protruding through the floor from where they'd originally stood. Because the house remained in the Kaufmann family until it was donated in 1963 to the Western Pennsylvania Conservancy, it also has all of their books, objets d'art, and an art collection including work by Audubon, Tiffany, Diego Rivera, and Picasso. Walking through Fallingwater, you get a visceral feeling of Wright's low-slung aesthetic, from the teeny-tiny bedrooms he insisted on to the low ceilings (they never bothered the 5-ft., 5-in. architect). Wherever you are in the house, stop for a moment and listen—you'll be able to hear the waterfall burbling below.

Make tour reservations in advance; few are offered in the winter months.

---

ⓘ **Fallingwater,** S.R. 381, Mill Run (ℂ **724/329-8501;** www.paconserve.org)

✈ Pittsburgh

🛏 $$ **The Historic Summit Inn,** 101 Skyline Dr. (ℂ **800/433-8594** or 724/438-8594; www.summitinnresort.com). $$$ **Nemacolin Woodlands Resort and Spa,** 1001 LaFayette Dr. (ℂ **800/422-2736** or 724/329-8555; www.nemacolin.com).

**417** Iconic Designs

# Cyclorama Center
## *Theater in the Round*
### Gettysburg, Pennsylvania

OF THE FEW REMAINING CYCLORAMA BUILDINGS—THREE OTHERS EXIST, IN BOSTON, BUFFALO, and Atlanta—this is the only modern one. But whether this particularly sleek and dramatic building will stay on its original site is still undecided.

Way back before 3-D IMAX movies, this was the ultimate in visual experiences: a 360-degree oil painting surrounding the spectator, putting you right in the middle of the artwork's setting. They were all the rage in Europe and America in the late 1800s, set up in special auditoriums with foreground props and landscaping to intensify the realistic impact. Once they fell out of fashion—superseded by moving pictures—most cycloramas were destroyed or rotted away in some damp cellar. But not the Gettysburg Cyclorama, one of the most stirring and effective cycloramas ever painted.

This elaborately detailed painting depicts Pickett's Charge, a valiant and ultimately hopeless Confederate attack on the Union forces, one of the most tragic chapters of the 4-day-long Battle of Gettysburg. Noted French cyclorama artist Paul Philippoteaux was commissioned in 1879 to come to the United States to paint Pickett's Charge for a special exhibition 1883 in Chicago. Even veterans of the battle praised Philippoteaux's meticulously researched representation. The Gettysburg version is a second copy, which was exhibited to admiring crowds for 20 years in a special round auditorium in Boston.

Moved to Gettysburg in 1913, it was acquired by the National Park Service in the 1940s and reopened in 1963 in a striking new visitor center, built to commemorate the battle's centennial. Famed Modernist architects Richard Neutra and Robert Alexander designed the building, a round white concrete drum with a long glass-sheathed causeway, tucked snugly into the rolling Pennsylvania farmland overlooking the battlefield. At the time the National Park Service praised the Cyclorama Center as the new prototype of national park visitor centers, heralding the future of the national park system.

The painting is 359 feet (180m) long, 27 feet (8.1m) high, and weighs around 3 tons, so of course every time it was moved it required extensive restoration and repair.

(The original Chicago version, owned by Wake Forest University, is in such poor condition it can't be displayed.) Since November 2005 the Gettysburg cyclorama has been closed for extensive rehabilitation, to be moved to a new visitor center projected to open in 2008.

But the fate of the old cyclorama building—nominated as a National Historic Landmark—is what concerns architectural historians. Neutra himself described the cyclorama as the building closest to his heart. Yet the National Park Service presently plans to raze it, despite its architectural significance. Pending lawsuits are urging the NPS to relocate the cyclorama if it can't be preserved on its old site. Battle is brewing again at Gettysburg.

ⓘ **Gettysburg National Military Park Battlefield,** 97 Taneytown Rd. (ⓒ **717/334-1124;** www.nps.gov/gett). **Mission 66** (www.mission66.com).

✈ Baltimore-Washington International

🛏 $$$ **Holiday Inn Battlefield,** 10800 Vandor Lane (ⓒ **717/334-6211**). $$ **Quality Inn,** 380 Steinwehr Ave. (ⓒ **800/228-5151** or 717/334-1103; www.gettysburg qualityinn.com).

**Iconic Designs** 418

# Malmi Airport Terminal
## *Sinking in Helsinki*
### Helsinki, Finland

FINLAND'S SECOND-BUSIEST AIRPORT, WITH ITS STUNNING TERMINAL BUILDING, IS ALSO A delightful, well-used recreational spot. However, the airport is slowly sinking into the swampland on which it was built.

When the Malmi airport was first conceived in the 1930s, Finnish authorities consulted aviation hero Charles Lindbergh about their proposed site. Lindbergh vetoed the location—its unstable clay soil wouldn't support heavy aircraft, he said. The Finns went ahead with Malmi anyway, though.

Sure it was a swamp, they reasoned, but since you couldn't build houses on a swamp, you might as well put an airport there.

They dressed it up, however, with a particularly handsome terminal building, a white three-story cylinder with continuous circling bands of windows, topped by a neat control tower and flanked by two low wings. This marvelously clean and economical design by architects Dag Englund and Vera Rosendahl was part of a showcase ensemble of functionalist buildings Finland could point to with pride when the 1940 Summer Olympics were suddenly switched from Tokyo to Helsinki.

Though the 1940 Olympics were eventually cancelled because of World War II, they finally came to Helsinki after the war, in 1952—by which time Lindbergh's prediction had proven all too true. A new main airport had to be built with runways strong enough to handle the international passenger planes that would be arriving for the games. (Malmi only had one hangar, anyway—they'd never been able to find a solid piece of land big enough to build a second one.) Malmi was henceforth relegated to light and mid-sized aircraft, including private planes, pilot training planes, taxi planes, aerial photographers, parachute jumpers, sea-rescue craft, Border Guard planes, and police and ambulance helicopters. It's still Finland's second-busiest airport, with nearly a million people moving in and out every year. The airfield also provides a green oasis in the spreading Helsinki metropolitan area, a nesting ground for several endangered bird species including the curlew, the corncrake, and the red-backed shrike. A popular jogging/cycling trail rings the airport, and model aircrafters and hot-air balloonists gather there on weekends.

Now, in a final ironic twist, the city wants that unusable swampland back again—to build houses after all. Despite the fact that Malmi is still a working airfield—and the only back-up to Helsinki-Vantaa International—Helsinki is trying to cancel its lease with the existing air operations, which should extend until 2034. The authorities claim they want to preserve the landmark terminal building (which has sunk nearly half a meter/1½ ft. into that shifting ground over the decades); they just want to close down the airfield. But for aviation enthusiasts, the whole point of the terminal is that it still is the center of a working airfield complex. What else should a functionalist gem do if not to serve its intended function?

ⓘ **Helsinki-Malmi Airport** (www.pelastamalmi.org/en)

✈ Helsinki-Vantaa International

🛏 $$$ **Hilton Helsinki Strand,** John Stenbergin Ranta 4 (✆ **800/445-8667** in the U.S. or 358/9/393-51; www.hilton.com). $$ **Martta Hotelli,** Uudenmaankatu 24 (✆ **358/9/618-74-00;** www.marttahotelli.fi).

**419** Iconic Designs

# TWA Terminal at JFK Airport
## *Come Fly with Me*
### New York, New York

JFK's Terminal 5 didn't seem so much a building as a boomerang or a seagull's wing, momentarily arrested in flight. Demolition has left only a few of its innovative features, and those that remain are left to their fate.

The streamlined white concrete parabolas of Eero Saarinen's TWA Flight Center at John F. Kennedy International Airport always looked ready for take off. Its aerodynamic curves outside were repeated inside as well, in a soaring lobby of smoked glass and smooth concrete where there didn't seem to be a straight line in sight.

When Saarinen's landmark was built in 1962, the airport was still called Idlewild and the building, prosaically, Terminal 5. In an architectural era dominated by the

# 10 | Ideas of a House

Four walls, a sloping roof, a door, square windows—we think we know what a house should look like. But throughout the ages, various people have found other creative housing solutions, responding to various environmental factors, like harsh weather, limited building materials, or the threat of invasion. Here are 10 examples that have survived into modern times:

**420 Barumini su Nuraxi, Sardinia, Italy**   Dating back to the Bronze Age, *nuraghe* are villages clustered around a central cone-shaped tower, built of huge rough-cut gray stones set on strategic high ground. Found only in Sardinia, these curious honeycomb settlements were apparently deserted and repopulated repeatedly during the Phoenician, Punic, and Roman invasions of the island. From the air, you can see the circular foundations of the tiny houses nested around the main tower and its four side towers. www.sardegna.com.

**421 Matera, Italy**   The word *sassi* literally means stones—as in the steep ravine walls that prehistoric southern Italians carved into these tiny windowless homes, with cisterns and canals nearby to collect water. During invasions, these protected dwellings offered safe refuge, and eventually an entire town. Today, these abandoned sassi have now been renovated into hotels, restaurants, and chic residences, becoming Matera's tourist claim to fame. ℂ *39/835/331983*. www.sassiweb.it.

Cappadocia.

**422 Cappadocia, Turkey**   The original inhabitants of this Turkish hinterland hollowed out shelters in eroded pillars of soft tufa rock; centuries later, they made great refuges for early Christians fleeing persecution. Basing yourself in the town of Ürgüp, head east to visit the nearby town of Goreme, with its open-air museum, or northwest to the Zelve Valley's open-air museum, three consecutive valleys whose walls are riddled with living quarters and passageways carved out of pink tufa. ℂ *90/384/4112525*.

**423 Matmâta, Southern Tunisia**   Filmmaker George Lucas discovered a ready-made sci-fi setting for his *Star Wars* in this small Berber village, where prehistoric ancestors built homes around a large circular pit, two stories deep, leading to each family's private network of cave chambers and connecting passageways (he shot the cantina scene here). Today's villagers are accustomed to floods of tourists; some of these underground homes have even been turned into hotels. *TunisUSA.* ℂ *800/474-5500*. www.tunisusa.com.

**424 Ksour, Western Tunisia**   "Ksour" is plural for *ksar*, the ancient Berbers' traditional mud-and-stone complexes of community granaries, or *ghurfas*—every family in a village had its own chamber for storing grain. As time passed, villagers walled these granaries to use them as forts in times of foreign invasion. Though their inhabitants had moved to modern towns, the crumbling abandoned *ksour* stand as haunting relics in the desert, viewable on a day trip out of the modern town of Tataouine. *TunisUSA.* ✆ *800/474-5500. www.tunisusa.com.*

**⊕ Ulan Bator, Mongolia**   The yurts themselves may not be ancient—how permanent could a dwelling of felt ever be?—but the concept is old indeed, a brilliant adaptation by Mongolian nomads to their peripatetic lives on the Central Asia steppes. Hung on a collapsible wood lattice, these round felt-covered homes (known as *ger* in Mongolian) could be packed onto a camel or yak for easy transport. Tours to outlying yurt settlements are popular tourist excursions from the capital today. *www.mongoliatourism.gov.mn.*

**⊕ Alberobello, Italy**   Beginning in the 13th century, the wily peasants of the rugged Apulia countryside built beehive-shaped trulli cottages, using whatever materials were easy to build with. The stones fit ingeniously together without a speck of mortar—that way, they could be swiftly dismantled if royal inspectors showed up. The town of Alberobello still has some 1,000 of these cozy storybook dwellings in a maze of curving cobble lanes. ✆ *39/80/4325171.*

Alberobello.

**⊕ Gjirokastra, Albania**   The word *gjirokastra* means "silver fortress"—an apt named for this historic Ottoman town in southern Albania, with its distinctive 17th-century Turkish *kule,* or tower houses. Piled on the steep hillsides surrounding a 13th-century citadel, these slate-roofed stone houses were stacked vertically. The entrance was through the top story, reached by ladders which the families could retract against enemies. *www.united-albania.com.*

**⊕ Shirakawago, Japan**   In the Japanese Alps of central Honshu, extended families bunked together in shared *gassho-zukuri*—snowfall-shedding houses with tall A-frame thatched roofs (the name translates to "hands joined in prayer," which is what the roofs resemble). Check out the hamlet of Ogimachi, which contains many 200- to 300-year-old thatched houses amid its rice paddies and mulberry orchards; the open-air museum Shirakawago Gassho Zukuri Minkaen features several. ✆ *81/5769/6-1231.*

**⊕ Coober Pedy, Australia**   Early-20th-century settlers in this colorful opal-mining town in Australia's rough-and-ready interior found a unique solution to the harsh heat and dust of Outback existence: live underground, in the holes left by earlier miners or the sun-bleached mullock heaps of mining waste. Even the hotels and restaurants here are mostly underground. It certainly gives new meaning to the term "Down Under." ✆ *1800/637 076 in Australia, or 61/8/8672 5298. www.opalcapital oftheworld.com.au.*

Coober Pedy.

glass-box skyscrapers of the International Style, Saarinen's sculptural terminal was a breathtaking leap forward. Among its innovative features were the airline industry's first electronic departure boards, closed-circuit television, and baggage carousels. Instead of plodding down ordinary hallways to catch their flights, passengers strolled into exotic red-carpeted tubes. Even the staircases, seating areas, recessed light fixtures, and counters were designed with distinctive sleek ovoid shapes, a look copied so often afterward that it's easy to forget how radical it was when it first appeared. Everything about the place trumpeted Trans World Airlines' sophistication and preeminence in the world of air travel. Sadly, Saarinen himself died in 1961 before he could see the acclaim instantly accorded to his creation.

When American Airlines bought out TWA in 2001, however, the iconic Terminal 5 ceased operations. The Port Authority of New York and New Jersey, which owns the airport, didn't quite know what to do with the terminal, which, having been named a National Historic Landmark, couldn't easily be razed. It stood abandoned for several years before relative newcomer JetBlue Airways, which now operates out of neighboring Terminal 6, agreed to use the front of Terminal 5 as an entry and ticketing area if it could build a huge new terminal expansion behind it.

Unfortunately, some structures on the airfield side had to be demolished—including the innovative satellite-like gate modules at the far end of those red-carpeted tubes. (The tubes themselves will be preserved as the connecting passages between the historic terminal and the new JetBlue terminal.) The hulking scale of the 26-gate addition will overshadow the Saarinen building, some architecture critics protest. Others are more philosophical, saying that at least Saarinen's lobby and roofline will be preserved and are being used for their original purpose. Next time you fly through New York, have a look for yourself and decide.

ⓘ **NYC & Company** (✆ **800/NYC-VISIT** [692-8474]; www.nycvisit.com)

✈ John F. Kennedy International

🛏 $ **Best Western Seaport Inn,** 33 Peck Slip (✆ **800/HOTEL-NY** [468-3569] or 212/766-6600; www.bestwestern.com)

**Iconic Designs** **430**

# 2 Columbus Circle
## *The Lollipop Building*
### New York, New York

A LONE EMPTY BEACON ON NEW YORK CITY'S FAMED COLUMBUS CIRCLE, REVILED WHEN IT was built, the Lollipop building sat neglected for years. Oddly enough, the public had grown fond of it and fought exterior revamping. Today, surrounded by glitzy towers, it now stands encased in scaffolding as a new facade is built.

New Yorkers had all sorts of wiseguy nicknames for the marble-clad modern building on the south side of Columbus Circle—the Lollipop Building, the Tennis Racket Museum, the Marble Juice Box. Designed by Edward Durrell Stone—a former International Style adherent who became enamored of classical ornamentation in reaction against the cold glass-box look of modern skyscrapers—this 12-story curiosity offered a blank white facade, one horizontal stripe of arched black windows toward the top, and a perforated strip of tiny portholes running up and down the corner edges. At street level, its most noticeable feature was a dotted line of lozenge-topped columns, supposedly echoing the Doge's Palace in Venice. It was a building that everybody loved to hate.

Situated on an awkwardly small trapezoid-shaped lot, 2 Columbus Circle was built in 1964 as an art museum, to exhibit the modern art collection of A&P grocery heir Huntington Hartford. But the idiosyncratic footprint and swanky interior design made it a bit of a white elephant once the art collection closed down in 1969. After a few years as Fairleigh-Dickinson University's New York Cultural Center, it fell into city ownership in 1980. With no other tenant available, the city's bureau of cultural affairs occupied it for a while, then vacated the premises. The building became run down through benign neglect.

Still, at that highly visible location—Columbus Circle sits at the southwest corner of Central Park—the Lollipop Building was a familiar element in the city's fabric, and over the years people became fond of its warmth, whimsy, and small scale amidst the shouldering crowd of Midtown behemoths. It became eligible for landmark designation in 1996, and most people assumed it would be a shoo-in or, at any rate, that the hearings would be lively and amusing.

This being New York City, however, all sorts of murky politics began to intervene. Somehow the landmark hearings never took place, igniting massive protests by a number of architects, artists, and urban scholars—protests that apparently came too late. In June 2005, a new owner—the Museum of Art and Design—received a city permit to strip off the curved marble facade and build an entirely new skin for the building.

By that time, the massive glass-walled hulk of the Time-Warner Center had gone up on the next block west, Donald Trump had rewrapped the former Paramount Building on the north side in glitzy bronze, and the Christopher Columbus statue at the center of the circle began to look tiny and forlorn indeed. Scaffolding encased the Lollipop Building, and the next thing you knew, the lollipops were gone for good.

ⓘ **NYC & Company** (ⓒ **800/NYC-VISIT** [692-8474]; www.nycvisit.com)

✈ John F. Kennedy International, Newark Liberty International, LaGuardia.

⌖ $ **Best Western Seaport Inn,** 33 Peck Slip (ⓒ **800/HOTEL-NY** [468-3569] or 212/766-6600; www.bestwestern.com)

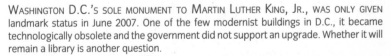

**431** Iconic Designs

# Martin Luther King, Jr., Library
## *An Open Book*
### Washington, D.C.

WASHINGTON D.C.'S SOLE MONUMENT TO MARTIN LUTHER KING, JR., WAS ONLY GIVEN landmark status in June 2007. One of the few modernist buildings in D.C., it became technologically obsolete and the government did not support an upgrade. Whether it will remain a library is another question.

Washington, D.C., has never been big on modern architecture—fluted white columns and massive neoclassical pediments are more its style. Still, the nation's capital does have one Modernist gem: the Martin Luther King, Jr., Memorial Library, the central building of D.C.'s public library system.

Designed by Ludwig Mies Van der Rohe, an undisputed master of the International Style, it was Mies's last building, though he never lived to see it completed (he died in 1969 at age 83). It's also Washington's only monument to the slain civil rights leader, though many cities across the country also dedicated libraries to Martin Luther King, Jr., after his assassination in 1968.

What appears at first to be a minimalist box of black-painted steel and bronze-tinted glass has much more character upon closer inspection. At street level, a loggia invites pedestrians inside, with the upper floors cantilevered overhead. Large as it is (400,000 sq. ft./37,000 sq. m), at only four stories high the library seems graceful rather than bulky, with the black girders of its exterior grid emphasizing its horizontal sweep. (Mies did include in his plans a possible fifth floor if the library ever needed to expand.) At night, the dark glass becomes transparent, letting passersby look right through an interior grid of black-girdered bookshelves and overhead light strips, seemingly suspended in mid-air. Many of the interior fittings, too, reflect Mies's Bauhaus sensibility—granite-topped circulation desks, Steelcase tables, chrome-plated hardware.

In the decades since it was built in 1972, however, the library—like many public buildings in this chronically underfunded city—has become considerably run down, requiring major overhauls of its air-conditioning system, elevators, lighting, and restrooms. The carpets are ragged and stained and the drinking fountains don't work. What's more, the advent of the digital age has radically redefined the space needs of a public library. (On the ground floor you'll notice a shadow on the floor where massive card catalogs once stood, before the circulation system went online.) The D.C. government has eyed the central library building's decay as an opportunity to build something new—something that might dovetail with redevelopment of the former Washington Convention Center nearby.

In a city with few Modernist buildings at all—the notorious Watergate apartment complex and the Kennedy Center are among the only others—winning historic recognition for 20th-century architecture is no easy task. However, the Martin Luther King, Jr., Memorial Library was finally granted landmark status, interior as well as exterior, in June 2007. And, as some skeptics have already noted, landmark status is no guarantee of safety—Washington, D.C., has razed certified landmarks before.

---

ⓘ 901 G Street NW, Washington, DC (🕾 **800/422-8644** or 202/789-7000; www.washington.org)

✈ Ronald Reagan Washington National, Dulles International, Baltimore-Washington International

🛏 $$$ **Hilton Washington,** 1919 Connecticut Ave. NW (🕾 **800/HILTONS** [445-8667] or 202/483-3000; www.washington.hilton.com). $$ **Embassy Suites Hotel Downtown,** 1250 22nd St. NW (🕾 **800/EMBASSY** [362-2779] or 202/857-3388; www.embassysuitesdcmetro.com).

---

**Iconic Designs**

**432**

# Salk Institute
## *Inspiring Science*
### La Jolla, California

THE SALK INSTITUTE HAS PERFORMED IMPORTANT RESEARCH ON CANCER, DIABETES, BIRTH defects, Alzheimer's disease, Parkinson's disease, and AIDS. Today, a struggle exists between the institution's need to expand and the need to preserve the uncluttered serenity of the original design. Thus, the landmark campus may get an update that could alter its original oceanview design.

When Dr. Jonas Salk—world famous for developing the polio vaccine in the 1950s—set out to found an independent research institute for biological science, he shrewdly recognized that a beautiful campus would help attract the best researchers around. He chose a breath-taking clifftop location on the Torrey Pines Mesa of La Jolla, San Diego's loveliest suburb, and hired noted modern architect Louis I. Kahn to design the complex.

But even Salk may not have imagined how triumphantly Kahn's design would succeed. Asked to provide laboratories for 56 faculty fellows to work in, Kahn made the lab areas open and flexible, to enhance the give-and-take of scientific collaboration—and then gave each scientist an individual study for privacy and reflection. He set them in a pair of mirror-image two-story-high buildings, 65 feet (20m) deep and 245 feet (74m) long, flanked by green lawns and facing each other congenially across a wide travertine-paved plaza open to the sky and sea. For the crowning touch, the courtyard is bisected with a single shimmering channel of water, flowing straight as an arrow toward the Pacific Ocean.

Classically simple and harmonious in design, the campus buildings are nevertheless anything but stark. Wood-framed windows and panels of sun-bleached shingles give texture to their exposed concrete facades. Instead of a regimented straight line, they're a succession of slightly angled modules, so that every fellow's office has an inspiring ocean view. Modern as it is in some respects, in others the complex demonstrates Kahn's reverence for the ancient architecture of Italy, Greece, and Egypt—the institute feels just like a modern Acropolis.

Over the years, the 27-acre (11-hectare) campus has worn incredibly well, winning historic landmark status in 1991. More laboratories and administrative offices were built in the 1990s, but that serene centerpiece was left untouched. But now, the Salk Institute has announced plans for a 240,000-square-foot (22,300-sq.-m) addition on the western side overlooking the ocean. In order to attract top research talent these days, the directors argue, they need to offer amenities like a fitness center, day care, and residences. And the only place left to build is at the open end of the central courtyard, even if it does spoil the harmony of Kahn's oceanview composition.

While the institute is still seeking planning approval, this may be your last chance to see the campus as Kahn built it. Free tours of the grounds are offered periodically throughout the week; call for a reservation.

ⓘ 10010 N. Torrey Pines Rd., La Jolla (✆ **858/453-4100**)

✈ San Diego

🛏 $$$ **Catamaran Resort Hotel,** 3999 Mission Blvd., San Diego (✆ **800/ 422-8386** or 858/488-1081; www.catamaran resort.com). $ **Park Manor Suites,** 525 Spruce St. (✆ **800/874-2649** or 619/291-0999; www.parkmanorsuites.com).

**433** Places of Worship

# St. Mary's Church
## *Quintessentially English*
### Stow-in-Lindsey, Lincolnshire, United Kingdom

POET LAUREATE SIR JOHN BETJEMAN ONCE CALLED THIS RUGGED GOLDEN STONE CHURCH THE "finest Norman church in Lincolnshire." And at over 1,000 years old, it still stands. But with crumbling stones and dwindling congregations, how long will it last?

Poet laureate Sir John Betjeman may have gotten the dates wrong—some historians believe that St. Mary's predates the Norman invasion, having been founded in A.D. 678, burned down by Danish invaders in 870, and rebuilt between 1034 and 1050. It's clearly one of the oldest parish churches in England, with a significant number of its early architectural elements intact—timber roof beams, tall rounded Saxon arches, even ancient graffiti depicting a Viking longboat scratched onto a stone wall.

St. Mary's was once the head church of the diocese of Lincolnshire—around town it's referred to as Stow Minster, and townsfolk still blame those upstart Normans for moving the cathedral to the nearby city of Lincoln. But despite its substantial size, today St. Mary's is just a rural parish church, and like many parish churches in the U.K., its dwindling congregation can't afford to keep up with repairs. And when your church is over 1,000 years old, expect a lot of repairs.

In the Victorian era, St. Mary's barely escaped demolition because its rector at the time had a personal fortune to spend on having it restored; today's rector has no such option. St. Mary's vestry estimates that it will take between £2 and £3 million to fix the church's lead roof, replace crumbling masonry, make the building watertight, and then hire skilled craftsmen to restore the historic decorative details inside, a project they hope to complete by 2015. Even with help from English Heritage and the World Monuments Fund—both of them concerned about losing such a quintessentially English treasure—that's a lot of money to raise.

Within the mottled stone walls of St. Mary's, you can trace a continuous tapestry of English history. Two early English saints, St. Hugh and St. Etheldreda, are associated with the church and depicted in its stained-glass windows. One of its earliest benefactors was the 11th-century Earl of Mercia, Leofric, and his wife Lady Godiva, famous for riding naked through the streets of Coventry to protest high taxes. There's a ghostly 13th-century wall painting of the great English martyr St. Thomas à Becket, an ornate 15th-century stone font with pagan symbols like a dragon and a Green Man carved around its base, and a fine Jacobean carved pulpit. Some of the Pilgrims who later colonized America worshipped here in the 16th century. In World War II, its square crenellated stone tower was used as a landmark for bomber pilots. It's more than just a village church—it's England in microcosm, and that's worth saving.

---

ⓘ Church St., Stow-in-Lindsey (16km/10 miles northwest of Lincoln; www.stow minster.org.uk)

✈ Heathrow

🚆 Lincoln

🛏 $$$ **White Hart Hotel,** Bailgate, Lincoln (✆ **44/1522/526222**). $$ **Hillcrest Hotel,** 15 Lindum Terrace, Lincoln (✆ **44/1522/510182;** www.hillcrest-hotel.com).

**Places of Worship** 434

# Church of the Holy Nativity
## *An Unstable Stable Scene*
### Bethlehem, Israel

WHILE GUIDED TOURS STILL COME DAILY FROM JERUSALEM TO SEE JESUS' BIRTHPLACE, THE locality is so drained by military turmoil that routine maintenance has been ignored in the decaying church guarding where he was born.

Church of the Holy Nativity.

Even if you're not a practicing Christian, you probably know where Jesus Christ was born—the story of his birth in a stable in Bethlehem has been told over and over again for 20 centuries now. But Bethlehem today is no simple village of shepherds, camels, and donkeys; it's a busy, modern town in the West Bank, that political tinderbox torn between Israel and Palestine.

Milling around a plaza called Manger Square, you'll notice different priests protecting their sects' claim to this sacred site—Franciscan priests in brown robes, Armenians in purple- and cream-colored robes, bearded Greeks in black robes with long hair tied into a bun. After being tussled over for centuries, it's no surprise that the ancient **Church of the Holy Nativity** looks dilapidated—competing priests may even come to blows over the right to scrub a certain section of the worn floors. (Having armed Palestinian soldiers occupy the church, as has happened recently, only aggravates the situation.) Though it was first built in A.D. 326 by the Roman emperor Constantine, and rebuilt

200 years later by Emperor Justinian, its present fortresslike facade was the work of 12th-century crusaders, aggressively reinforcing their claim to the site. Unlike the grand portals of most churches, this one has an odd low doorway—some say lowered by Christians to prevent Ottomans from riding their horses inside, others say built by post-crusade Muslins to humble Christian pilgrims.

Inside, the stately Corinthian pillars that line the basilica's naves bear faded paintings of apostles, bishops, saints, and kings; gilded lamps hang from the oak ceiling, and trapdoors in the stone-and-wood floor give mere glimpses of old Byzantine mosaic glories beneath. But the heart of the church lies not with its ornate gold-and-silver main altar, but down narrow staircases beside the altar: a subterranean marble grotto, draped in worn tapestries. According to ancient tradition, this shallow cave is where Mary gave birth to Jesus; altars mark nearby spots where the manger stood and where the Magi bowed to the baby Jesus. Historically accurate or not, after centuries of adoration this hushed grotto is full of spiritual aura.

While you're here, you should also visit the grand **Franciscan church** just north of the Church of the Holy Nativity, which offers a competing Nativity site: A stairway from the back of its nave leads to an underground maze of rock-hewn chambers that supposedly includes the stable where Joseph and Mary stayed the night of Jesus' birth. In the scrum of modern Bethlehem, finding not one but two holy retreats isn't a bad bargain at all.

ⓘ **The Church of the Holy Nativity,** Manger Square, Bethlehem (✆ 972/2/647-7050)

✈ Jerusalem

🛏 $$$ **Jerusalem Sheraton Plaza,** 47 King George St. (✆ **800/325-3535** or 972/2/629-8666; www.sheraton.com). $$ **King Solomon Hotel,** 32 King David St. (✆ **972/2/569-5555**).

**TOUR Egged Tours** (✆ **972/2/530-4422**). **United Tours** (✆ **972/2/625-2187**). **Alternative Tours** (✆ **972/52/864-205** or 02/628-3282, raed@jrshotel.com). **Heartland Christian Biblical Tours** (✆ **972/2/940-0422**).

# La Sagrada Familia
## The Flower of Modernismo
### Barcelona, Spain

THE UNFINISHED *LA SAGRADA FAMILIA* IS SCHEDULED TO BE FINALLY COMPLETED IN 2026. But will the proposed underground tunnel for a high-speed train, which may shake its foundations, be completed before the cathedral is finished?

Amid the massed Gothic cathedrals of Europe, *La Sagrada Família* rises like a breath of fresh air—the exuberantly un-Gothic masterpiece of the great 20th-century architect Antoni Gaudí. Begun in 1882, this church is the glorious flowering of Gaudí's signature style: modernismo, a romantic, voluptuous Catalonian offshoot of Art Nouveau that flourished in Barcelona from about 1890 to 1910.

But when Gaudí died in 1926, *La Sagrada Familia* (the Church of the Holy Family) was still far from done. Two portals were later completed, in startlingly contrasting styles by two different sculptors—the stark, blocky figures of the Passion facade and the more fanciful, Gaudí-like Nativity facade—but the Glory portal, the transepts, and several of its 18 spiky mosaic-crowned spires are still unfinished. The joyous flowerlike vaulting of the central nave wasn't completed until 2000. With no government or church funding, the project depends on tourism revenues and private donations; its projected 2026 completion date is seriously in doubt. And now, to cap it all off, an underground tunnel for the new high-speed train from Barcelona to Madrid has been proposed to be drilled only 4m (13 ft.) from the cathedral, shaking it to its intricately engineered foundations.

As it expanded beyond its historic core in the late 19th century, Barcelona offered a virtual blank slate for a gifted crew of architects eager to express their Catalan identity—and Gaudí stood head and shoulders above them all. (Other examples of his style can be found along the Passeig de Gràcia and out in the northern suburbs at Parc Güell.) Their *modernismo* rejected monumental symmetry and went instead for forms found in nature, with lots of hand-crafted decoration. Gaudí in particular loved drooping masses, melting horizontal lines, and giddy spirals. This cathedral erupts skyward with clusters of honeycombed spires, looking more like encrusted stalagmites than like traditional Gothic towers; its arches are neither pointed Gothic nor rounded Romanesque, but tapering curves of a certain *Star Trek*–ish flair. (Gaudí's versions of flying buttresses are definitely Space Age struts.) Sculpted figures seem to grow organically out of its portals and arches; brightly colored fruits and flowers sprout from the fanciful pinnacles. *La Sagrada Familia*'s rose windows really do look like roses, its fluted columns like flower stalks, rising to a vaulted ceiling pattern that looks like nothing more than a field spangled with daisies.

Gaudí's original plans were only discovered in 1950; with those in hand, the directors of the ongoing project hope to execute the cathedral just as he intended it. But unlike Europe's Gothic cathedrals, which took leisurely centuries to complete, *La Sagrada Familia* is in a race against time. Will that high-speed train beat it to the finish line?

ⓘ Carrer de Sardenya, Barcelona (ℂ **34/93-207-30-31;** www.sagradafamilia.org; www.sossagradafamilia.org)

✈ Barcelona

🛏 $$$ **Hotel Hespería Sarriá,** Los Vergós 20 (ℂ **34/93-204-55-51**). $$ **Duques de Bergara,** Bergara 11 (ℂ **34/93-301-51-51;** www.hoteles-catalonia.com).

---

**436** Places of Worship

# The Abbey of Mont-St-Michel
## *Time & Tide*
### Normandy, France

WHEN YOU THINK OF THE ENGINEERING REQUIRED TO BUILD THIS IMMENSE CHURCH ON THIS tide-scoured outcrop, it's a marvel it has stood this long. Short-sighted renovations that built the causeway and altered natural tidal patterns has exacerbated the silting up of the bay. Can the government reverse this?

Approaching across the coastal flatlands, you see its Gothic splendor erupt toward the sky, usually cloaked in dramatic fog. Set upon a massive rock just off the Normandy coast, the great Gothic abbey church of Mont-St-Michel rises dramatically from its rampart walls to an ethereal spire topped with a gilded statue of the archangel Michael, the abbey's guardian spirit.

Yet in the last couple of centuries, St. Michael seems to have let down his guard. The narrow land bridge that once connected Mont-St-Michel to the mainland, exposed only at low tide, was beefed up in 1879 into a permanent causeway, accessible at all hours. Meanwhile, the local folks kept on tinkering with the natural tidal processes—polderizing shallow parts of the bay to create pastureland, making a canal out of the Couesnon River—until the bay gradually silted up. Finally, in June 2006, the French government took action, initiating a hydraulic dam project to make Mont-St-Michel a true island again, by 2012 if all goes well.

In the Middle Ages, this was a popular pilgrimage site, founded in the 8th century by St. Aubert; medieval pilgrims could get here only at low tide, walking across treacherous tidal sands, a challenge that increased the spiritual value of the journey. Enhanced over the next few centuries, however, as the abbey's monks grew richer and more powerful, the abbey came to look more like a fortress than a holy retreat—a fact that served it well in the Hundred Years' War (1337–1451), when it almost miraculously resisted capture by the English. The rampart walls also made it easy to convert to a prison after the monks were disbanded, in the days of the French Revolution. Since the late 19th century it's been a national monument, not a church, although recently some new monks have settled in as well.

It's a steep walk to the abbey up Grande Rue, lined with half-timbered 15th- and 16th-century houses. Inside the abbey walls are more staircases to climb. But it's worth it to investigate the abbey's stunning Gothic interiors, most notably the Salle des Chevaliers (Hall of the Knights) and graceful cloisters with rosy pink granite columns. Crowning the summit is the splendid abbey church—note the round Romanesque arches in the 11th-century nave and transept, transitioning to the pointy Flamboyant Gothic arches of the 15th-century choir area. In the summer, if you're staying on the mount, you can visit the church at night—not a bad idea for avoiding hordes of day-trippers.

---

ⓘ **The Abbey of Mont-St-Michel** (✆ 33/ 2/33-89-80-00)

✈ Orly and Charles de Gaulle

🚎 Rennes

🛏 $$ **Les Terrasses Poulard,** Grande Rue (✆ **33/2/33-60-14-09;** www.mere-poulard.fr)

# The Painted Churches of Moldavia
## *Picture-Book Walls*
### Northern Romania

ONLY ABOUT A DOZEN OF THESE PAINTED CHURCHES REMAIN TODAY, TUCKED AWAY IN SMALL out-of-the-way towns near the Ukrainian border, reachable only by narrow roads and mountain passes. Often their congregations are too poor to properly restore and preserve these treasures.

In medieval northern Europe, those grand Gothic windows of stained glass had a purpose—to tell Bible stories to an illiterate congregation. In Greece and other Orthodox countries, intricate mosaics did the same job. But only in northern Romania, in a kingdom once known as Moldavia, even the simplest country church might be painted inside and out with vivid, dramatic narrative murals.

Amid the turmoil of Ottoman invasion, from 1522 to 1547 a handful of now-anonymous artists moved around this mountainous countryside painting frescoes on church after church. (Note the churches' distinctive regional architecture, with round towers and apses, octagonal steeples set on a star-shaped base, and wide-eaved roofs like brimmed hats clapped on top.) These itinerant artists used simple paints, easily manufactured from local minerals; if they were lucky, they were able to slip in a touch of gold leaf or precious lapis lazuli blue. Household ingredients like charcoal, egg, vinegar, and honey were thrown in to preserve the color, which evidently worked—they have withstood the rugged Carpathian climate for over 450 years. In fact, the outside frescoes often have fared better than the inside ones, which are darkened by centuries of incense fumes and candle smoke.

If you can only see one, make it **Voroneţ,** with its amazing *Last Judgment* on one large west wall; for some reason Voroneţ, nicknamed "the Sistine Chapel of the East," had access to plenty of lapis lazuli, and the blues glow richly here. But **Humor** is worth a detour for all the daring political references its artist slipped in—look for turbaned Turkish enemies in many of his murals. Green is the dominant color at charming little **Arbore,** which has a detailed painting of the story of Genesis. **Sucevita** is not just one church but an entire fortified monastery compound, with thousands of pictures—notice the one blank wall, which was left unfinished, the story goes, when the painter fell off his scaffolding to his death. **Moldovița** has a particularly panoramic depiction of the Siege of Constantinople, a major event for

the Greek Orthodox Church. All five can be visited in a few hours, on a loop of back roads west of Suceava. Catch them before they fade away.

✈ Suceava

$$$ **Best Western Hotel Bucovina,** 4 Bucovina Ave., Gura Humorului (✆ **40/ 230/32115;** www.bestwestern.com). $$ **Balada Hotel,** Str. Mitropoliei 3, Suceava (✆ **40/230/522146;** www.balada.ro).

# Ayasofya Mosque
## *The Model Mosque*
### Istanbul, Turkey

AS IF SURVIVING CENTURIES OF WAR, EARTHQUAKES, AND HUMID WEATHER WASN'T ENOUGH, when they put a railroad next to Little Hagia Sophia—that was the last straw.

You'd think a holy place this old would get a little more respect. After all, this is the oldest Byzantine monument in Istanbul, built as the Christian church of Sts. Sergios and Bacchos by Emperor Justinian in A.D. 527 to 536. Many architectural historians believe it was a working model for Justinian's later great church, Hagia Sophia (now the Ayasofya Mosque), which is why this one eventually became known as Little Hagia Sophia. Like the bigger Hagia Sophia, this smaller church was converted to a mosque in 1504 after the Moslem takeover of Istanbul, and the gold Byzantine mosaics that once glittered all over its interior were plastered over. Unlike big Hagia Sophia, though, it is still a working mosque, which you can visit (observe the usual etiquette for visiting mosques—remove your shoes, don't take flash photos, don't walk in front of worshippers, and dress modestly). Its lovely octagonal nave is surmounted by a broad dome, accented by slender columns of colored marble with ornately sculpted capitals; don't miss its especially serene and leafy garden outside.

Little Hagia Sophia is one of Istanbul's lesser known gems, tucked away by the southern city walls near the shore of the Sea of Marmara. The 20th century, however, has not been kind to it. It was once closer to the sea, until the 1950s, when a landfill project made room for a new coastal road routed close to the mosque. The railway came soon afterward, adding more vibrations to shake the ancient building. When rising damp became a problem, the foundation was raised in the 1970s—but a recently built sea wall nearby raised the water table and caused the damp to return worse than ever.

When the earthquake of 1999 widened existing cracks in the dome, rainwater seeped in and the mosque—which had just been restored in 1996—began to show serious signs of decay. Unless those unsteady foundations were finally shored up, there was every reason Little Hagia Sophia would collapse. The mosque was closed for major structural work beginning in 2002—but almost immediately, workers discovered ancient tombs under the site,

# 10 All-American Lighthouses

Throughout the 19th century, expanding America's bustling shipping corridors depended on a network of sturdy, often lonely lighthouses. Superseded by improved navigational technology, only about 600 of these romantic coastal towers are left; many face extinction. Here are 10 that preservationists are working to save:

White Island.

**439 White Island, New Hampshire**   On the Isle of Shoals, 10 miles off the New Hampshire coast, poet Celia Thaxter lived as a child in this white 1859 brick-and-stone lighthouse on White Island. It's still a working light (though now automated), but it was badly battered in storms in 1984, 1991, and 2007. However, an enthusiastic group of seventh-graders is working to restore its severely cracked interior. *www.lighthousekids.org.*

**440 Sankaty Head, Nantucket, Massachusetts**   New England's most powerful light shone since 1850 from this white-and-red-striped, brick-and-granite structure overlooking dangerous shoals on the outer end of Nantucket Island. Over the years it became a popular tourist attraction, with particularly breathtaking views from its 90-foot-high (70m) bluff. Erosion of the steep bluff threatened its existence, however, and in 2007 the entire lighthouse was moved 405 feet (122m) inland. *www.sconsettrust.org.*

**441 Esopus Lighthouse, Esopus, New York**   The Esopus Lighthouse—aka the Middle Hudson Lighthouse or "the Maid of the Meadows"—was opened in 1871 to warn Hudson River craft of treacherous mud flats. Growing out of the roof of a substantial white-frame house squeezed onto a granite pier in the middle of the river, it had become seriously dilapidated by 1990. A major restoration saved it from collapse; its light was finally turned back on in 2003. *www.esopuslighthouse.org.*

**442 Mispillion River Lighthouse, Delaware**   First lit in 1873, the Misipillion Lighthouse provided a beacon for sailors headed upriver to Milford, Delaware, its square-towered lantern room rising from a handsome L-shaped Carpenter Gothic house. In 1929, it was replaced by an unglamorous steel skeleton tower, and over decades of private ownership, its condition rapidly deteriorated. Struck by lighting in 2002, it was a mere shell when new owners in 2004 moved its remains, beacon and all, to rebuild it in Shipcarpenter Square in Lewes. *www.lighthousefriends.com.*

**443 Bodie Island Lighthouse, Cape Hatteras, North Carolina**   It's been built and rebuilt three times since 1847—first to correct a Pisa-like tilt, then to replace the tower blown up by Confederate soldiers in the Civil War. The third time was the charm, and now this 150-foot-high (45m), black-and-white banded stone tower can be seen for miles. Though it's not as tall as its famous neighbor, the Cape Hatteras Lighthouse, Bodie's light still operates, warning ships of the perilous Outer Banks waters. *www.nps.gov/caha.*

**444 Morris Island Lighthouse, Charleston, South Carolina**   A beloved landmark guarding the entrance to Charleston harbor, the Morris Island Light dates to 1876 (its predecessor was destroyed in the Civil War); it has survived many hurricanes and an earthquake, but time has taken its toll. The foundation is weakened, the tower leans, and beach erosion swept away its once-grand living quarters, leaving the lighthouse stranded alone 1,600 feet (5,250m) offshore. Walk over the dunes of Folly Beach to see this faded brown-and-white beauty. *www.savethelight.org.*

**445 Raspberry Island Lighthouse, Bayfield, Wisconsin**   The Great Lakes have their lighthouses too— rough waters made the shipping channel around Lake Superior's Apostle Islands particularly hazardous, creating a need for the Raspberry Island Light to be built in 1863. Touted as the Showplace of the Apostle Islands, the substantial red-roofed white-frame house below the light tower was repeatedly expanded for lightkeepers' families and assistants. But its bluff-top site faces serious erosion from Superior's pounding waves. *www.nps.gov/apis.*

Raspberry Island Lighthouse.

**446 Nottawasaga Island Lighthouse, Collinwood, Ontario**   One of six so-called "Imperial Towers" around Ontario's Georgian Bay, the 26m (85-ft.) limestone Nottawasaga Lighthouse was built in 1858 on an isolated Lake Huron island (today a bird sanctuary) prone to lightning storms. Fire gutted the keeper's house in 1958, after which the graceful conical white lighthouse was automated. It was decommissioned in 2003 after chunks of outer wall fell off—yet its solar-powered light continues to shine, without maintenance. *www.visitgeorgianbay.ca.*

**447 Sand Island Lighthouse, Alabama**   Standing 125 feet (38m) tall, this slim black tower near the mouth of Mobile Bay was the third built on this Gulf Coast island— once 400 acres (160 hectares), now eroded to a narrow strip of sand. Built of wood on a granite base, it was hit badly by hurricanes in 1906 and 1919. Left to crumble for many years, it now belongs to the nearby town of Dauphin Island. *www.sandislandlighthouse.com.*

**448 Isla de Mona Lighthouse, Puerto Rico**   Isla Mona, off Puerto Rico's west coast, has had a checkered history as a pirate hideout and smugglers' haven. When Puerto Rico was ceded to the U.S. after the Spanish-American War, a steel lighthouse was promptly erected in 1900— and not just any steel lighthouse, but one designed by Gustave Eiffel (yes, the designer of the Eiffel Tower). It worked steadily until 1976, when it was replaced by an automated light. Now abandoned, the rusting hulk of the original structure remains in disrepair. © **787/724-3724.**

Isla de Mona Lighthouse.

which ground work to a halt. Some international observers began to fear that the landmark mosque would be left to rot.

It's been a long haul, but the project was finally completed in 2007. The mosque, crisply repainted and plastered, looks in fine form again. After all it's gone through, it deserves a visit.

ⓘ Lower end of Küçük Ayasofya Cad

✈ Atatürk International, Istanbul

🛏 $$$ **Çiragan Palace Hotel Kempinski Istanbul,** Çiragan Cad. 84 (② **800/426-3135** in the U.S., 90/212/258-3377 in Istanbul; www.ciraganpalace.com). $$ **Mavi Ev (Blue House),** Dalbasti Sok. 14 (② **90/212/638-9010;** www.bluehouse.com.tr).

---

**Places of Worship** **449**

# The Mosques of Timbuktu
## *Melting into the Desert*
### Timbuktu, Mali

BUILT OF MUD, LIKE EVERY OTHER BUILDING IN TIMBUKTU, THESE THREE MEDIEVAL MOSQUES are susceptible to damage from nature's most common wrath—rain.

Yes, Timbuktu really does exist, although it was the early 19th century before any white European traveled there and lived to tell the tale. By then, this desert trading city—situated right where the Niger River flows into the southern edge of the Sahara desert—was long past its golden age, when it had a population of 100,000. Today's population is only about 32,000, but Timbuktu's skyline still boasts three towering medieval landmarks—a trio of mosques once renowned throughout the Islamic world.

There's just one catch: Those mosques are built entirely of mud. Every spring when the rains come, citizens pack fresh mud onto their rounded towers and sloping walls to keep them from dissolving back into the desert (even the streets here are nothing but drifting sand—camels and donkeys fare better than the few taxis). The tan walls of the taller sections bristle with the tips of dark wooden struts, but despite those supports, an unexpected thunderstorm could wipe out them out at any time. Only recently have they begun desperately needed structural reinforcement.

Dominating the intersection where Arabia's gold and ivory were traded for sub-Saharan Africa's salt and slaves—imagine the Sahara as an ocean, and Timbuktu as its biggest seaport—medieval Timbuktu used its wealth to become Africa's greatest Islamic center of learning. These aren't just any mosques—they were also universities, or *madrassahs*, with celebrated imams teaching in the courtyards, and libraries containing thousands of precious manuscripts. Most studies centered on the Koran, but related fields such as astronomy, history, and logic were also taught. The first mosque—**Djinguere Ber,** or the Friday Prayers Mosque—was built in 1327 by Emperor Mansa Mussa. (His Egyptian architect designed an even larger mosque in Djenné, still the largest mud-built structure in the world.) With its main tower like a tapering, stunted skyscraper, Djinguere Ber is big enough for 2,000 worshippers, and is still the central mosque of the city. The other two, **Sankore** and **Sidi Yahya,** were built in the 15th century. Pyramid-shaped Sankore developed into the epicenter of Islamic scholarship in all of Africa, and even today functions as a university.

Though non-Muslim visitors are no longer allowed inside, you can still marvel at the mosques' flowing exteriors (said to have inspired Antonin Gaudí in designing La Sagreda Familia). Today you'll see television aerials on Timbuktu's huddled mud houses; there's even an internet café on the high street. But it's still remote and desolate, and the heat is relentless (at midday, nobody ventures outdoors). Strolling around its soft sand streets between the uniformly tawny, low adobe buildings is like entering a dream world—don't miss it.

✈ Timbuktu International

⊨ $$ **Hendrina Khan Hotel,** off Route de Korioumé (✆ **223/292-16-81**). $$ **Hotel Colombe,** Blvd. Askia Mohamed (✆ **223/ 292-14-35**).

TOUR **World Heritage Tours** (✆ **800/ 663-0844** or 604/264-7378; www.world heritagetours.com). **Intrepid Travel** (✆ **800/970-7299;** www.intrepidtravel. com). **Palace Travel** (✆ **800/683-7731** or 215/471-8555; www.palacetravel.com).

# Ajanta Caves
## *Worshipping Art*
### Maharashtra, India

MORE THAN 2,000 YEARS OLD, THE AJANTA CAVES DISPLAY ROCK PAINTINGS THAT HAVE survived for centuries. However, clumsy restoration and the presence of so many admirers are hastening their decay.

It's quite a proposition, getting to the ancient cave temple of Ajanta, in far-flung Maharashtra, India, about 500km (300 miles) east of Mumbai. What makes it worth the trip is not just the beauty of this Buddhist worship site—though it certainly is beautiful, a horseshoe-shaped cliff above a hairpin bend in the Waghora River—it's the fact that it was chiseled patiently out of the cliff face, chip by chip, using nothing but handheld tools.

Remote as it is, thousands of visitors come here every year, particularly in the summer months. The crush inside the caves can be stifling. Visitors are asked to take their shoes off, photography is forbidden, and barriers prevent people from touching the artworks. The rock surfaces need to be treated to protect the art against inevitable water leakage. The painting in some caves survived the centuries better than in others, where only tantalizing fragments of images remain. Some earlier attempts at restoring the paintings have even worsened their condition. The sculptures have survived better—proof of

how hard this stone was to carve—though some are pitted with age.

Ajanta is an incredibly old site—begun in the 2nd century B.C. and executed over the next 700 years by Buddhist monks. Some of its 29 caves are *chaityas*— shrines—and others are *viharas*, or monasteries, where the artworks were meant to inspire spiritual contemplation on the life and teachings of Buddha. Cave 1 is perhaps the most famous vihara, renowned for the two fantastic murals of bodhisattvas (precursors of Buddha) flanking the doorway of the antechamber—on one side Avalokitesvara with his thunderbolt in hand, on the other Padmapani holding a water lily. The great *mandala*, or sacred meditative design, on the ceiling of Cave 2 is awesome. Cave 16 has a lovely painting of the princess Sundari, wife of the Buddha's half-brother (she's swooning at the news that her husband's becoming a monk); the most brilliantly painted is Cave 17, where maidens float overhead, accompanied by celestial musicians, lotus petals, and scroll work. Check out the huge

The Ajanta Caves.

sculpture of the reclining Buddha in the richly carved Cave 26.

It has been said that all Indian art stems from Ajanta—and yet, incredibly, for centuries it lay remote and forgotten, rediscovered accidentally by a boar-hunting British soldier in 1819. As you walk through, don't get overwhelmed by the sheer profusion of detail. Focus instead on imagining the anonymous monks long ago, tending to their devotions, and creating immortal art in the process.

✈ Aurangabad

🛏 $$ **The Ambassador Ajanta,** Jalna Rd., Aurangabad (✆ **0240/248-5211;** www.ambassadorindia.com). $$ **Quality Inn The Meadows,** Gat no. 135 and 136, Village Mitmita, Aurangabad (✆ **0240/267-7412;** meadows@gnbom.global.net.in).

**Places of Worship**

451

# The Great Stupa of Sanchi
## *In the Shadow of Bhopal*
### Madhya Pradesh, India

A THOROUGH 20TH-CENTURY RESTORATION BROUGHT THE GREAT STUPA BACK TO TOP CONDITION. But since the 1984 environmental disaster at nearby Bhopal, tourism has dried up. Is the Great Stupa facing a fourth chapter of decline?

Three times in its history, the Great Stupa of Sanchi was nearly destroyed—once by vandals in the 2nd century B.C.; a second time from the 13th through 18th centuries, when Buddhism withered in India; and a third time in the late 19th century when amateur archaeologists and treasure hunters ravaged the newly rediscovered ruins.

It's a shame, because there's something innately appealing about this plump domed Buddhist monument, set serenely on a hill with lovely views of the surrounding countryside. India's finest example of ancient Buddhist architecture, it's the centerpiece of a complex founded in the 3rd century B.C. by the Mauryan emperor Ashoka, who converted to Buddhism after massacring thousands in his military campaigns. Excavations to date have unearthed about 55 temples, pillars, stupas, and monasteries in the complex, an amazing continuum of Buddhist architectural styles. Yet it doesn't overwhelm the visitor—it's a low-rise site of gentle domes and spaces for contemplation.

The proportions of the Great Stupa itself are so harmonious, you're surprised when you get up close to see how big it actually is. At 16m (54 ft.) high, nearly eight stories tall, it anchors the center of the complex like a massive beehive, or maybe a flying saucer. The stupa may once have held inside some ashes of the Buddha, who died in 483 B.C. (smaller stupas alongside, like satellites around a mother ship, contain ashes of his disciples).Originally it was a smaller brick hemisphere; in the 2nd century B.C. the brick dome was enlarged considerably with a sandstone casing, and a balustrade was added. Later, around 25 B.C., four intricately carved gateways of finer-grained sandstone were placed around the stupa, facing the four points of the compass. Mounted on these gates are intricately carved story panels depicting episodes from the life of Buddha. (Notice that the Buddha is never pictured as a human—look for him instead as a lotus, a wheel, a bodhi tree, or a pair of feet.) As a classic stupa, it also has circling pathways designed for meditative circumambulations.

Originally the stupa was a much more gaudy affair—its dome and supporting plinth were coated with white-lime concrete, the railways and gateway painted red, and the surface of the stupa painted with swags and garlands. The antennalike spire on top would have been gilded, too. But it wears its present weathered look well—the peace of the centuries seems to settle upon it like the folds of a sari.

---

ⓘ **Madhya Pradesh State Tourism Development Corp.** (www.mptourism.com)

✈ Bhopal

🚐 $$ **Jehan Numa Palace,** 157 Shamla Hill, Bhopal (✆ **91/755/266-1100;** www.hoteljehanumapalace.com)

## Places of Worship
### 🔴452

# Borobudur
## *Ascending to Nirvana*
### Central Java, Indonesia

INDONESIAN ANTIQUITIES OFFICIALS, WORRIED THAT TOURIST FOOTPRINTS ARE WEARING DOWN the ancient stone, are now pressing to have the terraced walkways closed to visitors. Go before you lose your chance.

It was built to be walked on, after all—the winding pathway of this stepped pyramid was specifically designed for meditation, and you'll see hosts of saffron-robed Buddhist priests pacing along, chanting as they wind around the 3.2km-long (2-mile) route to the top. Set on a smooth green plain south of Magelang on the gardenlike island of Java, Borobudur is not only the largest Buddhist monument in the world, it is quite simply one of the most stunning architectural creations you'll ever see.

Some two million blocks of lava rock completed the original pyramidlike design, though some have been lost over the centuries. Seen from the ground, it looks like a mountain, bristling with odd little spires; seen from above, it looks like an open lotus blossom, the sacred expression of Buddhism.

But the true brilliance of Borobudur can only be understood if you walk around it. The first six levels (plus another one left underground to stabilize the pyramid) are rectangular in shape, decorated with sculpted bas-relief panels, 1,460 in all. Seen in order, the panels are more or less a spiritual textbook, depicting the life and lessons of Buddha. Each ascending level represents a higher stage of man's spiritual journey.

The top three levels, however, are circular terraces with no ornamentation—Buddhism considers simplicity far more virtuous than decoration. Instead, these upper levels hold a series of beehivelike stone stupas, their bricks arranged in perforated checkerboard patterns, with stone Buddhas tucked inside. Each inscrutable Buddha sits cross-legged, making a hand gesture that signifies one of five spiritual

attainments. At the top, one large central stupa crowns the pyramid, empty inside—scholars still debate whether it once contained a bigger Buddha, or whether its emptiness symbolizes the blessed state of nirvana.

One of the many mysteries of Borobudur is why it was ever abandoned. When Sir Thomas Stanford Raffles discovered it in 1814, Borobudur was buried under layers of ash from nearby Mount Merapi. Perhaps it was buried Pompeii-style; or maybe a series of eruptions brought famine to the region, causing the population to move away. Either way, Borobudur lay forgotten for centuries. Nowadays, it's Java's most popular tourist destination. Despite the level of visitor traffic, however, a meditative peace still holds sway. It would be a shame to lose it.

✈ Yogvakarta

🛏 $$$ **Sheraton Mustika,** JL Laksda Adisucipto, Yogyakarta (📞 **274/488588;** www.sheraton.com). $$ **Manohara Hotel,** Borobudur Archaeological Park, Magelang (📞 **361/731520;** www.bali www.com).

---

**Places of Worship** **453**

# Mission San Miguel Arcangel
## *Mission Accomplished*
### San Miguel, California

AFTER 4 YEARS OF INTENSIVE REPAIR AND EARTHQUAKE PROOFING, DUE TO THE DAMAGE sustained from a 2003 earthquake, the mission's courtyard and convent building have reopened, but the wooden-roofed main church is still closed, undergoing a seismic retrofitting—a building technique that the original friars surely never anticipated.

It was like a lifeline of civilization along the California coast—the string of adobe monasteries built between 1769 and 1823 by a crew of Franciscan friars, determined to convert the native Indians to Christianity. By the time the padres arrived to found Mission San Miguel Arcangel on July 25, 1797 (it was the 16th of 21 missions), the Indians

were eagerly awaiting them. They knew they'd find prosperity in the mission's vineyards, fields, and pastures, not to mention learning vital trades: carpentry, masonry, weaving, blacksmithing, leatherwork.

While many of the other missions have been turned into tourist sights, San Miguel still functions as a parish church—or at least it did until December 22, 2003. That's when the San Simeon earthquake rattled the central California coast, severely damaging the 200-year-old mission, its foundations already weakened by years of vibrations from the nearby Union Pacific Railroad.

Though San Miguel is one of only four missions owned today by the Franciscan order, it wasn't always so holy—during the California Gold Rush, it was a store, saloon, and dance hall, returned to the Franciscans only in 1928. But through all those years, local priests tended the plain, rectangular adobe main church; until the earthquake, it was judged to be the most authentically preserved of the 21 missions. In fact, its interior has never been repainted—especially important because its walls were elaborately decorated by Indian artisans, guided by a Spanish priest named Esteban Munras. The challenge of preserving those time-worn frescoes while making the necessary structural repairs infinitely complicates the job at Mission San Miguel, though techniques developed here will no doubt come in handy when the other California missions face their own restorations.

Although most of the missions were closer to the coast, the friars doggedly went where the Indians were, choosing this valley despite its poor soil and hot climate. Being relatively out of the way, it got less tourist traffic than the more famous missions in Santa Barbara, San Juan Capistrano, and Carmel, which accounts for its unrenovated, and therefore authentic, condition. While the wood-beamed main church with its historic frescoes is off limits, the Mission Museum in the convent building is still fascinating. Take the time to stroll along the cool arched cloister, overlooking its fine old cactus garden—like Mission San Miguel, those hardy cactuses are proven survivors.

---

ⓘ ✆ **805/467-2131**

✈ San Luis Obispo

⊨ $$ **Garden Street Inn,** 1212 Garden St., San Luis Obispo (✆ **800/488-2045** or 805/545-9802; www.gardenstreetinn. com). $$ **Best Western Cavalier Oceanfront Resort,** 9415 Hearst Dr. (Calif. 1), San Simeon (✆ **800/826-8168** or 805/927-4688; www.bestwestern.com).

---

**454** Places of Worship

# Prairie Churches of North Dakota
## *Lighthouses of the Prairie*
### North Dakota

THEIR STEEPLES ARE VISIBLE FOR MILES, RISING ABOVE THE WHEAT FIELDS AND ROLLING PASTURES of rural North Dakota—beacons of community in the treeless prairie landscape. They're the state's most distinctive architectural heritage—and they're fast disappearing due to dwindling congregations and aging structures.

Built in the late 19th and early 20th centuries, these austere frontier churches were the focal points of their farming communities, knitting together first-generation immigrants from Norway, Iceland, Germany, and Ukraine. While the farmers themselves may have lived in simple sod houses, they proudly poured communal labor into their houses of worship, mortaring together round gray fieldstones or cutting down scarce trees to provide wood siding.

A century later, those churches serve increasingly small, aging congregations, who can scarcely foot the repair bills for sagging roofs, tipping steeples, broken windows, splintered floors, wheezy pump organs, and coughing furnaces—let alone combat rising damp in basements that have hosted hundreds of church suppers. Given North Dakota's sweeping winds and blizzards, these buildings have had a hard life—and it shows.

North Dakota still has the nation's highest number of churches per capita, with 2,300 still standing, three fourths of them in rural areas. In some cases, a parish may rotate services around half a dozen old churches just to keep them all in operation. In others, churches are converted to museums or community centers. In all too many other cases, they simply stand empty, rotting away.

Just south of I-94, for example, in the town of Belfield, you can see the abandoned, weathered **Sts. Peter and Paul Ukrainian Orthodox Church,** a domed cruciform church built in 1917 and originally located in the aptly named Ukrainia, North Dakota (it was moved here in 1950). North of I-94, the soon-to-be-disused **Vang Lutheran Church** (12th St. SW, 12 miles/ 19km east of Manning) has a particularly fine white steeple with German-Hungarian detailing above the doorway. An even more evocative sight lies farther south in Grant County: small, spare **Hope Lutheran Church** (west of N.D. 49 in Elgin), standing alone among the wheat fields. It hasn't even got a steeple, only a plain white cross tacked onto its cedar-shingled roof. Built in 1903 to 1904 for $595, it hasn't been a church since 1956, but the Grant County Historical Society still opens it for special-occasion services. Or head east to Morton County, where the neat white-frame **Sims Scandinavian Evangelical Church**—the first Lutheran church west of the Missouri River, built in 1884—is all that's left of the vanished town of Sims (U.S. 10-BL, near Mandan). Services are still held here every other week, and descendants of the town's founders have restored the parsonage, which is now a museum.

---

(i) **Preservation North Dakota** (www. prairieplaces.org)

✈ Bismarck

🛏 $$ **Country Suites by Carlson,** 3205 N. 14th St., Bismarck (✆ **701/258-4200;** www.countryinns.com). $$ **Trapper's Inn,** I-94 and U.S. 85 N, Belfield (✆ **800/284-1855** or 701/575-4261).

*Wigwam Motels.*

455

# The Red Routemaster
## *Double-Decker Tradition*
### London, England

FOR HALF A CENTURY, THE RED DOUBLE-DECKER BUSES TRUNDLING AROUND LONDON WERE AN iconic sight—a visible symbol of the city as much as black-helmeted bobbies and Buckingham Palace guards. Accessibility requirements, fuel efficiency, and emission standards rendered the Routemasters obsolete. Now only two remain.

True, by the dawn of the 21st century the Red Routemasters were inadequate for new public transport standards—they couldn't accommodate wheelchairs, and they required new engines for fuel efficiency and emission controls. Nevertheless, it seemed unthinkable that they should be withdrawn from service entirely by 2006. On the last day of service, December 9, 2005, so many people lined the final route that traffic was stopped completely, making the usually timely bus 10 minutes late in reaching its garage.

The Routemaster was, in fact, a classic piece of British design, superbly fitted to carry a maximum of passengers and still negotiate London's narrow winding streets. Built of durable but light aluminum and easy to repair, it featured a rear open platform that made it easy to hop on and off, although that feature also increased labor costs, requiring a ticket-taking conductor on the bus as well as a driver. Not all were red, in fact; several green Routemasters were also in operation, mostly on outlying routes.

By the time of its demise, the Routemaster had already been replaced on many routes by single-level buses, and some were converted to private sightseeing operations with an open top deck (not practical otherwise—England is, after all, a country where it rains frequently). In all, nearly 3,000 Routemasters were built, and around 1,000 were still running in 2005. They were largely replaced by long articulated buses, slower and heavier than Routemasters and much less adept at steering around the London street maze (but easier for fare skippers to slip onto).

The outcry over withdrawal of the Routemaster was so great that London Mayor Ken Livingstone agreed to keep them on two short versions of regular routes, called Heritage Routes: Route 9, a 5km (3-mile) route which runs from Royal Albert Hall to Aldwych via Hyde Park corner and Piccadilly Circus, and Route 15, between Trafalgar Square and Tower Hill via St. Paul's Church and Charing Cross. Between these two routes, a significant number of tourist destinations will still be served by the red double-deckers.

✈ Heathrow International

🛏 $$ **Hart House Hotel,** 51 Gloucester Place, Marylebone (© **44/20/7935-2288;** www.harthouse.co.uk). $$ **Vicarage Private Hotel,** 10 Vicarage Gate, South Kensington (© **44/20/7229-4030;** www.londonvicaragehotel.com).

# 456

# The Last Supper
## *da Vinci's Wall*
### Santa Maria delle Grazie, Milano, Italy

IT'S A MASTERPIECE OF COMPOSITION, BOTH TECHNICAL AND DRAMATIC, AND NO MATTER HOW often it's parodied (Mel Brooks, Monty Python, and George Carlin have all had a go at it), the original still takes your breath away.

It's been said that all that's left of the original *Last Supper* is a "few isolated streaks of fading color"—everything else was layered on by later hands. Leonardo da Vinci's masterful picture of Jesus and his disciples at their Passover Seder began to disintegrate almost as soon as Leonardo finished it, for in executing this mural on the wall of a convent in Milan, he experimented with risky new paints and application techniques. But it is so clearly a work of genius that over the centuries artists and restorers felt drawn to save it, repainting it in the 1700s, the 1800s, and again quite recently; though modern techniques have improved the sensitivity of these repaintings, it's often impossible to tell what was painted by da Vinci and what was painted by later restorers. In 1943, a bomb demolished the roof—luckily that wall wasn't hit—and the painting stood exposed to the elements for 3 years. It just may be the master's greatest painting, but it's a wonder that anything is left of it at all.

Though born in Florence, Leonardo da Vinci spent many years in Milan (1482–99 and 1506–13), under the patronage of the dukes of Milan. The finicky da Vinci produced endless studies and sketches for projects he never finished; one he did complete, however, was this mural that Duke Ludovico commissioned for the convent of Santa Marie delle Grazie church.

Set above a doorway in what was once a dining hall, *The Last Supper (Il Cenacolo Vinciano)* is a huge artwork, 8.5km (28 ft.) wide and 4.6m (15 ft.) tall. There's nothing static about this scene: Jesus, hands outspread (as if to display his future wounds) has just announced that one of his followers will betray him, and the disciples all lean away, aghast, each in his own manner protesting his fidelity. (Judas is the one with his face in shadow, already clutching the bag of money he was paid to betray Jesus.) Christ's sorrowful figure is isolated, the curved pediment of a doorway over his head suggesting a halo; light streams in from the windows behind him, while darkness looms behind the disciples.

Only 25 viewers are admitted at a time (be prepared to wait in line), and you must pass through anti-pollutant chambers before you get your allotted 15 minutes in front of the painting. A lot to go through, but *The Last Supper* is worth it.

---

ⓘ Piazza Santa Maria delle Grazie (off Corso Magenta; ℂ **39/2/4987588**)

✈ Milan's Aeroporto di Linate or Aeroporto Malpensa

⊨ $$$ **Four Seasons Hotel Milano,** Via Gesú 8 (ℂ **39/2/77088;** www.four seasons.com). $$ **Antica Locanda Leonardo,** Corso Magenta 78 (ℂ **39/2/463317;** www.leoloc.com).

**457**

# Fenway Park
## *Granddaddy of All Ballparks*
Boston, Massachusetts

HAVING WON THE WORLD SERIES, IN BOTH 2004 AND 2007, THE BOSTON RED SOX ARE lovable underdogs no longer—now they are certified winners. And as a result, management has, at least temporarily, stopped making noises about replacing Fenway Park.

"Stadium" is almost too grand a term for Fenway, the oldest baseball park in the major leagues. Built in 1912, it's smaller than modern parks, and full of quirks that only add to its mystique. Seats are narrow, often wood-slatted chairs dating back to 1934; many have poor sightlines and no legroom. The scoreboard is still, incredibly, hand-operated; pitchers warm up in bullpens right on the edge of the diamond, in plain view of the spectators. And then there is the 37-foot-high (11m) left-field wall known as the "Green Monster" for its tendency to rob opposing hitters of their home runs. (During pitching changes, left fielders have been known to sneak inside the Green Monster to get relief from the sun.)

From management's perspective, it would be great to have more seats to sell—Fenway can only hold 36,298 spectators, or 34,482 for day games (one bleacher section has to be covered over to keep sun glare from distracting batters). It would be an enormous relief to replace the dingy, cramped locker rooms and have a drainage system that would keep the outfield playable during heavy rains. And so a number of different plans are on the table, everything from piecemeal renovations to building an entirely new stadium.

But current management acquired the Red Sox on a Save Fenway platform, and change isn't popular in Red Sox Nation. The 2005 movie *Fever Pitch* didn't exaggerate anything: Sit among Red Sox fans in the stands and you'll definitely remember that the word "fan" comes from "fanatic." The seats may be uncomfortable but they're gratifyingly close to the field, without the wide swaths of grass other parks have put between the fans and the players. In 2003 a new section of seats—more like barstools, at nosebleed heights—opened atop the Green Monster; uncomfortable as they are, they're the most sought-after seats in the park.

If you can't get tickets to a game—and in the heat of a pennant race, they're more scarce than Rs in a Boston accent—take a **Fenway Park** tour (conducted year-round, though there are no tours on game days or holidays). You actually get to peer inside the cramped space behind the Green Monster and walk out onto the warning track, stop in the press box, and visit the Red Sox Hall of Fame. Best of all, you get a running commentary on all the legends who've played here. Raze Fenway? Sacrilege.

Fenway Park.

ⓘ **Fenway Park,** 4 Yawkey Way, Boston, MA (ℂ **877/REDSOX-9** [733-7699] tickets, 617/226-6666 tours; www.redsox.com)

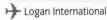 

 Logan International

🛏️ $$ **Doubletree Guest Suites,** 400 Soldiers Field Rd. (📞 **800/222-TREE** [222-7633] or 617/783-0090; www.doubletree.com). $ **The MidTown Hotel,** 220 Huntingdon Ave. (📞 **800/343-1177** or 617/262-1000).

## 458

# Wrigley Field
## *Cubs Losing Their Den?*
### Chicago, Illinois

UNLIKE THEIR COLLEAGUES IN BOSTON, THE CHICAGO CUBS HAVEN'T PLAYED IN THE WORLD Series since 1945 and haven't won the darn thing since 1908. But with new owners, the Cubs may have to move, thus leaving Wrigley Field.

Chicagoans love their Cubbies, champs or not, and they love their home field, one of baseball's classic venues. Built in 1914, Wrigley Field is the second oldest venue in baseball (after Fenway Park 457), although the Cubs didn't move in until 1916 (a decade after their last Series victory!). Back in 1988 lights were finally installed for night play, but they're rarely used—the Cubs still prefer to play mostly day games. With its ivy-covered outfield walls, hand-operated scoreboard, a view of Lake Michigan from the upper deck, and the El rattling past, it's old-fashioned baseball all the way.

After years, however, of being owned by the Chicago Tribune company, the Cubs were sold in 2007—and new owner Sam Zell has indicated his willingness to sell the team separately from its landmarked stadium. Could this mean that the Cubs find a new (larger, more modern) home? If so, what other fate might await Wrigley Field?

Wrigley is small enough that every seat is a decent seat, and the place truly earns its nickname the Friendly Confines—fans are passionate, friendly, well informed, and good natured (much more so than Red Sox fans). Riding the Red Line El to the Addison Street stop, you can look down into the park from the train, and hear the roar of the crowd as soon as you step onto the platform. During the regular season on nongame days, you can take a 90-minute tour of the vintage stadium, visiting the press box, dugouts, both visitors' and Cubs' clubhouses, and the playing field itself (📞 **773/404-CUBS** [404-2827]).

Officially, Wrigley Field can seat 39,600 fans, but the walls are so low that enterprising owners of surrounding houses have built stands on their roofs where they seat their own ticket holders. Other Wrigley quirks: Ground rules declare that if a ball gets stuck in the ivy, it's a double; a pennant is flown after every game with a big w or l to alert passers-by to the outcome of the game (so who needs the Internet?). Best of all, when the opposing team hits a home run out of the park, somebody on the sidewalk outside picks up the offending ball and throws it back in. You've gotta love a ballpark where that happens—and hope against hope it's not lost.

ⓘ **Wrigley Field,** 1060 W. Addison St., Chicago, IL (📞 **773/404-CUBS** [404-2827]; www.cubs.mlb.com)

✈️ O'Hare International

🛏️ $$ **Hotel Allegro Chicago,** 171 N. Randolph St. (📞 **800/643-1500** or 312/236-0123; www.allegrochicago.com). $$ **Homewood Suites,** 40 E. Grand St. (📞 **800/CALL-HOME** [225-5466] or 312/644-2222; www.homewoodsuiteschicago.com).

**459**

# Houston Astrodome
## *Under the Dome*
### Houston, Texas

STANDING EMPTY, THE ASTRODOME WAS PUT TO SUDDEN USE IN AUGUST 2005 WHEN SOME 25,000 Hurricane Katrina victims were housed there on an emergency basis for 2 weeks—a sad late chapter in the life of a building once called the Eighth Wonder of the World.

How could Houston possibly have a baseball team? Given the sweltering Texas heat and humidity, summer games would be brutal for spectators, let alone players.

But in the early 1960s, ex-mayor Judge Roy Hofheinz offered a stunning solution: Build an indoor stadium, complete with air-conditioning, enclosed under a giant skylit dome. And so major league baseball came to Houston with a team named the Colt .45s, soon renamed the Astros in recognition of Houston's growing role in the space program. Their $35-million new home opened in 1965, an 18-story-high domed circular stadium covering 9½ acres (3.8 hectares), with a stunning column-free span of 642 feet (193m). It wasn't just for baseball—the Astrodome could host football as well, with ingenious movable seating to accommodate up to 42,000 spectators (the parking lot held 30,000 cars). Not only that, the Astrodome boasted 53 luxury suites, a revenue-boosting innovation that ballparks across the country immediately coveted.

The Astrodome field was covered with a specially bred type of grass, but soon it became clear that the dome's 4,000-plus Lucite panes focused the sun's rays into a nasty glare. The window panes were painted white, the grass died, and the Astros played the rest of the season on green-painted dirt. A new type of green nylon artificial grass was then developed, which quickly earned the name AstroTurf. (It took several seasons for players to realize the toll that AstroTurf play took on their knees.)

Over the years, inevitably the Astrodome began to show its age, especially as the development of retractable roofs made its fixed ceiling seem quaint. In 1997 the Houston Oilers moved to Tennessee after their owner had repeatedly demanded a new stadium; when the Astros also threatened to leave, the city built Enron Field (now Minute Maid Park) downtown in 2000. Then Reliant Stadium went up next door to the Astrodome in 2002 to house a new football team, the Houston Texans. Soon the big rodeos and concerts also moved to Reliant, leaving the Astrodome empty except for high-school football games and business conventions.

Demolition seems inevitable, but at present, the city has rejected any such plans because the surrounding neighborhood is so dense. The latest scheme is to convert the Astrodome into a luxury hotel. It only took 35 years for America's Colosseum to become an outdated relic—that's progress for you.

---

ⓘ **Houston Astrodome,** 8400 Kirby Dr., Houston

✈ George Bush Intercontinental Airport

🛏 $$ **La Quinta Inn Reliant Center,** 9911 Buffalo Speedway (ⓒ **800/531-5900** or 713/668-8082; www.laquinta.com). $$ **Patrician Bed & Breakfast Inn,** 1200 Southmore Blvd. (ⓒ **800/553-5797** or 713/523-1114; www.texasbnb.com).

# Hialeah Park Race Track
## *Down to the Wire*
### Hialeah, Florida

HURRICANE DAMAGE IN 2005 HASTENED THE DETERIORATION OF THIS FLORIDA TRACK, already caught up in business problems, a long-term decline of horse racing, and competition from nearby Gulfstream Park. Being a listed landmark and bird sanctuary may have hurt more than it helped.

Though Hialeah was built for greyhound racing and evolved into a top track for thoroughbred horses, it'll always be remembered for its flamingoes, that dazzling flock of 300-plus stilt-legged pink beauties presiding over the infield's palm-bordered artificial lake. Hialeah's trademark, a distinctively Floridian touch, those flamingoes became so famous that the lake was designated an Audubon Society sanctuary. The rest of the park should be so lucky.

Here's Hialeah's history in a nutshell: opened in 1921 (greyhound track, amusement park, horse track), nearly wiped out by the great hurricane of 1926, reopened as a horse-racing track with a spectacular new grandstand and tropical landscaping in 1932. Add nearly 70 years of racing, with horses from Seabiscuit and War Admiral to Citation and Seattle Slew pounding the turf here, and you get what came to be the East Coast's most important winter meet. From there, however, you have to fast-forward to 2001, when the track was closed to the public; to 2005, when the already-empty and neglected facility was damaged by Hurricane Wilma; and 2007, when its stables were demolished despite landmark eligibility. The next chapter is still up in the air, as the city council reviews a proposal for a condo-retail-office development to be built where the track now stands.

There was a time when Hialeah mattered—when its Flamingo Stakes for 3-year-olds was a crucial lead-up to the Kentucky Derby, and its Widener Handicap for horses 4 years and older was paired with California's Santa Anita Handicap as the nation's two most essential winter races. As one of the earliest tourist attractions in south Florida, it helped to define the Sunshine State's charm for visitors from the 1930s on. Frequently described as the most beautiful racetrack ever built, Hialeah gave a touch of class to horse racing, a sport that has unfortunately declined in the United States over the second half of this century.

Although it's been listed on the National Register of Historic Places since the 1970s, and was deemed eligible for National Historic Landmark status in 1988, Hialeah's owner never pursued the landmark process—a common fate for sports facilities, whose owners are afraid that landmark status will prohibit renovations needed to increase profitability. When historic Hialeah began to lose money (competition from the more modern Gulfstream Park, up northeast in Hallandale, didn't help), it was easier just to shut it down. But the flamingoes are still there—along with the ghosts of many plucky jockeys and beautiful thoroughbreds. And the vintage track's still there, waiting for them.

---

ⓘ **Save Hialeah Park** (www.save hialeahpark.com)

✈ Miami International

🛏 $$$ **Sonesta Beach Resort Key Biscayne**, 350 Ocean Dr., Key Biscayne (ⓒ **800/SONESTA** [766-3782] or 305/361-2021; www.sonesta.com). $$ **Indian Creek Hotel**, 2727 Indian Creek Dr., Miami Beach (ⓒ **800/491-2772** or 305/531-2727; www.indiancreekhotel.com).

**461**

# National Tennis Center
## *Home of Real Tennis*
### Newport, Rhode Island

A RARE GEM FROM THE DAYS OF COURT TENNIS, PRECURSOR OF TODAY'S OUTDOOR GAME, THE Center is the only court tennis facility in the U.S. that is available to the public for viewing or playing.

When New York Herald publisher James Gordon Bennett, Jr., launched his own exclusive social club in 1880, called the Newport Casino, sports were a crucial element: archery, lawn bowling, and the new game called lawn tennis, which was all the rage in Newport's tony social circles. Just in case lawn tennis turned out to be a flash in the pan, Bennett also included a building for court tennis, the older European indoor game that had inspired the lawn tennis fad.

As it turned out, lawn tennis was no mere fad—though nowadays it's just called tennis and is rarely played on a lawn, the Casino's famously manicured Horseshoe Court being one of the nation's few remaining permanent grass courts. But what's even more of a relic is the Casino's surviving court tennis facility, one of only 10 in the United States, all on the East Coast. (There are another 25 courts around the rest of the world.)

A certain Gilded Age elegance still distinguishes the old Casino building, a McKim, Mead & White landmark with dark-green turrets and verandas and a jewel-like interior piazza. Trophies in mahogany cases line the grand staircase. Though the rambling shingle-style Casino is no longer a private club—since 1954 it has been the International Tennis Hall of Fame, where exhibits tell the history of lawn tennis—there is one private club housed within this landmark, the National Tennis Club,

devoted to court tennis. With a current membership of around 100, the NTC was formed in 1980 with the rebuilding of the original court tennis court, which had been destroyed by a series of fires in 1945 and 1946. Though the court is mostly new, the floor and some of the lower walls are the 1880 originals.

Played with tightly strung wooden racquets and heavy, unbouncy hand-sewn balls covered with woven cloth, court tennis is played on an enclosed concrete court surrounded on three sides by a "penthouse" or roofed shed. There are several windows in the penthouse as well; players can score points by knocking a ball into a window. Adherents say court tennis requires much more strategy than lawn tennis. It goes by many names—*jeu de paume* in France, royal tennis in Australia, or real tennis in England (which is either a corruption of the Spanish word for *royal,* or a term to distinguish it from upstart lawn tennis). Whatever the name, it's a rare relic of an earlier era of sportsmanship.

ⓘ **National Tennis Club,** 194 Bellevue Ave. (ⓒ **401/849-6672;** www.national tennisclub.org)

✈ Providence (28 miles/45km)

🛏 $$$ **Hyatt Regency Newport,** 1 Goat Island (ⓒ **800/233-1234** or 401/851-1234; www.hyatt.com). $$ **Mill Street Inn,** 75 Mill St. (ⓒ **800/392-1316** or 401/849-9500; www.millstreetinn.com).

The Tennis Hall of Fame.

# 462

# Coney Island
## *Last Act on the Brooklyn Boardwalk?*
### Brooklyn, New York

WHILE MASS-MARKET THEME PARKS LIKE SIX FLAGS AND BUSCH GARDENS PROLIFERATE, THE granddaddy of them all—Coney Island—struggles to survive, a string of small private amusements huddled at the end of New York's D and F subways.

All that's left of its glory days are two iconic rides, the eight-story-high Cylone wooden roller coaster (built in 1927) and the ingenious double Ferris wheel known as the Wonder Wheel (1920), both protected as historic landmarks. The Parachute Jump, a relic of the 1939 World's Fair, remains as an architectural landmark, but no longer operates as a ride.

Back in the summers before air-conditioning, families fled New York's tenement neighborhoods to find cool breezes at Coney Island beach, where snazzy amusement parks like Luna Park, Dreamland, and Steeplechase Park packed in the crowds. After World War II, however, rising crime and the spread of car culture sounded Coney Island's death knell. Originally the Cyclone was one of three 1920s-era roller coasters; the Tornado burned down in 1977 and Thunderbolt went out of business in 1983 and stood rusting for years before a mysterious late-night demolition in 2000. Astroland, which opened in 1962 with a futuristic space-age theme, closed in 2007. The minor parks that remain offer mostly kiddie rides, haunted houses, bumper cars, and cheesy game arcades. A handful of food stands and bars remain in business, most notably the original Nathan's hot dog outlet on Surf Avenue.

Some of the boardwalk's midway glamour was recently restored, however, with a postmodern hipster gloss. Brooklyn artists have painted retro murals on several side walls, and Coney Island USA (www.coneyisland.com) operates a museum and sideshow performances at West 12th Street and Surf Avenue every weekend, as well as organizing the kitschy Mermaid Parade every June. The New York City parks department has spruced up the wooden boardwalk itself and installed new facilities along the wide white-sand Atlantic beach. Only a short walk east, where Dreamland once stood, the New York Aquarium (Surf Ave. and W. 8th St.; © **718/265-3400;** www.nyaquarium.com) is a first-rate facility featuring dolphins, sea lions, seals, and walruses. Down the beach to the west, on the old Steeplechase Park site, KeySpan Park is home to the Mets' popular farm team, the Brooklyn Cyclones (© **718/449-8497;** www.brooklyncyclones.com). Plans are afoot to reopen the vintage B & B Carousel in a pavilion near KeySpan Park.

Developers, hungry to capitalize on this prime beachfront, are currently fighting to build hotels and residential high-rises along Surf Avenue. Would this bring prosperity to the neighborhood, or spoil its essential character? Coney Island has survived up to now, a grungy shadow of its former self—but the ball could drop at any moment.

---

ⓘ **Coney Island,** Surf Ave. between W. 10th and W. 12th sts., Brooklyn, NY (www.coneyisland.com)

✈ John F. Kennedy International, Newark Liberty International, LaGuardia.

🛏 $$$ **Le Parker Meridien,** 118 W. 57th St. (© **800/543-4300** or 212/245-5000; www.parkermeridien.com). $$ **Excelsior Hotel,** 45 W. 81st St. (© **800/368-4575** or 212/362-9200; www.excelsiorhotelny.com).

463

# Weeki Wachee Springs
## *The Mermaids' Tale*
### Weeki Wachee, Florida

AT 60 YEARS OLD, THIS RUN-DOWN RELIC OF A BYGONE ERA FACES EXTINCTION. HOWEVER, the new owner, the state of Florida, wants to preserve this park—and its mermaids.

Thanks to its quirky geology, the state of Florida has freshwater springs busting out all over, but of them all, Weeki Wachee Springs has to be the prize-winner. This booming natural spring, located just an hour north of St. Petersburg, pumps an incredible 170 million gallons of 72°F (22°C) water every day into the Weeki Wachee River. It's also the deepest naturally formed spring in the United States, with sections of underwater cavern as deep as 407 feet (122m) underwater.

Mermaids of Weeki Wachee.

Nowadays, a natural attraction like this would probably have been set aside in its pristine state, featured as the environmental wonder it is. But in 1947, an ex-Navy frogman named Newton Perry saw Weeki Wachee Springs and had one thought: mermaids.

Perry—who had developed an air hose that would allow swimmers to breathe underwater long stretches of time—correctly read the post-war hunger for entertainment and travel. He built an 18-seat amphitheater into the limestone shelf beside a spring and recruited comely young women to sheathe their legs in a fake tail and put on underwater mermaid ballet. By today's standards, the shows were fairly primitive—the shapely swimmers simply swirled around smiling, waving, drinking bottled soda, and eating—but they did it under water, an astonishing feat indeed. It also helped that Weeki Wachee was situated alongside two-lane Highway 19, a big road in those preinterstate days.

By the 1950s, Weeki Wachee was an extremely popular tourist stop, offering landscaped gardens, a beach, and "jungle cruise" rides as well as the mermaid show. The ABC television network bought it in 1959, expanded it, and promoted it heavily on its television shows. The mermaid shows became glossy extravaganzas, running up to 10 performances a day.

But when Disney World opened in 1971—located at a nexus of new interstate highways—mere mermaids began to seem old hat. A seasonal water park, fed by the springs, was added in 1982, but as the years passed Weeki Wachee's faded glories attracted fewer and fewer visitors. At the time of its 60th anniversary in 2007, the run-down park faced permanent closure. Rumors were that the land's owner, Southwest Florida Water Management District (nicknamed Swiftmud) was unable to sell the property to new owners and planned instead to turn it into a state park.

In 2008 the announcement came: The state of Florida would take over Weeki Wachee Springs in November 2008—but plans are to preserve the historic mermaid shows. Whether or not the state can pull this off remains to be seen, but surely it's worth saving this relic of an earlier—and more innocent—era of tourism.

ⓘ 6131 Commercial Way, Weeki Wachee (Hwy. 19 at Hwy. 50; ✆ **877/469-3354** or 352/596-2062; www.weekiwachee.com)

✈ Tampa International

🛏 $$ **Quality Inn Weeki Wachee Resort,** 6172 Commercial Way (✆ **352/596-2007**)

# Luna Park
## *Saving the Face*
### Sydney, Australia

UNLIKE MODERN "THEME" PARKS THAT TRY TO SIMULATE FOREIGN COUNTRIES OR MOVIE SETS, Luna Park remains an unabashed collection of straightforward rides (no movie tie-ins here) with just enough tawdriness to lend it a spark of nostalgic flavor.

No child who has ever walked into Luna Park, through the grotesque gaping grin of the Face, could fail to be wowed. First opened in 1935 and continually refurbished throughout the 1950s, Luna Park was Sydney's homegrown version of Disneyland, and while it may not have had the Disney imagination going for it, it made up for that with a sturdy Aussie sense of fun. Though its history from the 1970s on has been rocky—numerous redevelopment proposals, shutdowns, safety and noise violations, and the tragic death of 13 people on the Ghost Train in 1979—adults who were hooked as children have continually risen to save the park, through street protests, lawsuits, National Heritage Board actions, and, finally, specific government legislation on its behalf. (Copenhagen's Tivoli Gardens is the world's only other amusement park that's a government-legislated landmark.)

Luna Park's most recent reincarnation opened in April 2004 and so far is thriving, aside from a few lawsuits (almost de rigueur, considering Luna Park's history). The entrance is still through the Face, a giant smiling polyurethane mask nearly 9m (20 ft.) wide. Behind the Face, the Midway stretches through the park to Coney Island, the original 1930s funhouse—a cornucopia of vintage amusements like rotating barrels, moving platforms, and large slides (modified, of course, to meet modern safety standards) plus a bank of arcade games. Along the Midway, you'll find major rides like an antique carousel (the Racing Cockerels), a Ferris wheel, a flying saucer ride, and the 1960s-era Wild Mouse. A boardwalk ambles along the park's seaside edge. The Midway's heritage-listed Crystal Palace has been retrofitted as a function space, while an event venue called the Luna Circus replaces a beloved ride known as the Big Dipper, which was ruled too noisy to remain in this densely developed neighborhood.

You can ride to Luna Park via the Sydney Harbour ferry (Milsons Point is the stop) and there are even views across the harbor of Sydney's most iconic sight, the Opera House. It's not a perfect restoration, but it's enough to keep the Luna Park spirit alive—and that keeps the Face grinning.

ⓘ 1 Olympic Dr., Milson's Point (℃ **61/2/ 9922 6644;** www.lunaparksydney.com)

✈ Sydney International Airport

🛏 $$$ **North Sydney Harbourview Hotel,** 17 Blue St., North Sydney (℃ **61/2/ 9955 0499** or toll-free in Australia 300/785 453; www.viewhotels.com.au). $$ **Wattle Private Hotel,** 108 Oxford St., Darlinghurst (℃ **61/2/9332 4118;** www.thewattle.com).

# Schönbrunn Zoo
## *The Baroque Backyard Zoo*
Vienna, Austria

THE OLDEST ZOO IN THE WORLD, OPENED IN 1752 AND ALMOST CLOSED IN 1992, IS ALSO one of the only zoos in the world to house giant black-and-white pandas.

In the olden days—we're talking 18th century here—royalty had all the fun. Empress Maria Theresia, for example, wanted a little menagerie to entertain her children while they were at their summer palace, Schönbrunn; in 1752 her husband, Franz Stephan von Lothringen, built a baroque gem for her in the palace's formal gardens, painted in the ochre color favored by the Hapsburgs. It's the world's oldest zoo still in operation, and a beauty indeed.

Of course, theories of zookeeping have changed a lot since 1752, and this staid little zoo was sadly behind the times—almost on the point of closing—when ambitious new management in 1991 decided to turn things around. As this Cinderella story unfolded, such innovations as naturalistic environments, breeding programs, and ecosystem displays were brought to this little zoo. It has no less than 700 species on a tiny site, many of them small creatures like fish and

reptiles and insects, but there's a respectable number of the big animals as well, your crowd-pleasing lions, elephants, giraffes, and hippos.

Perhaps the most impressive of the new exhibits is the tropical Borneo rainforest, with orchids and mangrove forests—there's even a stage-set storm set off periodically, complete with pelting rain, cracks of lightning, thunder, and fog. Be sure to go up to the top level to walk at tree-canopy level with the flying foxes and bats. A nursery for exotic butterflies is connected to an aquarium that has a crocodile lagoon, an 80,000-liter (21,000-gallon) coral reef tank, and an underground glass tunnel (look up and you'll see stingrays) leading to a terrarium full of snakes and scorpions. In the Big Cat House, tigers and cheetahs now roam the outdoor areas where zoogoers used to stand, while humans crowd into the interiors that once confined the cats. The polarium is a popular stop, not only

A curious polar bear at Schönbrunn Zoo.

crowds come every day for the sea lion feedings. The new Desert House took over an old Art Deco greenhouse outside the zoo proper to recreate a desert ecosystem. An authentic antique Tyrolean farmhouse was transplanted stone by stone, timber by timber, to a hill at the back of the zoo, where a charming petting zoo was set up (as well as the best restaurant in the zoo).

The final vindication for the zoo's rescuers: In 2003 China chose Schönbrunn Zoo to receive a pair of giant black-and-white pandas for a 10-year loan, an honor conferred only upon the most respected zoos. Ja!

---

ⓘ **Tiergarten Schönbrunn,** Schönbrunn Schlosstrasse, Vienna (✆ **43/1/8779-2940;** www.zoovienna.at)

✈ Vienna International

🛏 $$$ **Hotel Römischer Kaiser,** Annagasse 16 (✆ **800/528-1234** or 43/1/512775113; www.bestwestern.com). $$ **Hotel am Schubertring,** Schubertring 11 (✆ **43/1/717020;** www.schubertring.at).

because it's cool inside in summer, but because visitors love to watch through a glass wall as penguins soar and dive;

# 466

# Tamansari Water Castle
## *The Sultan's Swimming Pool*
### Yogyakarta, Indonesia

THE RUINS OF THE SULTAN'S POOL HOUSE ARE ONE OF YOGYAKARTA'S CHIEF TOURIST DRAWS today. A 2006 earthquake, however, has put the fragile palace at risk.

Indonesia can get pretty steamy in the summertime, so naturally Sultan Hamengku Buwono I—an 18th-century Islamic ruler of Yogyakarta—needed a cool retreat. The design of his Tamansari water castle (the name means "perfumed garden") was totally up-to-date for 1758, an intricate nest of gleaming stone pavilions, fountains, and bathing pools where he and his family, including concubines, could beat the heat. The sultan had cleverly arranged it so that he could discreetly watch his concubines bathing below—and then invite anyone who caught his eye up to his own more secluded pool.

The original complex includes 59 structures—a mosque, meditation chambers, terraces, swimming pools, and a series of

18 water gardens and pavilions surrounded by ornamental lakes. After the plumbing was damaged by an earthquake in 1867, the lakes and pools stood dry for well over a century; squatters eventually moved in and dwelt among the deserted pavilions. Recent renovation brought back a taste of the pleasure palace's grandeur, with the central bathing complex opened to the public again in 2004. Another earthquake in 2006, however, dealt the site a serious setback; researchers are still investigating how to shore up the palace's aging stone to protect it from future quakes.

The central pool area has been filled with water again and smartened up for tourists, but wandering around the meandering passageways and tunnels of the rest of the complex is also an evocative experience. While its fountains and pools resemble European-style water gardens of the same era, these are heavily ornamented with Javanese motifs and distinctly Asian rooflines. Elaborate bas-reliefs are everywhere, many of them bearing inscriptions in an intricately symbolic script. It was said that some of the tunnels led the

sultan to his secret supernatural wife Nyai Roro Kidul (Queen of the South Sea); more likely they were an escape route or hiding place for the royal family in times of enemy attack. Though the outlying lakes and canals are still dry, you can see where an artificial island was raised in the middle of the lake, shaped like a lotus floating in the middle of the pond. Upon it stands a royal pavilion surrounded by flowering trees, wafting scent upon every breeze up to the sultan's bedroom.

It's also fun to explore the maze of back alleys and tiny houses that surround the many gates into the ruins (only the main gate charges admission). The water palace is also convenient to the city's atmospheric Ngasem bird market.

 Yogyakarta

 $$$ **Sheraton Mustika,** JL Laksda Adisucipto, Yogyakarta (© **274/488588;** www.sheraton.com). $$ **Manohara Hotel,** Borobudur Archaeological Park, Magelang (© **361/731520;** www.bali www.com).

# 467

# Flushing Meadows
## *All the World's a Fair*
### New York, New York

LOCAL RESIDENTS COME HERE TO JOG, ICE SKATE, AND VISIT THE QUEENS ZOO AND ART museum as if it were just another park—but the Unisphere tells us differently.

You can spot them from the Grand Central Parkway, wedged between LaGuardia Airport, the Mets' baseball stadium, and the tennis center where the U.S. Open is played: a slightly forlorn ensemble of Space Age structures stranded in the outer borough of Queens. There's a tall pair of concrete observation towers where the Jetsons would feel at home; a circular pavilion that looks like a sci-fi Stonehenge; and most distinctive of all, the Unisphere, a 140-foot-high (42m) globe of the world,

its oceans an airy grid of stainless steel with a couple of Telstar-like orbit rings.

Here, in a former city ash dump, New York City's powerful parks commissioner Robert Moses created a 1,200-acre (480-hectare) park to host the 1939 World's Fair. Coming at the end of the Depression and just before World War II—though no one know that at the time—it was a great declaration of faith in the future, with several corporations showing off American technology. It was also a

The Unisphere.

financial failure. The world was quite a different place by 1964, when yet another World's Fair was launched on the same site, this time promoting peace through international cooperation. Since the 1964 Fair wasn't officially sanctioned by the Bureau of International Expositions, many major countries didn't have pavilions there, but smaller countries filled the void, as did U.S. corporations. The Walt Disney company debuted several audio-animatronic displays later transplanted to Disneyland, including "It's A Small World" and a talking Abraham Lincoln statue. It was big, bold, and exciting—and it also lost money.

While many exhibits were shipped elsewhere or razed after the fair, strolling around the park today you can glimpse several World's Fair ghosts. The New York State Building from the 1939 Fair—which in the late 1940s was the United Nation's first home—became the 1964 Fair's New York City Pavilion; currently it's the Queens Museum of Art. Inside, you'll find the Panorama of New York, a 1964 scale model of the entire city, which is still updated every few years. Next to a weath-

ered sculpture of a supersonic jet and a gleaming pair of actual space rockets displayed in 1964, another building has become the New York Hall of Science. Several sculptures from 1964 stand marooned around the central plaza near the Unisphere; man-made Meadow Lake to the east remains a boating pond. The 1964 Fair's New York State Pavilion—that Stonehenge-like structure by the Unisphere—stands empty and decaying, though plans to make it an air and space museum float around.

It's tempting to view this collection of urban flotsam as a metaphor for our tarnished faith in the future, but the site also has a weird poetry all its own.

ⓘ **NYC & Company** (ⓒ **800/NYC-VISIT** [692-8474]; www.nycvisit.com)

✈ John F. Kennedy International, Newark Liberty International, LaGuardia

🛏 $ **Best Western Seaport Inn,** 33 Peck Slip (ⓒ **800/HOTEL-NY** [468-3569] or 212/766-6600; www.bestwestern.com)

## 468

# Wellfleet Drive-In
## *Steamy Summer Nights*
### Wellfleet, Massachusetts

WELLFLEET'S DRIVE-IN IS ONE OF THE LAST SURVIVORS OF THESE VINTAGE OUTDOOR MOVIE theaters. Given Cape Cod's seasonal swell in population and its appeal for vacationing families, it seemed natural that a drive-in would survive here.

Sooner or later, it was inevitable that someone would combine Americans' love affair with the automobile to their appetite for movies—and so was born the drive-in movie. The first drive-in opened in 1933 in Camden, New Jersey; in the baby boom years after World War II their numbers mushroomed, rising to nearly 5,000 nationwide by the late 1950s. The drive-in movie served two audiences: young parents, who wanted to catch a movie while their children slept in the back seat, and high schoolers, who took advantage of the car's privacy for make-out sessions.

But by the late 1960s, drive-ins were on the wane, for several reasons: They lacked air-conditioning; distributors often refused to give them first-run films, forcing managers to rely on slasher movies and X-rated films; and their large lots became increasingly desirable real estate as communities sprawled outwards. The rise of home video in the early 1980s killed off many more.

Built in 1957, the Wellfleet Drive-In is open from mid-April or early May through mid-October, showing first-run films after dark on a 100×44-foot (30×13m) outdoor screen. While moviegoers can get the film's soundtrack via old-fashioned monaural speakers you clip to your car window, you can also tune to a special frequency on your FM radio to pick up the soundtrack in stereo. The lines of sight were designed for 1950s-height vehicles, so SUVs and campers and pick-ups are restricted to the back of the lot. In keeping with drive-in movie tradition, a double feature is shown every week, with an intermission for trips to the snack bar (vintage ads seduce you with visions of dancing popcorn buckets). Kids can blow off steam at a playground on-site, and a 1961-vintage minigolf course next door makes a great preshow activity.

Part of the reason for the Wellfleet Drive-In's survival (two other Cape drive-ins, in Hyannis and Yarmouth, closed years ago) is that its longtime owner figured out ways to supplement drive-in revenues—a popular flea market occupies the parking lot on weekend days, and there's a year-round indoor movie theater next door. When the owner died in 1998, two longtime employees kept it going.

A recent resurgence of nostalgia for drive-ins has helped some defunct sites reopen, and even a few new drive-ins have been built, though there are still only 400 or so in the United States, half of them in California. But will the costs of converting from old celluloid projectors to new digital systems be too steep for vintage drive-ins? Don't wait to find out how this picture ends; grab a bucket of dancing popcorn and experience one now.

ⓘ **Wellfleet Drive-In,** Rte. 6, Eastham-Wellfleet (✆ **508/349-7176;** www.wellfleetdrivein.com)

✈ Hyannis

🛏 $$ **Viking Shores Motor Lodge,** Rte. 6, Eastham (✆ **800/242-2131;** www.vikingshores.com). $$ **Even'tide,** 650 Rte. 6, South Wellfleet (✆ **800/368-0007** in MA only, or 508/349-3410; www.eventidemotel.com).

## 469

# The Oldest McDonald's
## *Speedee the Chef's Drive-In*
### Downey, California

FOR THOSE WHO LOVE FAST FOOD AND AMERICAN KITSCH, THE OLDEST McDONALD'S IS STILL open. Though the food's much the same as at any other McDonald's, the packaging and the signs are totally retro.

This burger shack in Downey wasn't the McDonald's brothers' first restaurant (that was a hot-dog stand in Arcadia), the first place where they pioneered their "fast food" assembly-line operation (that would have been their San Bernardino burger bar), or even the first of their restaurants to have golden arches in its design (that was in Phoenix). But when this site—their fourth franchise outlet—opened in 1953, the formula was finally set, and this location has remained in business ever since—the oldest McDonald's still in operation.

There's something weirdly familiar and yet strange about its vintage red-and-white striped tile exterior and the pair of parabolic golden arches supporting its roof; the employees wear '50s-vintage uniforms with white shirts, paper hats, and bolo ties. Strictly a walk-up restaurant (no PlaySpace here), it has outdoor tables where you can take your burger and milkshake after you've ordered your food at the window. The roadside marquee is hard to miss, with its 60-foot-high (18m) neon-outlined figure of a chipper character named Speedee the Chef, the chain's long-retired early mascot, Ronald McDonald's great-grand-daddy.

A year after this restaurant opened, a milkshake-machine salesman named Ray Kroc saw the potential in the McDonalds brothers' formula, bought out their little chain, and the rest is history. The Downey restaurant is our last reminder of the modern megachain's simple beginnings. After it was damaged in the 1994 Northridge earthquake, this outlet—which had been losing money—was nearly closed down. Historic preservationists fought to keep it, and eventually in 1996 the McDonald's corporation woke up to an opportunity to honor its own past. Refurbishment restored the historic features, and a museum and gift shop were added (displays of vintage Happy Meal toys, anyone?). However you feel about the parent chain, there's something undeniably fascinating about seeing its 1950s incarnation, from long before the fast-food concept supersized into something entirely different.

---

ⓘ **Historic Speedee McDonald's,** 10207 Lakewood Blvd. (✆ **562/622-9248**)

✈ Los Angeles International

🛏 $$ **Roosevelt Hotel, Hollywood,** 7000 Hollywood Blvd. (✆ **800/950-7667** or 323/466-7000; www.hollywood roosevelt.com). $$ **Beverly Garland's Holiday Inn,** 4222 Vineland Ave., North Hollywood (✆ **800/BEVERLY** [238-3759] or 818/980-8000; www.beverlygarland. com).

# 10 Classic Movie Palaces

Though the first moving pictures were projected onto linen sheets hung on the walls of ordinary rooms, exhibitors soon realized that people came to the movies to escape reality—and they set upon extending the fantasy from the films to the theaters themselves. Many borrowed themes from world architecture, particularly exotic Chinese, Aztec, and Egyptian motifs, but the most popular look was Art Deco, with its streamlined chrome and sinuous curves. But with the rise of the suburban multiplex, these grand palaces were boarded up, used for other purposes, or demolished. Here are 10 palaces that have escaped the wrecking ball:

**470 Uptown Theater, Chicago, Illinois**  With nearly 4,500 seats, the Uptown Theater was the second-largest movie palace in the United States, after Radio City Music Hall. The design is Spanish Revival; a deliriously ornate five-story entrance lobby rests behind an eight-story facade. Initially built in 1921 for live performance (it had its own orchestra), by the 1940s it was mostly a movie house, though in the 1950s it did host the TV show *Queen for a Day* 1 week a year. A designated Chicago landmark, it's been closed since 1981. *www.uptowntheatre.com.*

**471 Gateway Theater, Chicago, Illinois**  When it opened in 1930, the Gateway featured the latest rage: "atmospheric-style" decor, with a dark-blue star-spangled ceiling like a sky over the 2,100-seat auditorium, and classical statuary and vines on the side walls. Praised for its acoustics, the Gateway remained an active single-screen cinema through the 1970s. In 1985 a Polish-American community group, the Copernicus Foundation, took over and restored the theater, using it for community gatherings and special events. © *773/777-8898. www.copernicusfdn.org.*

The Egyptian Theater.

**472 Loew's Jersey Theater, Jersey City, New Jersey**  This astonishing baroque theater opened its doors at 54 Journal Square in 1929, with a grand lobby dominated by a chandelier. Its large clock tower, featuring a copper statue of St. George and the dragon, is a local landmark. Slated for demolition in 1987, it was saved by a grass-roots campaign, and today shows vintage films and hosts live performances. © *201/798-6055. www.loewsjersey.org.*

**473 The Egyptian Theater, Hollywood, California**  This grand theater opened in 1922, the same year King Tut's tomb was found, inspiring its motif—a columned forecourt, hieroglyphics, murals, and a tiled fountain. Built by Sid Grauman as a palace fit for premieres, it continued to host premieres until 1968. Closed in 1992 and damaged in the 1994 Northridge earthquake, it was restored by the American Cinematheque in the late 1990s and now shows classic and indie films. *www.americancinematheque.com.*

**474 El Capitan, West Hollywood, California** When the El Capitan Theater opened in 1926, it featured a Spanish colonial exterior and an elaborate East Indian interior. Designed for live plays, the El Capitan gradually became a movie house; in 1941 the world premiere of *Citizen Kane* was held here. The declining El Capitan was bought in 1989 by the Walt Disney Company, which restored much of its original decor. ℂ *323/467-7674. www.disney.go.com/disneypictures/el_capitan.*

**475 The Alex Theatre, Glendale, California** Built in 1925, The Alex Theatre began as a vaudeville theater and first-run movie house, designed with Greek and Egyptian motifs. The atmospheric decor featured a stage set simulating an ancient garden. In 1940, a 100-foot-tall (30m) Art Deco neon tower topped by a spiked starburst was added. Renovation began in 1992, and today it hosts films and cultural events, but its future is uncertain. ℂ *818/243-7700. www.alextheatre.org.*

The Alex Theater.

**476 Tampa Theatre, Tampa, Florida** The Tampa Theatre opened in 1926 in downtown Tampa as a breathtaking example of an "atmospheric theater," simulating an immense Mediterranean courtyard with statues, flowers, and gargoyles under a "sky" of twinkling stars and floating clouds. Faced with demolition in 1973, it was rescued through community efforts and reopened in 1978. *711 N. Franklin St.* ℂ *813/274-8981. www.tampatheatre.org.*

Tampa Theatre.

**477 The YAM Movie Palace, Portales, New Mexico** This splendid example of geometric Art Deco architecture was Portales's pride when it opened as the Portola Theater in 1926. Like many small-town Art Deco beauties, its future was in question until recently, when a combination of private and state funds were raised to restore it and reopen as a performance space. *219 S. Main St. www.portalesnm.org/mainstreet/yam/theater.htm.*

**478 Coronet Cinema, London, England** Prime among new cinemas converted from existing theaters was the 1898 Coronet Theatre in Notting Hill Gardens, an imposing Palladian theater where, legend has it, Sir John Gielgud saw his first Shakespeare play. Converted to a movie house in 1923, this landmarked cinema has shown movies ever since. *www.coronet.org.*

**479 Capri Theater, Goodwood, South Australia** A sleek Art Deco palace built in this Adelaide suburb in 1941, the Capri's most outstanding feature is its classic Wurlitzer theater organ. The Capri, in fact, has the largest theater organ in the Southern Hemisphere, which is played before film screenings 3 nights a week. *141 Goodwood Rd.* ℂ *61/8/8272 1177. www.capri.org.au.*

## 480

# Trader Vic's
## *Death by Mai Tai*
### Beverly Hills, California

WITH ITS POTENT NEON-COLORED COCKTAILS ADORNED WITH UMBRELLAS AND SERVED OUT OF coconuts, and exotic menu items with creative Asian accents, Trader Vic's was the classy end of the food chains. Today, the flagship spot may be no longer.

Trader Vic's sat at the opposite end of the dining spectrum from McDonald's; it was a Special Occasion Restaurant, where mid-century cocktail-lounge hipness gave the concept of fine dining a unique twist. Spun off from a popular bar in Oakland, California, run by a raffish raconteur named Victor Bergeron, Trader Vic's developed into the ultimate Polynesian restaurant. The first branch was in Seattle, Washington, in 1949, but this one in the Beverly Hilton hotel, opened in 1955, was where the Trader Vic mystique really took hold.

The Beverly Hilton hotel was the Hilton chain's West Coast flagship, and as such it needed a classy restaurant for its patrons. Not only would hotel guests be guzzling mai tai cocktails—the legendary rum drink invented by Trader Vic himself—they'd be nibbling on pupu platters and crab rangoon, sitting in shadowy dining rooms under a thatched palm ceiling with fierce Tiki masks, fishnets, and outrigger paddles hung on grass-cloth walls. With its own separate entrance at the corner of Santa Monica and Wilshire boulevards, the Beverly Hills Trader Vic's had a stage-set presence, with that A-frame jutting out and an 8-foot-tall (2.4m) Tiki pole looming over the stairs, the front walls hand-carved with a strikingly primitive polychromed bas relief. Yes, it was kitschy, but the Beverly Hills Trader Vic's perfected the kitsch, setting off a nationwide Tiki-lounge craze in the late 1950s and early 1960s. Soon hundreds of Tiki bars opened all across America, but none of them was quite as stylish and self-assured as the Beverly Hills Trader Vic's.

Branches of the restaurant eventually opened all around the world—many of them in Hilton hotels—reaching a total of 25 by the end of the 1960s. In the 1970s and 1980s, however, the Polynesian theme lost its appeal and several branches closed. In the late 1990s the concept took off once more; there are now 25 restaurants again.

But sadly, the Beverly Hills branch is no longer one of them. In late 2006, the property's new owner announced plans to put up a Waldorf hotel tower at the corner of Santa Monica and Wilshire, knocking down the Hilton's east wing. Even though the wing remained open pending approval of the plans, Trader Vic's—obviously the chief landmark that would prevent demolition—was abruptly closed in April 2007, replaced by a "casual" poolside bar called Trader Vic's Lounge (hardly the same thing, as any Trader Vic's habitué could tell you). The Los Angeles Conservancy has vowed to fight the demolition—stay tuned.

ⓘ **Trader Vic's,** 9876 Wilshire Blvd., Beverly Hills (✆ **310/276-6345**). Los Angeles Conservancy (✆ **213/623-2489;** www.laconservancy.org)

✈ Los Angeles International

🛏 $$ **Roosevelt Hotel, Hollywood,** 7000 Hollywood Blvd. (✆ **800/950-7667** or 323/466-7000; www.hollywoodroosevelt.com). $$ **Beverly Garland's Holiday Inn,** 4222 Vineland Ave., North Hollywood ✆ **800/BEVERLY** [238-3759] or 818/980-8000; www.beverlygarland.com).

# 481

## Milestone Motel
### *An Overnight Sensation*
San Luis Obispo, California

CLOSED IN 1991, NOW EMPTY AND NEGLECTED, THE FIRST MOTOR INN STILL RETAINS THE design that has inspired roadside motels across the United States.

Architecturally, there's nothing distinguished about this low-slung set of stucco buildings, a vague pastiche of Mission architecture with a three-story tower meant to evoke the Santa Barbara mission's famous bell-tower. But back in 1926, motorists traveling between Los Angeles and San Francisco would have seen it as a rare destination, exactly halfway up the coast and located right on Highway 101 (the same El Camino Real route used by California's early Spanish settlers). It was neither a traditional hotel nor one of the rustic campgrounds that had recently begun to sprout around gas stations in the infancy of America's automotive age. This place even had a new sort of name: a motor hotel—or, to fit better on a roadside sign, a "mo-tel."

As the bronze plaque on its front wall attests, architect Arthur Heineman gets full credit for inventing the motel concept. His location was ideal: at the midway point in San Luis Obispo, right beside Highway 101, the main north-south road in those days. (It was also at the north end of Monterey St., up the road from where San Luis Obispo's own historic Spanish mission was located.) It cost $80,000 to build; guests were charged a stiff $1.25 a night for a two-room bungalow with a kitchenette, indoor bathroom (with a shower!), and parking conveniently located right outside the room. All the bungalows faced onto a central palm-lined courtyard with a pool and picnic tables. It combined a certain level of swanky comfort (car owners in the 1920s were, after all, among the more affluent citizens) with car-friendly efficiency. A restaurant and dance hall were included in the complex as well. Plans were to erect a whole chain of Milestone Motels up and down the California coast; the Depression, however, put an end to that scheme.

Though it was originally named the Milestone Mo-Tel, the motel was renamed the Motor Inn and had become severely run down by the time it closed in 1991. Since then it has sat empty, with boarded-up windows and a chain link fence hung with yellow warning signs surrounding the site. Various owners have proposed plans for a face-lift that never comes to fruition. Parts have already been demolished and other may soon go from sheer dilapidation; bringing the motel up to current building code would most likely be prohibitively expensive by this time. Even from outside the fence, though, you can see that classic design, adapted over the years to thousands of Travel-Lodges and Motel 6s and other roadside lodgings across the country. Heineman's brainstorm was an idea that worked.

---

(i) 2223 Monterey St., San Luis Obispo.

✈ San Luis Obispo

🛏 $$ **Garden Street Inn,** 1212 Garden St., San Luis Obispo ((C) **800/488-2045** or 805/545-9802; www.gardenstreetinn.com). $$ **Best Western Cavalier Oceanfront Resort,** 9415 Hearst Dr. (CA 1), San Simeon ((C) **800/826-8168** or 805/927-4688; www.bestwestern.com).

# 482

# Doo-Wop Motels
## *Catch the Kitsch*
### Wildwood, New Jersey

THE PANORAMA OF THE WILDWOOD STRIP IS LIKE A LOW-RENT VERSION OF EARLY LAS VEGAS. But with many of those classic 1950s hotels already demolished, this corner of the Jersey shore is a last holdout of the Rat Pack signature style.

By the mid–20th century, it wasn't enough for a motel just to have a room with attached bath, a parking space, and a pool; the joint had to have a *theme*. And along this strip of beach towns on the south Jersey Shore, the wackier the theme, the better. Jazz it up with pulsating neon, accent it with bright paint schemes, throw in zigzag rooflines and balconies, and slap on free-form arches, fins, and boomerangs, and there you'd have it: a Doo Wop motel.

A pack of these classic Doo Wop motels still stand, officially recognized by the State of New Jersey as the Wildwoods Shore Resort Historic District. Ocean Avenue in Wildwood Crest is the main drag, lined today with over 50 vintage motels. But another 50 or so were knocked down quite recently, between 2000 and 2005, victims of the area's real-estate boom. Historic preservationists in the area are vigilant about protecting what's left.

The Wildwood resort area really took off in the 1950s as the new Garden State Parkway made this coastal strip easily accessible to vacationers from New York City, Philadelphia, and Baltimore. Though the basic motel layout was the same, each establishment tried to lure motorists with color, light, and snazzy themes tied to pop songs, exotic travel destinations, and '50s movie extravaganzas. (Wildwood also bills itself as the birthplace of rock 'n' roll because Bill Haley's "Rock Around the Clock" was recorded here.)

In Wildwood Crest, the Caribbean Motel (5600 Ocean Ave.; www.caribbeanmotel.com) has a traffic-stopping sign in red neon script, a swooping front ramp, and fake palm trees by the pool. Then there's the Royal Hawaiian, which looks like a flying saucer landed atop a massive Tiki hut with lava rock walls (500 E. Orchid Rd.; www.royalhawaiianresort.com). A swashbuckling pirate strides over the yellow neon sign above the entrance of the Jolly Roger (805 Atlantic Ave.; www.jollyroger motel.com), while knights and coats-of-arms adorn the facade of the Crusader Motel (Cardinal Rd. and Beach). Follow Ocean Avenue north into Wildwood to see the Starlux, a silver-sheathed Space Age beauty with a soaring, glass-walled lobby (305 E. Rio Grande; www.thestarlux.com) and roll on into North Wildwood to see the futuristic arched carports and cool blue neon signs of the Chateau Bleu (911 Surf Ave.) and the classic Candyland-ish sign of the Lollipop Motel (23rd and Atlantic aves.; www.lollipopmotel.com).

Though some properties on the Wildwood Strip look a little faded, others have been spruced up, attracting a whole new generation of urban hipsters.

ⓘ **Greater Wildwoods Tourism Improvement and Development Authority** (ⓒ **800/WW-BY-SEA** [992-9732]; www.wildwoodsnj.com)

✈ Atlantic City or Philadelphia

# Gulf Boulevard's Vintage Motels
## *Retro by the Seaside*
### Treasure Island, Florida

THESE GULF BOULEVARD MOTELS MAY NOT BE AS ARCHITECTURALLY MODERN AS THE SPIFFY new condo towers and chain lodgings that surround them, but their vintage neon signs and sun-kissed charm persevere.

Back in the 1950s, trying to cash in on the post-war automotive travel boom, some civic booster for this 3¹/₂-mile-long (5.6km) Gulf Coast barrier island dreamed up a corny marketing stunt: Bury a couple chests full of money in the pearly-white sand and let some tourists dig them up. Cheesy as the stunt was, it worked—and the island got a new name out of it.

Connected to the St. Petersburg peninsula by three classic Art Moderne causeway bridges, this beachside community developed fast in the 1950s. Two-story stucco motels popped up all along Gulf Boulevard, their rooms overlooking central courtyards dominated by palm-shaded, turquoise swimming pools. Across the street, gulf beaches beckoned with their soft sands and amazing sunset views.

But then development blossomed elsewhere—farther south, in Naples, Sanibel, and Fort Myers, and then in central Florida, around Orlando. Busch Gardens went up in northeast Tampa. For years, all the action seemed to be somewhere else, and Treasure Island got left behind. No developers came along to raze those vintage mom-and-pop motels and replace them with chain lodgings, and they never lost their ocean views and beach access.

So far, so good, until the early 2000s, when property values soared and a wave of condo fever hit Treasure Island. Though local zoning laws only permit buildings to be five stories high—that's a lot higher than these classic motels—many motel owners, faced with the high costs of maintaining aging buildings, allowed their motels to be replaced with boxy five-story condo towers. The first significant loss was the stylishly angular Surf Motel in 2004, but more followed.

These Gulf Boulevard motels may not be as architecturally goofy as their contemporaries on the Jersey Shore—their basic shapes are simpler and sturdier, built to withstand the occasional hurricane—but instead of razzmatazz each motel offers its own pastel color scheme, neat landscaping, pool, striped beach umbrellas and chaise lounges, and in many cases a shuffleboard court. Though most are air-conditioned, they still have casement windows that you can open to catch gulf breezes. Vintage neon signs have been preserved outside a few of the motels, notably the Sands Beach Resort and the Thunderbird. The palm trees here are real, and brilliant hibiscus spills from the planters.

But walk along the beach and you'll see the beachfront skyline disrupted more and more by condo towers. The essential character of Treasure Island already seems lost, but enough may be left to turn back the clock.

---

ⓘ **Treasure Island Friends** (www. recentpast.org/groups/treasure)

✈ Tampa International

🛏 **The Sands Beach Resort,** 11800 Gulf Blvd. (© **727/367-1969;** www.surf andsands.com). **Thunderbird Beach Resort,** 10700 Gulf Blvd. (© **800/367-2473;** www.thunderbirdflorida.com). **Tahitian Resort,** 11320 Gulf Blvd. (© **888/606-5809** or 727/360-6264; www.tahitianresort.com).

# 10 Signs That Go Blink in the Night

The beauty of the neon sign was that you could twist those glass tubes into any shape you wanted. And as America took to the highways in the 1950s and 1960s, advertisers took advantage of that, spangling the nighttime streetscape with colorful whimsies touting everything from bowling alleys to ice-cream stands to Tiki bars.

Good old-fashioned neon lighting has been outmoded by fiber-optic technology. The good news is that preservationists are working to save neon signs for future generations, either on-site or in museums. After all, what would America be without a few giant neon donuts around?

**484 Electric City, Scranton, Pennsylvania**   In 1910, in the pre-neon age, this flashing electric crest was erected eight stories high atop the steep-gabled Victorian-era Scranton Electric Building on Linden Street at Courthouse Square. Its purpose: to promote the fact that Scranton was the first U.S. city to install electric streetcars. The sign went dark in 1972, but it was restored and relit in 2004. © *570/963-5901*. www.scrantontomorrow.org.

**485 The Stinker Station, Twin Falls, Idaho**   Opened in 1936, this Idaho gas station chain made the most of its era's penchant for whimsical roadside advertising. Original owner Farris Lind based his success on low prices that undersold the competition, so naturally he developed as his mascot a black-and-white neon skunk. There are still neon skunks adorning a few outlets around the state, but the biggest and best is at 1777 Kimberly Rd. in Twin Falls. © *208/734-6560*.

**486 The East Gate, Los Angeles, California**   This pagoda-shaped California landmark turns on enough lights to illuminate a small town in China. It opened in 1938 in Los Angeles in an enclave modeled by a Hollywood set designer to serve Chinese-Americans displaced by the building of Union Station. The East Gate was the entrance to a mini-mall that housed 18 stores (now known as Old Chinatown Plaza, 1100 N. Broadway). There are other vintage neon buildings on-site, making it a bright destination for travelers stopping in Los Angeles. www.oldchinatownla.com.

**487 Leon's Frozen Custard, Milwaukee, Wisconsin**   It's said that this vintage burger and custard stand at 3131 S. 27th St., opened in 1942, was the model for Al's Diner in the TV show *Happy Days*. While other local eateries dispute this fact, this Milwaukee landmark with its radiating strips of neon under the carports and its unmissable roadside marquee is worth visiting just for the signage, though the burgers and malts are a delicious bonus. © *414/383-1784*.

**488 Superdawg Drive-In, Chicago, Illinois**   With its neon-studded canopies, the Superdawg drive-in—founded in 1948 at 6363 N. Milwaukee Ave.—features more than a delicious snack: It's a local landmark, known for the two tall hot dogs cavorting on its roof. The male hot dog is for some reason wearing a loincloth. Modesty, perhaps? Whatever the reason, this drive-in's an excellent example of mascots gone wild. www.superdawg.com.

**489 The Seven Dwarfs, Wheaton, Illinois**   Though several tubes are burned out, the fabulous neon sign at the Seven Dwarfs Restaurant and Fountain, 917 E. Roosevelt Rd., still welcomes customers with a friendly waving pig wearing a chef's hat. As for Snow White and the dwarves, they show up on murals inside this friendly-family diner. ✆ **630/653-7888.**

The Seven Dwarfs.

**490 The Elephant Car Wash, Seattle, Washington**   With 380 blinking lights, the big pink elephant in the jaunty hat on the Elephant Car Wash sign at 616 Battery St. in downtown Seattle has been a source of delight since the early 1950s. While the car wash chain now has nine locations in the Seattle area, the downtown branch is the one with that iconic revolving sign. www.elephantcarwash.com.

Elephant Car Wash.

**491 Rancho Grande Mexican Restaurant, Tulsa, Oklahoma**   Along Route 66—a grand thoroughfare of neon signage during its heyday—several fascinating neon relics remain. One of these sits above the Mexican restaurant at 1629 E. 11th St., Route 66's in-town route through Tulsa. Built in 1953, it features a dapper black-hatted caballero slinging a yellow neon lasso around the name of the restaurant. ✆ **918/584-0816.**

**492 Western Hills Motel, Flagstaff, Arizona**   Neon was the perfect medium for beckoning weary drivers off the road at night into roadside motels. Farther west along Route 66, this low-slung fieldstone motel (with a pool!) is still in operation at 1580 E. Rte. 66 behind its classic roadside marquee featuring a red covered wagon and horses, which apparently were once animated. The name of the motel glows blue above the unmistakably huge word "motel" in yellow. ✆ **928/774-6633.** www.westernhillsmotel.com.

**493 Crescent Bowl, Bowling Green, Kentucky**   In a town named Bowling Green, you'd expect a few bowling alleys, right? Well, bowling is by no means as popular a sport as it was in the mid–20th century, and those old lanes are fast disappearing, along with their vintage neon signs. This old-school establishment at 2724 Nashville Rd. may have seen better days inside, but outside a vintage big tenpin glows for all to see, perhaps the most popular neon icon of all. ✆ **270/843-6021.**

Crescent Bowl.

## 494

# Wigwam Motels
## *Teepee Time*
### Kentucky/Arizona/California

FRANK REDFORD WAS SO FASCINATED WITH INDIANS THAT HE DECIDED TO BUILD A CHAIN OF wigwam-shaped motor courts across America. True, the shape he actually used for his tiny tourist cabins wasn't a wigwam at all, it was a teepee. But as wacky roadside themes went out of style, these curiosities became anachronisms.

Like many other such establishments built in the dawn of the automobile travel age, the 1930s and 1940s, Redford's Wigwam Villages offered overnight guests privacy with tiny separate lodgings, marked by kitschy themes that emphasized the character of the region. In the end, only seven Wigwam Villages were built, but cramped and quirky as they are, they have so much character that three remain perfectly preserved today.

Redford's first village went up in 1934 near Horse City, Kentucky, built to house his collection of Native American relics. Intrigued (obsessed, frankly) with his idea, he patented the design in 1937, closed the small Horse City site, and built a larger Wigwam Village in Cave City, near the popular tourist attraction of Mammoth Cave. Later branches went up in 1940 in New Orleans (closed in 1954) and Bessemer, Alabama (closed in 1964); after the war in the late 1940s three more went up, in Orlando (the largest of the chain, razed in 1974), and two more which have survived along Route 66, the United State's main east-west highway in the preinterstate era, known for its wacky themed restaurants, motels, and gas stations.

The concept was fairly standard: 15 to 20 white stucco teepees, 30 feet (9m) tall, decorated with red zigzag stripes. Somehow a tiny bathroom was squeezed into the cone-shaped huts, and diamond-shaped windows were discreetly spaced around the base (real teepees, of course, don't have windows). The original exterior design also featured red swastikas, a traditional Indian motif, but when that symbol became associated with Nazi Germany in the late 1930s, the swastikas were painted over. A 50-foot-tall (15m) teepee contains the motel office/gift shop/restaurant; guest teepees are clustered around a central court (the California one has a kidney-shaped swimming pool). The California and Kentucky motels have been updated with satellite TV and internet access, but the Arizona branch—run by the same family that's owned it since the late 1940s—doesn't even have phones in the rooms. Both the Kentucky and Arizona Wigwam Villages still boast the original 1930s-vintage cane-and-hickory lodgepole-style furnishings.

Be sure to reserve well in advance if you want to stay in these teepee lodgings. The rooms may be tiny and inconvenient, the kitschy Indian theme politically incorrect, but as nostalgic artifacts they can't be beat, and they're very much in demand.

✈ Louisville, KY; Flagstaff, AZ; San Bernardino, CA

🛏 $ **Wigwam Village Motel,** 601 N. Dixie Hwy, Cave City, KY (✆ **270/773-3381;** www.wigwamvillage.com). $ **Wigwam Village Motel,** 811 W. Hopi Dr., Holbrook, AZ (✆ **928/524-3048;** www.wigwam-motel-arizona.com). $ **Wigwam Motel,** 2728 W. Foothill Blvd., Rialto, CA (✆ **909/875-3005;** www.wigwammotel.com).

# 495

# Googie Design
## *Cruising Space-Age Googieland*
### Orange County, California

FOR YEARS SERIOUS ARCHITECTS LOOKED DOWN ON GOOGIE ARCHITECTURE, WITH ALL ITS POP-culture-styled curves and cantilevers and bold colors. Today preservationists are scrambling to save what's left.

A close cousin of New Jersey's Doo-Wop style, even in its 1950s Southern California heyday Googie architecture was considered way too commercial, a design style fit only for bowling alleys, motels, coffee shops, strip malls, liquor stores, and car washes—surely not anything with substance.

Well, times change, tastes change; Googie design now has picked up a gloss of hipster cachet. Unfortunately, most of it was carelessly razed in the past few decades as road construction and suburban redevelopment spiraled in Orange County.

The name "Googie" was eventually applied to the whole movement, derived from the inventive design of Googie's Coffee Shop at Sunset Boulevard and Crescent Heights in Los Angeles. The hotbed of Googie, though, was here in Orange County, where a late 1950s real-estate boom was jump-started by Disneyland's 1955 opening. The futuristic promise of Tomorrowland echoed over and over outside the park as well, with Sputnik-shaped signs and launchpadlike roofs. Starbursts, boomerangs, and amoebas replaced rectilinear forms; cartoonish lettering replaced formal typefaces on signs. Neon was an essential ingredient; so were chrome details (not surprising, in midcentury car culture) and Formica and fiberglass accents in bold colors. Advances in plateglass technology allowed vast expanses of windows, too, making the most of California's sunshine in those presmog years.

Postwar fascination with South American and South Pacific motifs was thrown in as well, courtesy of the many returning servicemen who settled in sunny Southern California.

The Anaheim Convention Center in Anaheim (800 W. Katella) is a big-scale Googie example, its domed white roofline and swoops of glass looking distinctly flying-saucer-like. Take Katella east to State College Boulevard and go south 2 blocks to Angel Stadium, where a tall green roadside with a rakish halo sets a Googie keynote for the ballpark. Then retrace your route on Katella west to South Harbor Boulevard, turn right, and cruise northward to Lincoln Avenue; head west on Lincoln to Brookhurst, turn right and go south on Brookhurst to Garden Grove Boulevard, where a left-hand turn will take you east back to Harbor Boulevard. These are all traffic-clogged major thoroughfares—exactly where you can still hope to find a few roadside signs and small businesses that sport the vintage Googie look. They're still there, but every year, you have to look harder and harder.

---

✈ John Wayne Airport in Santa Ana

🛏 $$$ **Disney's Grand Californian Hotel,** 1600 S. Disneyland Dr. (📞 **714/956-MICKEY** [956-6425] or 714/635-2300; www.disneyland.com). $ **Candy Cane Inn,** 1747 S. Harbor Blvd. (📞 **800/345-7057** or 714/774-5284; www.candycaneinn.net).

## 496

# Coral Castle
## *Memorial to a Broken Heart*
### Homestead, Florida

YOU DON'T COME HERE FOR THRILLS, DEEP MEANING, OR ARTISTIC EXCELLENCE—YOU COME here for its sheer randomness. Coral Castle is simply a weird collection of rough-hewn outdoor sculptures made of pastel-tinted coral rock, hand-carved by one solitary folk artist.

In our postmodern age, it's not easy to retrieve the innocent mindset that vacation travel used to operate on. Nobody went online to book advance admission tickets or downloaded four-color brochures. You simply drove down a highway, saw a sign for something offbeat, pulled off, and paid a few cents to spend half an hour there. No big deal.

That's the sort of tourist attraction Coral Castle is. Over the course of 28 years, its creator, Latvian immigrant Edward Leedskalnin, eventually transformed 1,100 tons of rock into a variety of shapes—a moon fountain, a rocking chair, a table shaped like a heart, another table shaped like the state of Florida. The carving's so crude, it almost looks prehistoric. Though it's called a "castle," no one could ever live in this roofless structure, not even in subtropical Florida. It serves no purpose whatsoever, which is ultimately what makes it so cool.

Leedskalnin began this massive project in 1923, suffering from a broken heart after his 16-year-old fiancée left him at the altar. (Perhaps she could tell there was something a little off about the groom.) Leedskalin was a tiny guy, only 5 feet (1.5m) tall and no more than 100 pounds (45kg); after the breakup, he plunged himself obsessively into working at night on this project, using only tools he'd made himself from junk parts. He began in

Florida City, his first home in the Miami area, but later spent 3 years moving the gigantic work-in-progress to his new home in Homestead, using a friend's tractor to haul it on his small trailer. Then in 1940, somewhat improbably, he erected a coral-rock wall around it and began charging visitors 10 cents to see it.

Leedskalin's motivations for building Coral Castle were never clear, and the construction of this folly remains shrouded in mystery. In fact, nobody ever actually saw Ed working on Coral Castle at all—how could such a small man, working alone, move such huge boulders? Ed himself, being from a family of stone masons in Latvia, swore he used secret techniques passed down through the ages, the same techniques that allowed slaves to build the Great Pyramids. Well, it makes a good story.

(i) 28655 S. Dixie Hwy., Homestead, FL (✆ **305/248-6345;** www.coralcastle.com)

✈ Miami International

🛏 $$$ **Sonesta Beach Resort Key Biscayne,** 350 Ocean Dr., Key Biscayne (✆ **800/SONESTA** [766-3782] or 305/361-2021; www.sonesta.com). $$ **Indian Creek Hotel,** 2727 Indian Creek Dr., Miami Beach (✆ **800/491-2772** or 305/531-2727; www.indiancreekhotel.com).

# 497

# Paul Bunyan Statues
## *Roadside Giants*
### Minnesota Lake Country

WHILE ROADSIDE KITSCH SEEMS TO BE DISAPPEARING ACROSS THE COUNTRY, IT'S STILL ALIVE and well along the secondary highways of northern Minnesota. Here is where the legend of Paul Bunyan resides.

It seems that every small town has some plaster animal mounted on a pole outside of town—a rainbow trout, a beaver, a moose—to proclaim itself to visitors. But why mess around with a mere animal when you could have the North Woods' most enduring legend—the King of the Lumberjacks, Paul Bunyan, and his big blue ox, Babe?

You really know you've hit the North Woods when you arrive in Brainerd, Minnesota, and see the 11½-foot-tall (3.5m) fiberglass Paul Bunyan statue beside the tourist information stand on Highway 371 just south of town. Brainerd's city fathers apparently aren't too cool for the old Bunyan image, because they commissioned this statue recently, after failing to acquire a much larger seated Paul Bunyan figure from the now-defunct Paul Bunyan Center. That statue wound up at This Old Farm, 17553 Hwy. 18, Brainerd (*©* **218/764-2524**), an endearing mishmash of old-style attractions which combines a restored 1940s farm, a corn maze, an arcade (where Paul sits), and a small ho-hum amusement park.

Brainerd, in fact, has established itself as the anchor for a 100-mile (161km) paved Paul Bunyan Trail that winds through lake country. And some 70 miles (113km) farther upstate, in the town of Akeley, on Main Street you'll find the next Paul Bunyan statue, a really big one—he'd be 25 feet (7.5m) tall if he stood up. Instead he crouches down kindly, resting his axe beside him, with his hand gently cupped

Paul Bunyan and Friend.

to hold tourists for photo ops. The black beard on this one is seriously impressive.

Forty miles (64km) north of Akeley, you come to Bemidji—purportedly Bunyan's birthplace—where the granddaddy of all Paul Bunyan statues stands downtown, next to the tourist office, on the pine-edged shore of Lake Bemidji (created, so the folklore goes, by one of Paul's footprints). Eastman Kodak once named this America's second-most photographed roadside icon, a classic piece of Americana erected in 1937. This rather crude Paul Bunyan figure stands 18 feet (5.4m) high and weighs 2½ tons; oddly, instead of the classic black beard, he has a Snidely-Whiplash-like handlebar mustache. Next to him stands a 5-ton Babe the Blue Ox.

There's also a Paul Bunyan Amusement Park beside the statues, and south of town is the Paul Bunyan Animal Farm, 3857 Animal Land Dr. (*©* **218/759-1533**), a small petting zoo. It might as well cash in on the name—everybody else up here does!

ⓘ **Visit Bemidji,** Paul Bunyan Dr., Bemidji, MN (✆ **218/759-0164;** www.visit bemidji.com)

✈ Brainerd Regional Airport, Bemidji Regional Airport

🛏 $$$ **Hampton Inn,** 1019 Paul Bunyan Dr. S., Bemidji (✆ **800/HAMPTON** [426-7866] or 218/751-3600; www. hamptoninn.hilton.com). $$ **AmericInn,** 1200 Paul Bunyan Dr. NW, Bemidji (✆ **800/ 634-3444** or 218/751-3000).

## 498

# Watts Tower
## *Folk-Art Fanatic*
### Los Angeles, California

SOMETHING REMAINS INDOMITABLE ABOUT WATTS TOWERS, THE LARGEST PIECE OF FOLK ART ever created by a single person. It's as if the sheer human will that built them imbued these skeletal steel fantasies with their own will to survive.

A gritty inner-city neighborhood threatened to engulf them; earthquakes have shaken their foundations; their own creator abandoned them years ago, leaving them to rack and ruin until art lovers "discovered" them and opened the site to the public in 1960.

Simon Rodia, an immigrant Italian tile setter, began this project—calling it Nuestro Pueblo, or Our Town—sometime in the early 1920s, working on it in his spare time for the next 33 years. Nine intricate cement-and-steel structures gradually rose to the sky, as high as 99 feet (30m), from the tiny yard of his cottage by the streetcar tracks. Though Rodia had no engineering degrees and used the simplest of tools, he was a skilled craftsman with an old-world pride in his handiwork. The towers are surprisingly strong, though even they sustained some damage in the 1994 Northridge earthquake.

As times passed the childless recluse became compulsively devoted to the project. Neighborhood punks tried to vandalize it and he built a wall; during World War II local gossips sought to raze the towers, accusing Rodia of using them to transmit secret information to the Japanese. Rodia persisted—until 1954 when he abruptly quit the project and moved out, offhandedly leaving his property to a neighbor. He claimed to have lost all interest and would not give interviews, except to say, "I had in mind to do something big and I did it." We'll never know what inspired him.

Topped with futuristic-looking spires, these steeples of interlaced steel are encrusted with a zany profusion of brightly colored mosaics, created out of anything that came to hand—seashells, pottery, mirrors, you name it. Look for chips of green glass (which came from old 7-Up bottles) and blue glass (from Milk of Magnesia bottles). Rodia's day job was at the legendary Malibu Potteries, so it seems likely that many fragments of valuable Malibu tile are embedded in the towers. Tours are offered every half-hour on a first-come, first-served basis.

ⓘ **Watts Towers,** 1727 E. 107th St., Los Angeles (✆ **213/847-4646;** www.watts towers.us)

✈ Los Angeles International

🛏 $$ **Beverly Garland's Holiday Inn,** 4222 Vineland Ave., North Hollywood (✆ **800/BEVERLY** [238-3759] or 818/ 980-8000; www.beverlygarland.com). $$ **Roosevelt Hotel, Hollywood,** 7000 Hollywood Blvd. (✆ **800/950-7667** or 323/ 466-7000; www.hollywoodroosevelt.com).

# 499

# The Death of the High Street
## *Working on the Chain Gang*
### The United Kingdom

"THE HIGH STREET"—IN ENGLAND, THE TERM IS SHORTHAND FOR CONSUMER CULTURE, STILL envisioned in the U.K. as something that takes place in historic town-center shopping streets. But with the proliferation of chain stores, few authentic high streets remain.

Over 5,000 streets are actually named High Street throughout the United Kingdom, and each one is expected to have its own character, set by local tradesmen selling regionally made products.

But judging by the number of chain stores along today's high streets, the cherished image of England as a nation of shopkeepers is long dead. A 2004 report by the New Economics Foundation titled "Clone Town Britain" rated English towns and cities according to the number of chain stores occupying their central retail district. The worst case was the cathedral town of Exeter, which had only one independent store in its entire shopping district; other extreme examples cited were Stafford, Middlesbrough, Weston-super-Mare, and Winchester. In 2007 a group of MPs organized as the All-Party Parliamentary Group for Small Shops predicted that small and independent shops could vanish entirely from the high street by 2015.

It's not just a question of American-style shopping malls displacing downtown retail, although the number of such malls quadrupled between 1986 and 1997. Even in the downtowns, chain stores have been pushing out independent merchants. Instead of local chemists, there are Boots Pharmacies; instead of an independent newsagent there's a W H Smith's; instead of butchers and greengrocers, there's a Tesco supermarket (an average of 23 butcher's shops have closed every month since 2000). Marks and Spencer's replaces the local clothing boutique, and multinational brand-name eateries like McDonald's, Pizza Hut, and Starbucks have driven out individual cafes. A comparison of Yellow Pages listings between 1992 and 2003 showed that the number of separate listings for fruit and vegetable shops had declined nearly 60%, butchers 40%, hardware shops 34%, bakers 20%.

So where can one find an authentic high street? One example might be Gloucester Road, a northern artery (A38) that curves through the Bristol suburb of Bishopston, half a mile north of the city center. There's nothing twee or stage-set perfect about it, just a series of tidy two-story terraces housing small merchants—a couple of butchers, a bakery, a fruit store, greengrocers, newsagents, clothing boutiques, a spirits shop, coffee bars, pubs, and takeaway shops. You won't see instantly recognizable logos on the neat hand-painted signs over shop entrances; catering to a largely middle-class neighborhood, Gloucester Road's shops basically serve residents' day-to-day needs, rather than being a shopping destination in and of itself. The opening of a Tesco Express in 2005 stirred a few feathers, however; since then a Pizza Hut and a small branch of Sainsbury's supermarket have also opened.

Best run down to the shops while you still can.

✈ Bristol

🛏 $$ **Tyndall's Park Hotel,** 4 Tyndall's Park Rd., Clifton (© **44/1179/735407;** www.tyndallsparkhotel.co.uk). $ **Downlands House,** 33 Henleaze Gardens, Henleaze (© **44/1179/621639;** www. downlandshouse.co.uk).

## 500

# Back Beat on the Reeperbahn
## *Hamburg's Music Clubs*
### Hamburg, Germany

OF THE FOUR VENUES THE BEATLES PLAYED IN HAMBURG, ONLY THE KAISERKELLER REMAINS, and even that has been vastly altered. What hasn't changed, though, is the raw energy of the Hamburg music scene, thriving alongside the Reeperbahn's X-rated sleaze.

It's an essential pilgrimage for Beatle fans: touring Hamburg's red-light district, where the fledgling English band played several gigs in 1960, 1961, and 1962. The infamous Reeperbahn, main drag of the St. Pauli red-light district, is undeniably rough and sleazy—Hamburg's tourism officials are well aware that its gritty atmosphere attracts tourists. (Amsterdam's equally famous red-light district, in contrast, seems sanitized.) But the music clubs are still there, sandwiched in among sex clubs, brothels, and bars. Whether they're the same clubs where the Beatles played is another question.

The Beatles' first Hamburg gig, starting in July 1960, was at the Indra Club, a shabby girlie lounge with worn red carpeting on a Reeperbahn side street called Grosse Freiheit. Around the corner at 33 Paul-Roosen Strasse is the former Bambi Kino, a run-down cinema where club owner Bruno Koschmider housed the Beatles in squalid cubicles behind the screen. The Indra Club at Grosse Freiheit 64 today is a modern renovation, so named to capitalize on the Beatles' fame—the original Indra abruptly closed in October 1960, after which the Beatles were shifted to Koschmider's other club, the Kaiserkeller, at 38 Grosse Freiheit, much closer to the Reeperbahn action. Here they performed on a makeshift stage, alternating with Rory Storm and the Hurricanes, whose drummer was Ringo Starr (Pete Best was still the Beatles' drummer). Extensively revamped since then, the Kaiserkeller is now owned by the next-door venue, Grosse Freiheit 36 (© **49/40/317778-0**), a prominent live-music venue which opened in 1985.

A month after debuting at the Kaiserkeller, the Beatles were lured to the Top Ten Club, a brassy new nightspot right on the main drag, at Reeperbahn 136, where they played back-up to headliner Tony Sheridan. Though legal problems soon sent them home, they returned in March 1961 for a 3-month engagement. The Top Ten Club survived for years, but finally closed; from outside the building, you can see the attic windows where the Beatles lived during that 1961 gig.

Returning to Hamburg in April 1962, the Beatles were popular enough to be booked at the hot new nightclub the Star Club, across from the Kaiserkeller at 39 Grosse Freiheit (go through the archway into the courtyard). The Star Club closed in 1969, was converted to a sex club, then burned down; the Star Club Hof cafe that's there now is another attempt to cash in on Beatle fame. You can, however, get a cheap meal at the Gretel & Alfons cafe, a few doors down from the Star Club, where the Beatles hung out between gigs.

It was an overnight education in rock 'n' roll for those Liverpool youngsters—an experience that helped to change pop music forever.

✈ Hamburg

🛏 $$$ **East,** Simon-von-Utrecht Strasse 31 (© **49/40/309930;** www.east-hotel.de). $ **Fritzhotel,** Schanzenstrasse 101–103 (© **49/40/8222-28322;** www.fritzhotel. com).

# Resource Index
## *Conservation Resources*

In researching this book, I discovered an encouraging number of organizations around the world who are actively working to preserve endangered natural, historical, and cultural treasures. While I've mentioned several in specific write-ups throughout this book, here's a list of important organizations I've come to depend upon—invaluable resources to anybody who cares about conservation and the environment.

## International

**Conservation International**
2011 Crystal Drive, Suite 500
Arlington, VA 22202
United States
☏ 703/341-2400
www.conservation.org

**Friends of the Earth International**
PO Box 19199
1000 GD
Amsterdam, The Netherlands
☏ 31/20 622 1369
www.foei.org

**Greenforce**
11-15 Betterton Street,
Covent Garden
London WC2H 9BP
United Kingdom
☏ 44/207 470 8888
www.greenforce.org

**Greenpeace International**
Ottho Heldringstraat 5
1066 AZ Amsterdam, The Netherlands
☏ 31/20 7182000
www.greenpeace.org

**The Nature Conservancy**
4245 North Fairfax Drive, Suite 100
Arlington, VA 22203-1606
United States
☏ 703/841-5300
www.nature.org

**Wetlands International**
PO Box 471
6700 AL Wageningen
The Netherlands

☏ 31/317 486774
www.wetlands.org

**Wildlife Conservation Society**
2300 Southern Boulevard
Bronx, New York 10460
United States
☏ 718/220-5100
www.wcs.org

**World Wide Fund for Nature/
World Wildlife Fund**
Av. du Mont-Blanc 1196
Gland, Switzerland
www.panda.org

**WWF United States**
1250 24th Street NW
PO Box 97180
Washington, DC 20090-7180
United States
☏ 202/293-4800

**WWF Canada**
245 Eglinton Avenue East Suite 410
Toronto, Ontario M4P 3J1
☏ 416/489 8800

**WWF United Kingdom**
Panda House Weyside Park
Godalming
☏ 44/1483 426 444

**WWF Australia**
Level 13 235 Jones Street
Ultimo NSW 2007
☏ 61/2 9281 5515

# United States

**Defenders of Wildlife**
1130 17th Street NW
Washington, DC 20036
United States
✆ **800/385-9712**
www.defenders.org

**Environment America**
44 Winter Street, 4th Floor
Boston, MA 02108
United States
✆ **617/747-4449**
www.environmentamerica.org

**Environmental Defense Fund**
257 Park Avenue South
New York, NY 10010
United States
✆ **800/684-3322**
www.edf.org

**National Audubon Society**
225 Varick Street, 7th floor
New York, NY 10014
United States
✆ **212/979-3000**
www.audubon.org

**National Wildlife Federation**
11100 Wildlife Center Dr.
Reston, VA 20190
United States
✆ **800/822-9919**
www.nwf.org

**The Sierra Club**
85 Second Street, 2nd Floor
San Francisco, CA 94105
United States
✆ **415/977-5500**
www.sierraclub.org

**The Wilderness Society**
1615 M St., NW
Washington, DC 20036
United States
✆ **800/THE-WILD**
www.wilderness.org

# Canada

**Nature Canada**
85 Albert St, Suite 900
Ottawa, Ontario
K1P 6A4, Canada
✆ **800/267-4088** or 613/562-3447
www.naturecanada.ca

# United Kingdom

**English Heritage**
Freepost WD214
PO Box 569
Swindon, Wiltshire, SN2 2UR
United Kingdom
✆ **44/870 333 1181**
www.english-heritage.org.uk

**Natural England**
1 East Parade
Sheffield, S1 2ET
United Kingdom
✆ **44/114 241 8920**
www.naturalengland.org.uk

**The Wildlife Trusts**
The Kiln, Waterside, Mather Road
Newark, Nottinghamshire NG24 1WT
United Kingdom
✆ **44/1636 677711**
www.wildlifetrusts.org

# Australia

**Australian Conservation Foundation**
Floor 1, 60 Leicester St.
Carlton, Vic 3053
Australia
℗ **61/3/9345 1111**
www.acfonline.org.au

**Australian Wildlife Conservancy**
PO Box 1897
West Perth, WA 6872
Australia
℗ **61/8/9380 9633**
www.australianwildlife.org

# New Zealand

**Royal Forest and Bird Protection Society**
Level One, 90 Ghuznee Street
PO Box 631
Wellington, New Zealand
℗ **64/4/385 7374**
www.forestandbird.org.nz

# Indexes

## Geographical Index

# Alphabetical Index

# Photo Credits